AutoCAD 2023 For Beginners (For Mac users)

CADFolks

© Copyright 2022 by Kishore

This book may not be duplicated in any way without the express written consent of the publisher, except in the form of brief excerpts or quotations for review. The information contained herein is for the personal use of the reader. It may not be incorporated in any commercial programs, other books, databases, or any software without the written consent of the publisher. Making copies of this book or any portion for a purpose other than your own is a violation of copyright laws.

Limit of Liability/Disclaimer of Warranty:
The author and publisher make no representations or warranties concerning the accuracy or completeness of the contents of this work and expressly disclaim all warranties, including without limitation warranties of fitness for a particular purpose. The advice and strategies contained herein may not be suitable for every situation. Neither the publisher nor the author shall be liable for damages arising there onwards.

Trademarks:
All brand names and product names used in this book are trademarks, registered trademarks, or trade names of their respective holders. The author and publisher are not associated with any product or vendor mentioned in this book.

For Resource files, visit:

https://autocadforbeginners.weebly.com

For Technical Support, contact us at:
online.books999@gmail.com

Table of Contents

Scope of this Book x

Chapter 1: Introduction to AutoCAD 2023 1

    Introduction 1
    System requirements 1
    Starting AutoCAD 2023 1
    AutoCAD user interface 2
        Changing the Color Theme 3
        Tool sets in AutoCAD 4
        Toolbar 7
        File tabs 7
        Drawing area 7
        ViewCube 8
        Command line 8
        Status Bar 9
        Menu Bar 13
        Changing the display of the Tool set 13
        Dialogs and Palettes 14
        Shortcut Menus 14
        Selection Window 16
    Starting a new drawing 18
        Templates on the Welcome Screen 18
        The Select Template dialog 18
    Opening an existing drawing file 19
    Help 20
    Command List 20
        3D Commands 31

Chapter 2: Drawing Basics 38

    Drawing Basics 38
        Drawing Lines 38
        Erasing, Undoing and Redoing 41
        Drawing Circles 42
        Drawing Arcs 45
        Drawing Polylines 47
        Drawing Rectangles 48
        Drawing Polygons 50
        Drawing Splines 51
        Drawing Ellipses 53
        Exercises 55

Chapter 3: Drawing Aids 58

    Drawing Aids 58
        Setting Grid and Snap 58

    Setting the Limits of a drawing 59

    Setting the Lineweight 59

    Using Ortho mode and Polar Tracking 60

    Using Layers 61

    Using Object Snaps 63

    Running Object Snaps 66

    Cycling through Object Snaps 67

    Using Object Snap Tracking 67

    Linetype gap selection 69

    Using Zoom tools 69

    Panning Drawings 72

Exercises 72

Chapter 4: Editing Tools 74

Editing Tools 74

    The Move tool 74

    The Copy tool 75

    The Rotate tool 75

    The Scale tool 76

    The Trim tool 77

    The Cut with Base Point Tool 78

    The Fillet tool 79

    The Chamfer tool 80

    The Mirror tool 81

    The Explode tool 82

    The Stretch tool 83

    The Polar Array tool 84

    The Offset tool 86

    The Path Array tool 87

    The Rectangular Array tool 88

    Editing Using Grips 90

    Modifying Rectangular Arrays 95

    Modifying Polar Arrays 99

    Revision Clouds 101

    Example 1 102

Exercises 107

Chapter 5: Multi View Drawings 115

Multi-view Drawings 115

    Creating Orthographic Views 115

    Creating Auxiliary Views 122

    Creating Named views 128

Exercises 129

    Exercise 1 129

  Exercise 2 130
  Exercise 3 130
  Exercise 4 130

Chapter 6: Dimensions and Annotations 133

 Dimensioning 133
  Creating Dimensions 133
  Creating a Dimension Style 147
  Adding Leaders 150
  Adding Dimensional Tolerances 152
  Geometric Dimensioning and Tolerancing 153
  Editing Dimensions by Stretching 156
  Modifying Dimensions by Trimming and Extending 157
  Using the DIMEDIT command 158
  Using the Update tool 158
  Using the Oblique tool 159
  Editing Dimensions using Grips 162
  Modifying Dimensions using the Properties palette 163
  Matching Properties of Dimensions or Objects 164
 Exercises 165
  Exercise 1 165
  Exercise 2 165
  Exercise 3 166
  Exercise 4 166
  Exercise 5 167

Chapter 7: Parametric Tools 169

 Parametric Tools 169
  Geometric Constraints 169
  Dimensional Constraints 178
  Creating equations using the Parameters Manager 180
  Creating Inferred Constraints 181
 Exercises 182
  Exercise 1 182
  Exercise 2 183

Chapter 8: Section Views 185

 Section Views 185
  The Hatch tool 185
  Setting the Properties of Hatch lines 190
  Island Detection tools 193
  Text in Hatching 194
 Exercises 195
  Exercise 1 195
  Exercise 2 195

Chapter 9: Blocks, Attributes, and Xrefs ... 197

Introduction ... 197
- Creating Blocks ... 197
- Inserting Blocks ... 198
- Redefining Blocks ... 199
- Creating Annotative Blocks ... 201
- Exploding Blocks ... 201
- Using the Purge tool ... 202
- Using the Divide tool ... 202
- Renaming Blocks ... 203
- Inserting Blocks in a Table ... 204
- Inserting Multiple Blocks ... 205
- Editing Blocks ... 205
- Using the Write Block tool ... 206
- Defining Attributes ... 207
- Inserting Attributed Blocks ... 209
- Working with External references ... 210
- Fading an Xref ... 212
- Clipping External References ... 212
- Editing the External References ... 213
- Binding the External References ... 213
- Adding Balloons ... 214
- Creating the Part List ... 215
- Exercise ... 216

Chapter 10: Layouts & Annotative Objects ... 218

Drawing Layouts ... 218
- Working with Layouts ... 218
- Creating Viewports in the Paper space ... 220
- Changing the Layer Properties in Viewports ... 223
- Creating the Title Block on the Layout ... 223
- Working with Annotative Dimensions ... 223
- Scaling Hatches relative to Viewports ... 226
- Working with Annotative Text ... 227

Exercises ... 228
- Exercise 1 ... 228

Chapter 11: Templates and Plotting ... 230

Plotting Drawings ... 230
- Creating Plot Style Tables ... 230
- Creating Templates ... 231
- Plotting/Printing the drawing ... 232
- Exporting to PDF ... 233
- Importing a PDF ... 233

  Compare Drawings..234
  Exporting the Compared results to a new drawing 236
  Batch Publish..237
  Package Drawing..238
  Exercise 238

Chapter 12: 3D Modeling Basics..240

 Introduction...240
  The Modeling tool set 240
  The Box tool...243
  Creating the User Coordinate System 243
  Creating a Wedge 244
  Creating a Cylinder 245
  Using Dynamic User Coordinate System..249
  Model Space Viewports for 3D Modeling 250
 Creating Other Primitive Shapes 251
  Creating Cones 251
  Creating a Sphere 251
  Creating a Torus 252
  Creating a Pyramid..252
  Using the Polysolid tool 252
  Using the Extrude tool...253
  Using the Revolve tool 254
  Using the Sweep tool...256
  Using the Loft tool 258
  Using the Presspull tool...260
  Performing the Boolean Operations..261
  Using the Helix tool 266
  Exercises..267

Chapter 13: Solid Editing & generating 2D views 270

 Introduction...270
  Using the Move tool..270
  Using the 3D Move tool..271
  Using the Array tool..271
  Using the 3D Align tool..272
  Using the 3D Mirror tool...274
  Using the Fillet Edge tool..276
  Using the Taper Faces tool..277
  Using the Offset Faces tool...278
  Using the 3D Rotate tool...279
  Using the 3D Polyline tool..280
  Creating a 3D Polar Array...280
  Using the Shell tool...281

  Using the Chamfer Edge tool...281
  Using the Section Plane tool..282
  Using the Live Section tool..282
  Exercises..283

Chapter 14: Creating Architectural Drawings...288
 Example 1..288
  Creating Outer Walls..288
  Creating Inner Walls...290
  Creating Openings and Doors..292
  Creating Kitchen Fixtures...298
  Creating Bathroom Fixtures...301
  Adding Furniture using Blocks..303
  Adding Windows..305
  Arranging Objects of the drawing in Layers...308
  Creating Grid Lines..311
  Adding Dimensions..313
 Example 2..318
  Creating the Stairs..318
  Creating the Section elevation of the Staircase...320
  Creating the Handrail...327
 Example 3..337
 Example 4..347
 Example 5..353
  Creating the Brick Venner..355
  Creating the Brick Tie..358
  Creating the Insulation...360
  Creating the Roof Detail..366
  Adding Annotations...375
 Exercise...379

Index..380

Introduction

CAD is an abbreviation for Computer-Aided Design. It is the process used to design and draft components on your computer. This process includes creating designs and drawings of the product or system. AutoCAD is a CAD software package developed and marketed by Autodesk Inc. It can be used to create two-dimensional (2D) and three-dimensional (3D) models of products. These models can be transferred to other computer programs for further analysis and testing. Also, you can convert these computer models into numerical data. This numerical data can be used in manufacturing equipment such as machining centers, lathes, mills, or rapid prototyping machines to manufacture the product.

AutoCAD is one of the first CAD software packages. It was introduced in the year 1982. Since that time, it has become the industry leader among all CAD products. It is the most widely used CAD software. Other systems utilize the commands and concepts introduced by AutoCAD. As a student, learning AutoCAD provides you with a more significant advantage as compared to any other CAD software.

Scope of this Book

The *AutoCAD 2023 For Beginners (For Mac Users)* book provides a learn-by-doing approach for users to learn AutoCAD. It is written for students and engineers who are interested to learn AutoCAD 2023 for creating designs and drawing of components or anyone who communicates through technical drawings as part of their work. The topics covered in this book are as follows:

- Chapter 1, "Introduction to AutoCAD 2023", gives an introduction to AutoCAD. The user interface and terminology are discussed in this chapter.

- Chapter 2, "Drawing Basics," explores the essential drawing tools in AutoCAD. You will create simple drawings using the drawing tools.

- Chapter 3, "Drawing Aids," explores the drawing settings that will assist you in creating drawings.

- Chapter 4, "Editing Tools," covers the tools required to modify drawing objects or create new objects using the existing ones.

- Chapter 5, "Multi View Drawings," teaches you to create multi-view drawings standard projection techniques.

- Chapter 6, "Dimensions and Annotations," teaches you to apply dimensions and annotations to a drawing.

- Chapter 7, "Parametric Tools," teaches you to create parametric drawings. Parametric drawings are created by using the logical operations and parameters that control the shape and size of a drawing.

- Chapter 8, "Section Views," teaches you to create section views of a component. A section view is the inside view of a component when it is sliced.

- Chapter 9, "Blocks, Attributes, and Xrefs," teaches you to create Blocks, Attributes, and Xrefs. Blocks are a group of objects in a drawing that can be reused. Attributes are notes or values related to an object. Xrefs are drawing files attached to another drawing.

- Chapter 10, "Layouts and Annotative Objects," teaches you to create layouts and annotative objects. Layouts are the digital counterparts of physical drawing sheets. Annotative objects are dimensions, and notes, which change their sizes to drawing scale.

- Chapter 11, "Templates and Plotting," teaches you to create drawing templates and plot drawings.

- Chapter 12, "3D Modeling Basics," explores the necessary tools to create 3D models.

- Chapter 13, "Solid Editing Tools," covers the tools required to edit solid models and create new objects by using the existing ones.

- Chapter 14, "Creating Architectural Drawings," introduces you to architectural design in AutoCAD. You will design floor plan, staircase, elevations, roof plan, and roof and wall details.

Chapter 1: Introduction to AutoCAD 2023

In this chapter, you will learn about:

- **AutoCAD user interface**
- **Customizing user interface**
- **Important AutoCAD commands**

Introduction

AutoCAD is a legendary software in the world of Computer Aided Designing (CAD). It has completed 38 years by 2020. If you are a new user of this software, then the time you spend on learning this software will be a wise investment. If you have used previous versions of AutoCAD, you will be able to learn the new enhancements. I welcome you to learn AutoCAD using this book through step-by-step examples to learn various commands and techniques.

System requirements

The following are system requirements for running AutoCAD smoothly on your system.

Operating System: Apple® macOS® Monterey v12, Apple® macOS® Big Sur v11, and Apple macOS Catalina v10.15

- **Model:**
    Basic: Apple Mac Pro® 4.1, MacBook Pro 5.1, iMac® 8.1, Mac mini® 3.1, MacBook Air®, MacBook® 5.1

    Recommended: Apple Mac® models supporting Metal Graphics Engine Apple Mac models with M series chip are supported under Rosetta 2 mode.

- CPU Type: 64-bit Intel CPU, Apple M series CPU
- 4 GB of RAM (8 GB Recommended).
- Resolution 1280 x 800 or **High Resolution**: 2880 x 1800 with Retina Display
- 5 GB of free space for installation.
- Apple-compliant Mouse, Apple-compliant Trackpad, Microsoft-compliant mouse
- Mac native installed graphics cards
- Disk Format: APFS, APFS(Encrypted), Mac OS Extended (Journaled), Mac OS Extended (Journaled, Encrypted)

Starting AutoCAD 2023

To start **AutoCAD 2023**, click the **AutoCAD 2023** icon on the Dock.

AutoCAD 2023 For Beginners (For Mac Users)

AutoCAD user interface

When you click the AutoCAD 2023 icon on the Dock, the **Welcome** screen will appear.

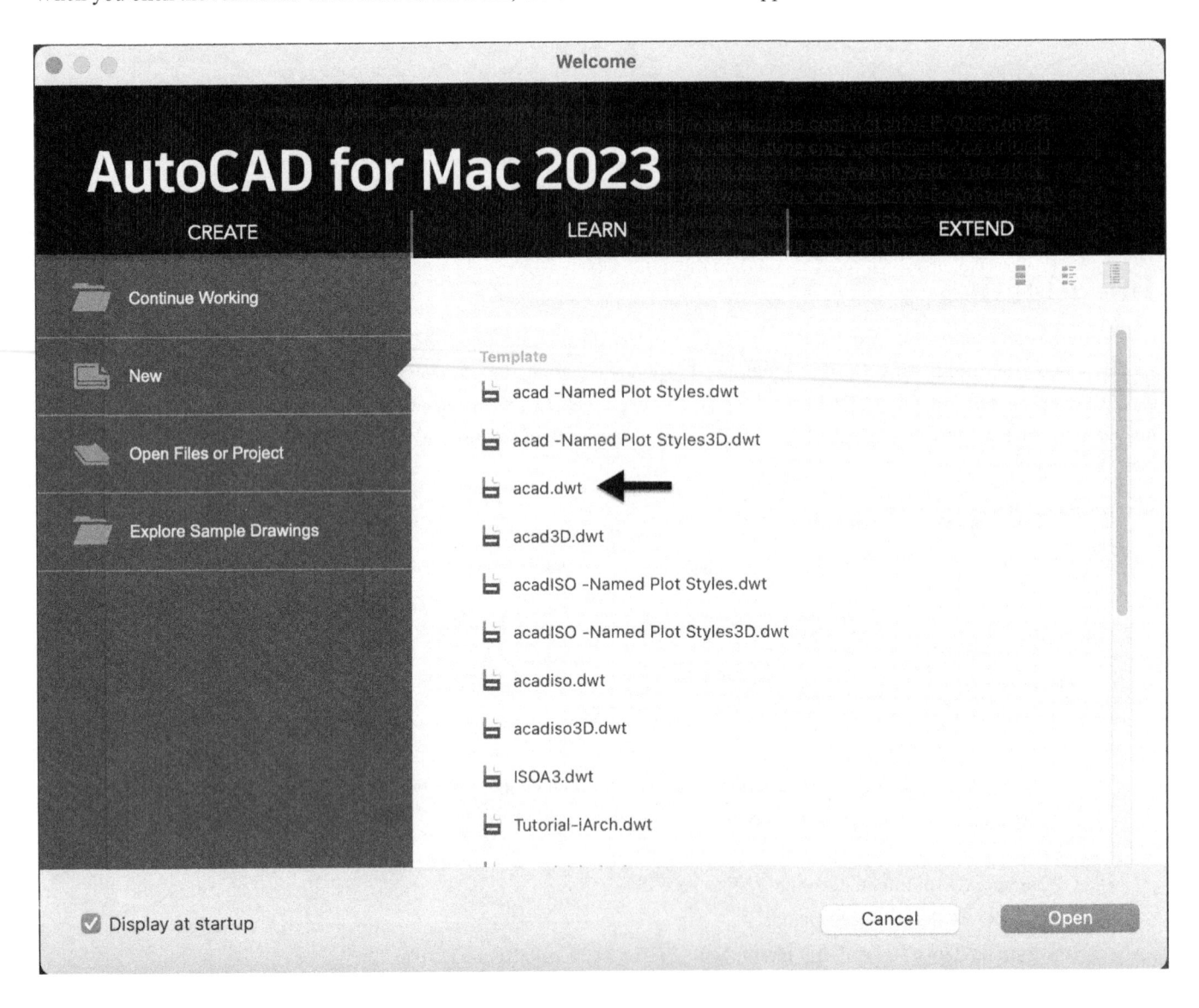

On the **Welcome** Screen, click **Create > New** and select a drawing template. Next, click the **Open** button to open a new drawing file. The drawing file consists of a drawing area, tool sets, menu bar, toolbar, command line, and other screen components.

AutoCAD 2023 For Beginners (For Mac Users)

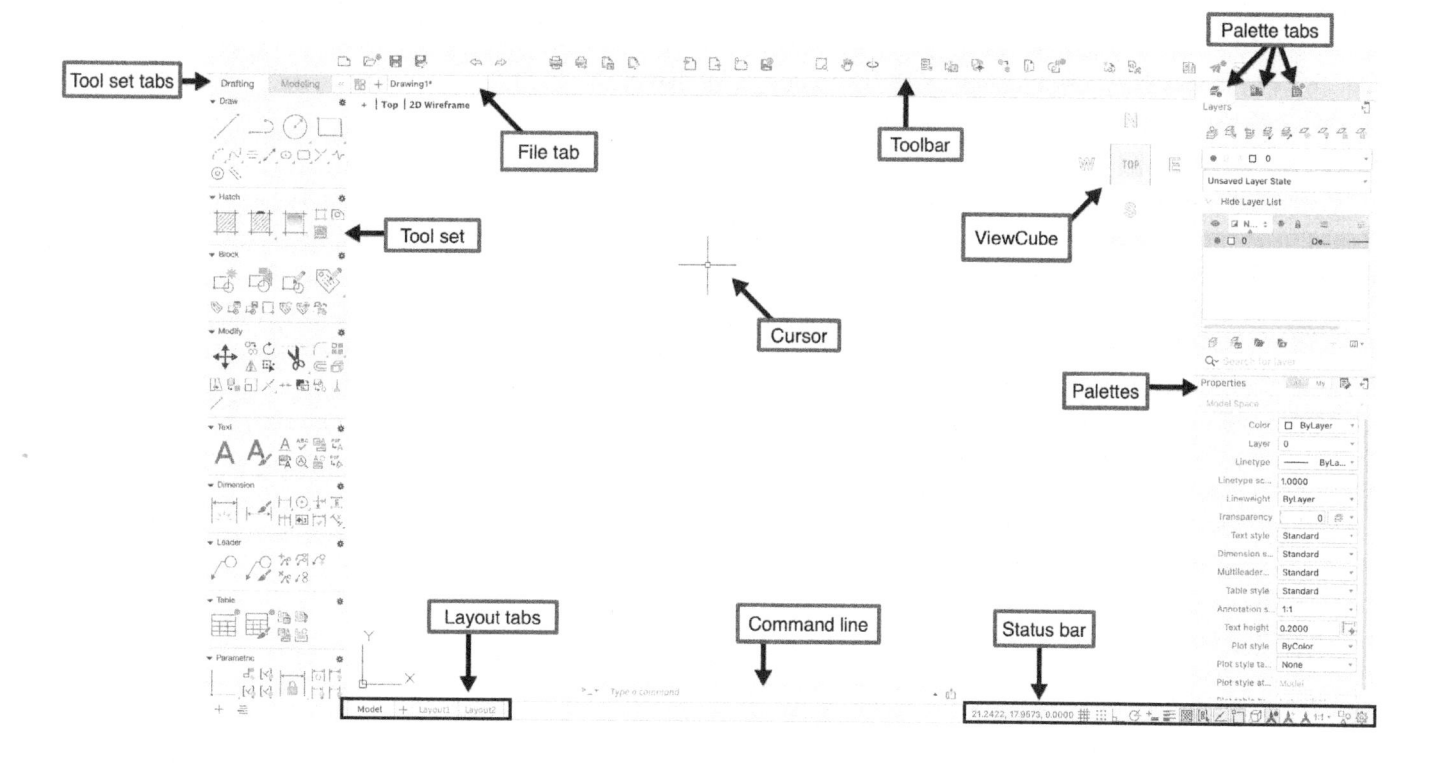

Changing the Color Theme

AutoCAD 2023 is available in two different color themes: **Dark** and **Light**. You can change the color theme by using the **Application Preferences** dialog. Click the right mouse button and select **Preferences** from the shortcut menu. On the **Application Preferences** dialog, click the **Look & Feel** tab and select an option from the **Themes** drop-down.

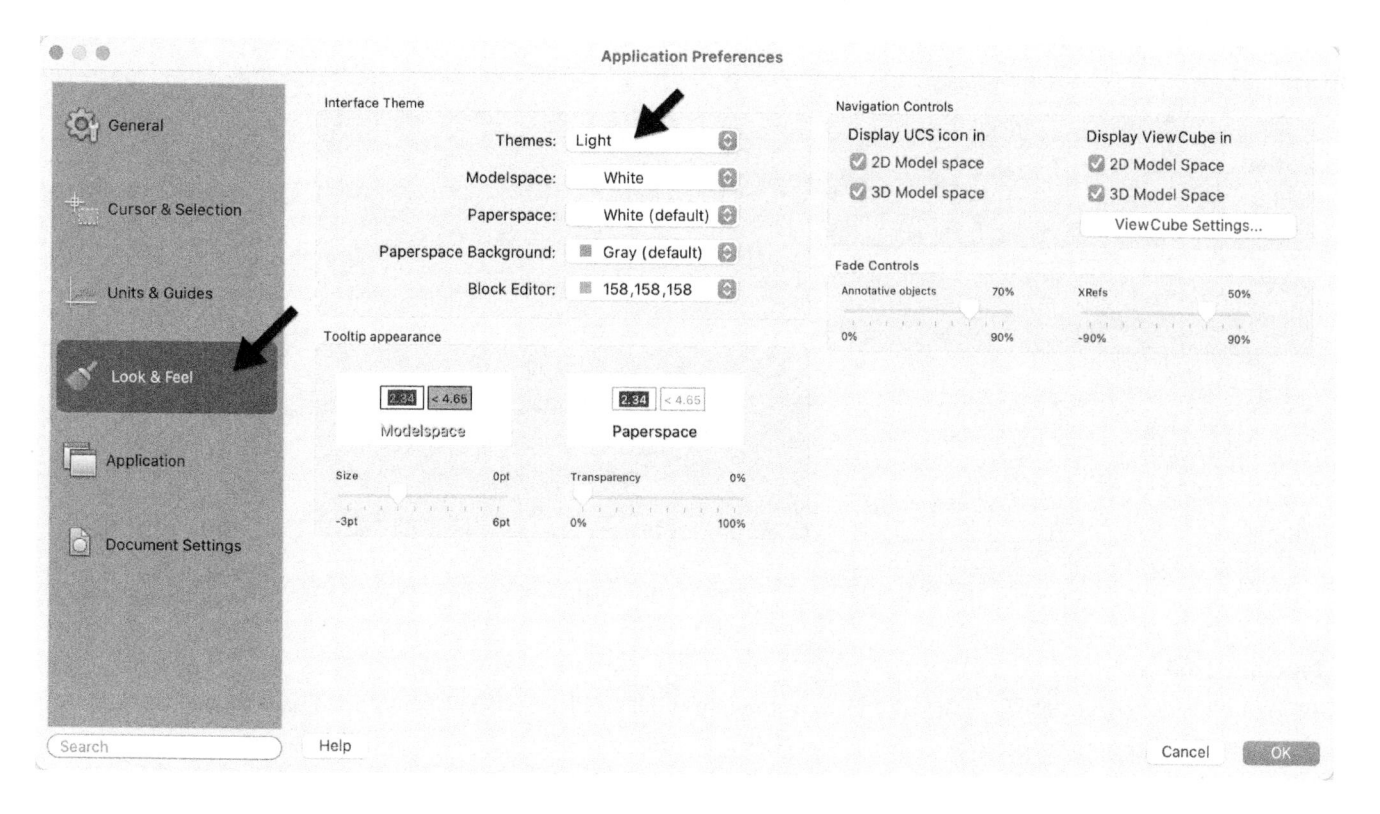

3 | Introduction to AutoCAD 2023

AutoCAD 2023 For Beginners (For Mac Users)

Tool sets in AutoCAD

There are two tool sets available in AutoCAD: **Drafting**, and **Modeling**.

Drafting Tool set

This Tool set has all the tools to create a 2D drawing. It is located at the left side of the drawing area. The tool set is divided into different panels. Panels such as **Draw**, **Hatch, Block**, **Modify**, and **Text** consist of tools which are grouped based on their usage.

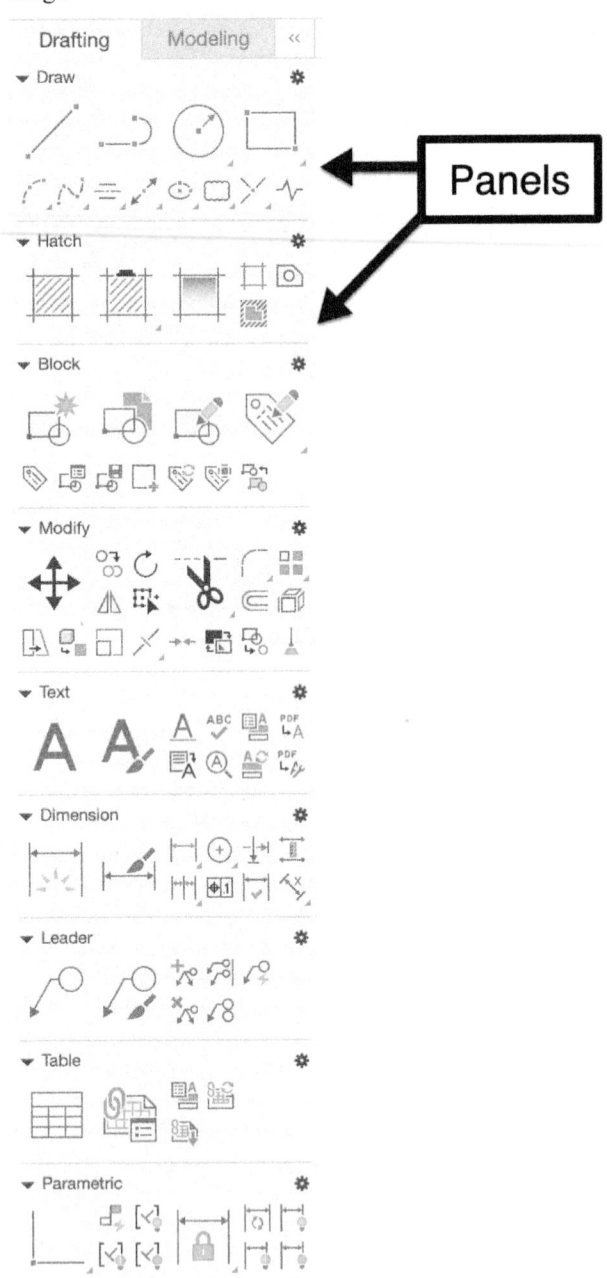

Modeling Tool set

This Tool set is used to create 3D models. You will learn more about this Tool sets in Chapter 12. The other components of the user Interface are discussed next.

4 | Introduction to AutoCAD 2023

AutoCAD 2023 For Beginners (For Mac Users)

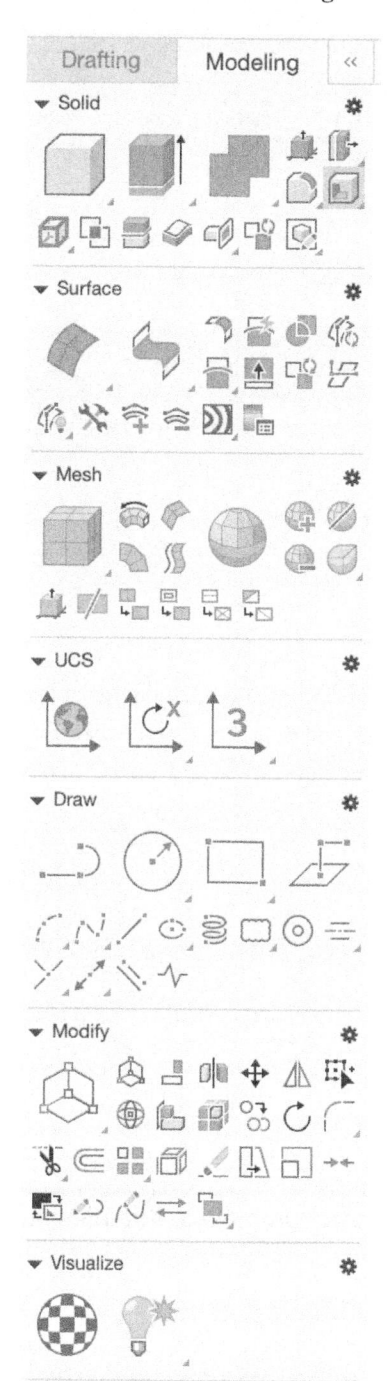

Customizing a Tool set

You can customize a panel by clicking the **Customize panel** icon available on the top-right corner of the panel. Next, select or deselect the check boxes next to the tools available on the menu. The selected tools will be displayed on the panel.

AutoCAD 2023 For Beginners (For Mac Users)

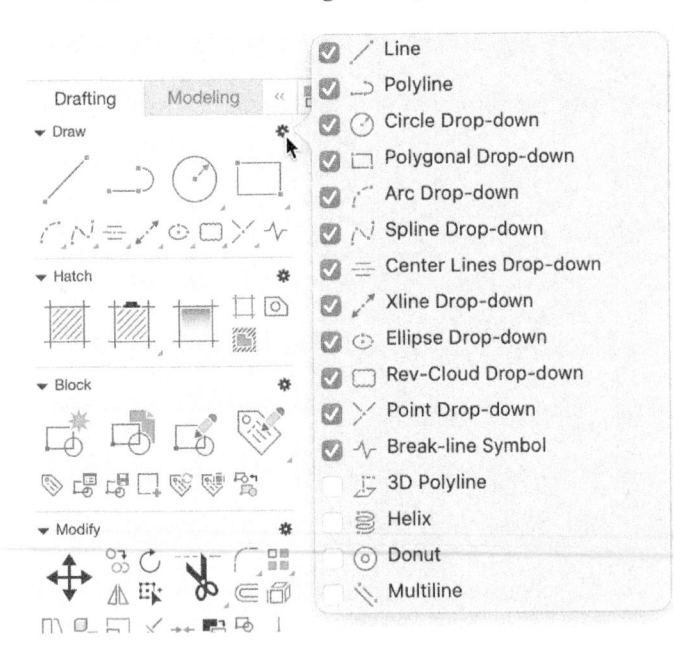

In addition to that, you can create new panels by clicking the **Create a new panel** icon located at the bottom left corner of the tool set. Next, type-in the name of the panel in the box available on the top of the dialog. Click and drag the desired tools from the tool list available on the right-side of the dialog. You can also search the required tool using the search bar available at the bottom.

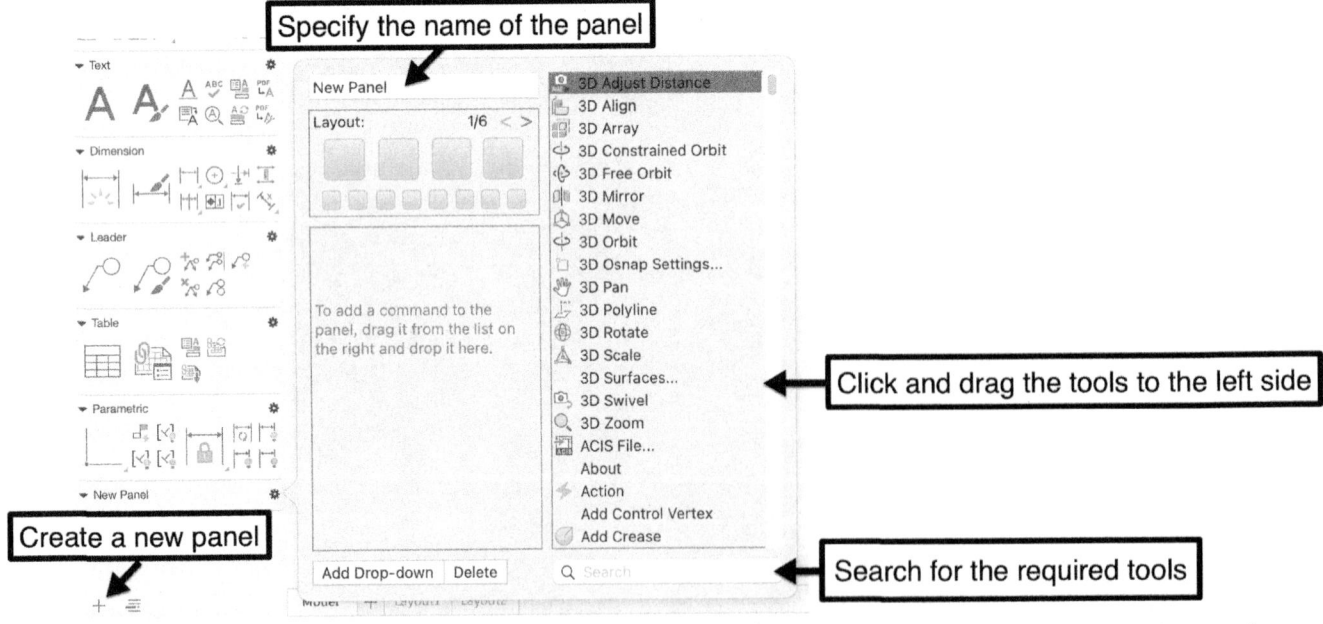

Click the **Add Drop-down** button to add a drop-down to the panel. Next, right-click on the newly added drop-down and change its name. Drag the required tools from the tools list and drop it under the drop-down. Next, select the desired layout by clicking the arrows available in the **Layout** section. Click in the drawing area to close the dialog.

Introduction to AutoCAD 2023

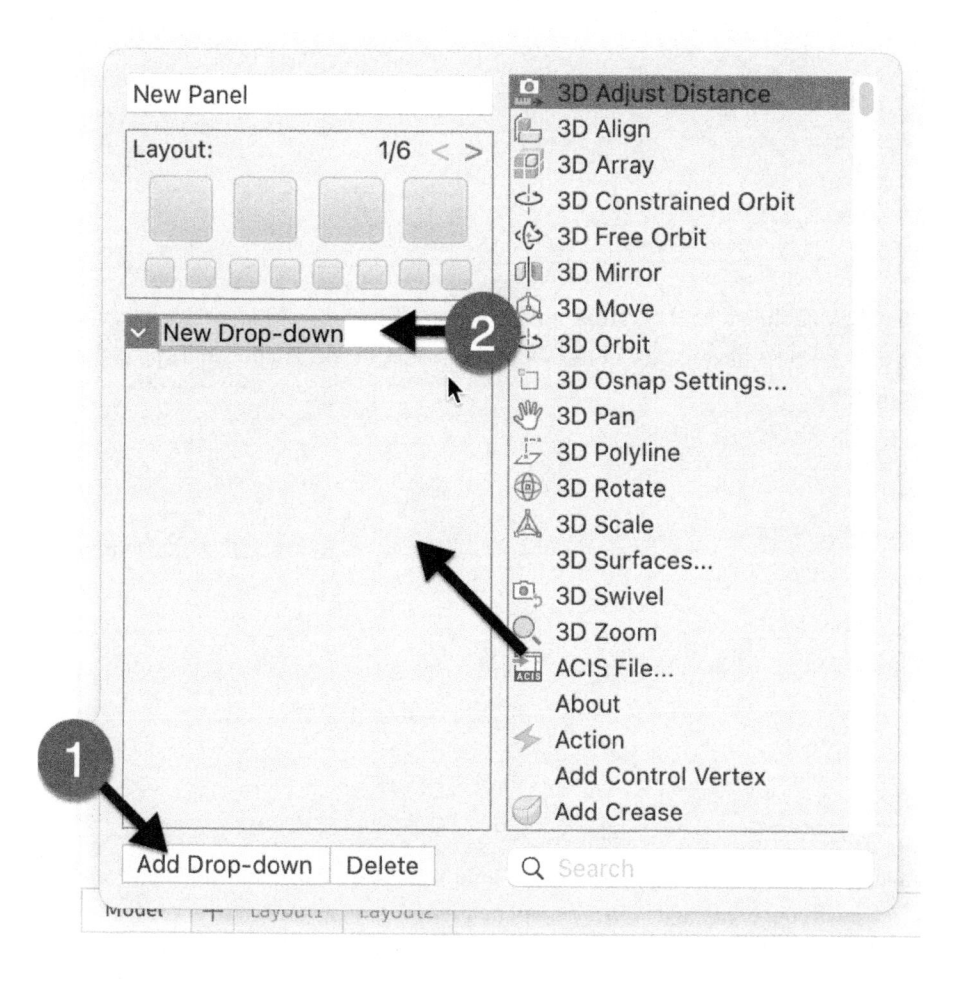

Toolbar

This is located at the top of the window and helps you to access commands quickly. It consists of commonly used commands such as **New**, **Save**, **Open**, **Save As**, **Plot**, and so on.

File tabs

The File tabs are located below the toolbar. You can switch between different drawing files by using the file tabs. Also, you can open a new file by using the + button, easily.

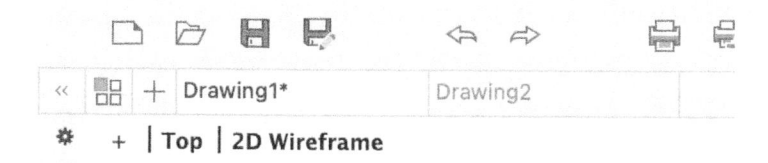

Drawing area

Drawing area is the blank space located below the file tabs. You can draw objects and create 3D graphics in the drawing area. The top left corner of the drawing area has **Viewport Label Menus**. Using this menu, you can set the orientation and display style of the model.

Introduction to AutoCAD 2023

ViewCube

The ViewCube allows you to navigate in the 3D Modeling and 2D drafting environments. Using the ViewCube, you can set the orientation of the model. For example, you can select the top face of the ViewCube to set the orientation to Top. You can click the corner points to set the view to Isometric.

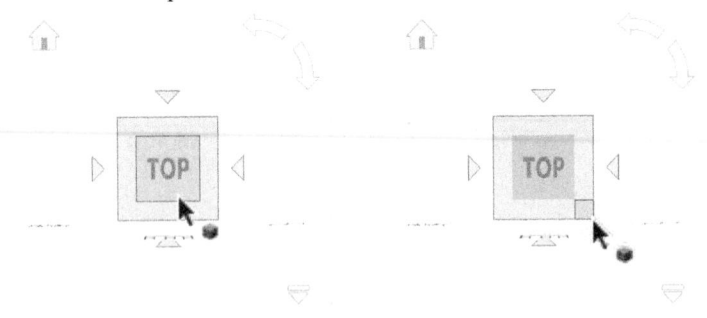

Command line

The command line is located below the drawing area. It is effortless to execute a command using the command line. You can just type the first letter of a command, and it lists all the commands starting with that letter. This helps you to activate commands very quickly and increases your productivity.

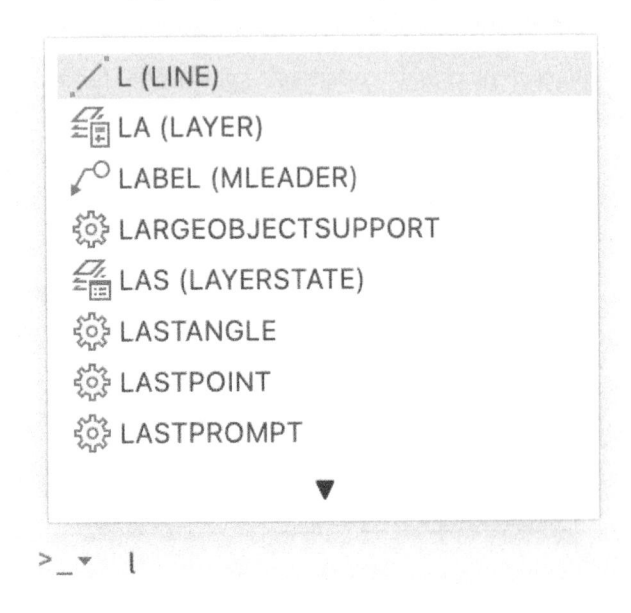

Also, the command line shows the current state of the drawing. It shows various prompts while working with any command. These prompts are a series of steps needed to execute a command successfully. For example, when you activate the LINE command, the command line displays a prompt, "Specify the first point." You need to click in the drawing area to specify the first point of the line. After defining the first point, the prompt, "Specify next point or [Undo]:" appears. Now, you need to determine the next end of the line. It is recommended that you should always have a look at the command line to know the next step while executing a command.

Status Bar

Status Bar is located at the bottom of the AutoCAD window. It contains many buttons which help you to create a drawing very easily. You can turn ON or OFF these buttons just by clicking on them. Some buttons are hidden by default. You can display more buttons on the status bar by clicking the **Customization** button at the bottom right corner and selecting the options from the menu. The buttons available on the status bar are briefly discussed in the following section.

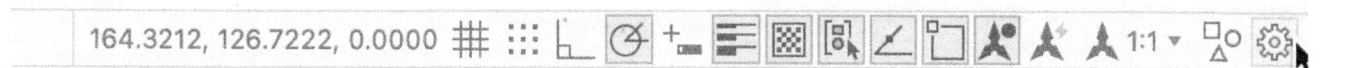

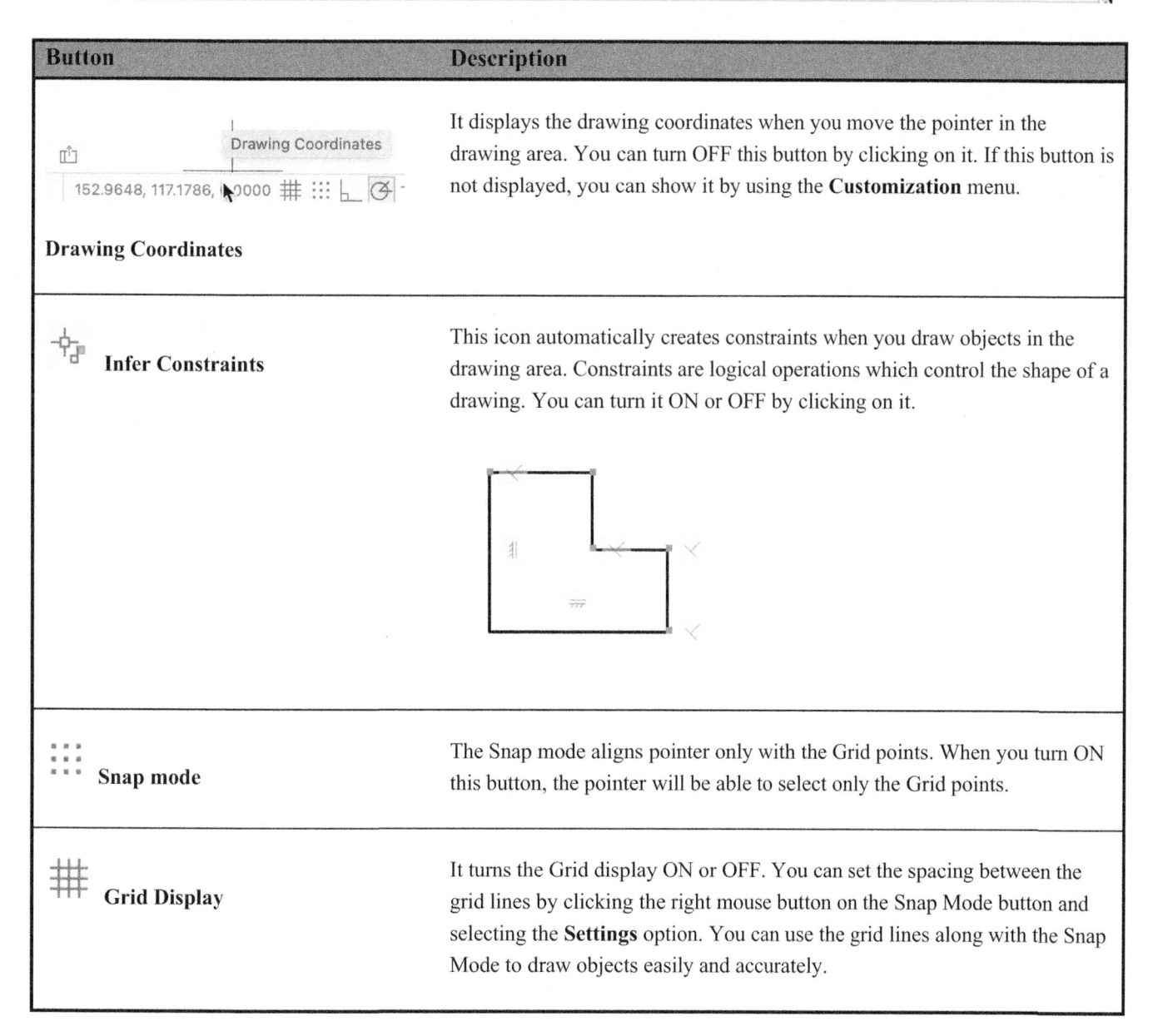

Button	Description
Drawing Coordinates	It displays the drawing coordinates when you move the pointer in the drawing area. You can turn OFF this button by clicking on it. If this button is not displayed, you can show it by using the **Customization** menu.
Infer Constraints	This icon automatically creates constraints when you draw objects in the drawing area. Constraints are logical operations which control the shape of a drawing. You can turn it ON or OFF by clicking on it.
Snap mode	The Snap mode aligns pointer only with the Grid points. When you turn ON this button, the pointer will be able to select only the Grid points.
Grid Display	It turns the Grid display ON or OFF. You can set the spacing between the grid lines by clicking the right mouse button on the Snap Mode button and selecting the **Settings** option. You can use the grid lines along with the Snap Mode to draw objects easily and accurately.

⌐	**Ortho Mode**	It turns the Ortho Mode ON or OFF. When the Ortho Mode is ON, only horizontal or vertical lines can be drawn.
⌀	**Polar Tracking**	This icon turns ON or OFF the Polar Tracking. When the Polar Tracking is turned ON, you can draw lines easily at regular angular increments, such as 5, 10, 15, 23, 30, 45, or 90 degrees. You will notice that a trace line is displayed when the pointer is at a particular angular increment. You can set the angular increment by clicking the down arrow next to this button and selecting the required angle.
		Polar: 8.4848 < 60°
⌁	**Object Snap**	This icon turns ON or OFF the Object Snap mode. When this mode is turned ON, you can easily select the key points of objects such as endpoints, midpoint, and center point and so on.
		Midpoint / Endpoint
⌂	**3D Object Snap**	This icon turns ON or OFF the 3D Object Snap. The 3D Object Snap is used to select the key points of 3D objects.
∠	**Object Snap Tracking**	This icon is used to turn ON or OFF the Object Snap Tracking mode. When this mode is turned ON, you can easily select points by using the trace lines originating from the key points.

AutoCAD 2023 For Beginners (For Mac Users)

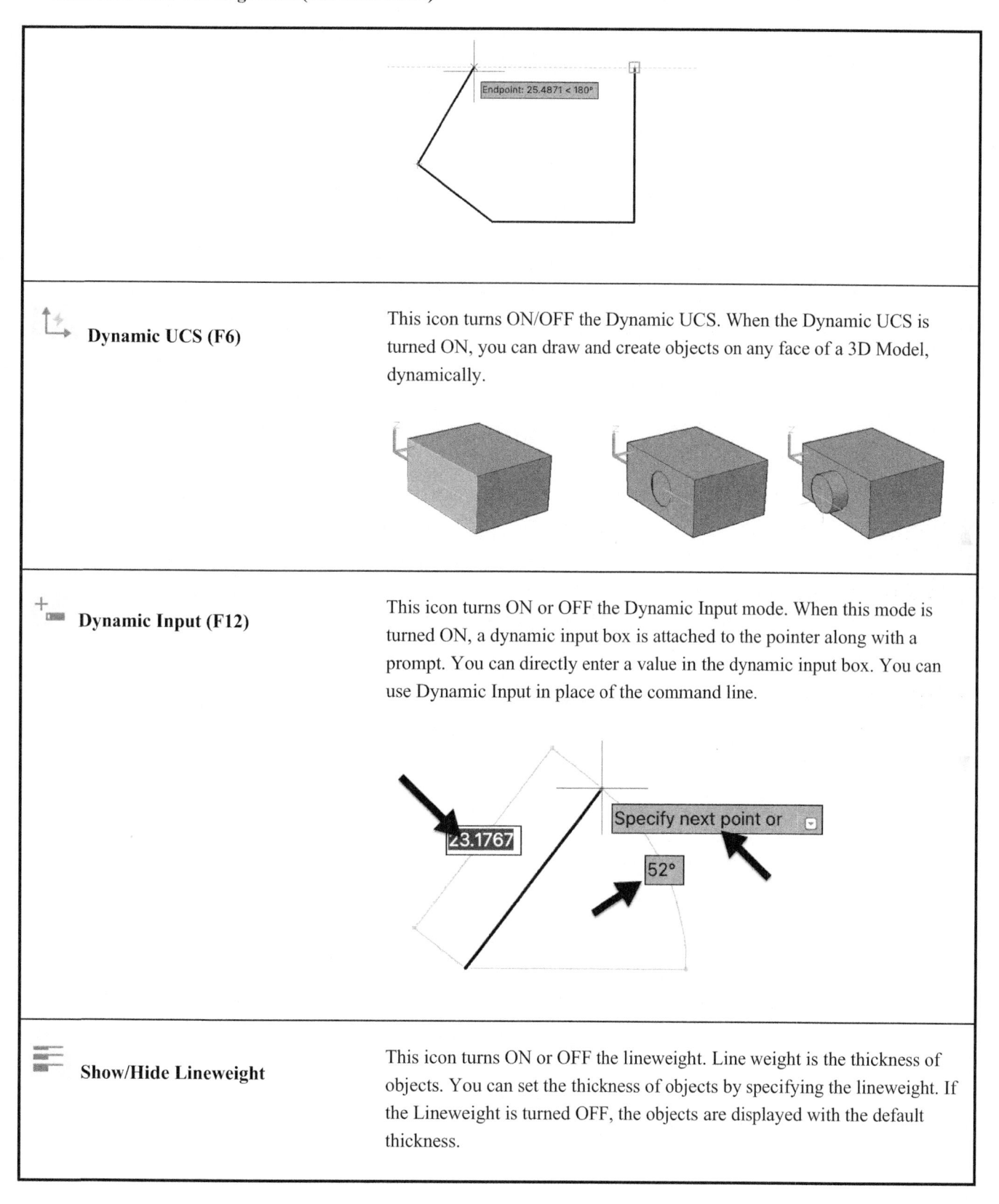

	Dynamic UCS (F6)	This icon turns ON/OFF the Dynamic UCS. When the Dynamic UCS is turned ON, you can draw and create objects on any face of a 3D Model, dynamically.
	Dynamic Input (F12)	This icon turns ON or OFF the Dynamic Input mode. When this mode is turned ON, a dynamic input box is attached to the pointer along with a prompt. You can directly enter a value in the dynamic input box. You can use Dynamic Input in place of the command line.
	Show/Hide Lineweight	This icon turns ON or OFF the lineweight. Line weight is the thickness of objects. You can set the thickness of objects by specifying the lineweight. If the Lineweight is turned OFF, the objects are displayed with the default thickness.

11 | Introduction to AutoCAD 2023

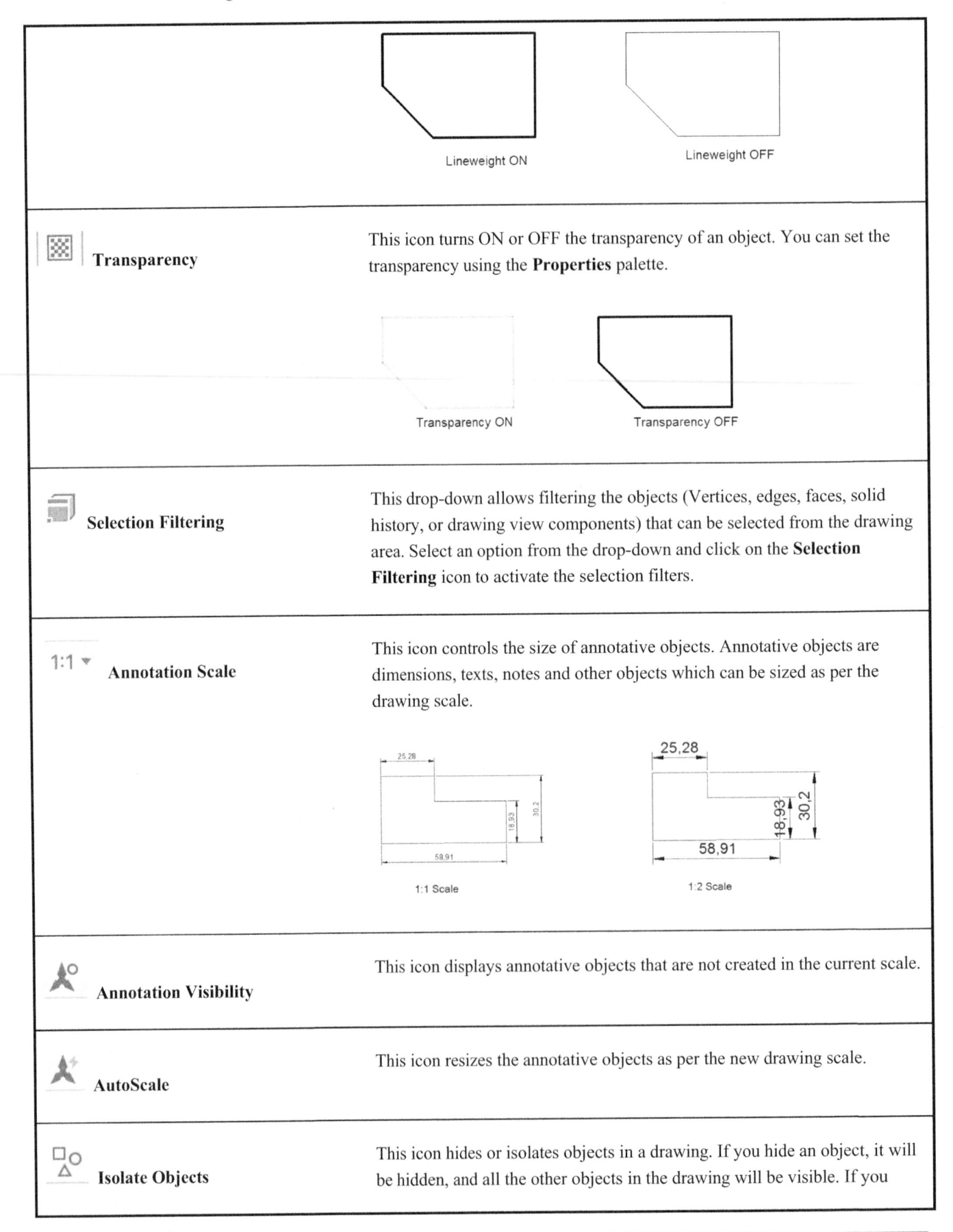

		Lineweight ON Lineweight OFF
	Transparency	This icon turns ON or OFF the transparency of an object. You can set the transparency using the **Properties** palette. Transparency ON Transparency OFF
	Selection Filtering	This drop-down allows filtering the objects (Vertices, edges, faces, solid history, or drawing view components) that can be selected from the drawing area. Select an option from the drop-down and click on the **Selection Filtering** icon to activate the selection filters.
1:1 ▼	**Annotation Scale**	This icon controls the size of annotative objects. Annotative objects are dimensions, texts, notes and other objects which can be sized as per the drawing scale. 1:1 Scale 1:2 Scale
	Annotation Visibility	This icon displays annotative objects that are not created in the current scale.
	AutoScale	This icon resizes the annotative objects as per the new drawing scale.
	Isolate Objects	This icon hides or isolates objects in a drawing. If you hide an object, it will be hidden, and all the other objects in the drawing will be visible. If you

Introduction to AutoCAD 2023

> isolate an object, the other objects in the drawing will be hidden, and the selected object will be visible.

Menu Bar

The Menu Bar is located at the top of the window just below the title bar. It contains various menus such as File, Edit, View, Insert, Format, Tools, Draw, Dimensions, Modify, and so on. Clicking on any of the words on the Menu Bar displays a menu. The menu contains various tools and options. There are also sub-options available on the list. These sub-options are displayed if you click on an option with an arrow. If you click on an option with (…), a dialog will appear.

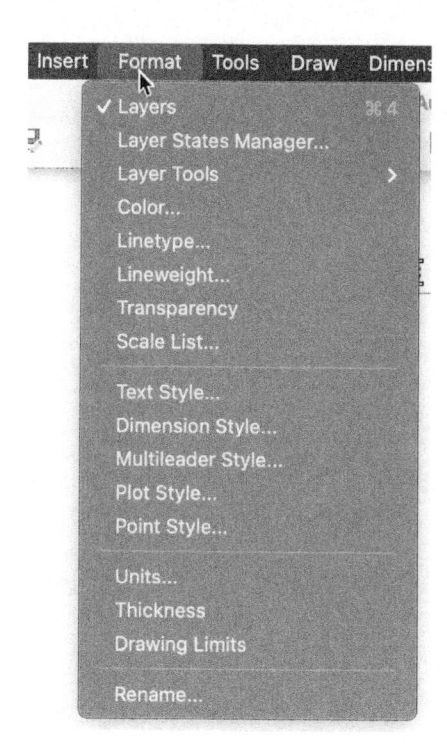

Changing the display of the Tool set

You can change the presentation of the tool set by clicking the arrow button located at the top of it. The tool set can be displayed in two different modes, as shown below.

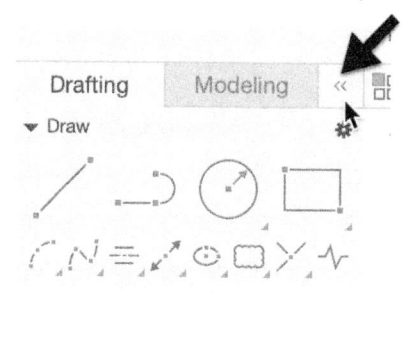

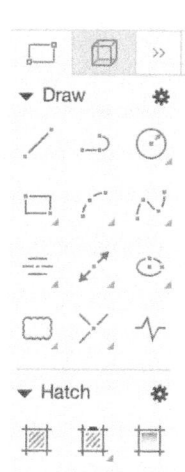

AutoCAD 2023 For Beginners (For Mac Users)

Dialogs and Palettes

Dialogs and Palettes are part of the AutoCAD user interface. Using a dialog or a palette, you can easily specify many settings and options at a time. Examples of dialogs and palettes are as shown below.

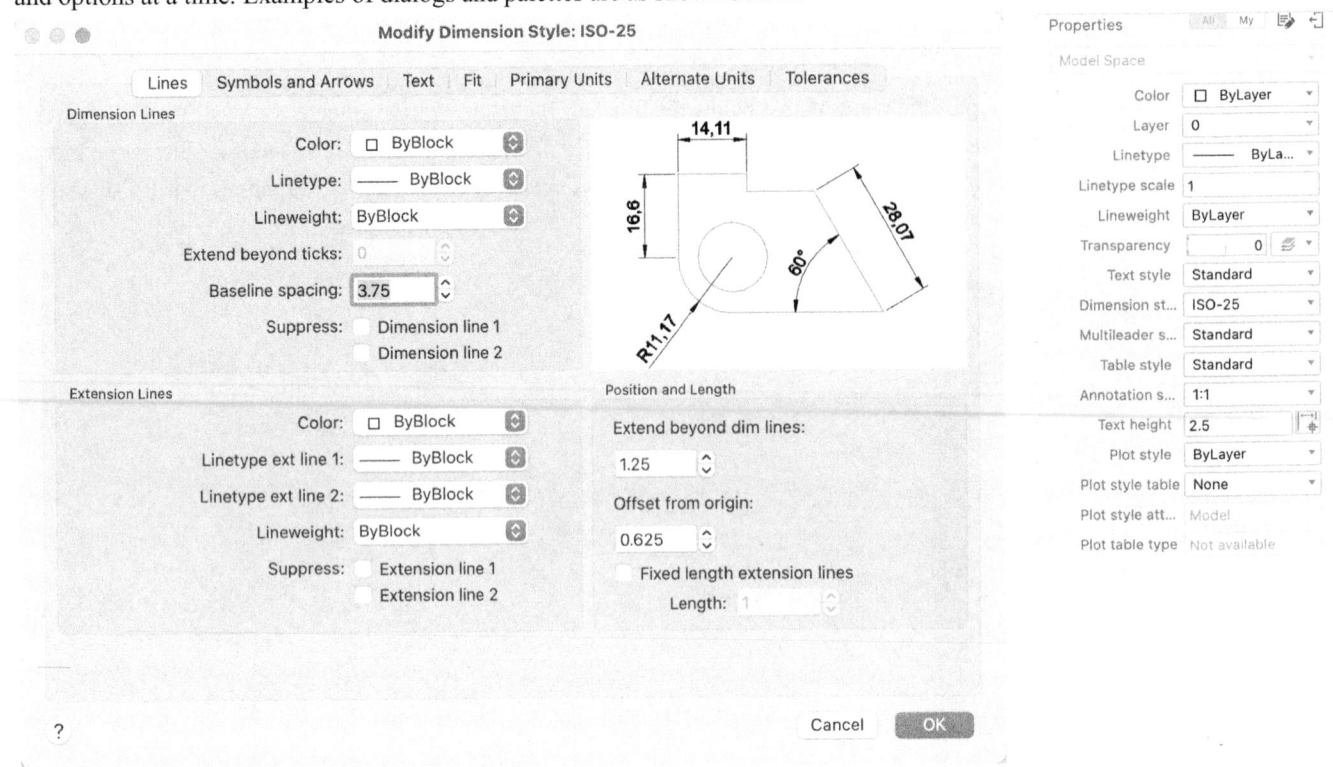

Shortcut Menus

Shortcut Menus appear when you right-click in the graphics window. AutoCAD provides various shortcut menus to help you access tools and options very easily and quickly. There are multiple types of shortcut menus available in AutoCAD. Some of them are discussed next.

Right-click Menu

This shortcut menu appears whenever you right-click in the graphics window without activating any command or selecting an object.

Select and Right-click menu

This shortcut menu appears when you select an object from the graphics window and right-click. It consists of editing and selection options.

Command Mode shortcut menu

This shortcut menu appears when you activate a command and right-click. It shows options depending upon the active command. The shortcut menu below shows the options related to the RECTANGLE command.

---

14 | Introduction to AutoCAD 2023

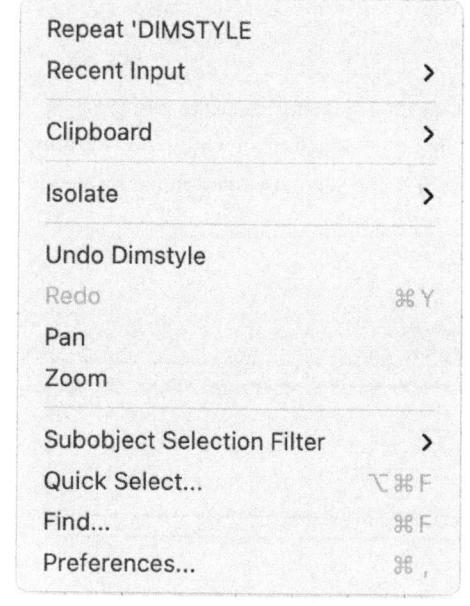

AutoCAD 2023 For Beginners (For Mac Users)

Right-click menu	Select and right-click menu	Command mode Shortcut menu
Repeat 'DIMSTYLE Recent Input > Clipboard > Isolate > Undo Dimstyle Redo ⌘Y Pan Zoom Subobject Selection Filter > Quick Select... ⌥⌘F Find... ⌘F Preferences... ⌘,	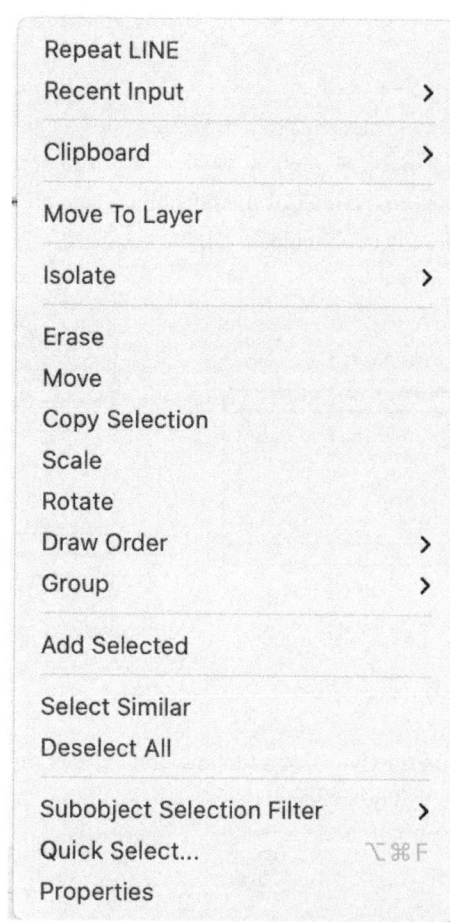 Repeat LINE Recent Input > Clipboard > Move To Layer Isolate > Erase Move Copy Selection Scale Rotate Draw Order > Group > Add Selected Select Similar Deselect All Subobject Selection Filter > Quick Select... ⌥⌘F Properties	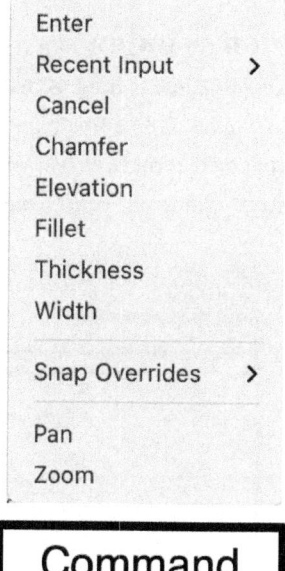 Enter Recent Input > Cancel Chamfer Elevation Fillet Thickness Width Snap Overrides > Pan Zoom

Grip shortcut menu

This shortcut menu is displayed when you select a grip of an object, move the pointer and right-click. It shows various operations that can be performed using grips.

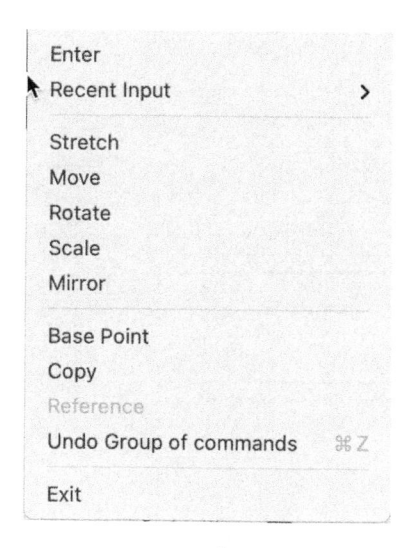

```
Enter
Recent Input            >
Stretch
Move
Rotate
Scale
Mirror
Base Point
Copy
Reference
Undo Group of commands  ⌘Z
Exit
```

15 | Introduction to AutoCAD 2023

Selection Window

A selection window is used to select multiple elements of a drawing. You can select various elements by using two types of selection windows. The first type is a rectangular selection window. You can create this type of selection window by defining its two diagonal corners. When you set the first corner of the selection window on the left and second corner on the right side, the elements which fall entirely under the selection window will be selected.

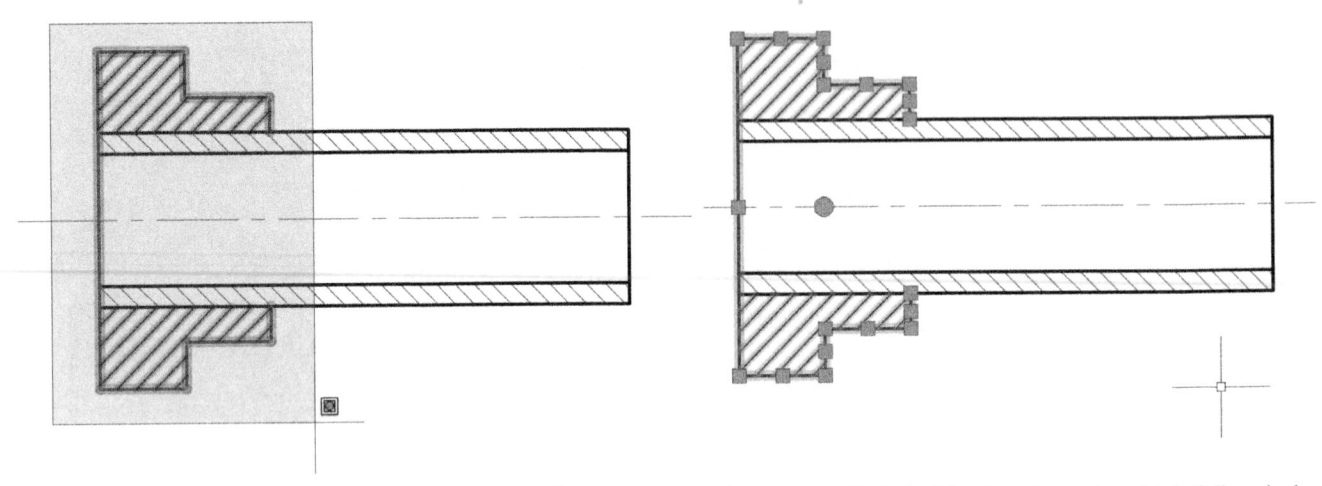

However, if you define the first corner on the right side and the second corner on the left side, the elements, which fall entirely or partially under the selection window, will be selected.

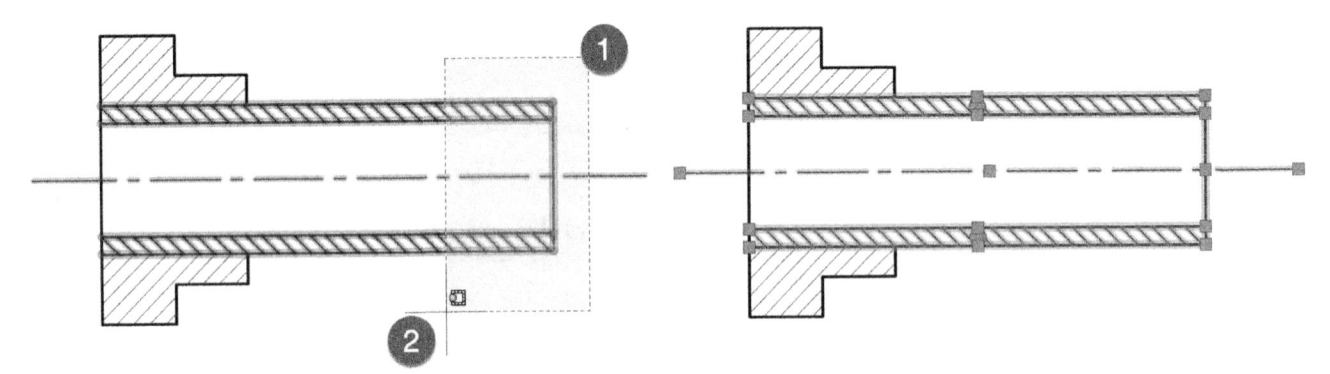

The second type of selection window is Lasso. Lasso is an irregular shape created by holding the left mouse button and dragging the pointer across the elements to select. If you drag the pointer from left to right, the elements falling entirely under the lasso will be selected.

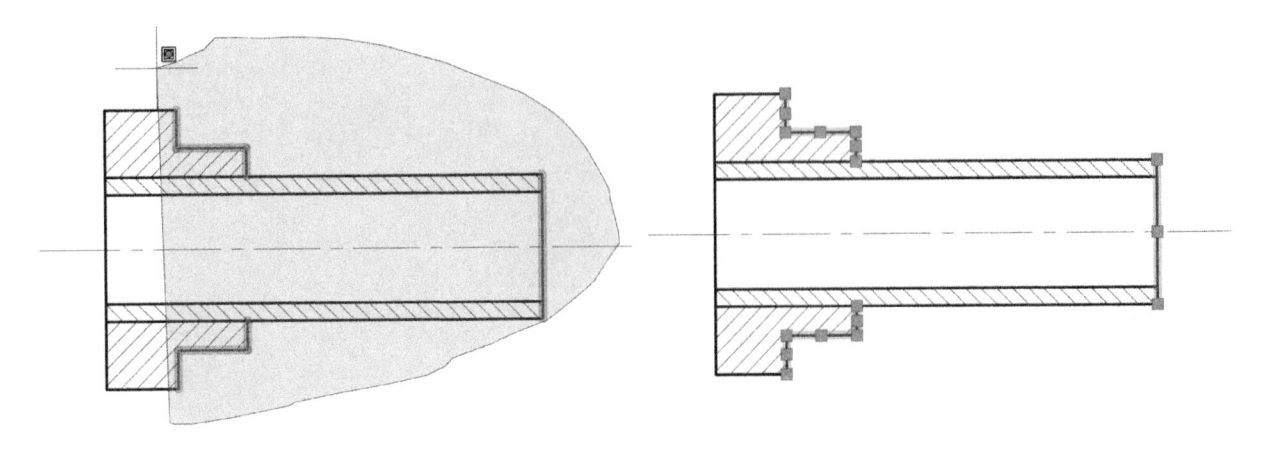

16 | Introduction to AutoCAD 2023

If you drag the pointer from right to left, the elements which fall wholly or partially under the lasso will be selected.

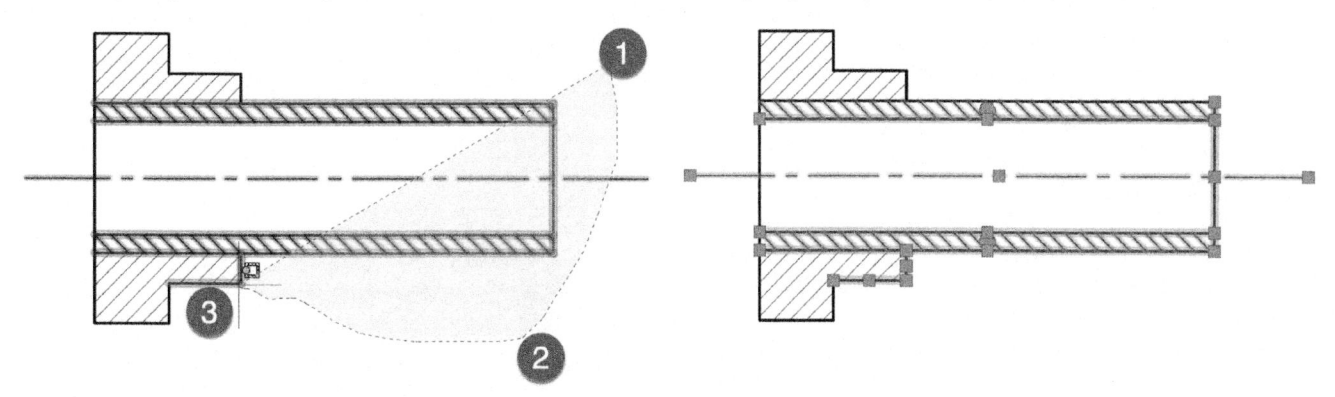

In AutoCAD, you can specify the first corner of the selection window at one portion of a large drawing. Next, zoom and pan to the rest of the drawing, and then specify the second corner of the selection window. By doing so, you can select the portion of the drawing, which is currently not visible on the screen.

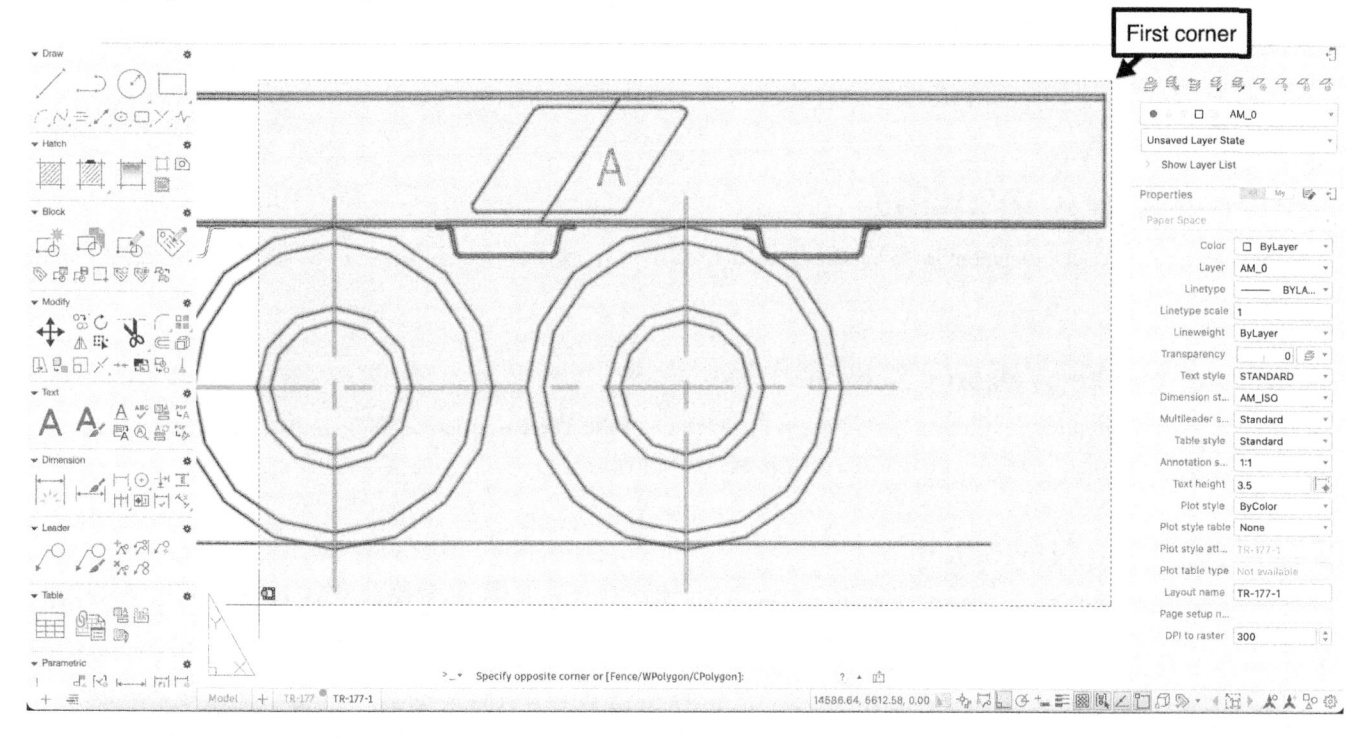

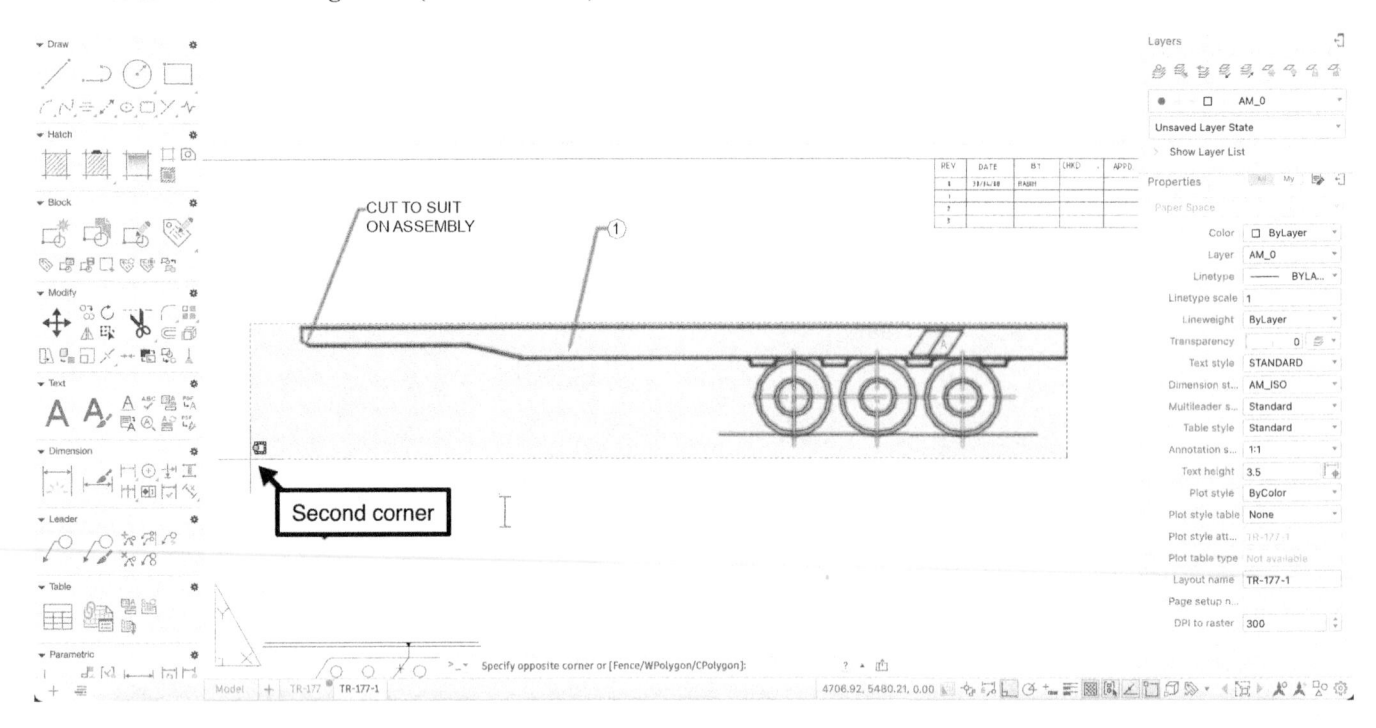

Starting a new drawing

You can start an AutoCAD document by using the templates available on the Welcome screen or by using the **Select template** dialog.

Templates on the Welcome Screen

To start a new drawing, click the **Create** tab > **New** at the left side of the **Welcome** screen. Next, select the acadiso.dwt template from the template list to start a new drawing in the ISO format.

The Select Template dialog

To start a new drawing using the **Select Template** dialog, click the **New** button on the Toolbar (or) click **File > New Drawing** on the Menu bar.

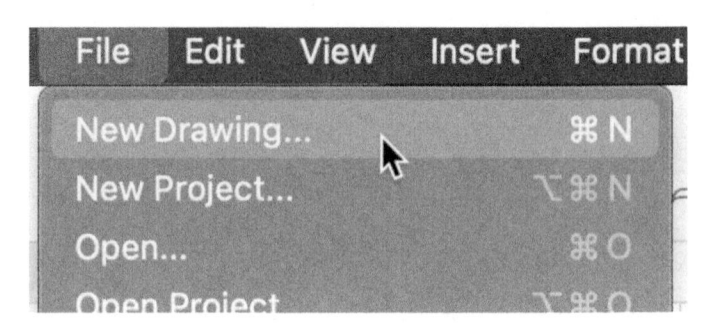

On the **Select Template** dialog, select the **acad.dwt** (inch units) or **acadiso.dwt** (metric units) template for creating a 2D drawing. Select the **acad3D.dwt** or **acadiso3D.dwt** template for creating 3D models.

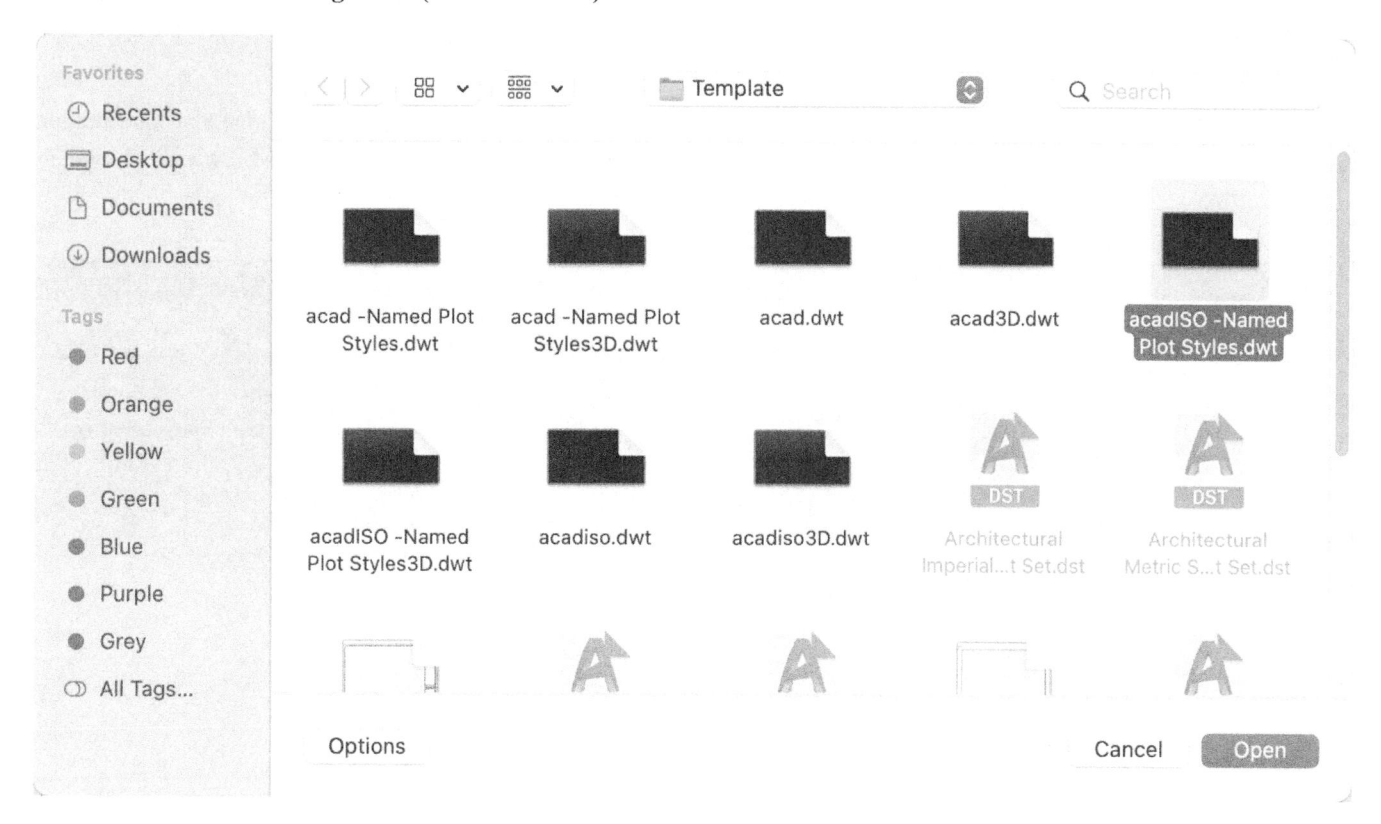

Opening an existing drawing file

If you open an existing drawing file, first start the AutoCAD application. Next, click the Open Files or Project tab on the Welcome window. However, if you already have a drawing file opened but you want to open another file, then click the **Open** button on the Toolbar (or) click **File > Open** on the Menu bar. Next, browse the desired location and double-click on the drawing file. You can also search the drawing file by typing its name in the Search box available at the top-right corner of the dialog.

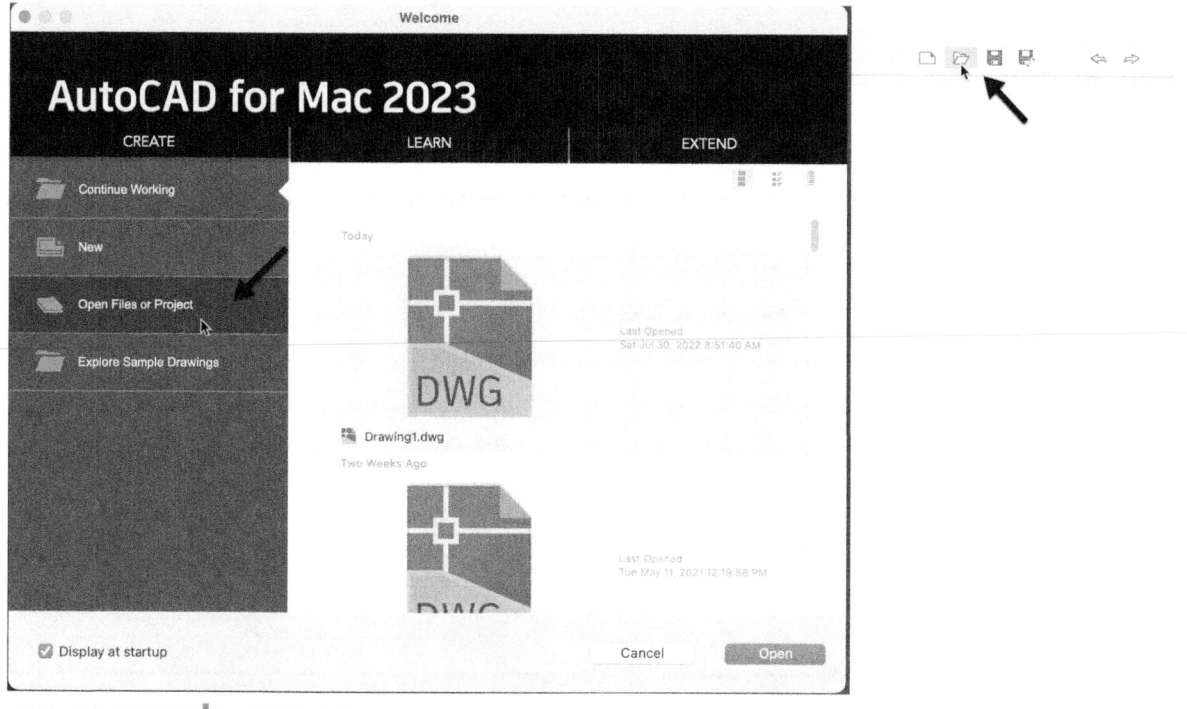

Help

Press F1 to get help for any topic. You can also click the **Help** option on the Menu bar and type-in the name of a command or option. Next, place the cursor on anyone of the search results; the selected search result is highlighted in the menu bar with an arrow.

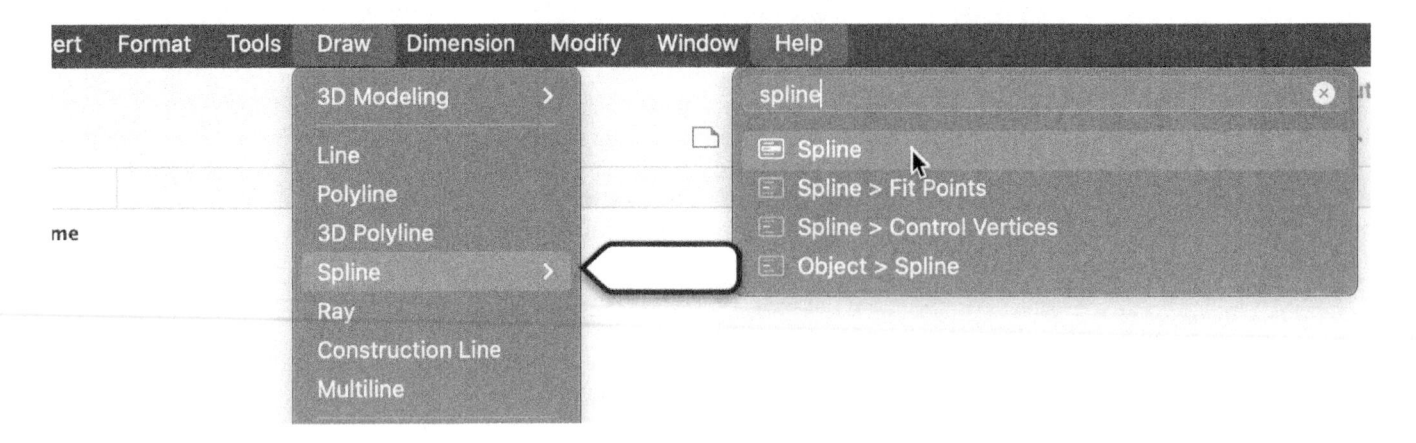

Command List

Various commands in AutoCAD are given in the table below:

Command	Alias	Description
APPLOAD		This command activates the **Load/Unload Applications** dialog.
ALIGN	AL	It is used to align objects with other objects.
ARC	A	It is used to create an arc.
AREA		This command displays the area of a selected closed object.
ARRAY	AR	Creates Rectangular, Path, or Polar 2D arrays.
ATTDEF	ATT	It displays the **Attribute Definition** dialog.
ATTEDIT	ATE	It is used to edit Attributes.
AUDIT		It is used to check and fix errors.

Introduction to AutoCAD 2023

AUTOCONSTRAIN		It is used to apply constraints automatically.
AUTOPUBLISH		It is used to create a DWF file.
BACTION	**AC**	It is used to add an action to a dynamic block. This command is available in Block Editor.
BLOCK		It is used to create a block.
BMAKE	**B**	It is used to create a block.
BMPOUT		It is used to create a Raster image out of the drawing.
BOUNDARY	**BO**	It is used to create a hatch boundary.
BREAK	**BR**	It is used to break an object.
CAL		It is used to calculate mathematical expressions.
CHAMFER	**CHA**	It is used to create chamfers.
CHPROP		This command changes the properties of a selected object.
CIRCLE	**C**	It is used to create a circle.
COLOR	**COL**	This command displays the **Color Palette** dialog.
COPY	**CO**	It is used to copy objects inside a drawing.
COPYCLIP		It is used to copy objects from one drawing to another.
CUSTOMIZE		It is used to customize the commands, menus, aliases, and shortcuts.

DDEDIT	**ED**	It is used to edit a note or annotation.
DIMSTYLE	**D**	It is used to create or modify a dimension style.
DDMODIFY		Displays the Properties palette.
DELCONSTRAINT		It is used to delete constraints.
OSNAP	**OS**	It is used to set the **Object Snap** settings.
DDPTYPE		It is used to set the point style and size.
VIEW	**V**	It is used to save views by names.
DIMCONSTRAINT	**DCON**	It is used to apply dimensional constraints to objects.
DIMLINEAR	**DLI**	It is used to create a linear dimension.
DIMALIGNED	**DAL**	It is used to create an aligned dimension.
DIMARC	**DAR**	It is used to dimension the arc length.
DIMRADIUS	**DIMRAD**	It is used to create a radial dimension.
DIMJOGGED	**JOG**	It is used to create a jogged dimension.
DIMDIAMETER	**DIMDIA**	It is used to create a diameter dimension.
DIMANGULAR	**DAN**	It is used to create an angular dimension.
DIMORDINATE	**DOR**	It is used to create an ordinate dimension.

DIMCONTINUE	**DIMCONT**	It is used to create continuous dimensions from an existing one.
DIMBASELINE	**DIMBASE**	It is used to create baseline dimensions.
DIMINSPECT		It is used to create an inspection dimension.
-DIMSTYLE		Update a dimension according to the current dimension style.
DIMSPACE		It is used to adjust the space between dimensions.
DIMBREAK		It is used to break the extension line of a dimension when it intersects with another dimension.
DIMOVERRIDE		It is used to override the system variables of a selected dimension.
DIMCENTER		It is used to create a center mark of a circle.
DIMEDIT	**DIMED**	It is used to edit a dimension.
DIMTEDIT	**DIMTED**	It is used to edit the dimension text.
DIMDISASSOCIATE		This command disassociates a dimension from the object.
DIST	**DI**	It is used to measure the distance between two points.
DISTANTLIGHT		It is used to create a distant light.
DIVIDE	**DIV**	Places evenly spaced objects on a line segment
DONUT	**DO**	It is used to create a donut.

DVIEW		It is used to get the aerial view of a drawing.
DXBIN		It is used to open a DXB file.
DXFIN		It is used to open a DXF file.
DXFOUT		It is used to save a file in the DXF format.
ELLIPSE	EL	It is used to create an ellipse.
ERASE	E	It is used to erase objects.
EXIT		It is used to close AutoCAD.
EXPLODE	X	It is used to explode or ungroup objects.
EXPORT	EXP	It is used to export data.
EXTEND	EX	It is used to extend an object up to another.
FILLET	F	It is used to create a fillet at the corner.
GEOMCONSTRAINT	GCON	It is used to apply geometric constraints.
GRADIENT		It is used to apply the gradient to a closed area.
GROUP	G	It is used to group objects.
HATCH	H	It is used to apply hatch to a closed area.
HATCHEDIT	HE	It is used to edit hatch.

HELP		Display the Help window.
HIDE	HI	This command changes the Visual Style to Hidden.
ID		This command displays the coordinate values of a selected point.
IMAGE, IMAGEATTACH	IM	It is used to attach an Image reference.
IMAGEADJUST	IAD	It is used to adjust images.
IMAGECLIP		It is used to crop an image.
IMPORT	IMP	It is used to import other forms of CAD data.
INSERT	I	It is used to insert a block.
ISOPLANE		It is used to set the current isometric plane.
JOIN	J	It is used to join the endpoints of two linear or curved objects.
LAYCUR		The Layer of the selected objects will be made current.
LAYER	LA	It is used to create a new layer and modify its properties.
LAYFRZ		It is used to freeze the layer of a selected object.
LAYISO		This command isolates the layer of a selected object.
LAYOUT		It is used to modify layouts.
LAYOFF		It is used to turn off the layer of a selected object.

LAYON		It is used to turn ON all the layers.
LENGTHEN	LEN	It is used to increase the length of an object.
LIMITS		It is used to set the drawing limits.
LIMMAX		It is used to set the maximum limit of a drawing.
LINE	L	It is used to create a line.
LINETYPE	LT	It is used to set the line type.
LIST	LI	This command lists the properties of a selected object in the text window.
LOAD		This command imports the shapes that can be used by the SHAPE command.
LTSCALE	LTS	It is used to set the linetype scale.
MEASURE	ME	It is used to place points or blocks at regular intervals on an object.
MIRROR	MI	It is used to create a mirror image of an object.
MLEDIT		It is used to edit a multiline.
MLINE	ML	It is used to create multiple parallel lines.
MOVE	M	It is used to move selected objects.
MSPACE	MS	I used to switch from paper space to model space.

MTEXT	MT or T	It is used to write text in multiple lines.
MVIEW	MV	It is used to create and modify viewports.
MVSETUP		It is used to set drawing specifications for printing purposes.
NEW	COMMAND+N	It is used to open a new file.
OFFSET	O	This command creates a parallel copy of a selected object at a specified distance.
OOPS		It is used to undo the ERASE command.
OPEN		It is used to open an existing file.
OPTIONS	OP	It is used to set various options related to the drawing.
ORTHO		This command turns ON/OFF the Ortho Mode.
OSNAP	OS	It is used to change the **Object Snap** settings.
PAGESETUP		It is used to specify the printing properties of a layout.
PAN	P	It is used to drag a drawing to view its different portions.
PARAMETER	PAR	It is used to assign expressions to a dimensional constraint.
PEDIT	PE	It is used to edit polylines.
PLINE	PL	It is used to create a polyline. A polyline is a single object which can have continuous lines and arcs.
PLOT	CONTROL+P	It is used to plot a drawing.

POINT	PO	It is used to place a point in the drawing.
POLYGON	POL	It is used to create a polygon.
PREVIEW	PRE	It is used to preview the plotted drawing.
PROPERTIES	PR	Displays the **Properties** palette.
PSOUT		It is used to create a postscript file.
PURGE	PU	It is used to remove unwanted data from the drawing.
QDIM		It is used to create a quick dimension.
QSAVE		It is used to save the current drawing.
QUIT		It is used to close the current drawing session.
RAY		It is used to create a line that starts from a selected point and extends up to infinity.
RECOVER		It is used to repair and open the damaged files.
RECTANG		It is used to create a polyline rectangle.
REDEFINE		It is used to restore an AutoCAD command, which has been overridden.
REDRAW	R	Refreshes the current viewport.
UNDEFINE		It is used to override an existing command with a new one.
REDO		It is used to cancel the previous UNDO command.

REDRAWALL	**RA**	This command refreshes all the viewports in a drawing.
REGEN	**RE**	This command regenerates the current viewport of a drawing.
REGENALL	**REA**	This command regenerates all the viewports of a drawing.
REGION	**REG**	This command converts the area enclosed by objects into a region.
RENAME	**REN**	It is used to rename blocks, viewports, and dimension styles.
REVCLOUD		It is used to highlight a portion of drawing by creating a cloud around it.
TOOLSETS		This command displays the tool set.
TOOLSETSCLOSE		This command hides the tool set.
SAVE	**COMMAND+S**	This command saves the currently opened drawing.
SAVEAS		This command saves the drawing with another name and location.
SCALE	**SC**	It is used to increase or decrease the size of a drawing.
SCRIPT	**SCR**	It is used to load a script file. A script is used to run various commands sequentially.
SETVAR	**SET**	It is used to list or change a system variable.
SHAPE		It is used to insert a shape into a drawing.
SHELL		It is used to enter SHELL OS commands.

SKETCH		It is used to draw freehand sketches.
SOLID	**SO**	It is used to create filled triangles or quadrilaterals.
SPELL	**SP**	It is used to check the spelling of a text.
SPLINE	**SPL**	It is used to create a spline (curved object).
SPLINEDIT	**SPE**	It is used to edit a spline.
STATUS		It is used to display the details of a drawing, such as limits, model space usage, and layers.
STRETCH	**S**	It is used to stretch objects.
STYLE	**ST**	It is used to create or modify the text style.
TEXT		It is used to enter text in the drawing.
THICKNESS	**TH**	It is used to set a thickness value to 2D objects.
TOLERANCE		It is used to apply geometric tolerances to the drawing.
TOOLBAR		It is used to display the toolbar.
TOOLBARCLOSE		It is used to hide the toolbar.
TRIM	**TR**	It is used to trim unwanted portions of an object.
UCS		It is used to specify the location of the user coordinate system.
UNDO	**CONTROL+Z**	It is used to undo the last operation.

UNITS	UN	Set the units of the drawing
VIEW		It is used to save and restore the model space, layout, and preset views.
VPLAYER		It is used to control layer visibility in paper space.
VPORTS		It is used to create multiple viewports in model space of paper space.
WBLOCK	W	It is used to convert objects or entire drawing into block.
WIPEOUT		It is used to wipe out a portion of the drawing.
XATTACH	XA	It is used to attach a drawing as an external reference.
XLINE	XL	It is used to create construction lines. Construction lines extend to infinity and help in drawing objects.
XREF	XR	It is used to attach a drawing as an external reference.
ZOOM	Z	It is used to Zoom in or out of a drawing.

3D Commands

Command	Shortcut	Description
3DARRAY	3A	It is used to create three-dimensional arrays of an object.
3DALIGN	3AL	It is used to align 3D objects.
3DFACE	3F	It is used to create a three or four-sided 3D surface.

3DMESH		It is used to create a freeform 3D mesh.
3DCORBIT		It is used to rotate a view in the 3D space with continuous motion.
3DDISTANCE		It is used to control the distance.
3DEDITBAR		It is used to add and edit control vertices on a NURBS surface or spline.
3DFLY		It is used to view the 3D model as if you are flying through.
3DFORBIT		It is used to rotate a view in 3D space freely.
3DMOVE	3M	It is used to move the objects in 3D space.
3DORBIT	3DO	It is used to rotate the view constrained along the horizontal or vertical axis.
3DORBITCTR		It is used to set the center for rotating the view in 3D space.
3DPAN		It is used to pan the 3D models horizontally or vertically. This is used when working in perspective view.
3DPOLY	3P	It is used to create a 3D polyline.
3DPRINT	3DP	It is used to print the model in 3D (plastic prototype).
3DROTATE		It is used to rotate 3D objects in 3D space.
3DSCALE	3S	It is used to increase or decrease the size of a 3D object along the X, Y, Z directions.

3DWALK		It is used to view the 3D model as if you are walking through it.
BOX		It is used to create a 3D box.
CONE		It is used to create a 3D cone.
CONVTONURBS		It is used to convert a surface to NURBS. You can easily edit a NURBS by using control vertices displayed on it.
CONVTOSOLID		It is used to convert 3D meshes, polylines, and circles to 3D solids.
CONVTOSURFACE		It is used to convert objects to surfaces.
CVADD		It is used to add control vertices to a NURBS surface or spline.
CVREMOVE		It is used to remove control vertices from a NURBS surface or spline.
CVHIDE		It is used to hide the control vertices of a NURBS surface or splines,
CVSHOW		It is used to display the control vertices of a NURBS surface or splines.
CVREBUILD		It is used to rebuild the control vertices of a NURBS surface.
CYLINDER		It is used to create a Cylinder.
EDGESURF		It is used to create a mesh surface from four adjacent edges.
EXTRUDE	EXT	It is used to extrude a closed region or polyline.

FILLETEDGE		It is used to blend an edge of a 3D object.
FLATSHOT		It is used to create a 2D representation of a 3D model.
FREEPOINT		It is used to create point light that emits light in all directions.
FREESPOT		It is used to create a spotlight without any target.
HELIX		It is used to create a helical or spiral curve.
INTERFERE		It is used to create a 3D solid at the interference point of the various solid objects.
INTERSECT	IN	It is used to create a 3D solid at the intersection portion of solid.
LIGHT		It is used to create a light.
LOFT		It is used to create a 3D solid or surface between various cross-sections.
MATERIALS		This command displays the Material Browser.
MATERIALASSIGN		It is used to assign a material to the model.
MESH		It is used to create 3D mesh objects.
MESHREFINE		It is used to refine the mesh of 3D mesh objects.
MESHSMOOTH		It is used to increase the smoothness of mesh objects.
MIRROR3D		It is used to mirror 3D objects in 3D space.

OFFSETEDGE		It is used to create a parallel copy of an edge at a specified distance.
PFACE		It is used to create a 3D Polyface mesh by specifying vertices.
PLAN		This command displays the top view of the 3D model.
PLANESURF		It is used to create a planar surface.
POINTLIGHT		It is used to create point light that emits light in all directions.
PRESSPULL		It is used to extrude or subtract material.
PYRAMID		It is used to create a pyramid.
REVOLVE	REV	It is used to create a revolved solid.
REVSURF		It is used to create a revolved surface.
RMAT		This command displays the Material Browser.
SECTION	SEC	It is used to create a section plane in a 3D model.
SLICE	SL	It is used to slice a 3D model.
SOLPROF		Create a profile from a 3D model in the paper space.
SOLIDEDIT		It is used to edit faces and edges of a 3D solid.
SPHERE		It is used to create a sphere.
SPOTLIGHT		It is used to create a spotlight that emits light like a torch.

STLOUT		It is used to export a file to STL format.
SURFBLEND	**BLENDSRF**	It is used to create a continuous blend surface between two surfaces.
SURFEXTEND		It is used to lengthen a surface up to another surface.
SURFEXTRACTCURVE		It is used to create Isoline curves on a surface, solid, or a face in U and V directions.
SURFFILLET		It is used to create a surface fillet between two surfaces.
SURFOFFSET		It is used to create a parallel surface at a specified distance.
SURFNETWORK		It is used to create a surface from various curves in U and V directions.
SURFPATCH		It is used to create a surface using the edges, forming a closed loop.
SURFSCULPT		It is used to create a closed surface by trimming and combining the surfaces that form a region together.
SURFTRIM		It is used to trim portions of a surface at intersections with other surfaces.
SURFUNTRIM		It is used to untrim the trimmed surface.
SWEEP		It is used to create a 3D solid or surface by sweeping a profile along a path.
TABSURF		It is used to create a mesh from a line or curve swept along a straight path

TORUS	**TOR**	It is used to create a torus.
UNION	**UNI**	It is used to combine various solids into one.
VISUALSTYLES		It is used to create and modify visual styles.
VPOINT		It is used to set the viewing direction of the 3D model.
WEDGE	**WE**	It is used to create a wedge shape.
XEDGES		It is used to create a 3D wireframe from a 3D solid.

AutoCAD 2023 For Beginners (For Mac Users)

Chapter 2: Drawing Basics

In this chapter, you will learn to do the following:

- Draw lines, rectangles, circles, ellipses, arcs, polygons, and polylines
- Use the Erase, Undo and Redo tools
- Draw entities using the absolute coordinate points
- Draw objects using the relative coordinate points
- Draw objects using the tracking method

Drawing Basics

This chapter teaches you to create simple drawings. You will create these drawings using the essential drawing tools. These tools include **Line**, **Circle**, **Polyline**, and **Rectangle**, and they are available in the **Draw** panel of the **Drafting** tool set, as shown below. You can also activate these tools by typing them in the command line.

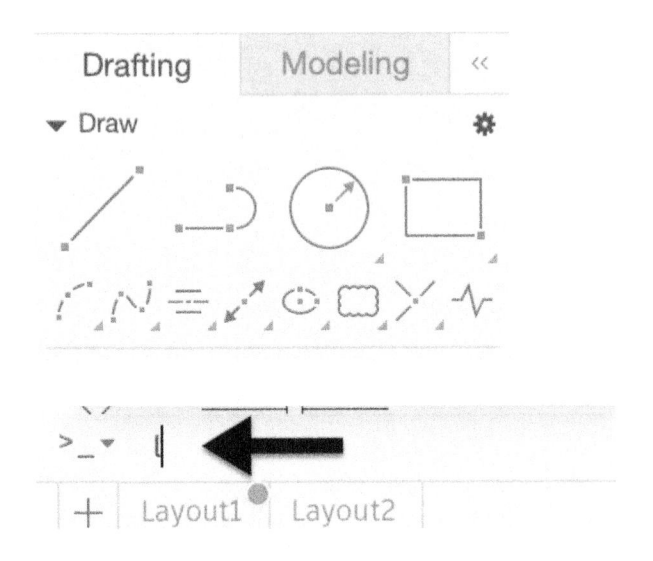

Drawing Lines

You can draw a line by specifying its start point and endpoint using the **Line** tool. However, there are various methods to specify the start and endpoint of a line. These methods are explained in the following examples.

Example 1 (using the Absolute Coordinate System)

In this example, you will create lines by specifying points in the absolute coordinate system. In this system, you specify the points with respect to the origin (0, 0). A point will be defined by entering its X and Y coordinates separated by a comma, as shown in the figure below.

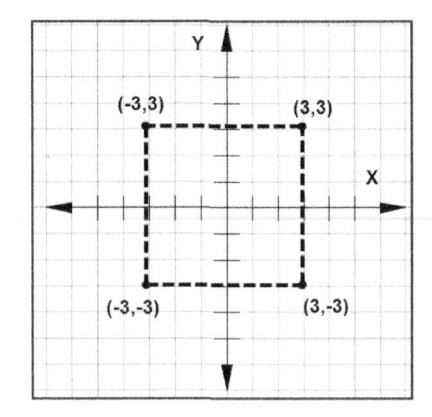

- Start AutoCAD 2023 by clicking the **AutoCAD 2023** icon on the Dock.
- On the Welcome screen, click **Create > New > acadiso.dwt**. This starts a new drawing using the ISO template.

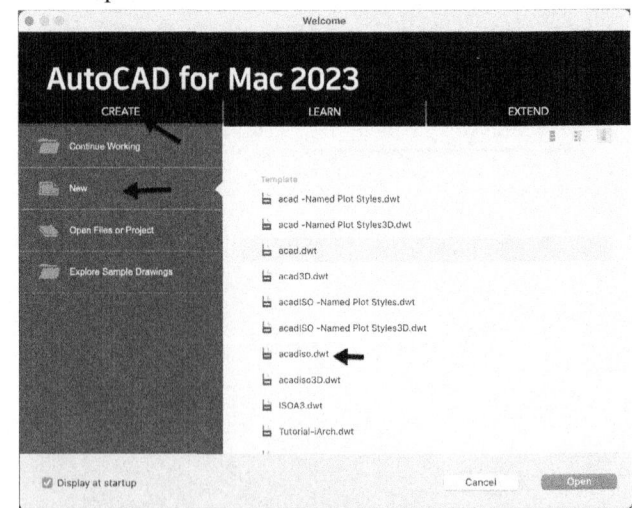

- Type Z in the command line and press RETURN.
- Type A in the command line and press RETURN; the entire area in the graphics window will be displayed.
- Turn OFF the **Grid Display** by pressing the CONTROL+G on your keyboard.
- Click the **Customization** button on the status bar, and then select **Dynamic Input** from the flyout. This displays the **Dynamic Input** icon on the status bar.

38 | Drawing Basics

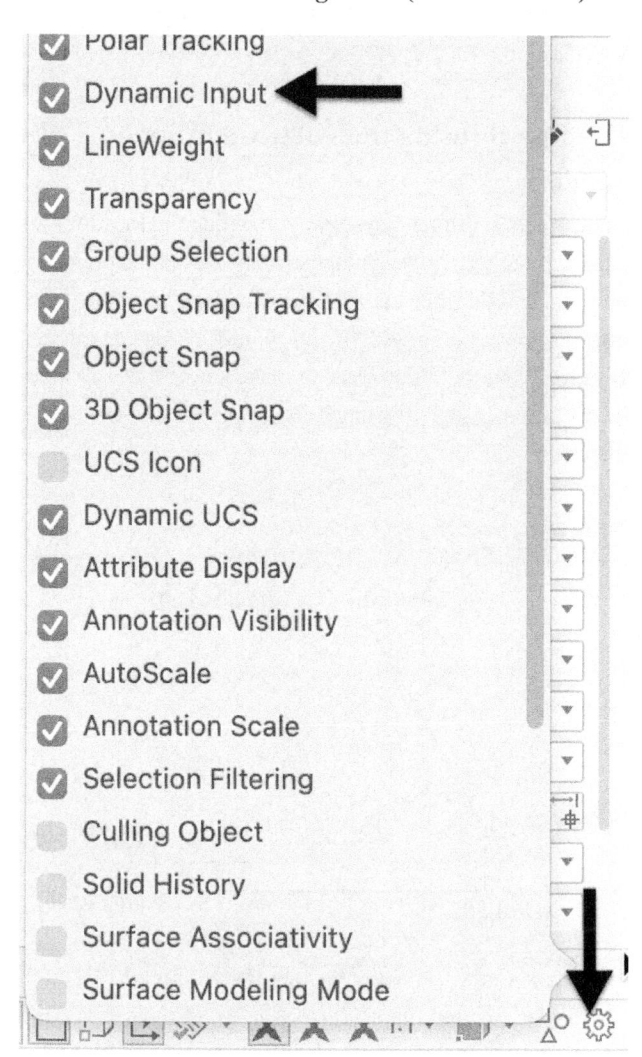

AutoCAD 2023 For Beginners (For Mac Users)

creates a rectangle, as shown below.

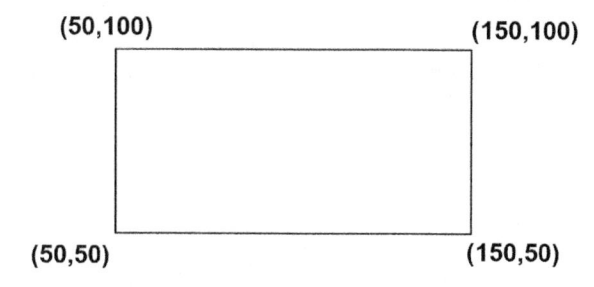

(50,100)   (150,100)

(50,50)   (150,50)

- Click **Save** on the **Toolbar**. 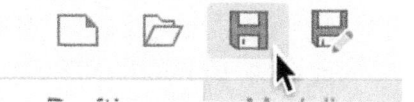
- Browse to a location on your computer using the down arrow next to the **Where** box.
- Type **Line-example1.dwg** in the **Save As** box.
- Click **Save**. 
- Close the file by closing the file tab, as shown.

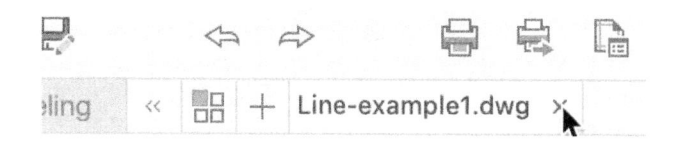

Example 2 (using the Relative Coordinate system)

In this example, you will draw lines by defining its endpoints in the relative coordinate system. In the relative coordinate system, you define the location of a point with respect to the previous point. For this purpose, the symbol, '@' is used before the point coordinates. This symbol means that the coordinate values are defined in relation to the previous point.

- Turn OFF the **Dynamic Input** icon. You will learn about **Dynamic Input** later in this chapter.

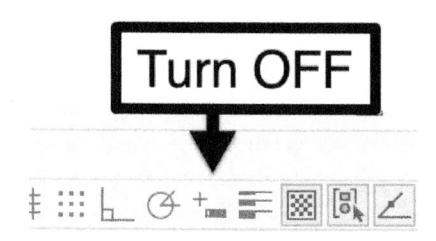

- To draw a line, click **Drafting > Draw > Line** on the tool set, or enter **LINE** or **L** in the command line.
- Type **50, 50**, and press RETURN.
- Type **150, 50**, and press RETURN.
- Type **150,100** and press RETURN.
- Type **50,100** and press RETURN.
- Type **C** in the command line and press RETURN. It

39 | Drawing Basics

(@-50,0) (@0,20)   (@-50,0)   (@0,120)

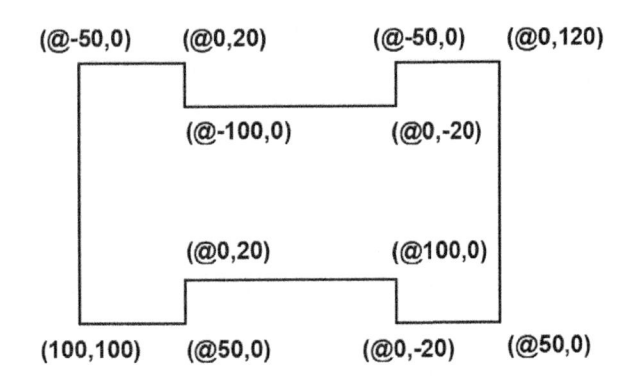

(@-100,0)   (@0,-20)

(@0,20)   (@100,0)

(100,100) (@50,0)   (@0,-20)   (@50,0)

- Click the **AutoCAD 2023** icon on the Dock.
- Click **Create > New** on the **Welcome** screen.
- Select the **acadISO-Named Plot Styles** template.
- Click **Open**.
- Type-in **Z** in the command line.
- Press RETURN to activate the **ZOOM** command.
- Type **A** in the command line. It displays the entire area in the graphics window.
- Turn OFF the **Grid** icon on the status bar.

Turn OFF

- Turn OFF the **Dynamic Input** mode, if active.
- Click **Drafting > Draw > Line** on the tool set, or enter **LINE** or **L** in the command line.
- Type **100,100** and press RETURN. It defines the first point of the line.
- Type **@50,0** and press RETURN.
- Type **@0,20** and press RETURN.
- Type **@100,0** and press RETURN.
- Type **@0,-20** and press RETURN.
- Type **@50,0** and press RETURN.
- Type **@0,120** and press RETURN.
- Type **@-50,0** and press RETURN.
- Type **@0,-20**, and press RETURN.
- Type **@-100,0** and press RETURN.
- Type **@0,20** and press RETURN.
- Type **@-50,0** and press RETURN.
- Type **C** in the command line and press RETURN.
- Save the file as **Line-example2.dwg**.

- Close the file.

Example 3 (using the Polar Coordinate system)

In the polar coordinate system, you define the location of a point by entering two values: distance from the previous point and angle from the zero degrees. You enter the distance value along with the @ symbol and angle value with the < symbol. You have to make a note that AutoCAD measures the angle in the anti-clockwise direction.

Drawing Task

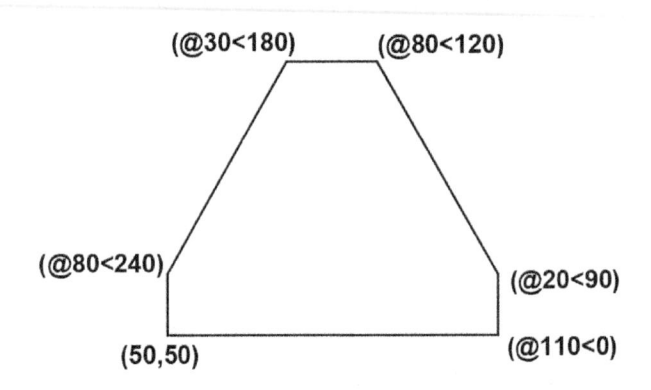

(@30<180)   (@80<120)

(@80<240)   (@20<90)

(50,50)   (@110<0)

- Open a new file using the **acadISO-Named Plot Styles.dwt** template.
- Type Z in the command line and press RETURN.
- Type A in the command line and press RETURN.
- Turn OFF the **Grid Display** icon on the status bar.
- Turn OFF the **Dynamic Input** icon, if active.
- Click **Drafting > Draw > Line** on the tool set, or enter **LINE** or **L** in the command line.
- Type **50,50** and press the RETURN key.
- Type **@110<0** and press RETURN.
- Type **@20<90** and press RETURN.
- Type **@80<120** and press RETURN.
- Type **@30<180** and press RETURN.
- Type **@80<240** and press RETURN.
- Type **C** in the command line and press RETURN.
- Save the file as **Line-example3.dwg**.
- Close the file.

Example 4 (using the Dynamic Input method)

In the dynamic input method, you draw a line by entering its distance and angle values. You use the **Dynamic Input** mode in this method.

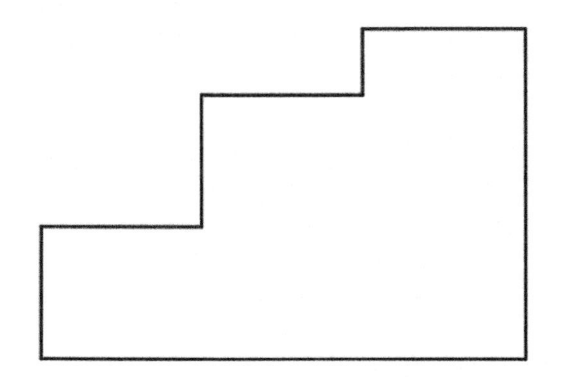

- Open a new file using the **acadISO-Named Plot Styles.dwt** template.
- Turn OFF the **Grid Display**  and **Snap Mode** icons on the Status Bar.
- Type Z and press RETURN.
- Type A and press RETURN.
- Activate the **Dynamic Input** icon on the Status Bar.
- Click **Drafting > Draw > Line** on the tool set, or enter **LINE** or **L** in the command line. 
- Define the first point of the line by typing 50,50 and pressing RETURN.
- Move the pointer horizontally toward right and type in 150 in the length box.
- Press the TAB key and type 0 as the angle. Next, press RETURN.
- Move the pointer vertically upwards and type-in 100 as length. 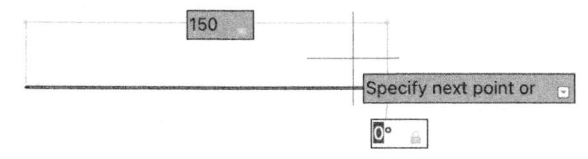
- Press the TAB key and type 90 as the angle — next, press RETURN.
- Move the pointer horizontally toward left and type 50.
- Press the TAB key and type 180 as the angle — next, press RETURN.
- Move the pointer vertically downwards and type 20.
- Press the TAB key and type 90 as the angle — next, press RETURN.
- Move the pointer horizontally toward left and type 50.
- Press the TAB key and type 180 as the angle — next, press RETURN.
- Move the pointer vertically downwards and type 40.
- Press the TAB key and type 90 as the angle — next, press RETURN.
- Move the pointer horizontally toward left and type 50.
- Press the TAB key and type 180 as the angle — next, press RETURN.
- Type C in the command line and press RETURN.
- Save and close the file.

Erasing, Undoing and Redoing

- Draw the sketch shown below using the **Line** tool. You can use the Dynamic Input method to create this sketch. Do not dimension the drawing. 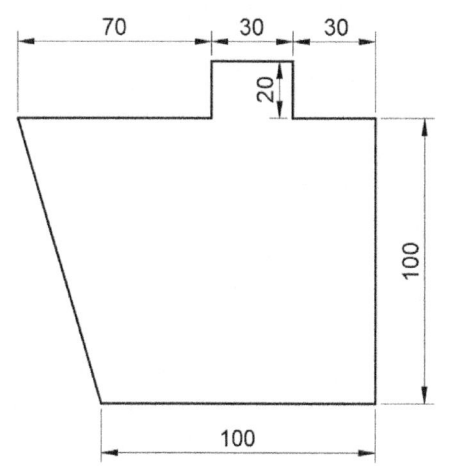
- Click the **Customize** panel icon on the **Modify** panel and select the **Erase** option; the **Erase** tool is displayed on the **Modify** panel.

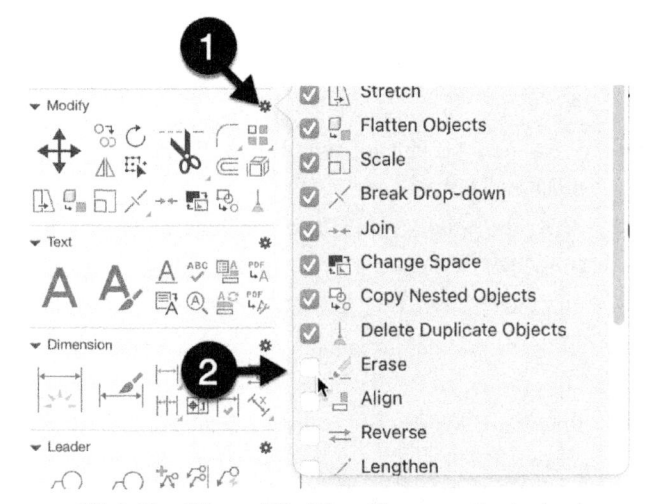

- Click **Drafting > Modify > Erase** on the tool set or Enter **ERASE** or **E** in the command line.

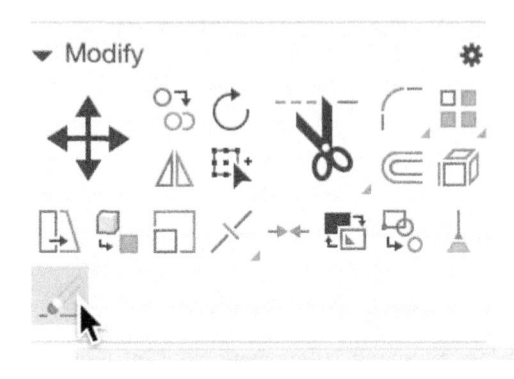

- Select the lines shown below and press RETURN. It erases the lines.

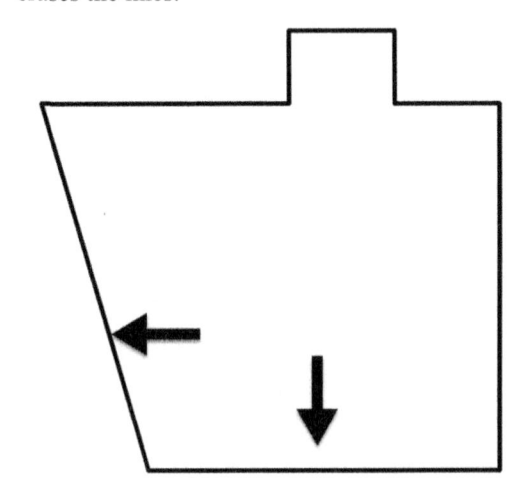

- Click the **Undo** button on the **Toolbar**. This action restores the lines.

- Click the **Redo** button on the **Toolbar**. This action erases the lines again.

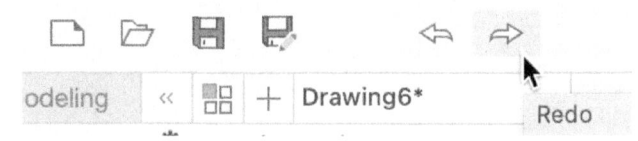

- Type **E** in the command line and press the SPACEBAR; the **ERASE** command will be activated.

- Drag a selection lasso as shown below and press RETURN; the entities will be erased. (Refer to the Selection Window section in Chapter 1 to learn about the selection lasso)

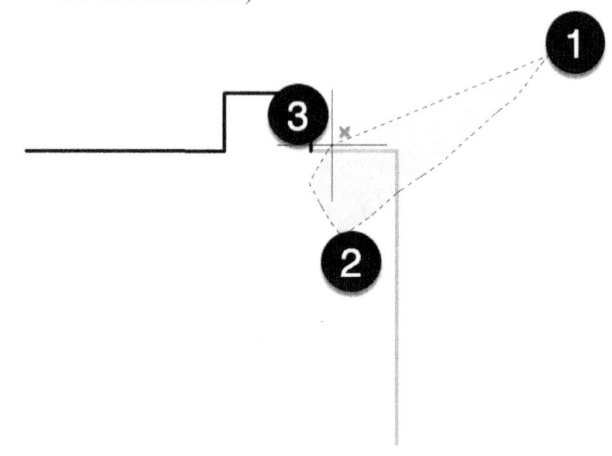

Drawing Circles

The tools in the **Circle** drop-down on the **Draw** panel can be used to draw circles. You can also type-in the **CIRCLE** command in the command line and create circles. There are various methods to create circles. These methods are explained in the following examples.

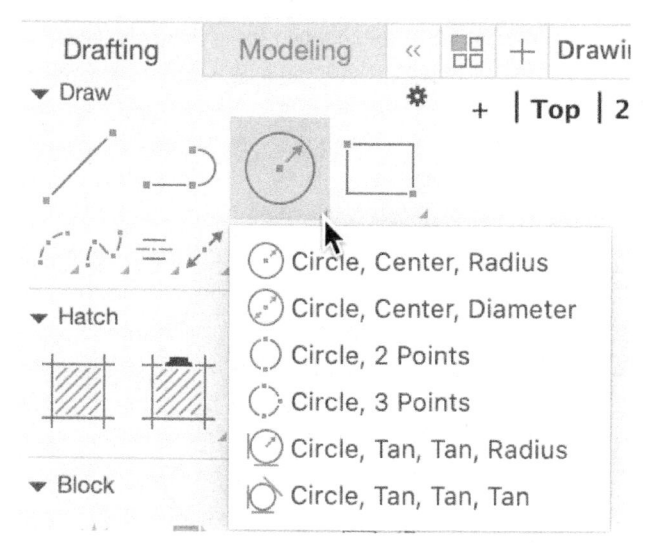

AutoCAD 2023 For Beginners (For Mac Users)

Example 1(Circle, Center, Radius)
In this example, you will create a circle by specifying its center and radius value.

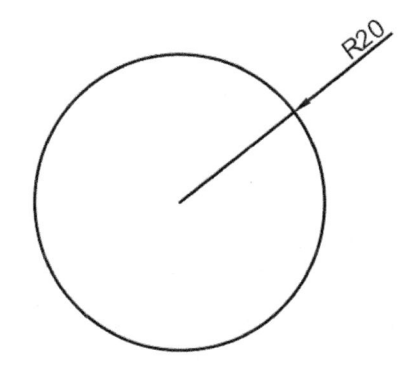

- Click **Drafting > Draw > Circle** drop-down > **Circle, Center, Radius**  on the tool set.
- Click in the graphics window.
- Type 20 as the radius and press RETURN.

Example 2(Circle, Center, Diameter)
In this example, you will create a circle by specifying its center and diameter value.

- Click **Drafting > Draw > Circle > Center, Diameter**  on the tool set. The message, "Specify center point for circle or [3P/2P/Ttr (tan tan radius)]:" appears in the command line.
- Pick a point in the graphics window, which is approximately horizontal to the previous circle. 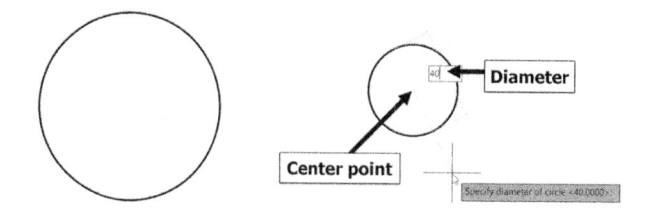
- Type 40 as the diameter and press RETURN; the circle will be created.

Example 3(Circle, 2 Points)
In this example, you will create a circle by specifying two points. The first point is to specify the location of the circle, and the second defines the diameter.

- Click the right mouse button on the **Object Snap** 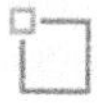 icon on the status bar. A flyout appears. The options in this flyout are called Object Snaps. You will learn about these Object Snaps later in Chapter 3.
- Activate the **Center** option, if it is not already active.
- Now, you will create a circle by selecting the center points of the previous circles.
- Click **Drafting > Draw > Circle > Circle, 2 Points**  on the tool set. The message, "Specify the first endpoint of circle's diameter:" appears in the command line.
- Select the center point of the left side circle; the message, "Specify the second endpoint of circle's diameter:" appears in the command line.
- Select the center point of the right-side circle; the circle will be created, as shown below.

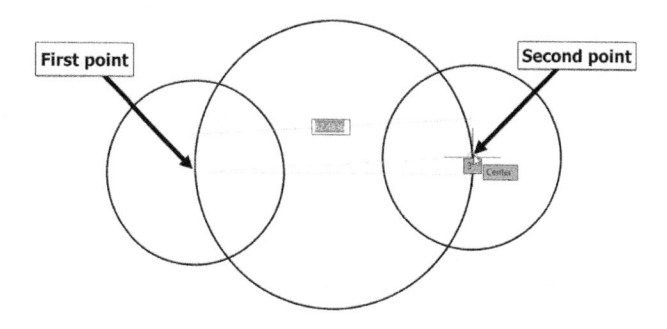

Example 4(Circle, 3 Points)
In this example, you will create a circle by specifying three points. The circle will pass through these three points.

43 | Drawing Basics

- Open a new drawing file.
- Use the **Line** tool and create the drawing shown in the figure below. The coordinate points are also given in the figure.

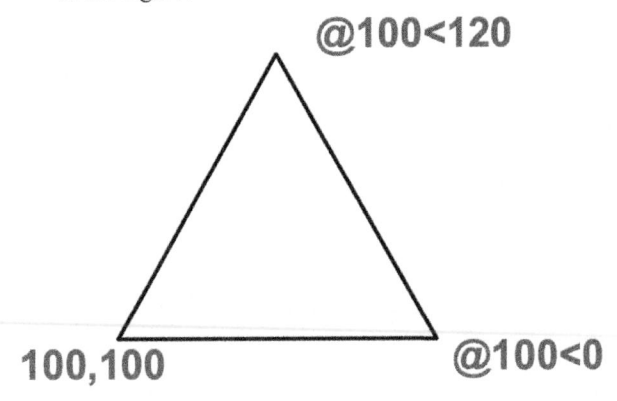

@100<120
100,100
@100<0

- Click **Drafting > Draw > Circle > Circle, 3 Points** on the tool set.
- Select the three vertices of the triangle; a circle will be created, passing through the selected points.

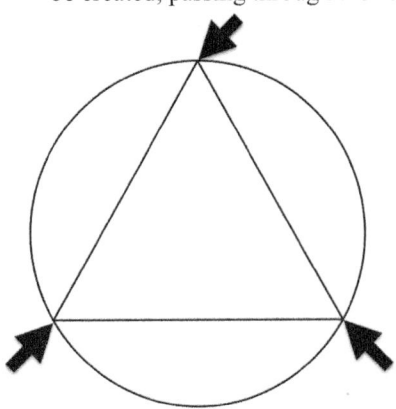

Example 5 (Tan, Tan, Radius)

In this example, you will create a circle by selecting two objects and then specifying the radius of the circle. A circle is created tangent to the selected objects.

- Click **Drafting > Draw > Circle > Tan, Tan, Radius** on the tool set; the message, "Specify point on the object for first tangent of circle:" appears in the command line.
- Select the horizontal line of the triangle; the message, "Specify point on object for second tangent of circle:" appears in the command line.
- Select any one of the inclined lines; the message, "Specify radius of circle," appears in the command line.
- Place the cursor on the outer circle; the center point of the circle is displayed.
- Select the center point of the circle.

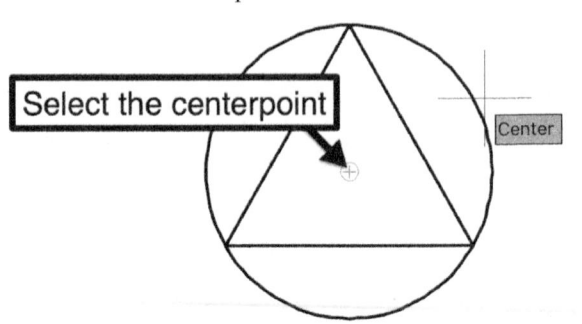

Select the centerpoint

- Move the cursor downward and select the midpoint of the horizontal line, as shown.

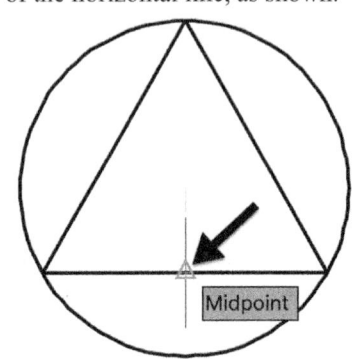

The circle will be created, touching all three sides of the triangle.

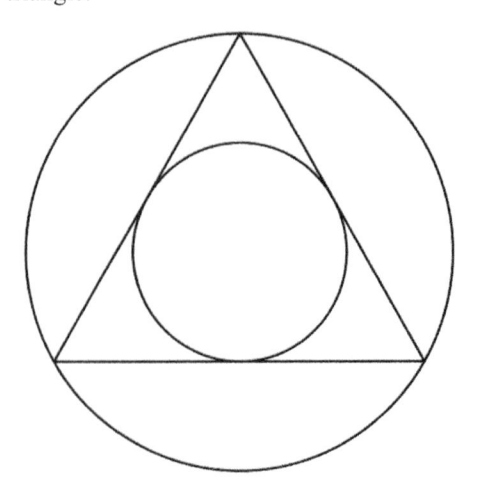

- Save and close the file.

Example 6 (Circle, Tan, Tan, Tan)

In this example, you will create a circle by selecting three objects to which it will be tangent.

44 | Drawing Basics

- Click the **Open** button on the **Toolbar**.

- Browse to the location of the **Line-example3.dwg** file and double-click on it; the file will be opened.
- Click **Drafting > Draw > Circle > Tan, Tan, Tan** on the tool set.
- Select the bottom horizontal line of the drawing.
- Select the two inclined lines. This creates a circle tangent to the selected lines.

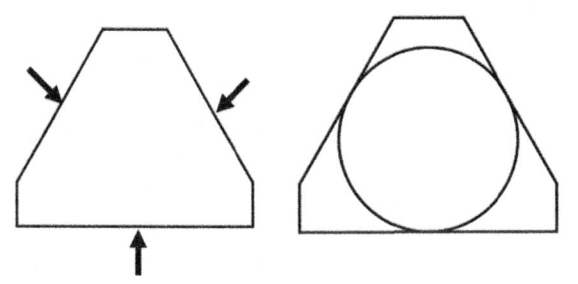

- Save and close the file.

Drawing Arcs

An arc is a portion of a circle. The total angle of an arc will always be less than 360 degrees, whereas the total angle of a circle is 360 degrees. AutoCAD provides you with eleven ways to draw an arc. You can draw arcs in different ways by using the tools available in the **Arcs** drop-down of the **Draw** panel. The usage of these tools will depend on your requirement. Some methods to create arcs are explained in the following examples.

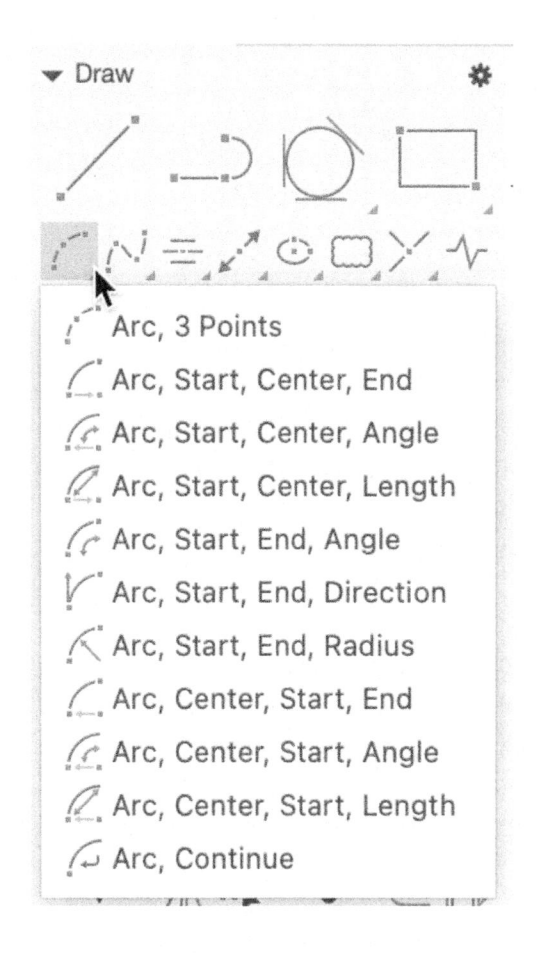

Example 1 (Arc, 3 Points)

In this example, you will create an arc by specifying three points. The arc will pass through these points.

- Open the **Line-example1.dwg** file.
- On the **Draw** panel, click **Point** drop-down > **Single Point**.

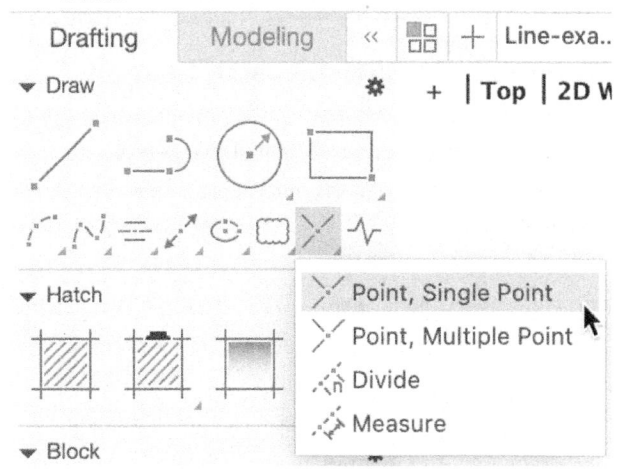

- Type 100,120 in the command line and press RETURN. It places a point above the rectangle.

45 | Drawing Basics

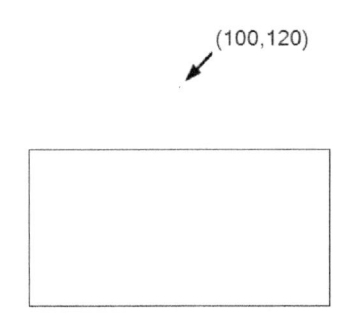

(100,120)

- Press ESC.
- Click the right mouse button on the **Object Snap** icon on the status bar, and then select the **Node** option from the menu.
- Click **Drafting > Draw > Arc > 3 Points** on the tool set. The message, "Specify start point of arc or [Center]:" appears in the command line.
- Select the top left corner of the rectangle.
- Select the point located above the rectangle.
- Select the top right corner of the rectangle; the three-point arc will be created.

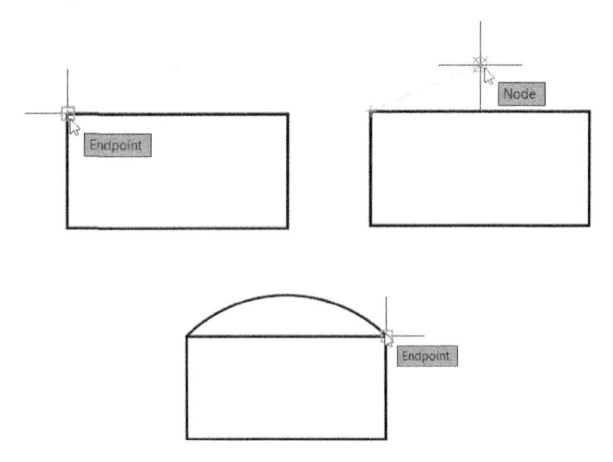

Example 2 (Arc, Start, Center, End)

In this example, you will draw an arc by specifying its start, center, and endpoints. The first two points define the radius of the arc, and the third point defines its included angle.

- Click **Drafting > Draw > Arc > Start, Center, End** on the tool set. The message, "Specify start point of arc or [Center]:" appears in the command line.
- Pick an arbitrary point in the graphics window to define the start point of an arc. The message, "Specify center point of arc:" appears.
- Pick a point to define the radius of the circle. You can also type in the radius value and press RETURN; the message, "Specify end point of arc or [Angle/chord Length]:" appears.

You will notice that, as you move the pointer, the included angle of the arc changes. The included angle of the arc is measured in the counter-clockwise direction. Press and hold the CONTROL key if you want to reverse the direction.

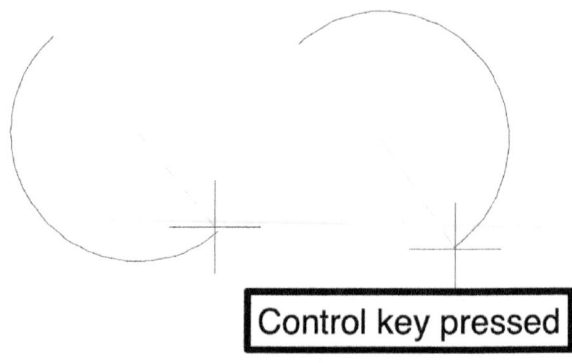

Control key pressed

- Pick a point to define the included angle of the arc. You can also type the angle value and press RETURN.

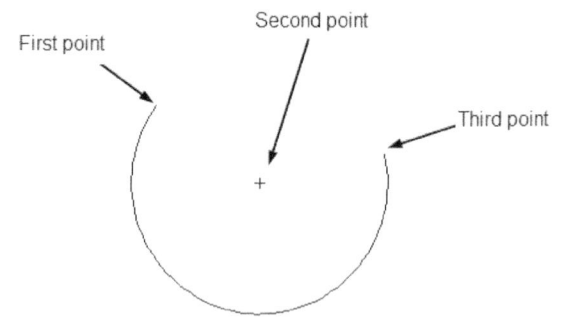

Example 3 (Arc, Start, End, Direction)

- Use the **Line** tool and create the drawing shown in the figure below. The dimensions are also given in the figure. (Use any one of the procedures given in the **Drawing Lines** section)

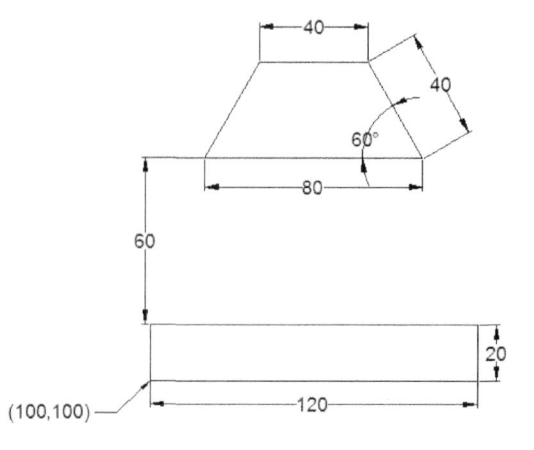

46 | Drawing Basics

- Click **Drafting > Draw > Arc > Start, End, Direction** on the tool set.
- Select the start and end points of the arc, as shown in the figure.

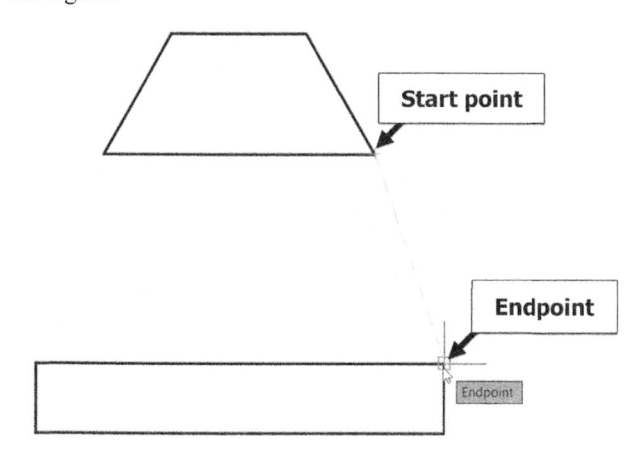

- Activate the **Ortho Mode** icon on the status bar.
- Move the pointer vertically downward and click to specify the direction.

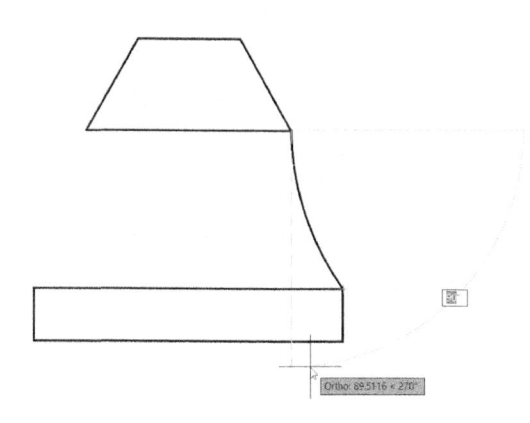

- Likewise, create another arc.

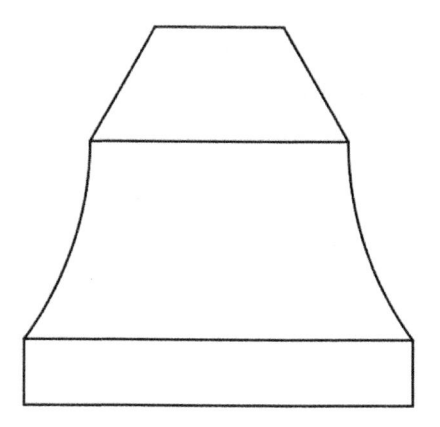

Drawing Polylines

A Polyline is a single object that consists of line segments and arcs. It is more versatile than a line, as you can assign a width to it. In the following example, you will create a closed polyline.

Example 1

- Activate the **Ortho Mode** on the Status Bar.
- Click **Drafting > Draw > Polyline** on the tool set or enter **PLINE** or **PL** in the command line; the message, "Specify start point:" appears in the command line.
- Select an arbitrary point in the graphics window.
- Move the pointer horizontally toward right and type 100 — next, press RETURN.
- Type **A** in the command line and press RETURN.
- Move the pointer vertically upward and type **50** — next, press RETURN.
- Type **L** in the command line and press RETURN.
- Move the pointer horizontally toward left and type **50** — next, press RETURN.
- Move the pointer vertically upward and type **50** — next, press RETURN.
- Type **A** in the command line and press RETURN.
- Move the pointer horizontally toward left and type **50** — next, press RETURN.
- Type **C** in the command line and press RETURN.

Now, when you click on a line segment from the sketch, the whole sketch will be selected. It is because the polyline created is a single object.

Drawing Rectangles

A rectangle is a four-sided single object. You can create a rectangle by just specifying its two diagonal corners. However, there are various methods to create a rectangle. These methods are explained in the following examples.

Example 1

In this example, you will create a rectangle by specifying its corner points.

- Open a new file.
- Click **Drafting > Draw > Rectangle** on the tool set, or enter **RECTANG** or **REC** in the command line; the message, "Specify first corner point or [Chamfer/Elevation/Fillet/Thickness/Width]:" appears in the command line.
- Pick an arbitrary point in the graphics window; the message "Specify other corner point or [Area/Dimensions/Rotation]:" appears in the command line.
- Move the pointer diagonally toward the right and click to create a rectangle.

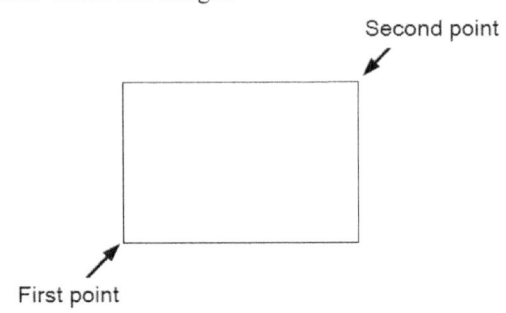

Example 2

In this example, you will create a rectangle by specifying its length and width.

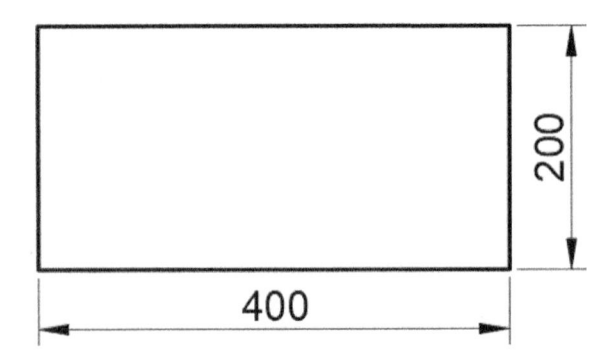

- Click **Drafting > Draw > Rectangle** on the tool set, or enter **RECTANG** or **REC** in the command line.
- Specify the first corner of the rectangle by picking an arbitrary point in the graphics window.
- Follow the prompt sequence given next:
  Specify other corner point or [Area/Dimensions/Rotation]: Type **D** in the command line and press RETURN.
  Specify length for rectangles: Type **400** and press RETURN.
  Specify width for rectangles: Type **200** and press RETURN.
  Specify other corner point or [Area/Dimensions/Rotation]: Move the pointer upward and click to create the rectangle.

Example 3

In this example, you will create a rectangle by specifying its area and width.

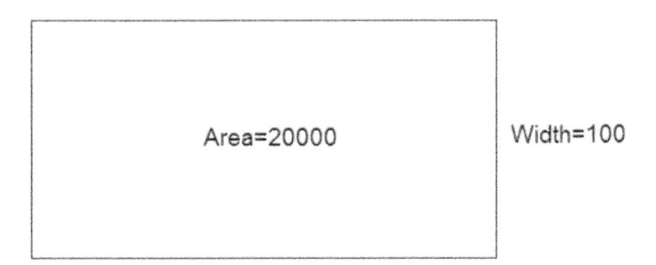

- Click **Drafting > Draw > Rectangle** on the tool set, or enter **RECTANG** or **REC** in the command line.
- Specify the first corner of the rectangle by picking an arbitrary point.
- Follow the prompt sequence given next:
  Specify other corner point or [Area/Dimensions/Rotation Type **A** in the command line and press RETURN.

  Enter area of rectangle in current units: Type **20000** and press RETURN.
  Calculate rectangle dimensions based on [Length/Width] <Length>: Type **W** in the command line and press RETURN.
  Enter rectangle width: Type **100** and press RETURN; the length will be calculated automatically.

Example 4

In this example, you will create a rectangle with chamfered corners.

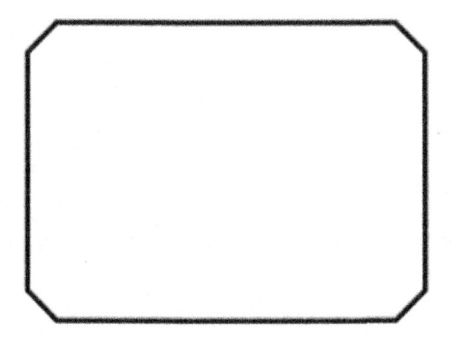

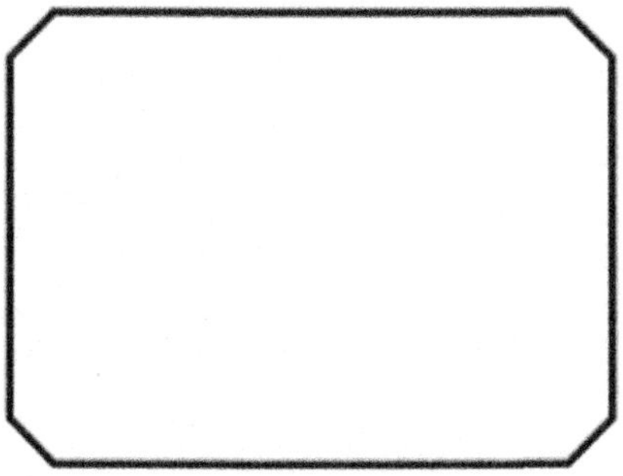

- Click **Drafting > Draw > Rectangle** on the tool set, or enter **RECTANG** or **REC** in the command line.
- Follow the prompt sequence given next:
  Specify first corner point or [Chamfer/Elevation/Fillet/Thickness/Width]: Type **C** in the command line and press RETURN.
  Specify first chamfer distance for rectangles: Type **20** and press RETURN.
  Specify second chamfer distance for rectangles: Type **20** and press RETURN.
  Specify first corner point or [Chamfer/Elevation/Fillet/Thickness/Width]: Click at an arbitrary point in the graphics window to specify the first corner.
  Specify other corner point or [Area/Dimensions/Rotation]: Move the pointer diagonally toward the right and click to specify the second corner.

Example 5

In this example, you will create a rectangle with rounded corners.

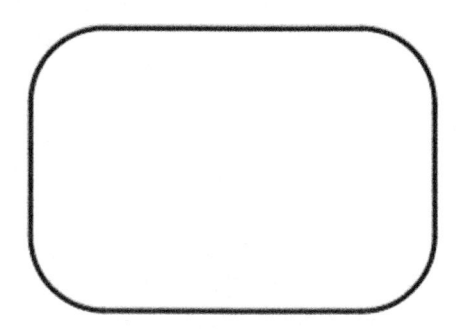

- Click **Drafting > Draw > Rectangle** on the tool set, or enter **RECTANG** or **REC** in the command line.
- Follow the prompt sequence given next:
  Specify first corner point or [Chamfer/Elevation/Fillet/Thickness/Width]: Type **F** in the command line and press RETURN.
  Specify fillet radius for rectangles: Type **50** and press RETURN.
  Specify first corner point or [Chamfer/Elevation/Fillet/Thickness/Width]: Click at an arbitrary point in the graphics window to specify the first corner.
  Specify other corner point or [Area/Dimensions/Rotation]: Move the pointer diagonally toward the right and click to specify the second corner.

Example 6

In this example, you will create an inclined rectangle.

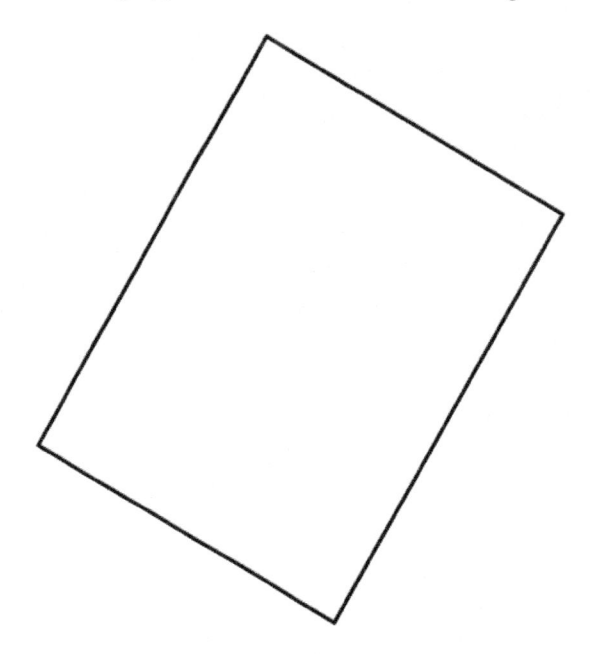

- Click **Drafting > Draw > Rectangle** on the tool set, or enter **RECTANG** or **REC** in the command line.
- Type **F** in the command line and press RETURN.
- Type **0** and press RETURN.
- Specify the first corner of the rectangle by picking an arbitrary point.
- Follow the prompt sequence given next:

Specify other corner point or [Area/Dimensions/Rotation]: Type **R** in the command line and press RETURN.
Specify rotation angle or [Pick points]: Type **60** and press RETURN.
Specify other corner point or [Area/Dimensions/Rotation]: Type **D** in the command line and press RETURN.
Specify length for rectangles: Type **400** and press RETURN.
Specify width for rectangles: Type **300** and press RETURN.

- Move the pointer toward the right and click to position the rectangle.

Drawing Polygons

A Polygon is a single object having many sides ranging from 3 to 1024. In AutoCAD, you can create regular polygons having sides with equal length. There are two methods to create a polygon. These methods are explained in the following examples.

Example 1

In this example, you will create a polygon by specifying the number of sides and then determining the length of one side.

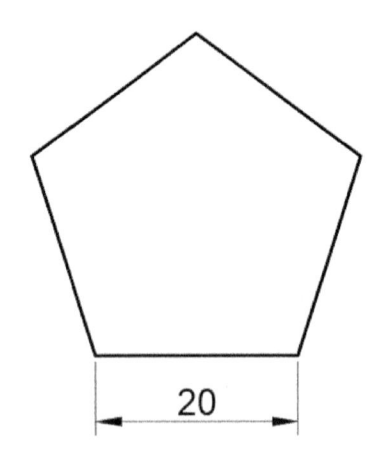

- Click **Drafting > Draw > Rectangle > Polygon** on the tool set.

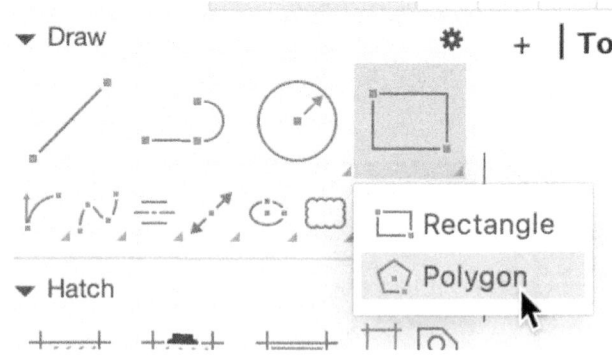

- Follow the prompt sequence given next.

  Enter number of sides <4>: Type **5** and press RETURN.
  Specify center of polygon or [Edge]: Type **E** in the command line and press RETURN.
  Specify first endpoint of edge: Select an arbitrary point.
  Specify second endpoint of edge: Move the pointer horizontally toward the right. Next, type **20**, and press RETURN.

Example 2

In this example, you will create a polygon by specifying the number of sides and drawing an imaginary circle (inscribed circle). The polygon will be created with its corners located on the imaginary circle. You can also create a polygon with the circumscribed circle. A circumscribed circle is an imaginary circle which is tangent to all the sides of a polygon.

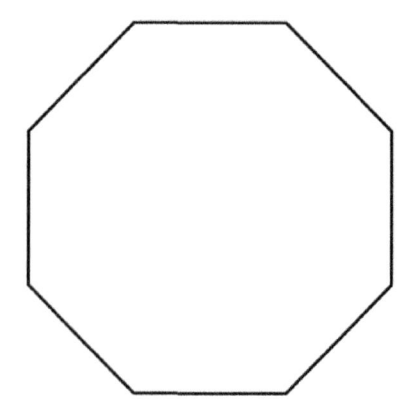

- Type **POL** in the command line and press RETURN; the **POLYGON** command will be activated.
- Follow the prompt sequence given next:

Enter number of sides <5>: Type **8** and press RETURN.
Specify center of polygon or [Edge]: Select an arbitrary point
Enter an option [Inscribed in circle/Circumscribed about circle] <C>: Type **I** in the command line and press RETURN.
Specify radius of circle: Type **20** and press RETURN; a polygon will be created with its corners touching the imaginary circle.

Drawing Splines

Splines are non-uniform curves, which are used to create irregular shapes. In AutoCAD, you can create splines by using two methods: **Spline Fit** and **Spline CV**. These methods are explained in the following examples:

Example 1: (Spline Fit)

In this example, you will create a spline using the **Spline Fit** method. In this method, you need to specify various points in the graphics window. The spline will be created, passing through the specified points.

- Start a new drawing file.
- Use the **Line** tool and create a sketch similar to the one shown below.

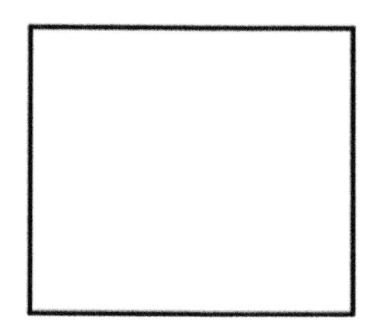

- On the **Drafting** tool set, click **Draw** panel > **Spline** drop-down > **Spline Fit**; the message, "Specify first point or [Method/Knots/Object]:" appears in the command line.

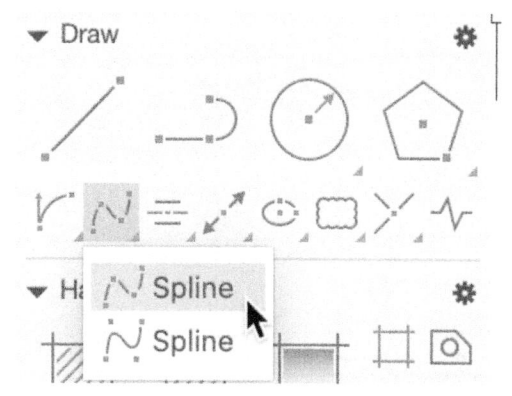

- Select the lower-left corner of the sketch; the message, "Enter next point or [start Tangency/toLerance]:" appears in the command line.

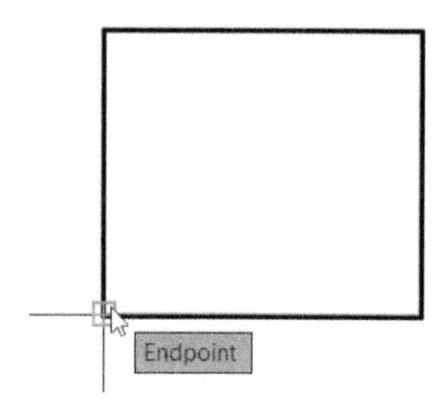

- Select the top-left corner point of the sketch.

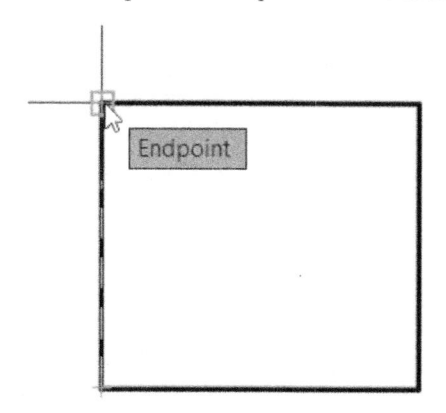

- Similarly, select the top-right and lower-right corners; a spline will be attached to the pointer.
- Press RETURN.

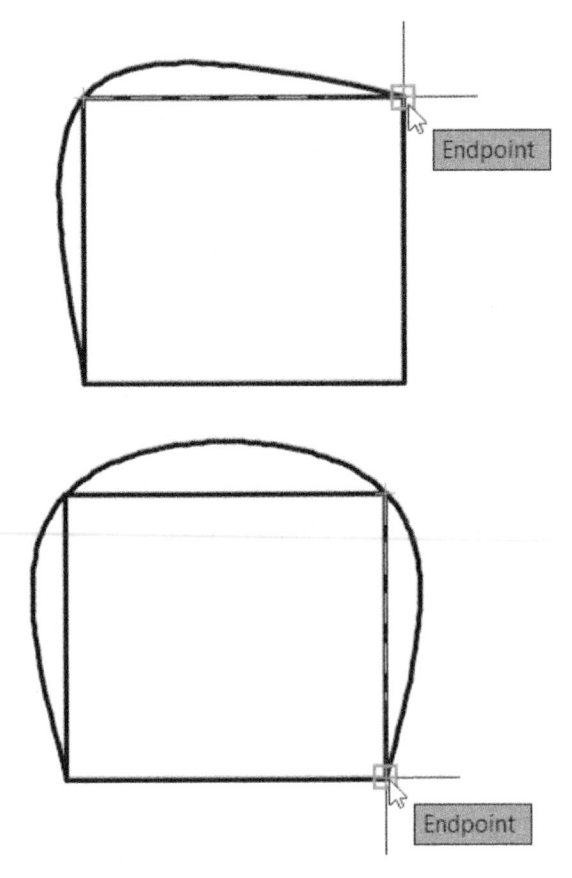

Example 2: (Spline CV)

In this example, you will create a spline by using the **Spline CV** method. In this method, you will specify various points called control vertices. As you specify the control vertices, imaginary lines are created connecting them. The spline will be drawn tangent to these lines.

- On the **Drafting** tool set, click **Draw** panel > **Spline** drop-down > **Spline CV**.

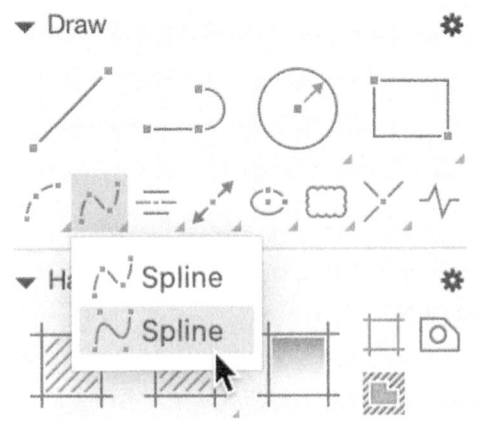

- Select the four corners of the sketch in the same sequence as in the earlier example.

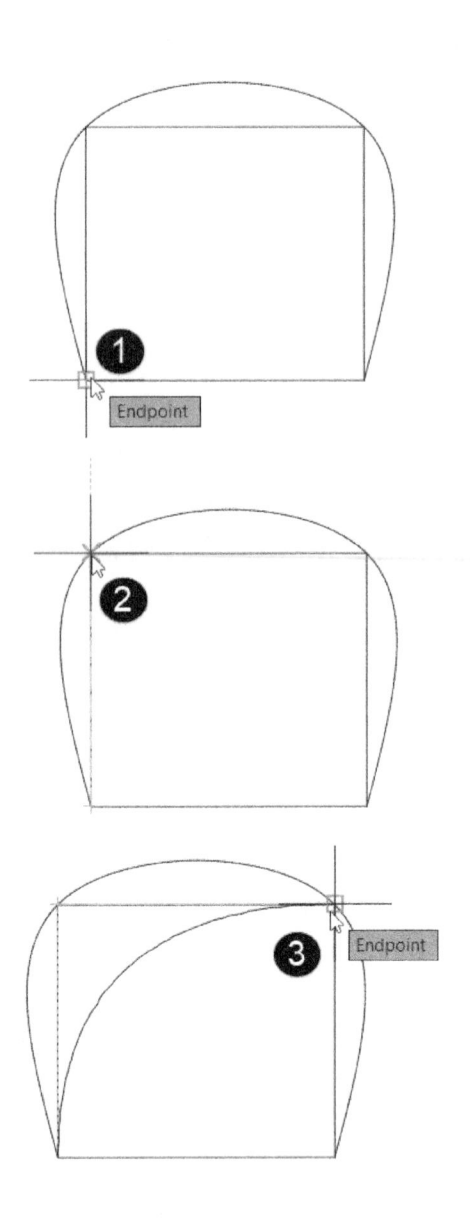

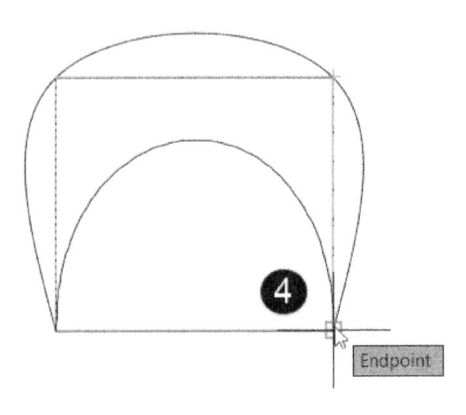

- Press RETURN; a spline with control vertices will be created.

AutoCAD 2023 For Beginners (For Mac Users)

Example 3:
- Create a polyline, as shown.

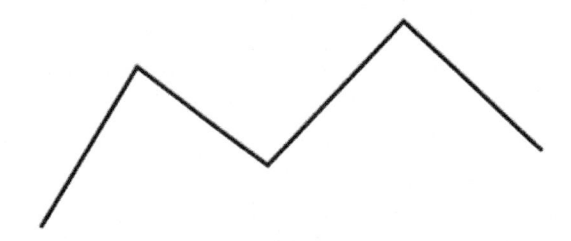

- Activate the **Spline CV** command.
- Type **O** in the command line and press RETURN.
- Select the polyline and press RETURN; the polyline is converted into a spline.

Drawing Ellipses

Ellipses are also non-uniform curves, but they have a regular shape. They are actually splines created in a proper closed shape. In AutoCAD, you can draw an ellipse in three different ways by using the tools available in the **Ellipse** drop-down of the **Draw** panel. The three different ways to draw ellipses are explained in the following examples.

Example 1 (Center)

In this example, you will draw an ellipse by specifying three points. The first point defines the center of the ellipse. The second and third points define the two axes of the ellipse.

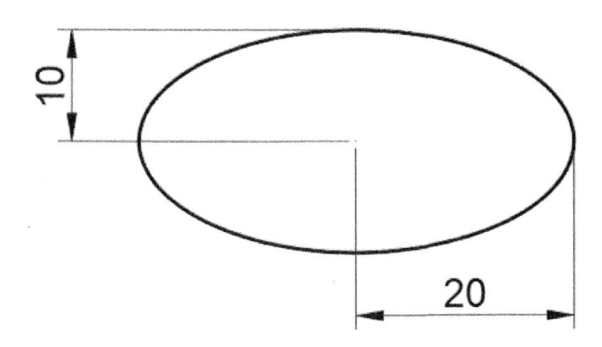

- Click **Drafting > Draw > Ellipse > Center** on the tool set; the message, "Specify center of ellipse:" appears in the command line.

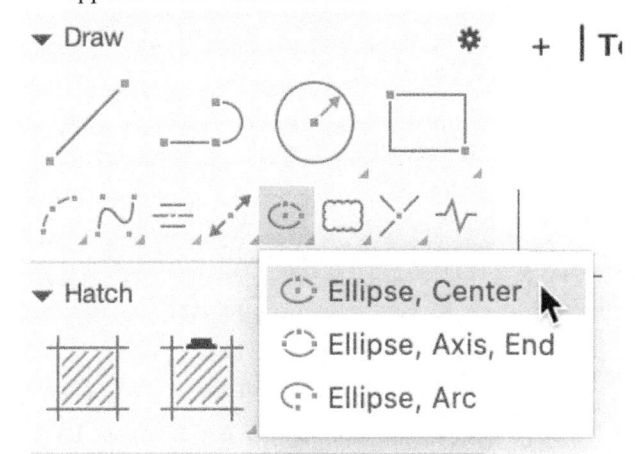

- Select an arbitrary point in the graphics window; the message, "Specify endpoint of axis:" appears in the command line.
- Move the pointer horizontally and type 20. Next, press RETURN; the message, "Specify distance to other axis or [Rotation]:" appears in the command line.
- Type 10 and press RETURN; the ellipse will be created.

Example 2 (Axis, End)

In this example, you will draw an ellipse by specifying three points. The first two points define the location and length of the first axis. The third point defines the second axis of the ellipse.

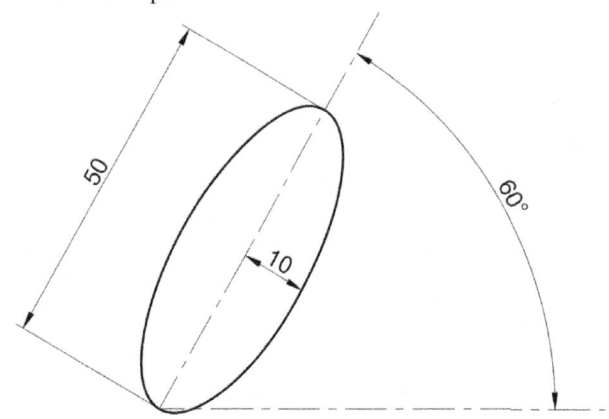

- Activate the **Dynamic Input** icon on the status bar, if it is not active.
- Click **Drafting > Draw > Ellipse > Axis, End** on the tool set.

53 | **Drawing Basics**

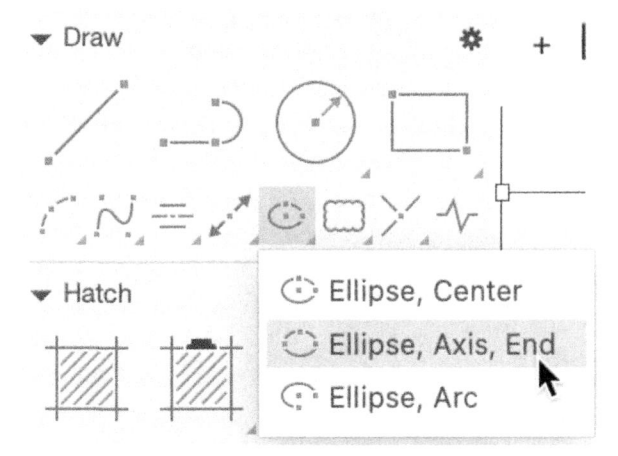

- Select an arbitrary point to specify an axis endpoint.
- Type **50** as the length of the first axis and press TAB.
- Type **60** as angle and press RETURN.
- Type **10** as the radius of the second axis and press RETURN; the ellipse will be created inclined at a 60-degree angle.

Example 3 (Elliptical Arc)

In this example, you will draw an elliptical arc. To draw an elliptical arc, first, you need to define the location and length of the first axis. Next, set the radius of the second axis; an ellipse will be displayed. Next, you need to set the start angle of the elliptical arc. The start angle can be any angle between 0 and 360. After defining the start angle, you need to specify the end angle of the elliptical arc.

- Select an arbitrary point to specify an axis endpoint.
- Move the pointer horizontally toward left and type **60**. Next, press RETURN to specify the axis length.
- Move the pointer upward and type **15**. Next, press RETURN to specify the length of another axis.
- Type **0** and press RETURN to specify the start angle.
- Type **240** and press RETURN to specify the end angle.

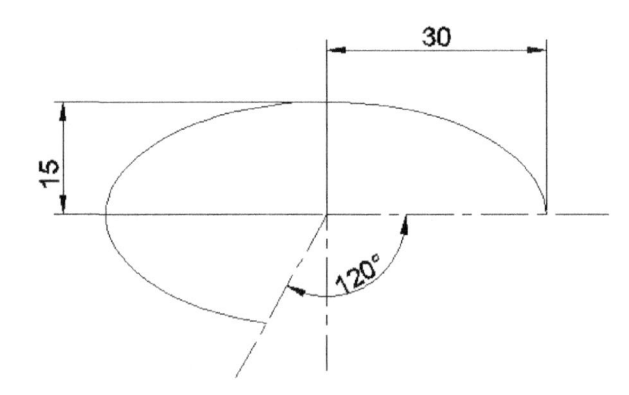

- Turn on the **Ortho Mode** on the Status bar.
- Click **Drafting > Draw > Ellipse > Elliptical Arc** on the tool set.

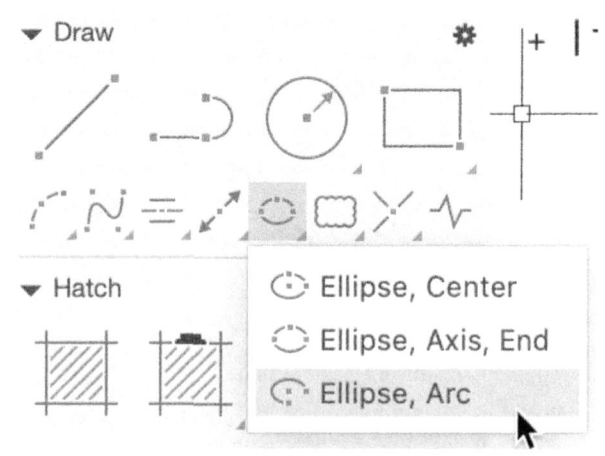

54 | Drawing Basics

Exercises

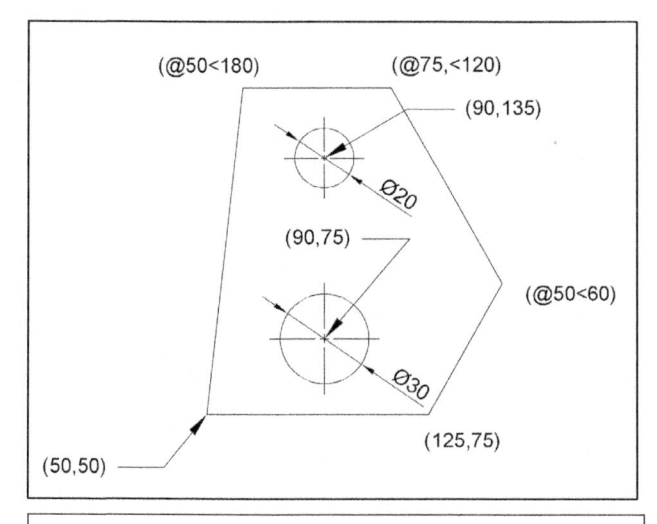

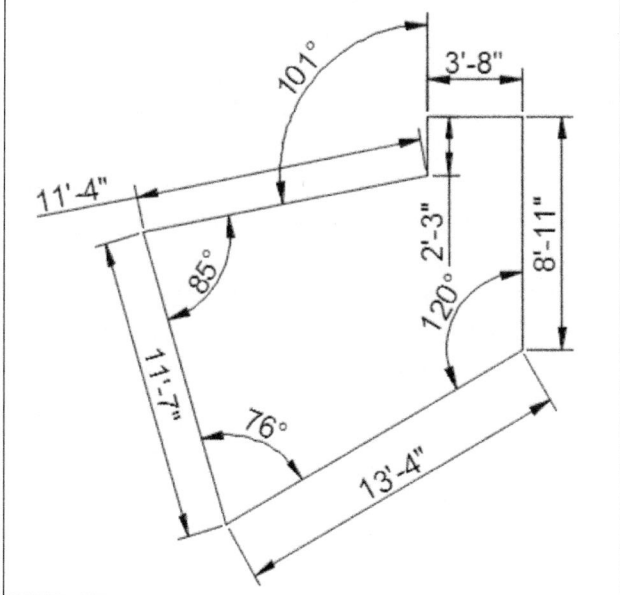

Direct Input Method

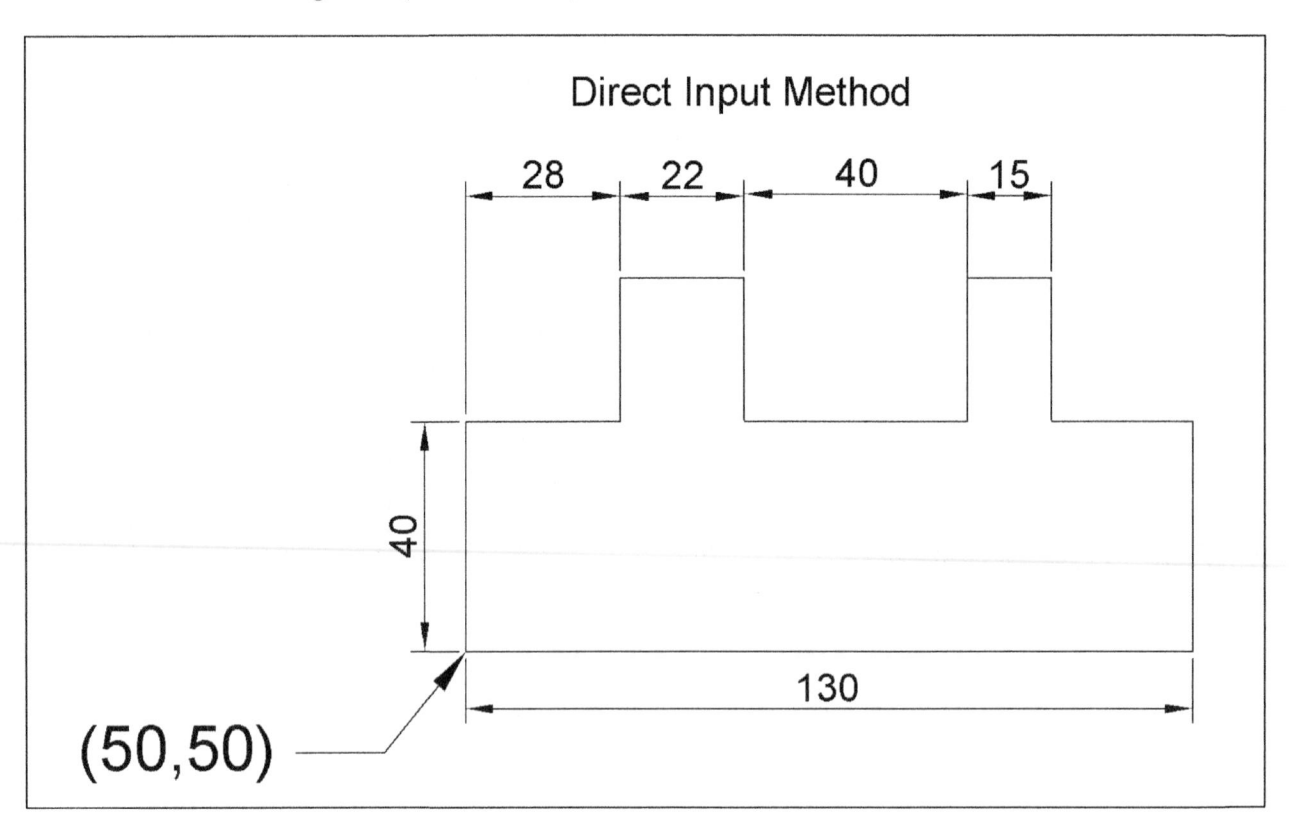

28 | 22 | 40 | 15

40

(50,50)

130

AutoCAD 2023 For Beginners (For Mac Users)

Chapter 3: Drawing Aids

In this chapter, you will learn to do the following:

- **Use Grid and Snap**
- **Use Ortho Mode and Polar Tracking**
- **Use Object Snaps and Object Snap Tracking**
- **Create Layers and assign properties to it**
- **Zoom and Pan drawings**

Drawing Aids

This chapter teaches you to define the drawing settings, which will assist you in creating a drawing in AutoCAD quickly. Most drawing settings can be turned on or off from the status bar. You can also access additional drawing settings by right-clicking on the button located on the status bar.

Setting Grid and Snap

Grid is the primary drawing setting. It makes the graphics window appear like a graph paper. You can turn ON the grid display by clicking the **Grid** icon on the status bar.

Snap is used for drawing objects by using the intersection points of the grid lines. When you turn the Snap Mode ON, you will be able to select only grid points. In the following example, you will learn to set the grid and snap settings.

Example:

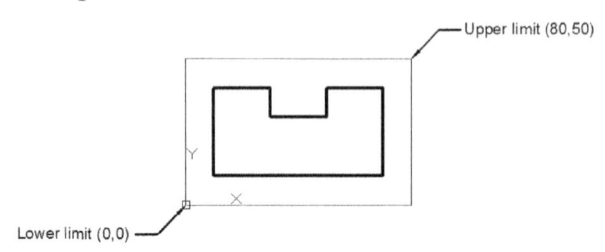

- Click **File > New Drawing** on the menu bar.
- Select the **acadISO-Named Plot Styles** template. Click **Open**.
- On the Status bar, click the right-mouse button on the **Snap Mode** icon and select **Settings**. The **Drafting Settings** dialog appears.
- Click the **Snap & Grid** tab on the dialog.
- Set **Grid X spacing** to **10** and press the TAB key; the **Grid Y spacing** is updated with the same value.
- Set **Major line every** to **10**.

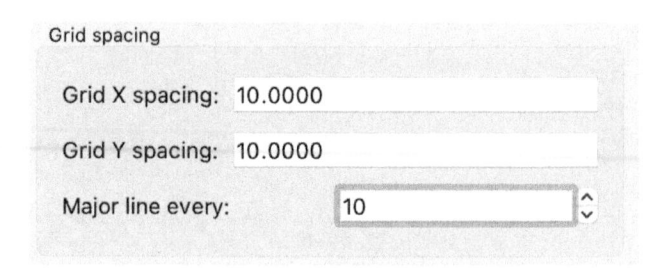

- Select the **Snap On** checkbox.
- Make sure that **Snap X spacing** and **Snap Y spacing** is set to **10**.

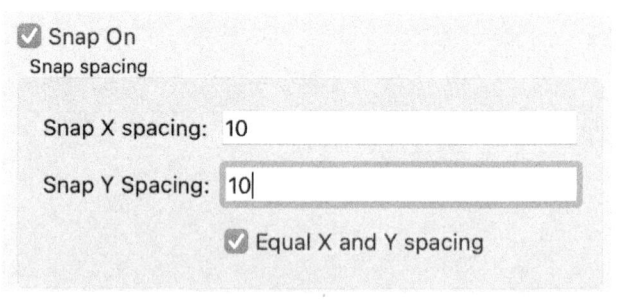

- Make sure that the **Grid snap** option is selected in the **Snap type** group.

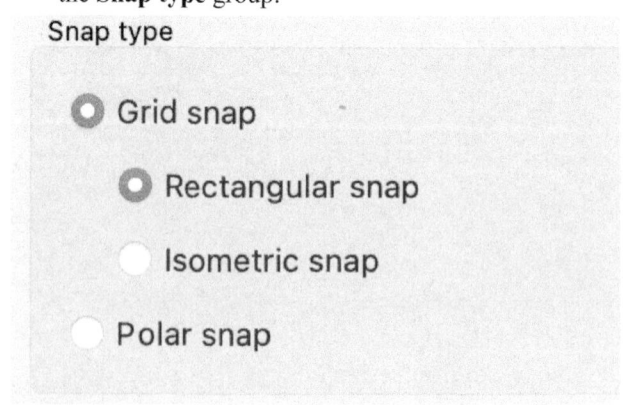

- Select the **Rectangular snap** option under **Grid snap**.
- Click **OK** on the dialog.
- Activate the **Grid** icon on the Status Bar.

Drawing Aids

AutoCAD 2023 For Beginners (For Mac Users)

Setting the Limits of a drawing

You can set the limits of a drawing by defining its lower-left and top-right corners. By setting Limits of a drawing, you will determine the size of the drawing area. In AutoCAD, limits are set to some default values. However, you can redefine the limits to change the drawing area as per your requirement.

- Type **Limits** at the command line and press RETURN.

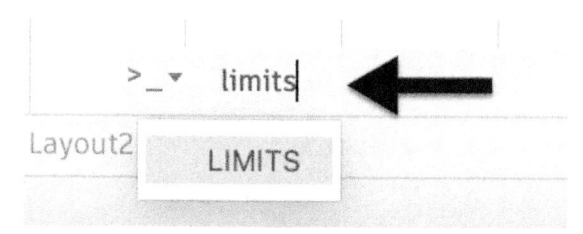

- Type 0,0 and press RETURN to define the lower limit.
  Now, you need to define the upper limit.
- Type 80,50 and press the RETURN key.
- Type Z and press RETURN.
- Type A and press RETURN; the graphics window will be zoomed to the limits.

Setting the Lineweight

Line weight is the thickness of the objects that you draw. In AutoCAD, there is a default lineweight assigned to objects. However, you can set a new lineweight. The method to set the lineweight is explained below.

- On the Status bar, click the **Customization** option, and then select **LineWeight** from the flyout. This shows the **LineWeight** icon on the status bar.
- Activate the **Show/Hide Lineweight** icon located on the status bar.
- Right click on the **Show/Hide Lineweight** icon, and then select **Settings**. The **Lineweight Settings** dialog appears.
- On the **Lineweight Settings** dialog, select **0.40** mm from the **New layer default** drop-down.

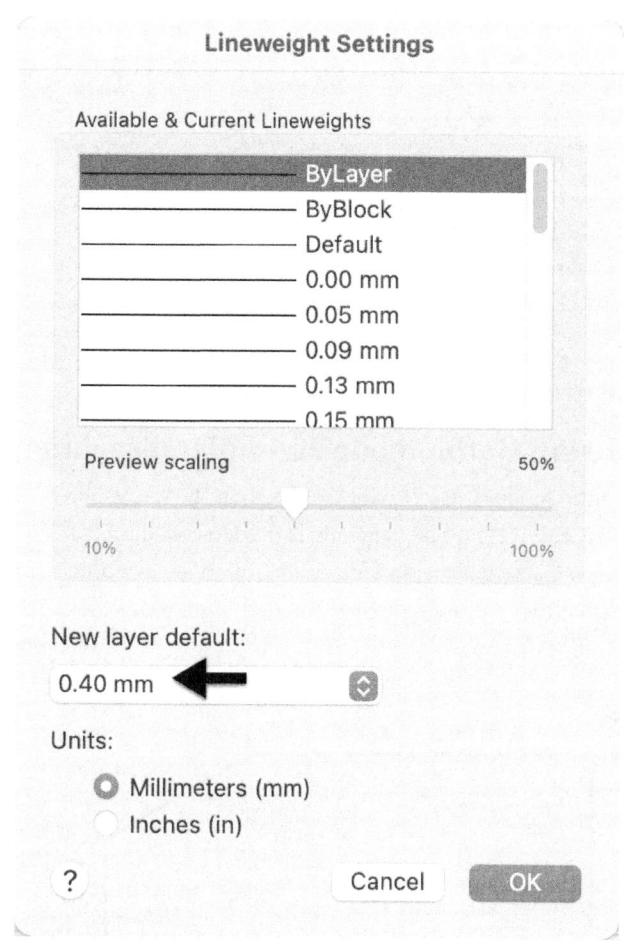

- Click **OK**.
- Type **L** in the command line and press RETURN.
- Type 10,10 and press RETURN to define the first point.
- Move the pointer horizontally toward the right and click on the sixth grid point from the first point.
- Move the pointer vertically upwards and select the third grid point from the second point.
- Move the pointer horizontally toward the left and select the second grid point from the previous point.
- Move the pointer vertically downwards and select the grid point next to the previous point.
- Move the pointer horizontally toward the left and select the second grid point from the previous point.
- Move the pointer vertically upwards and select the grid point next to the previous point.
- Move the pointer horizontally toward the left and select the second grid point from the previous point.
- Right-click and select **Close**.

Drawing Aids

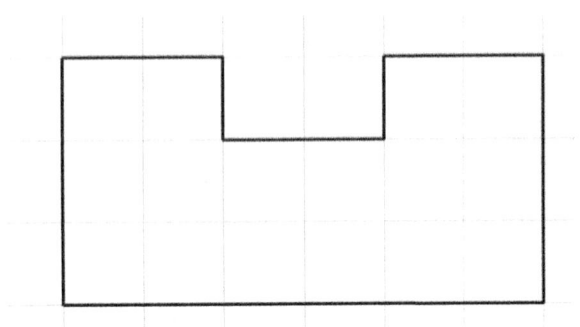

- Save and close the file.

Using Ortho mode and Polar Tracking

Ortho mode is used to draw orthogonal (horizontal or vertical) lines. Polar Tracking is used to constrain the lines to angular increments. In the following example, you will create a drawing with the help of Ortho Mode and Polar Tracking.

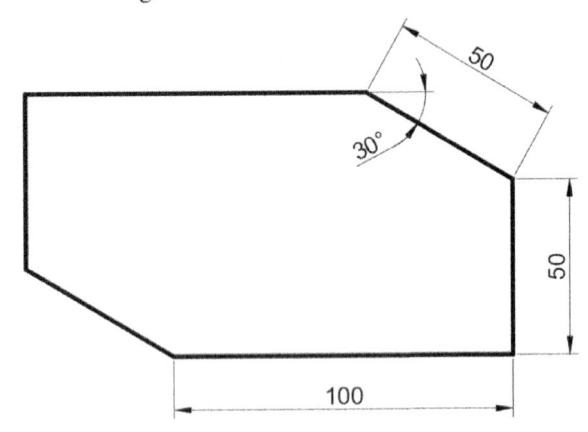

- Open a new AutoCAD file.
- Deactivate the **Grid Display** and **Snap Mode** icons on the status bar.
- Click the **Ortho Mode** icon on the status bar.
- Type Z and press RETURN.
- Type A and press RETURN.
- Click the **Line** button on the **Draw** panel.
- Select an arbitrary point to define the starting point.
- Move the pointer toward the right, type 100, and press RETURN; you will notice that a horizontal line is created.
- Move the pointer upwards, type 50, and press RETURN; you will notice that a vertical line is created.
- Click the **Polar Tracking** icon on the status bar.
- Click the right mouse button on the **Polar tracking** icon and select **30** from the menu.

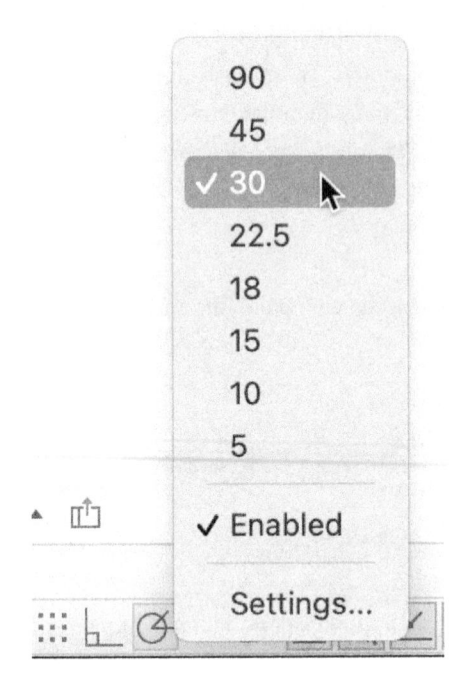

You will notice a track line at 30-degree increments when you rotate the pointer.

- Move the pointer and stop when the tooltip displays <150 angle value.
- Type 50 and press RETURN when the tooltip displays <150°.
- Move the pointer toward left.
- Type 100 and press RETURN when the tooltip displays <180°.
- Move the pointer vertically downward.
- Type 50 and press RETURN when the tooltip displays <270°.
- Right-click and select **Close**.

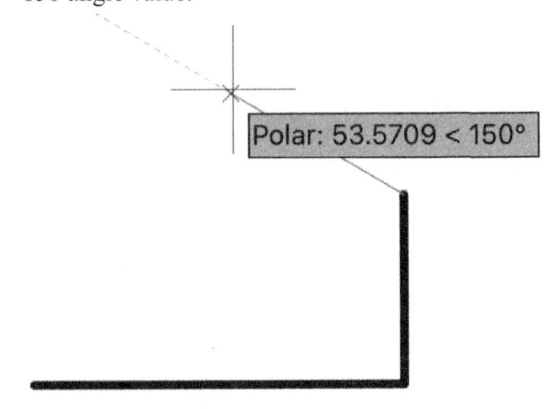

60 | Drawing Aids

Using Layers

Layers are like a group of transparent sheets that are combined into a complete drawing. The figure below displays a drawing consisting of object lines and dimension lines. In this example, the object lines are created on the 'Object' layer, and dimensions are created on the layer called 'Dimension.' You can easily turn-off the 'Dimension' layer for a more unobstructed view of the object lines.

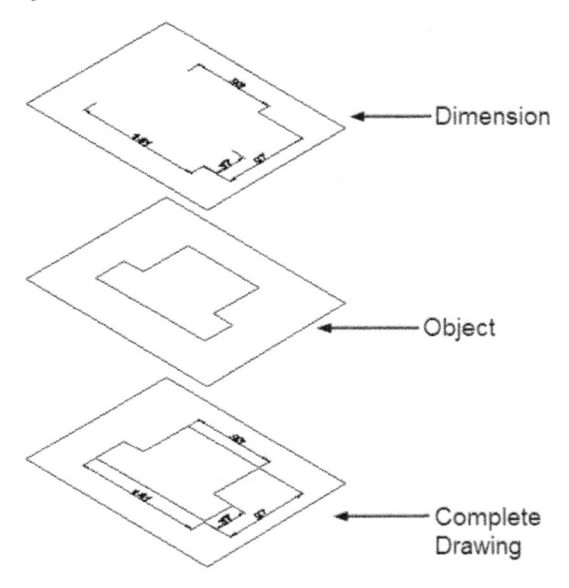

Layer palette

The **Layers** palette is used to create and manage layers. It is displayed at the right-side of the drawing area. You can undock the Layers palette by clicking the Undock icon located at its top-right corner.

The **List View** section is the main body of the **Layers** palette. It lists the individual layers that currently exist in the drawing.

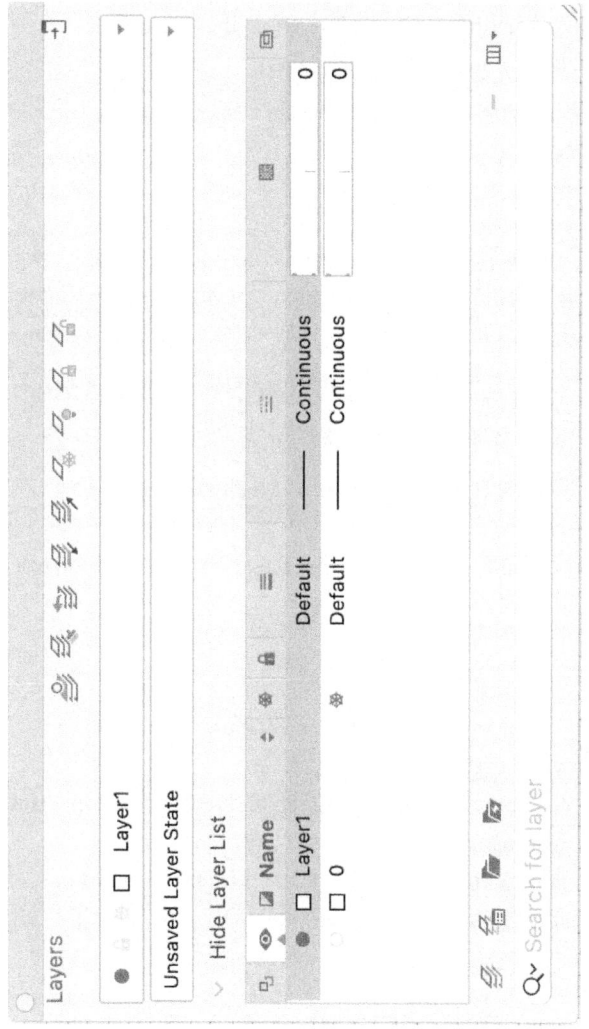

The **List View** section contains various properties. You can set layer properties and perform multiple operations in the **List View** section. A brief explanation of each layer property is given below.

Visibility – It is used to turn on/off the visibility of a layer. When a layer is turned on, it shows a grey circular dot. When you turn off a layer, white circular dot.

Name - Shows the name of the layer. Also, you can change the layer color using the Color drop-down available in this column.

Freeze – It is used to freeze the objects of a layer so that they cannot be modified. Also, the visibility of the object is turned off.

Lock - It is used to lock the layer so that the objects on it cannot be modified.

Lineweight – It is used to define the lineweight (thickness) of objects on the layer.

Linetype – It is used to assign a linetype to the layer.

New VP Freeze – It is used to create and freeze a layer in any new viewport.

Transparency – It is used to define the transparency of the layer. You set a transparency level from 0 to 90 for all objects on a layer.

Plot Style – It is used to override the settings such as color, linetype, and lineweight while plotting a drawing.

Plot – It is used to control which layer will be plotted.

Description – It is used to enter a detailed description of the layer.

Creating a New Layer

You can create a new layer by using any one of the following methods:

1. Click the **New Layer** button on the **Layer Properties Manager**; a new layer with the name '**Layer1**' appears in **Name** field. Next, enter the name of the layer in the **Name** field.

2. Right-click in the **Name** field and select **New Layer** from the shortcut menu.

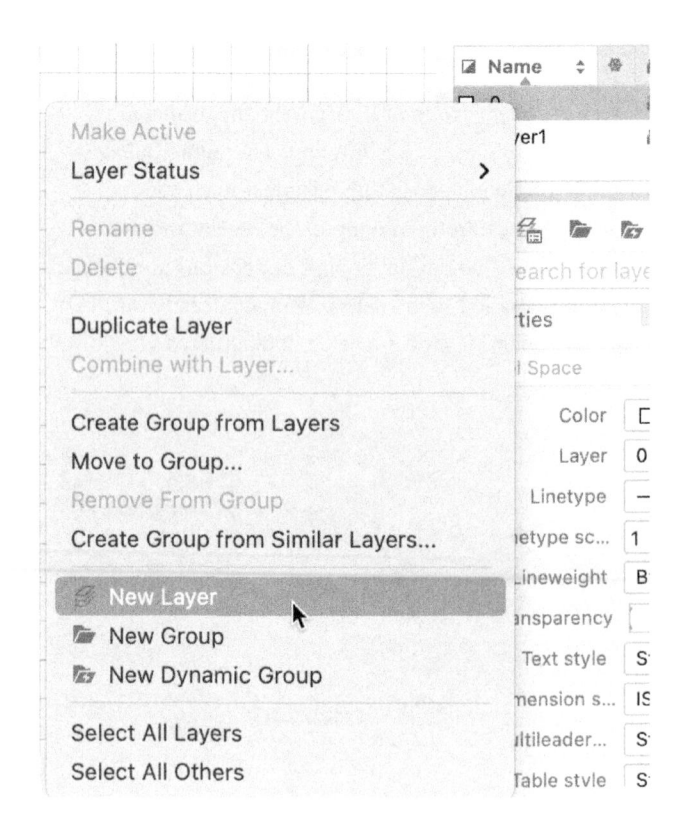

Making a layer active

If you want to draw objects on a particular layer, then you have to make it current. You can make a layer current using the methods listed below.

1. Double-click on the **Name** field of the layer.
2. Right-click on the layer and select **Make active**.
3. Select the layer from the **Layer** drop-down of the **Layers** palette.

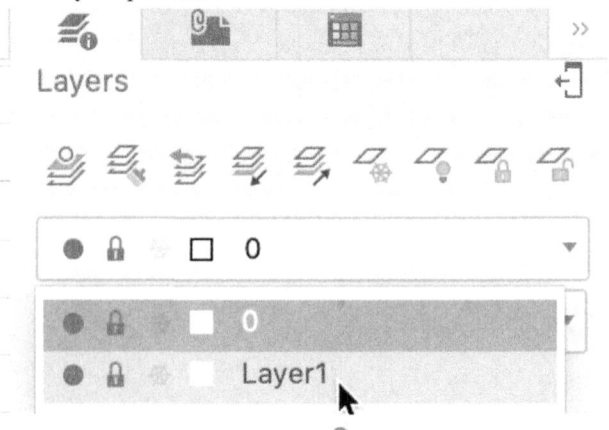

4. Click the **Make Current** button on the **Layers** palette. Next, select an object from the graphics window; the layer related to the selected object will become current.

---

62 | Drawing Aids

Deleting a Layer

You can delete a layer by using any one of the following methods:

1. Click the **Delete Layer** button.

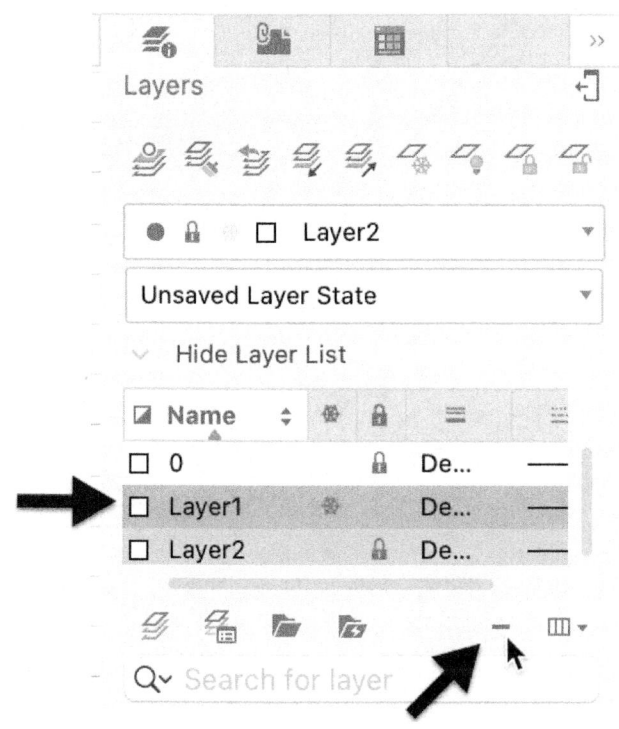

2. Right-click in the **Name** field and select **Delete** from the shortcut menu.

You will learn more about layers in later chapters. You can find an example related to layers in the **Offset** tool section of chapter 4.

Using Object Snaps

Object Snaps are essential settings that improve your performance and accuracy while creating a drawing. They allow you to select key points of objects while creating a drawing. You can activate the required Object Snap by using the **Object snap** shortcut menu. Press and hold the SHIFT key and right-click to display this shortcut menu. Note that the object snaps can be used only when a drawing command is active.

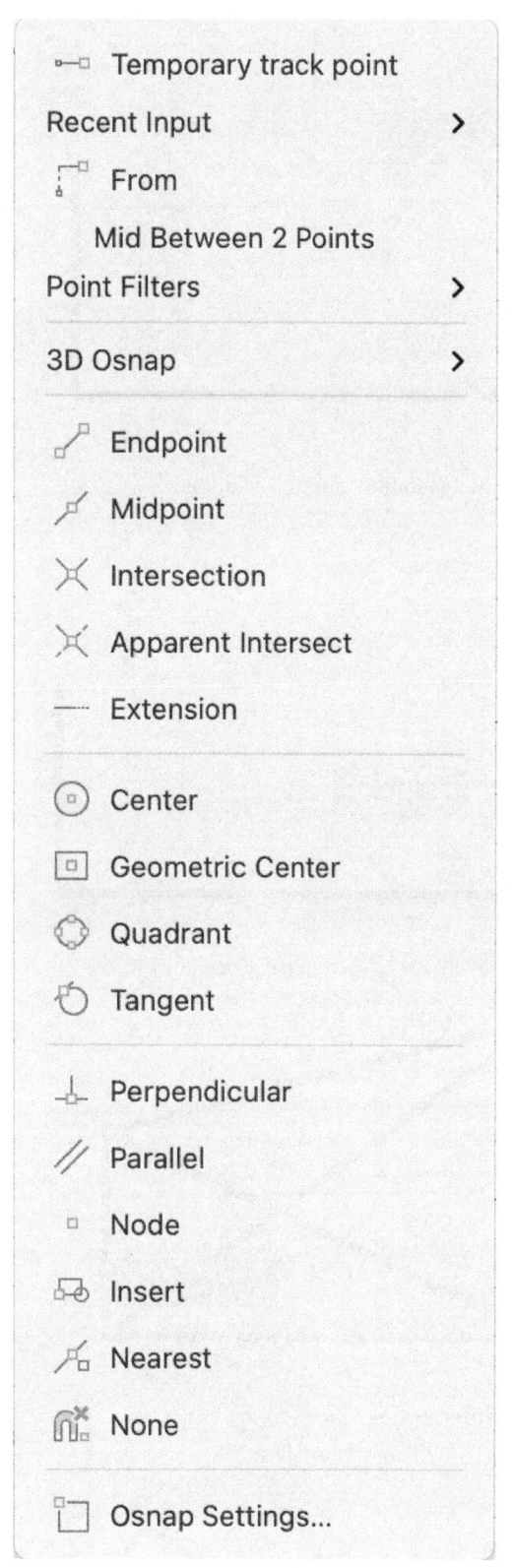

The functions of various Object Snaps are explained next.

Endpoint: Snaps to the endpoints of lines and arcs.

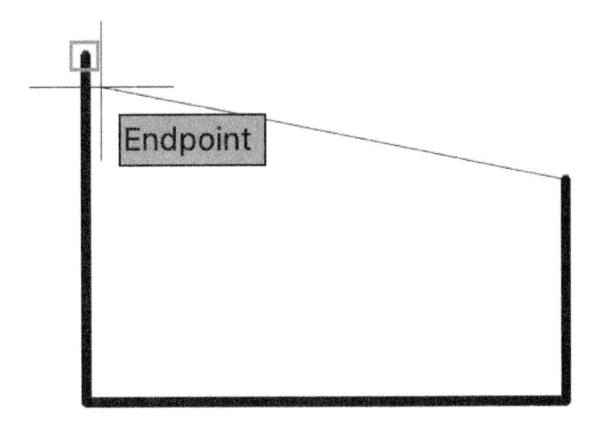

Midpoint: Snaps to the midpoint of a line.

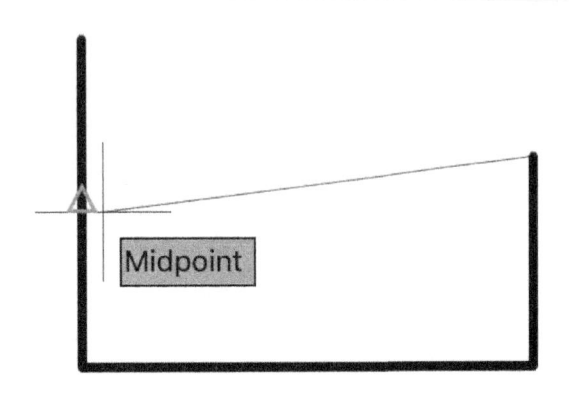

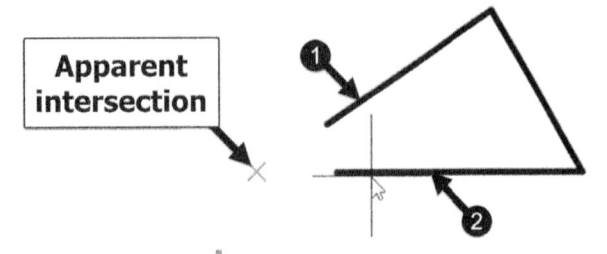

Extension: Creates a temporary extension line when the pointer passes through the endpoints of a line or an arc. You can pick points along the temporary extension lines.

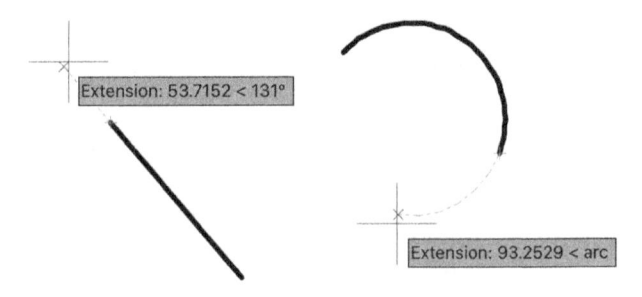

Center: Snaps to the centers of circles and arcs.

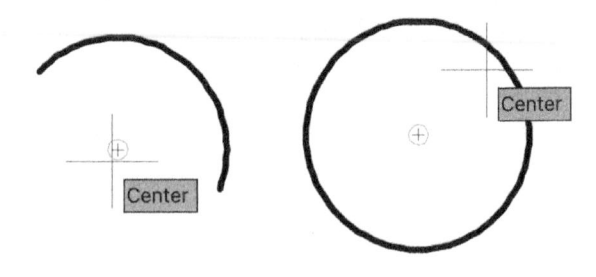

Geometric Center: Snaps to the center point of a closed geometry created by a single object such as polyline, rectangle, or polygon.

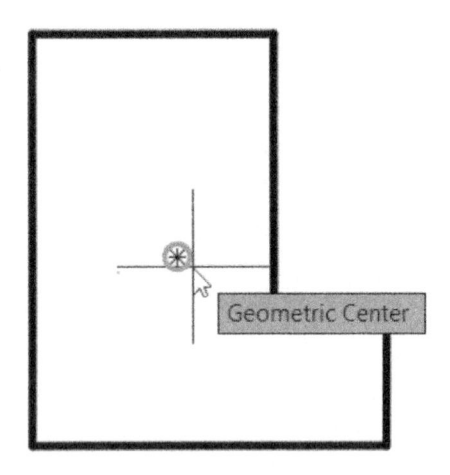

Intersection: Snaps to the intersections of objects.

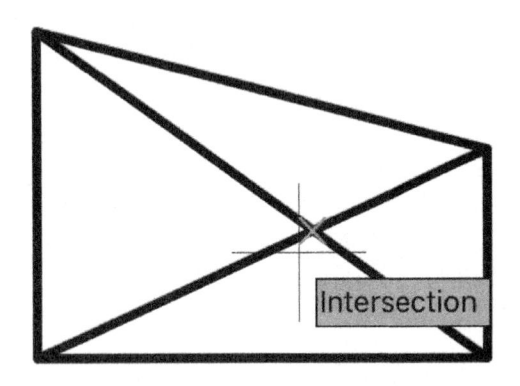

Apparent Intersection: Snaps to the projected intersection of two objects in 3D space.

Quadrant: Snaps to four key points located on a circle.

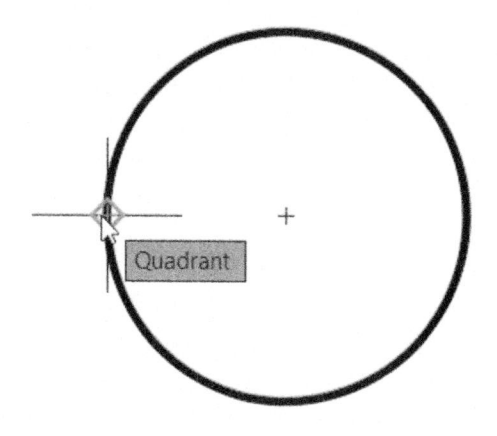

Tangent: Snaps to the tangent points of arcs and circles.

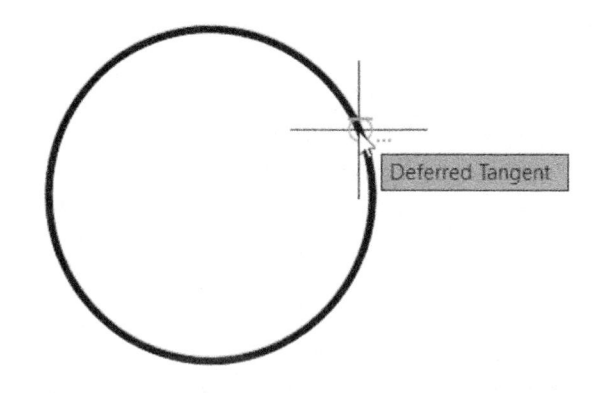

Perpendicular: Snaps to a perpendicular location on an object.

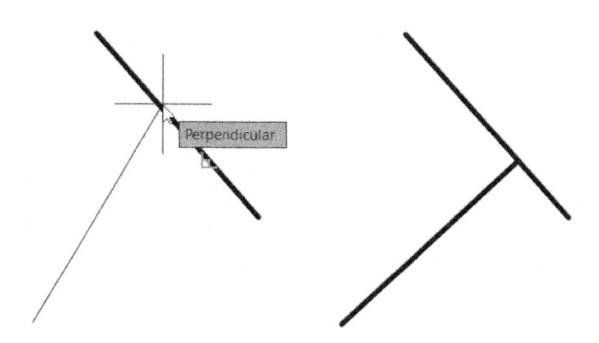

Parallel: It is used to draw an object parallel to another object. Select this option and place the pointer on the first line. Next, move the pointer and notice the track line parallel to the first object. Move along the track line and click to create a line parallel to the first line.

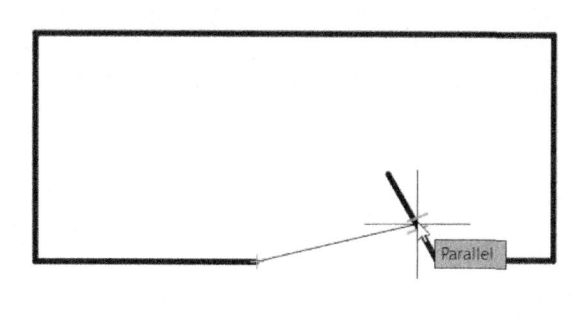

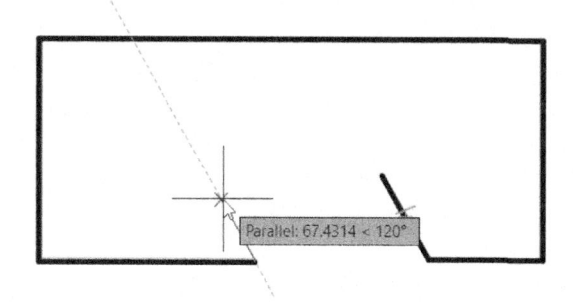

Node: Snaps to points of dimension` lines, text objects, and dimension text.

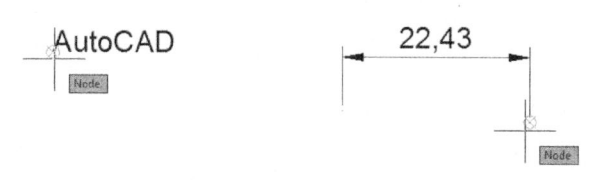

Insert: Snaps to the insertion point of blocks, shapes, and text.

Nearest: Snaps to the nearest point found along with any object.

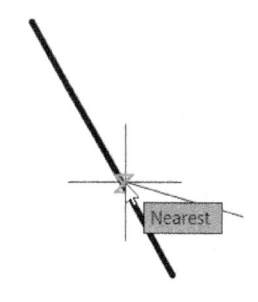

None: Deactivates the Object Snap.

65 | Drawing Aids

Temporary Track Point: It is used to locate a point by using trace lines from a reference point.

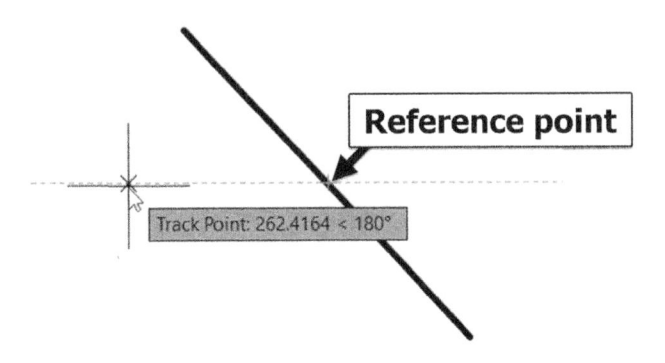

From: Locates a point at a specified distance and direction from a selected reference point.

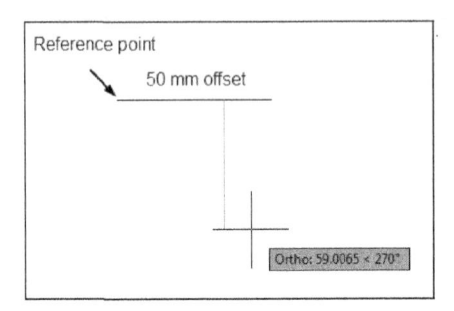

Midpoint Between 2 Points: Snaps to the middle point of two selected points.

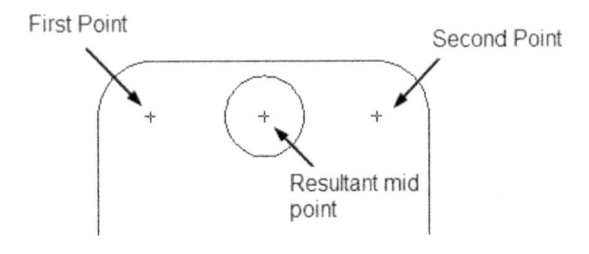

Running Object Snaps

Previously, you have learned to select Object Snaps from the shortcut menu. However, you can make Object Snap modes available continuously instead of picking them every time. You can do this by using the **Running Object Snaps**. To use the Running Object Snaps, click the right-mouse button on the **Object Snaps** button on the status bar and select the required object snap from the menu.

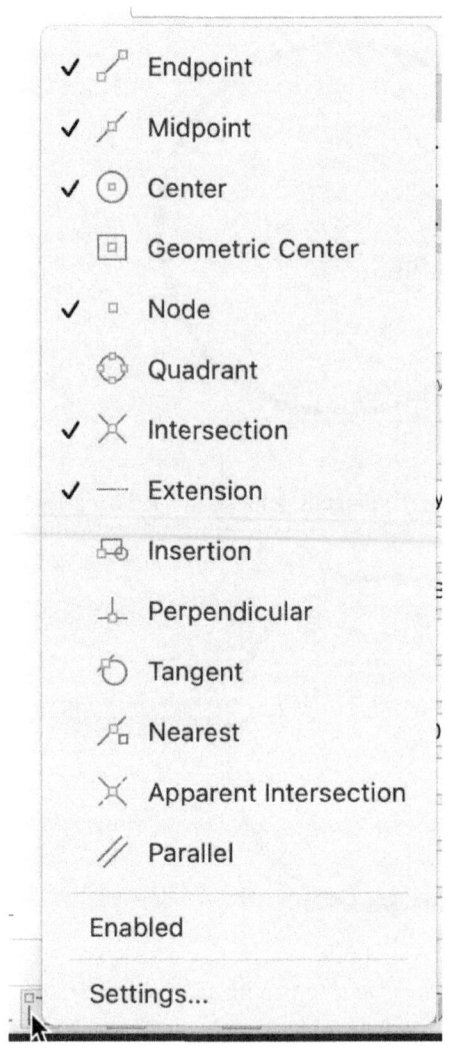

You can also select the **Settings** option from the menu to open the **Drafting Settings** dialog. In this dialog, you can choose the required Object Snaps by selecting checkboxes.

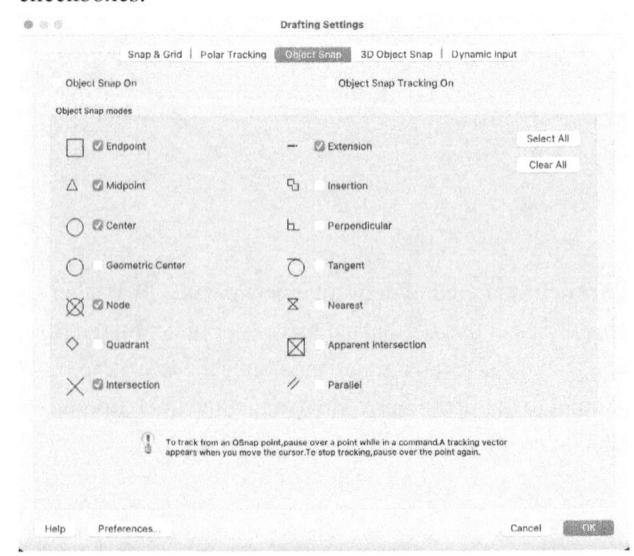

Cycling through Object Snaps

After setting the Running Object Snap settings, AutoCAD displays object snaps depending on the shape of the object. However, you can cycle through the object snaps by pressing the TAB key. In the following example, you will learn to cycle through different object snaps.

Example:

- Click the right mouse button on the **Object Snap** button and select the **Settings** option; the **Drafting Settings** dialog appears.
- Click the **Select All** button and click the **OK** button.
- Draw the objects, as shown below.

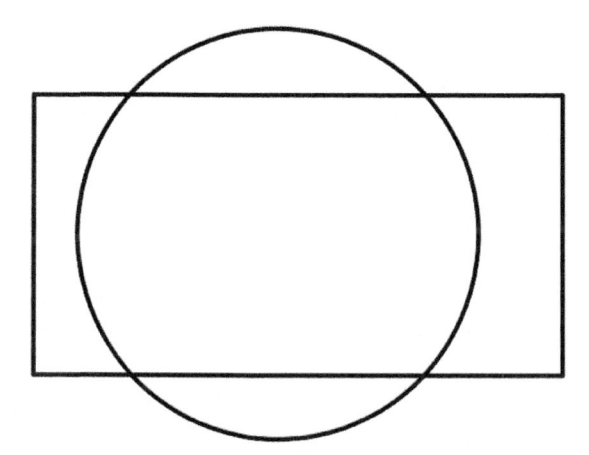

- Click the **Circle** button on the **Draw** panel.
- Place the pointer on the intersection point of the circle and rectangle. Press the TAB key; you will notice that the object snaps change.

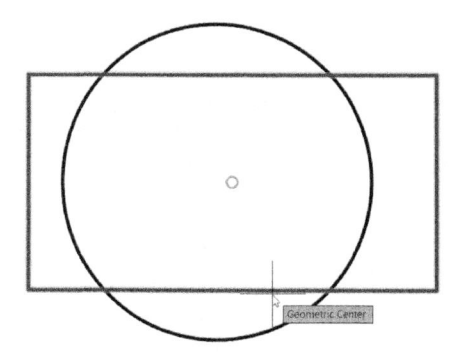

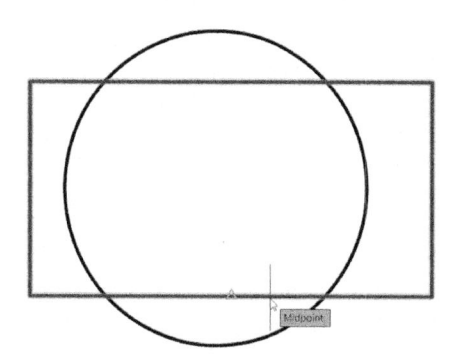

- Click when the **Center** snap is displayed and draw a circle.

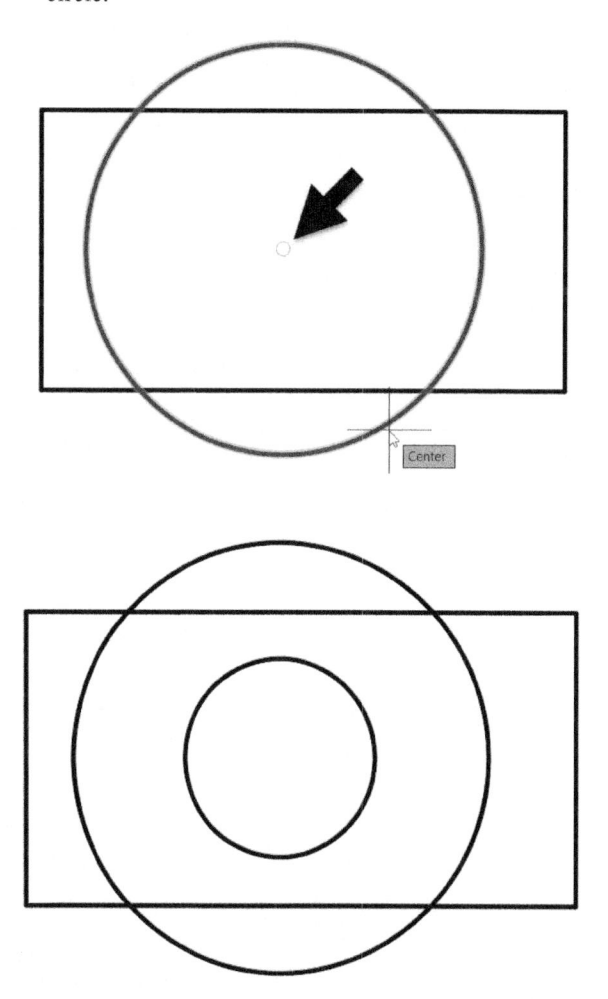

Using Object Snap Tracking

Object Snap tracking is the movement of the pointer along the trace lines originating from the key points of objects. Object Snap Tracking works only when the **Object Snap** mode is turned on. In the following example, you will learn to use Object Snap Tracking for creating objects.

AutoCAD 2023 For Beginners (For Mac Users)

Example:
- Select the **Object Snap Tracking** button from the Status bar.

(OR)
- Open the **Drafting Settings** dialog and click the **Object Snap** tab.
- Select the **Object Snap Tracking On** checkbox.

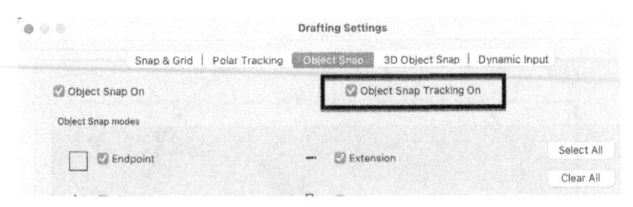

- Click **OK**.
- Use the **Line** tool and draw the objects, as shown below.

- Press the RETURN key twice to start drawing lines from the last point.
- Move the pointer and place it on the endpoint of the lower horizontal line.

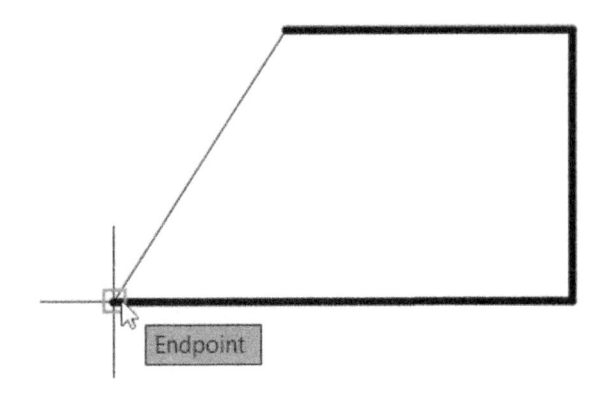

- Move the pointer vertically upward; you will notice the trace line, as shown below.

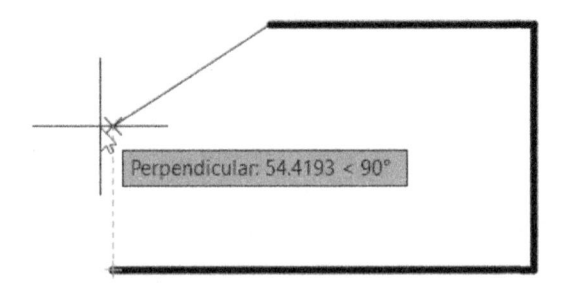

- Click on the trace line to create an inclined line.
- Snap the pointer to the endpoint of the lower horizontal line and click.

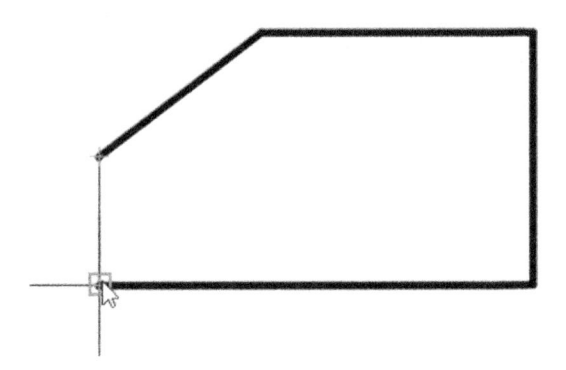

- Right-click and select Enter.
- Click the **Circle** button on the **Draw** panel of the tool set.
- Place the pointer over the lower endpoint of the inclined line and move horizontally; you will notice that a trace line is displayed.
- Place the pointer on the midpoint of the lower horizontal line; a vertical trace line is displayed from the midpoint of the horizontal line, as shown below.

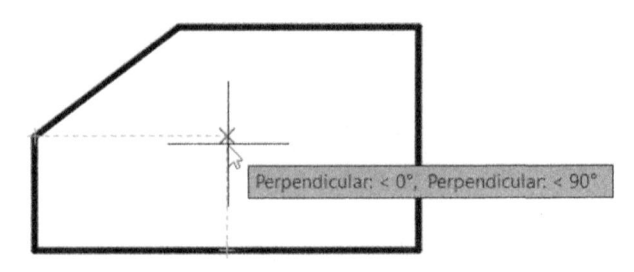

- Click at the point where the horizontal and vertical trace lines intersect. Next, create a circle, as shown below.

68 | Drawing Aids

AutoCAD 2023 For Beginners (For Mac Users)

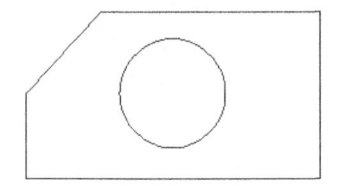

Linetype gap selection

AutoCAD makes it easy to select line types such as centerlines, dashed-dotted lines, hidden, and phantom. Earlier, it was difficult to select these linetypes by clicking in the gaps. Now, you can select them by clicking on the gaps.

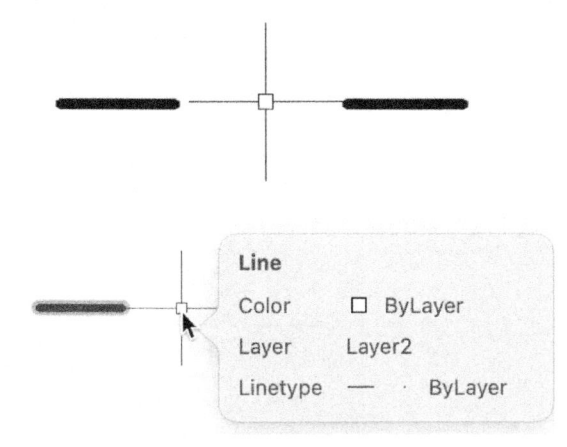

You can also snap to the line at the gaps.

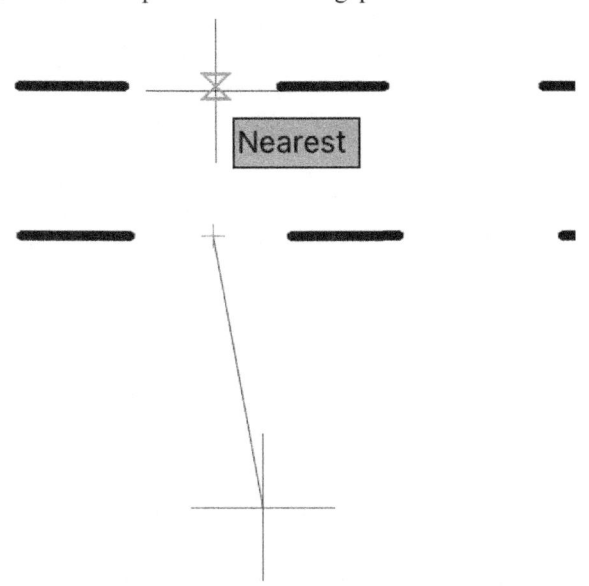

The LTGAPSELECTION system variable, when set to 1, helps you to select the line by clicking in the gaps. You can turn OFF this feature by setting the LTGAPSELECTION system variable to 0.

Using Zoom tools

Using the zoom tools, you can magnify or reduce a drawing. You can use these tools to view the minute details of a very complicated drawing. The Zoom tools can be accessed from the Command line and Menu Bar.

Menu Bar

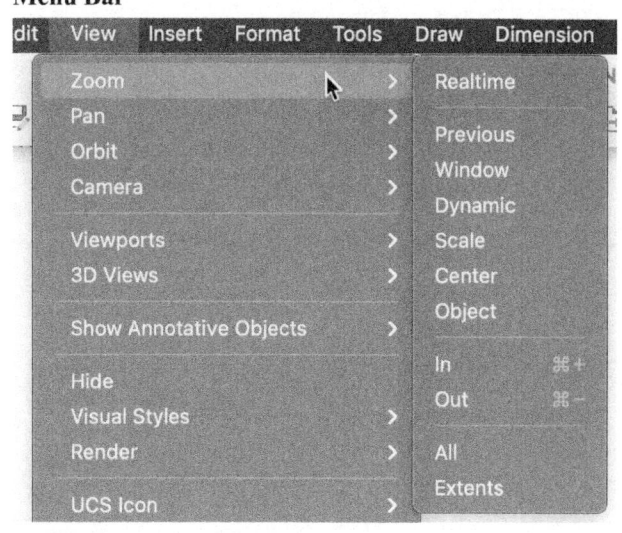

Command line

ZOOM [All/Center/Dynamic/Extents/Previous/Scale/Window/Object] <real time>:

Zooming with the Mouse Wheel

Zooming using the mouse wheel is one of the easiest methods.

- Roll the mouse wheel forward to zoom into a drawing.
- Roll the mouse wheel backward to zoom out of the drawing.
- Press the mouse wheel and drag the mouse to pan the drawing.

Using Zoom Extents

Using the **Zoom Extents** tool, you can zoom to the extents of the largest object in a drawing.

- Click **View > Zoom > Extents** on the Menu bar.
- You can also double-click on the mouse wheel to zoom to extents.

Drawing Aids

Using Zoom-Window

Using the **Zoom-Window** tool, you can define the area to be zoomed by selecting two points representing a rectangle.

- Click **View > Zoom > Window** on the Menu Bar (or) click the **Zoom Window** icon on the toolbar.
- Specify the first point of the zoom window, as shown.
- Move the pointer diagonally toward the right, and then specify the second point, as shown.
  The area inside the window will be zoomed.

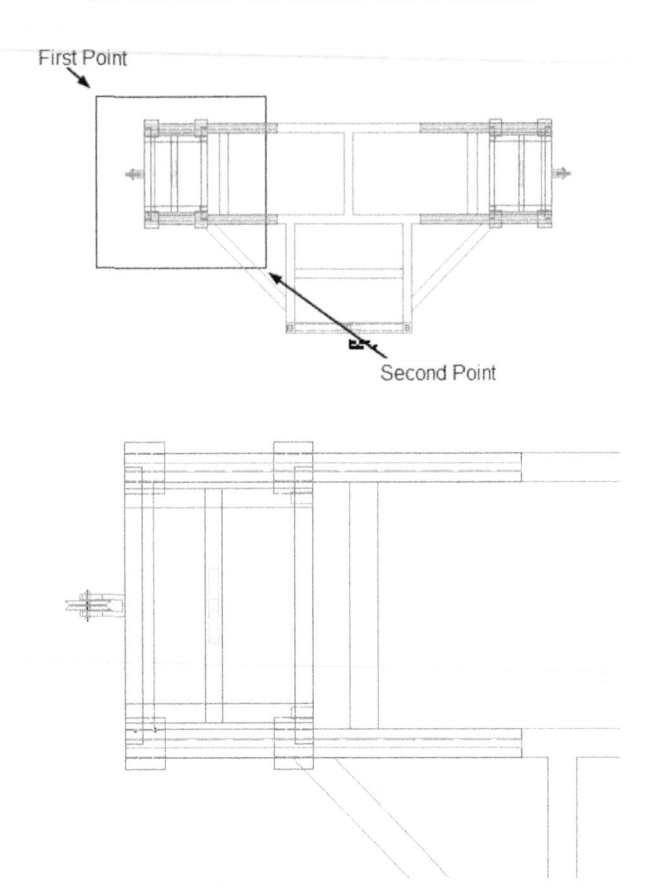

Using Zoom-Previous

After magnifying a small area of the drawing, you can use the **Zoom-Previous** tool to return to the previous display.

- Click **View > Zoom > Previous** on the Menu Bar.

Using Zoom-Realtime

Using the **Zoom-Realtime** tool, you can zoom in or zoom out of a drawing dynamically.

- Click **View > Zoom > Realtime** on the **Menu Bar** (or) right-click and select **Zoom** from the shortcut menu; the pointer is changed to a magnifying glass with plus and minus symbols.
- Press and hold the left mouse button and drag the mouse forward to zoom into the drawing.
- Drag the mouse backward to zoom out of the drawing.

Using Zoom-All

The **Zoom All** tool is used to adjust the drawing space to the limits set by using the LIMITS command.

- Click **View > Zoom > All** on the **Menu Bar**; the drawing will be zoomed to its limits.

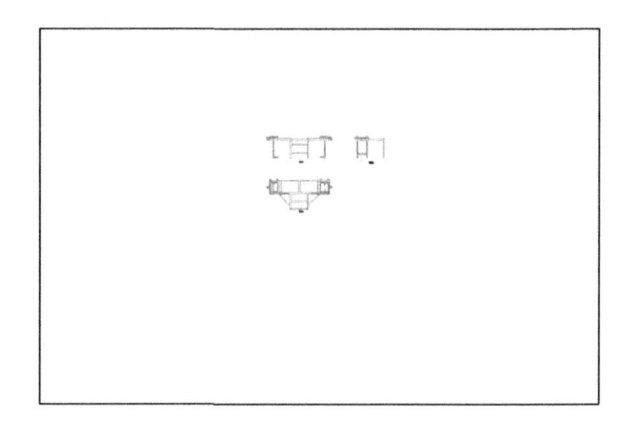

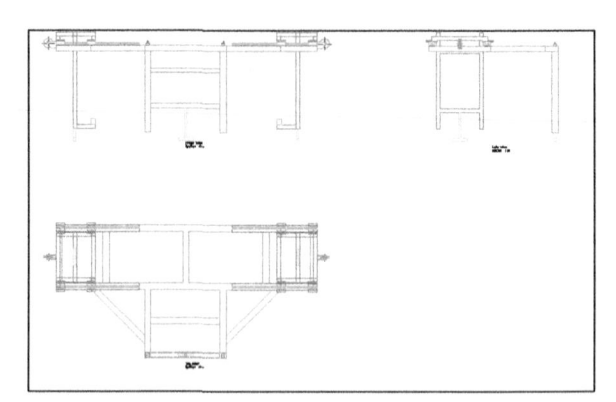

Using Zoom Dynamic

With the **Zoom Dynamic** tool, you can zoom to a particular portion of a drawing by using a viewing box.

- Click **View > Zoom > Dynamic** on the Menu Bar; the drawing will be zoomed to its limits. Also, a viewing box is attached to the pointer.

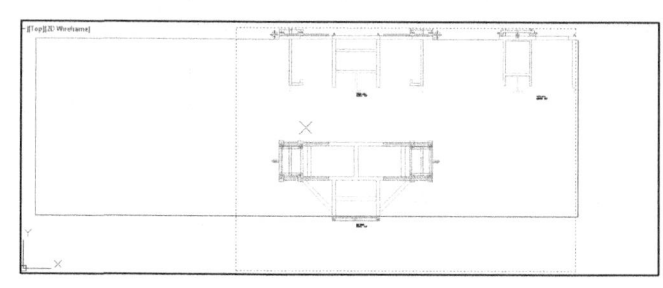

- Click and drag the pointer to define the size of the viewing box.
- Left-click and move the pointer to the area to be zoomed.

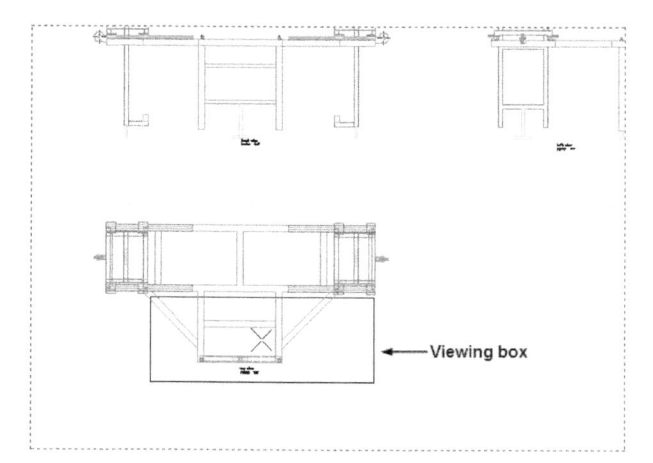

- Press RETURN. The area covered by the viewing box is magnified.

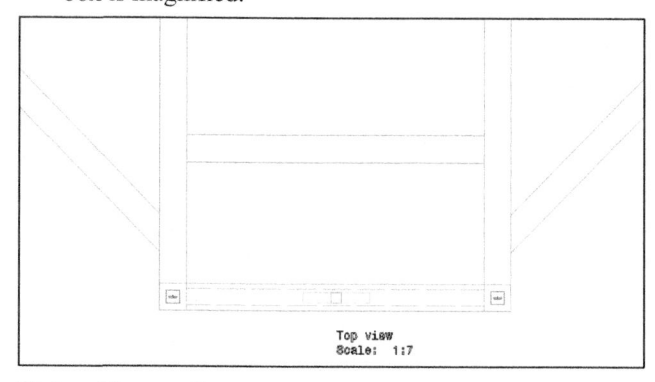

Using Zoom-Scale

Using the **Zoom-Scale** tool, you can zoom in or zoom out of a drawing by entering zoom scale factors directly from your keyboard.

- Click the **View > Zoom > Scale** on the Menu Bar. The message, "**Enter a scale factor (nX or nXP)**," appears in the command line.
- Enter the scale factor 0.25 to scale the drawing to 25% of the full view.
- Enter the scale factor 0.25X to scale the drawing to 25% of the current view.
- Enter the scale factor 0.25XP to scale the drawing to 25% of the paper space.

Using Zoom-Center

Using the **Zoom Center** tool, you can zoom to an area of the drawing based on a center point and magnification value.

- Click **View > Zoom > Center** on the Menu bar; the message, "**Specify Center point**," appears in the command line.
- Select a point in the drawing to which you want to zoom in; the message, "**Enter magnification or height**," appears in the command line.

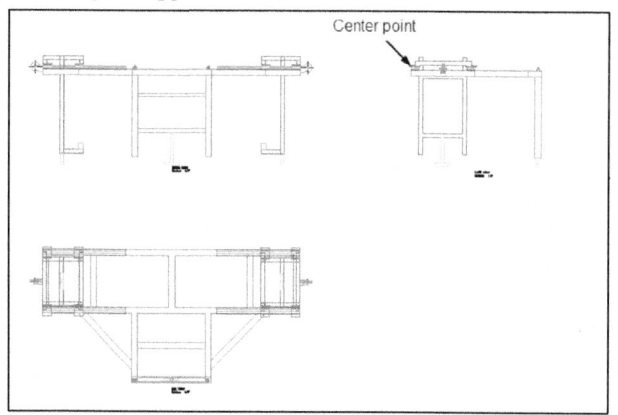

- Enter 10X in the command line to magnify the location of the point by ten times.

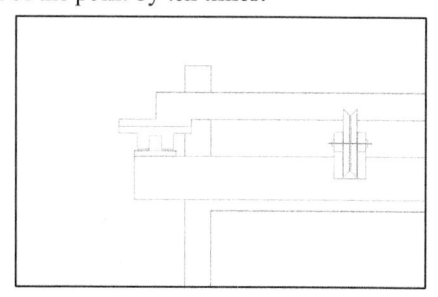

Using Zoom-Object

Using the **Zoom Object** tool, you can magnify a portion of the drawing by selecting one or more objects.

- Click **View> Zoom > Object** on the Menu Bar.
- Select one or more objects from the drawing and press RETURN; the objects will be magnified.

Drawing Aids

Using Zoom-In

Using the **Zoom In** tool, you can magnify the drawing by a scale factor of 2.

- Click **View > Zoom > In** on the Menu Bar; the drawing is magnified to double.

Using Zoom-Out

The **Zoom-out** tool is used to de-magnify the display screen by a scale factor of 0.5.

Panning Drawings

After zooming into a drawing, you may want to view an area that is outside the current display. You can do this by using the **Pan** tool.

- Click **Pan** on the Toolbar.

- Press and hold the left mouse button and drag the mouse; a new area of the drawing, which is outside the current view, is displayed.

Exercises

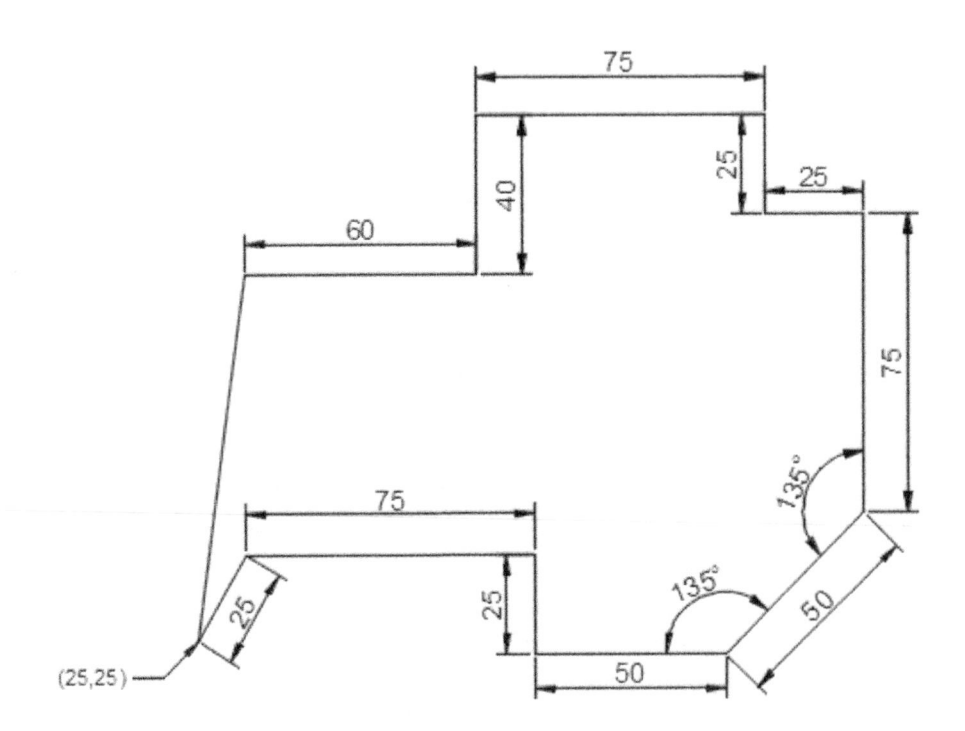

Drawing Aids

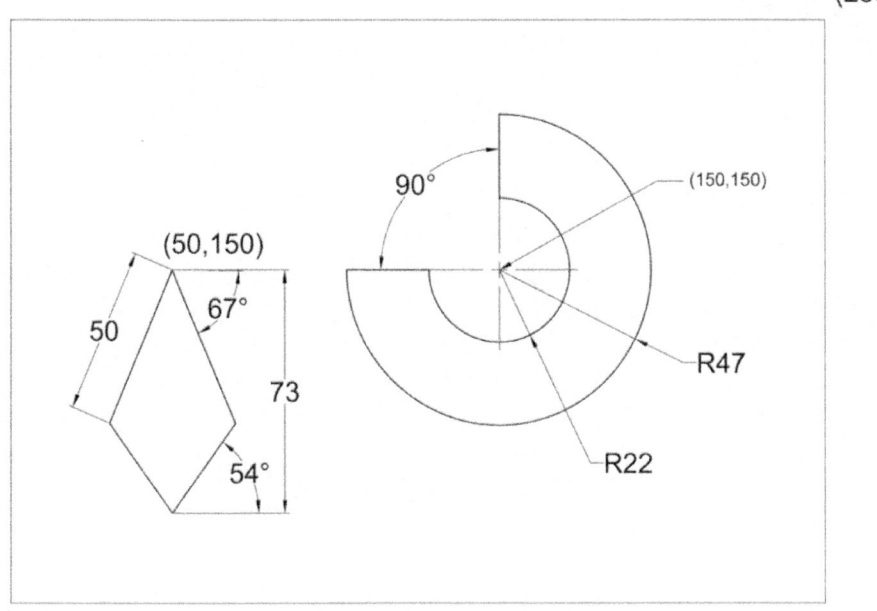

Chapter 4: Editing Tools

In this chapter, you will learn the following tools:

- The **Move** tool
- The **Copy** tool
- The **Rotate** tool
- The **Scale** tool
- The **Trim** tool
- The **Extend** tool
- The **Fillet** tool
- The **Chamfer** tool
- The **Mirror** tool
- The **Explode** tool
- The **Stretch** tool
- The **Polar Array** tool
- The **Offset** tool
- The **Path Array** tool
- The **Rectangular Array** tool

Editing Tools

In previous chapters, you have learned to create some simple drawings using the basic drawing tools. However, to create complex drawings, you may need to perform various editing operations. The tools to perform the editing operations are available in the **Modify** panel on the **Drafting** tool set. You can click the down arrow on this panel to find more editing tools. Using these editing tools, you can modify existing objects or use existing objects to create new or similar objects.

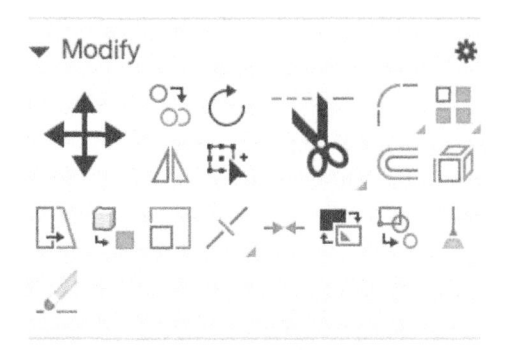

The Move tool

The **Move** tool moves a selected object(s) from one location to a new location without changing its orientation. To move objects, you must activate this tool and select the objects from the graphics window. After selecting the objects, you must define the 'base point' and the 'destination point.'

Example:

- Create the drawing, as shown below.

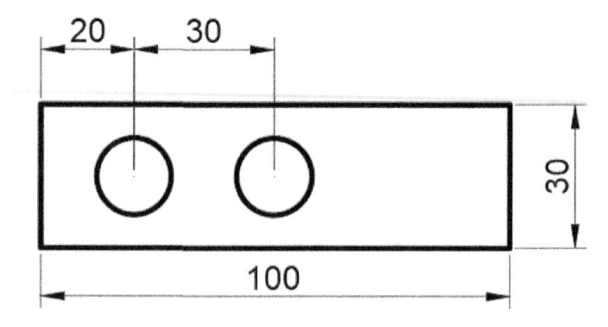

- Click **Drafting > Modify > Move** on the tool set (or) type **M** in the command line and press RETURN.
- Click on the circle located at the right side, and then right-click to accept the selection.

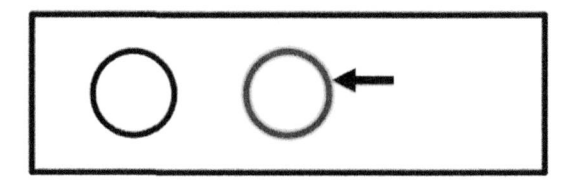

- Select the center of the circle as the base point.

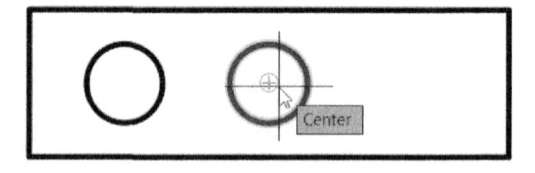

- Make sure that the **Ortho Mode** is activated.
- Move the pointer toward the right, type 30, and then press RETURN. It moves the circle to the new location.

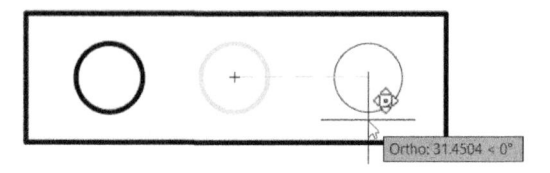

The Copy tool

The **Copy** tool is used to copy objects and place them at a required location. This tool is similar to the **Move** tool, except that the object will remain at its original position, and a copy of it will be placed at the new location.

Example:
- Draw two circles of 40 mm and 70 mm radii, respectively.

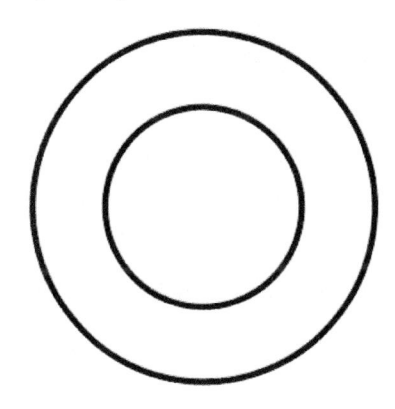

- Click **Drafting > Modify > Copy** on the tool set (or) type **CO** in the command line and press RETURN.
- Select the two circles and then right-click to accept the selection.
- Select the center of the circle as the base point.

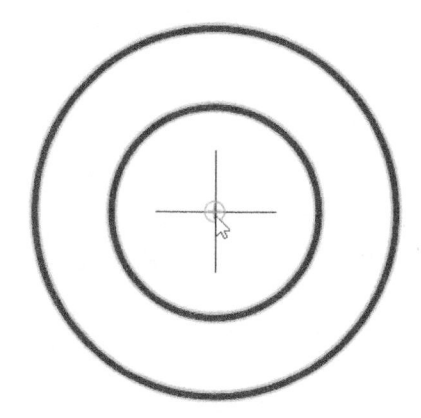

- Make sure that the **Ortho Mode** is active.
- Move the pointer toward the right.
- Type 200 and press RETURN. This action creates a copy of the circles at the new location

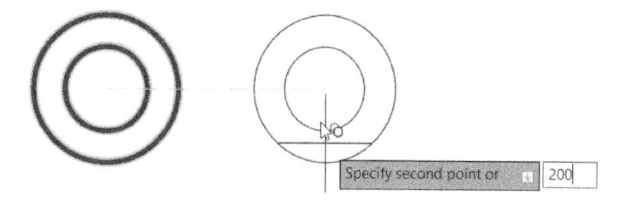

- Right-click and select **Exit** from the shortcut menu.

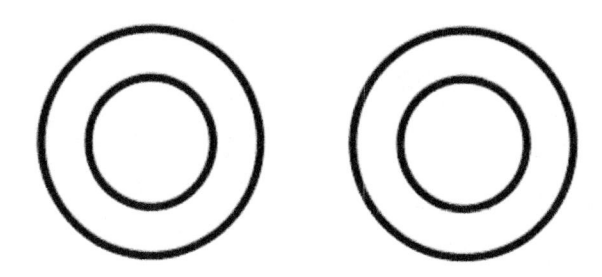

The Rotate tool

The **Rotate** tool rotates an object or a group of objects about a base point. Activate this tool and select the objects from the graphics window. After selecting objects, you must define the 'base point' and the angle of rotation. It rotates the object(s) about the base point.

- Click **Drafting > Modify > Rotate** on the tool set (or) type **RO** in the command line and press RETURN.
- Select the circles as shown below, and then right-click to accept.

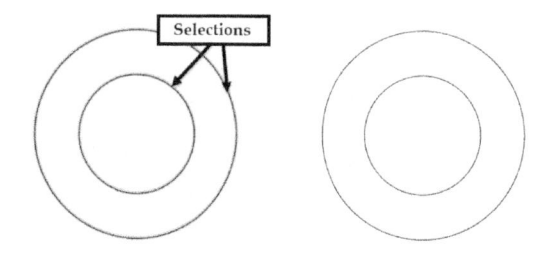

- Select the center of the other circle as the base point.

Editing Tools

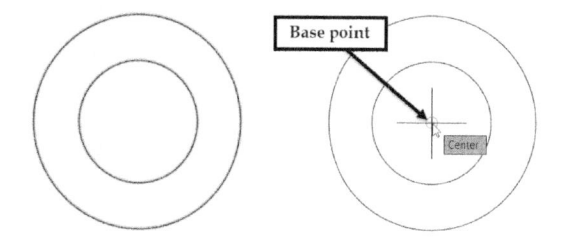

AutoCAD 2023 For Beginners (For Mac Users)

- Right-click and select **Copy** from the shortcut menu.
- Type -90 as the rotation angle and press RETURN; the selected objects are rotated by 90 degrees.

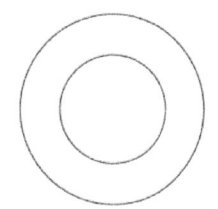

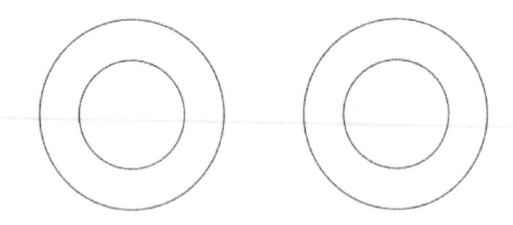

The Scale tool

The **Scale** tool changes the size of objects. It reduces or enlarges the size without changing the shape of an object.

- Click **Drafting > Modify > Scale** on the tool set (or) type **SC** in the command line and press RETURN.
- Select the circles as shown below and right-click to accept the selection.

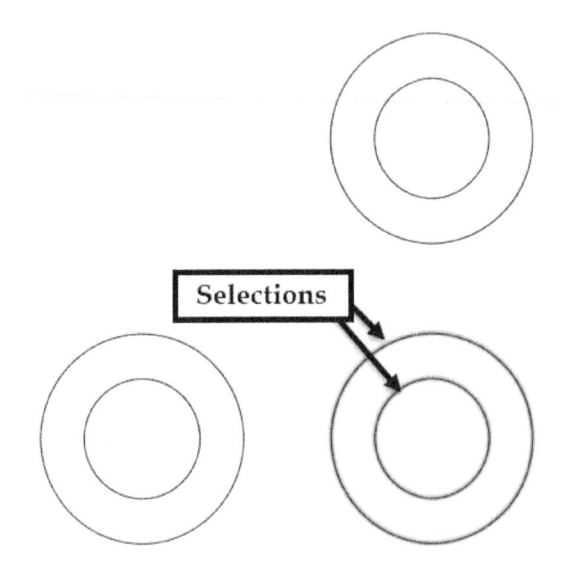

- Select the center point of the selected circles as the base point.
- Type 0.8 as the scale factor and press RETURN.

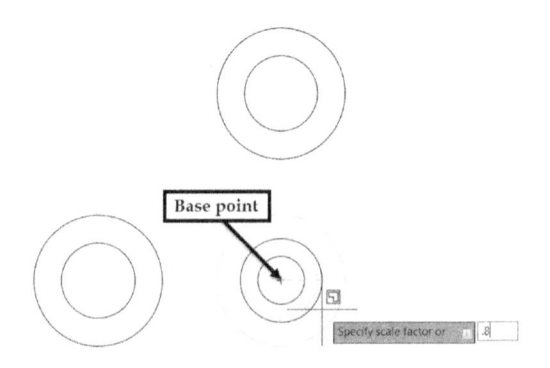

- Likewise, scale the circles located at the top to 0.7.

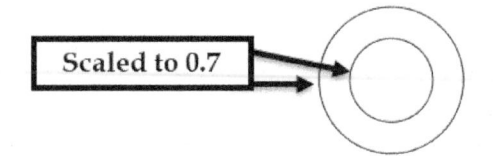

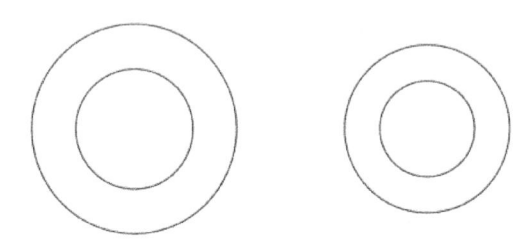

- Click **Drafting > Draw > Circle > Tan, Tan, Radius** on the tool set.
- Select the two circles shown below to define the tangent points.

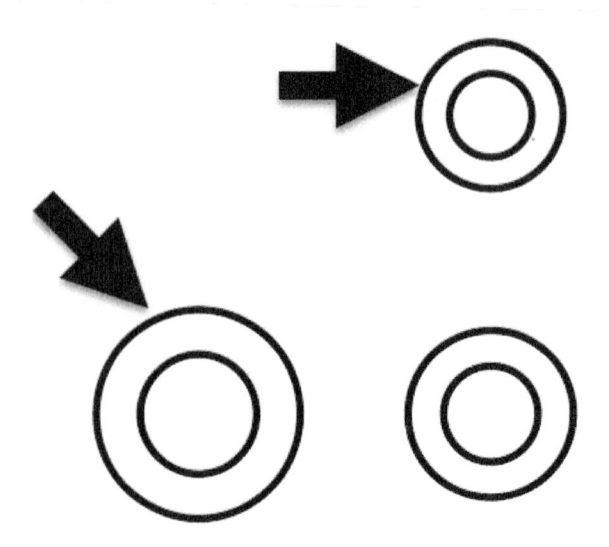

- Type 150 as the radius of the circle and press RETURN.

76 | Editing Tools

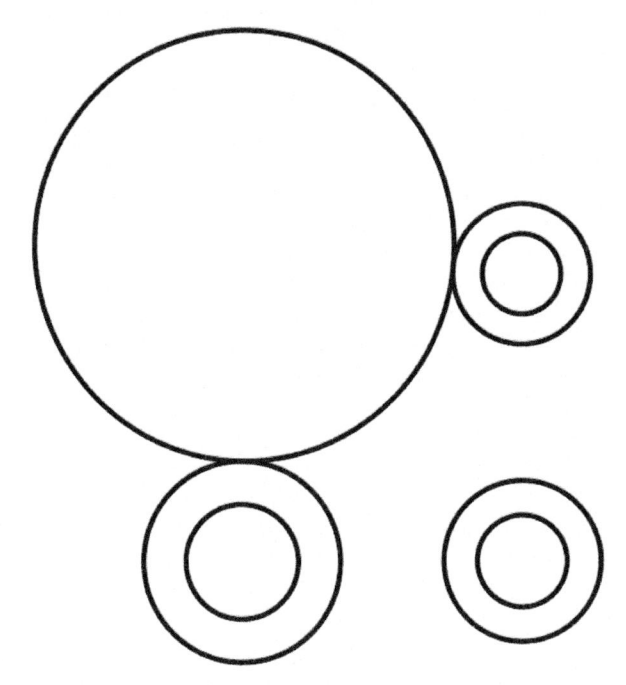

- Likewise, create other circles of radius 100 and 120.

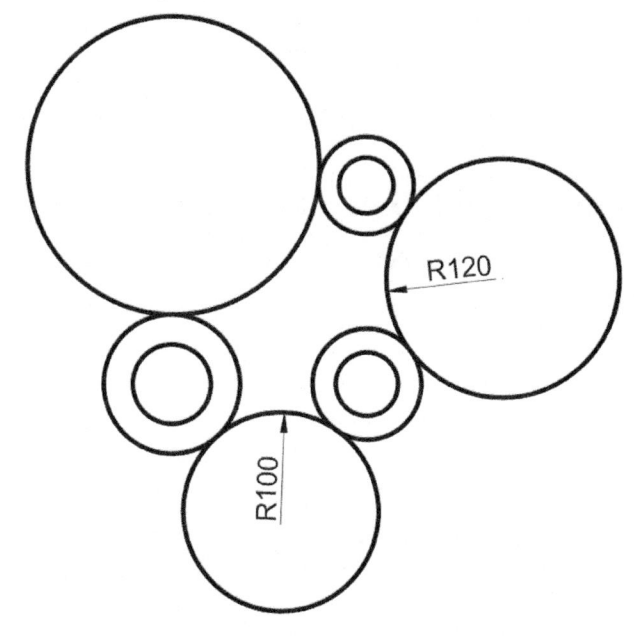

The Trim tool

When an object intersects with another object, you can remove its unwanted portion by using the **Trim** tool. To trim an object, you must first activate the **Trim** tool, and then select the elements to be trimmed. You can also select the elements to trim by dragging the cursor across them.

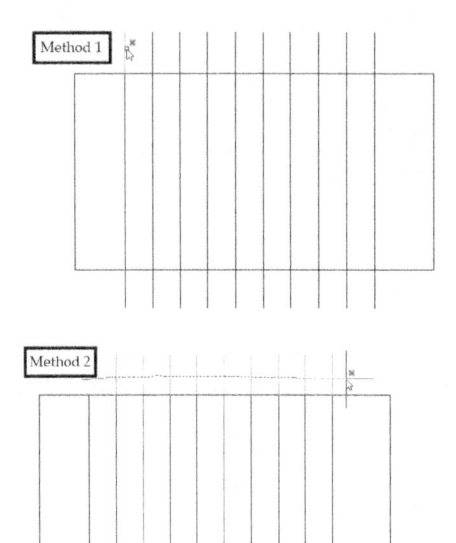

Click and move the pointer across the elements to trimmed. Next, click again to select them.

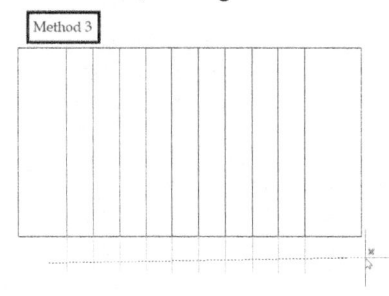

However, if you want to trim the elements using an intersecting object, then right-click and select **cuTting edges** option from the shortcut menu. Next, select the cutting edges (intersecting objects). Next, press RETURN and select the portions to be removed.

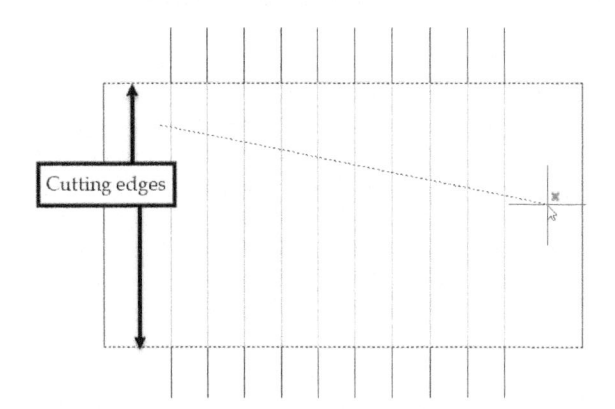

- Click **Drafting > Modify > Trim** on the tool set (or) type **TR** in the command line and press RETURN. Now, you must select the objects to be trimmed.

77 | Editing Tools

- Select the large circles one by one; the circles will be trimmed.

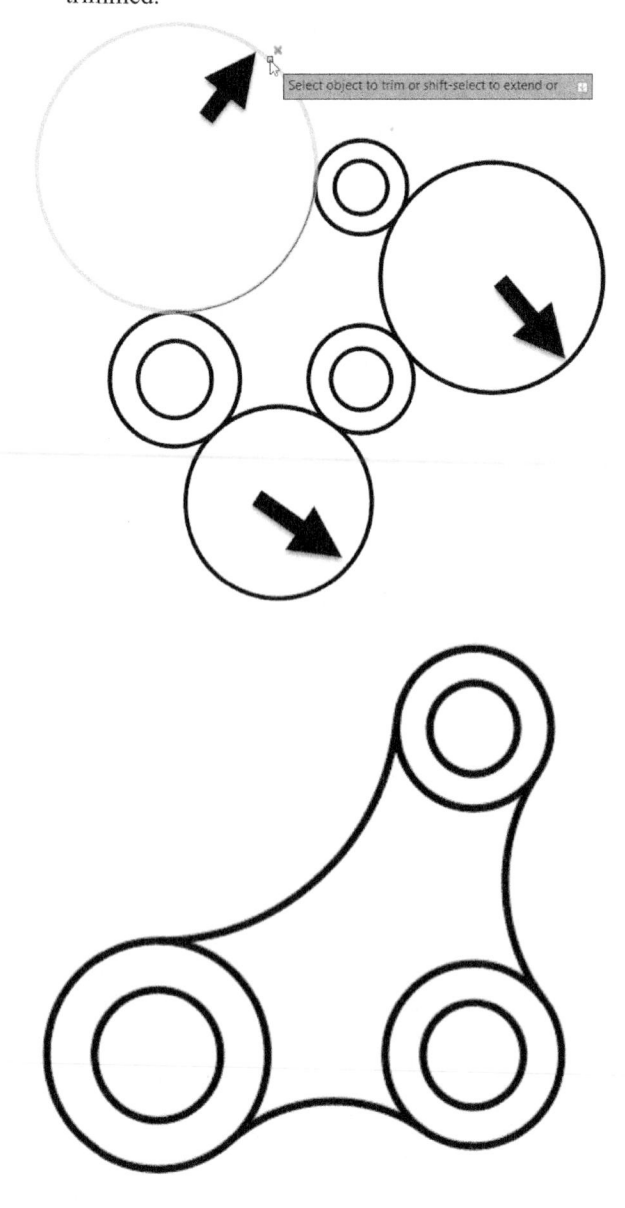

- Likewise, trim the other circles, as shown below.

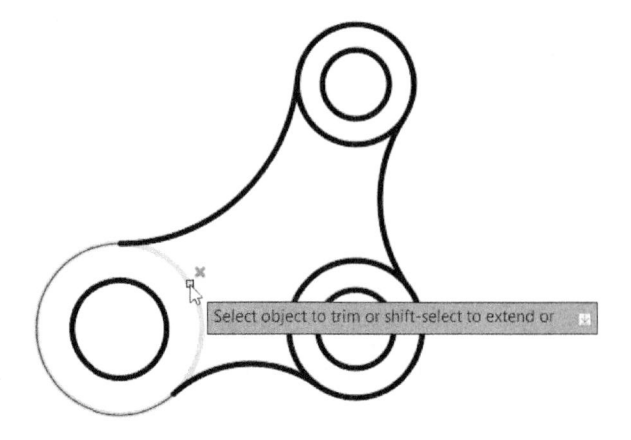

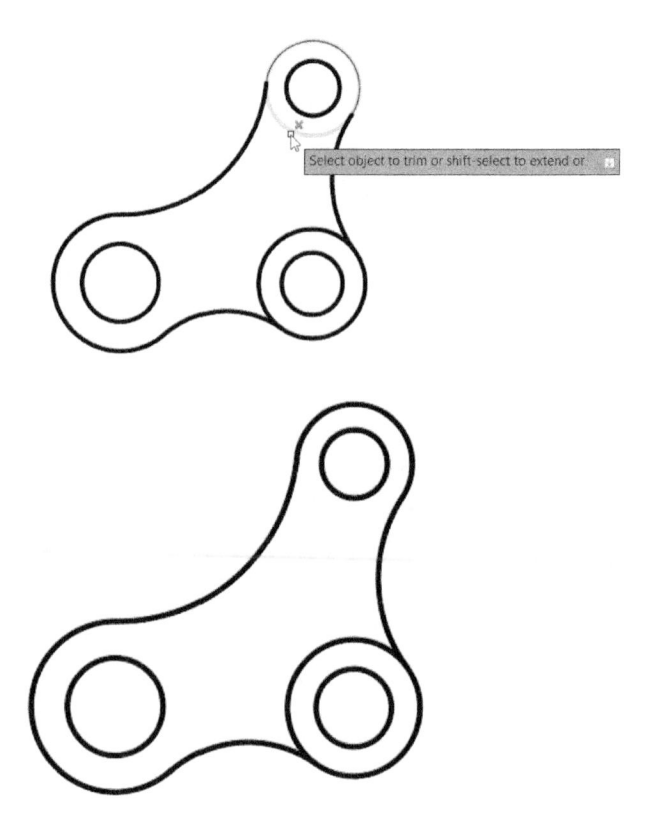

- Save and close the drawing.

The Cut with Base Point Tool

The **Cut With Base Point** tool allows you to cut and paste the selected objects using a base point. You can paste the cut objects within a drawing or in another drawing.

- Click **Edit > Cut With Base Point** on the menu bar.

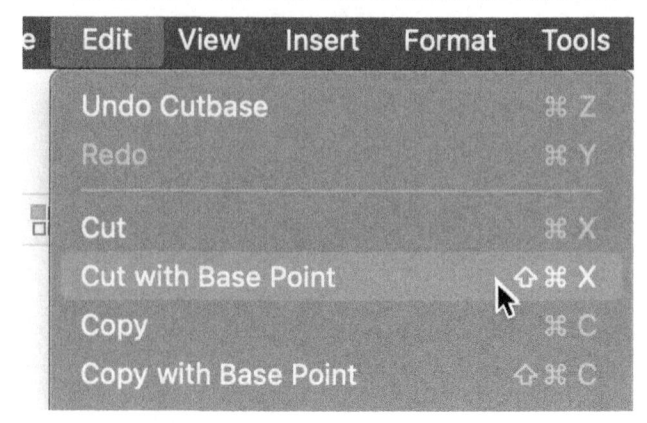

- Select the base point of the selection.

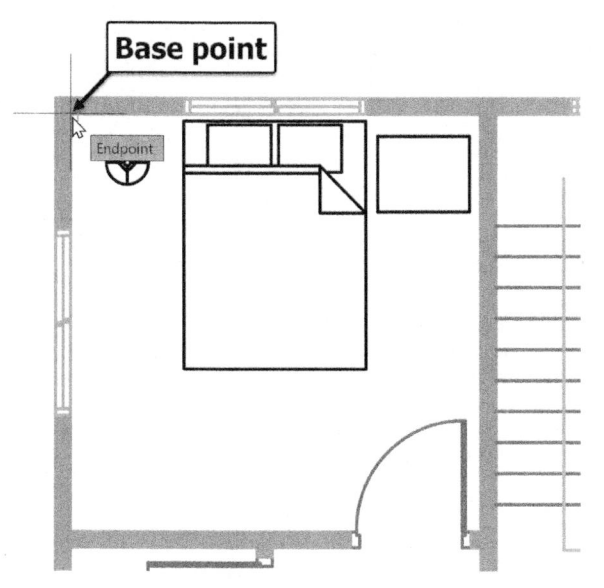

- Create a selection window across all the objects to be moved. Next, press ENTER.

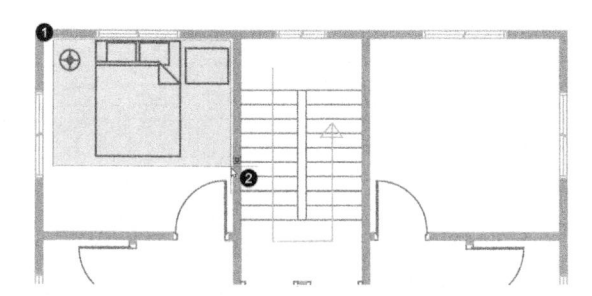

- Click **Edit > Paste** on the menu bar.
- Select the destination point.

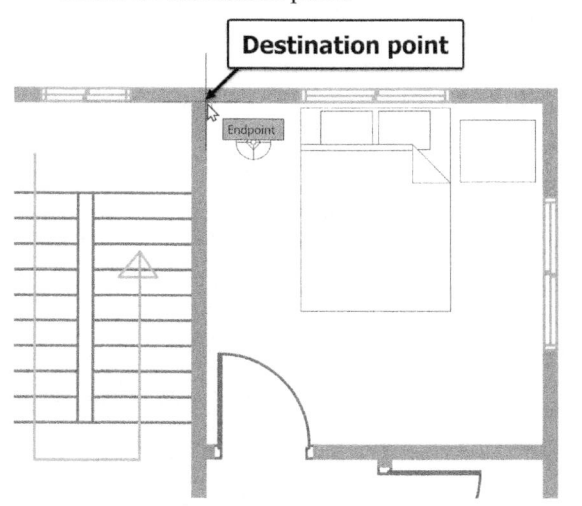

The Extend tool

The **Extend** tool is similar to the **Trim** tool, but its use is the opposite of it. This tool is used to extend lines, arcs, and other open entities to connect to other objects.

- Start a new drawing.
- Create a sketch, as shown below, using the **Line** tool.

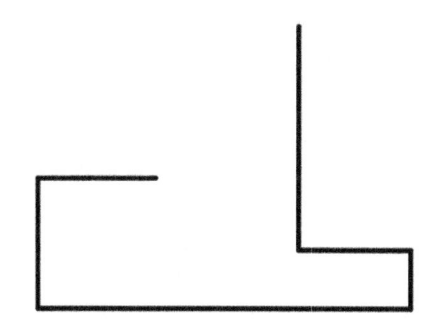

- Click **Drafting > Modify > Trim > Extend** on the tool set (or) type **EX** in the command line and press RETURN.
- Select the horizontal open line. It will extend the line up to the next element.

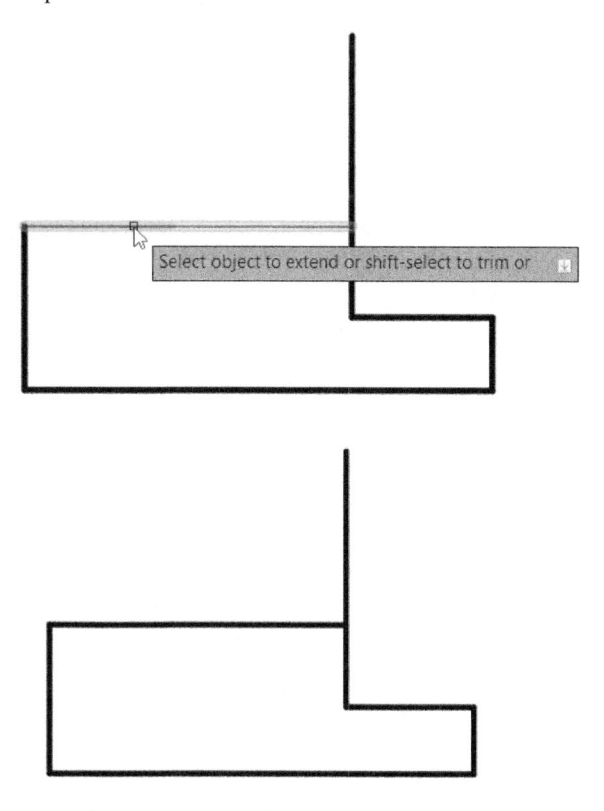

The Fillet tool

The **Fillet** tool converts the sharp corners into round corners. You must define the radius and select the objects forming a corner. The following figure shows some examples of rounding the corners.

AutoCAD 2023 For Beginners (For Mac Users)

Before   After

- Start a new drawing.
- Type **Limmax** in the command line and press RETURN.
- Set the maximum limit to 100,100 and press RETURN.
- Click **View > Zoom > All** on the Menu Bar.
- Click **Drafting > Draw > Polyline** on the tool set.
- Define the start point as 20, 50.
- Draw the lines, as shown below.

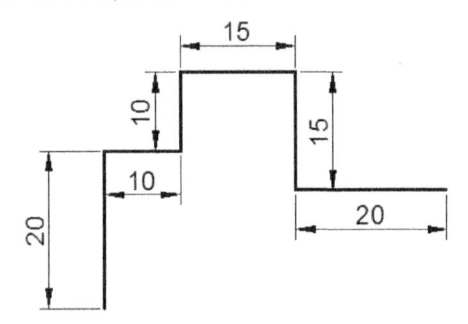

- Right-click and select RETURN.
- Click **Drafting > Modify > Fillet** on the tool set (or) type **F** in the command line and press RETURN.
- Right-click and select the **Radius** option from the shortcut menu.
- Type **5** and press RETURN.
- Select the vertical and horizontal lines, as shown below.

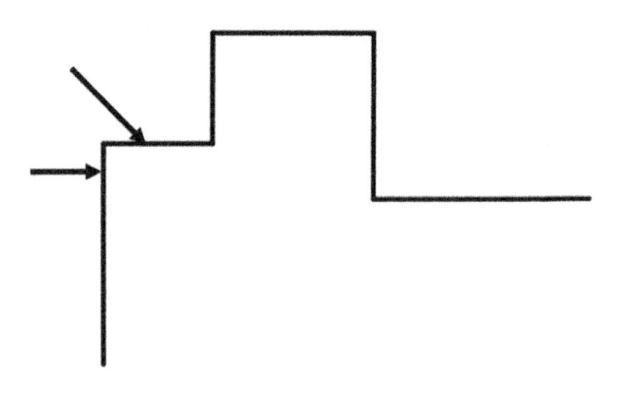

- Notice that a fillet is created.

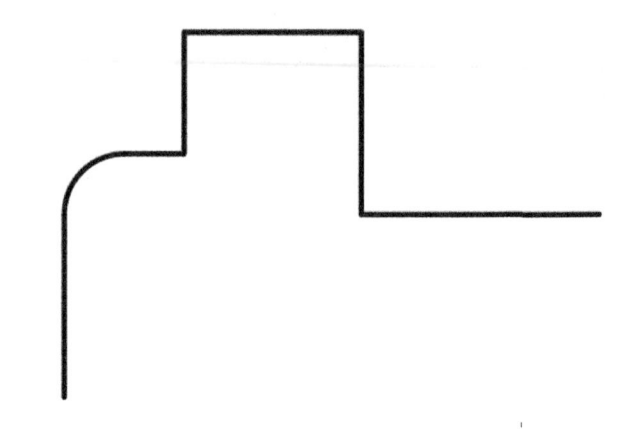

The Chamfer tool

The **Chamfer** tool replaces the sharp corners with an angled line. This tool is similar to the **Fillet** tool, except that an angled line is placed at the corners instead of rounds.

- Click **Drafting > Modify > Fillet > Chamfer** on the tool set (or) type **CHA** in the command line and press RETURN.
- Follow the prompt sequence given next:

Select first line or [Undo/Polyline/Distance/Angle/Trim/mEthod/Multiple]: Type D in the command line and press RETURN.

Define first chamfer distance <0.0000>: Enter **8** as the first chamfer distance and press RETURN.

80 | Editing Tools

AutoCAD 2023 For Beginners (For Mac Users)

Define second chamfer distance <8.0000>: Press RETURN to accept 8 as the second chamfer distance.

Select first line or [Undo/Polyline/Distance/Angle/Trim/mEthod/Multiple]: Select the vertical line on the right-side.

Select second line or shift-select to apply corner or [Distance/Angle/Method]: Select the horizontal line connected to the vertical line.

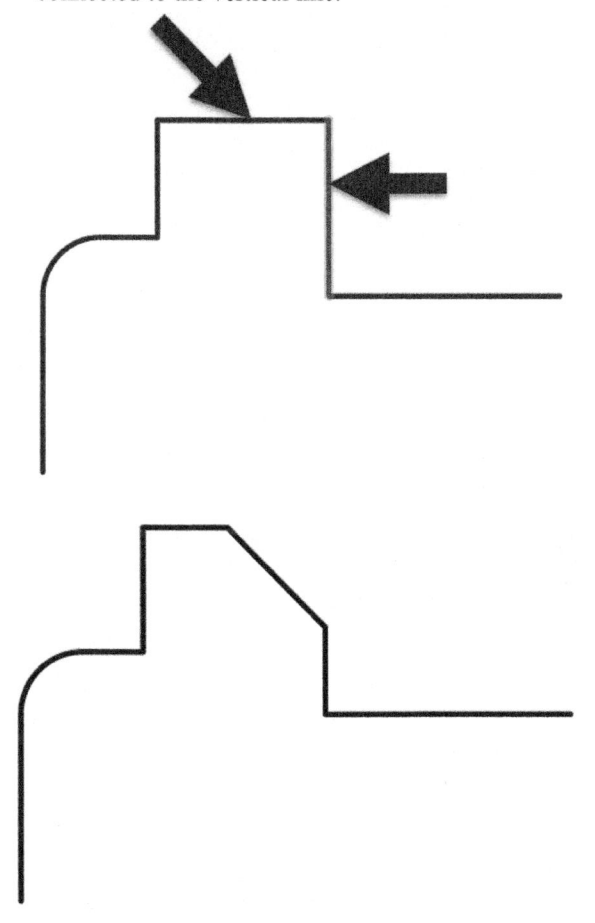

The Mirror tool

The **Mirror** tool creates a mirror image of objects. You can create symmetrical drawings using this tool. Activate this tool and select the objects to mirror, and then define the 'mirror line' about which the objects will be mirrored. You can define the mirror line by either creating a line or selecting an existing line.

- Click **Drafting > Modify > Mirror** on the tool set (or) type **MI** in the command line and press RETURN.

- Select the drawing by clicking on it, and then press RETURN.

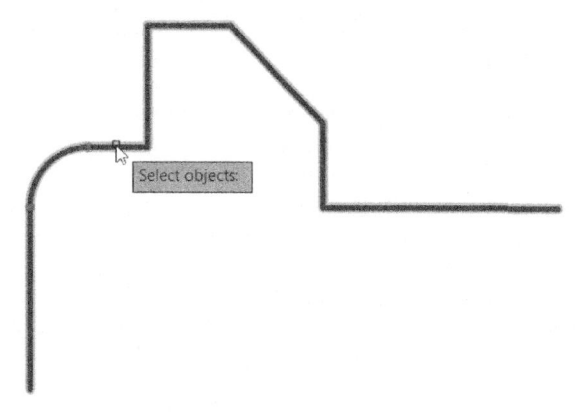

- Select the first point of the mirror line, as shown below.

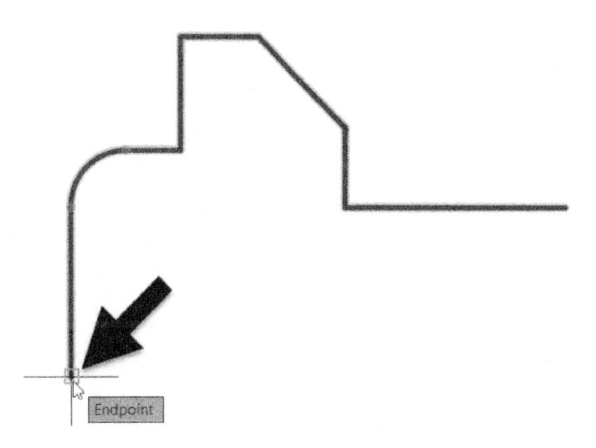

- Make sure that the **Ortho Mode** on the status bar is active.
- Move the pointer toward the right and click.

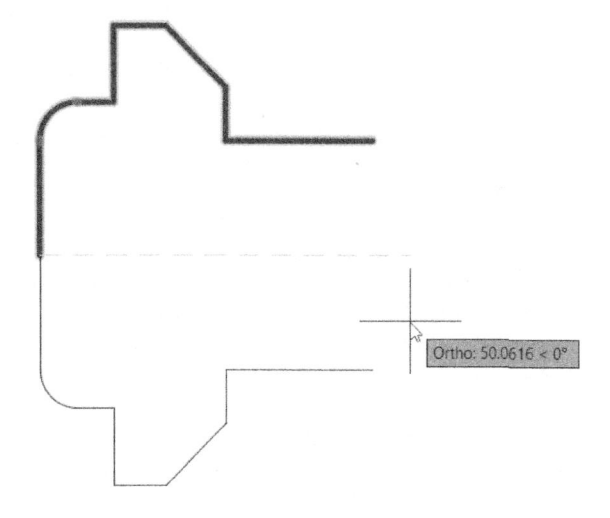

- Right-click and select the **No** option from the shortcut menu to retain the source objects.

Editing Tools

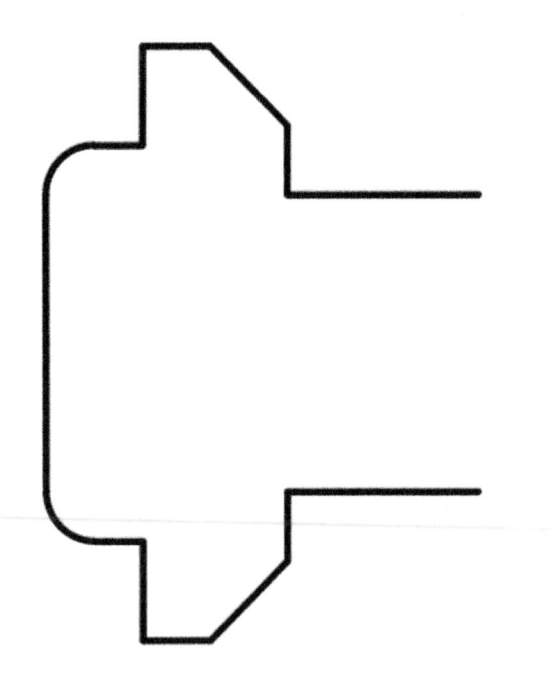

- Click **Drafting > Draw > Arc > Start, End, Direction** on the tool set.
- Select the start point of the arc, as shown.
- Select the endpoint of the arc, as shown.

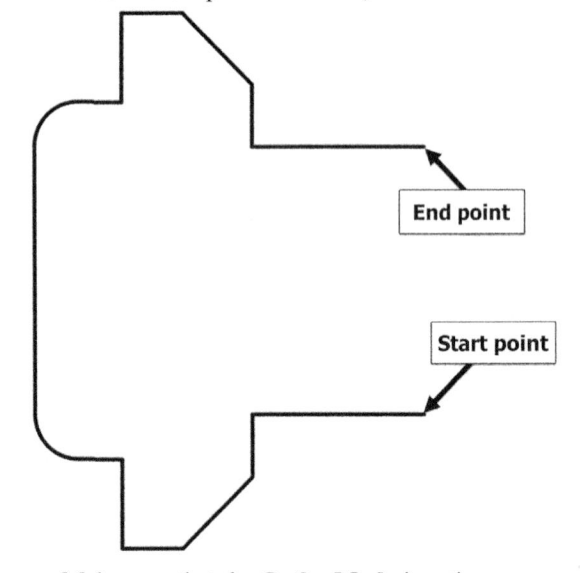

- Make sure that the **Ortho Mode** is active.
- Move the pointer toward the right and click.

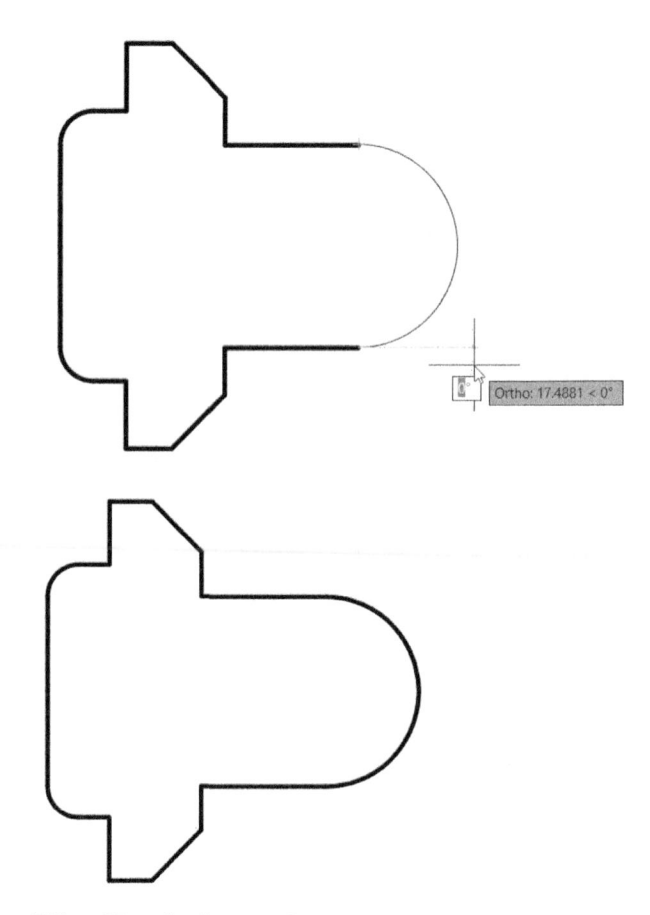

The Explode tool

The **Explode** tool explodes a group of objects into individual objects. For example, when you create a drawing using the **Polyline** tool, it acts as a single object. You can explode a polyline or rectangle or any group of objects using the **Explode** tool.

- Click on the portion of the drawing created using the **Polyline** tool; you will notice that the complete polyline is selected as a single object.

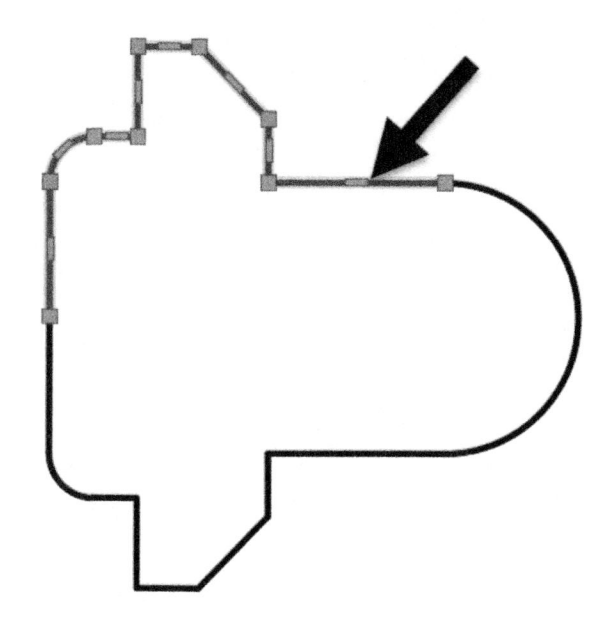

- Click **Drafting > Modify > Explode** on the tool set (or) type **X** in the command line and press RETURN.
- Select the polylines from the drawing.

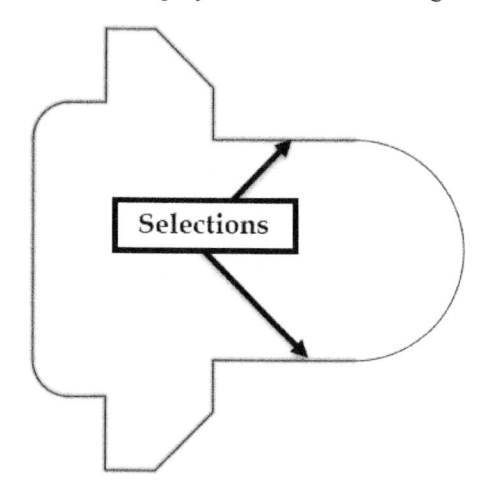

- Press RETURN; the polyline is exploded into individual objects.

Now, you can select the individual objects of the polyline.

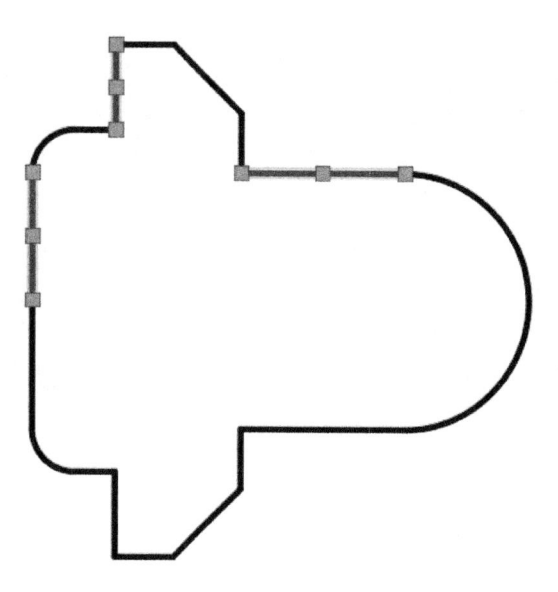

The Stretch tool

The **Stretch** tool lengthens or shortens drawings or parts of drawings. Note that you cannot stretch circles using this tool. Also, you must select the portion of the drawing to be stretched by dragging a window.

- Click **Drafting > Modify > Stretch** on the tool set (or) type **STRETCH** in the command line and press RETURN.
- Create a crossing window to select the objects of the drawing.

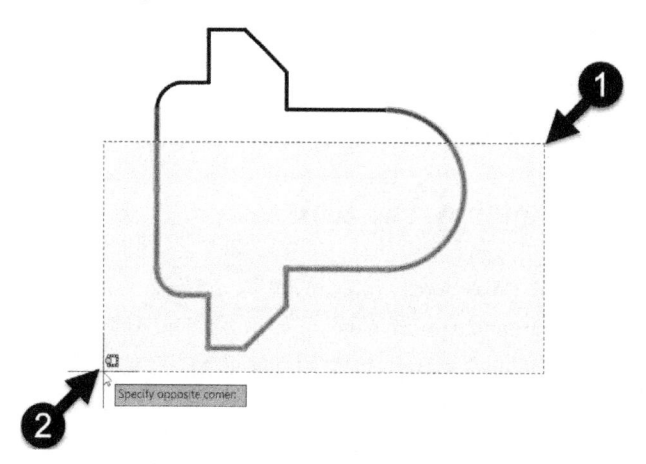

- Press RETURN (or) right-click to accept the selection.
- Select the base point, as shown below.

83 | Editing Tools

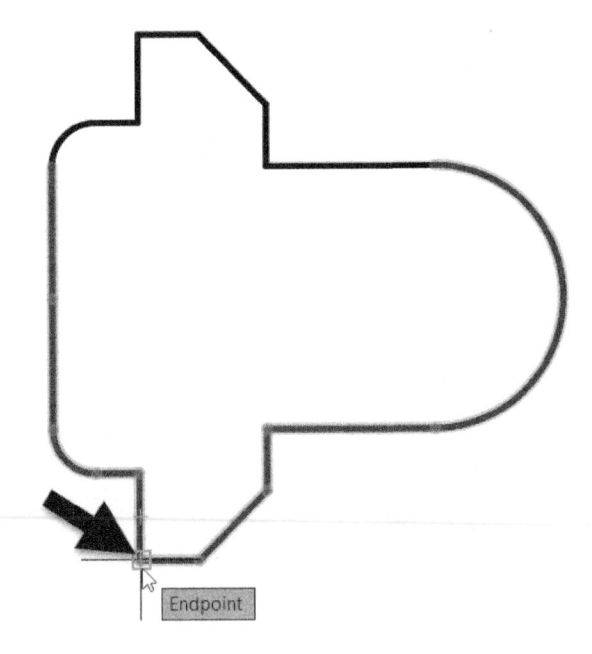

- Move the pointer downward and click to stretch the drawing.

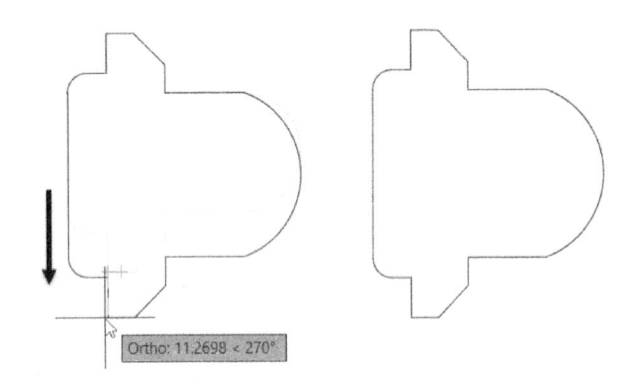

- Save and close the file.

The Polar Array tool

The **Polar Array** tool creates an arrangement of objects around a point in a circular form. The following example shows you to create a polar array.

- Create two concentric circles of 140 and 50 diameters.

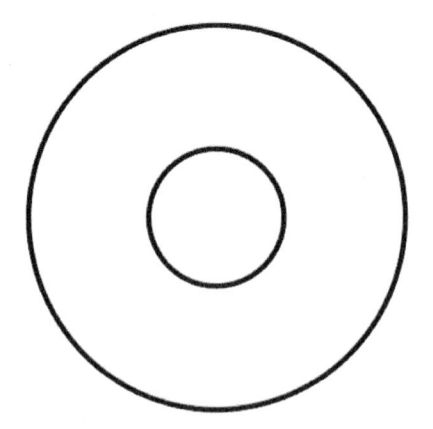

- Type **C** in the command line and press RETURN.
- Press and hold the Shift key, right-click, and select **Quadrant** from the shortcut menu.
- Select the quadrant point of the circle, as shown below.

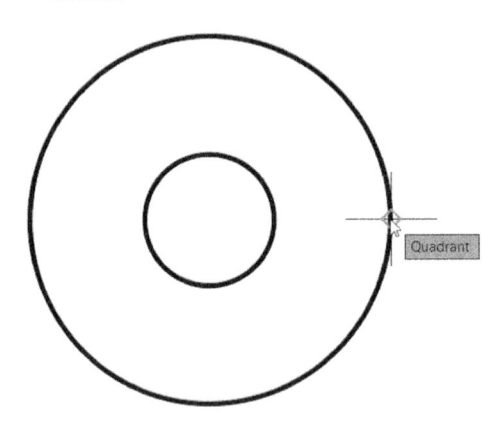

- Type 30 as radius and press RETURN.

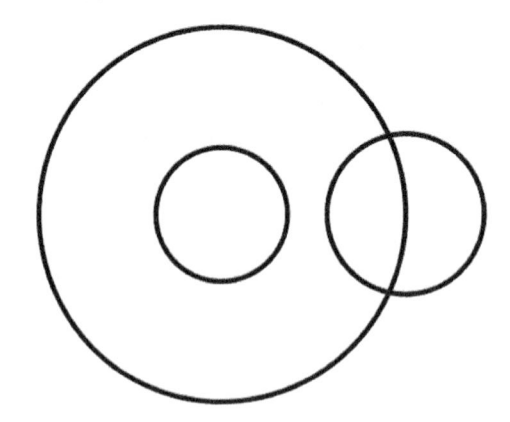

- Click **Drafting > Modify > Trim** on the tool set.
- Select the circle on the quadrant as the object to be trimmed.

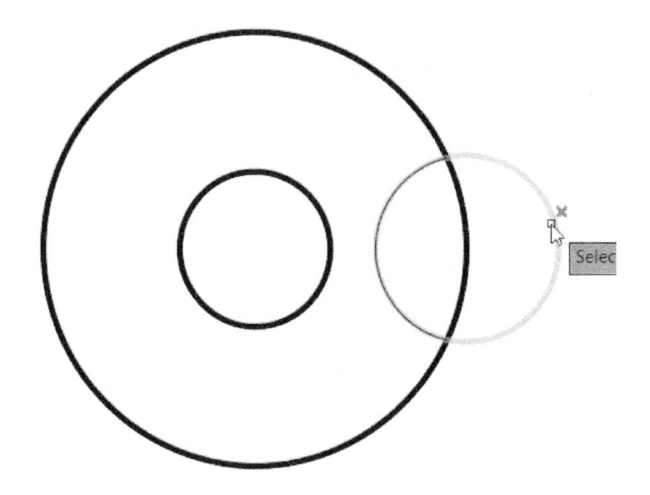

- Press RETURN.
- Click **Drafting > Modify > Array > Polar Array** on the tool set (or) type **ARRAYPOLAR** in the command line and press RETURN.
- Select the arc created after trimming the circle. Next, right-click to accept the selection.

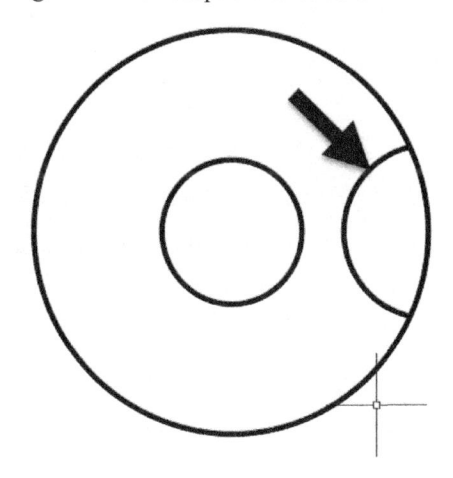

- Make sure that **Object Snap** is activated.
- Select the center of the large circle as the center of the array; the **Polar Array** visor appears.
- On the **Polar Array** toolbar, set the **Number of Items** value to 4.

- Right-click and select the **ROTate Items** option.
- Type **Yes** and press RETURN; it rotates the objects of the polar array. If you type **No** and press RETURN, the polar array is created without rotating the objects, as shown in the figure.

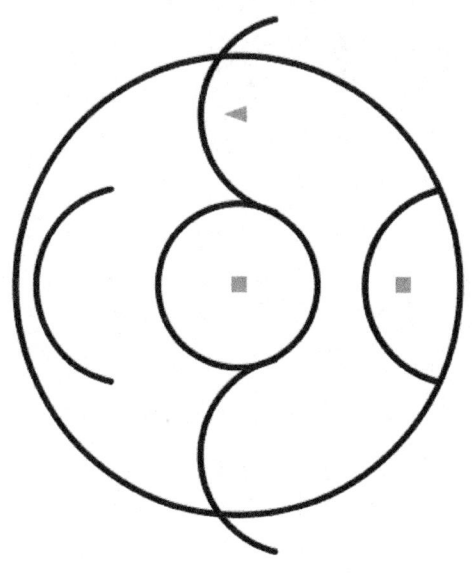

- Right-click and select the **ASsociative** option.
- Type **Yes** and press RETURN; it ensures that you can edit the array after creating it. If you type **No** and press RETURN, you will not be able to modify the array after creating it.
- Type 360 in the **Degrees to fill** box on the **Polar array** visor.
- Click the **Close array and close visor** icon.

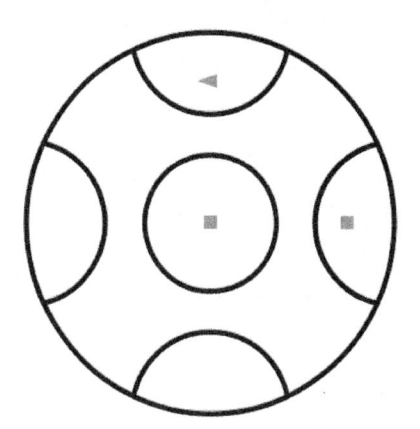

- Click the **Trim** button on the **Modify** panel.
- Trim the unwanted portions, as shown below.

Editing Tools

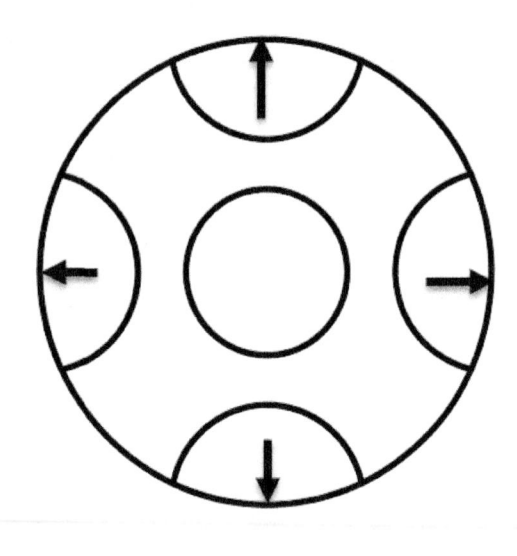

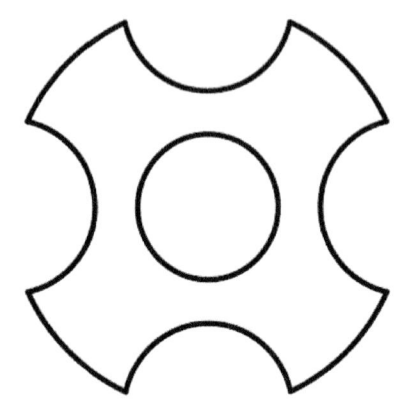

- Type **20** as the offset distance and press RETURN.
- Select the polyline loop.
- Click outside the loop to create a parallel copy. 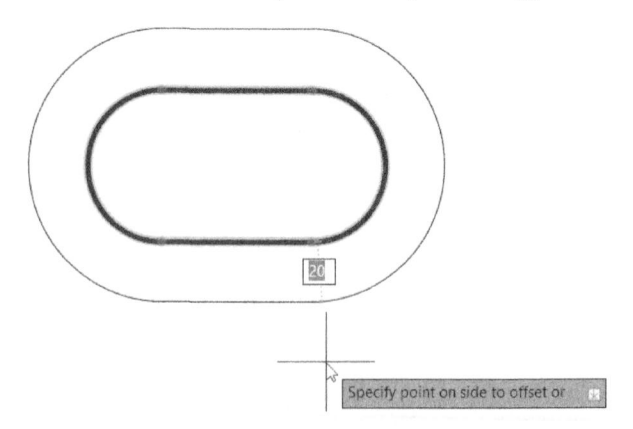
- Right-click and select **Exit** from the shortcut menu.
- On the **Layers** palette, click the arrow next to the **Show Layer List** option.
- Click the **New layer** icon on the **Layer** palette.
- Enter **Centerline** in the **Name** field. 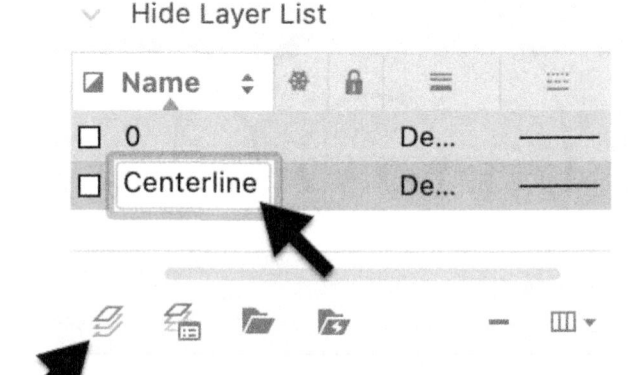
- Double-click on the newly created layer. It activates the new layer.
- Click in the **Linetype** field of the current layer and select the **Manage** option; the **Select Linetype** dialog appears.

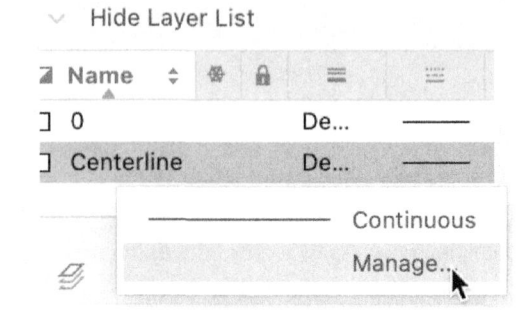

The Offset tool

The **Offset** tool creates parallel copies of lines, polylines, circles, and arcs. To create a parallel copy of an object, first, you must define the offset distance and then select the object. Next, you must define the side in which the parallel copy will be placed.

- Create the drawing shown below using the **Polyline** tool. Do not add dimensions.
- Click **Drafting > Modify > Offset** on the tool set (or) type **O** in the command line and press RETURN.

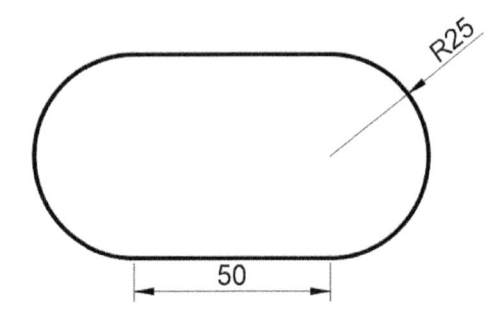

- On the **Select Linetype** dialog, click the **Load** button; the **Load or Reload Linetypes** dialog appears.

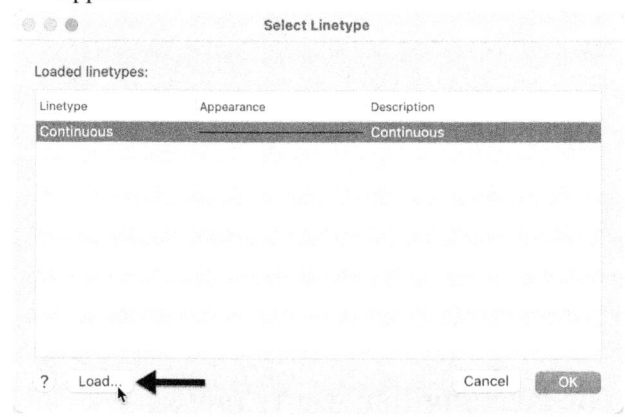

- Select the **CENTER2** Linetype from this dialog. Click **Add**. It adds the linetype to the **Select Linetype** dialog.

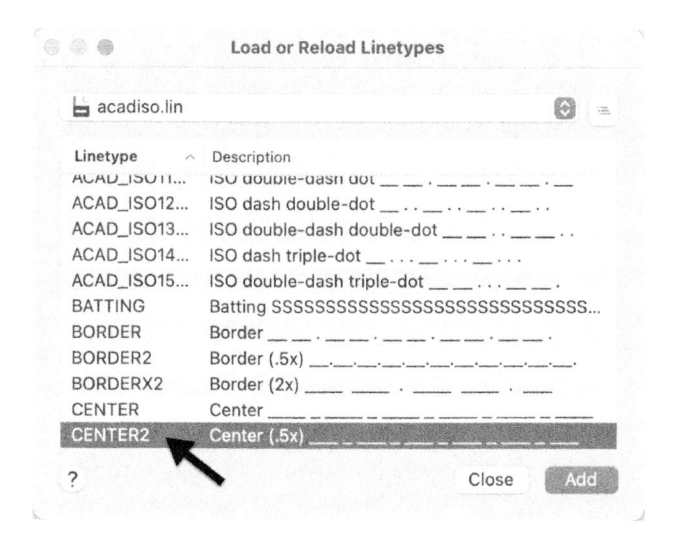

- Select the **CENTER2** linetype from the **Select Linetype** dialog and click **OK**.
- Click the **Offset** button on the **Modify** panel.
- Right-click and select the **Layer** option from the shortcut menu.
- Right-click and select the **Current** option from the shortcut menu; this ensures that the offset entity will be created with the currently active layer properties. If you select the **Source** option, the offset entity will be created with the properties of the source object.
- Type **10** as the offset distance and press RETURN.
- Select the outer loop of the drawing.
- Move the pointer inwards and click to create the offset entity.

- Right-click and select **Exit** from the shortcut menu.

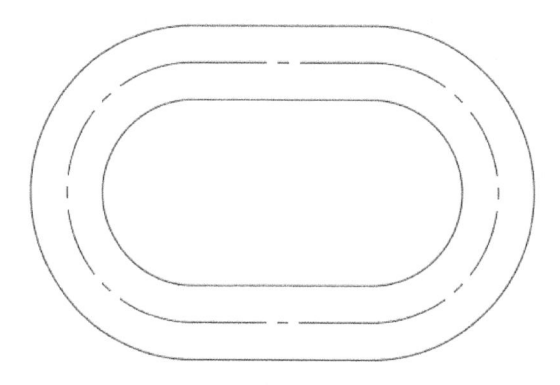

- Select the **0** layer from the drop-down on the Layers palette.

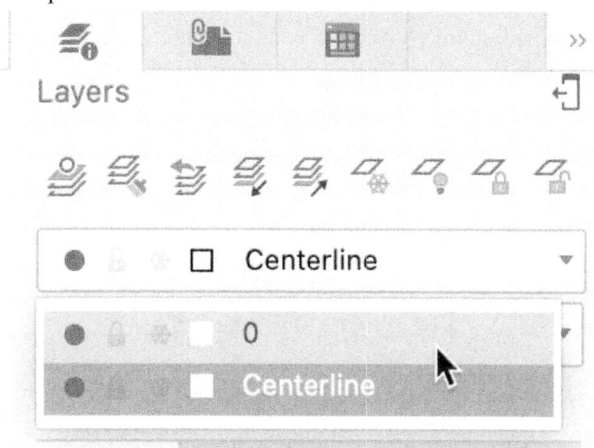

- Create a circle of 6 mm in radius, as shown.

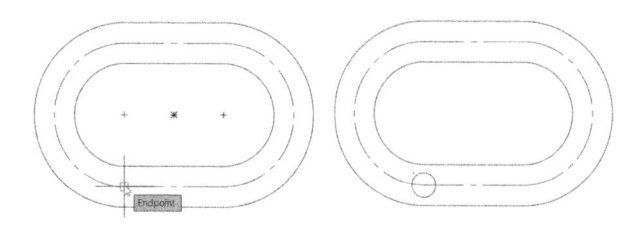

The Path Array tool

The **Path Array** tool creates an array of objects along a path (line, polyline, circle, helix, and spline).

- Click **Drafting > Modify > Array > Path Array** on the tool set (or) type **ARRAYPATH** in the command line and press RETURN.
- Select the circle and right-click.
- Select the centerline as the path; the preview of the path array appears.

87 | Editing Tools

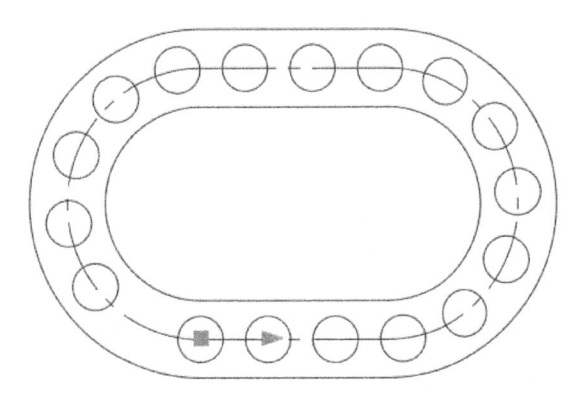

- On the **Path Array** visor, click **Method** > **Divide**
  . The number of items that you specify will be filled on the path. Now, you must enter the number of items in the path array.

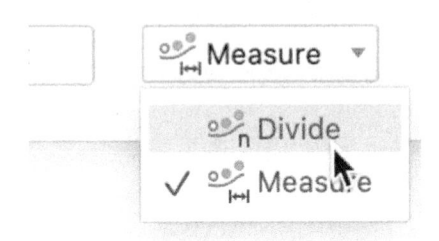

If you select the **Measure** method, you must enter the distance between the items in the path array.

- Type **12** in the **Number of items** box.
- Right-click and select the Align Items option.
- Type Yes in the command line and press RETURN. As a result, the items are aligned with the path. If you type No and press RETURN, the items will not be aligned with the path.

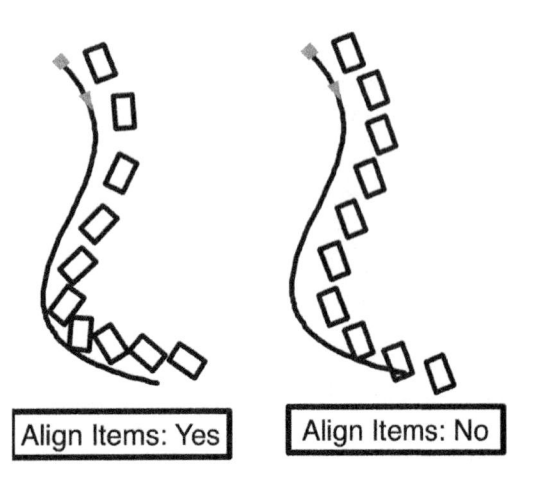

- Click the **Close array and close visor** button.

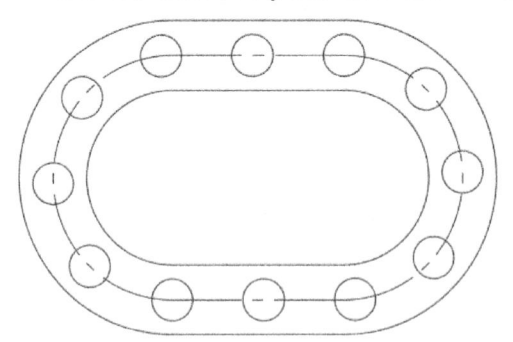

- Save and close the file.

The Rectangular Array tool

The **Rectangular Array** tool creates an array of objects along with the X and Y directions.

- Open a new AutoCAD file and draw the sketch shown below. Do not add dimensions. (refer to the **Drawing Rectangles** and **Drawing Circles** section in Chapter 2 to know the procedure to draw the rectangle and circle)

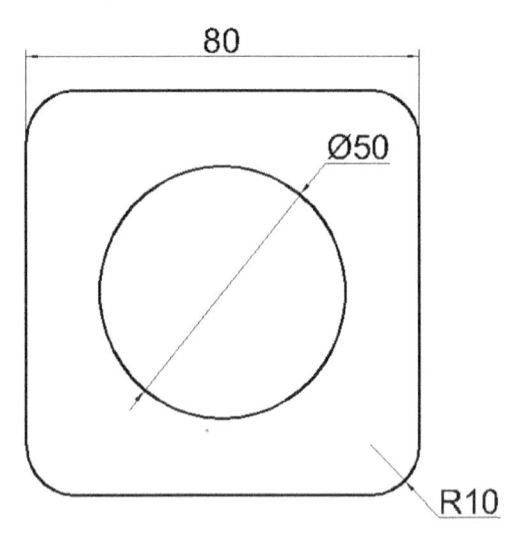

- Click **Drafting** > **Draw** > **Circle** drop-down > **Center, Radius** on the tool set.
- Select the center point of the lower-left fillet.

88 | Editing Tools

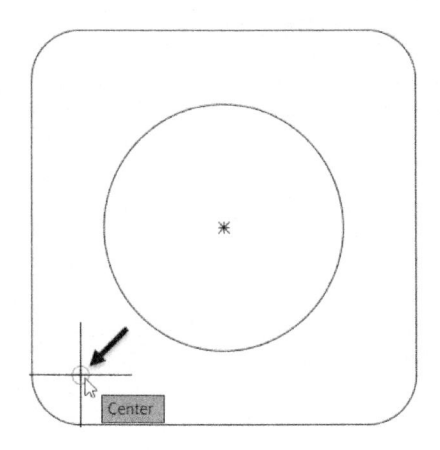

AutoCAD 2023 For Beginners (For Mac Users)

- Type 5 and press RETURN.

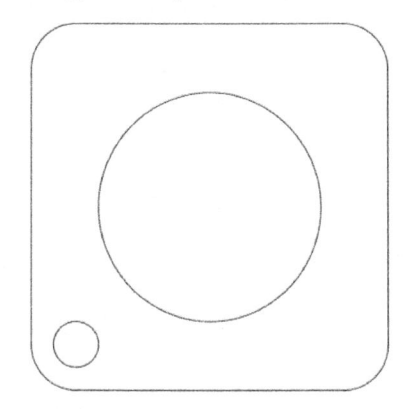

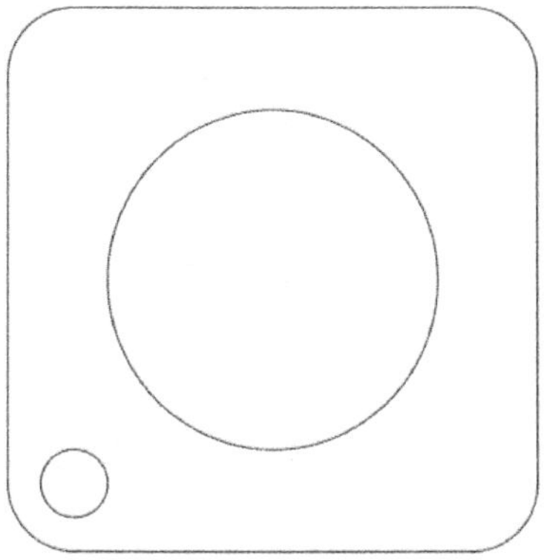

- Click **Drafting > Modify > Array > Rectangular Array** on the tool set (or) type **ARRAYRECT** in the command line and press RETURN.
- Select the small circle and right-click; a rectangular array with default values appears.

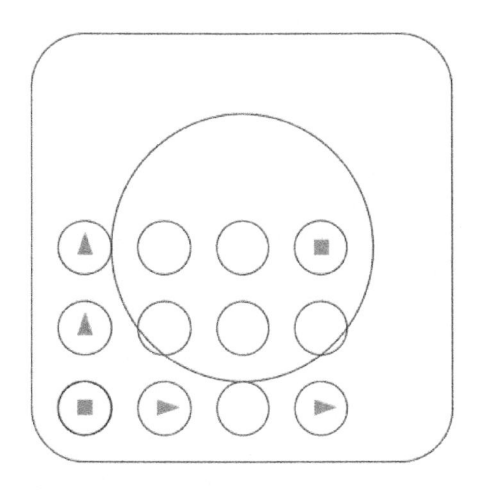

Also, the **Rectangular Array** visor appears.

- Type 2 in the **Number of columns** box.

- Type 2 in the **Number of rows** box.

- Right-click and select **Spacing**.
- Type 60 as the spacing between the columns, and then press RETURN.
- Type 60 as the spacing between the rows, and then press RETURN.
- Click the **Close array and close visor** button.

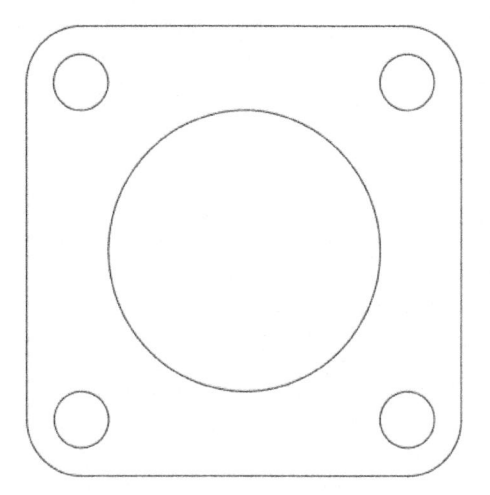

- Click the right mouse button on the toolbar, and then select **Customize Toolbar**.

- Drag and drop the **Inquiry** tools on to the toolbar.

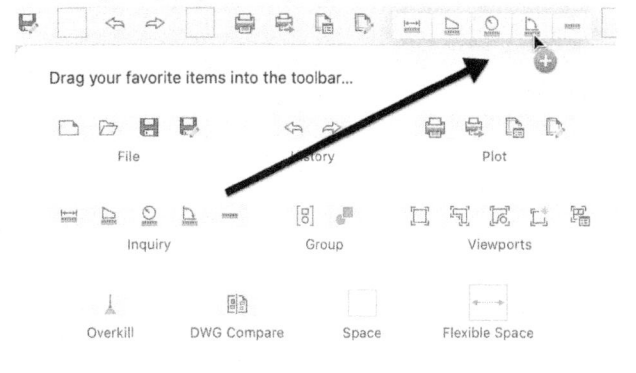

89 | Editing Tools

AutoCAD 2023 For Beginners (For Mac Users)

- Click the **Quick Measure** icon on the toolbar.

- Place the cursor inside the circle located at the center; the radius of the circle is displayed.

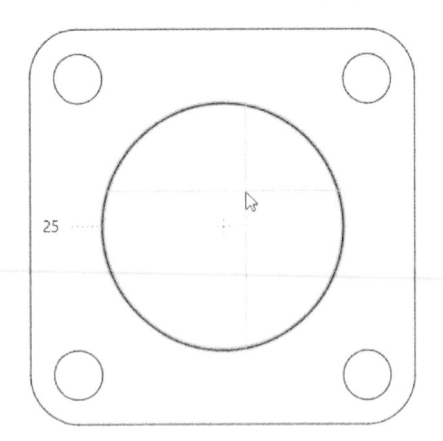

- Place the cursor between the two circles located at the bottom; the measurements of the objects located in four directions of the cursor are displayed.

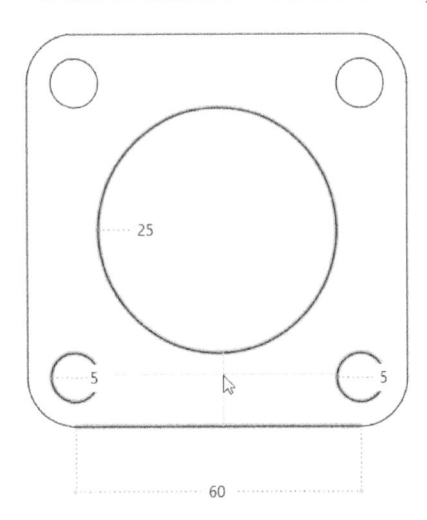

Editing Using Grips

When you select objects from the graphics window, small squares appear on them. These squares are called grips. You can use these grips to stretch, move, rotate, scale and mirror objects, change properties, and perform other editing operations. Grips displayed on selecting different objects are shown below.

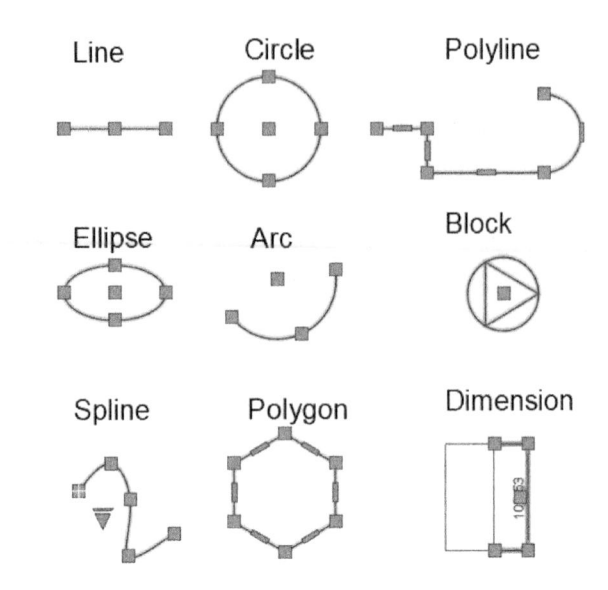

Line   Circle   Polyline

Ellipse   Arc   Block

Spline   Polygon   Dimension

The following table gives you the details of the editing operations that can be performed when you select and drag grips.

Object	Grip	Editing Operation
Circle	Grip on circumference	**Scale**: Select any one of the grips on the circumference and move the pointer to scale a circle.

Editing Tools

Arc		**Move**: Select the center grip of the circle and move the pointer.
	Center point grip	
	Grip on circumference	**Stretch**: Select the grip on the circumference and move the pointer.
	Center point grip	**Move**: Select the center grip of the arc and move the pointer.
Line	Midpoint Grip	
		Move: Select the Midpoint grip and move the pointer.

	Endpoint Grip	**Stretch/Lengthen**: Select an endpoint grip and move the pointer.
Polylines, Rectangles, Polygons	Corner Grips	**Stretch**: Select the corner grips and move the pointer.

Extend: Place the pointer on the endpoint grip and select the **Extend Vertex**. Next, move the pointer and click to create a new line attached to previous line.

Add/Remove Vertex: Place the pointer on the corner grip and select Add Vertex/Remove Vertex. |

		Stretch Vertex / Add Vertex / Remove Vertex
	Midpoint Grips	**Convert to Arc**: Place the pointer on the midpoint grip and select **Convert to Arc**.

Stretch / Add Vertex / Convert to Arc

Convert to Line: Place the pointer on the midpoint grip of a polyline arc and select **Convert to Line**.

Stretch / Add Vertex / Convert to Line |
| Ellipse | Center Grip | **Move**: Select the center grip and move the pointer. |

Editing Tools

	Grips on circumference	**Stretch**: Select a grip on the circumference and move the pointer.
Spline	Fit Points	**Stretch**: Select a grip on the spline and move the pointer.

Add/Remove Fit Point: Place the pointer on a fit point and select **Add Fit Point** or **Remove Fit Point**. |
| | Control Vertices | **Stretch Vertices**: Select the control vertices of a CV spline and move the pointer. |

Add/Remove Vertex: Place the pointer on a control vertex and select **Add Vertex** or **Remove Vertex**.

Refine Vertices: Place the pointer on a control vertex and select **Refine Vertices**.

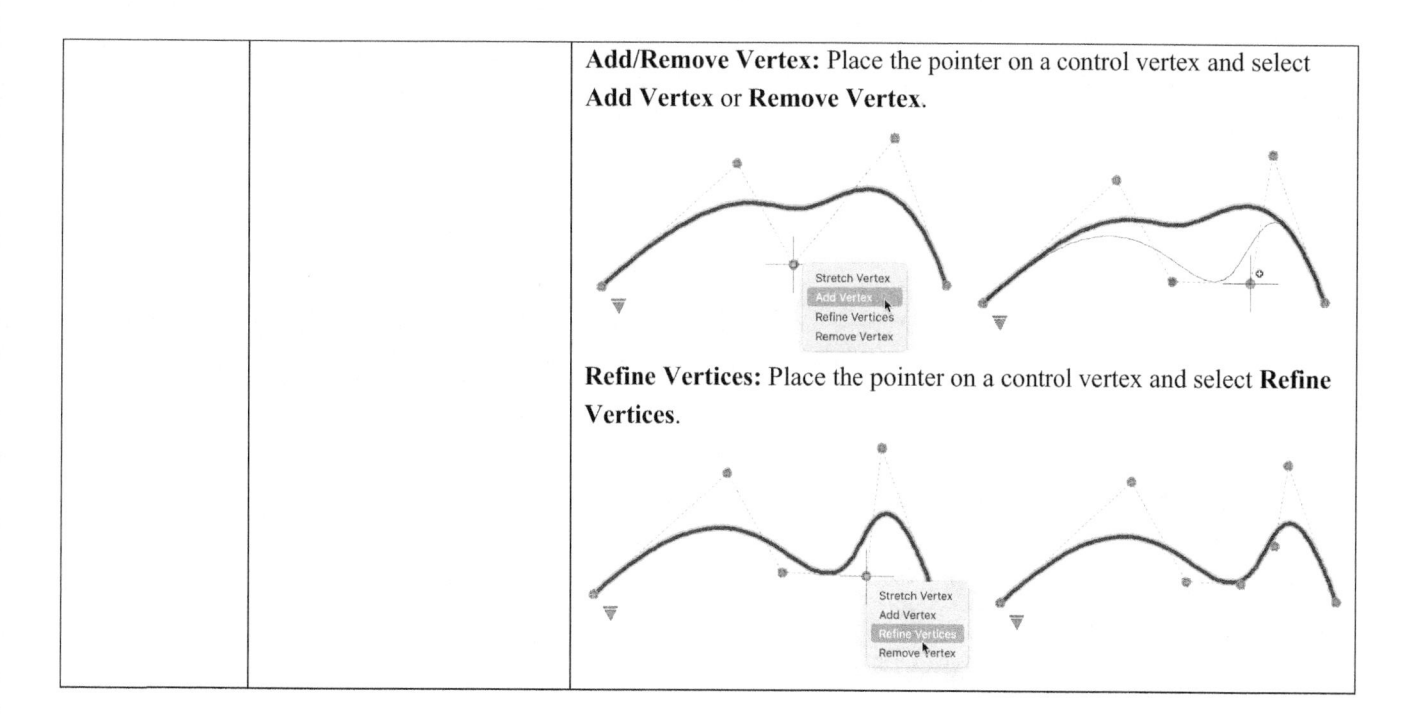

Modifying Rectangular Arrays

You can use grips to edit rectangular arrays dynamically. Various array editing operations using grips are given next.

Moving a Rectangular array

- Create a rectangular array, as shown below.

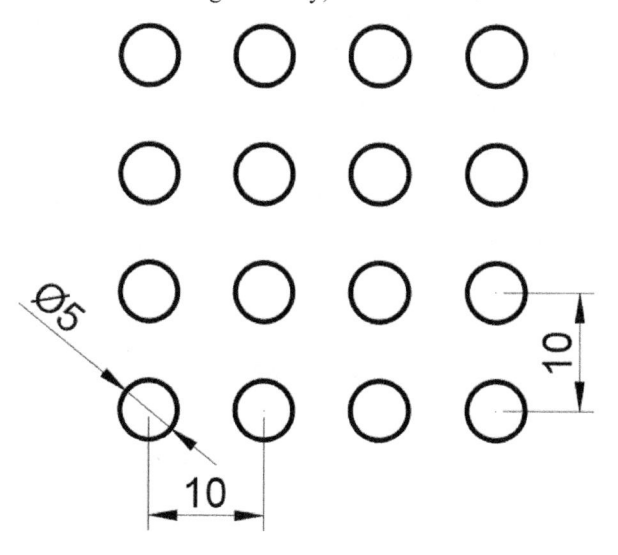

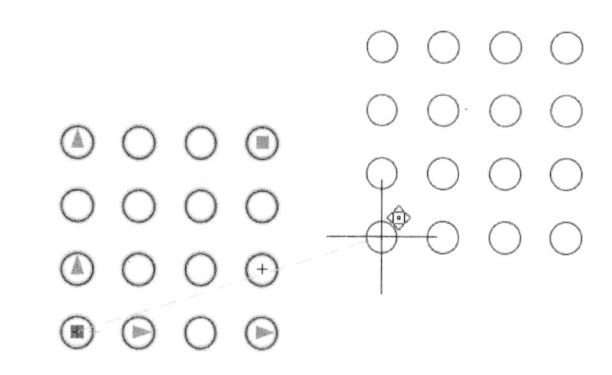

Adding/Removing Level to a Rectangular array

- Place the pointer on the lower left grip of the rectangular array; a shortcut menu appears.
- Select **Level Count** from the shortcut menu; the message, "**Specify number of levels**," appears in the command line.
- Type 3 and press RETURN.
- Press ESC.
- Click the **Home** button near the ViewCube to view the levels.

- Select the array; you will notice that grips are displayed on it.
- Select the grip located at the lower-left corner and move the array, as shown below.

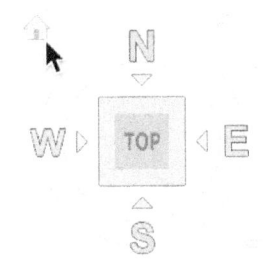

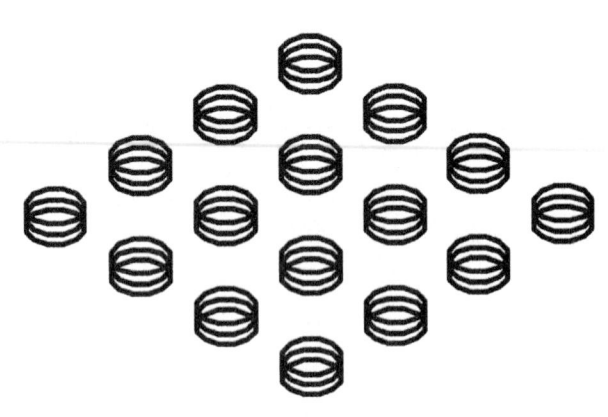

- Change the view to Top view by using the **Viewport Label Menus**.

Changing the Column and Row Count

- To change the column and row count, place the pointer on the top right corner grip; a shortcut menu appears.

- Select **Row and Column Count** from the shortcut menu; the message, "**Specify number of rows and columns**," appears in the command line.
- Type **5** in the command line and press RETURN; the number of rows and columns is changed to 5.
- If you only want to change the column count, place the pointer on the lower right corner grip of the array.

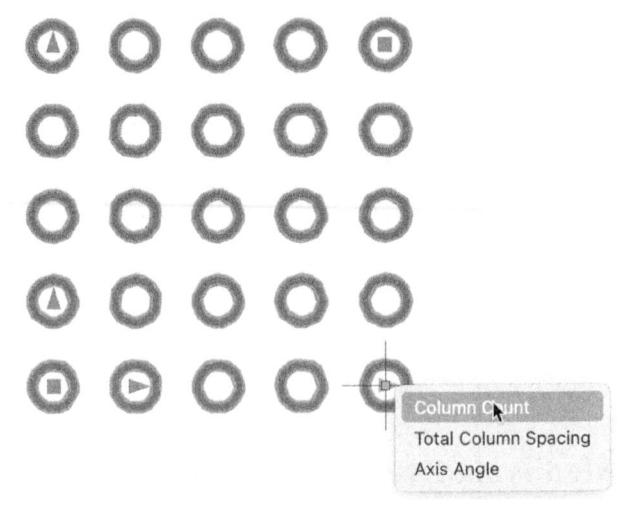

- Select **Colum Count** from the shortcut menu.
- Next, enter the number of columns or drag the pointer and click.

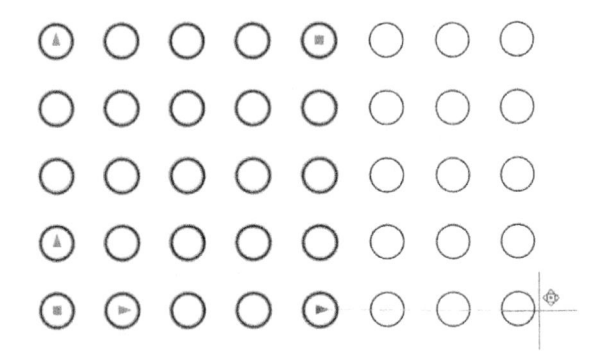

- To change the row count only, click the top left corner grip and drag the pointer. You can also enter the row count in the command line.

96 | Editing Tools

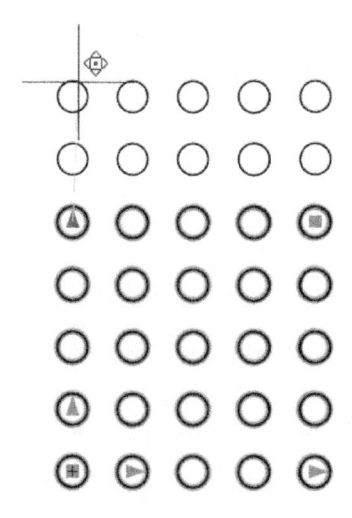

Changing the Column and Row Spacing

- To change the total column and row spacing, place the pointer on the top right corner grip and select **Total Row and Column Spacing** from the shortcut menu.

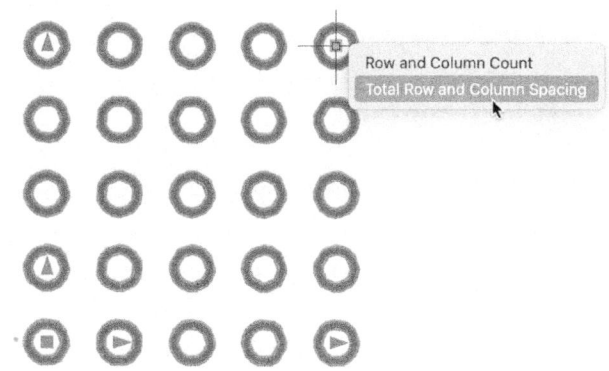

- Type 80 in the command line; the spacing between the columns and rows is adjusted to fit the total length.

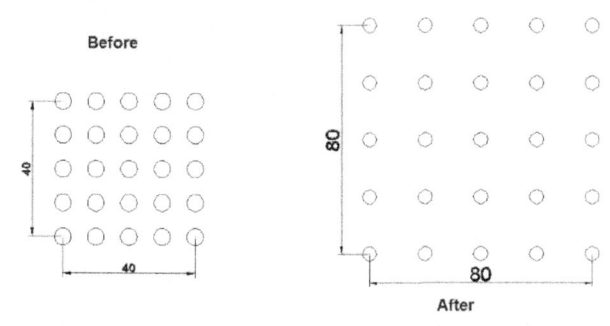

- To change the total column spacing only, place the pointer on the lower right corner grip and select **Total Column Spacing** from the shortcut menu.

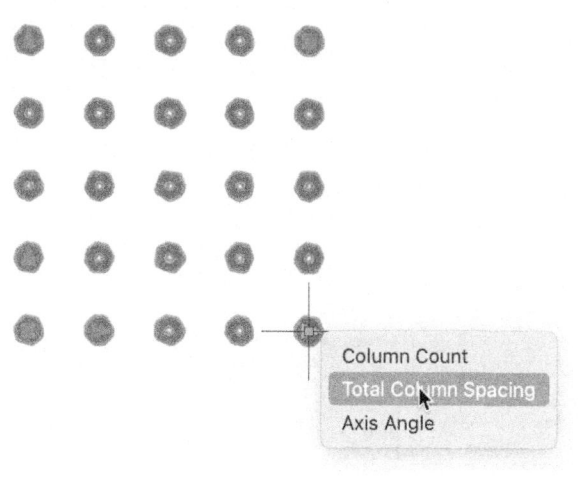

- Next, enter the total column distance or drag the pointer and click.

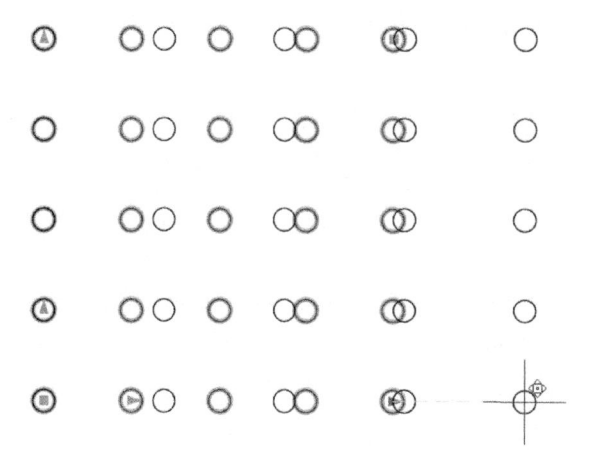

- If you want to change the distance between the individual columns, click the second column grip and drag the pointer.

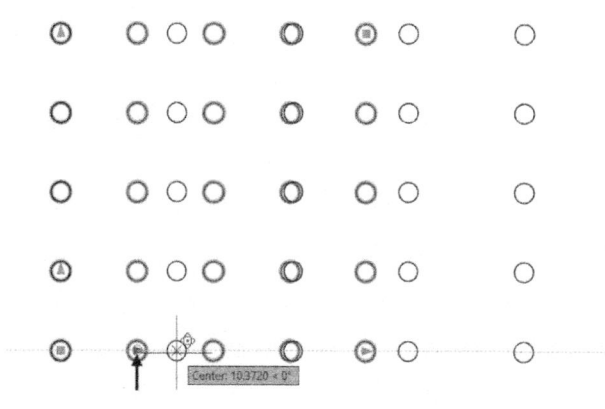

- You can also enter the distance in the command line.

- Likewise, you can change the total row spacing and distance between the individual rows by using the grips shown below.

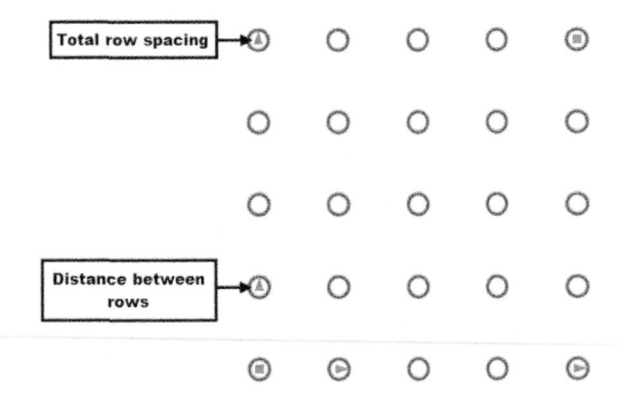

Changing the Axis Angle of the Rectangular Array

- To change the Axis angle of the rows, place the pointer on the lower right corner grip and select the **Axis angle** option from the shortcut menu.
- Type the angle and press RETURN. Note that the angle is calculated from the first column of the array. For example, if you enter 60 as the axis angle, the rows will be inclined by 60 degrees from the first column.

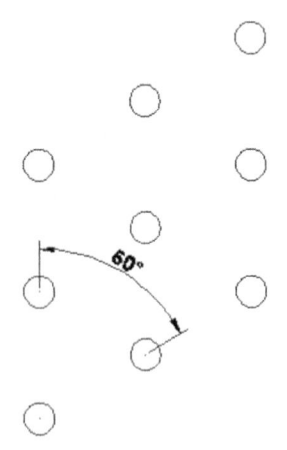

- Likewise, you can change the axis angle of the columns by using the top left corner grip.

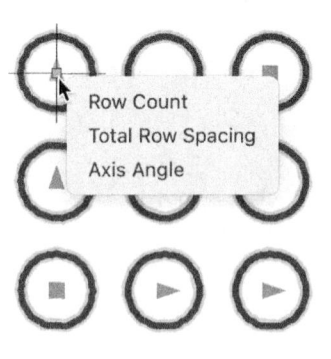

Editing the Source Item of the Rectangular Array

- Create a rectangular array, as shown below. 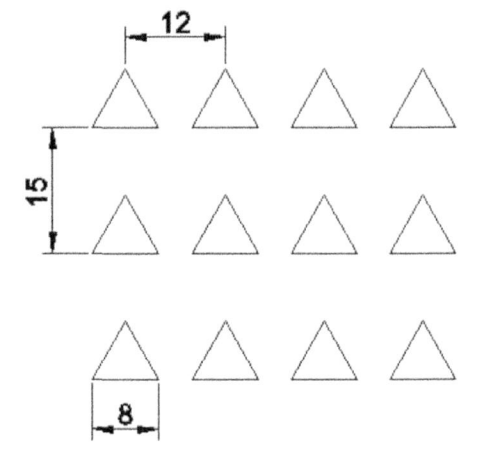
- Click **Close array and close visor**.
- Select the rectangular array; the **Rectangular Array** visor appears.
- Click the **Edit Source** button on the **Rectangular Array** visor; the message, "**Select item in array**" message appears in the command line. 
- Select the lower left triangle of the rectangular array; the **Array Editing State** message box appears.

98 | Editing Tools

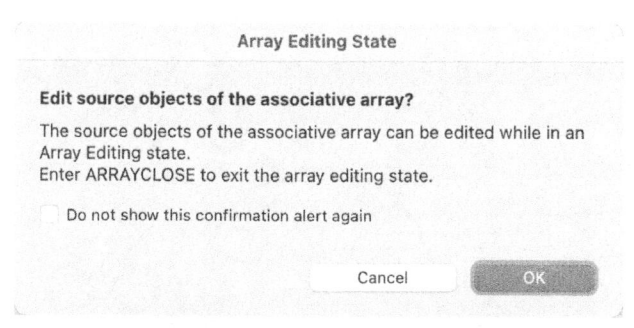

- Click **OK**; the array editing state is activated.
- Draw a circle and trim the unwanted portion, as shown below.

- Click **Save Changes** on the **Edit Array** visor.

Modifying Polar Arrays

Similar to editing rectangular arrays, you can also edit a polar array by using grips. Various array editing operations using grips are given next.

Changing the Radius of a Polar array
- Create the polar array, as shown in the figure.

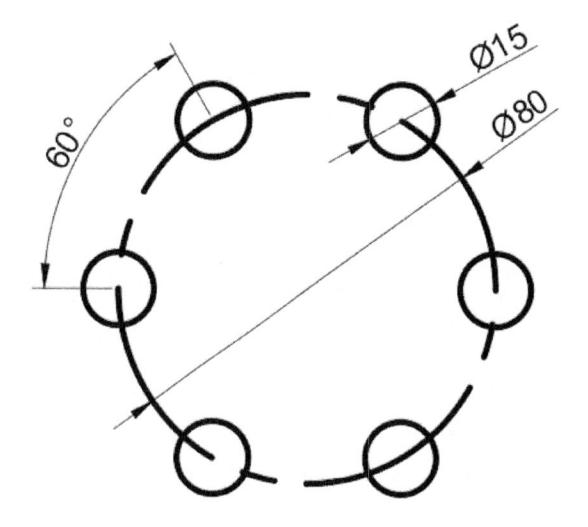

- Select the polar array; grips will be displayed on it.
- Place the pointer on the base grip, as shown in the figure.
- Select **Stretch Radius** from the shortcut menu.

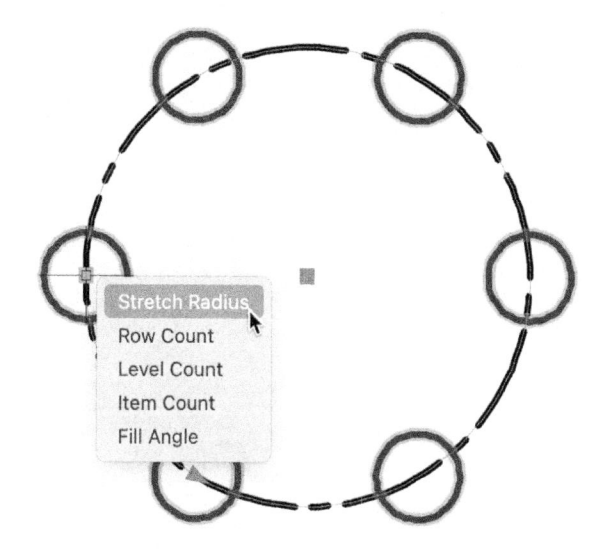

- Move the pointer outward or inward and click. You can also enter a new radius value of the polar array.

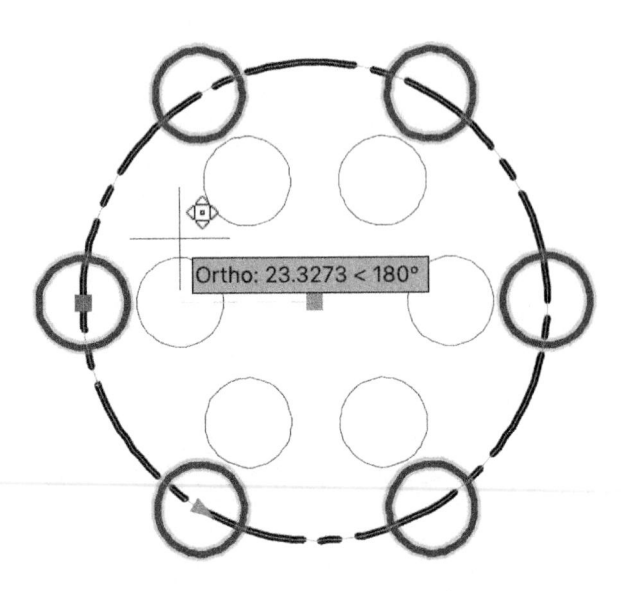

Changing the Row Count of a Polar array

- Place the pointer on the base grip of the array and select **Row Count** from the shortcut menu.
- Move the pointer outward and click. You can also enter the number of rows in the command line.

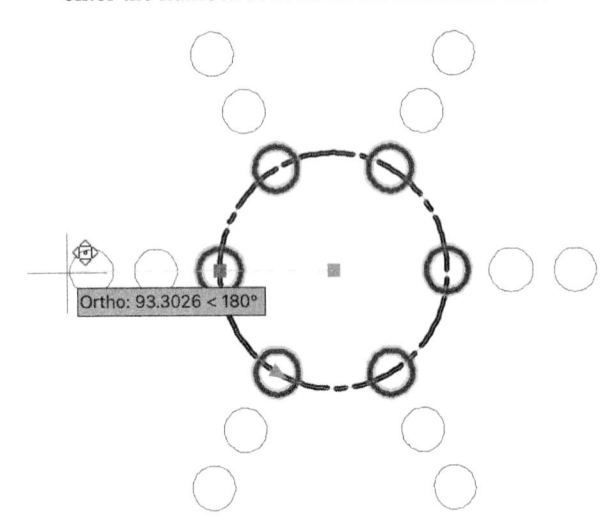

- You can again change the **Row Count** by using the last row grip.

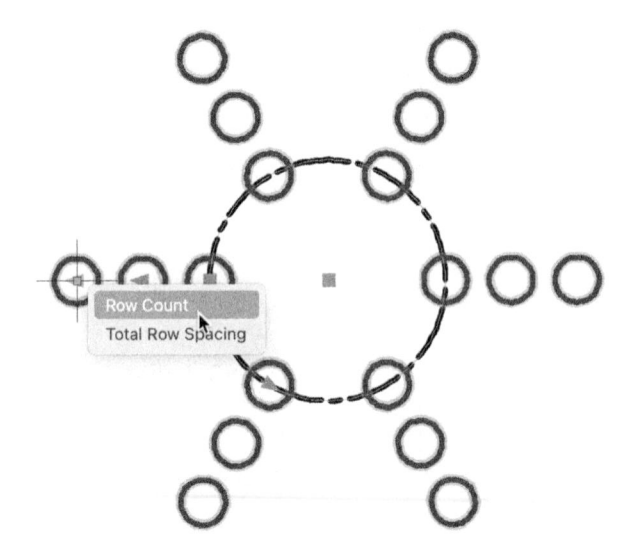

Changing the Row Spacing

- To change the total row spacing, place the pointer on the last row grip and select **Total Row Spacing**.

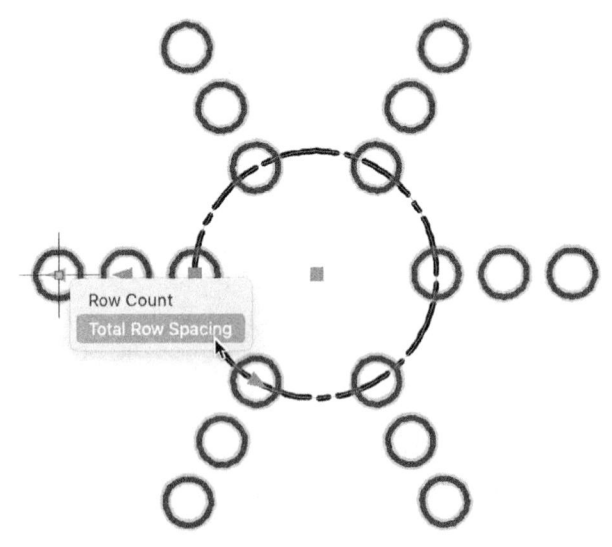

- Next, move the pointer and click. You can also enter the total row spacing value in the command line.
- To change the distance between the individual rows, click the second-row grip and move the pointer outward. You can also enter the distance in the command line.

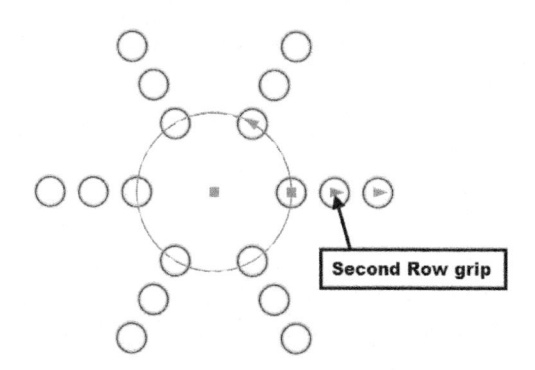

Changing the Angle between the Items

- To change the angle between the items, click the second radial grip, and enter the new angle value.

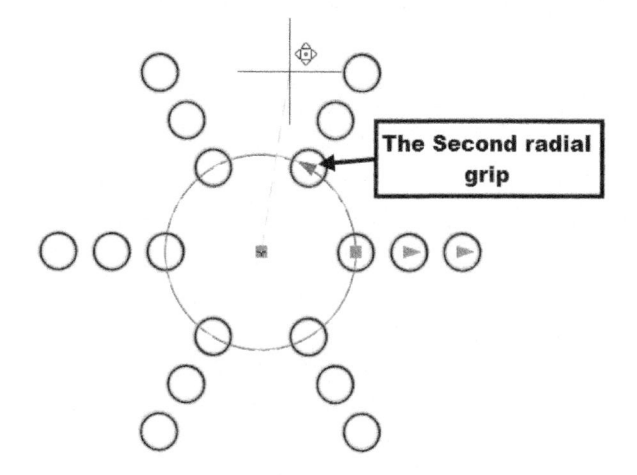

Changing the Fill angle of the array

- The default fill angle of a polar array is 360 degrees. To change the fill angle, place the pointer on the base grip and select **Fill Angle** from the shortcut menu.

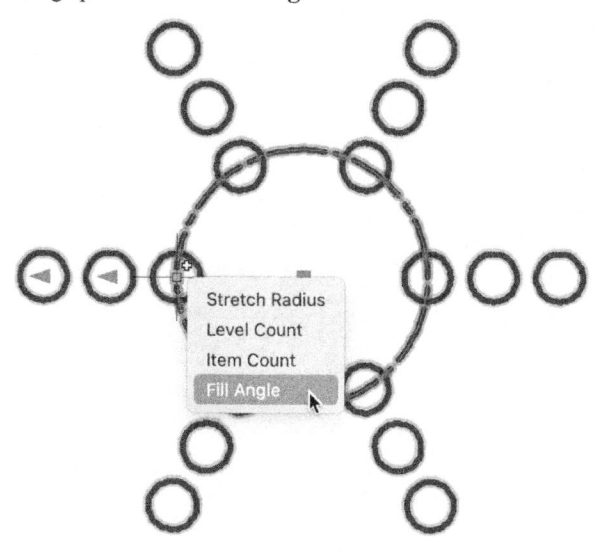

- Enter a new value for the fill angle or drag the pointer and click.

Changing the Item count of a Polar array

- Select the polar array and right-click and select **Array > Items**.
- Type the new item counts value and press RETURN.
- Press RETURN to exit the command.

Revision Clouds

Revision clouds are used to highlight the areas in a drawing. You can create revision clouds using three different tools.

Example 1:

- Start a new drawing using the acadISO template.
- On the tool set, click **Drafting > Draw > Revision Cloud** drop-down > **Rectangular Revision Cloud**.

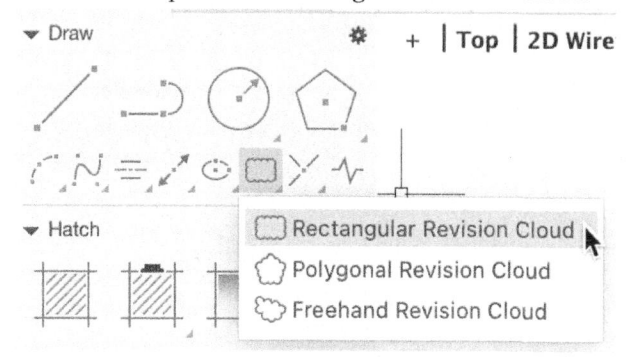

- Right-click and select **Arc Length** from the shortcut menu.
- Type 3 and press RETURN to specify the approximate arc length.
- Specify the first and second corners of the revision cloud. You can also select the **Object** option from the shortcut menu and select an object from the graphics window. The selected object will be converted into a revision cloud.

Editing Tools

- Select the revision cloud and notice the grips. You can use the midpoint grip to stretch or add new vertices to the revision cloud.

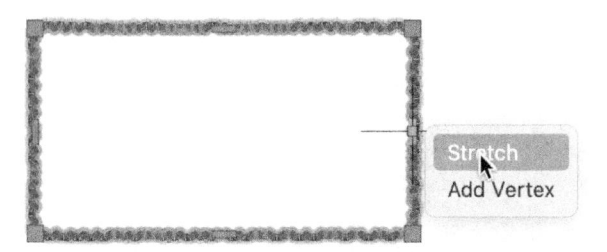

You can use the corner point grip to stretch, add, or remove vertices.

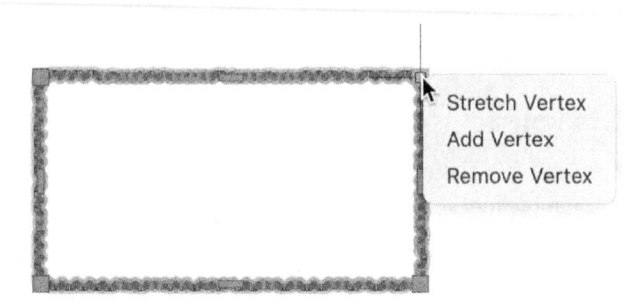

- Select the revision cloud, right-click, and select **Properties**. Notice that object type is displayed at **Revcloud** in the drop-down displayed at the top of the **Properties** palette.
- Scroll down on the **Properties** palette.
- Click in the **Arc Length** box, type **5**, and press RETURN. The arc length is changed.

Example 2:
- On the tool set, click **Drafting > Draw > Revision Cloud** drop-down **> Polygonal Revision Cloud**.
- Right-click and select **Style** from the shortcut menu.
- Right-click and select **Calligraphy** from the shortcut menu.

- Specify the corners of the revision cloud and press RETURN.

Example 3:
- On the tool set, click **Drafting > Draw > Revision Cloud** drop-down **> Freehand Revision Cloud**.
- Specify the start point of the revision cloud.
- Move the pointer around the area to be highlighted.
- Move the pointer onto the start point to close the cloud.

Example 1
In this example, you will create the drawing shown in the figure.

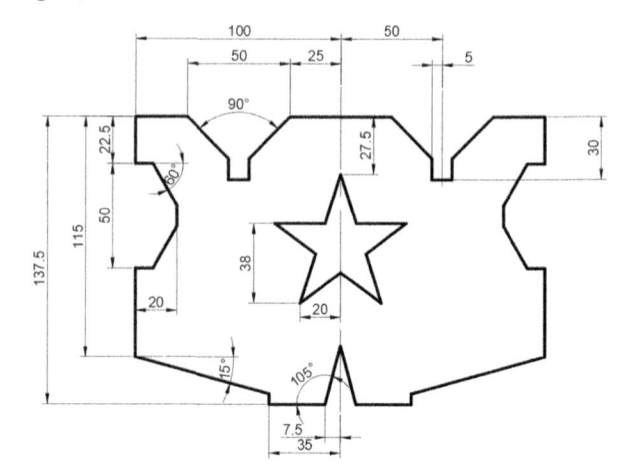

- Start a new drawing file using the acadISO-Named Plot Styles.dwt.
- Type LIMMAX in the command line and press RETURN.
- Type 200,200 and press RETURN.
- Click **View** > **Zoom** > **All** on the Menu bar.
- Click the **Ortho Mode** icon on the Status bar.
- Click the **Line** tool on the **Draw** panel of the **Drafting** tool set.
- Pick a point in the graphics area.
- Move the pointer toward the right.
- Type 35 and press RETURN.
- Move the pointer upward.
- Type 22.5 and press RETURN.
- Move the pointer toward the right.
- Type 65 and press RETURN.
- Move the pointer upward.
- Type 42.5 and press RETURN.
- Move the pointer toward left.
- Type 20 and press RETURN.
- Move the pointer upward.
- Type 50 and press RETURN.
- Move the pointer toward the right.
- Type 20 and press RETURN.
- Move the pointer upward.
- Type 22.5 and press RETURN.
- Move the pointer toward left.
- Type 45 and press RETURN.
- Move the pointer downward.
- Type 30 and press RETURN.
- Move the pointer toward left.
- Type 10 and press RETURN.
- Move the pointer upward.
- Type 30 and press RETURN.
- Move the pointer toward left.
- Type 45 and press RETURN.
- Move the pointer downward and select the start point of the drawing.

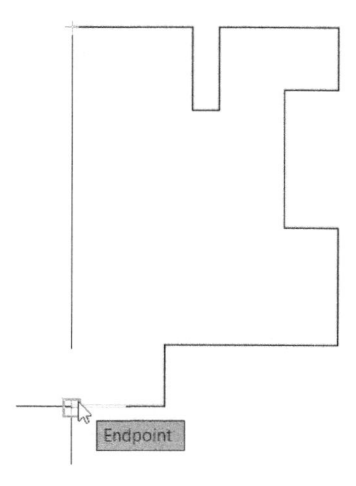

- Click **Fillet** drop-down > **Chamfer** on the **Modify** panel of the **Drafting** tool set.
- Right-click and select **Angle** from the shortcut menu.
- Type 20 as the chamfer distance.
- Type 45 as the chamfer angle.
- Select the horizontal and vertical lines, as shown in the figure.

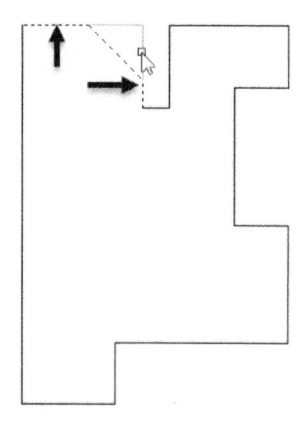

- Press RETURN to activate the **Chamfer** tool.
- Select the horizontal and vertical lines, as shown.

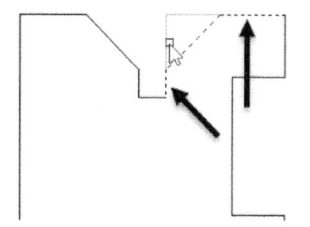

- Press RETURN to activate the **Chamfer** tool.
- Right-click and select **Angle** from the shortcut menu.
- Type 20 as the chamfer distance.

- Type 30 as the chamfer angle.
- Select the vertical and horizontal lines, as shown in the figure.

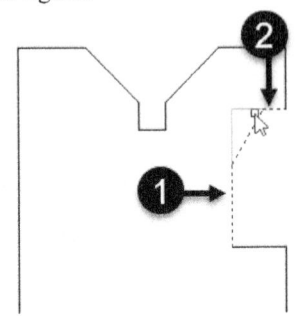

- Press RETURN to activate the **Chamfer** tool.
- Select the vertical and horizontal lines, as shown in the figure.

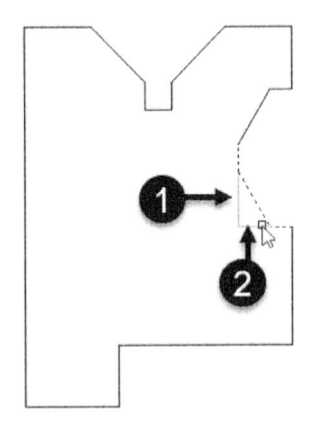

- Press RETURN to activate the **Chamfer** tool.
- Right-click and select **Angle** from the shortcut menu.
- Type 65 as the chamfer distance.
- Type 15 as the chamfer angle.
- Select the horizontal and vertical lines, as shown in the figure.

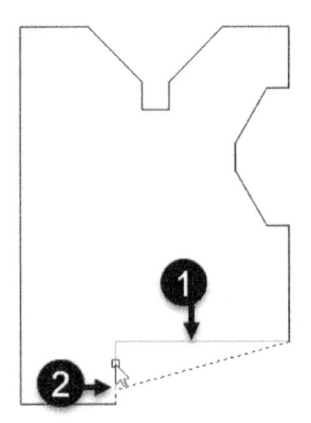

- Press RETURN to activate the **Chamfer** tool.
- Right-click and select **Angle** from the shortcut menu.
- Type 7.5 as the chamfer distance.
- Type 75 as the chamfer angle.
- Select the horizontal and vertical lines, as shown in the figure.

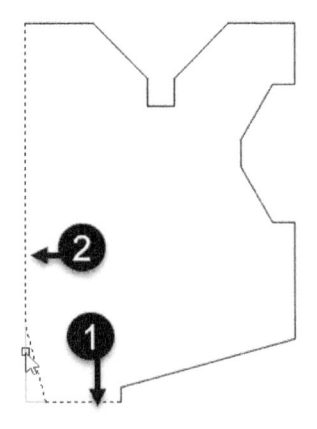

- Select the left vertical line and press Delete.

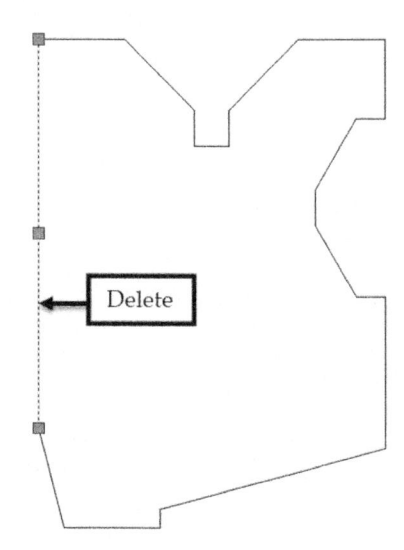

- Create a selection window across all the objects.

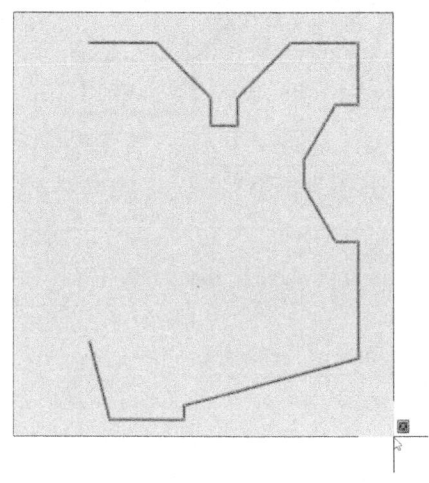

- Click **Mirror** on the **Modify** panel of the **Drafting** tool set.
- Select the points, as shown. The mirror line is defined.

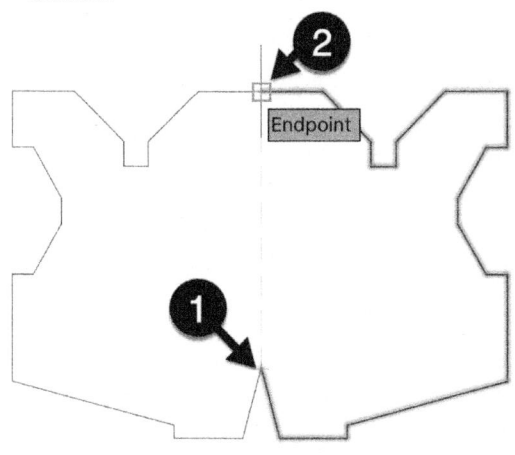

- Right-click and select **No** from the shortcut menu. The selected objects are mirrored about the mirror line.
- Click **Rectangle** drop-down > **Polygon** on the **Draw** panel of the **Drafting** tool set.
- Type 5 and press RETURN.
- Right-click and select the **Edge** option from the shortcut menu.
- Click in the empty area.
- Move the pointer toward the right.

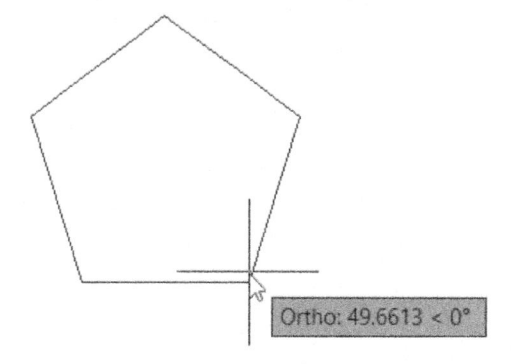

- Type **40** and press RETURN.
- Select the polygon and click the **Move** icon on the **Modify** panel of the **Drafting** tool set.
- Select the vertex point of the polygon, as shown.

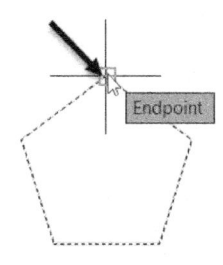

- Move the pointer and select the endpoint of the line, as shown.

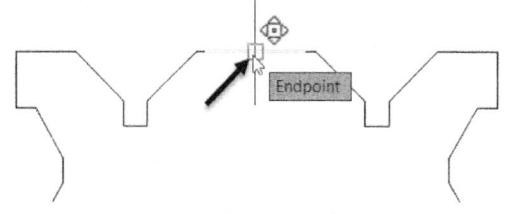

- Select the polygon and click the **Move** icon on the **Modify** panel of the **Drafting** tool set.
- Select the vertex point of the polygon, as shown.

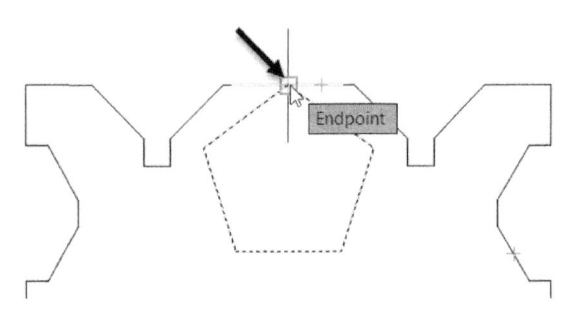

AutoCAD 2023 For Beginners (For Mac Users)

- Move the pointer downward.
- Type 27.5 and press RETURN.

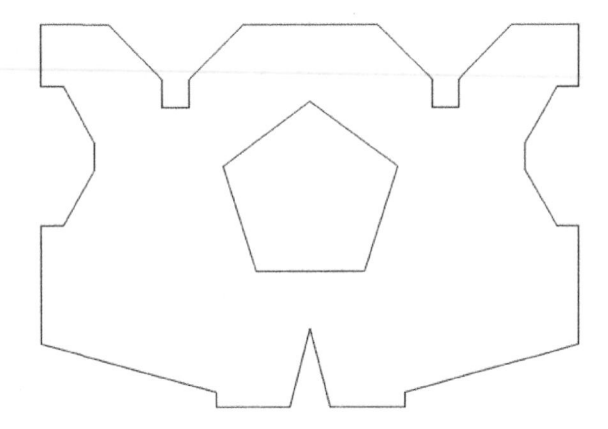

- Click the **Line** icon on the **Draw** panel of the **Drafting** tool set.
- Deactivate the **Ortho Mode** icon on the status bar.
- Select the vertices of the polygon, as shown.

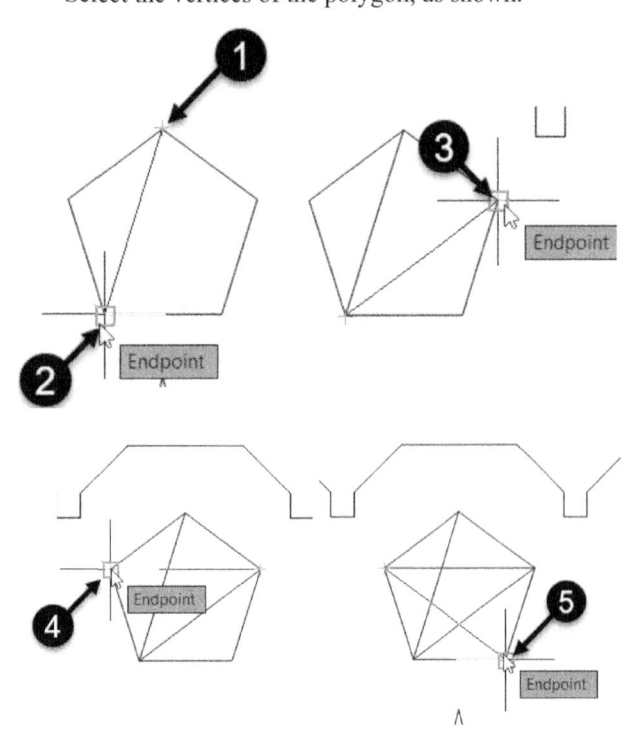

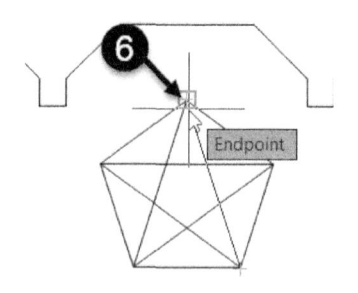

- Press ESC.
- Select the polygon and press Delete.

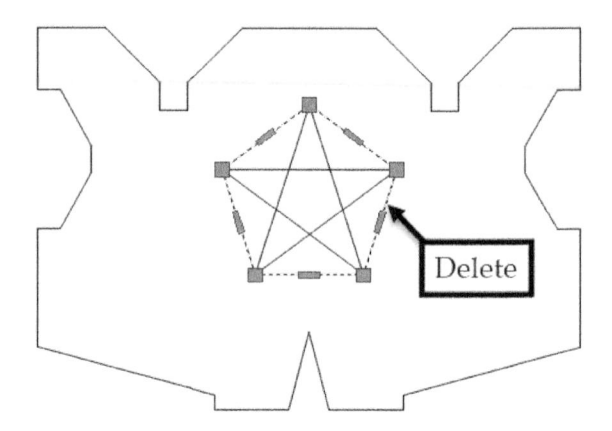

- Click the **Trim** icon on the **Modify** panel of the **Drafting** tool set.
- Select the inner lines of the star, as shown.

- Save and close the drawing file.

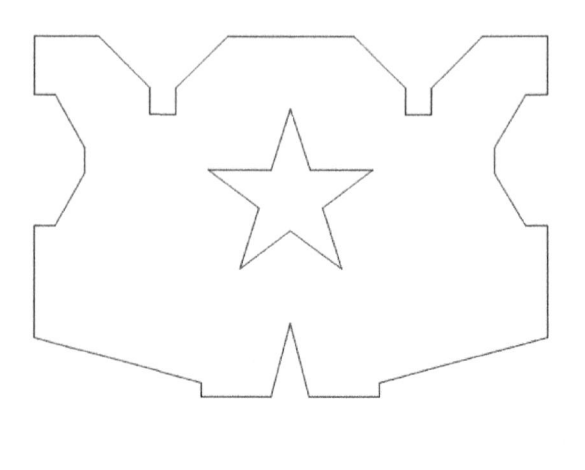

106 | Editing Tools

Exercises

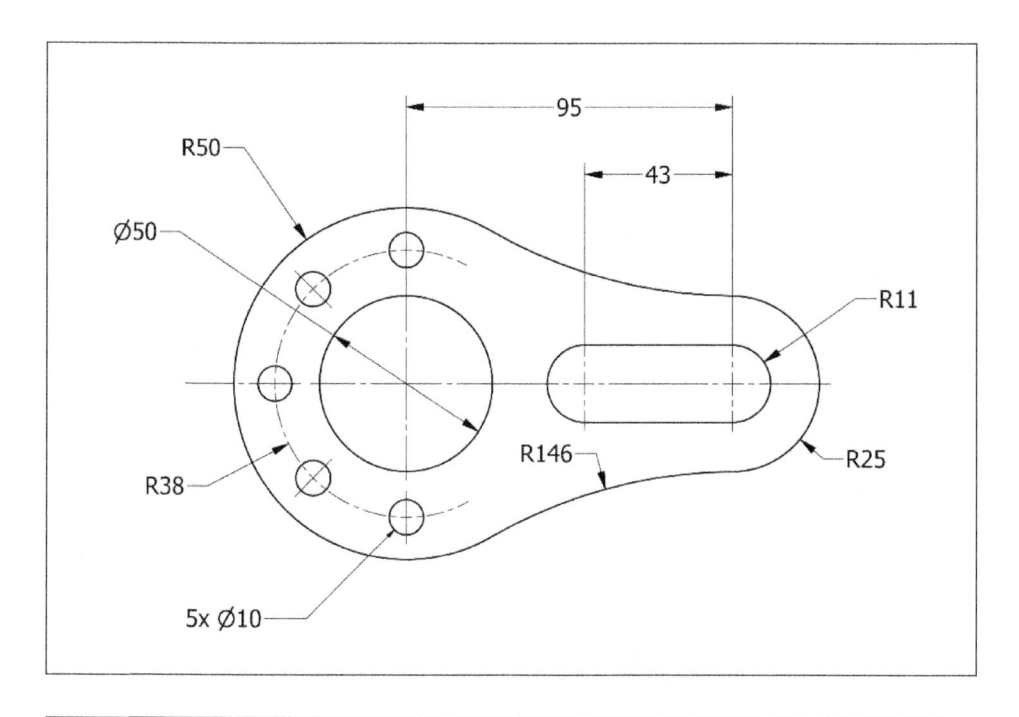

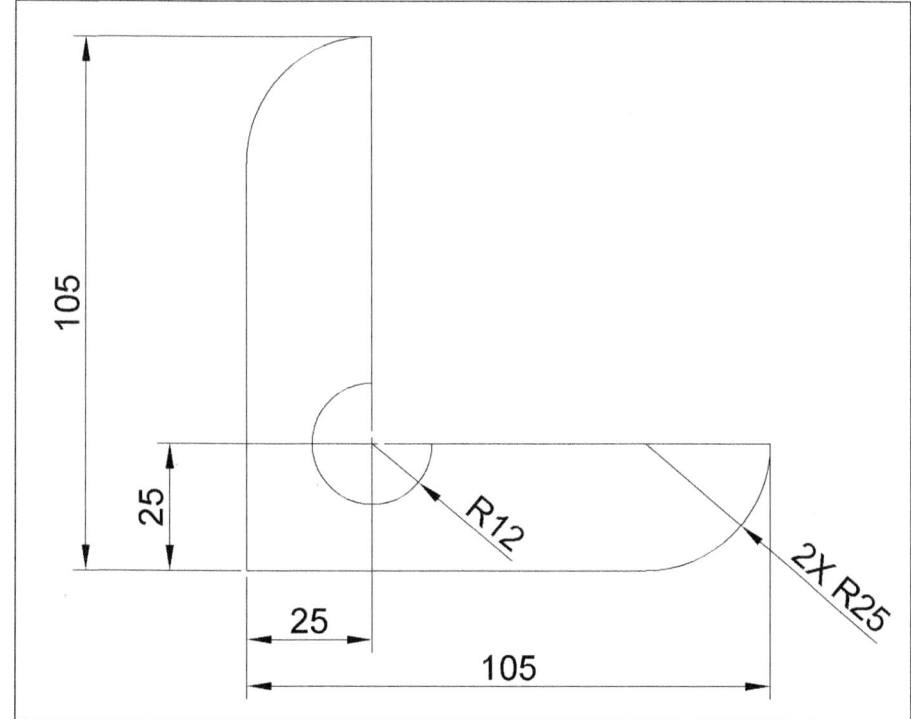

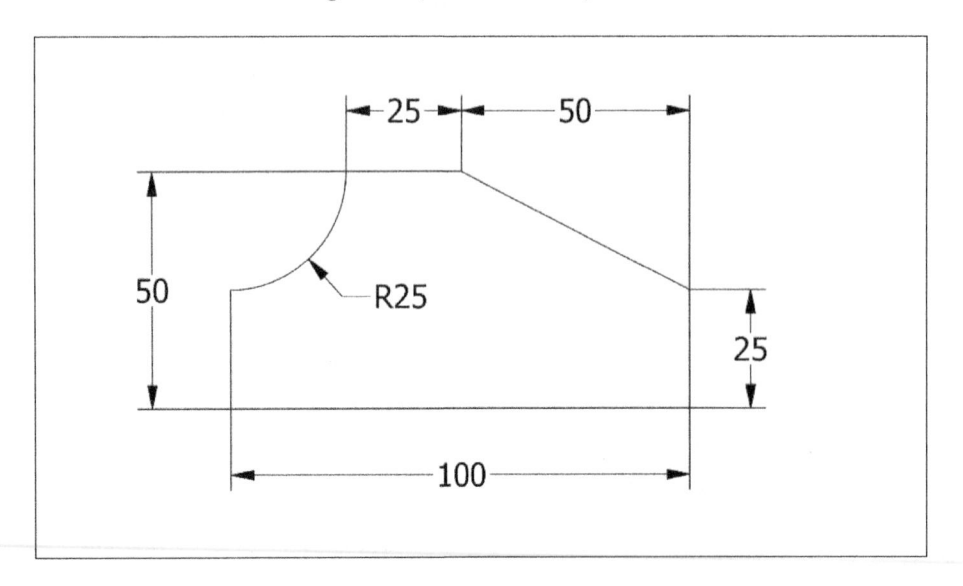

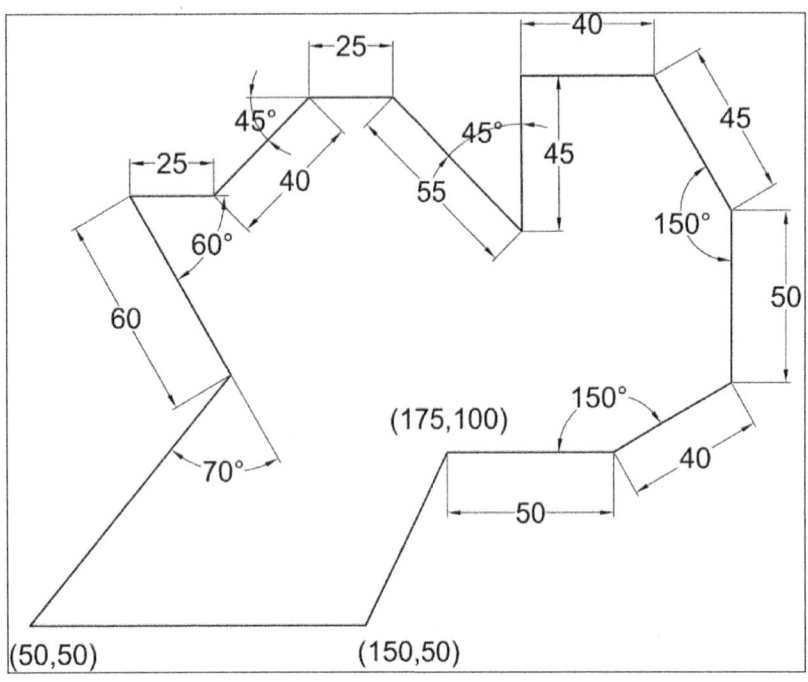

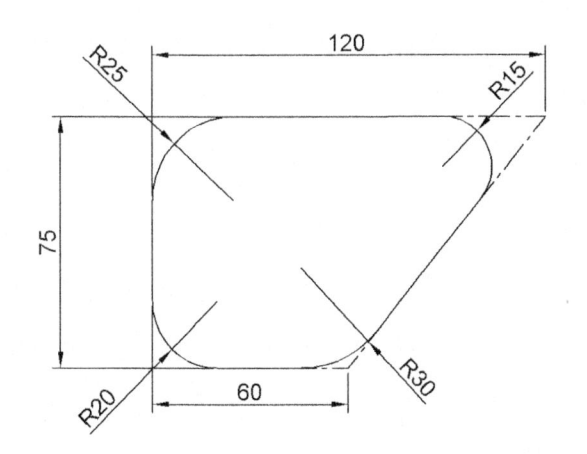

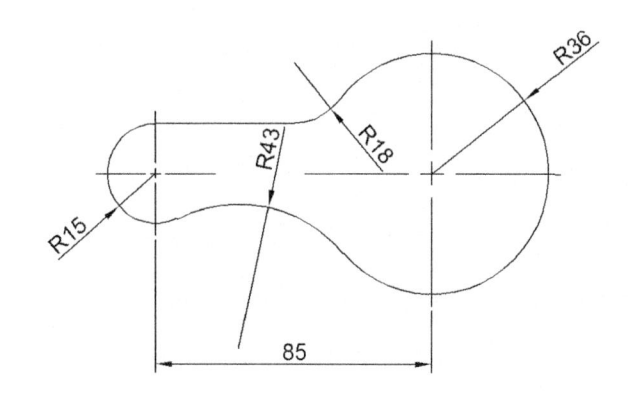

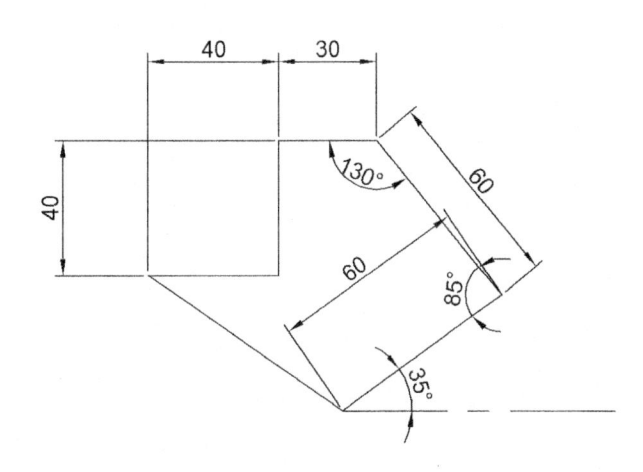

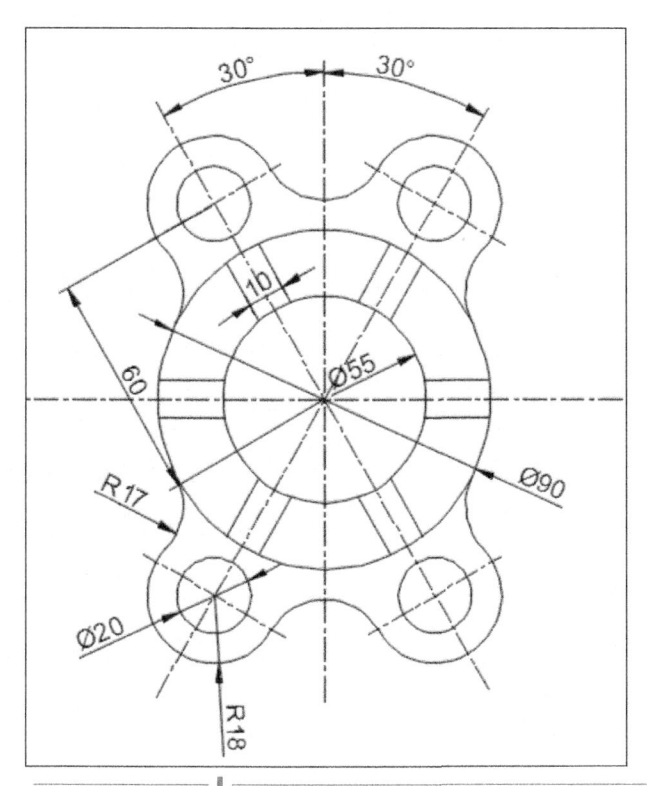

AutoCAD 2023 For Beginners (For Mac Users)

109 | Editing Tools

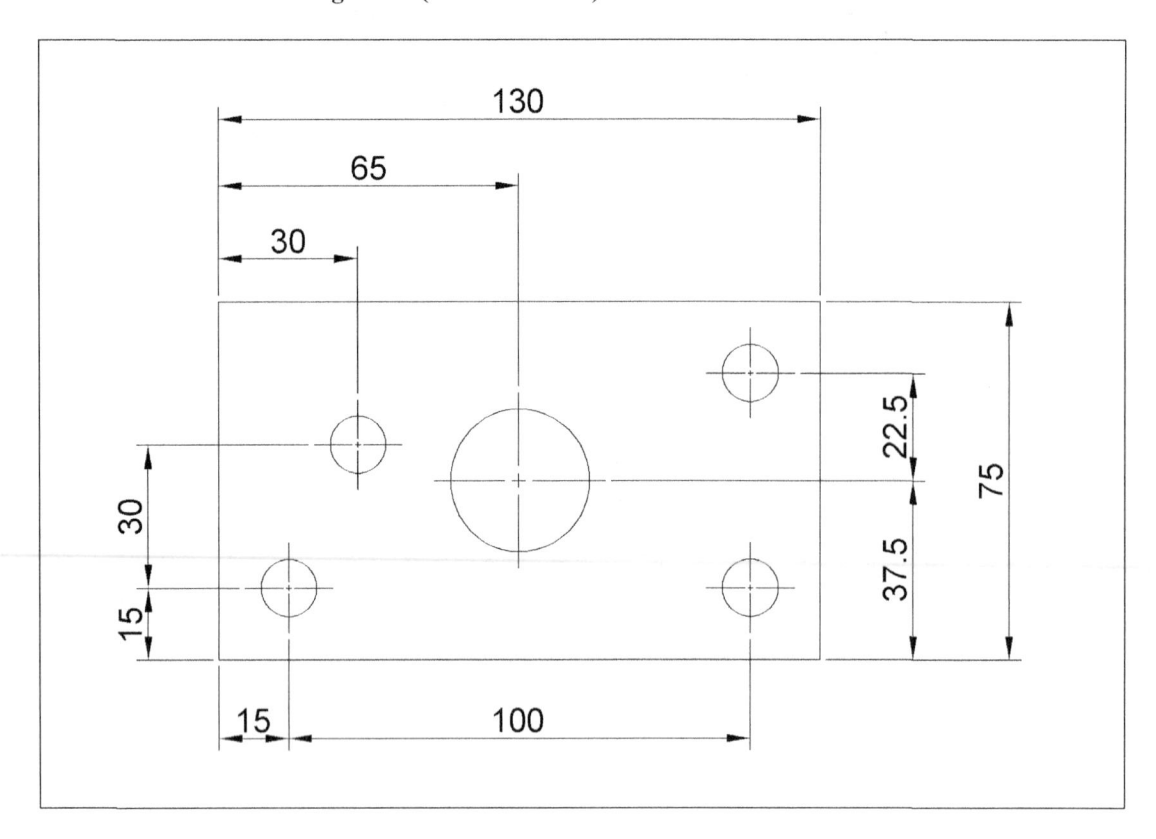

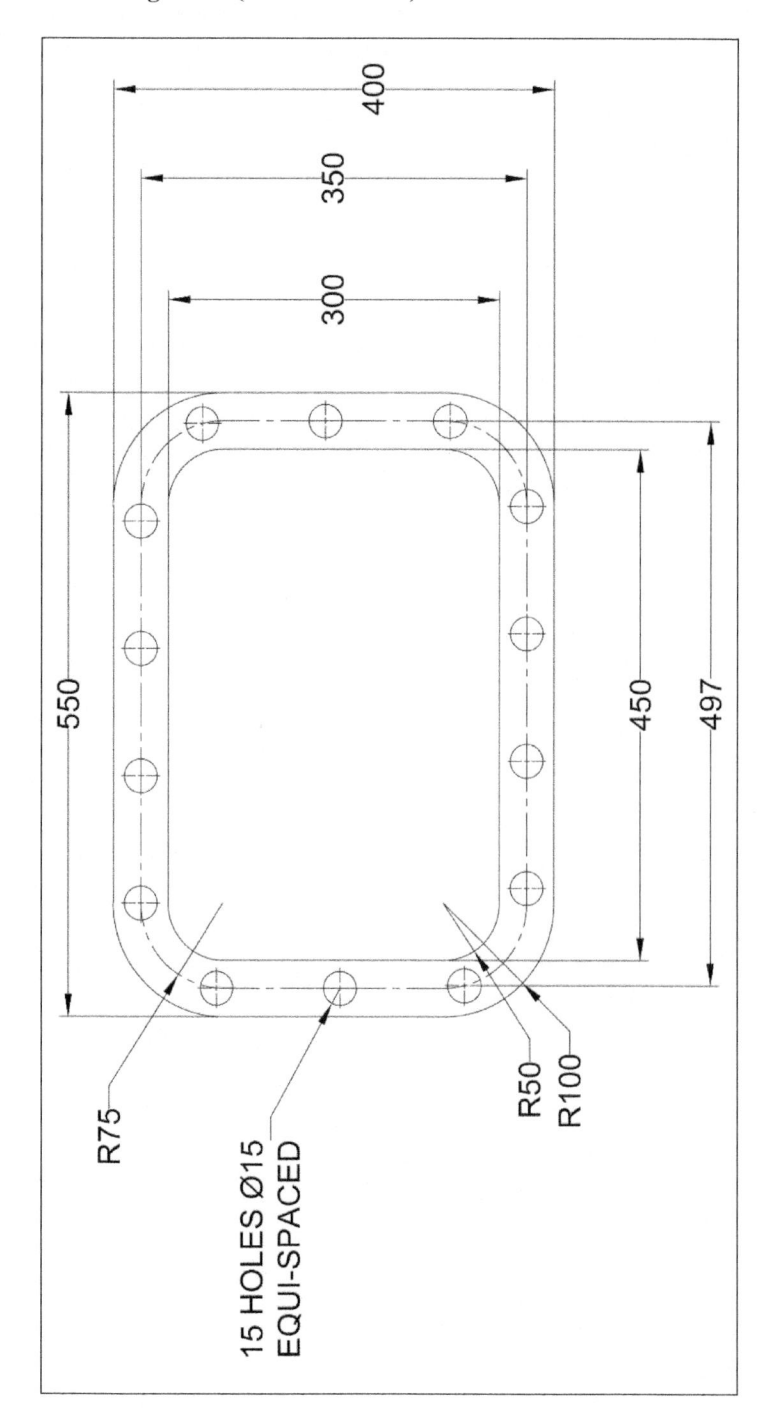

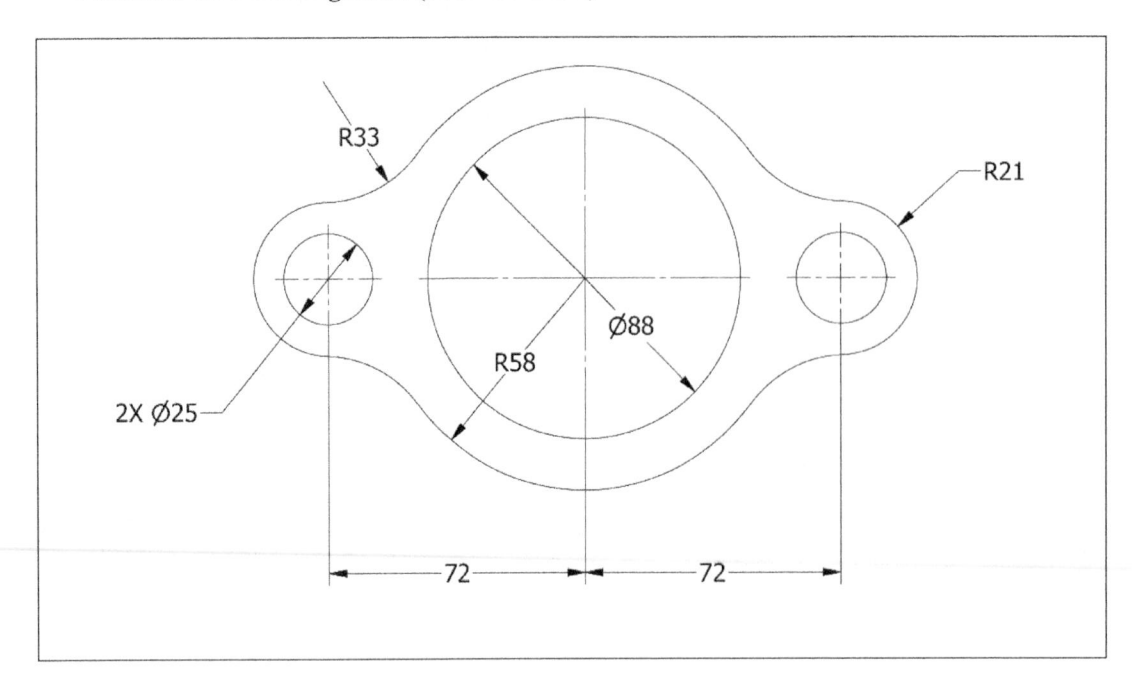

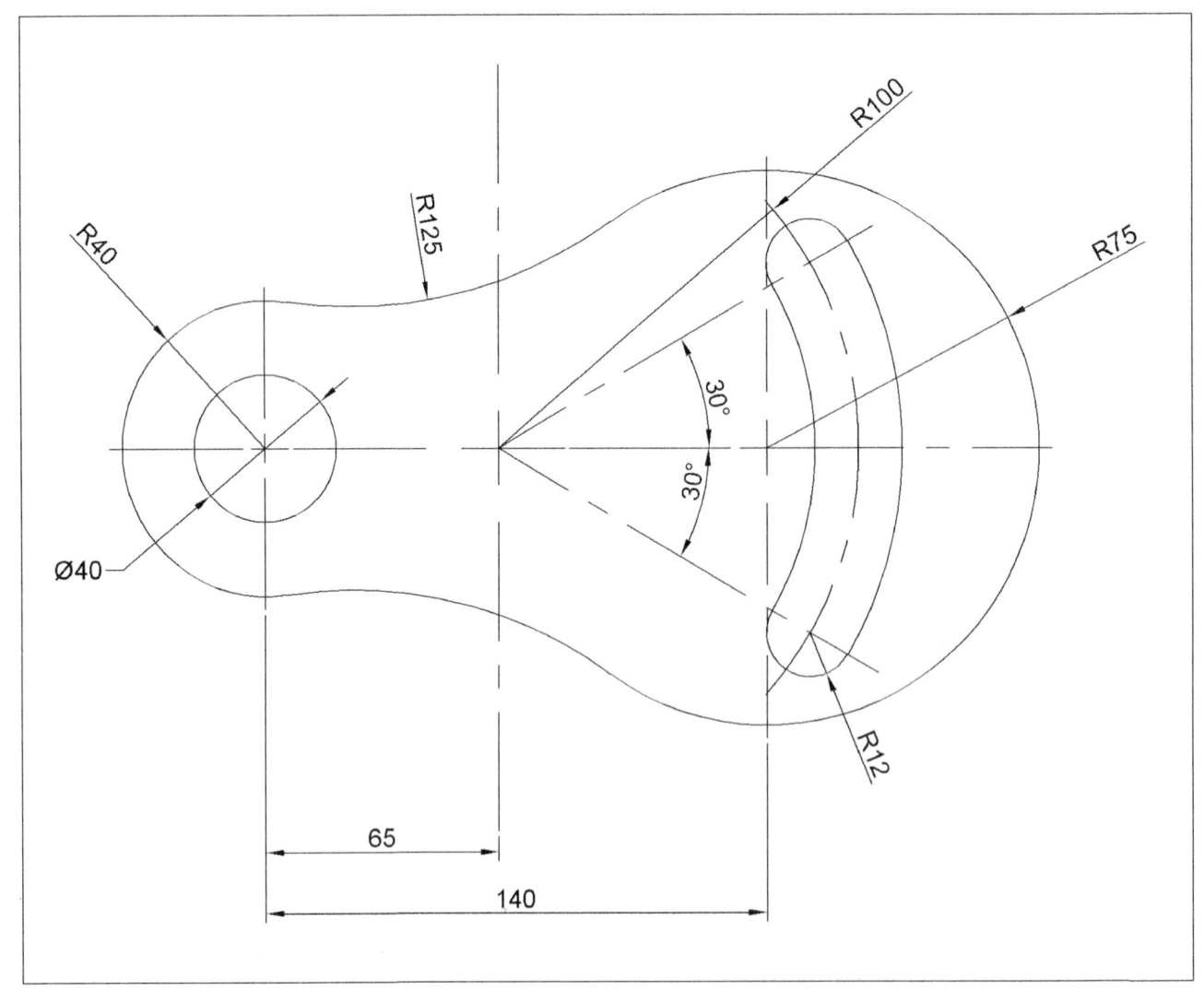

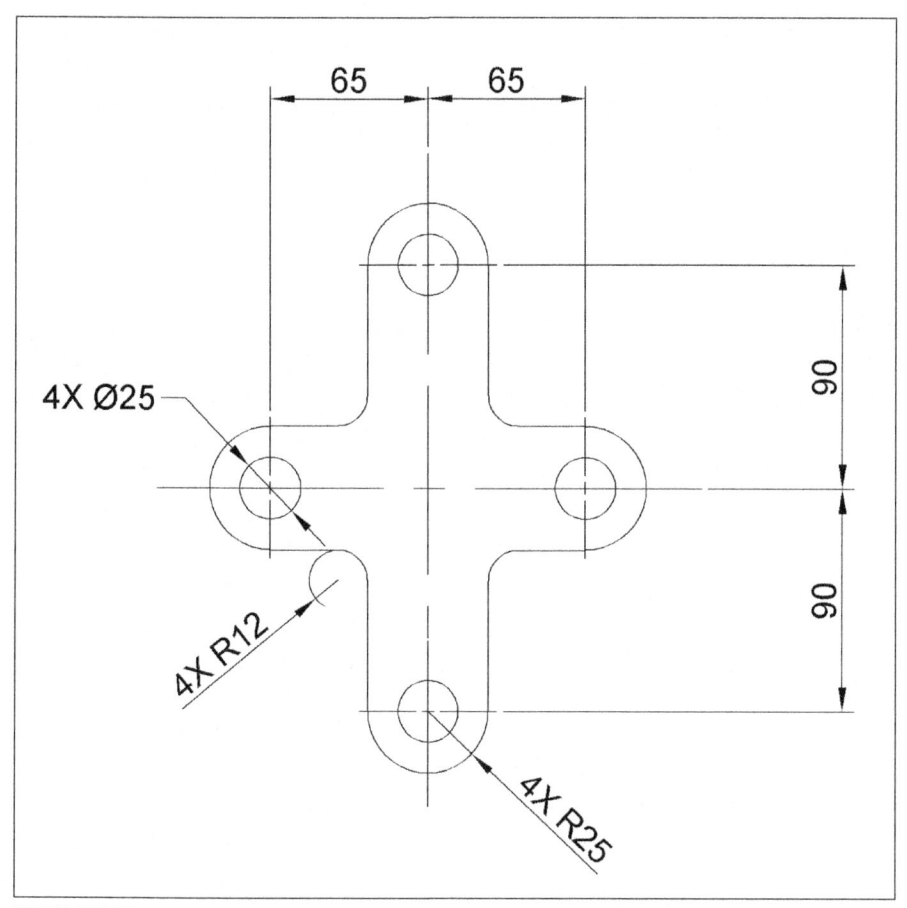

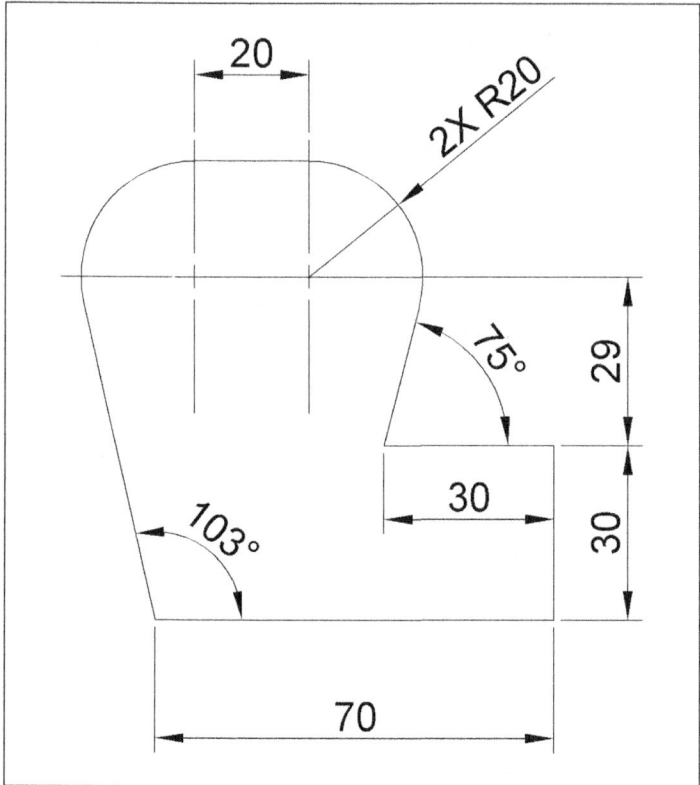

AutoCAD 2023 For Beginners (For Mac Users)

Chapter 5: Multi View Drawings

In this chapter, you will learn to create:

- **Orthographic Views**
- **Auxiliary Views**
- **Named Views**

Multi-view Drawings

To manufacture a component, you must create its engineering drawing. The engineering drawing consists of various views of the object, showing its true shape and size so that it can be dimensioned. It can be achieved by creating the orthographic views of the object. In the first section of this chapter, you will learn to create orthographic views of an object. The second section introduces you to auxiliary views. The auxiliary views clearly describe the features of a component, which are located on an inclined plane or surface.

Creating Orthographic Views

Orthographic Views are standard representations of an object on a sheet. These views are created by projecting an object onto three different planes (top, front, and side planes). You can project an object by using two different methods: **First Angle Projection** and **Third Angle Projection**. The following figure shows the orthographic views that will be created when an object is projected using the **First Angle Projection** method.

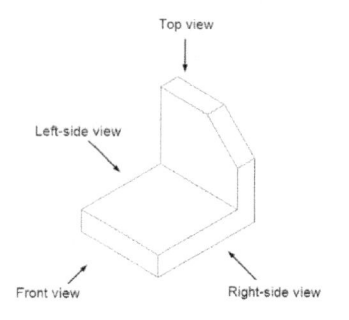

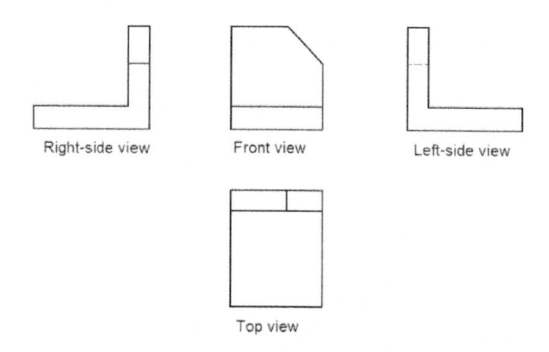

The following figure shows the orthographic views that will be created when an object is projected using the **Third Angle Projection** method.

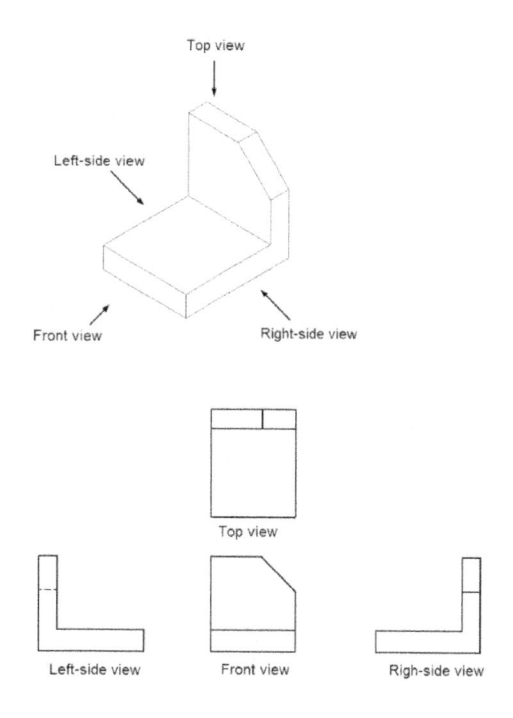

Example:

In this example, you will create the orthographic views of the part shown below. The views will be created by using the **Third Angle Projection** method.

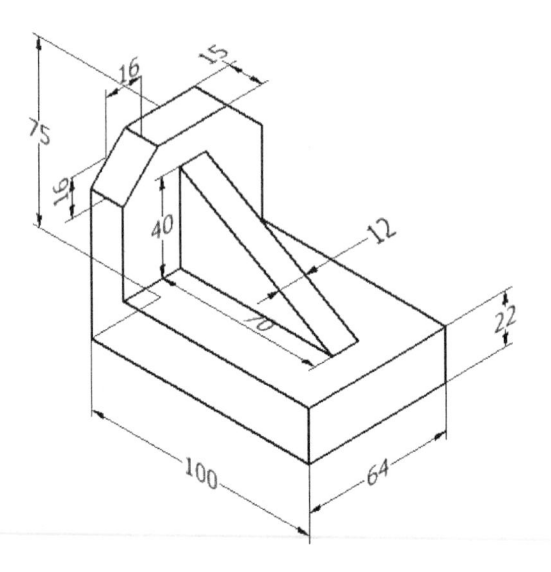

- Open a new drawing using the **acadISO –Named Plot Styles.dwt** template.
- On the **Layers** palette, click the arrow next to the **Show Layer List** option.
- Use the **New layer** icon on the **Layer** palette to create new layers.
- Create two new layers with the following properties.

Layer Name	Lineweight	Linetype
Construction	0.00 mm	Continuous
Object	0.30 mm	Continuous

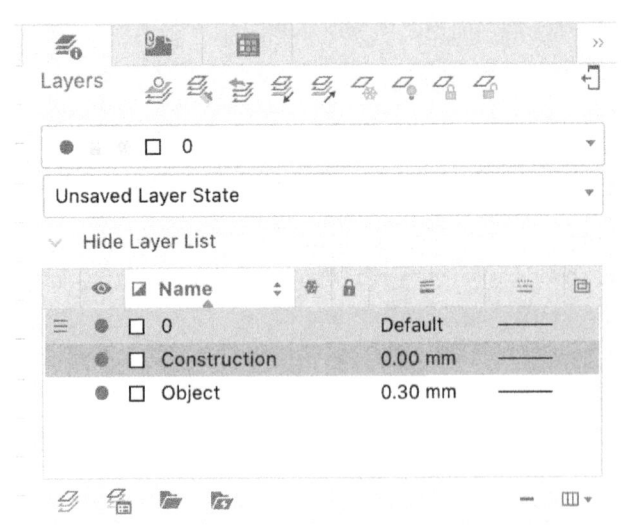

- Right-click on the **Construction** layer and select **Make active**.
- Activate the **Ortho Mode** icon on the status bar.
- Click **View > Zoom > All** on the Menu Bar.

Next, you need to draw construction lines. They are used as references to create actual drawings. You will create these construction lines on the **Construction** layer so that you can hide them when required.

- Click **Drafting > Draw > Construction** line on the tool set or enter **XLINE** in the command line. 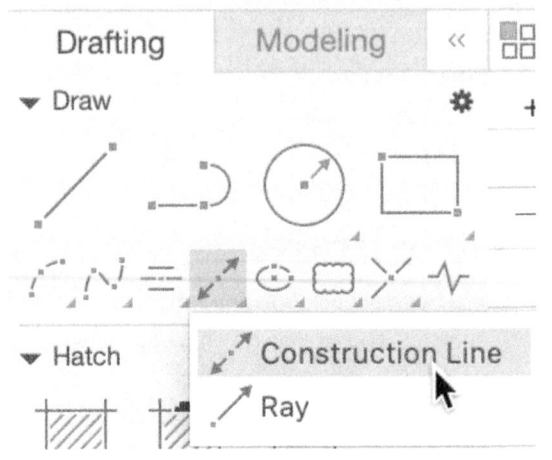
- Click anywhere in the lower-left corner of the graphics window.
- Move the pointer upward and click to create a vertical construction line.
- Move the pointer toward the right and click to create a horizontal construction line. 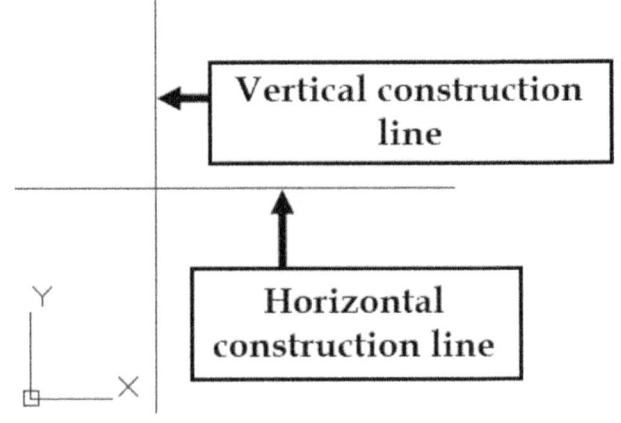
- Press RETURN to exit the tool.
- Click the **Offset** button on the **Modify** panel.
- Type 100 as the offset distance and press RETURN.
- Select the vertical construction line.
- Move the pointer toward the right and click to create an offset line.

116 | Multi View Drawings

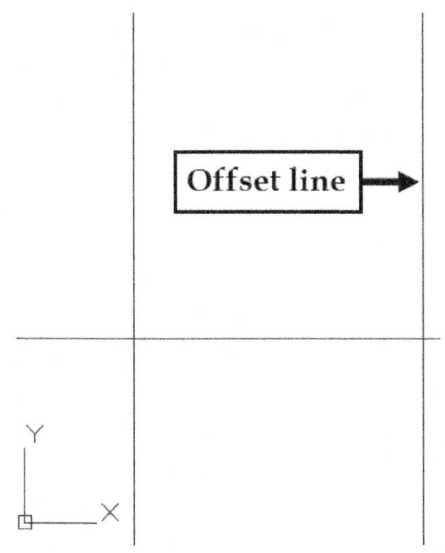

- Right-click and select **Enter** to exit the **Offset** tool.
- Press the SPACEBAR on the keyboard to start the **Offset** tool again.
- Type 75 as the offset distance and press RETURN.
- Select the horizontal construction line.
- Move the pointer above and click to create the offset line. 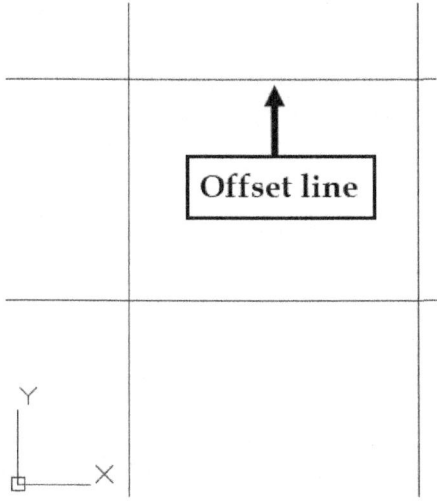
- Press RETURN to exit the **Offset** tool.
- Likewise, create other offset lines, as shown below. The offset dimensions are displayed in the image. Do not add dimensions to the lines.

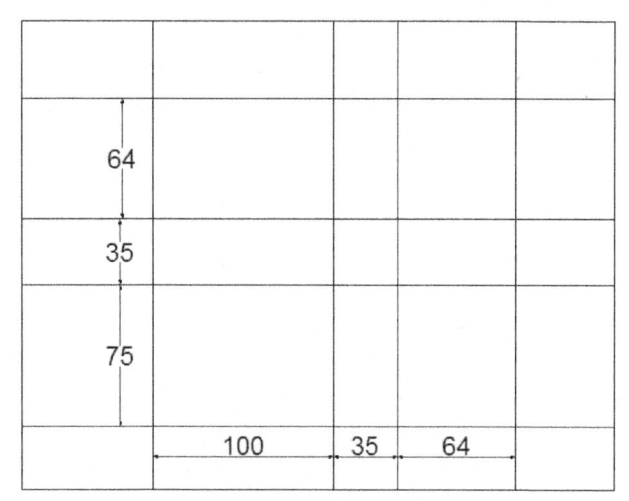

- Activate the **Object** layer.

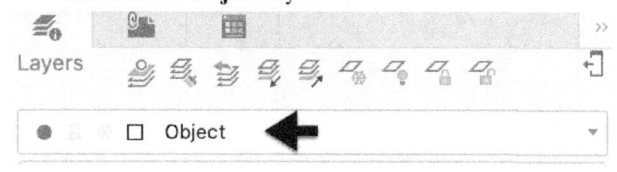

  Now, you must create the object lines.

- Activate the **Show/Hide Lineweight** button on the status bar.
- Click the **Line** button on the **Draw** panel.
- Select the intersection points of the construction lines, as shown. 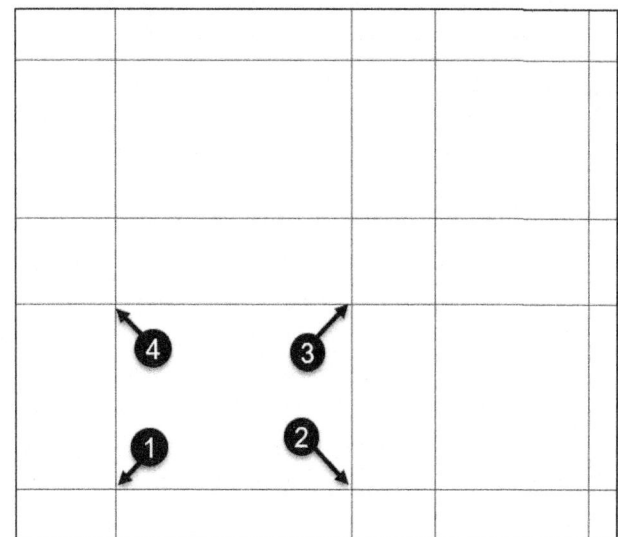
- Right-click and select the **Close** option from the shortcut menu to create the outline of the front view.

117 | Multi View Drawings

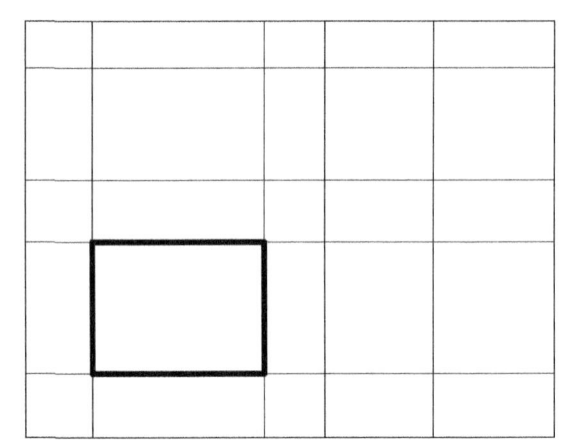

- Likewise, create the outlines of the top and side views.

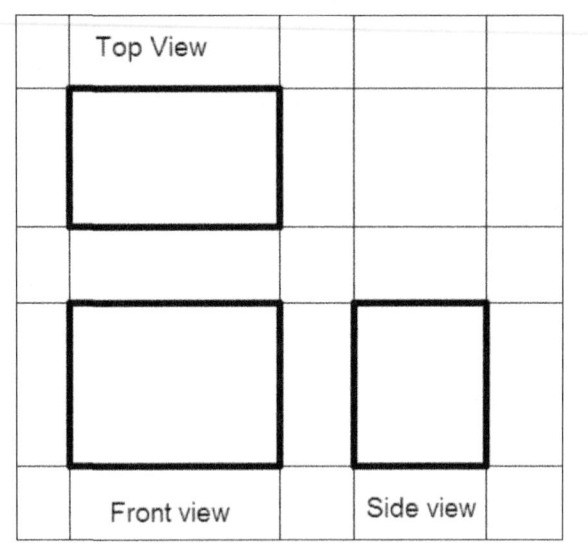

Next, you must turn off the **Construction** layer.
- Click on the **Layer** drop-down in the **Layers** palette.
- Click the circular dot of the **Construction** layer; the layer will be turned off.

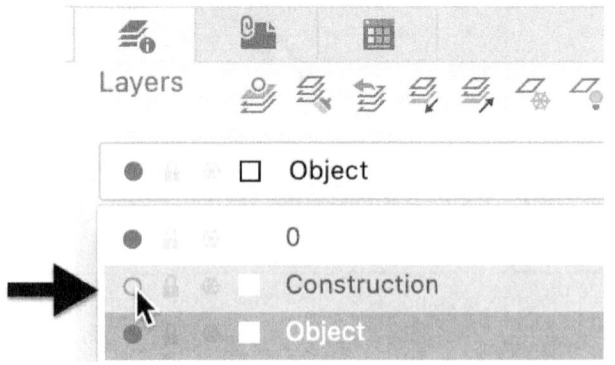

- Use the **Offset** tool and create two parallel lines on the front view, as shown below.

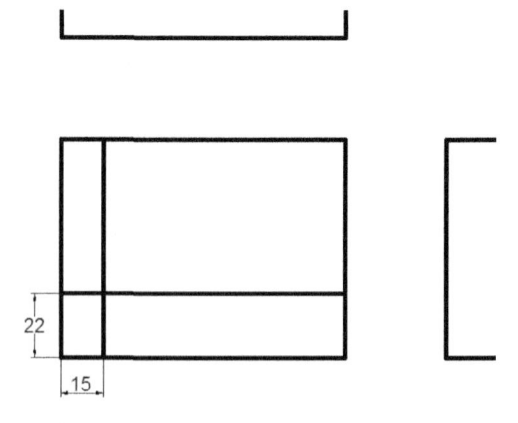

- Use the **Trim** tool and trim the unwanted lines of the front view, as shown below.

- Use the **Offset** tool to create the parallel line, as shown below.

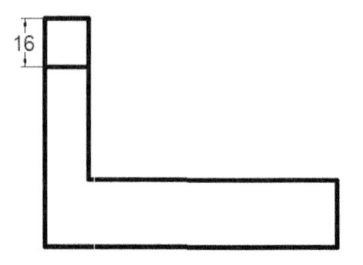

- Use the **Offset** tool and create offset lines in the Top view, as shown below.

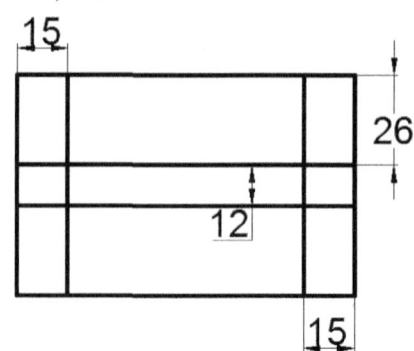

- Use the **Trim** tool and trim unwanted objects.

118 | Multi View Drawings

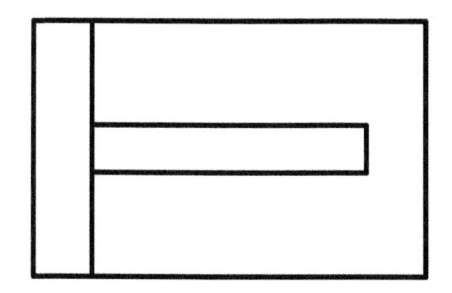

- Create other offset lines and trim the unwanted portions, as shown below.

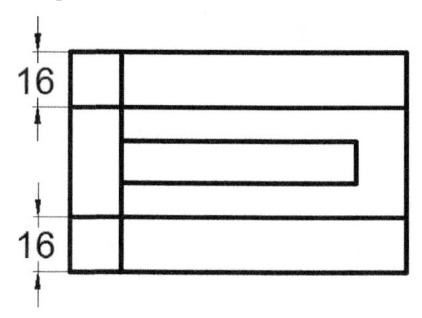

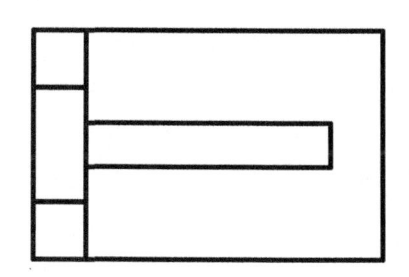

- Deactivate the **Ortho Mode** icon on the status bar.
- Click the **Line** button on the **Draw** panel.
- Press and hold the SHIFT key and right-click. Select the **From** option.

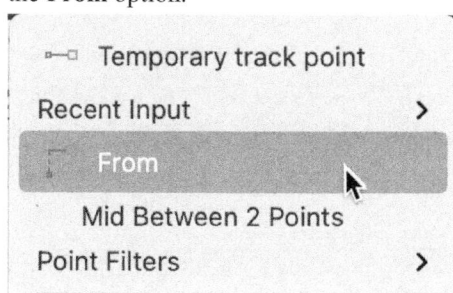

- Select the endpoint of the line in the front view, as shown below.

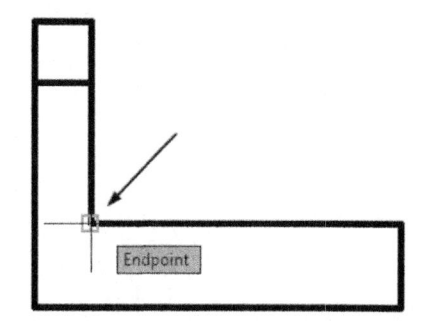

- Move the pointer on the vertical line and enter **40** in the command line; the first point of the line is specified at a point 40 mm away from the endpoint. Also, a rubber band line will be attached to the pointer.

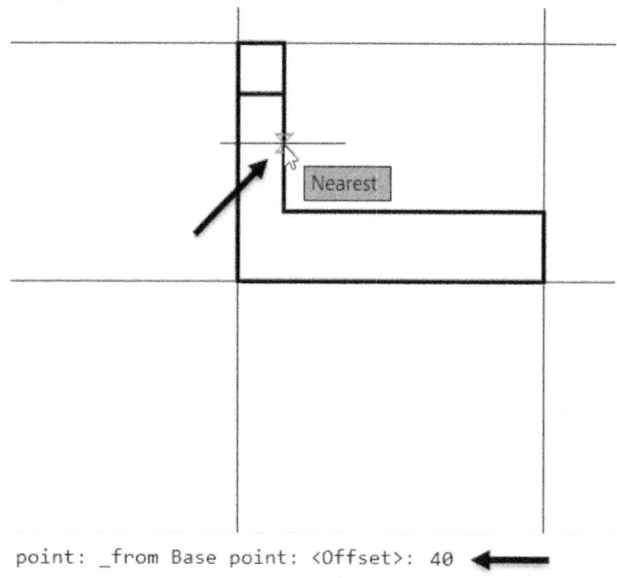

```
point: _from Base point: <Offset>: 40
```

- Move the pointer onto the endpoint on the top view, as shown below.

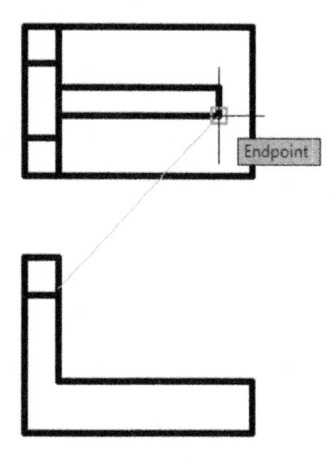

- Move the pointer vertically downward; you will notice the track lines.

Multi View Drawings

AutoCAD 2023 For Beginners (For Mac Users)

- Move the pointer near the horizontal line of the front view and click at the intersection point, as shown below. Press RETURN to exit the tool.

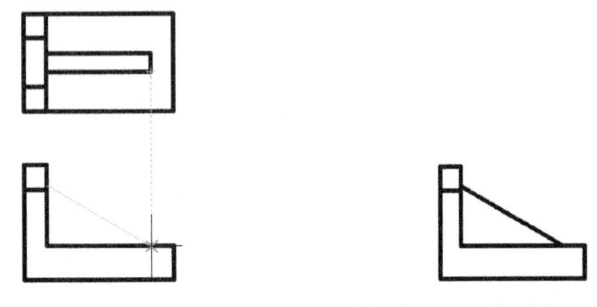

Next, you must create the right-side view. To do this, you must draw a 45-degree miter line and project the measurements of the top view onto the side view.

- Click on the **Layer** drop-down in the **Layers** palette.
- Click the circular dot of the **Construction** layer; the **Construction** layer is turned on.

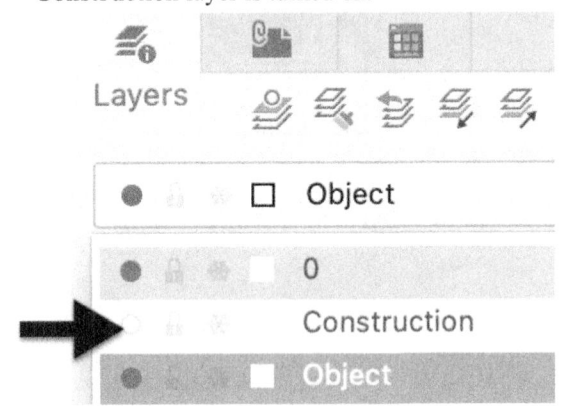

- Select the **Construction** layer from the **Layer** drop-down to set it as the current layer.
- Draw an inclined line by connecting the intersection points of the construction lines, as shown below.

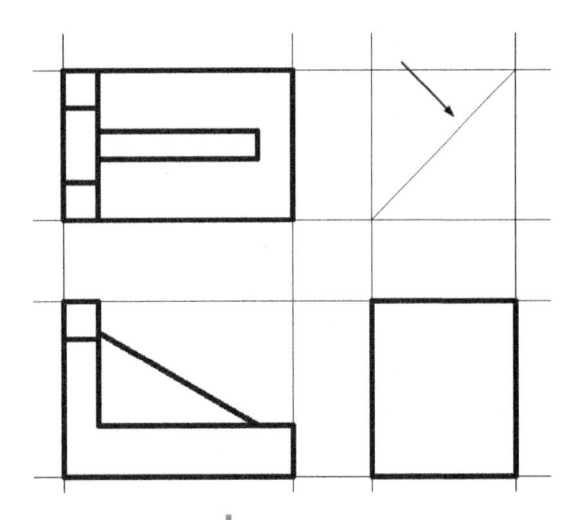

- Click the **Construction Line** button on the **Draw** panel.
- Right-click and select the **Hor** option from the shortcut menu.
- Select the points on the top and front views, as shown below.

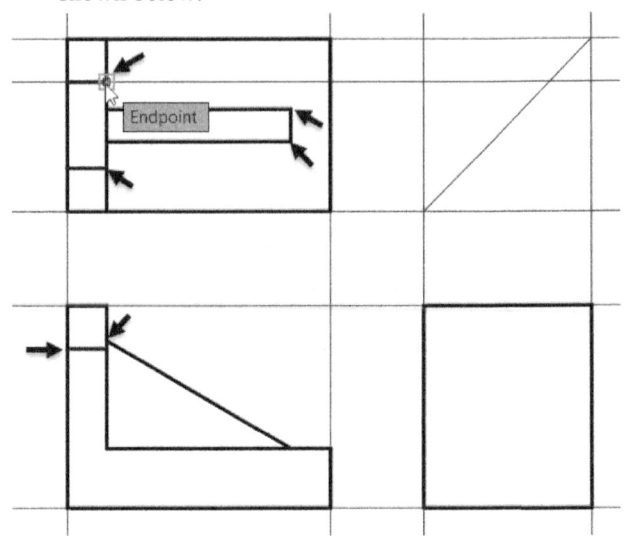

The projection lines are created, as shown below.

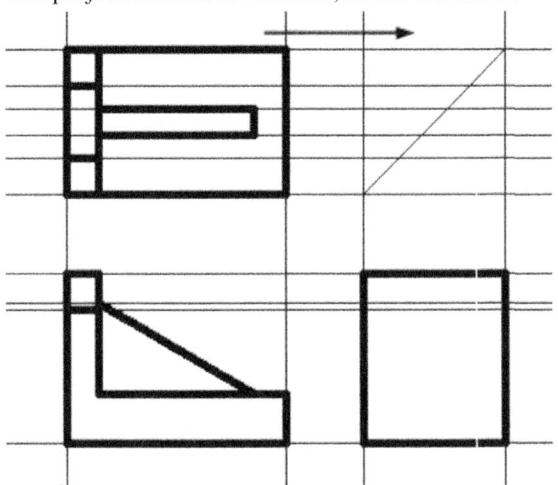

- Right-click to exit the **Construction Line** tool.
- Press RETURN.
- Right-click and select the **Ver** option.
- Create vertical projection lines, as shown below.

Multi View Drawings

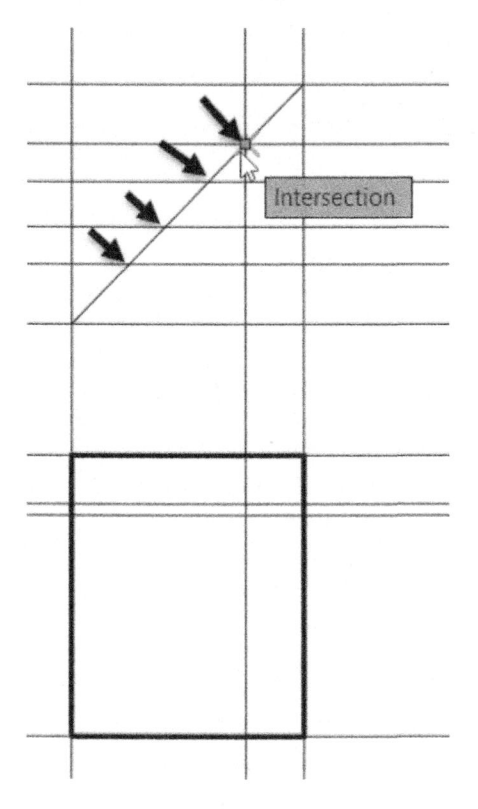

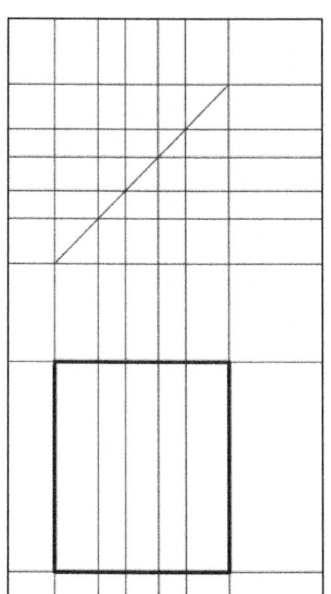

- Use the **Trim** tool and trim the extended portions of the construction lines.

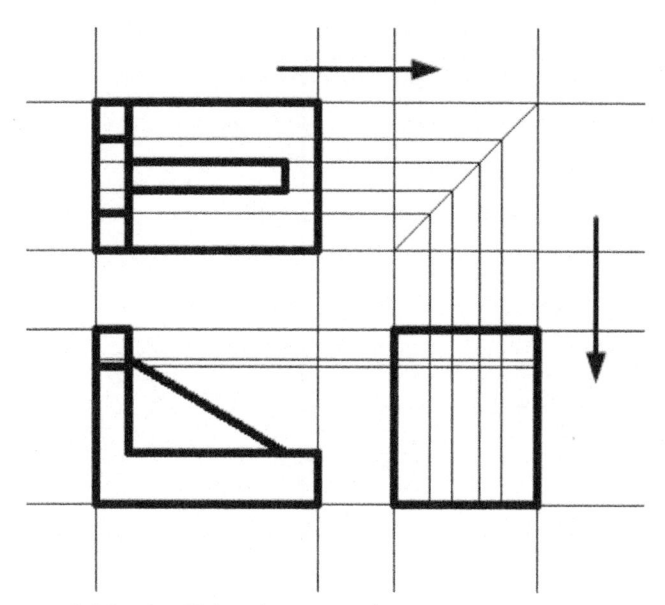

- Make the **Object** layer as active.
- Click the **Offset** button on the **Modify** panel.
- Right-click and select the **Through** option from the shortcut menu.
- Select the lower horizontal line of the side view.
- Select the endpoint on the front view, as shown below. 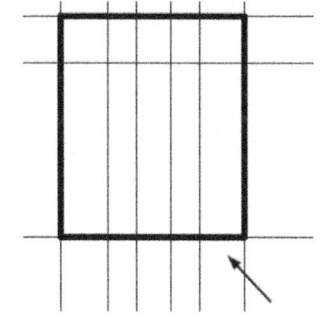
- Right-click and select **Exit** from the shortcut menu. 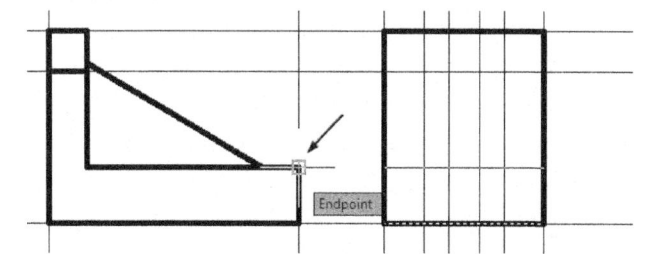
- Use the **Line** tool and create the objects in the side view, as shown below.

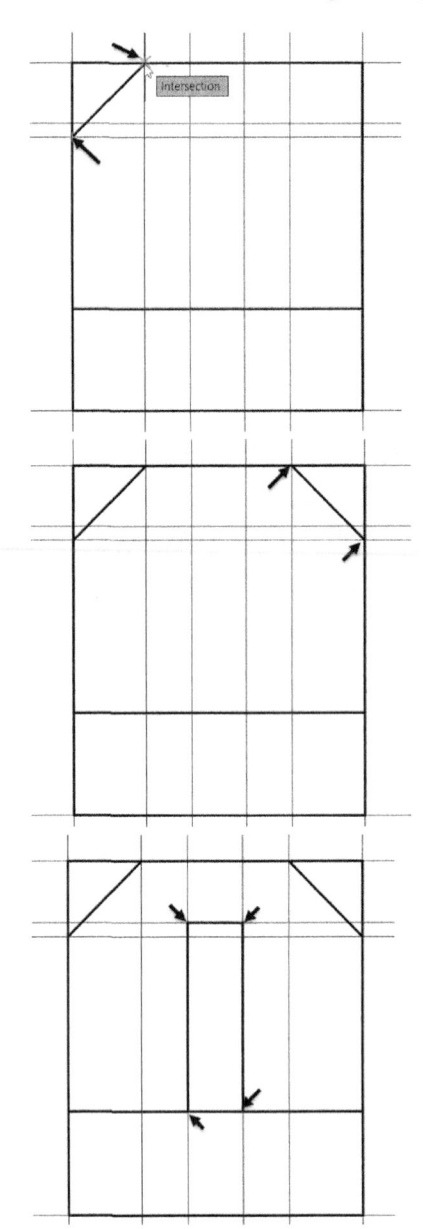

- Turn off the **Construction** layer by clicking on the circular dot of the **Construction** layer.
- Trim the unwanted portions on the right side view.

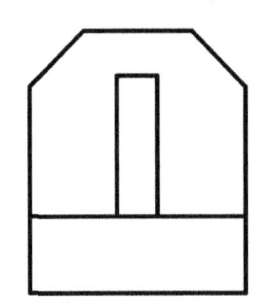

The drawing after creating all the views is shown below.

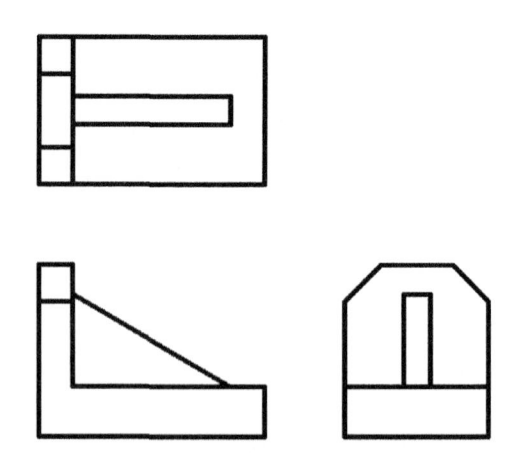

- Save the file as **ortho_views.dwg**. Close the file.

Creating Auxiliary Views

Most of the components are represented by using orthographic views (front, top and side views). But many components have features located on inclined faces. You cannot get the true shape and size for these features by using the orthographic views. To see an accurate size and shape of the inclined features, you must create an auxiliary view. An auxiliary view is created by projecting the component onto a plane other than horizontal, front, or side planes. The following figure shows a component with an inclined face. When you create orthographic views of the component, you will not be able to get the true shape of the hole on the inclined face.

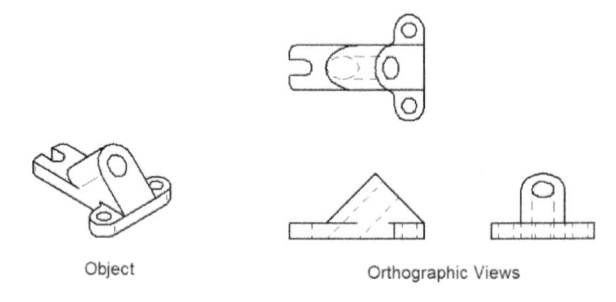

Object   Orthographic Views

To get the actual shape of the hole, you must create an auxiliary view of the object, as shown below.

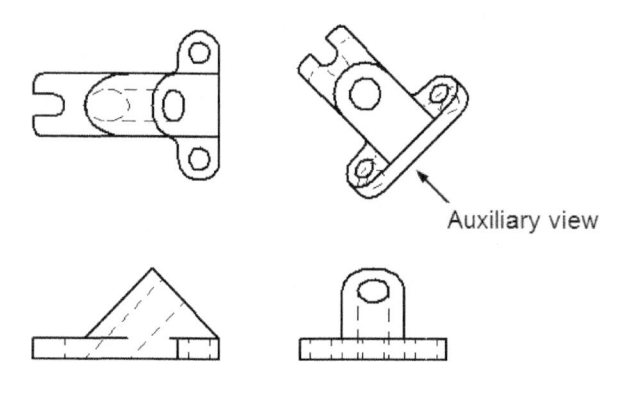

AutoCAD 2023 For Beginners (For Mac Users)

Example:

In this example, you will create an auxiliary view of the object shown below.

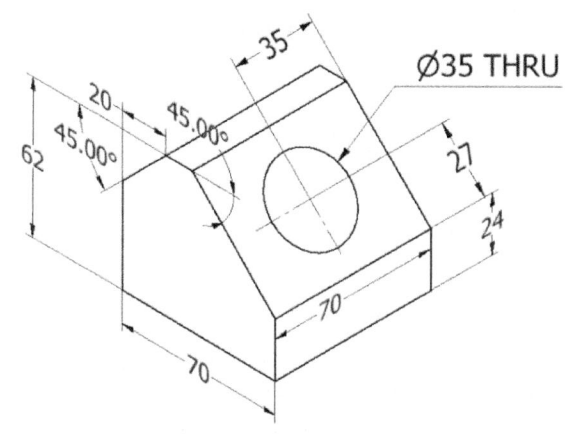

- Open a new AutoCAD file.
- Create four new layers with the following properties.

Layer Name	Lineweight	Linetype
Construction	0.00 mm	Continuous
Object	0.50 mm	Continuous
Hidden	0.30 mm	HIDDEN
Centerline	0.30 mm	CENTER

- Select the **Construction** layer from the **Layer** drop-down in the **Layers** palette.
- Create a rectangle at the lower-left corner of the graphics window, as shown in the figure.

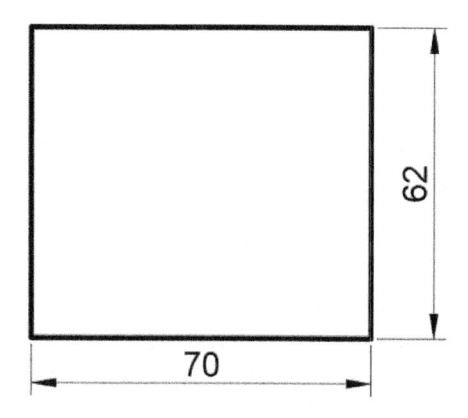

- Select the rectangle and click the **Copy** button on the **Modify** panel.
- Select the lower-left corner of the rectangle as the base point.
- Make sure that the **Ortho mode** is activated.
- Move the pointer upward and type **25** in the command line — next, press RETURN.
- Press ESC to exit the **Copy** tool.

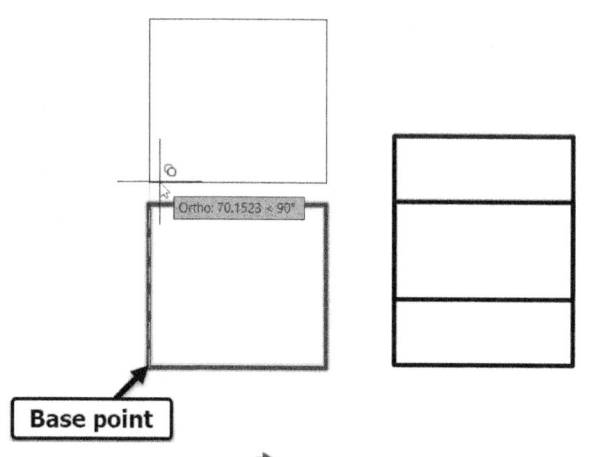

- Click the **Rotate** button on the **Modify** panel and select the copied rectangle. Press RETURN to accept.
- Select the lower right corner of the copied rectangle as the base point.
- Type 45 as the angle and press RETURN.

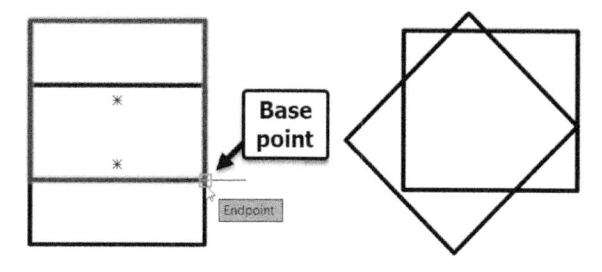

123 | Multi View Drawings

- Click the **Object Snap Tracking** icon on the Status Bar.
- Right-click on the **Object Snap** icon, and then select **Endpoint** from the list.
- Activate the **Rectangle** command.
- Place the pointer on the top left corner of the existing rectangle.
- Move the pointer vertically upward, and then notice a vertical tracking line from the top left corner of the rectangle.
- Move the pointer along the tracking line up to an approximate distance of 60 mm.

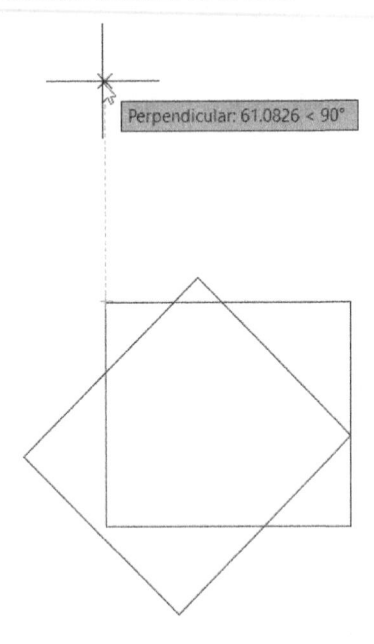

- Click to specify the first corner of the rectangle.
- Right-click and select **Dimensions** from the shortcut menu.
- Type 70 and press RETURN to specify the length of the rectangle.
- Again, type 70 and press RETURN to specify the width of the rectangle.
- Move the pointer up and click to position the rectangle.

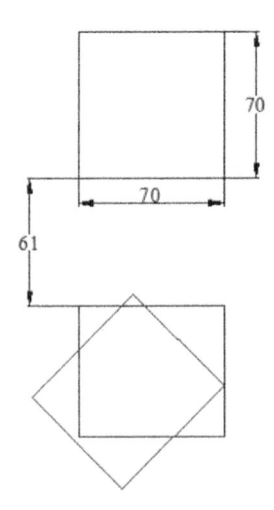

The rectangle located at the top is considered as top view and the below one as the front view.

- Click the **Explode** button on the **Modify** panel and select the newly created rectangle. Next, right-click to explode the rectangle.
- Activate the **Offset** tool.
- Right-click and select the **Through** option from the shortcut menu.
- Select the left vertical line of the top rectangle.
- Select any one of the through points, as shown; the selected vertical line is offset through the selected point.
- Again, select the left vertical line.
- Move the pointer, and then select the remaining through point.

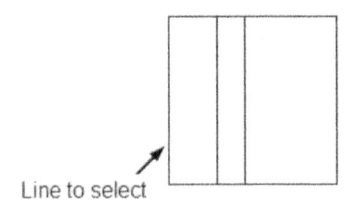

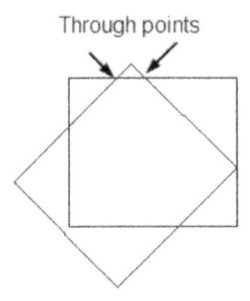

Line to select

Through points

- Press Esc to deactivate the **Offset** tool.

124 | Multi View Drawings

- Select the **Object** layer from the **Layer** drop-down in the **Layers** palette.
- Activate the **Show/Hide Lineweight** button on the status bar.
- Activate the **Line** tool and select the intersection points on the front view, as shown.
- Right-click and select **Close**. 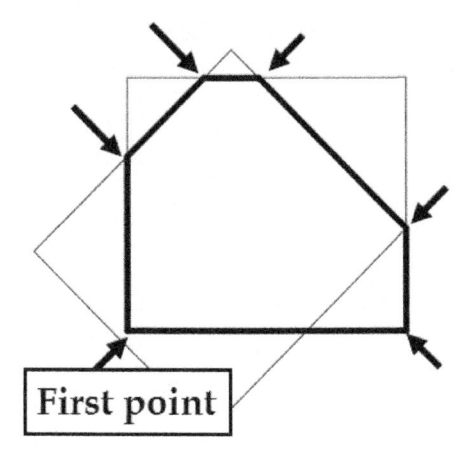
- Likewise, create the object lines in the top view, as shown below. 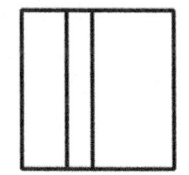 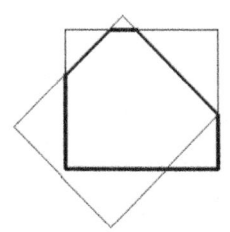
- Select the **Construction** layer from the **Layers** palette.
- Click the **Construction Line** button on the **Draw** panel.
- Right-click and select the **Offset** option from the shortcut menu.
- Right-click and select the **Through** option.
- Select the inclined line on the front view. Next, select the intersection point, as shown below.

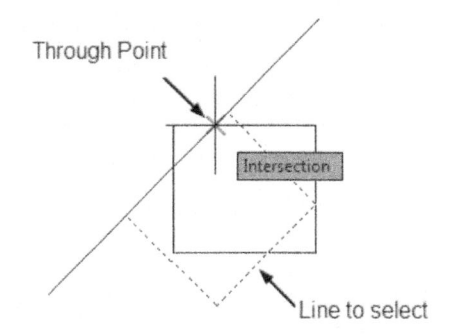

- Likewise, create other construction lines, as shown below.

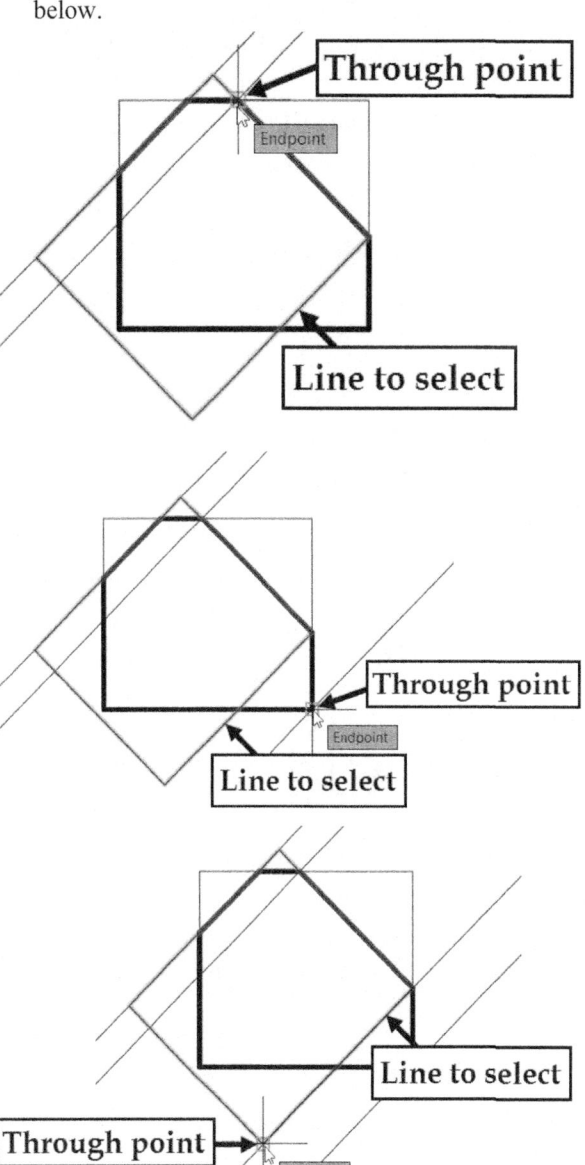

125 | Multi View Drawings

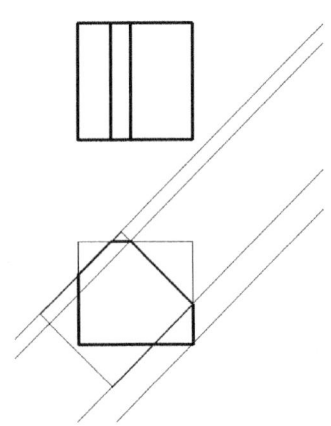

- Press Esc to deactivate the **Construction Line** command.
- Activate the **Construction Line** command.
- Right-click and select **Offset** from the shortcut menu.
- Type 80 and press RETURN.
- Select the inclined line of the front view, as shown.
- Move the pointer toward the right and click to create the construction line.

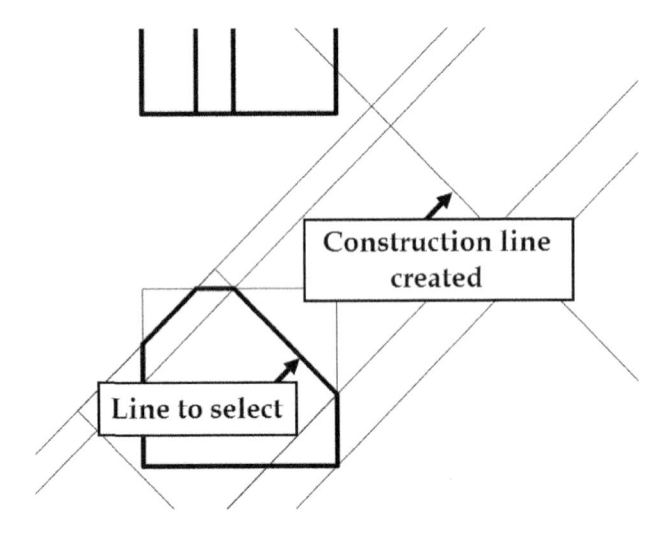

- Create other construction lines, as shown. The offset dimensions are given in the figure.

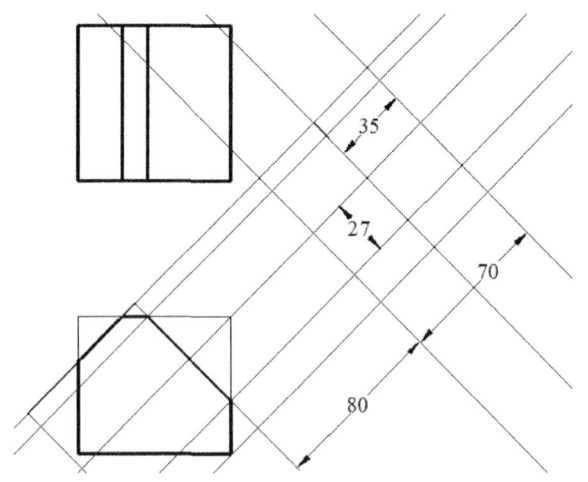

- Set the **Object** layer as the active layer. Next, create the object lines using the intersection points between the construction lines.
- Use the **Circle** tool and create a circle of 35 mm in diameter.

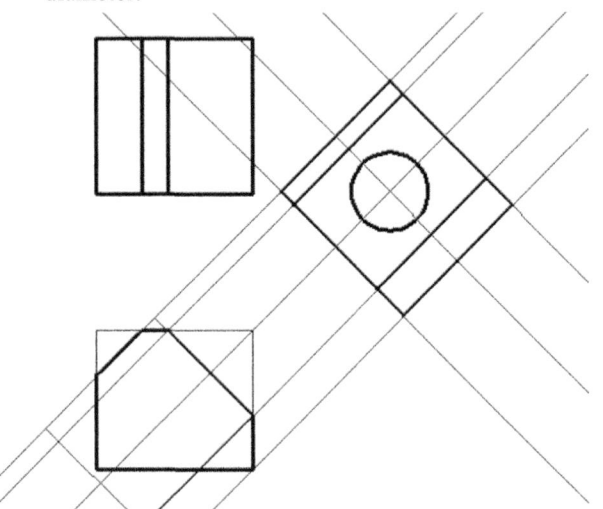

- Set the **Construction** layer as the active layer.
- Create projection lines from the circle.

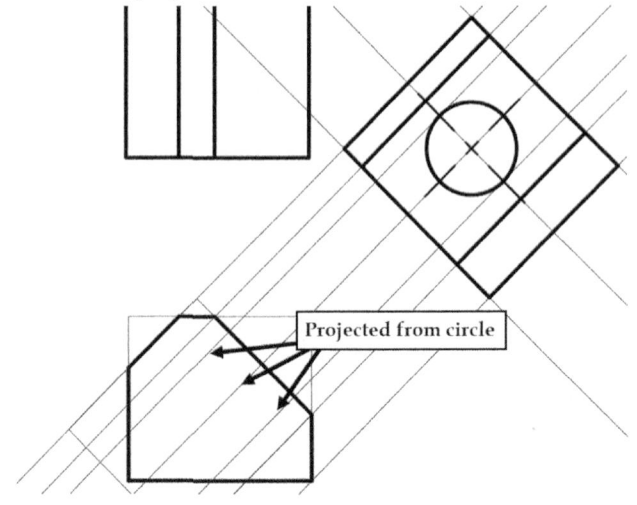

126 | Multi View Drawings

- Set the **Hidden** layer as the current layer,
- Create the hidden lines, as shown.

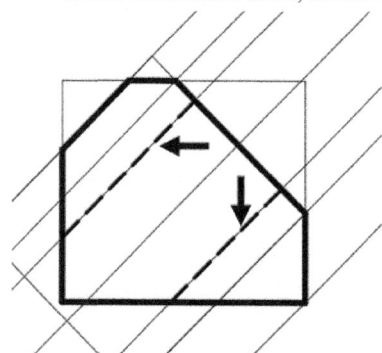

- Set the **Centerline** layer as the current layer.
- Activate the **Line** tool.
- Create the centerlines, as shown.

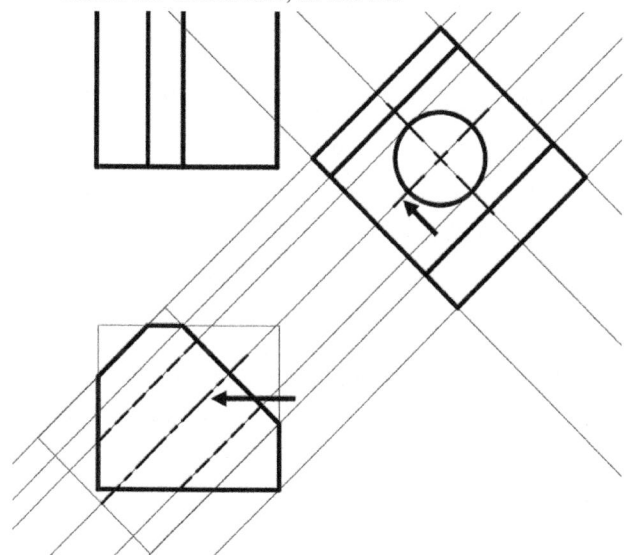

- Set the **Construction** layer as the active layer.
- On the tool set, click **Drafting > Draw > Construction** drop-down > **Ray**.
- Select the intersection point of the centerline and object line, as shown.
- Move the pointer upward and click to create a ray.

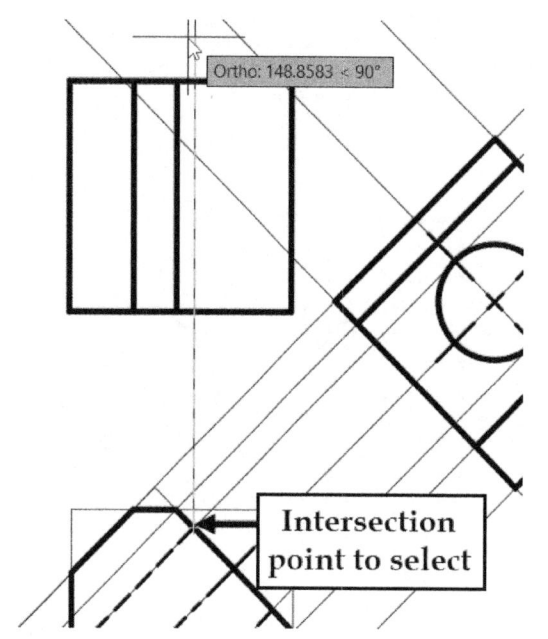

- Press RETURN twice.
- Likewise, create two more rays, as shown.

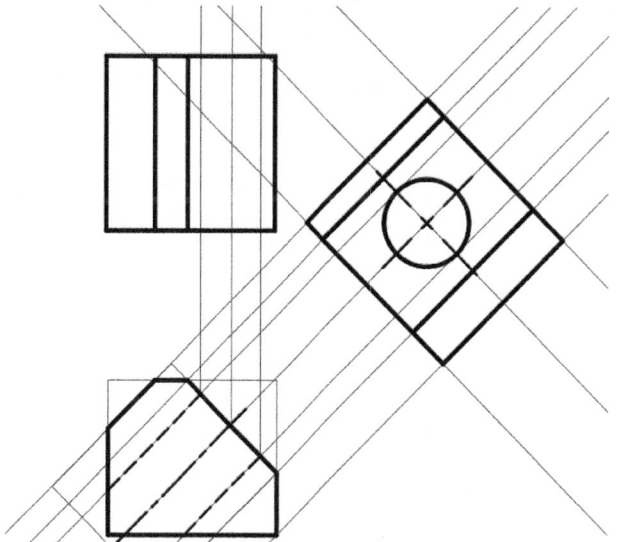

- Create a horizontal construction line passing through the midpoint of the top view, as shown.

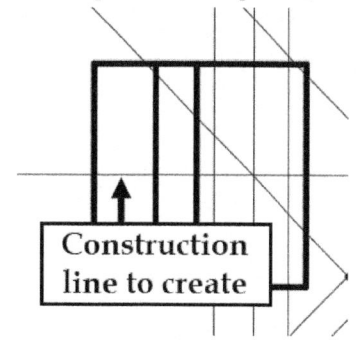

- Set the **Object** layer as the active layer,

- On the tool set, click **Drafting > Draw > Ellipse drop-down > Axis, End**.
- Specify the first and second points, as shown.

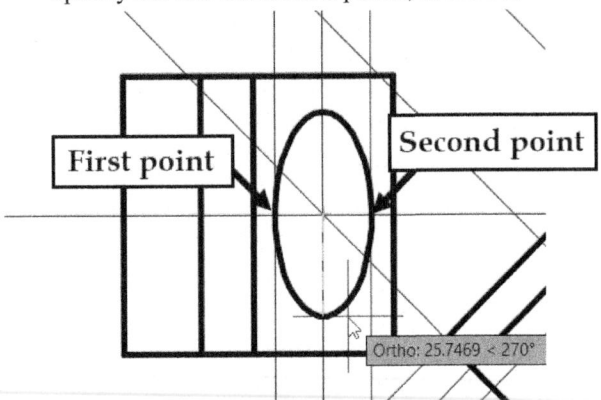

- Move the pointer downward, type-in 17.5, and then press RETURN.

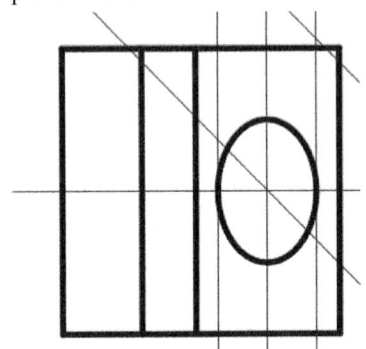

- Set the **Centerline** layer as an active layer,
- Create the remaining centerlines.
- The drawing after hiding the **Construction** layer is shown next.
- Save the file as auxiliary_views.dwg.

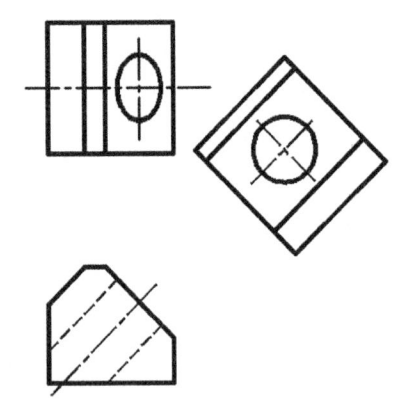

Creating Named views

While working with a drawing, you may need to perform numerous zoom and pan operations to view key portions of a drawing. Instead of doing this, you can save these portions with a name. Then, restore the named view and start working on them.

- Open the **ortho_views.dwg** file (The drawing file created in the Orthographic Views section of this chapter).
- Click the **New View** icon on the toolbar; the **New View** dialog appears.
- Select the **Define Window** option from the **Boundary** section of the **New View/Shot Properties** dialog.
- Create a window on the front view, as shown below.

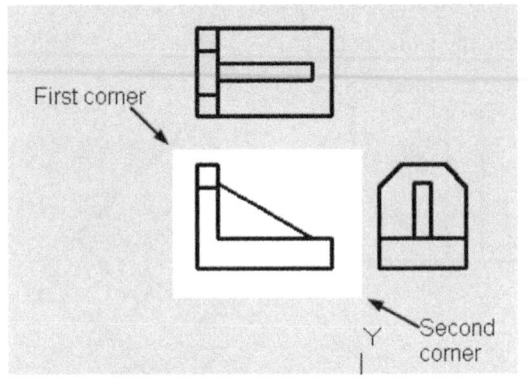

- Press RETURN to accept.
- Enter **Front** in the **View name** box.

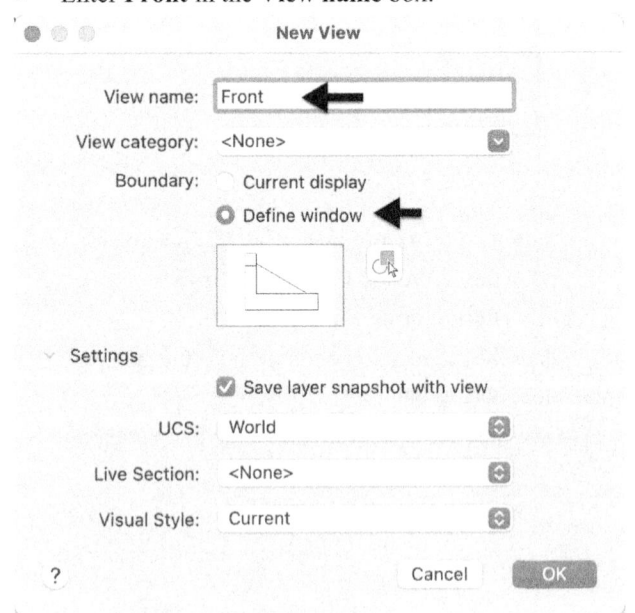

- Click **OK** on the **New View** dialog.
- Likewise, create the named views for the top and right views of the drawing.
- On the toolbar, click the **Insert View** icon; the three views are displayed.

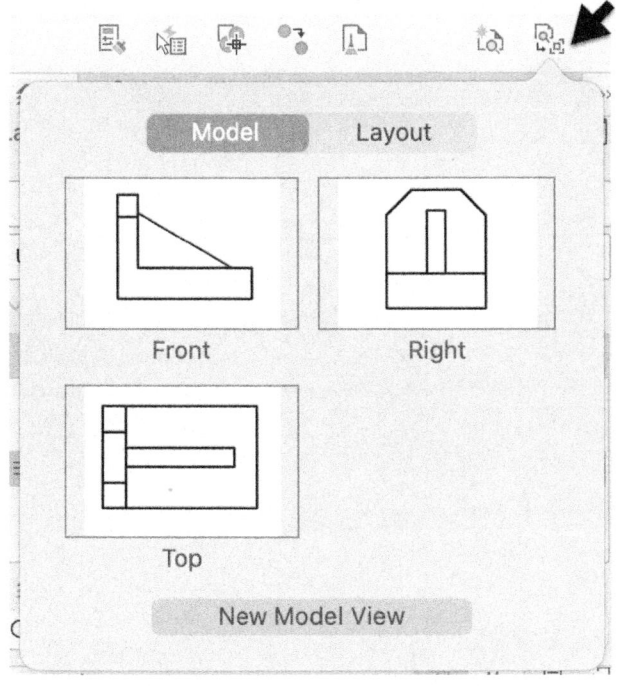

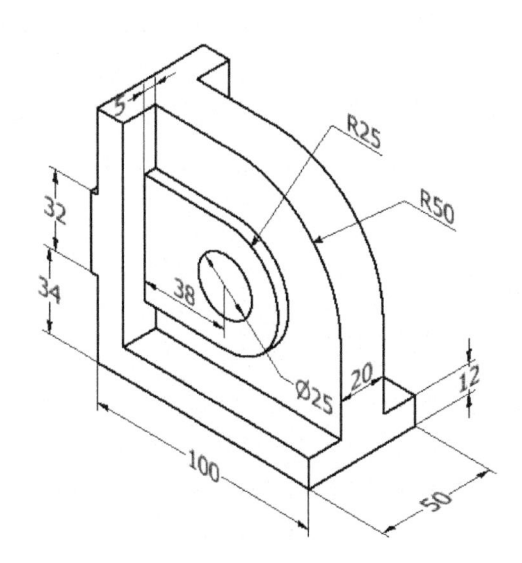

- To set the **Top** view to current, select it from the **Insert View** tree; the **Top** view will be zoomed and fitted to the screen.

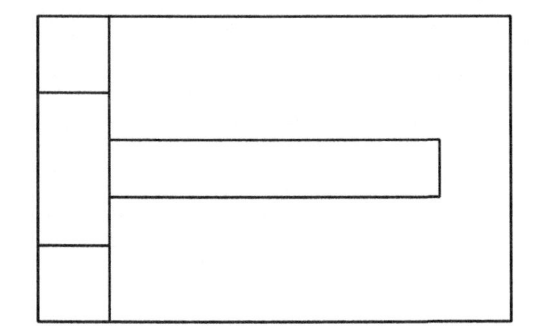

- Save and close the file.

Exercises

Exercise 1

Create the orthographic views of the object shown below.

Exercise 2

Create the orthographic views of the object shown below.

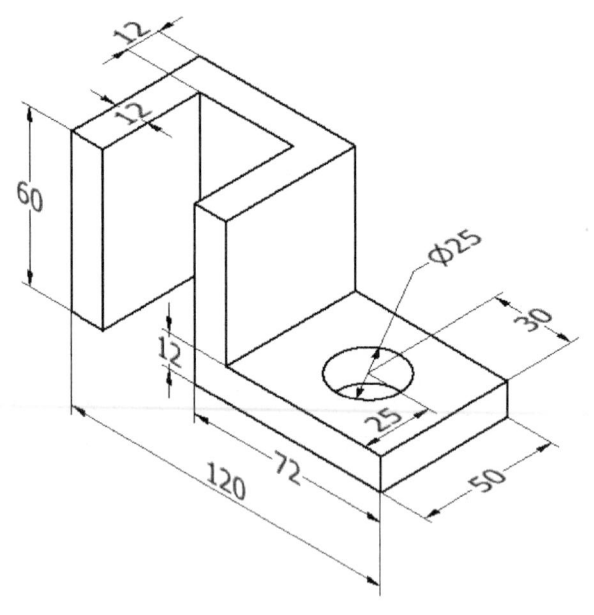

Exercise 3

Create the orthographic and auxiliary views of the object shown below.

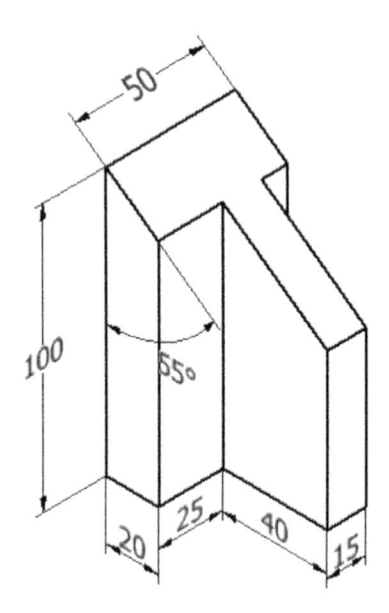

Exercise 4

Create the orthographic and auxiliary views of the object shown below.

Multi View Drawings

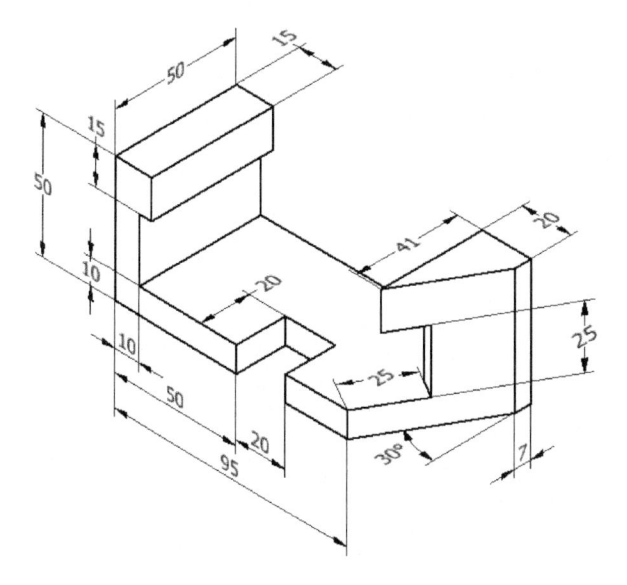

AutoCAD 2023 For Beginners (For Mac Users)

Chapter 6: Dimensions and Annotations

In this chapter, you will learn to do the following:

- **Create Dimensions**
- **Create Dimension Style**
- **Add Leaders**
- **Create Centerlines**
- **Add Dimensional Tolerances**
- **Add Geometric Tolerances**
- **Edit Dimensions**

Dimensioning

In previous chapters, you have learned to draw shapes of various objects and create drawings. However, while creating a drawing, you also need to provide the size information. You can provide the size information by adding dimensions to the drawings. In this chapter, you will learn how to create various types of dimensions. You will also learn about some standard ways and best practices of dimensioning.

Creating Dimensions

In AutoCAD, there are many tools available for creating dimensions. You can access these tools from the Tool set, Command line, and Menu Bar.

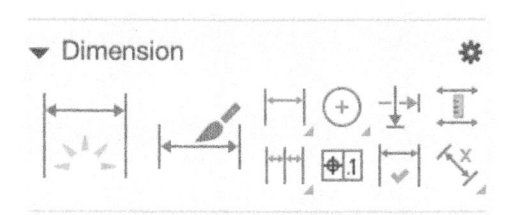

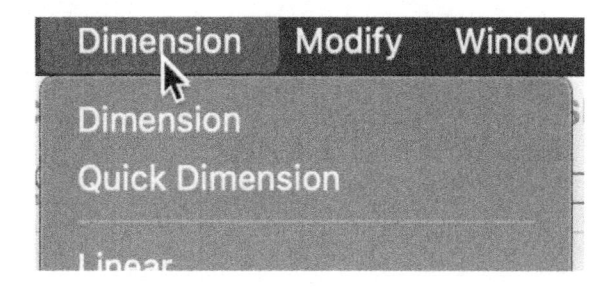

The following table gives you the functions of various dimensioning tools.

Tool	Shortcut	Function
Dimension	DIM	This tool creates a dimension based on the selected geometry.

133 | Dimensions and Annotations

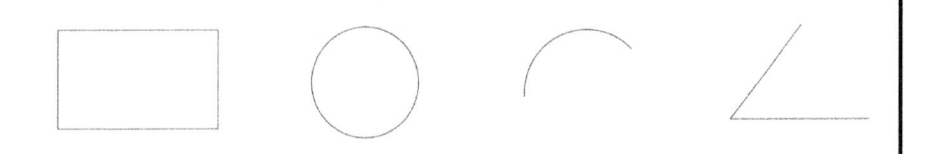

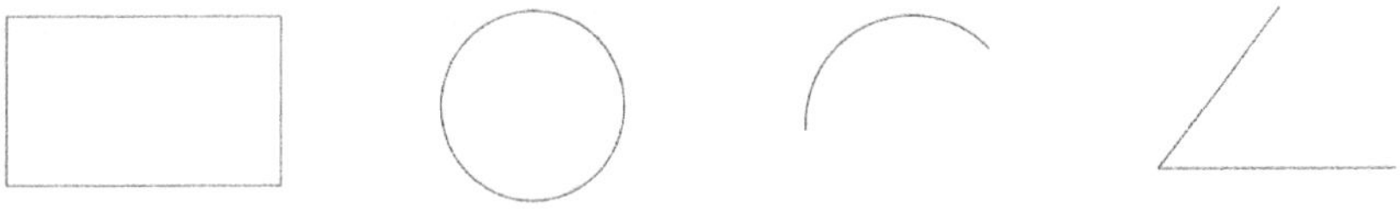

- Create a rectangle, circle, arc, and two intersecting lines, as shown in the previous figure.
- Click **Drafting > Dimension > Dimension** on the tool set.
- Select a line, move the pointer, and click to create the linear dimension.
- Select a circle, move the pointer, and click to position the diameter dimension. 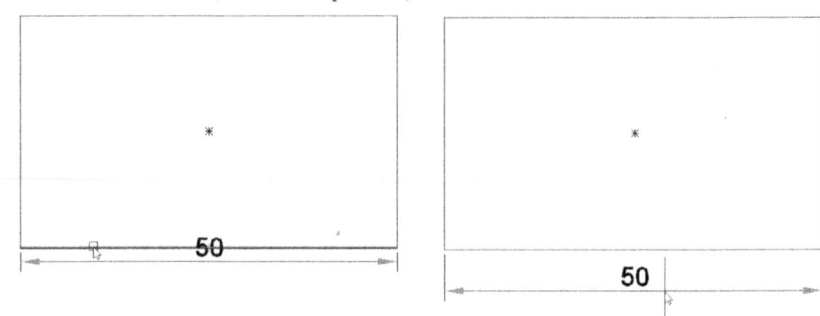
- Select an arc, move the pointer, and click to position the radial dimension. 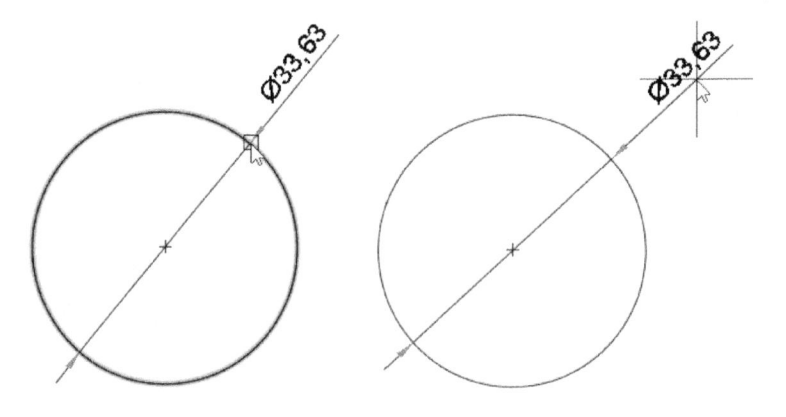 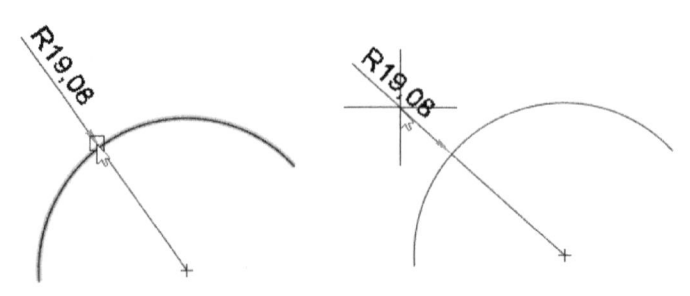
- Place the pointer on the arc, type L, and press RETURN. Select the arc, move the pointer, and click to position the arc length dimension.

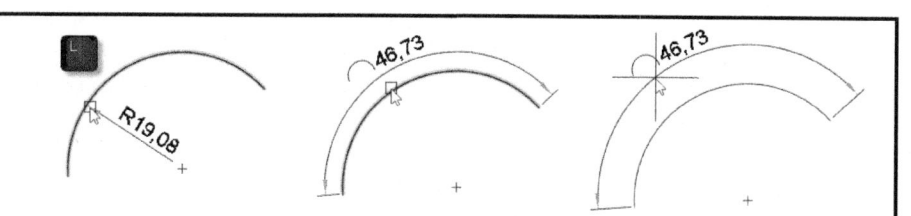

- Place the pointer on the arc, type A, and press RETURN. Select the arc, move the pointer, and click to position the angle of the arc.

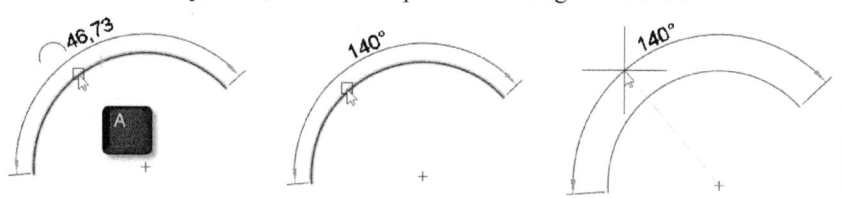

- Select two non-parallel lines and position the angular dimension between them.

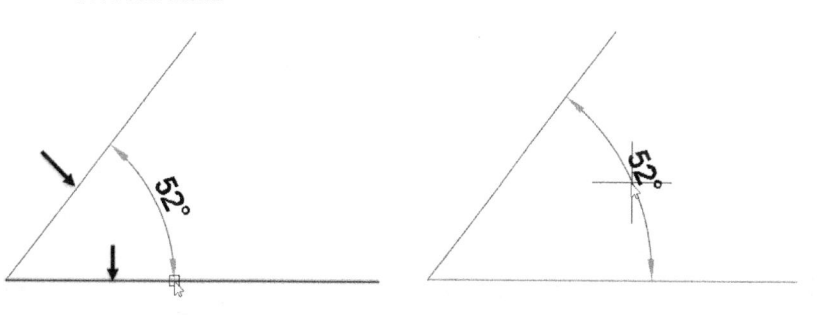

Likewise, you can create other types of dimensions using the **Dimension** tool.

Linear	DLI	This tool creates horizontal and vertical dimensions.

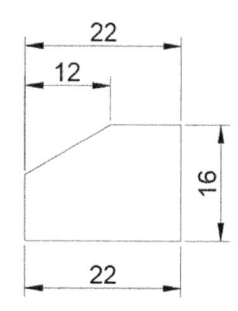

- Click **Drafting > Dimension > Dimension** drop-down > **Linear** on the tool set.

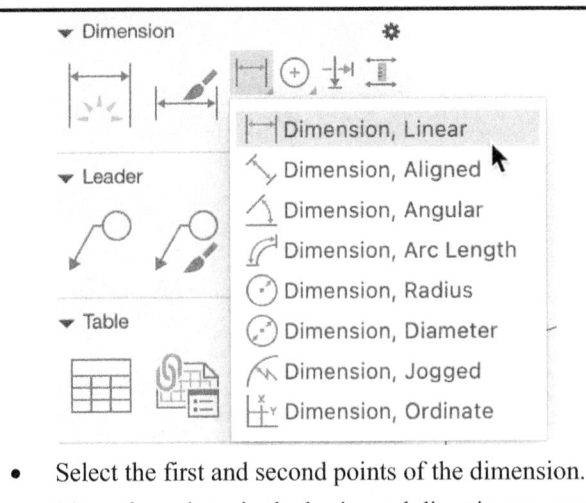

- Select the first and second points of the dimension.
- Move the pointer in the horizontal direction to create a vertical dimension (or) move in the vertical direction to create a horizontal dimension.
- Click to position the dimension.

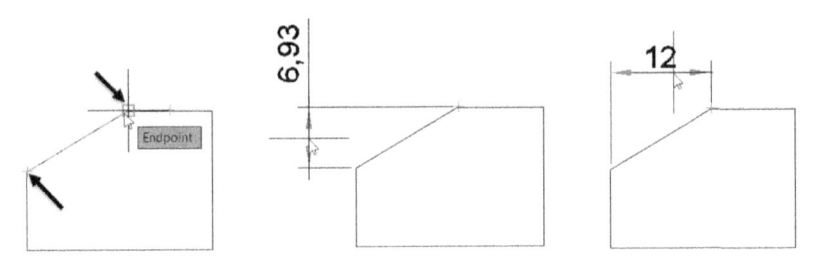

Aligned	DAL	This tool creates a linear dimension parallel to the object. 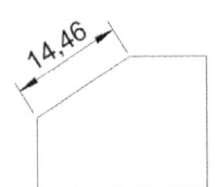

- Click **Drafting** > **Dimension** > **Dimension** drop-down > **Aligned** on the tool set.
- Select the first and second points of the dimension line.

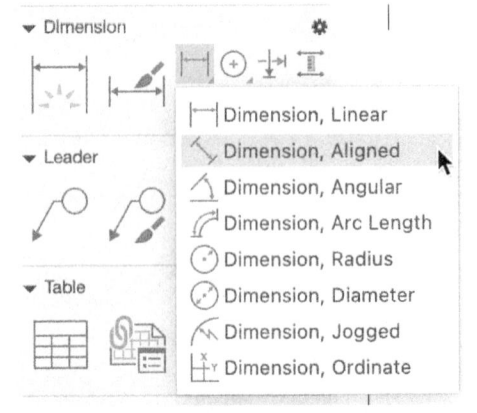

136 | Dimensions and Annotations

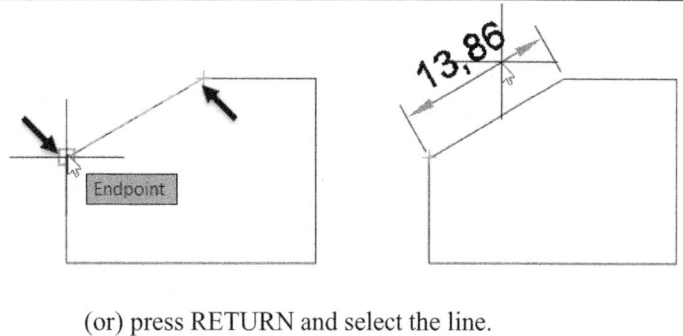

(or) press RETURN and select the line.

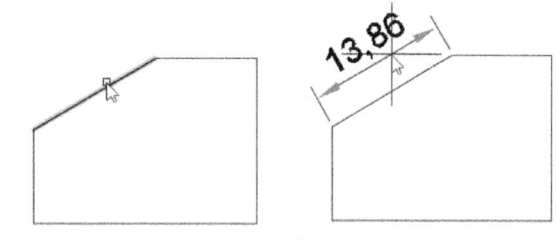

- Move the pointer and click to position the dimension.

Arc Length DAR It dimensions the total or partial length of an arc.

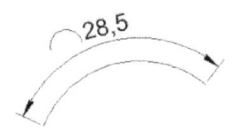

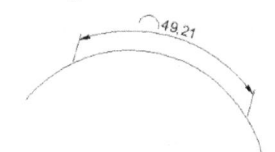

- Click **Drafting** > **Dimension** > **Dimension** drop-down > **Arc Length** on the tool set.
- Select an arc from the drawing. 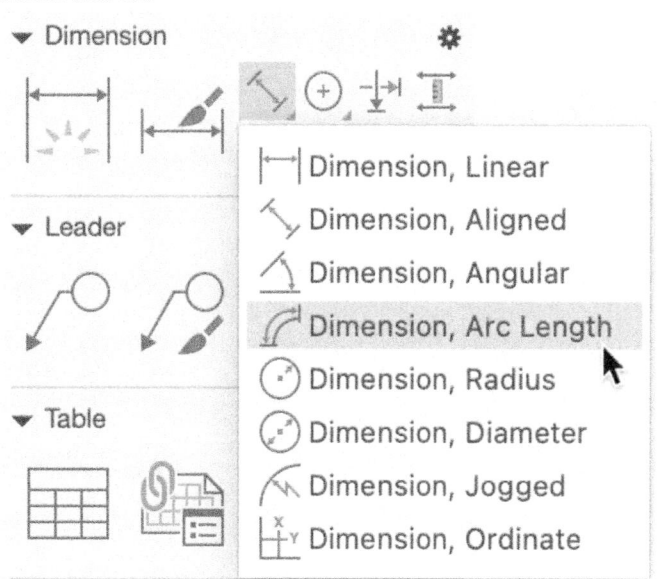
- If you want to dimension only a partial length of an arc, right-click and select **Partial** option. Next, select the two points on the arc.

137 | **Dimensions and Annotations**

- Move the pointer and click to position the dimension.

Continue	DCO	It creates a linear dimension from the second extension line of the previous dimension.

- Create a linear dimension by selecting the first and second points.

- Click **Drafting > Dimension > Continue** on the tool set; a chain dimension is attached to the pointer.

- Select the third and fourth points of the chain dimension.

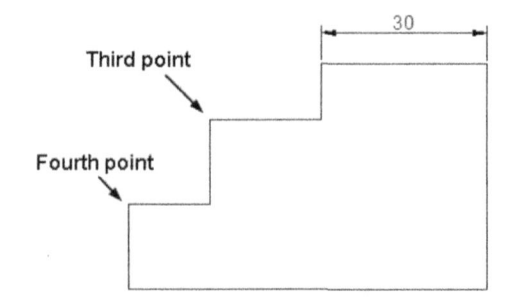

- Position the chain dimension. Next, right-click and select RETURN.

138 | Dimensions and Annotations

Baseline   DBA   It creates dimensions by using the previously created dimension, as shown below.

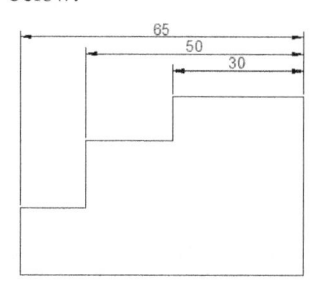

- Create a linear dimension by selecting the first and second points.

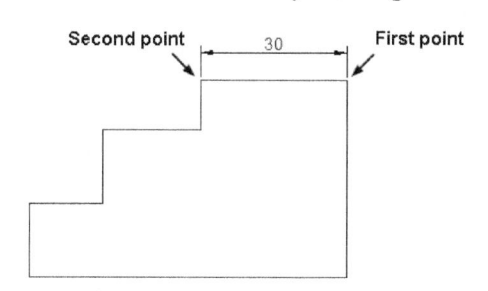

- Click **Drafting > Dimension > Continue > Baseline** on the tool set.

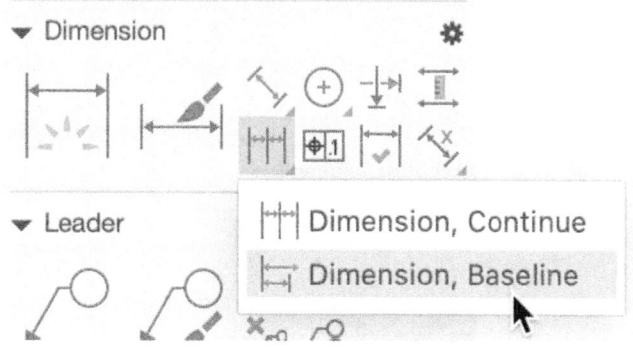

- Select the third and fourth points of the baseline dimension. Next, right-click and select RETURN.

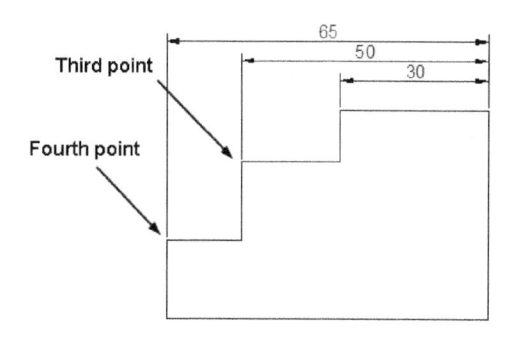

Angular   DAN   It creates an angular dimension.

139 Dimensions and Annotations

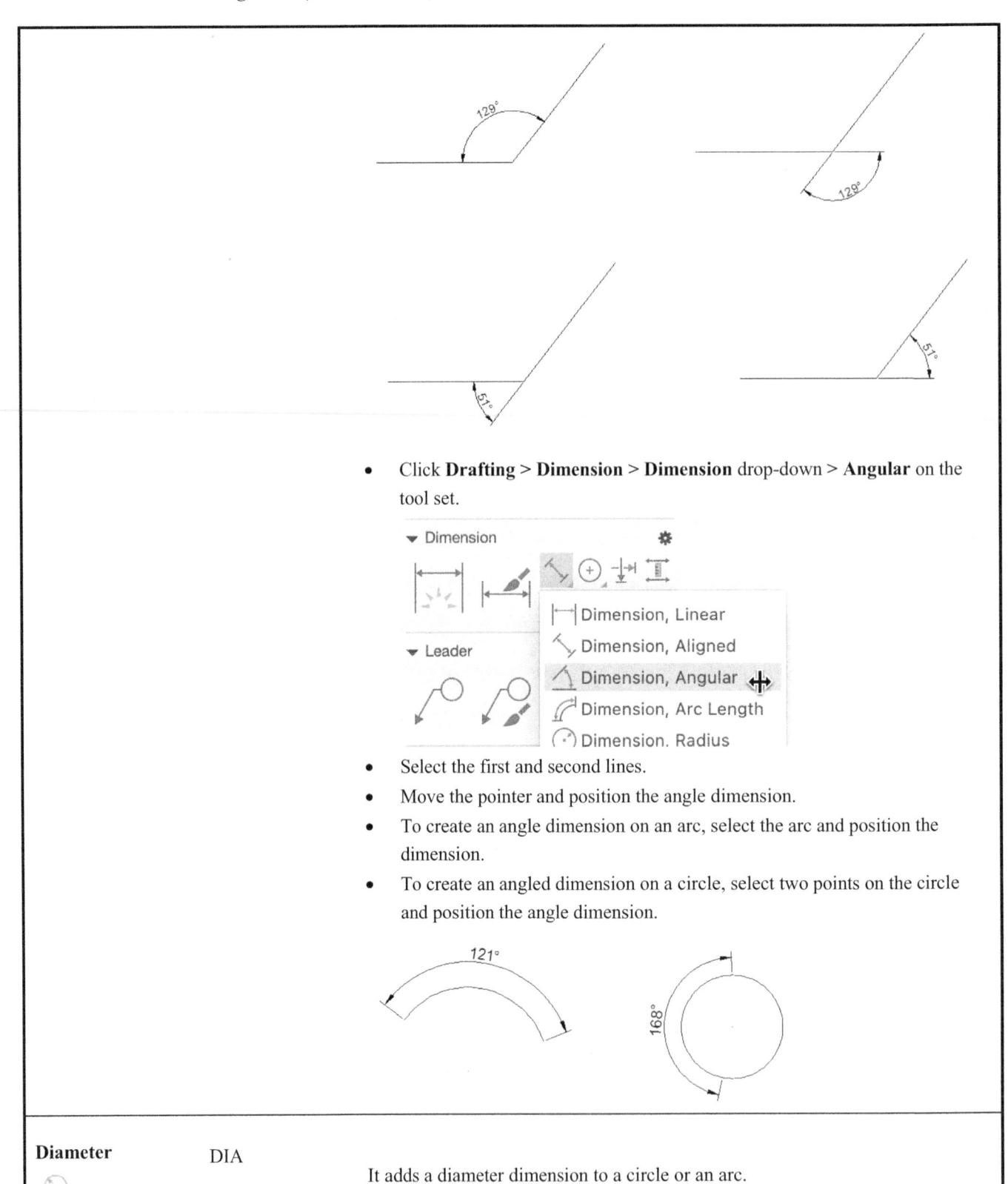

- Click **Drafting > Dimension > Dimension** drop-down > **Angular** on the tool set.
- Select the first and second lines.
- Move the pointer and position the angle dimension.
- To create an angle dimension on an arc, select the arc and position the dimension.
- To create an angled dimension on a circle, select two points on the circle and position the angle dimension.

Diameter   DIA

It adds a diameter dimension to a circle or an arc.

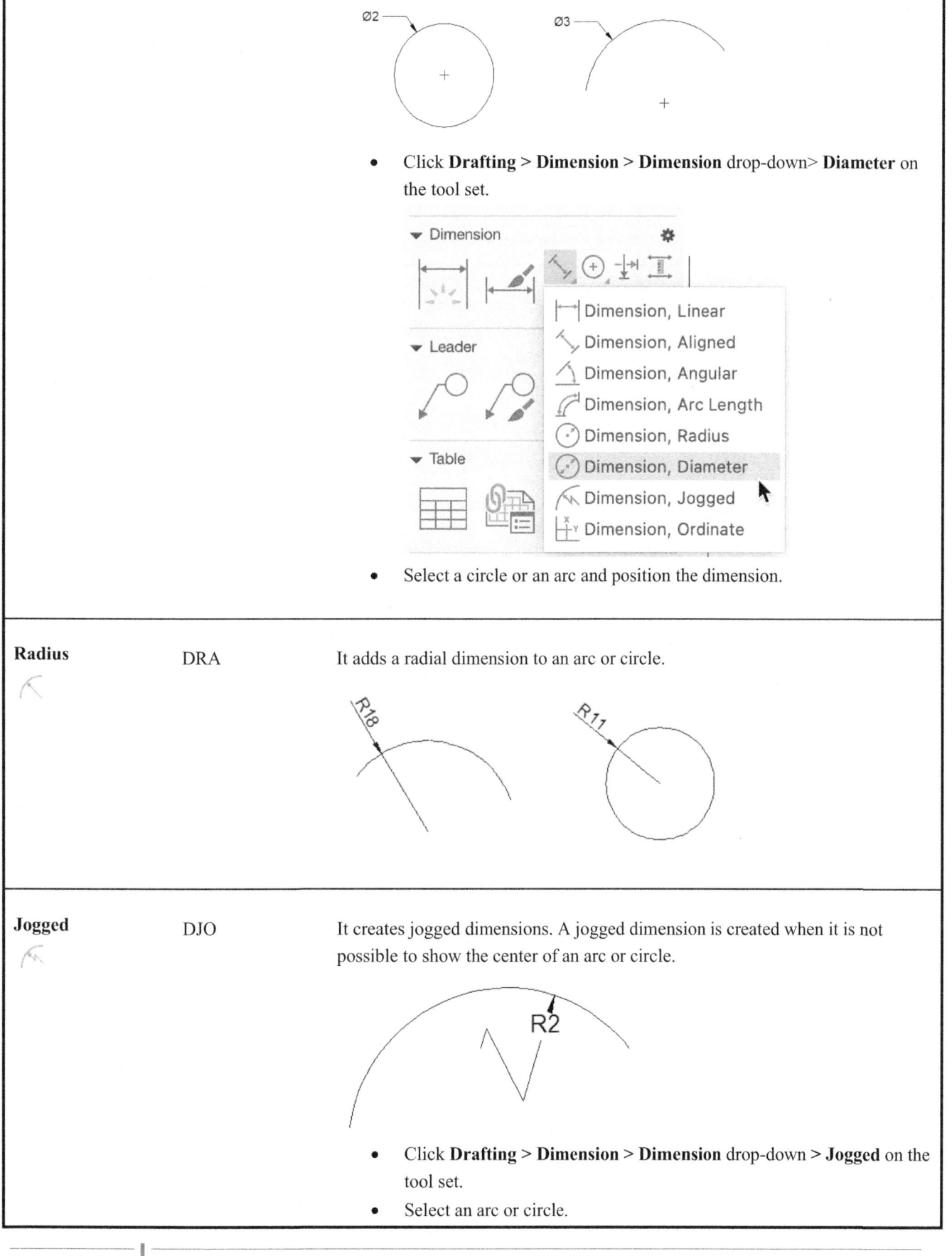

- Click **Drafting > Dimension > Dimension** drop-down> **Diameter** on the tool set.

- Select a circle or an arc and position the dimension.

Radius	DRA	It adds a radial dimension to an arc or circle.
Jogged	DJO	It creates jogged dimensions. A jogged dimension is created when it is not possible to show the center of an arc or circle.

- Click **Drafting > Dimension > Dimension** drop-down > **Jogged** on the tool set.
- Select an arc or circle.

141 | Dimensions and Annotations

- Select a new center point override.
- Locate the dimension and the jog location.

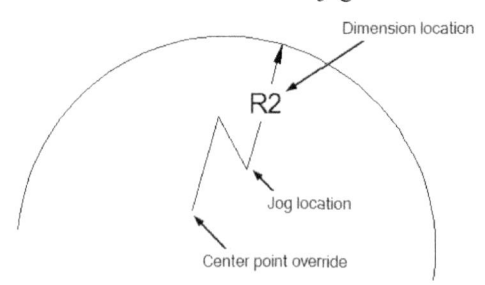

| **Dimension, Dimjogline** | DJL | It creates a jogged linear dimension. |

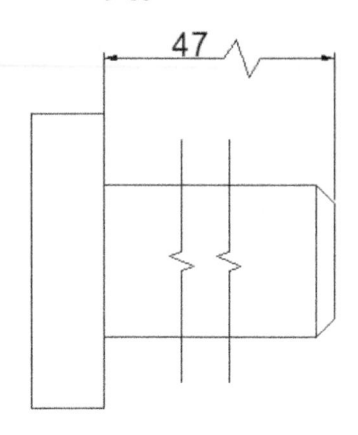

- Click the **Customize panel** icon on the **Dimension** panel and check the **Dimension, Dimjogline** option; the tool is displayed on the **Dimension** panel.

- Click **Drafting > Dimension > Dimension, Dimjogline** on the tool set.

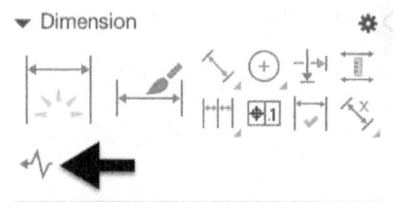

- Select the linear dimension to add a jog.
- Define the location of the jog on the dimension.

Center Mark	CENTERMARK		It adds a center mark to a circle or an arc.

- Click **Drafting > Dimension > Centerlines > Center Mark** on the tool set.
- Select an arc or a circle; the center mark will be positioned at its center.

Centerline	CENTERLINE		It creates a centreline between two lines. The centreline has the associative property. It changes with the position of the lines

- Click **Drafting > Dimension > Centerlines > Centerline** on the tool set.
- Select two lines that are parallel or non-parallel to each other; a centreline is created between them.

- Change the position of the lines; the centreline also changes.

Ordinate	DOR		It creates ordinate dimensions based on the current position of the User Coordinate System (UCS).

- Click **Drafting > Dimension > Dimension** drop-down > **Ordinate** on the tool set.
- Select the point of the object.
- Move the pointer in the vertical direction and click to position the X-Coordinate value.
- Select the point of the object.
- Move the pointer in the horizontal direction and click to position the Y-Coordinate value.

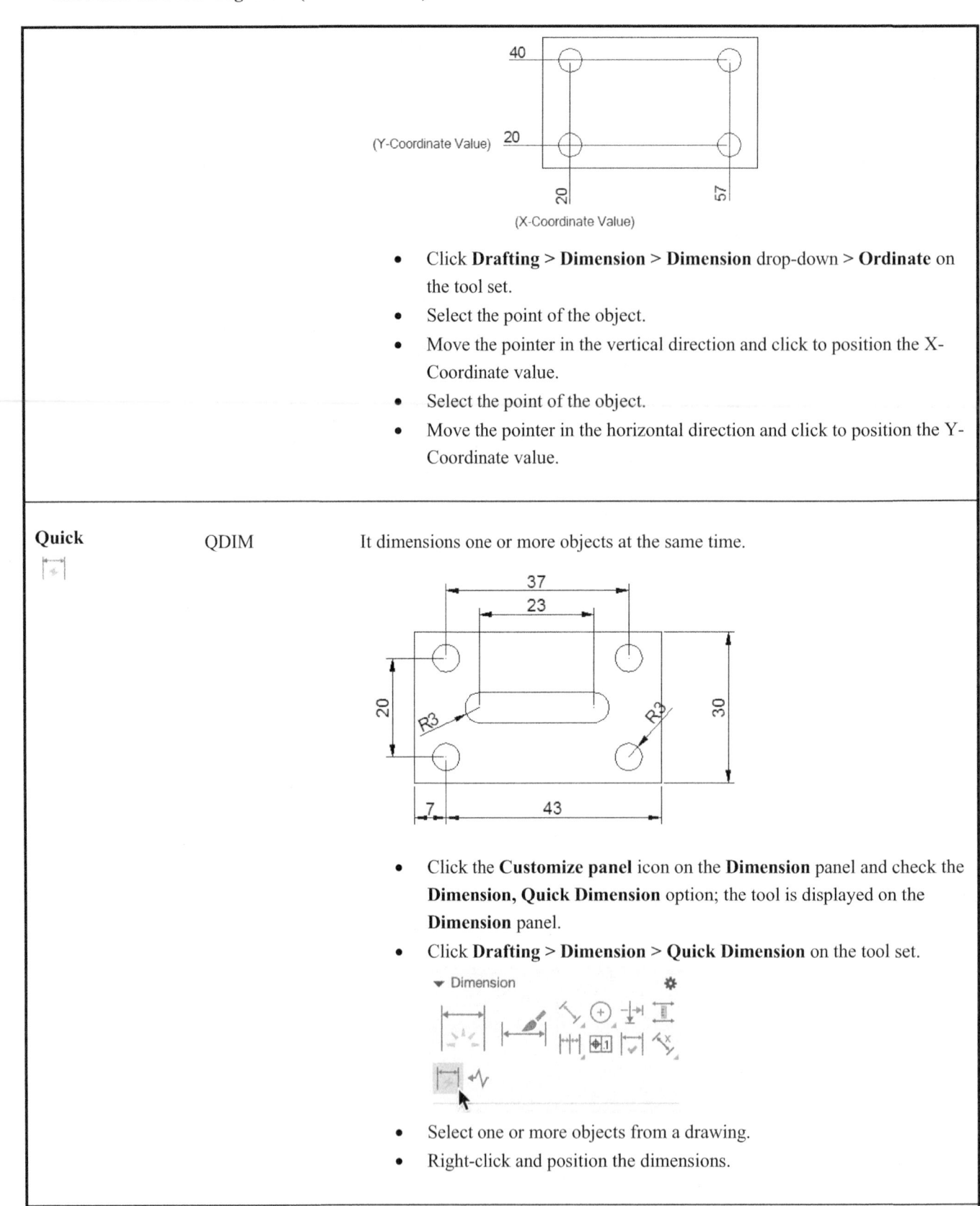

Quick	QDIM	It dimensions one or more objects at the same time.

- Click the **Customize panel** icon on the **Dimension** panel and check the **Dimension, Quick Dimension** option; the tool is displayed on the **Dimension** panel.
- Click **Drafting > Dimension > Quick Dimension** on the tool set.
- Select one or more objects from a drawing.
- Right-click and position the dimensions.

Adjust Space	DIMSPACE

144 Dimensions and Annotations

In the following figure, the drawing on the left side has congested dimensions, whereas the right side drawing has dimensions with ample space between them. You can use the **Adjust Space** tool to adjust the space between the dimensions.

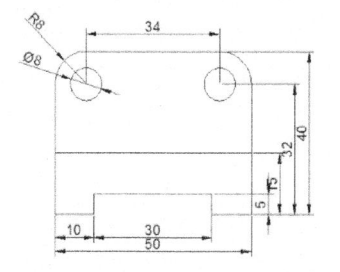

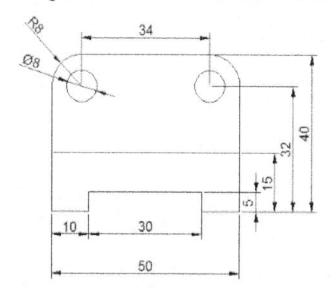

- Click **Drafting > Dimension > Adjust Space** on the tool set.
- Select the base dimension from which the other dimensions are to be adjusted.
- Select the dimensions to adjust.
- Right-click to accept.
- Enter the value of the spacing between the dimensions (or) right-click and select the **Auto** option; the dimensions will be adjusted with respect to the base dimension.

Break	DIMBREAK	It adds breaks to a dimension, extension, and leader lines.

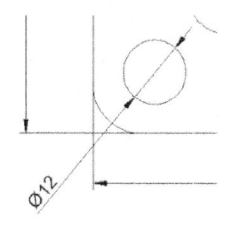

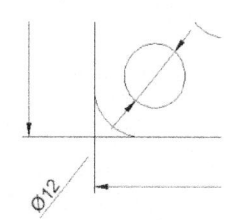

- Click **Drafting > Dimension > Break** on the tool set.
- Select the dimension to add a break.
- Select the dimension or object intersecting the dimension selected in the previous step. It breaks the dimension by the intersecting object.
- Right-click to exit the tool.

Inspect	DIMINSPECT	It creates an inspection dimension. The inspection dimension describes how frequently the dimension should be checked during the inspection process to ensure the quality of the component.

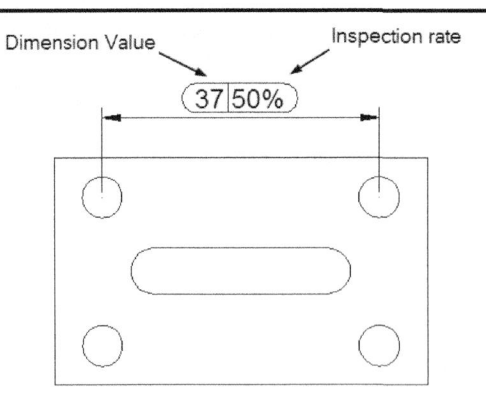

- Click **Drafting > Dimension > Inspect** on the tool set; the **Inspection Dimension** dialog appears.

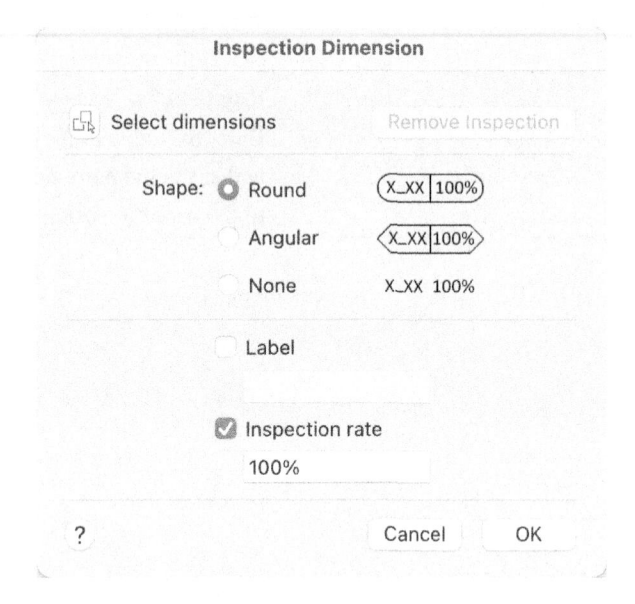

- Click the **Select dimensions** button on the dialog and select the dimension to apply the inspection rate.
- Right-click to accept.
- Select the shape of the inspection from the **Shape** section.
- Enter the **Inspection rate**. 100% means that the value will be checked every time during the inspection process. 50% means half the time.
- If required, select the **Label** checkbox and enter the inspection label.
- Click **OK**.

Example:

In this example, you will create the drawing, as shown in the figure, and add dimensions to it.

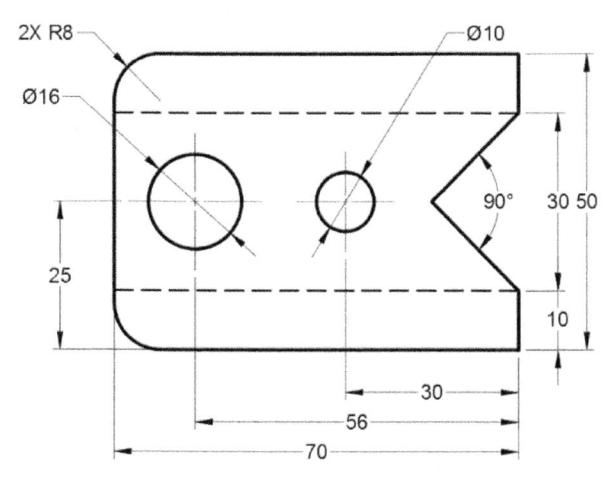

- Create four new layers with the following settings.

Layer	Lineweight	Linetype
Construction	0.00 mm	Continuous
Object	0.50 mm	Continuous
Hidden	0.30 mm	HIDDEN2
Dimensions	0.30 mm	Continuous

- Type LIMMAX and press RETURN.
- Type 100, 100, and press RETURN to set the maximum limit of the drawing.
- Click **View > Zoom > All** on the **Menu Bar**.
- Create the drawing on the **Object** and **Hidden** layers.

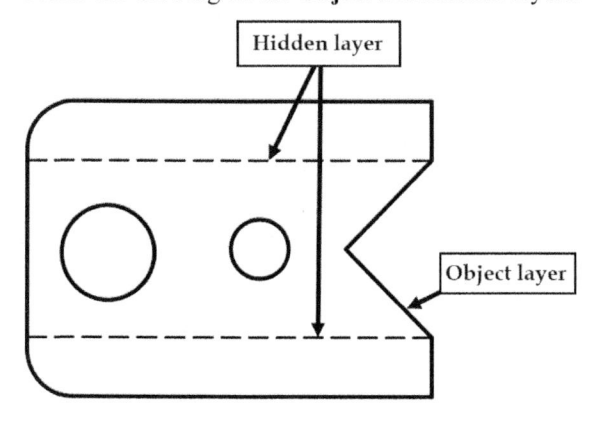

- Select the **Dimensions** layer from the **Layer** drop-down in the **Layers** palette.

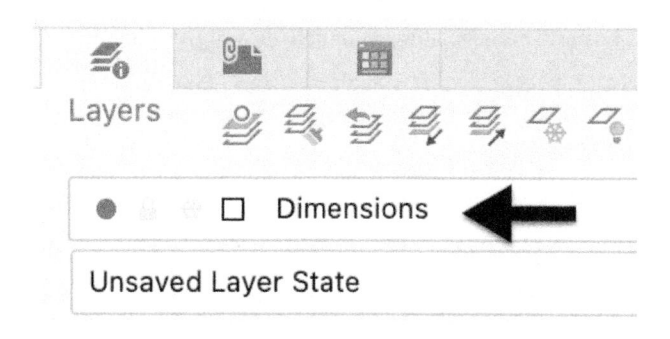

Creating a Dimension Style

The appearance of the dimensions depends on the dimension style that you use. You can create a new dimension style using the **Dimension Style Manager** dialog. In this dialog, you can specify various settings related to the appearance and behaviour of dimensions. The following example helps you to create a dimension style.

- Click **Dimension Style** on the **Dimension** panel on the **Drafting** tool set.

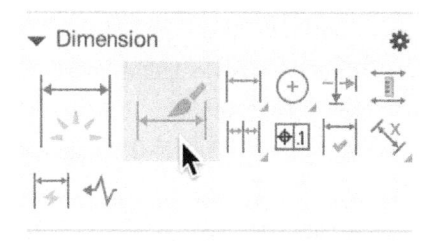

The **Dimension Style Manager** dialog appears.

147 Dimensions and Annotations

The basic nomenclature of dimensions is given below.

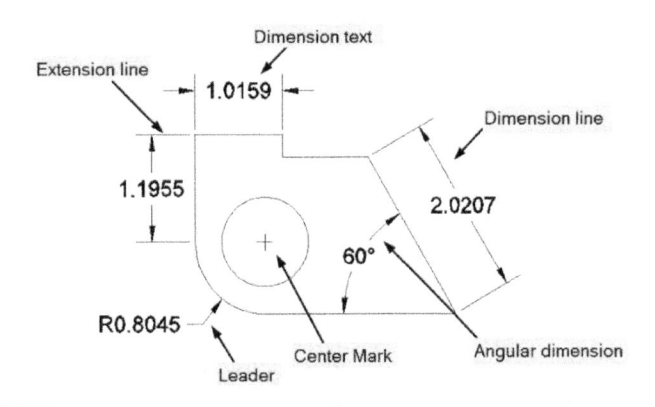

By default, the **ISO-25** or the **Standard** dimension style is active. If the default dimension style does not suit the dimensioning requirement, you can create a new dimension style and modify the nomenclature of the dimensions.

- To create a new dimension style, click the **Plus** button on the **Dimension Style Manager** dialog; the **Create New Dimension Style** dialog appears.
- In the **Create New Dimension Style** dialog, enter **Mechanical** in the **New Style Name**.
- Select **ISO-25** from the **Start With** drop-down and click **Continue**.

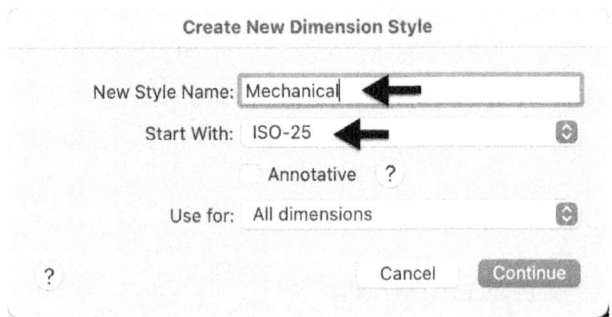

- In the **New Dimension Style** dialog, click the **Primary Units** tab.
- Ensure that the **Unit Format** is set to **Decimal**.
- Set **Precision** to **0**.
- Select **Decimal separator** > '**.**'(Period).

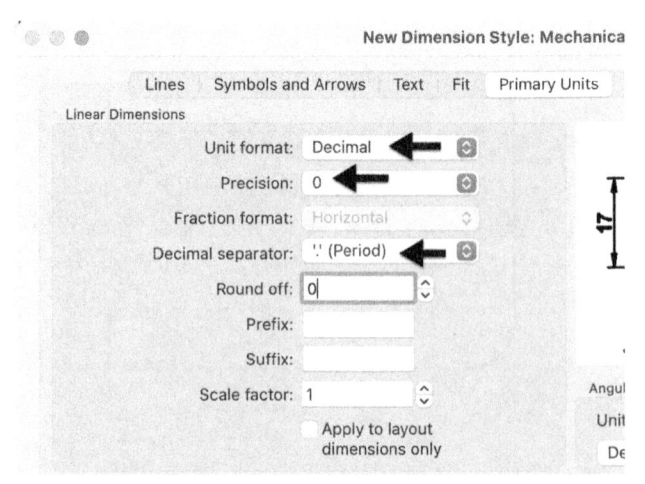

Study the other options in the **Primary Units** tab. Most of them are self-explanatory.

- Click the **Text** tab.
- Ensure that the **Text height** is set **2.5**.
- In the **Text placement** section, set the **Vertical** and **Horizontal** values to **Centered**.
- Select **Text alignment** > **Horizontal**.

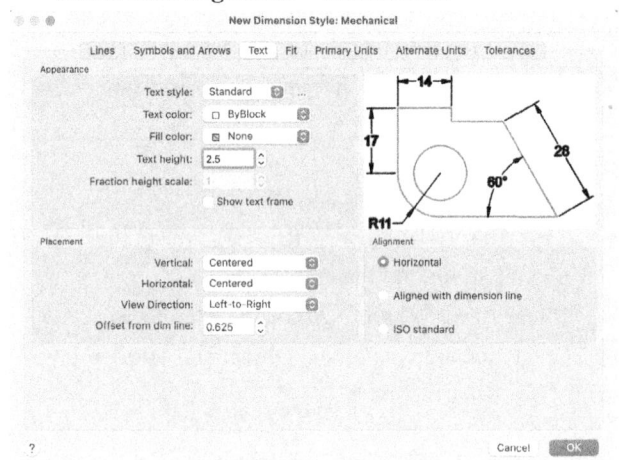

Study the other options in the **Text** tab. These options let you change the appearance of the dimension text.

- Click the **Lines** tab on the dialog.
- In this tab, notice the two options in the **Extension lines** section: **Extend beyond dim lines** and **Offset from origin**.

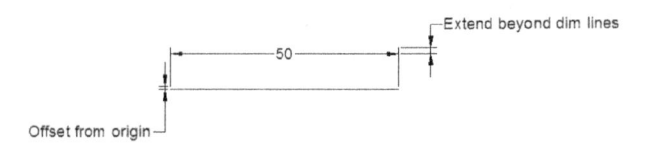

148 | Dimensions and Annotations

- Set **Extend beyond dim lines** and **Offset from origin** to **1.25**.
- Set the **Baseline spacing** in the **Dimension lines** section to **5**.

Study the different options in this tab. The options in this tab are used to change the appearance and behavior of the dimension lines and extension lines.

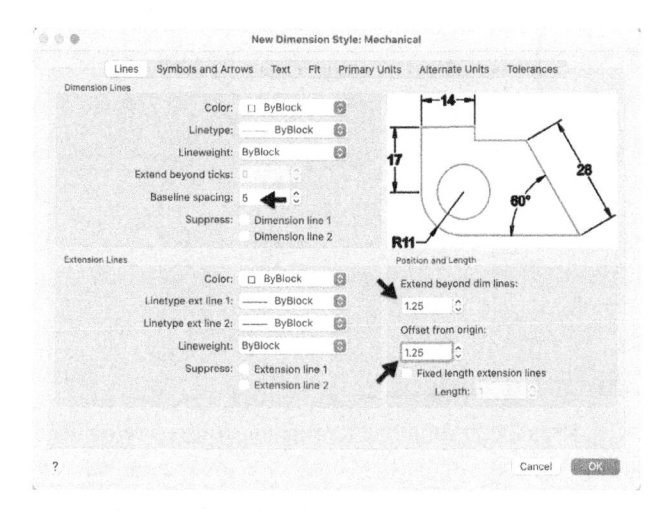

- Click the **Symbols and Arrows** tab, and then set **Arrow size** and **Center Marks** to 3.
- Select the **Line** option in the **Center marks** section.

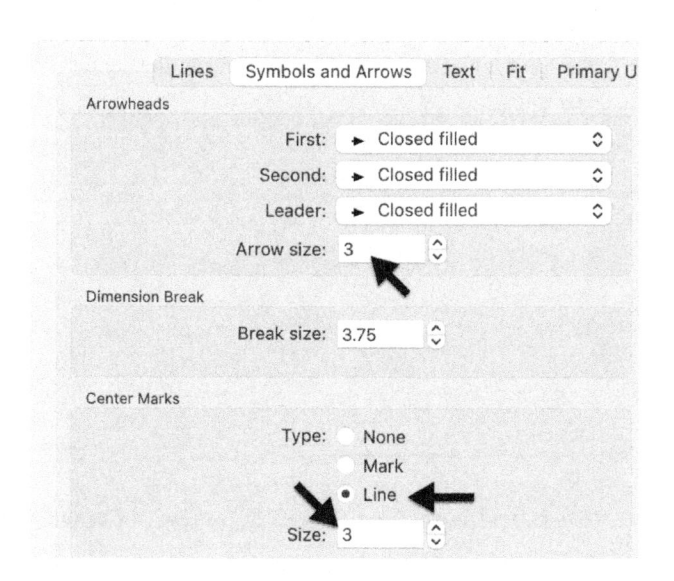

Notice the different options in this tab. The options in this tab are used to change the appearance of the arrows and symbols. Also, you can set the appearance of the center marks and centerlines of circles and arcs.

- Click **OK** to accept the settings.
- Right-click on the Mechanical dimension style and select **Set Current**; the **Mechanical** dimension style will be set as current.
- Click **Close** to close the dialog.
- On the **Drafting** tool set, click **Dimension > Centerlines** drop-down > **Center Mark**.
- Select the circles from the drawing to apply the center mark to them.

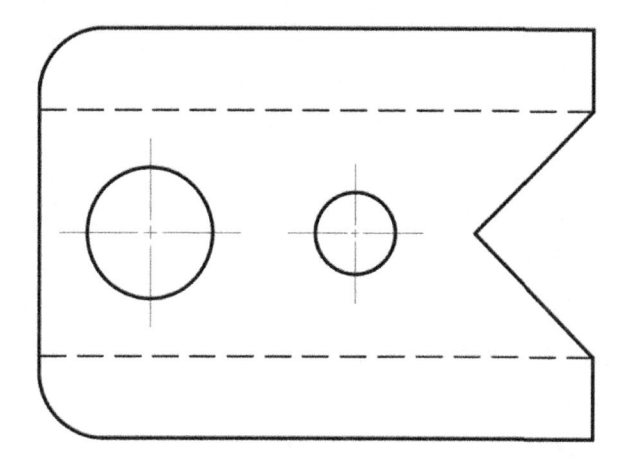

- On the **Drafting** tool set, click **Dimension > Dimension**.
- Make sure that the **Object Snap** icon is turned on the status bar.
- Select the lower right corner of the drawing.
- Select the endpoint of the center mark of the small circle; the dimension is attached to the pointer.
- Move the pointer vertically downwards and position the dimension, as shown below.

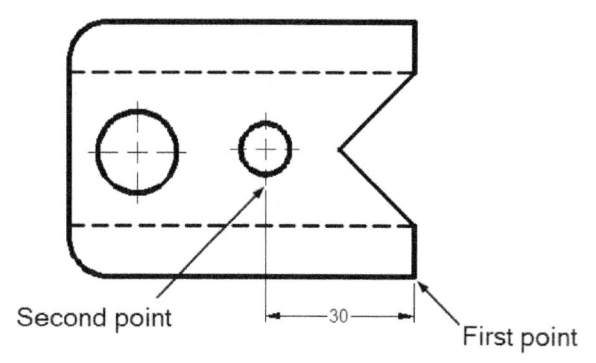

- Click **Continue > Baseline** on the **Dimension** panel.

149 | **Dimensions and Annotations**

- Select the right extension line of the linear dimension; a dimension is attached to the pointer.
- Select the endpoint of the center mark of the large circle; another dimension is attached to the pointer.
- Select the lower-left corner of the drawing.
- Press RETURN.

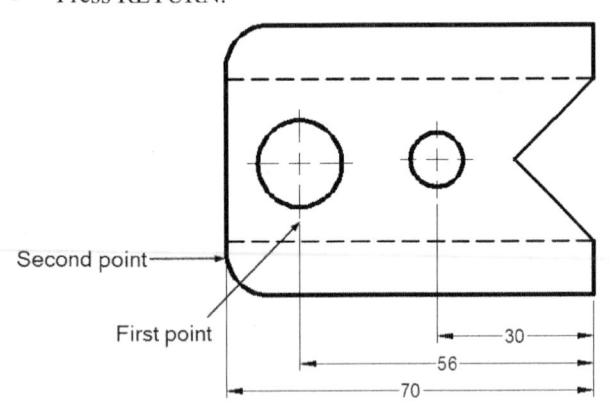

- Click **Dimension** drop-down > **Angular** on the **Dimension** panel.
- Select the two angled lines of the drawing and position the angle dimension.

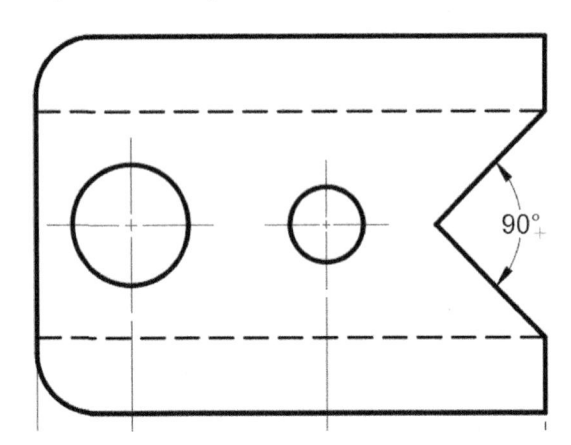

- Click **Dimension** drop-down > **Diameter** on the **Dimension** panel.
- Select the large circle and position the diameter dimension.
- Press RETURN.
- Select the small circle and position the dimension.
- Click **Dimension** drop-down > **Radius** on the **Dimension** panel.
- Select the fillet located at the top left corner; the radial dimension is attached to the pointer.
- Right-click and select **Mtext** from the shortcut menu.
- Type **2X** and press SPACEBAR.

- Click in the graphics window to update the dimension text.
- Next, position the radial dimension approximately at 45 degrees.
- Likewise, apply the other dimensions, as shown.
- Save and close the drawing.

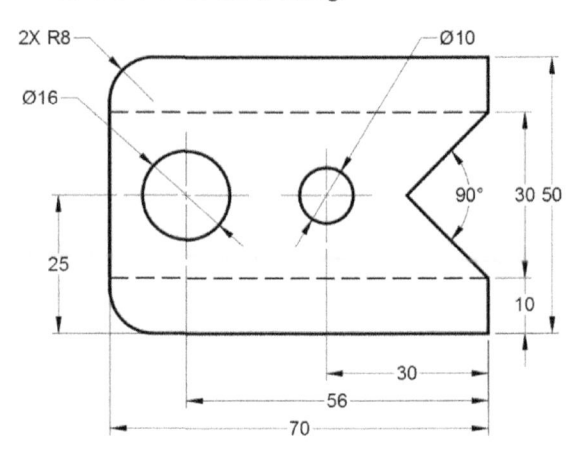

Adding Leaders

A leader is a thin solid line terminating with an arrowhead at one end and a dimension, note, or symbol at the other end. In the following example, you will learn to create a leader style and then create a leader.

Example 1:
- Draw a square of 24 mm side length.
- Create a circle of 10.11 mm diameter at the center of the square.

- Click **Drafting** > **Draw** > **Arc** drop-down > **Center, Start, Angle** on the tool set.
- Select the center point of the circle.
- Move the pointer horizontally toward the right.
- Type 6 as the radius and press RETURN.

150 | Dimensions and Annotations

- Move the pointer vertically downward and click.

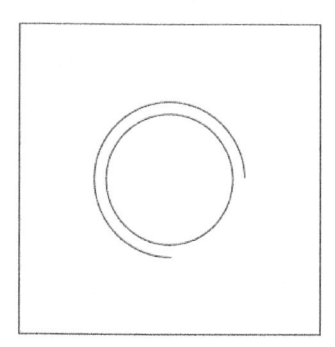

- On the **Drafting** tool set, click the **Multileader Style Manager** icon on the **Leader** panel.

- In the **Multileader Style Manager** dialog, click the **Plus** button; the **Create New Multileader Style** dialog appears.

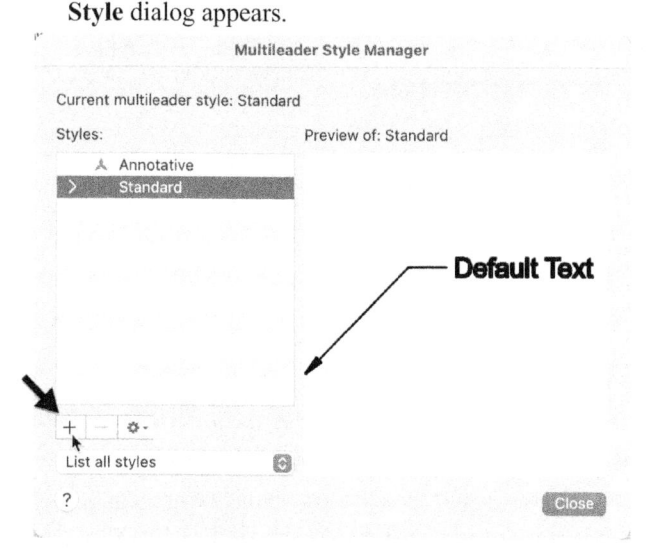

- In the **Create New Multileader Style** dialog, enter **Hole callout** in the **New style name** box and select **Standard** from the **Start with** drop-down.

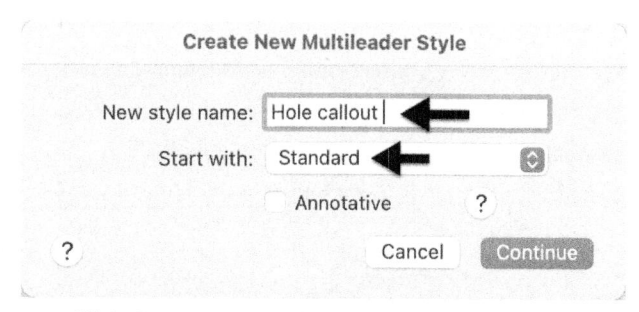

- Click **Continue**; the **Modify Multileader Style** dialog appears.
- Click the **Leader Format** tab and set the **Arrowhead Size** to **2.5**.

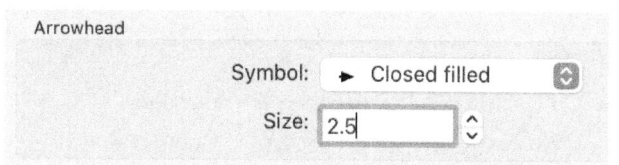

Also, notice the other options in this tab. They are used to set the appearance of the multileader lines and the arrowhead.

- Click the **Leader Structure** tab and set the **Landing distance** to **5**.

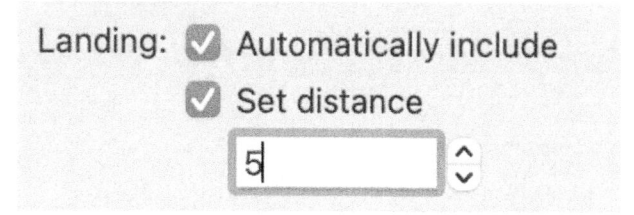

- Click the **Content** tab and set the **Text height** to **2.5**.

The other options in this tab are used to define the appearance of the text or block that will be attached at the end of the leader line.

- Click **OK** on the **Modify Multileader Style** dialog.
- Click **Close** to close the dialog.
- Click **Drafting** > **Leader** > **Multileader** on the tool set.

- Click the right mouse button on the **Polar tracking** button on the status bar and select **45** from the menu.

- Activate the **Polar tracking** button on the status bar.
- Select a point in the first quadrant of the arc.
- Move the pointer in the top-right direction and click to create the leader.

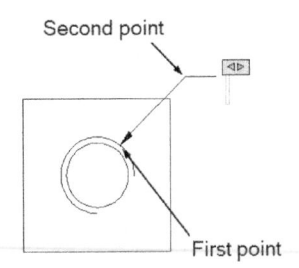

- Type **M12x1.75 – 6H 16** in the text editor. Next, you must insert the depth symbol before 16.
- Position the pointer before 16 and click the **Symbol** button on the **Text Editor** visor; a menu appears.

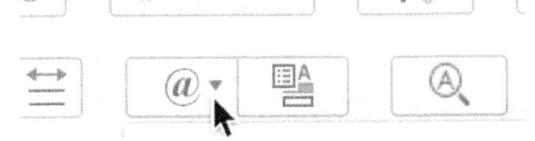

- Click **Other** on the menu; the **Character Map** dialog appears.

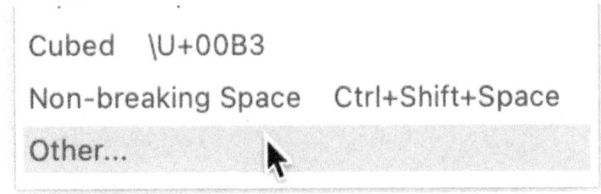

- In the **Character Map** dialog, type **U+21A7** in the search bar; the hole depth symbol appears.
- Select the Hole Depth symbol from the dialog, and then close it.

- Click in the graphics window.

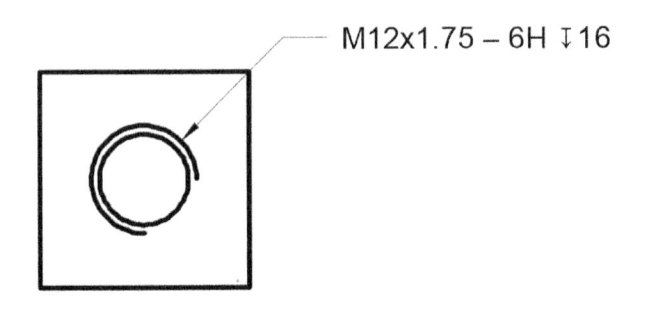

Adding Dimensional Tolerances

During the manufacturing process, the accuracy of a part is an important factor. However, it is impossible to manufacture a part with the exact dimensions. Therefore, while applying dimensions to a drawing, we provide some dimensional tolerances, which lie within acceptable limits. The following example shows you to add dimension tolerances in AutoCAD.

Example:

- Create the drawing, as shown below. Do not add dimensions to it.

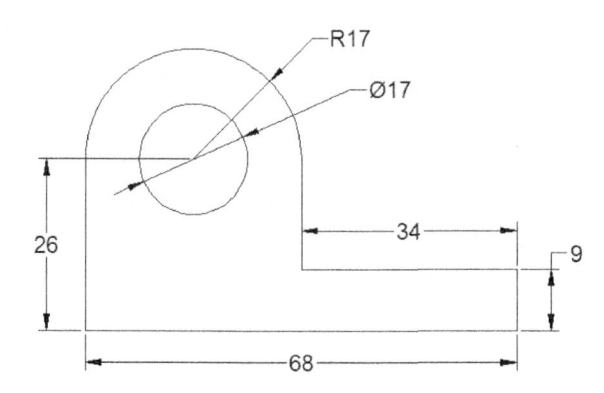

- Create a new dimension style with the name **Tolerances**.
- In the **New Dimension Styles** dialog, click the **Tolerances** tab.
- In the **Tolerances** tab, set the **Method** as **Deviation**.
- Set **Precision** as **0.00**.
- Set the **Upper Value** and **Lower Value** to **0.05**.
- Set the **Vertical position** as **Middle**.
- Specify the following settings in the **Primary Units**, **Text**, and **Symbols and Arrows** tab:

    The **Primary Units** tab:
    Unit format: Decimal
    Precision: 0.00
    Decimal Separator: '.' Period

    The **Text** tab:
    Text Height: 2.5
    Text placement:
        Vertical: Centered
        Horizontal: Centered
    Text alignment: Horizontal

    The **Symbols and Arrows** tab:
    Arrow Size: 2.5
    Center Marks: Line

- Click **OK** on the **New Dimension Styles** dialog.
- Right-click on the **Tolerances** dimension style and select **Set Current**.
- Click **Close** on the **Dimension Style Manager** dialog.

- Apply dimensions to the drawing.

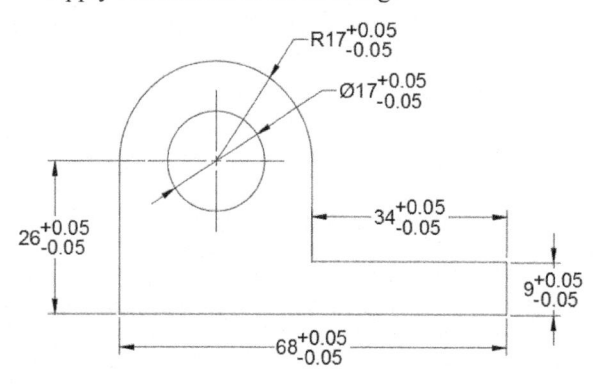

Geometric Dimensioning and Tolerancing

Earlier, you have learned how to apply tolerance to the size (dimensions) of a component. However, the dimensional tolerances are not sufficient for manufacturing a component. You must give tolerance values to its shape, orientation, and position as well. The following figure shows a note which is used to explain the tolerance value given to the shape of the object.

Note: The vertical face should not taper over 0.08 from the horizontal face

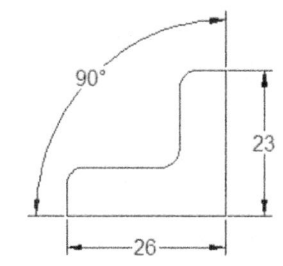

Providing a note in a drawing may be confusing. To avoid this, we use Geometric Dimensioning and Tolerancing (GD&T) symbols to specify the tolerance values to shape, orientation, and position of a component. The following figure shows the same example represented by using the GD&T symbols. In this figure, the vertical face to which the tolerance frame is connected must be within two parallel planes 0.08 apart and perpendicular to the datum reference (horizontal plane).

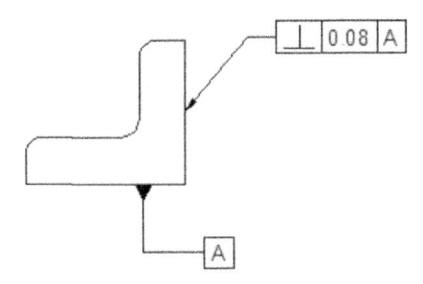

The Geometric Tolerancing symbols that can be used to interpret the geometric conditions are given in the table below.

Purpose		Symbol
To represent the shape of a single feature.	Straightness	—
	Flatness	▱
	Cylindricity	⌭
	Circularity	○
	Profile of a surface	⌒
	Profile of a line	⌒
To represent the orientation of a feature with respect to another feature.	Parallelism	//
	Perpendicularity	⊥
	Angularity	∠
To represent the position of a feature with respect to another feature.	Position	⌖

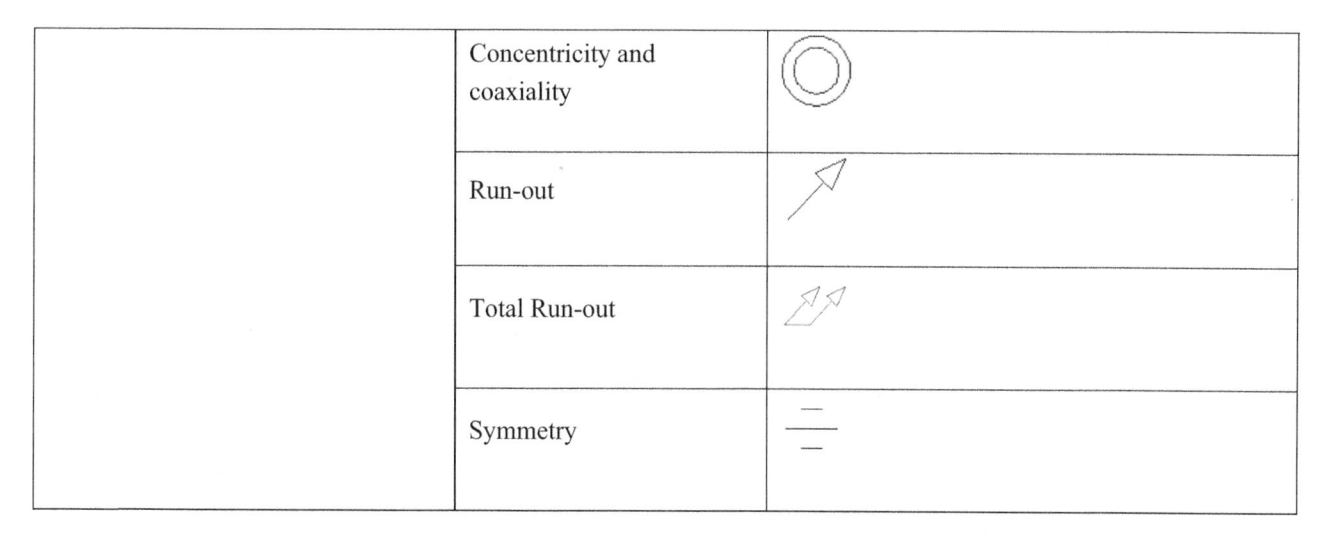

	Concentricity and coaxiality	⊚
	Run-out	↗
	Total Run-out	↗↗
	Symmetry	⩵

Example 1:

In this example, you will apply geometric tolerances to the drawing shown below.

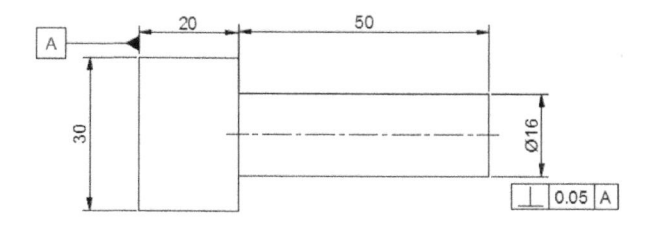

- Create the drawing, as shown below.

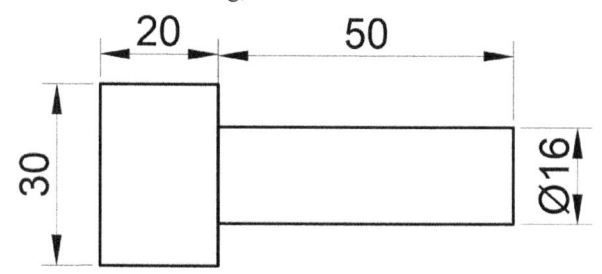

- Click **Drafting > Dimension > Tolerance** on the tool set; the **Geometric Tolerance** dialog appears.

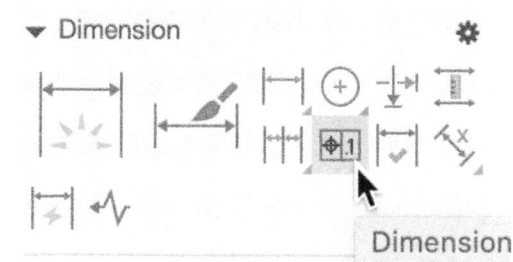

- In the **Geometric Tolerance** dialog, click the upper box of the **Sym** group. The **Symbol** dialog appears.

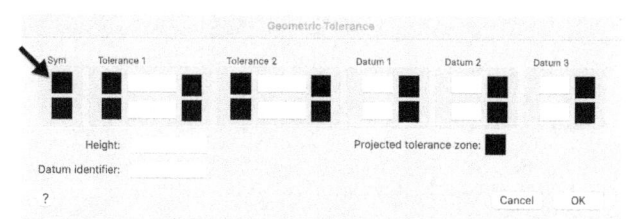

- In the **Symbol** dialog, click the **Perpendicularity** symbol. The symbol appears in the **Sym** group.

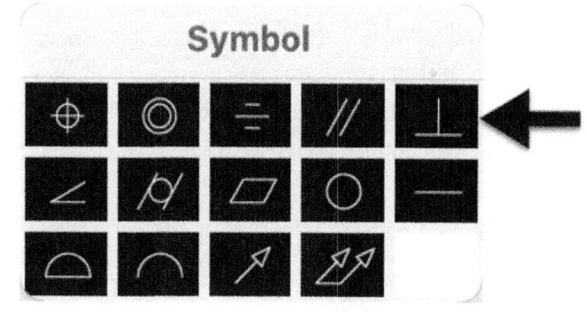

- Click in the top left box in the **Tolerance 1** group. The diameter symbol appears in the box.
- Enter **.05** in the box next to the diameter symbol.

- Enter **A** in the upper box of the **Datum 1** group.

155 | **Dimensions and Annotations**

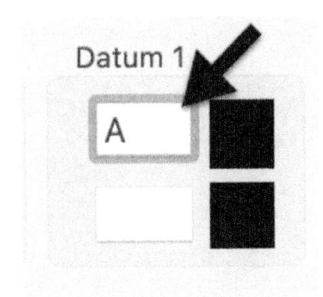

- Click **OK** and position the **Feature Control frame**, as shown below.

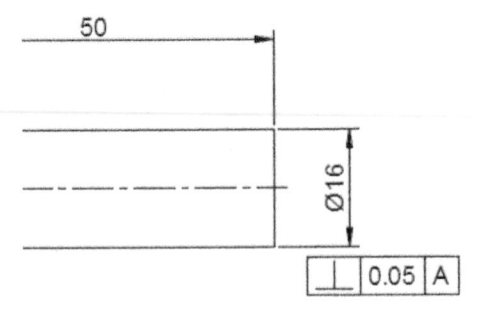

Next, you must add the datum reference.

- On the **Drafting** tool set, click **Multileader Style** on the **Leader** panel.
- Click the **Plus** + button.
- On the **Create New Multileader Style** dialog, type **Tolerance** in the **New Style name** box, and click **Continue**.
- Click the **Leader Format** tab and select **Arrowhead > Symbol > Datum triangle filled**.
- Set the **Size** to 2.5.
- On the **Leader Structure** tab, set **Maximum leader points** to **2**.
- Click the **Content** tab and select **Type > Block**.
- Select **Source block > Box**.
- Set the **Scale** value to 0.75.
- Click **OK**.
- Right-click on the Tolerance style and select **Set Current**.
- Click **Close**.
- On the **Drafting** tool set, click **Leader > Multileader**.
- Specify the first and second points of the datum reference, as shown.

- On the **_TagBox** dialog, type **A** in the **Enter tag number** box.
- Click **Confirm**.

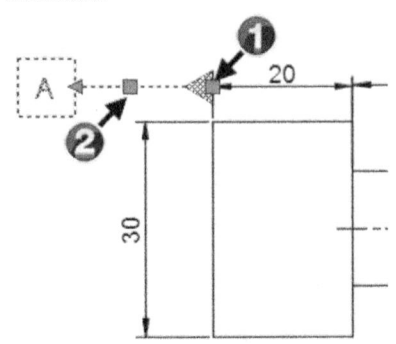

Editing Dimensions by Stretching

In AutoCAD, the dimensions are associated with the drawing. If you modify a drawing, the dimensions will be modified automatically. In the following example, you will stretch the drawing to modify the dimensions.

Example:

- Create the drawing, as shown below, and apply dimensions to it.

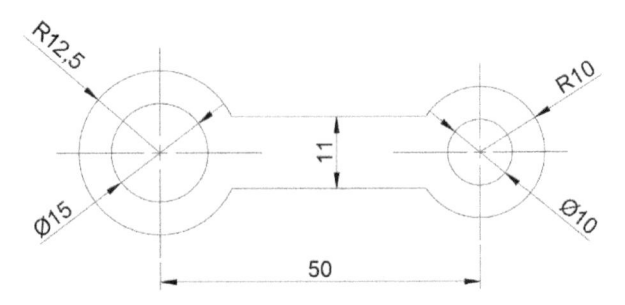

- Click **Drafting > Modify > Stretch** on the tool set.
- Drag a window and select the right-side circles and the horizontal lines.

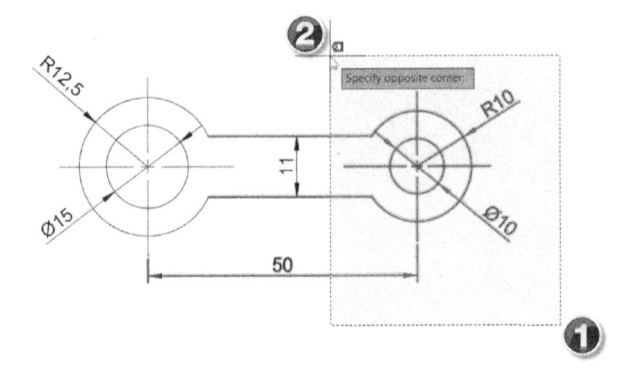

156 | Dimensions and Annotations

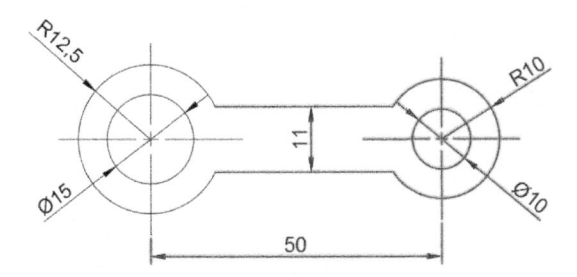

- Right-click and select the center point of the right-side circles.
- Move the pointer to stretch the drawing; you will notice that the horizontal dimension also changes.
- Type **30** and press RETURN; the horizontal dimension is updated to 80.

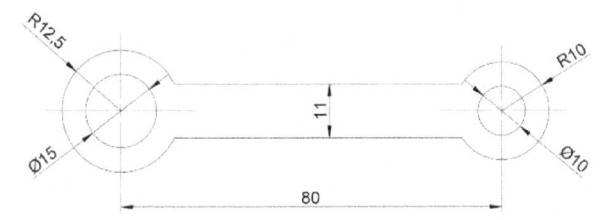

Modifying Dimensions by Trimming and Extending

In earlier chapters, you have learned to modify drawings by trimming and extending objects. In the same way, you can modify dimensions by trimming and extending. The following example shows you to modify dimensions by this method.

Example:
- Create a drawing, as shown below, and add dimensions to it.

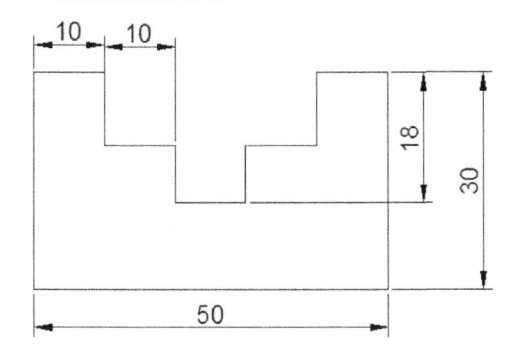

- Click **Drafting > Modify > Trim** on the tool set.

- Right-click and select the **cuTting edges** option from the shortcut menu.
- Select the horizontal edge, as shown in the figure, to define the cutting edge.
- Right-click to accept.

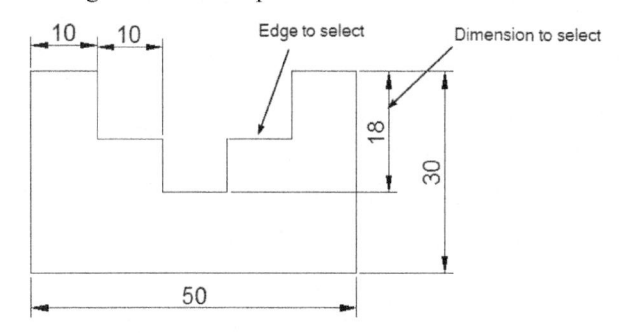

- Select the vertical dimension with the value 18. It trims the dimension up to the selected edge.

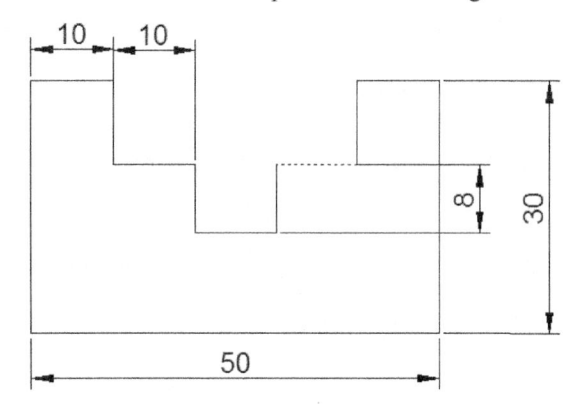

- Press ESC.
- Click **Drafting > Modify > Trim > Extend** on the tool set.
- Right-click and select the **Boundary edges** option from the shortcut menu.
- Select the vertical edge as the boundary, as shown below. Next, right-click to accept.

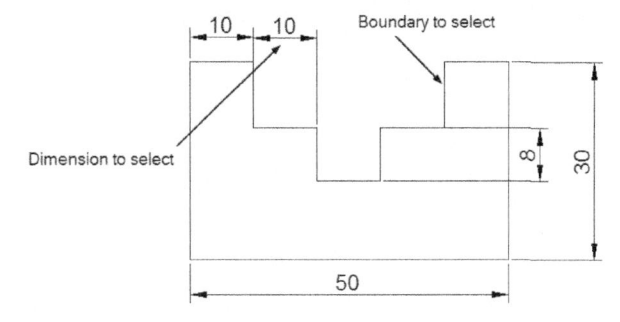

- Select the horizontal dimension with the value 10. It will extend the dimension up to the selected boundary.

- Press Esc.

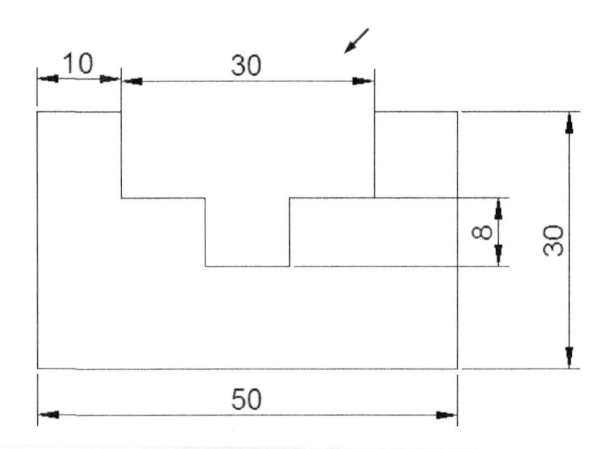

Using the DIMEDIT command

The **DIMEDIT** command can be used to modify dimensions. Using this command, you can add text to a dimension, rotate the dimension text and extension lines, or reset the position of the dimension text.

Example 1: (Adding Text to the dimension)

- Type **DED** in the command line and press RETURN.
- Right-click and select the **New** option from the shortcut menu; a text box appears.
- Enter **TYP** in the text box and press the SPACEBAR.

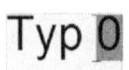

- Left-click and select the dimension with value 10.

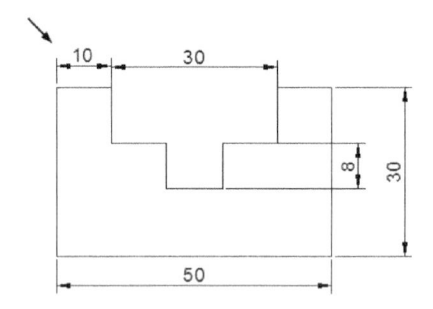

- Press RETURN; the dimension text will be changed.

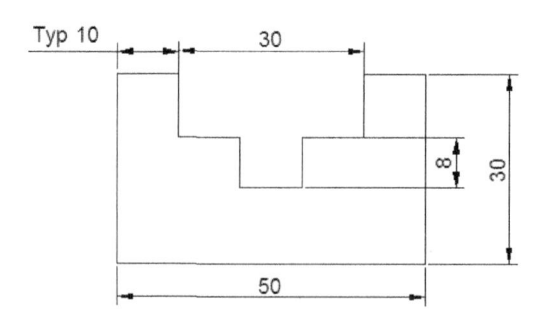

Example 2: (Rotating the dimension text)

- Type **DED** in the command line and press RETURN.
- Right-click and select the **Rotate** option; the message, "Specify angle for dimension text," appears in the command line.
- Type **30** and press RETURN.
- Select the dimension with the value 50 and right-click. The angle of the dimension text is changed to 30 degrees. Note that the angle is measured from the horizontal axis (X-axis).

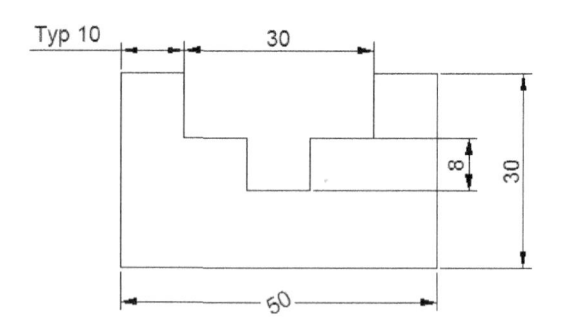

Using the Update tool

The **Update** tool is used to update a dimension with the currently active dimension style. For example, if you have created a new dimension style, you can apply it to an already existing dimension using the **Update** tool. The following example shows you to update a dimension.

- Type **D** in the command line and press RETURN; the **Dimension Style Manager** dialog appears.
- In the **Dimension Style Manager** dialog, select **Standard** from the **Styles** list
- Click the down-arrow next the gear icon and select **Modify**.

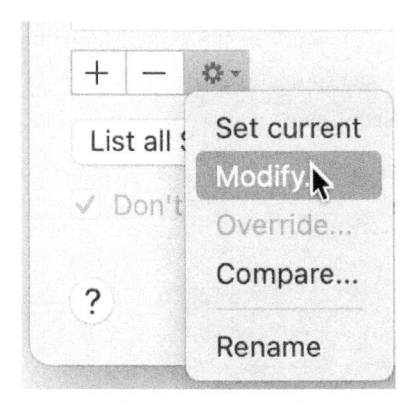

- In the **Modify Dimension Style** dialog, click the **Text** tab, and then set the **Text height** to **2.5**.
- Click the **Text Style** button; the **Text Style** dialog appears. 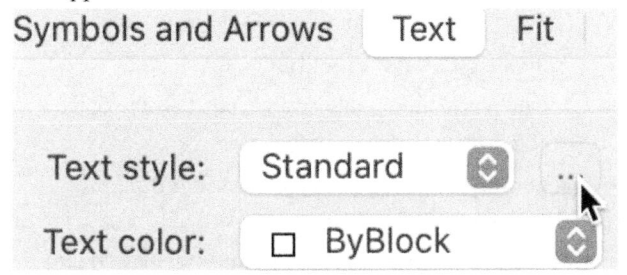
- In the **Text Style** dialog, change the **Typface** to **Italic**. 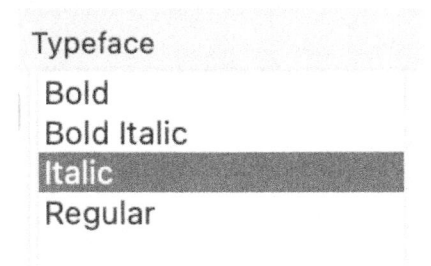
- Click **Apply** and close the **Text Style** dialog.
- Click **OK** on the **Modify Dimension Style** dialog.
- Right-click on the **Standard** dimension style and select **Set current**.
- Click **Close** on the **Dimension Style Manager** dialog.
- Type **-DIMSTYLE** in the command line and press RETURN.
- Select the horizontal dimension with the value 30. Next, right-click; the dimension will be updated with the current dimension style.

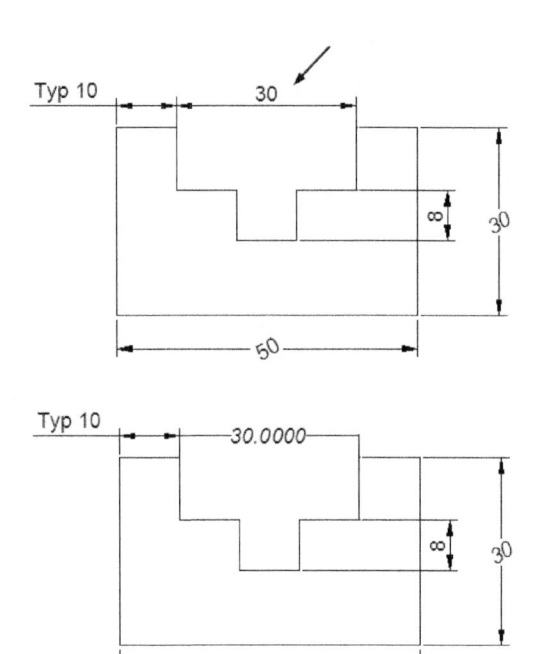

Using the Oblique tool

The **Oblique** tool is used to incline the extension lines of a dimension. This tool is very useful while dimensioning the isometric drawings. It can also be used in 2D drawings when the dimensions overlap with each other.

Example:

In this example, you will create an isometric drawing and add dimensions to it. Next, you will use the **Oblique** tool to change the angle of the dimension lines.

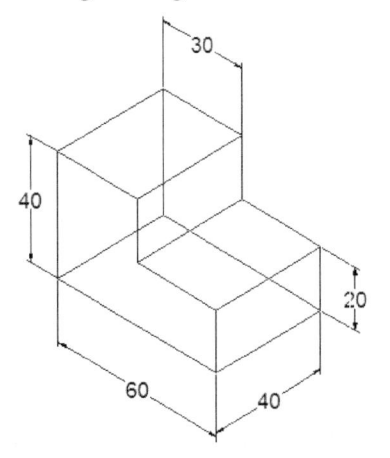

- Type-in **DS** in the command line, and then press RETURN.
- On the **Drafting Settings** dialog, click the **Snap & Grid** tab.

- In the **Drafting Settings** dialog, set **Snap type** to **Isometric snap** and click **OK**.

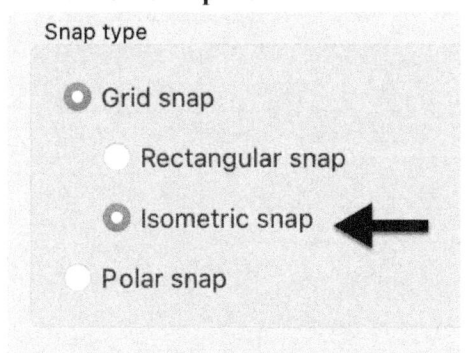

- Turn on the **Snap Mode** and the **Ortho Mode**. Also, turn on the **Dynamic Input**.
- Click **View > Zoom > All** on the Menu Bar.
- Type **L** in the command line and press RETURN.
- Click at a random point and move the pointer vertically upward.
- Type 40 in the command line and press RETURN; a vertical line will be created.
- Move the pointer toward the right; you will notice that an inclined line is attached to the pointer.

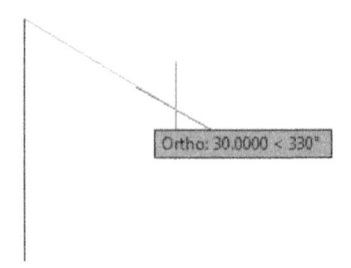

- Type 30 and press RETURN; an inclined line is drawn.
- Move the pointer downward.
- Type 20 and press RETURN.

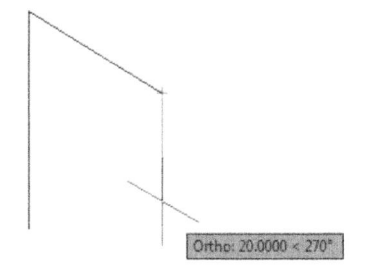

- Move the pointer toward the right.
- Type 30 and press RETURN.
- Move the pointer downward, type 20, and then press RETURN.

- Move the pointer toward the left and click on the start point of the sketch.
- Right-click select Enter.

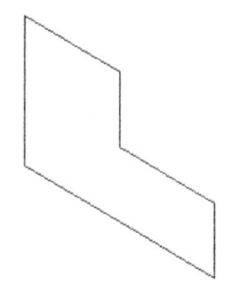

- Turn off the **Ortho Mode**.
- Right-click on the **Polar Tracking** icon on the Status bar, and then select **30** from the flyout.
- Activate the **Polar Tracking** icon.
- Create a selection window and select all the objects of the sketch.
- Right-click and select **Copy-Selection** from the shortcut menu.
- Select the lower-left corner point as the base point.

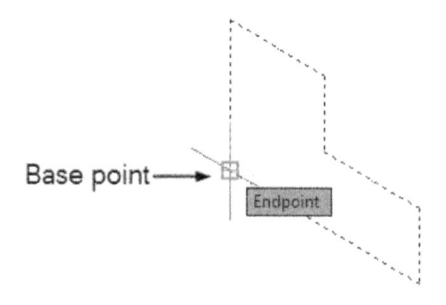

- Move the pointer in the direction perpendicular to the drawing; the track line is displayed.
- Move the pointer along the track line.

Dimensions and Annotations

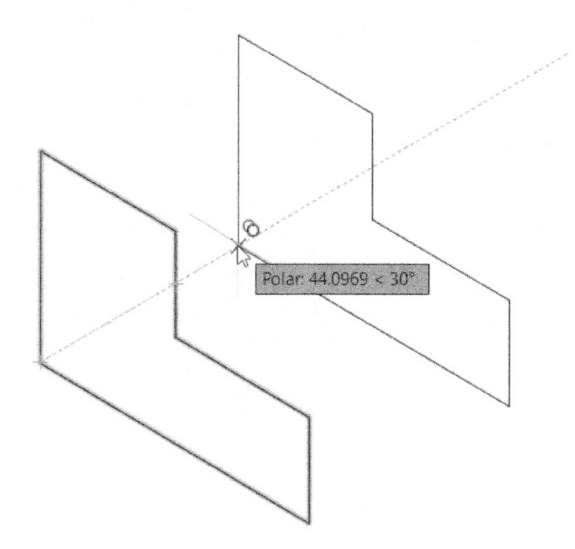

- Use the dimensioning tools and apply dimensions to the sketch.

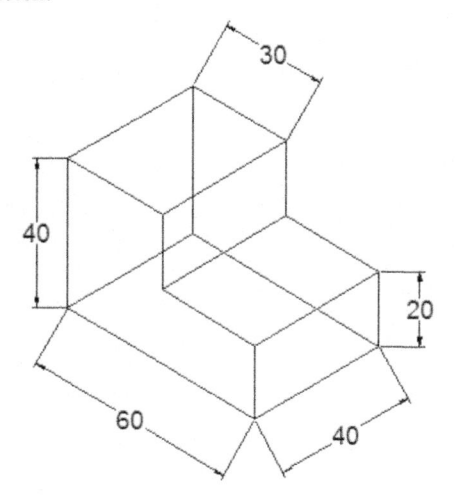

- Type 40 and press RETURN.
- Right-click and select Enter.

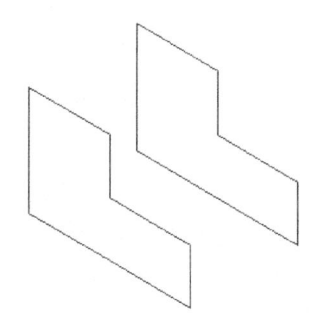

- Type DIMEDIT in the command line and press RETURN.
- Right-click and select **Oblique** from the shortcut menu.
- Select the vertical dimensions and right-click to accept; the message, "**Enter obliquing angle,**" appears in the command line.

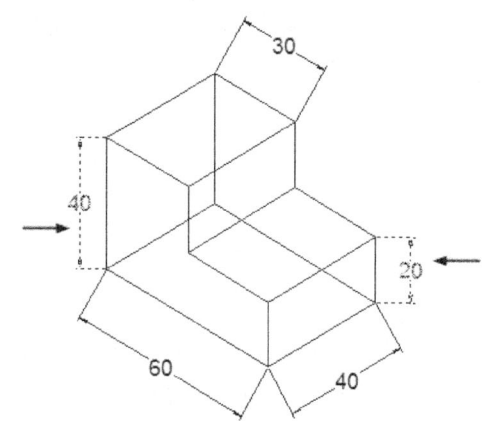

- Use the **Line** tool and connect the endpoints of the two sketches.

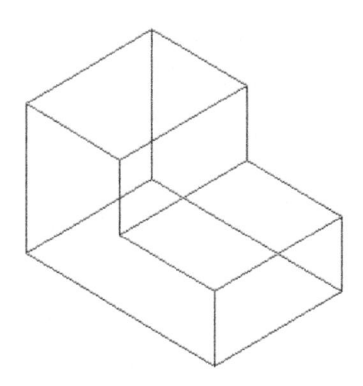

- Type 150 as the oblique angle and press RETURN; the dimensions are oblique, as shown below.

- Type **DS** and press RETURN.
- On the **Drafting Settings** dialog, click the **Snap & Grid** tab.
- In the **Drafting Settings** dialog, set **Snap type** to **Rectangular snap** and click **OK**.
- Deactivate the **Snap Mode** icon on the status bar.

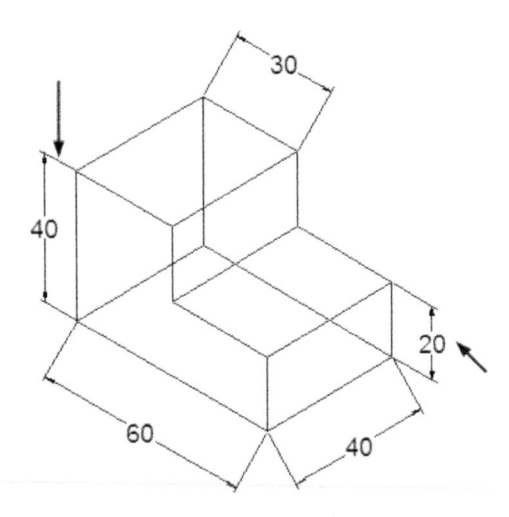

- Type DIMEDIT and press RETURN.
- Type O and press RETURN.
- Select the aligned dimensions. Next, right-click to accept.

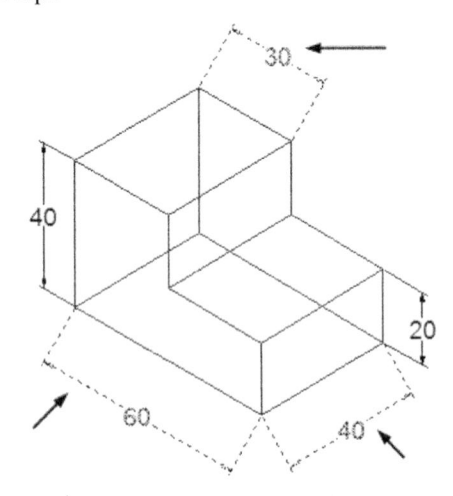

- Type 90 as the oblique angle and press RETURN; the dimensions will be oblique, as shown below.

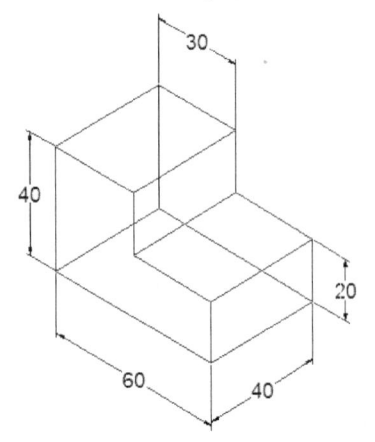

Editing Dimensions using Grips

In Chapter 4, you have learned to edit objects using grips. In the same way, you can edit dimensions using grips. The editing operations using grips are discussed next.

Example 1: (Stretching the Dimension)

- Select the dimension to display grips on it.
- Select the endpoint grip of the dimension.
- Next, move the pointer and select a new point; the dimension value will be updated automatically.

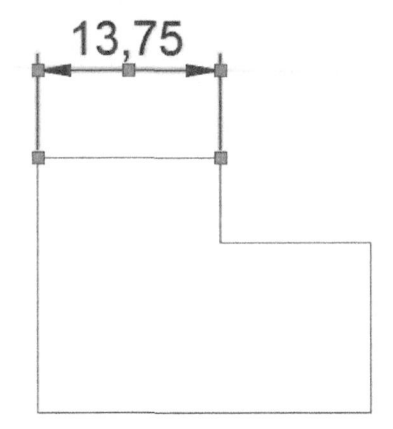

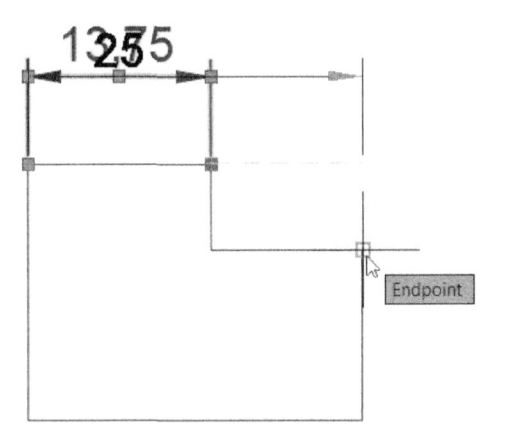

- You can also stretch the angular or radial dimensions.

162 | Dimensions and Annotations

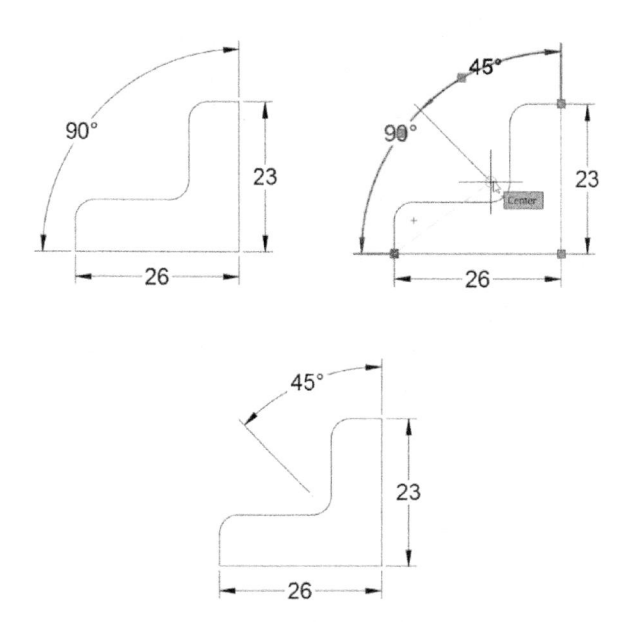

Example 2: (Moving the Dimension)

- To move a linear dimension, select the middle grip and move the pointer.

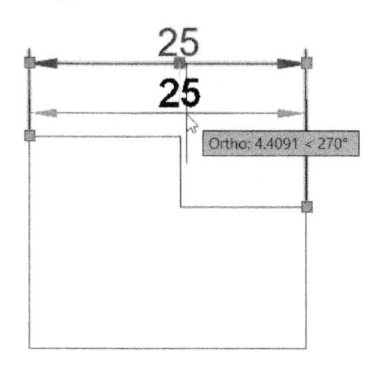

- Likewise, you can move the angular and radial dimensions.

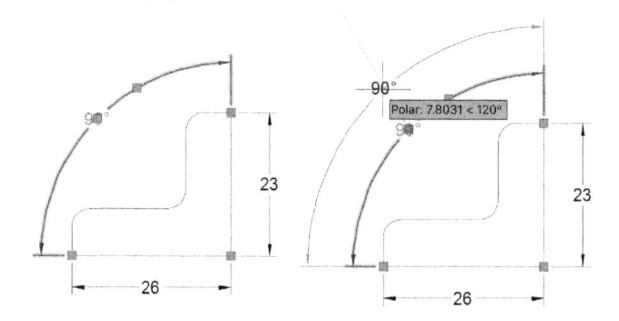

Example 3: (Modifying the Dimension text)

- Select the dimension and position the pointer on the middle grip; a shortcut menu appears as shown below.

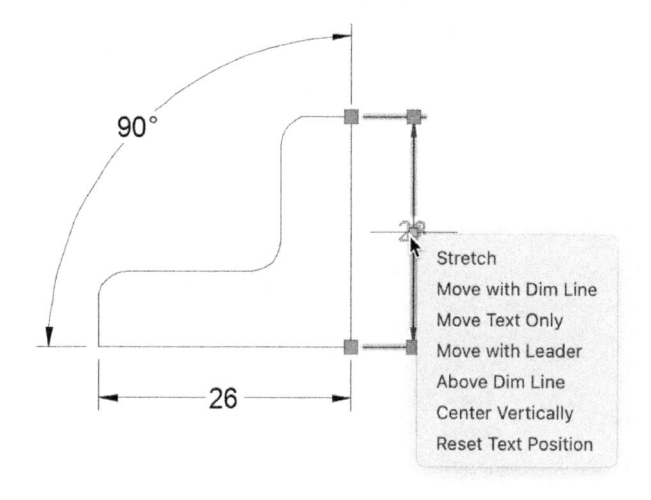

The options in the menu are self-explanatory. You can perform the required operation by selecting the corresponding option.

- Likewise, position the pointer on the endpoint of the dimension line and select the required option from the menu.

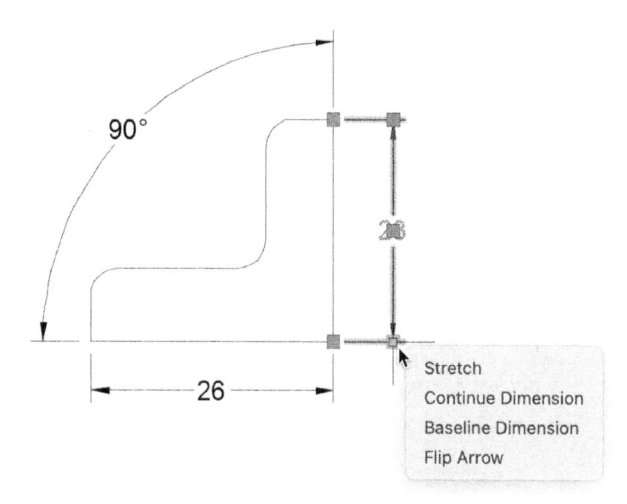

Modifying Dimensions using the Properties palette

Using the **Properties** palette, you can modify the dimensional properties such as text, arrow size, precision, linetype, and lineweight. The **Properties** palette comes in handy when you want to modify the properties of a particular dimension only.

163 | Dimensions and Annotations

Example:

- Create the drawing shown in the figure and apply dimensions to it.

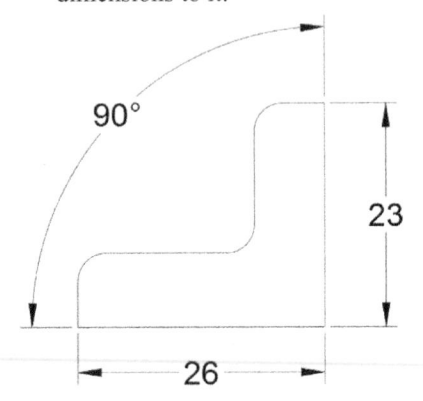

- Select the vertical dimension.
- Click the **All** tab on the **Properties** palette.

- In the **Properties** palette, under the **Lines & Arrows** section, set the **Arrow size** to **2**.

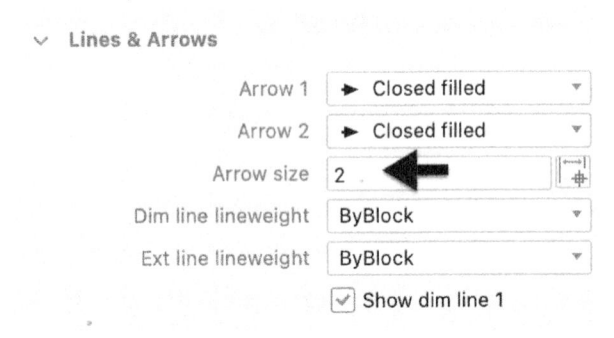

- Under the **General** section, set **Color** to **Blue**.

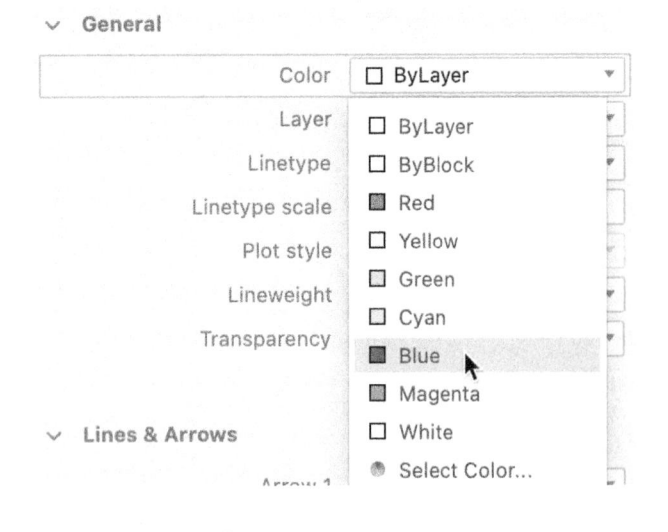

- In the **Properties** palette, under the **Lines & Arrows** section, set the **Ext line offset** value to **1.25**.
- Scroll down to the **Text** section and set **Text height** to **2**.

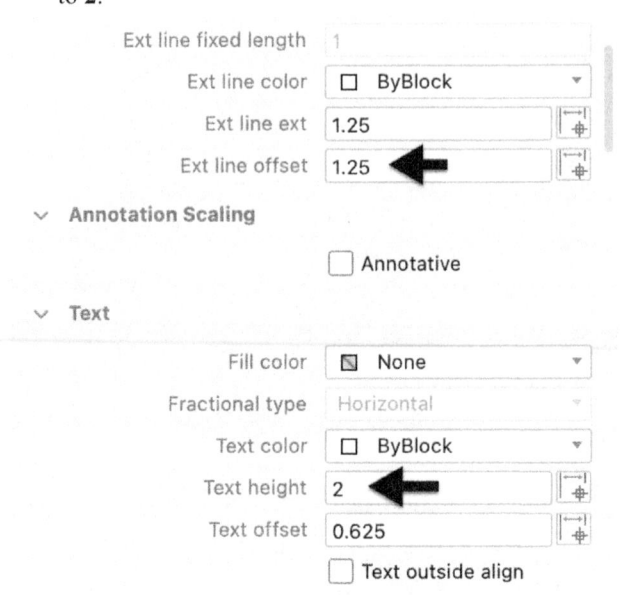

- Press ESC; you will notice that the properties of the dimension are updated as per the changes made.

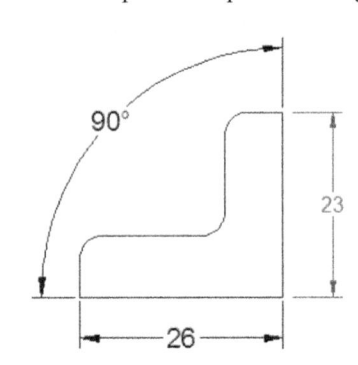

Matching Properties of Dimensions or Objects

In the previous section, you have learned to change the properties of a dimension. Now, you can apply these properties to other dimensions by using the **Match Properties** tool.

- Click **Match Properties** on the toolbar or type **MA** and press RETURN; the message, "Select source object," appears in the command line.

164 | Dimensions and Annotations

- Select the vertical dimension from the drawing; the message, "Select destination object(s) or [Settings]:" appears in the command line.

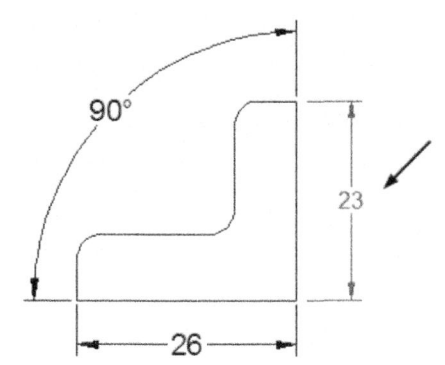

- Right-click and select the **Settings** option from the shortcut menu; the **Match Properties Settings** dialog appears.

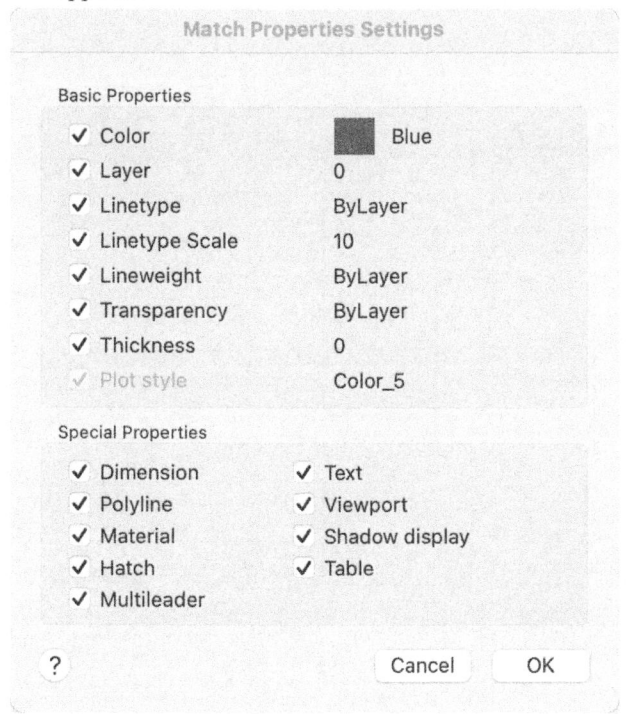

In this dialog, you can select the settings that can be applied to the destination dimensions or objects. By default, all the options are selected in this dialog.

- Click **OK** on the **Match Properties Settings** dialog. Next, you must select the destination objects.

- Select the other dimensions from the drawing; the properties of the source dimension are applied to other dimensions.

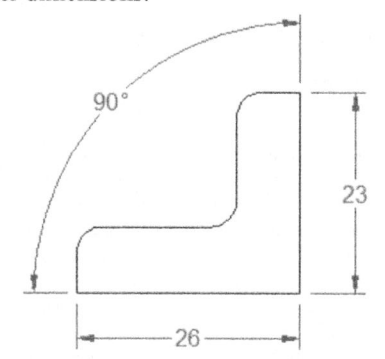

- Right-click and select Enter.

Exercises

Exercise 1

Create the drawing shown below and create hole callouts for different types of holes. Assume missing dimensions.

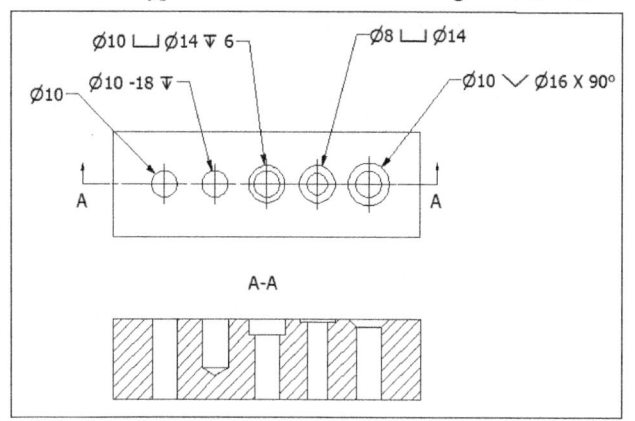

Exercise 2

Create the following drawings and apply dimensions and annotations. The Grid Spacing X= 10 and Grid Spacing Y=10.

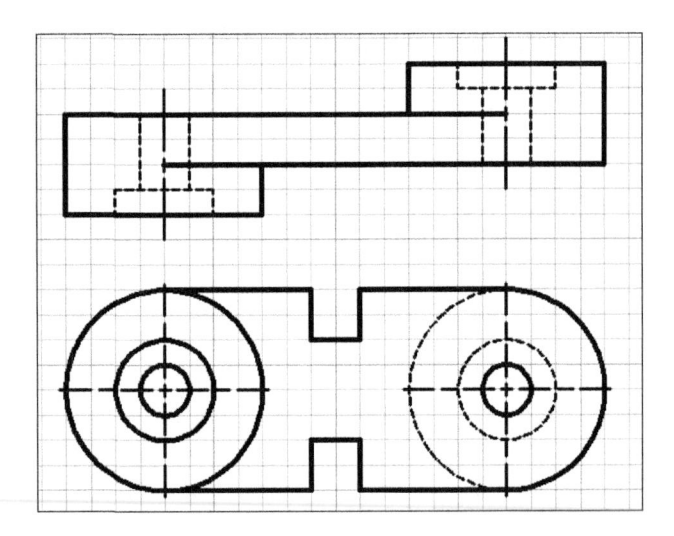

Exercise 3

Create the drawing shown below. The Grid spacing is 10 mm. After creating the drawing, apply dimensional tolerances to it. The tolerance specifications are given below.

Method: Limits
Precision: 0.00
Upper Value: 0.05
Lower Value: 0.05

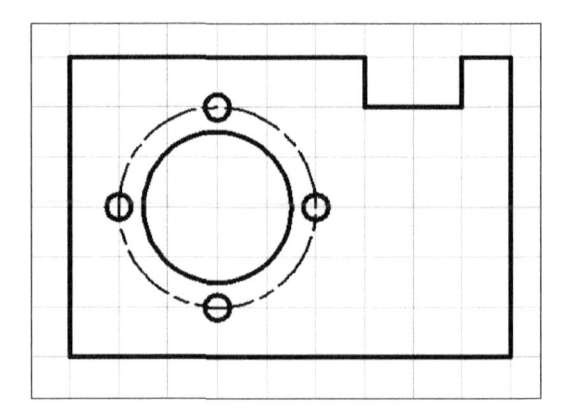

Exercise 4

Create the drawing shown below.

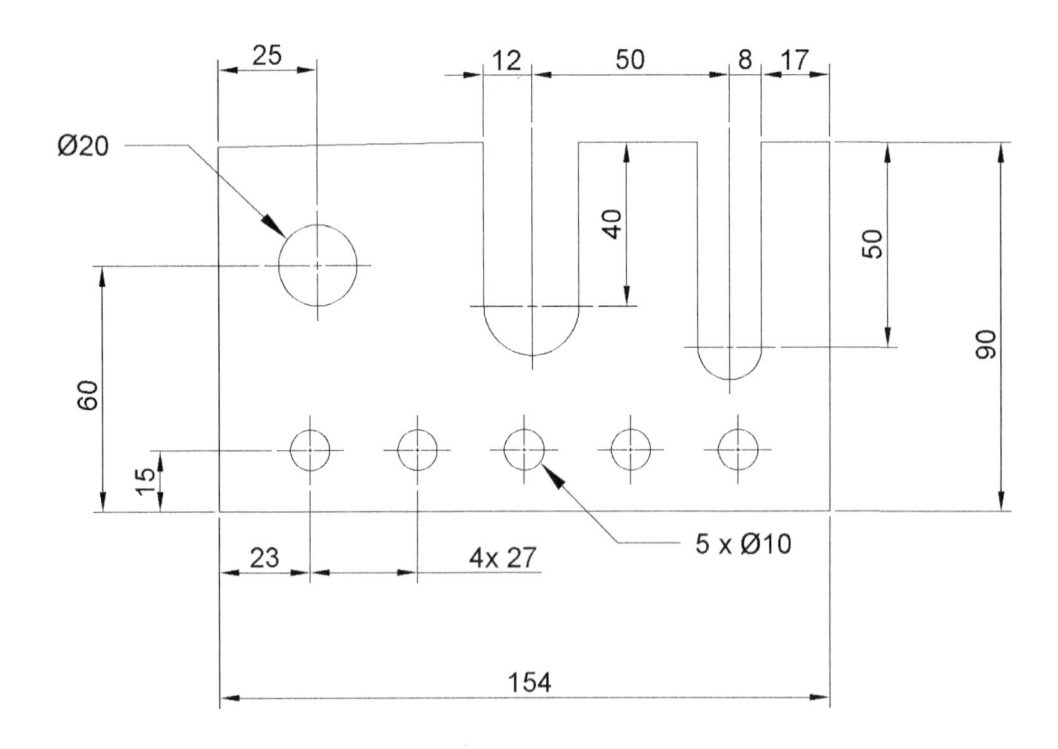

Exercise 5

Create the drawing shown below.

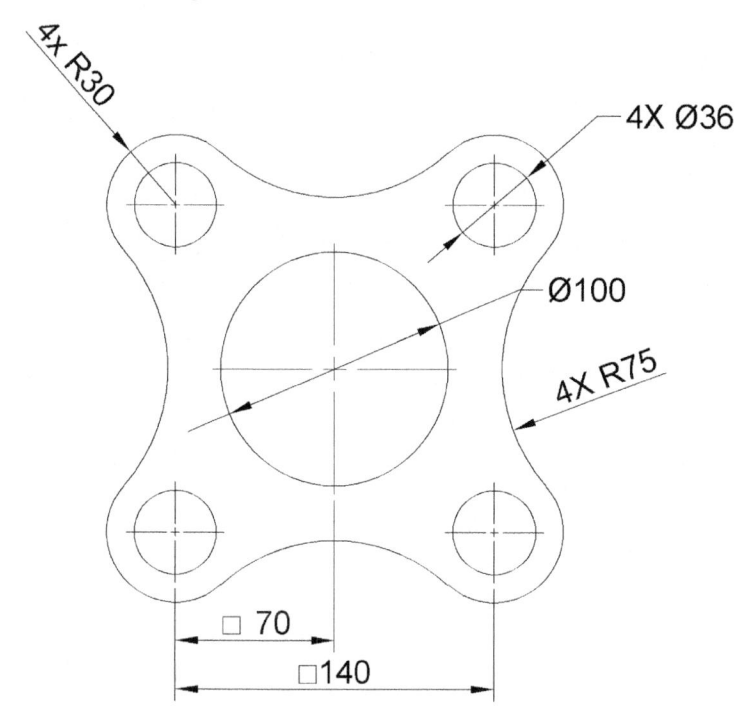

Chapter 7: Parametric Tools

In this chapter, you will learn to do the following:

- **Apply Geometric and Dimensional Constraints**
- **Create Equations using the Parameter Manager**
- **Create Inferred Constraints**

Parametric Tools

Parametric tools are one of the main advancements in Computer-Aided Design. Using the parametric tools, you can define the shape and size of a drawing by applying relations and dimensions between the objects. You can also use equations in place of dimensions. Changing one parameter of an equation would change the entire shape and size of the drawing. It makes it easy to modify the design.

The parametric tools can be accessed from the Tool set, Command line, and Menu Bar.

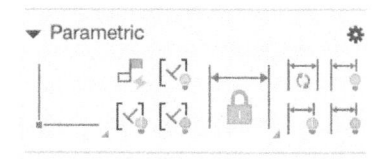

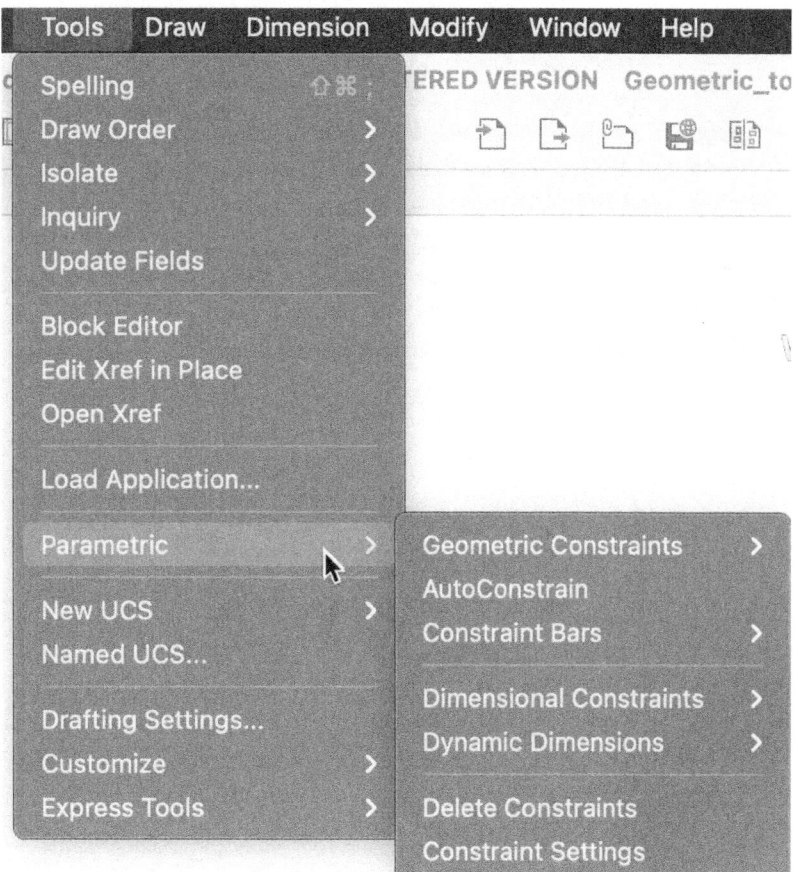

Geometric Constraints

Geometric Constraints are used to control the shape of a drawing by applying geometric relationships between the objects. For example, you can apply the **Tangent** constraint to make a line tangent to a circle. You can use the **Equal** constraint to make two lines equal in length.

The following table shows various geometric constraints and their functions.

Constraint	Function
Coincident	It is used to constrain a point to lie on another point or an object. • Click **Parametric > Geometric Constraint** drop-down > **Coincident** on the **Drafting** tool set. • Select a point on a line or arc. • Select a point on another object; the two points will coincide with each other.
Collinear	It is used to constrain a line along another line. The lines are not required to touch each other. • Click **Parametric > Geometric Constraint** drop-down > **Collinear** on the **Drafting** tool set. • Select the first line and the second line; the second line will be made collinear with the first line.
Concentric	It is used to make the center points of arcs, circles, or ellipses coincident.

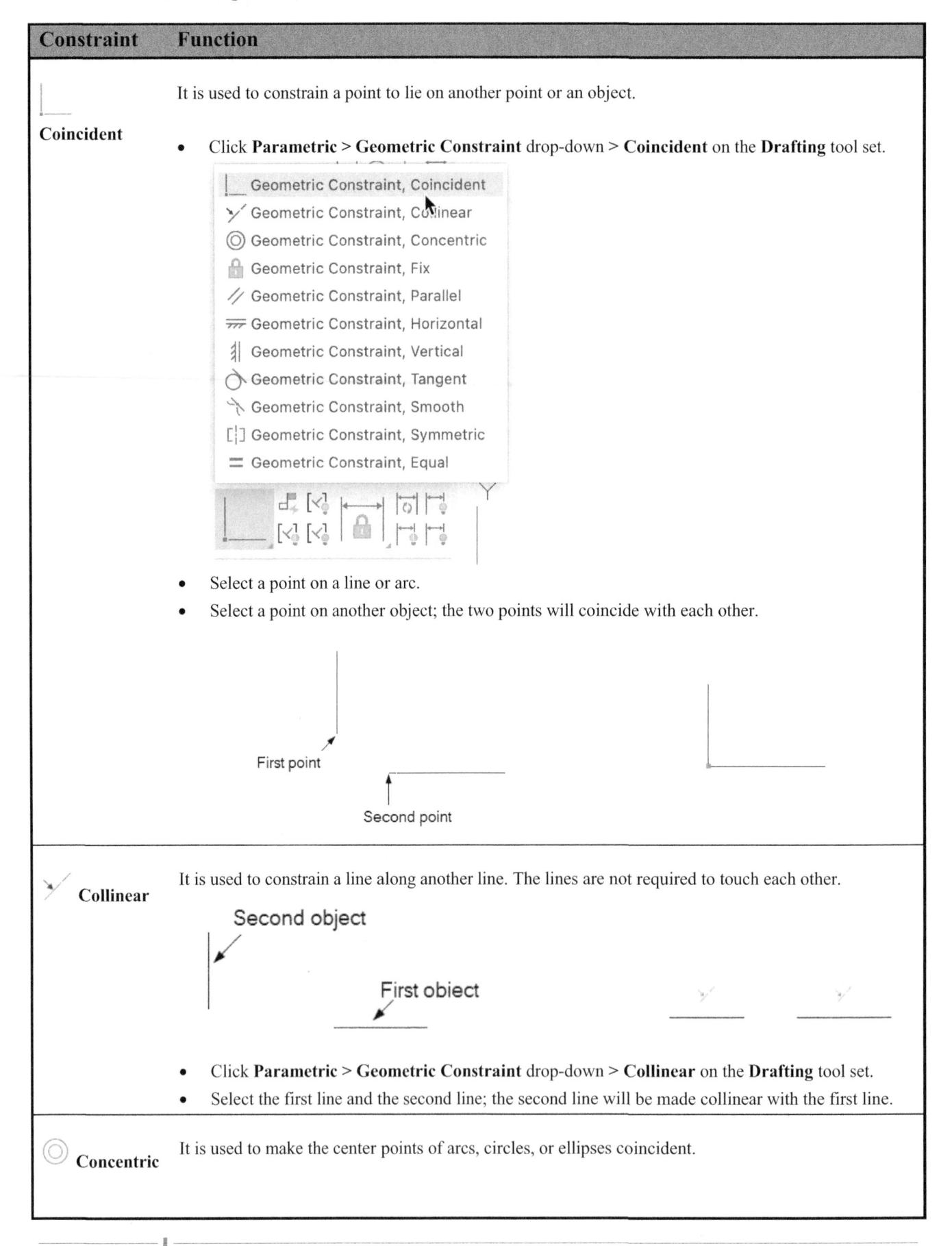

170 Parametric Tools

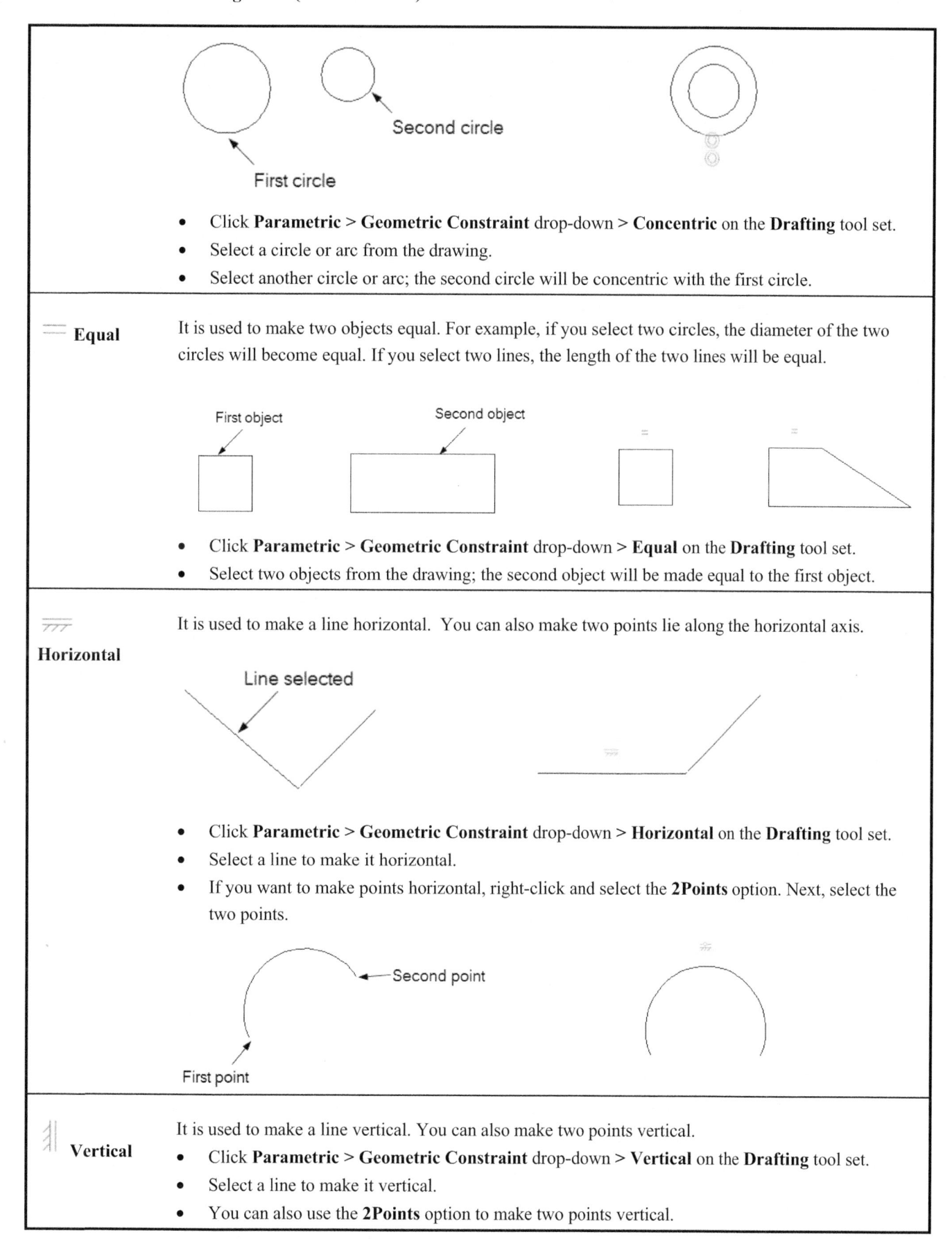

- Click **Parametric** > **Geometric Constraint** drop-down > **Concentric** on the **Drafting** tool set.
- Select a circle or arc from the drawing.
- Select another circle or arc; the second circle will be concentric with the first circle.

Equal

It is used to make two objects equal. For example, if you select two circles, the diameter of the two circles will become equal. If you select two lines, the length of the two lines will be equal.

- Click **Parametric** > **Geometric Constraint** drop-down > **Equal** on the **Drafting** tool set.
- Select two objects from the drawing; the second object will be made equal to the first object.

Horizontal

It is used to make a line horizontal. You can also make two points lie along the horizontal axis.

- Click **Parametric** > **Geometric Constraint** drop-down > **Horizontal** on the **Drafting** tool set.
- Select a line to make it horizontal.
- If you want to make points horizontal, right-click and select the **2Points** option. Next, select the two points.

Vertical

It is used to make a line vertical. You can also make two points vertical.
- Click **Parametric** > **Geometric Constraint** drop-down > **Vertical** on the **Drafting** tool set.
- Select a line to make it vertical.
- You can also use the **2Points** option to make two points vertical.

Fix 🔒	It is used to fix a point or an object at a particular location. • Click **Parametric > Geometric Constraint** drop-down **> Fix** on the **Drafting** tool set. • Select a point to make it fixed at its location. • You can also use the **Object** option to select objects from the drawing.
Perpendicular	It is used to make two lines perpendicular to each other. *Second object* *First object* • Click **Parametric > Geometric Constraint** drop-down **> Perpendicular** on the **Drafting** tool set. • Select two lines from the drawing; the second line is made perpendicular to the first line.
Smooth	It is used to make a spline continuous with another spline or arc. *First point* *Second point* • Click **Parametric > Geometric Constraint** drop-down **> Smooth** on the **Drafting** tool set. • Select a spline curve. • Select another spline or arc; the first curve will become continuous with the second curve.
Parallel	It is used to make two lines parallel to each other.

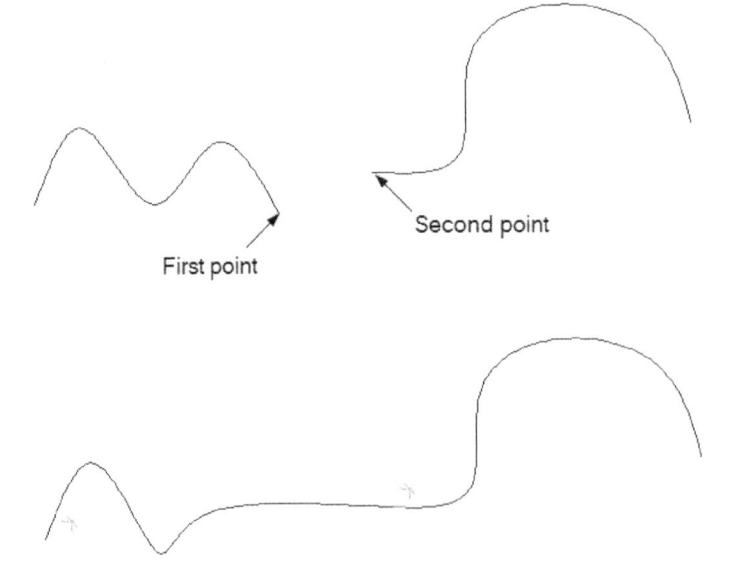

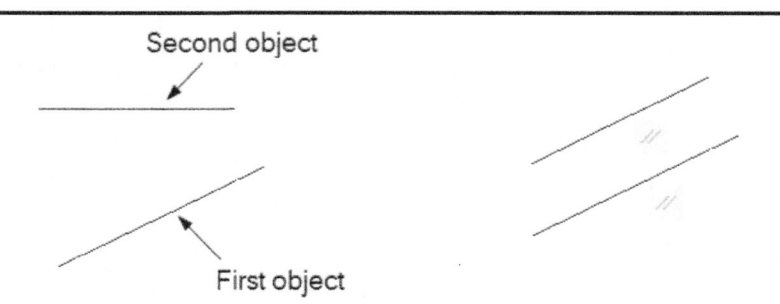

- Click **Parametric > Geometric Constraint** drop-down > **Parallel** on the **Drafting** tool set.
- Select two lines from the drawing; the second line is made parallel to the first line.

Symmetric

It is used to make two objects symmetric about a line. The objects will have the same size, position, and orientation about a line.

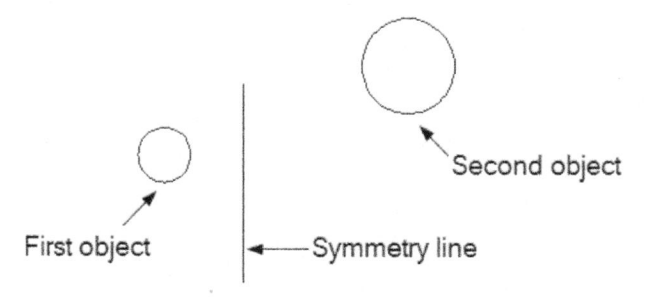

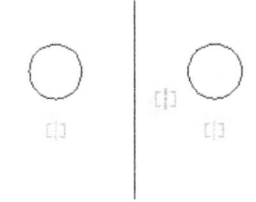

- Click **Parametric > Geometric Constraint** drop-down > **Symmetric** on the **Drafting** tool set.
- Select two objects from the drawing.
- Select the symmetry line; the objects will be made symmetric about the selected line.
- You can also use the **2Points** option to make two points symmetric about a line.

Tangent

It is used to make an arc, circle, or line tangent to another arc or circle.

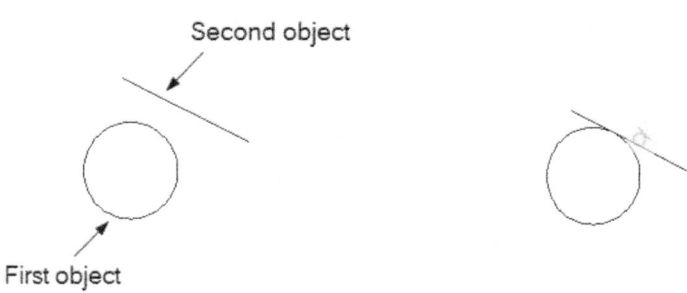

- Click **Parametric > Geometric Constraint** drop-down > **Tangent** on the **Drafting** tool set.

	• Select a circle, arc, or line. • Select another circle, arc, or line; the second object will be tangent to the first object.
Auto Constrain	The **Auto Constrain** tool is used to apply constraints to the objects automatically. • Click **Parametric > Auto Constrain** on the **Drafting** tool set. • Right-click and the **Settings** option from the shortcut menu; the **Constraint Settings** dialog appears. *Constraint Settings dialog shown with Geometric, Dimensional, AutoConstrain tabs. Applied constraints listed: Collinear, Parallel, Perpendicular, Tangent, Concentric, Horizontal, Vertical. Constraint Tolerances & Rules: Distance: 0.05, Angle: 1.0. Tangent objects must intersect (checked), Perpendicular objects must intersect (unchecked). Cancel / OK buttons.* • In this dialog, select the constraints that you want to apply. You can also select the **Tangent objects must intersect**, and **Perpendicular objects must intersect** option. • Click **OK**. • Select multiple objects by clicking on them or by dragging a selection window. • Right-click and select **Enter**; geometric constraints are applied to the objects based on their geometric condition.

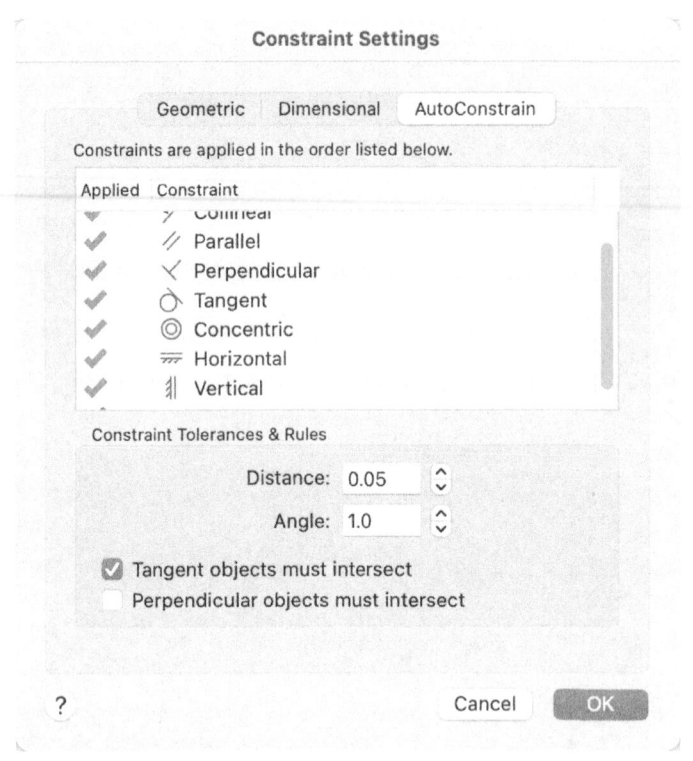

Example:

In this example, you will create the following drawing by
using the drawing and parametric tools.

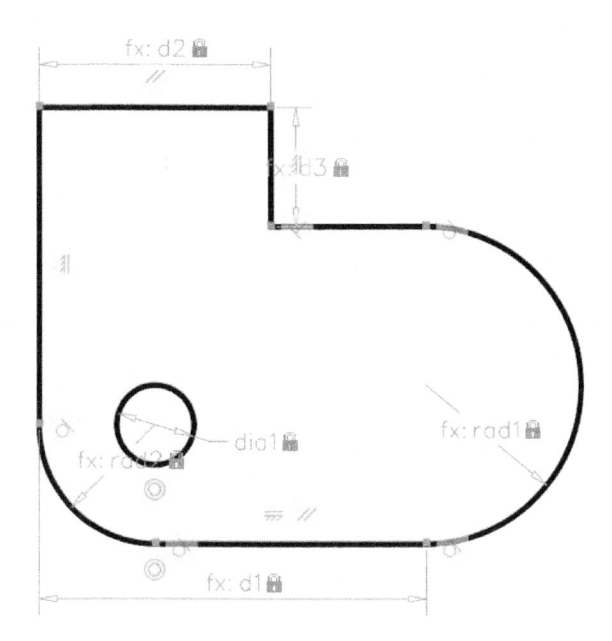

- Open a new AutoCAD file.
- Create two circles and a line, as shown in the figure.

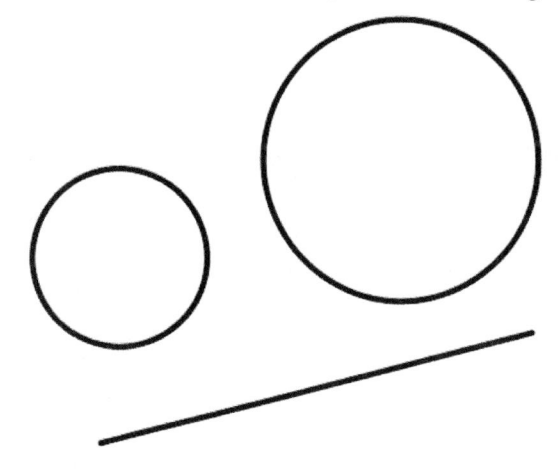

- Click **Parametric > Geometric Constraint** drop-down > **Horizontal** on the **Drafting** tool set.
- Select the line to make it horizontal.

- Press the SPACEBAR.
- Right-click and select **Horizontal**.
- Right-click and select the **2Points** option from the shortcut menu.
- Select the large circle and the small circle; the center points of the two circles will be horizontal.

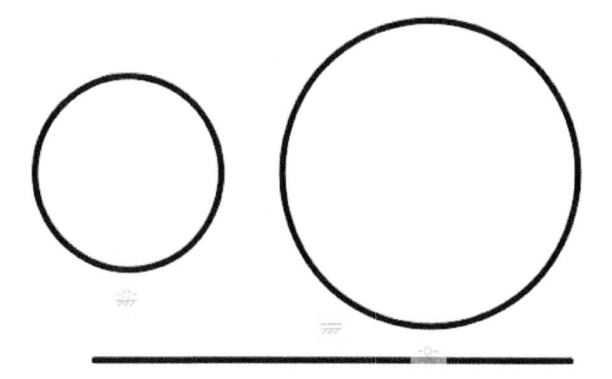

- Create four lines, as shown below.

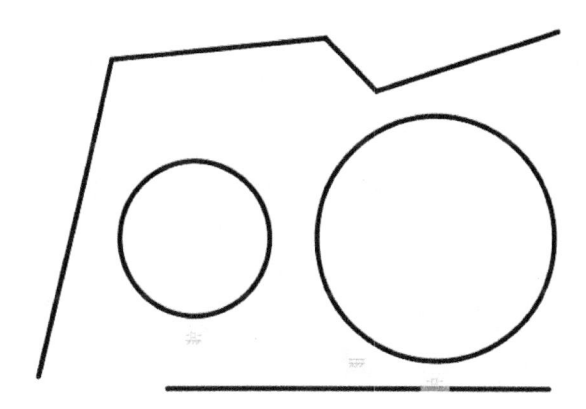

- Click the **Geometric Constraint** drop-down > **Coincident** button on the **Parametric** panel and select the two endpoints of the lines as shown below; the endpoints will be made coincident.

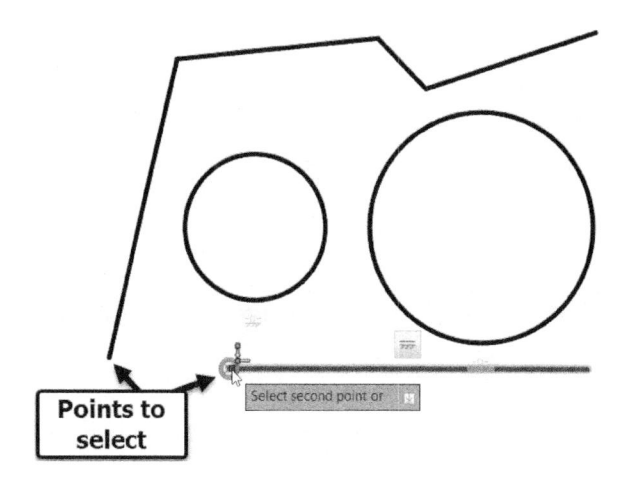

Parametric Tools

- Click the **Auto Constrain** button on the **Parametric** panel and select the four lines, as shown below.

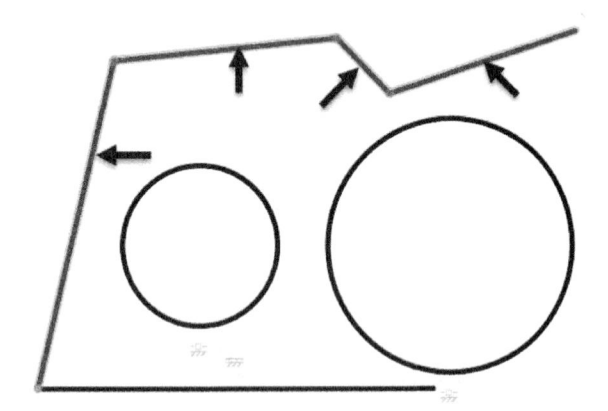

- Right-click and select **Enter**; constraints are applied to the selected objects, automatically.

- Click the **Geometric Constraint** drop-down > **Vertical** button on the **Parametric** panel and select the line as shown below; the line will become vertical.

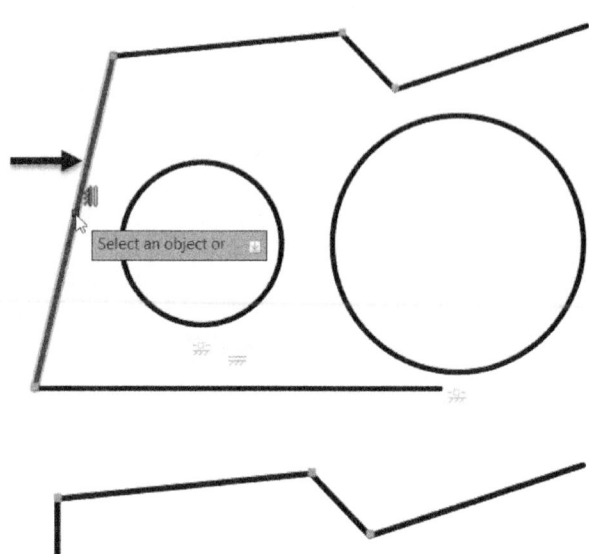

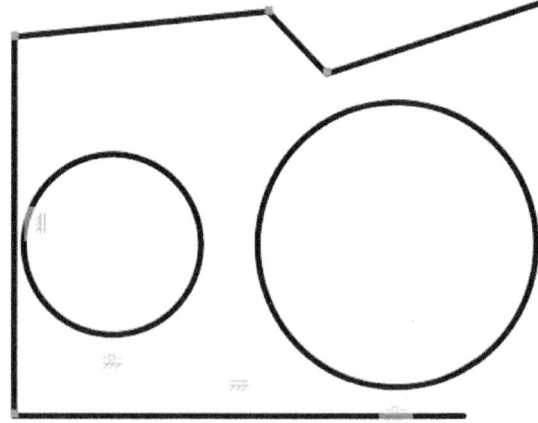

- Click the **Geometric Constraint** drop-down > **Parallel** tool and make the two lines parallel to each other, as shown below.

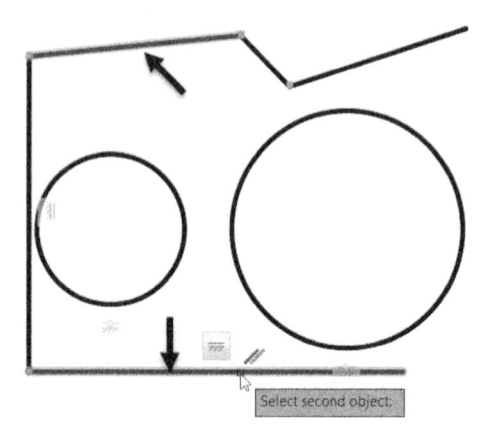

176 | Parametric Tools

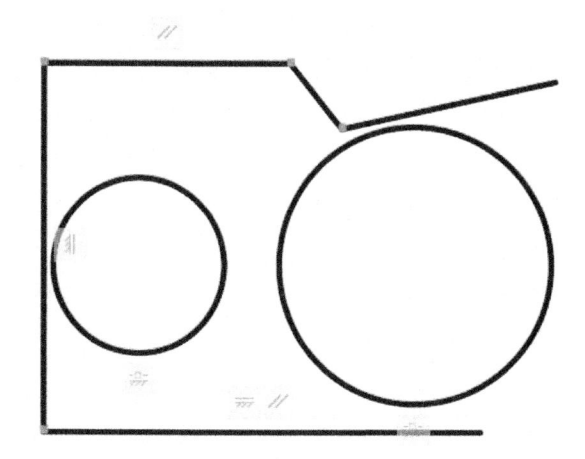

- Use the **Tangent** tool and make the two lines tangent to the large circle, as shown below.

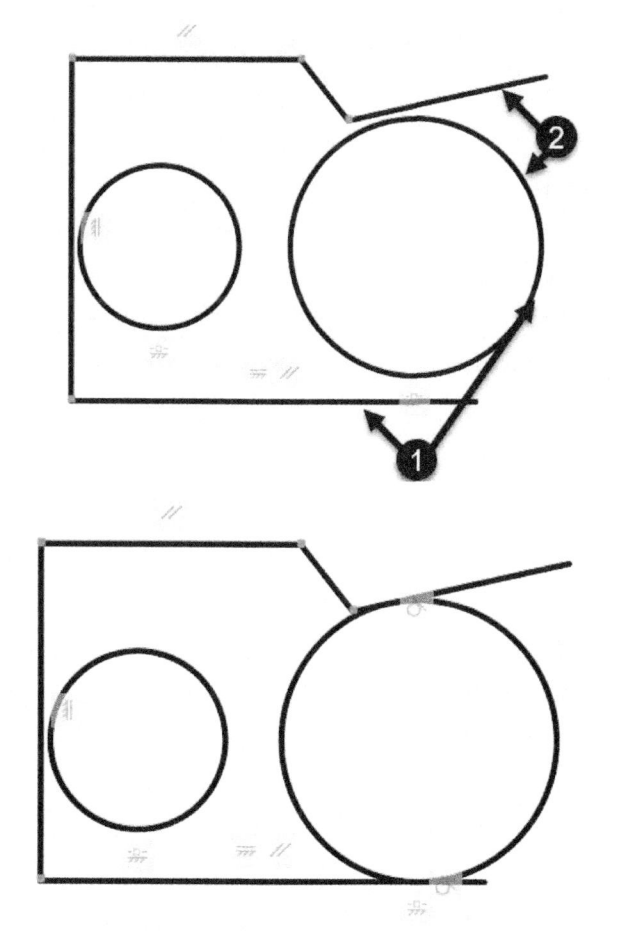

- Click the **Geometric Constraint** drop-down > **Coincident** button on the **Parametric** panel.
- Right-click and select the **Object** option.
- Select the large circle.

- Select the endpoint of the lower horizontal line to make it coincident with the circle.

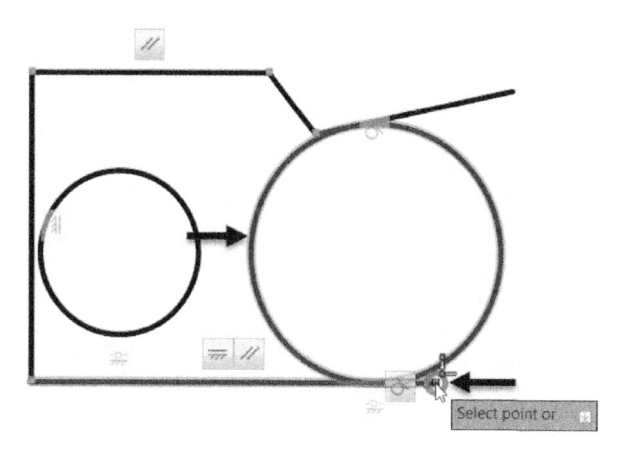

- Likewise, apply the **Coincident** constraint between the large circle and the upper horizontal line.

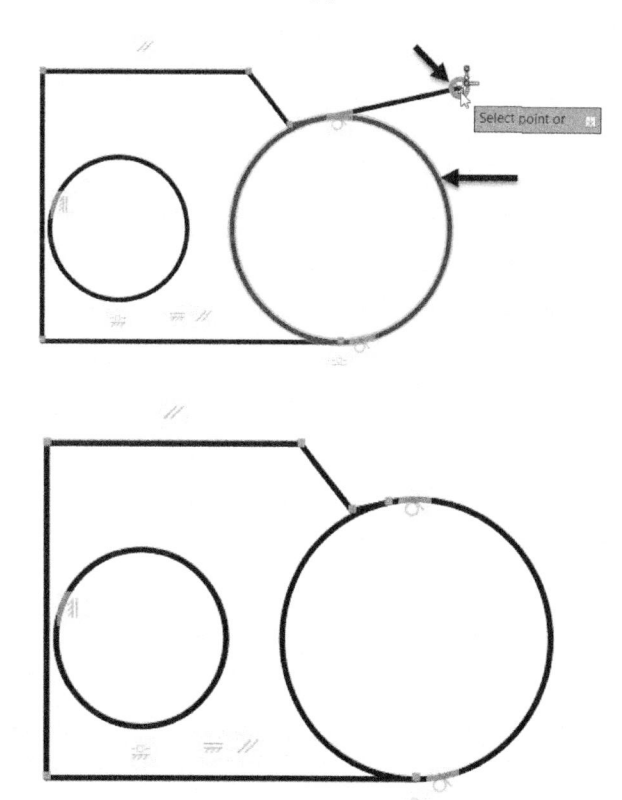

- Use the **Trim** tool and trim the unwanted portion of the circle.

177 | Parametric Tools

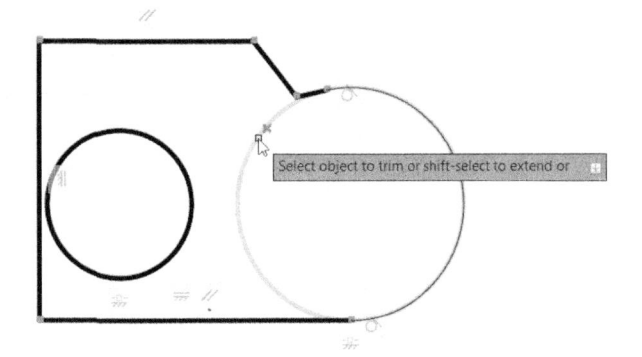

Follow the next three steps if the **Tangent** and **Coincident** constraints are deleted.

- Click the **Auto Constrain** button on the **Parametric** panel.
- Drag a window around the arc and lines, as shown.
- Right-click and select **Enter**; the **Tangent** and **Coincident** constraints are applied between the arc and the horizontal lines.

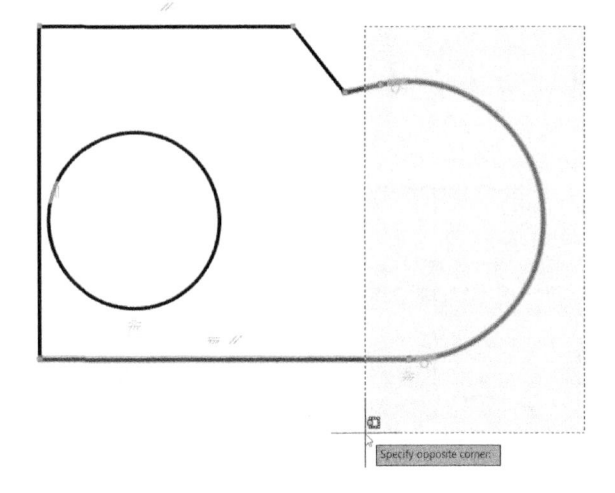

- Click **Tools** > **Parametric** > **Geometric Constraint** drop-down > **Perpendicular** button on the menu bar.
- Select the two lines, as shown.

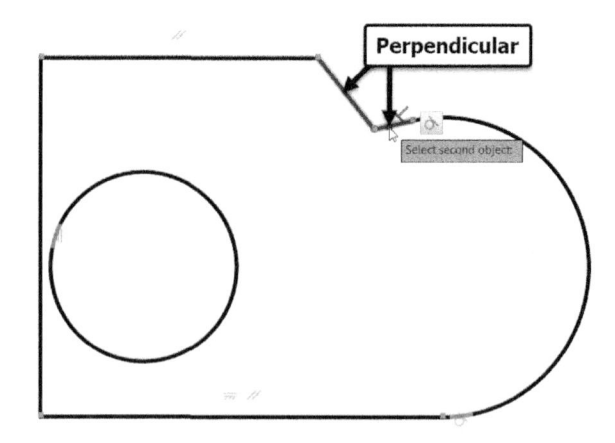

- Click **Geometric Constraint** drop-down > **Vertical** button on the **Parametric** panel.
- Select the line, as shown.

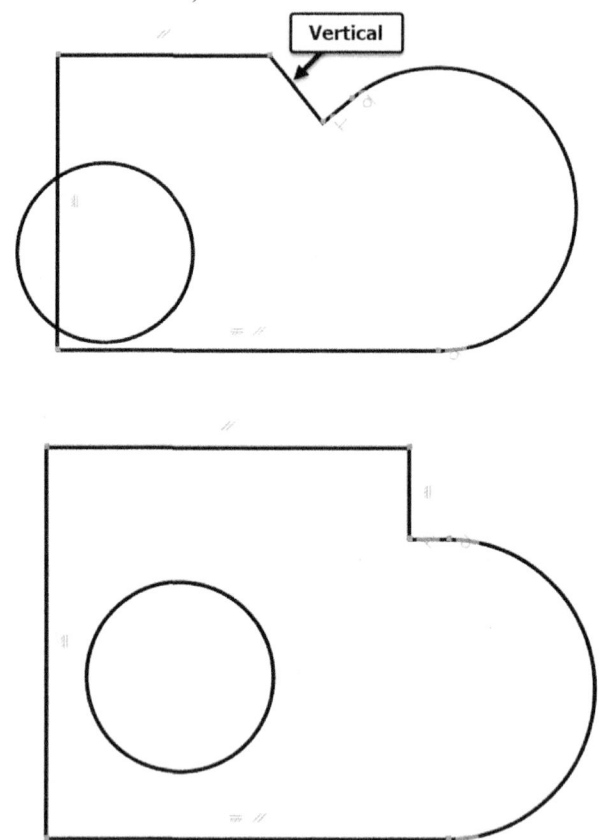

Dimensional Constraints

Dimensional constraints are applied to a drawing after applying the Geometric constraints. They are used to control the size and position of the objects in a drawing. You can apply the dimensional constraints using the tools available in the **Parametric** panel of the **Drafting** tool set.

- Click the **Customize** panel icon on the **Parametric** panel.
- Check the **Constraint Settings** option; the **Constraint Settings** icon is displayed on the **Parametric** panel.
- Click the **Constraint Settings** icon on the **Parametric** panel; the **Constraint Settings** dialog appears.
- On the **Constraint Settings** dialog, click the **Dimensional** tab.
- set **Constraint format** to **Name only**.

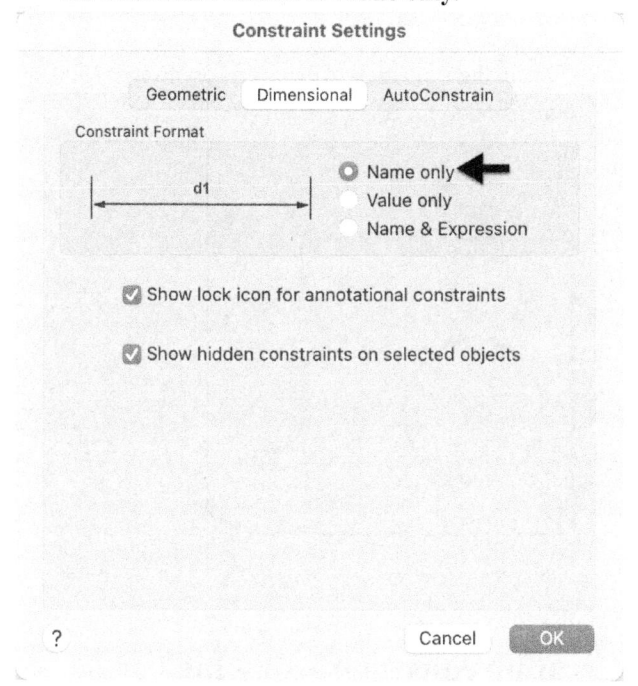

- Click the **OK** button.
- Click **Parametric > Dimensional Constraint** drop-down **> Linear** on the tool set.

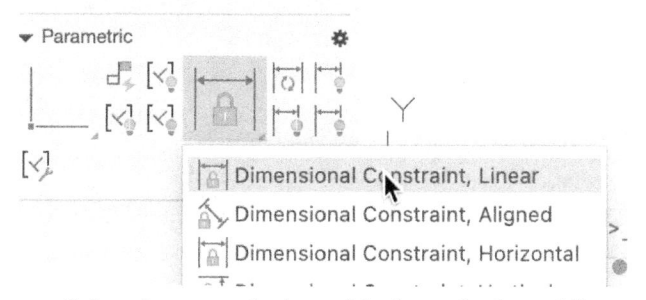

- Select the two endpoints of the lower horizontal line; the dimensional constraint is attached to the pointer.

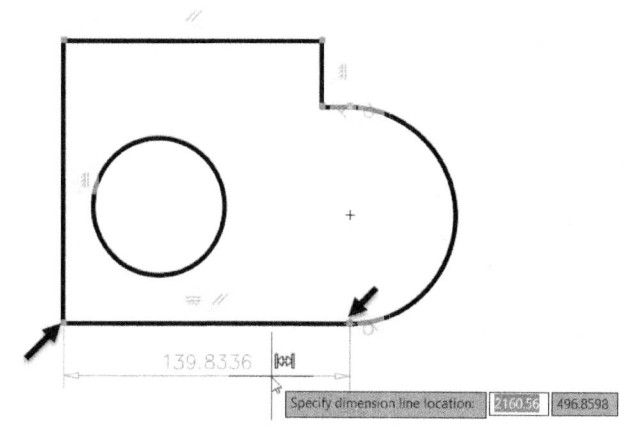

- Place the dimension constraint and left-click.

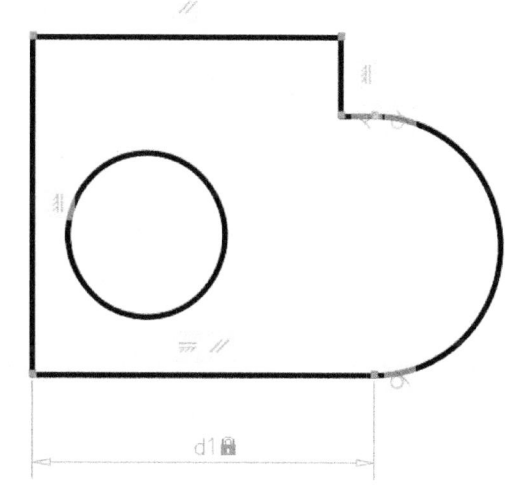

- Similarly, apply linear dimensions to other lines, as shown below.

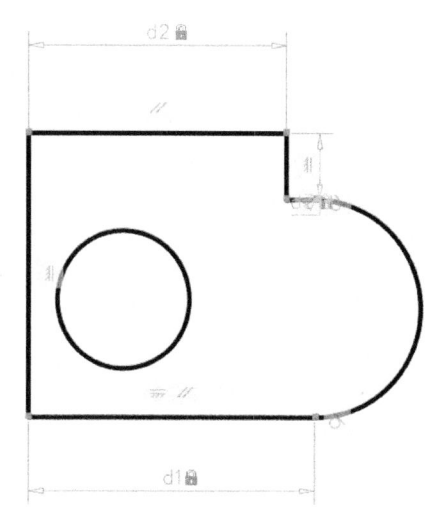

You will notice that when you try to apply the dimensional constraint to the horizontal line connected to the arc, the **Dimensional Constraints** message box

179 | Parametric Tools

appears. It shows that the dimension will over-constrain the geometry. In an over-constrained geometry, there are conflicting dimensions or relations or both. Click the **Cancel** button on the **Dimensional Constraints** message box.

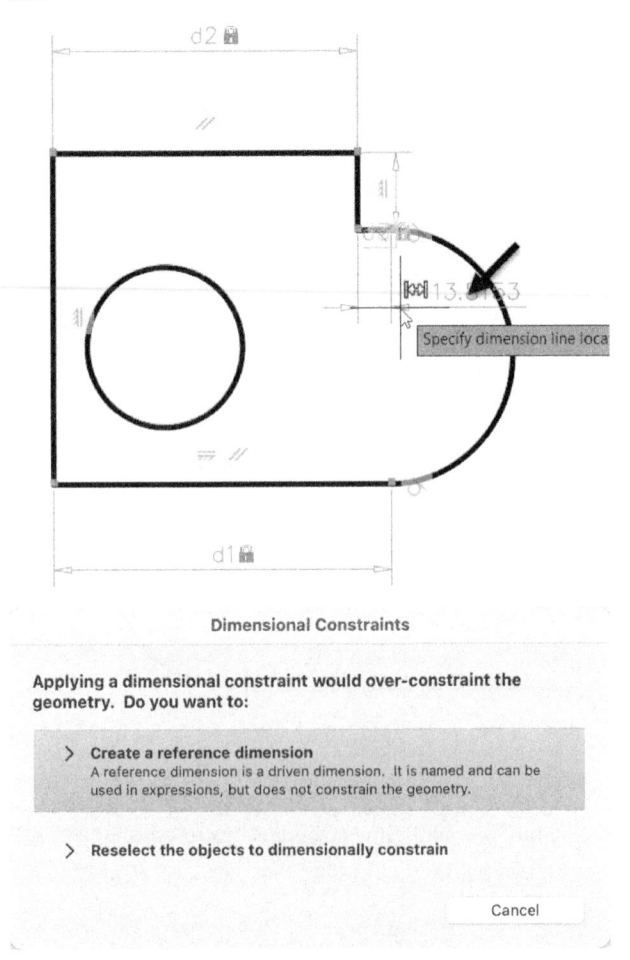

- Click the **Dimensional Constraint** drop-down > **Diameter** on the **Parametric** panel and apply the diameter dimension to the circle located on the left side.

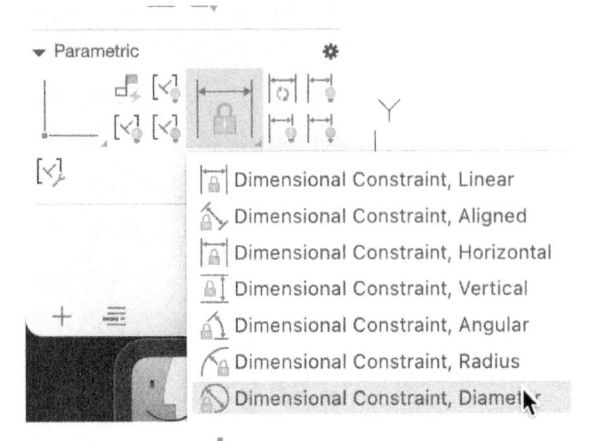

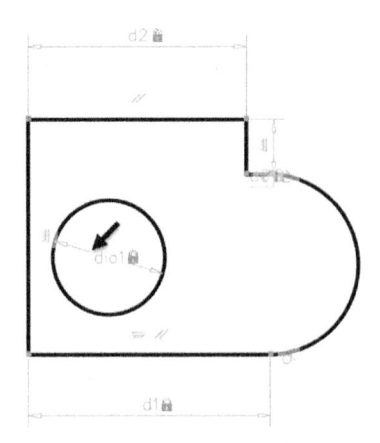

- Click **Dimensional Constraint** drop-down > **Radius** on the **Parametric** panel and apply the radial dimension to the arc.

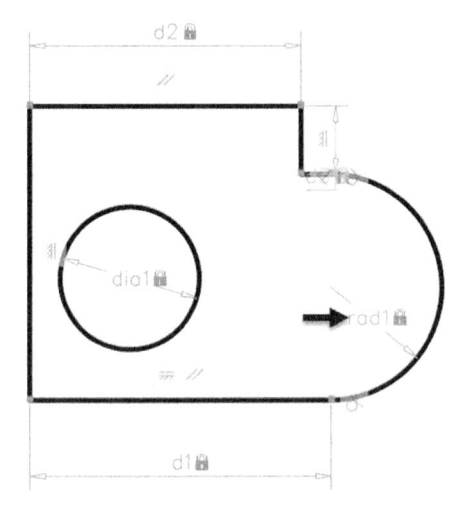

Creating equations using the Parameters Manager

Equations are relations between the dimensional constraints. Look at the drawing given below. In this drawing, all the dimensions are controlled by the diameter of the hole. In AutoCAD, you can create this type of relations between dimensions very easily using the -**PARAMETERS** command.

180 | Parametric Tools

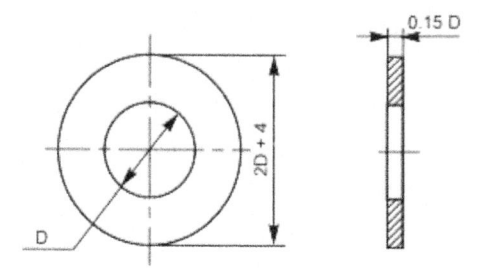

- Type **-PARAMETERS** in the command line and press RETURN.
- Right-click and select **Edit** from the shortcut menu.
- Type **dia1** and press RETURN.
- Type **50** and press RETURN twice.
- Type **E** and press RETURN.
- Type **d1** and press RETURN.
- Type **3*dia1+100** and press RETURN twice.
- Type **E** and press RETURN.
- Type **d2** and press RETURN.
- Type **3*dia1** and press RETURN twice.
- Type **E** and press RETURN.
- Type **d3** and press RETURN.
- Type **3*dia1/2** and press RETURN twice.
- Type **E** and press RETURN.
- Type **rad1** and press RETURN.
- Type **2*dia1** and press RETURN.

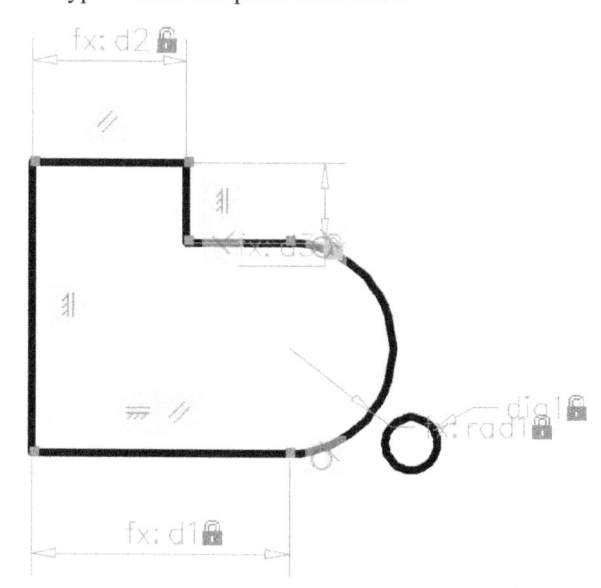

You will notice that the circle is placed outside the loop.

- Click **View > Zoom > All** on the **Menu Bar** to view the circle.

Creating Inferred Constraints

The **Infer Constraints** button helps you to create constraints automatically. With this button active on the status bar, you can automatically create constraints while drawing a sketch.

- On the status bar, click the **Customization** button and select **Infer Constraints** from the flyout. It adds the **Infer Constraints** button to the status bar.
- Activate the **Infer Constraints** button on the status bar. 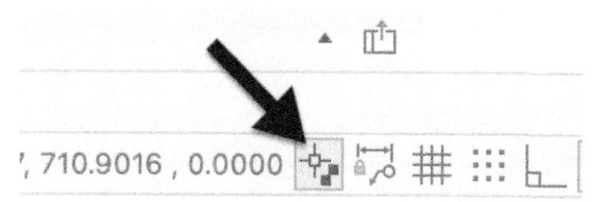
- Click the **Fillet** button on the **Modify** panel of the **Drafting** tool set.
- Right-click and select the **Radius** option from the shortcut menu.
- Type **50** as the radius and press RETURN.
- Create a fillet at the lower-left corner of the sketch.

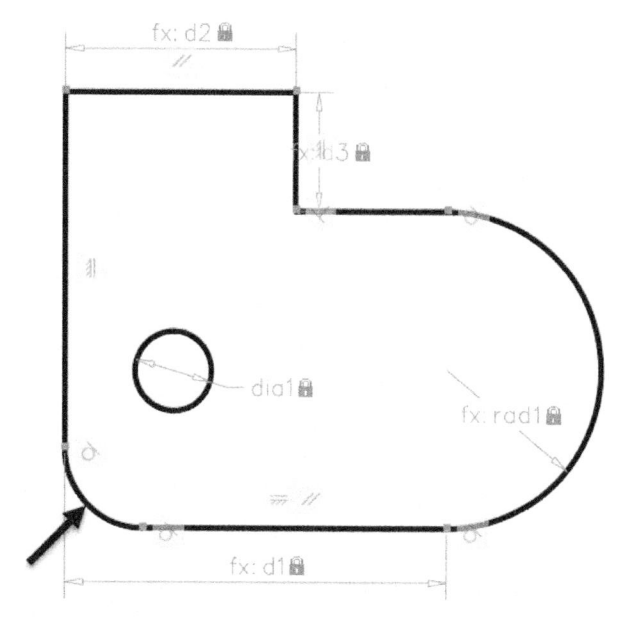

You will notice that the **Tangent** and **Coincident** constraints are applied automatically.

- Click **Geometric Constraints** drop-down > **Concentric** button on the **Parametric** panel.

Parametric Tools

- Select the circle located outside the loop and the fillet; they both will be concentric.

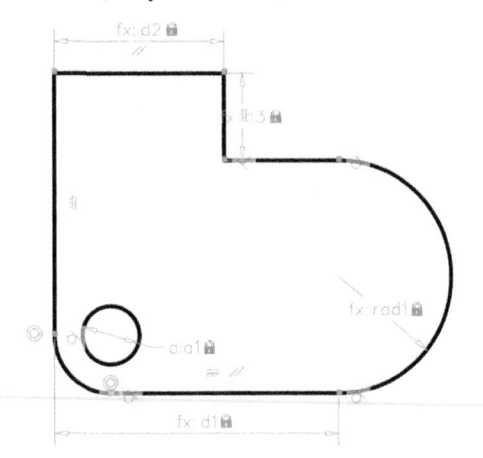

- Click **Dimensional Constraint > Radius** on the **Parametric** panel and apply the dimensional radius constraint to the fillet.
- Type **-PARMETERS** in the command line and press RETURN.
- Type **E** and press RETURN.
- Type **rad2** and press RETURN.
- Type **3/2*dia1** and press RETURN.

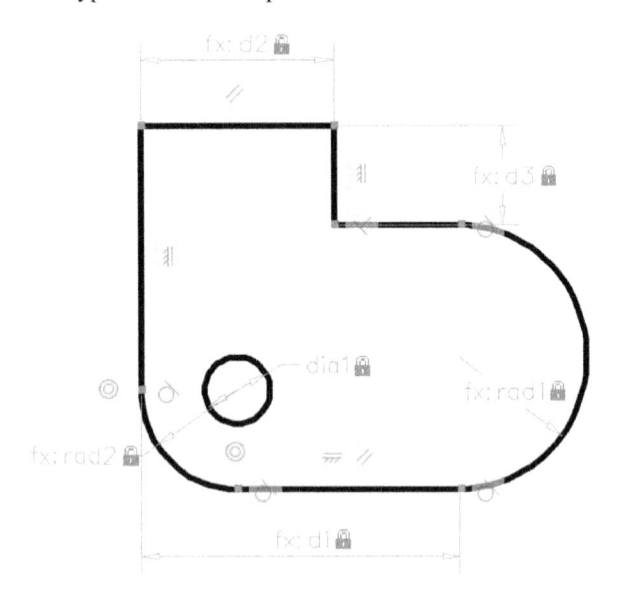

- To hide all the Geometric Constraints, click the **Hide All Geometric Constraints** button on the **Parametric** panel.

- Similarly, click **Hide All Dynamic Constraints** on the **Parametric** panel to hide all the dimensional constraints.

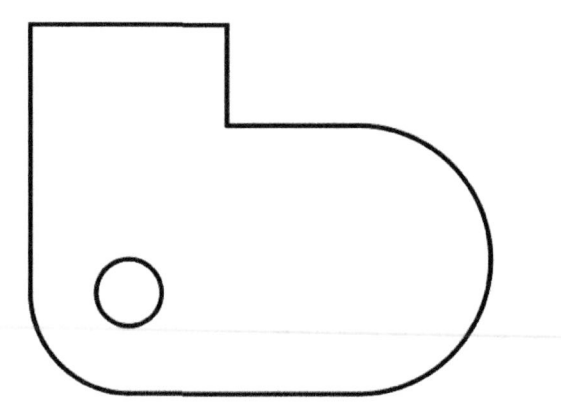

- To modify the size of the drawing, change the value of **dia1** using the **-PARAMETERS** command; you will notice that all the values will be changed automatically.
- Save and close the file.

Exercises

Exercise 1

In this exercise, you need to create the drawing shown in the figure and apply geometric and dimensional constraints to it.

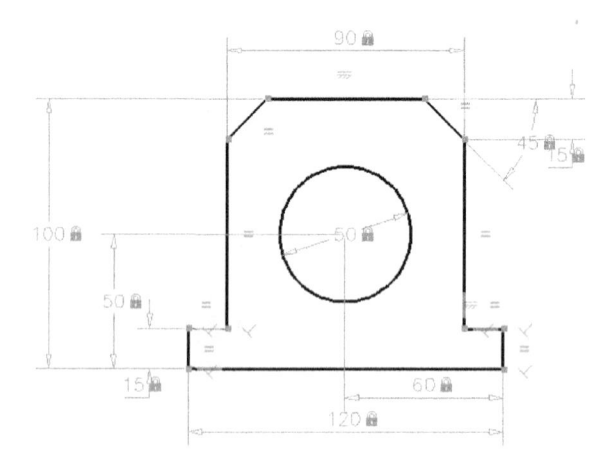

Exercise 2

In this exercise, you need to create the drawing as shown below and apply geometric and dimensional constraints to it. Also, create relations between dimensions using the -**PARAMETERS** command.

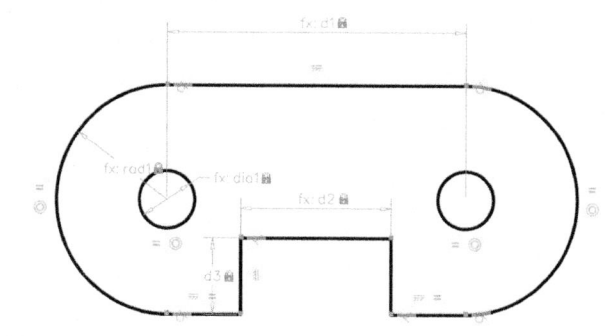

Name	Expression	Value
d1	2*d2	100
d2	2*d3	50
d3	25	25
dia1	¾*d3	18.75
rad1	2*dia1	37.5

AutoCAD 2023 For Beginners (For Mac Users)

Chapter 8: Section Views

In this chapter, you will learn to:

- **Create Section Views**
- **Set Hatch Properties**
- **Use Island Detection tools**
- **Create text in Hatching**
- **Edit Hatching**

Section Views

In this chapter, you will learn to create section views. You can create section views to display the interior portion of a component that cannot be shown clearly using hidden lines. It can be done by cutting the component using an imaginary plane. In a section view, section lines, or cross-hatch lines are added to indicate the surfaces that are cut by the imaginary cutting plane. In AutoCAD, you can add these section lines or cross-hatch lines using the **Hatch** tool.

The Hatch tool

The **Hatch** tool is used to generate hatch lines by clicking inside a closed area. When you click inside a closed area, a temporarily closed boundary will be created using the PLINE command. The closed boundary will be filled with hatch lines, and then it will be deleted.

Example 1:

In this example, you will apply hatch lines to the drawing, as shown in the figure below.
- Open a new AutoCAD file.
- Create four layers with the following properties.

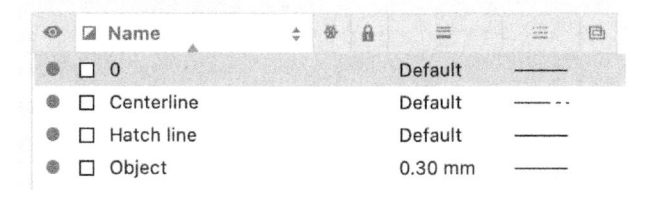

- Create the drawing, as shown below. Do not apply dimensions.

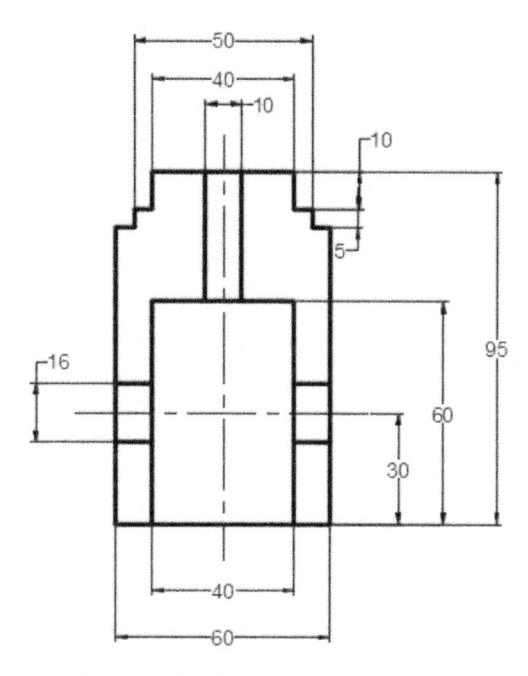

- Select the **Hatch lines** layer from the **Layer** drop-down of the **Layers** palette.
- Click **Drafting > Hatch > Hatch** on the tool set (or) type **H** in the command line and press RETURN; the **Hatch Editor** visor appears in the tool set.

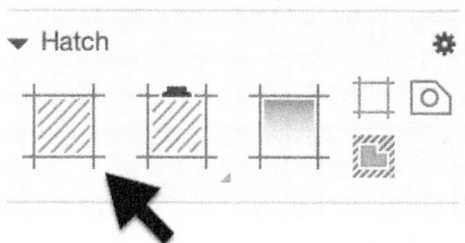

- Click the **Hatches** drop-down > **Hatches**; the **Hatch Library** appears.

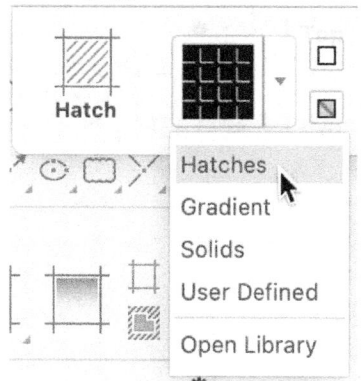

- Select ANSI from the drop-down located at the top on the Hatch library.

AutoCAD 2023 For Beginners (For Mac Users)

- Select **ANSI31** from the **Hatch Library**.

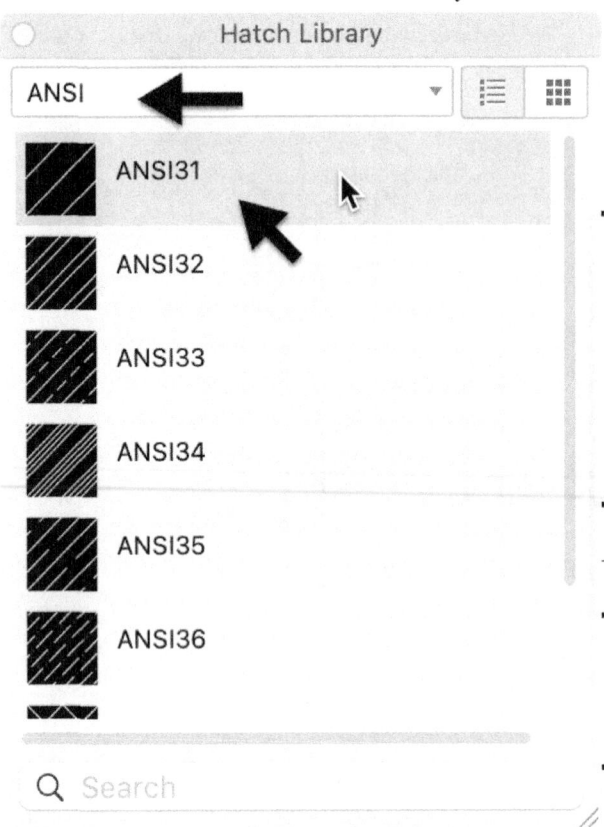

- Click on the four regions of the drawing, as shown below.

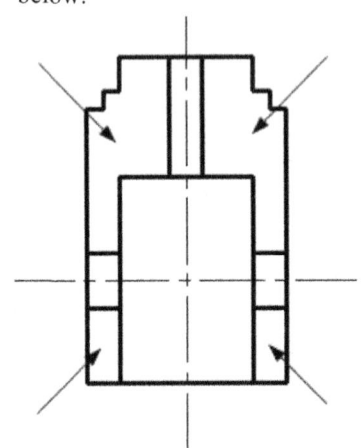

- Click the **Exit Hatch Editor and close the visor** button.

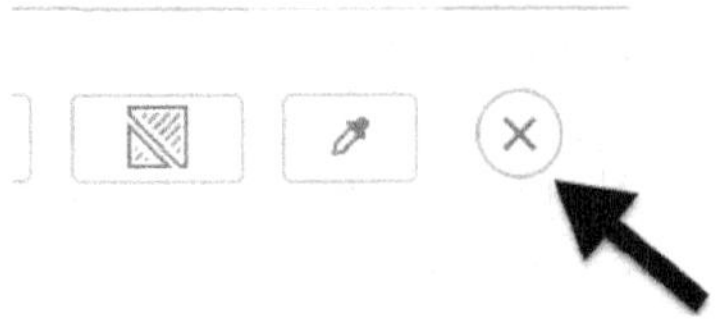

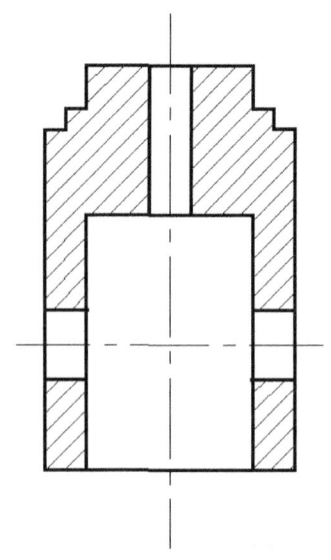

Example 2:

In this example, you will create the front and section views of a crank.

- Create five layers with the following settings:

Layer	Lineweight	Linetype
Construction	0.00 mm	Continuous
Object	0.30 mm	Continuous
Centerline	0.00 mm	CENTER
Hatch lines	0.00 mm	Continuous
Cutting Plane	0.30 mm	PHANTOM

- Activate the **Construction** layer and create construction lines, as shown.

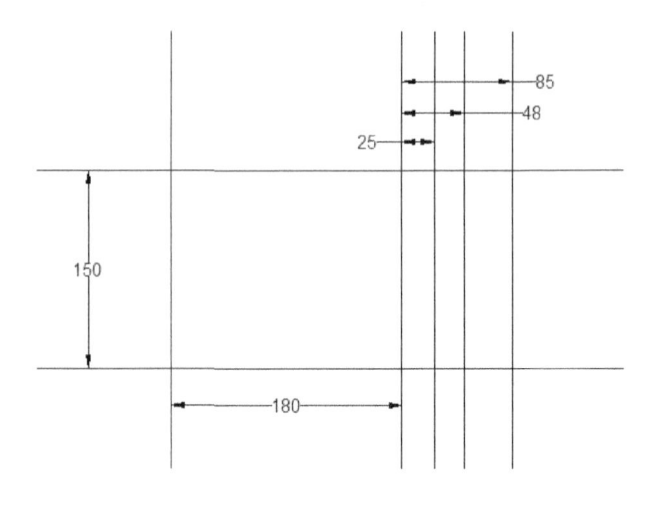

186 Section Views

AutoCAD 2023 For Beginners (For Mac Users)

- Activate the **Object** layer and create circles, as shown below.

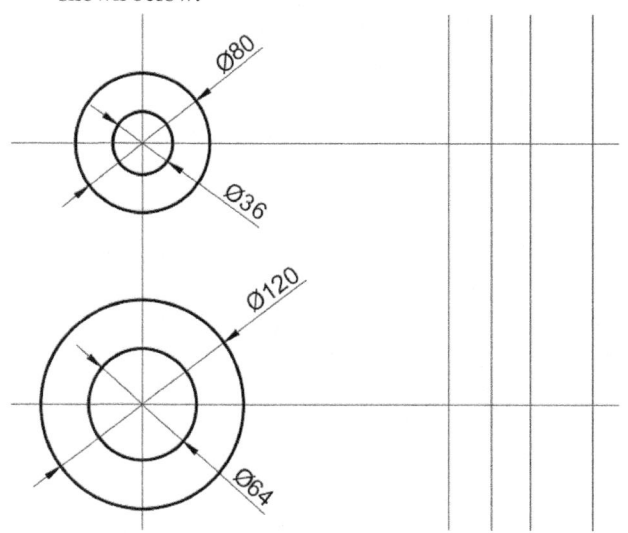

- Activate the **Construction** layer and create construction lines, as shown.

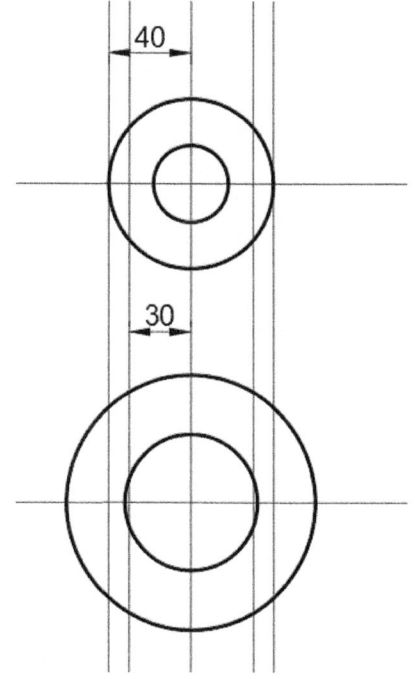

- Activate the **Object** layer and create two lines, as shown.

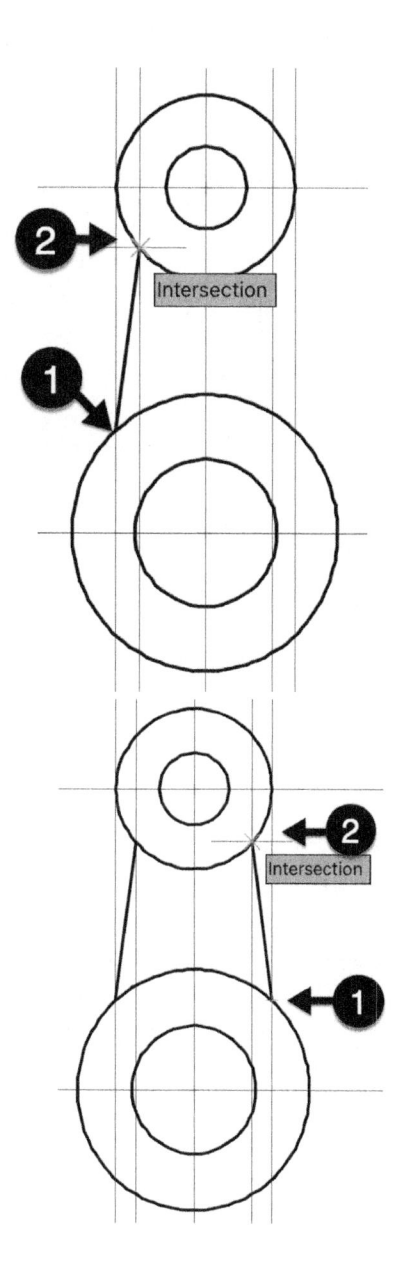

- Create the fillets at the corners, as shown.

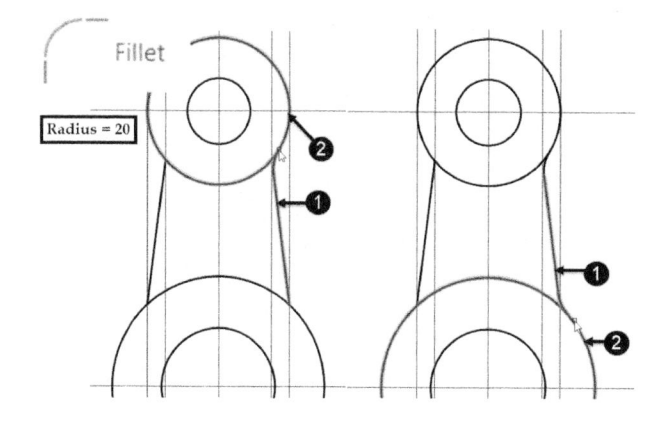

187 | Section Views

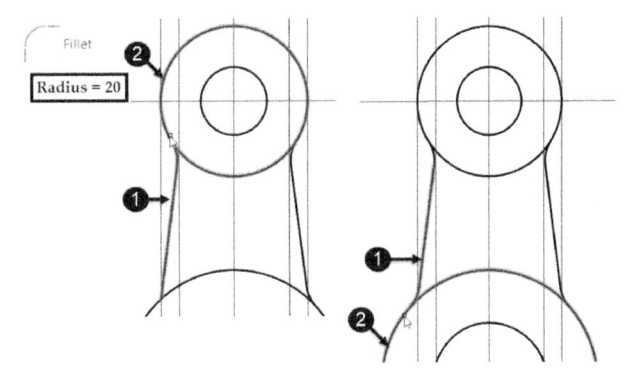

- Create a 16X38 rectangle, as shown.

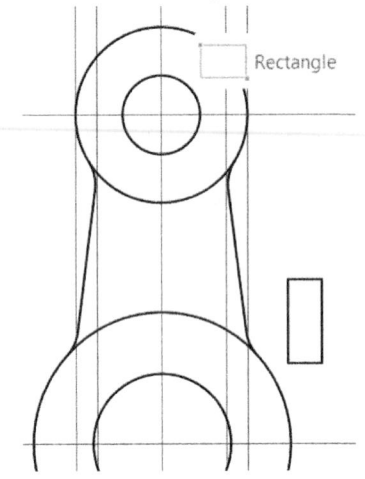

- Move the rectangle and place it at the centerpoint of the bottom circle, as shown.

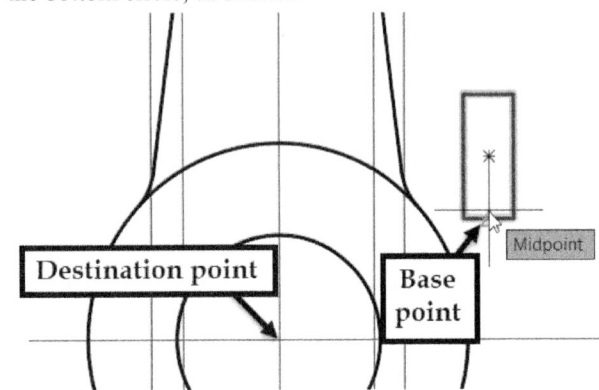

- Trim the unwanted entities of the rectangle, as shown.

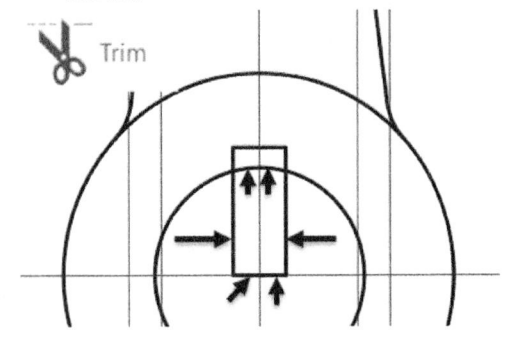

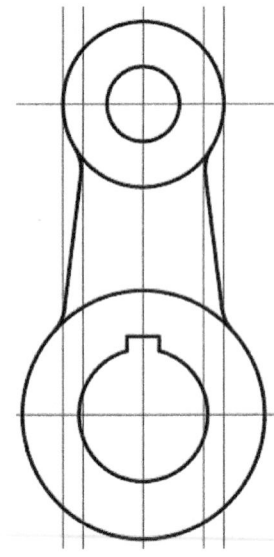

- On your own, create the objects of the section view, as shown below. (For any help, refer to the **Multi view Drawings** section of Chapter 5)

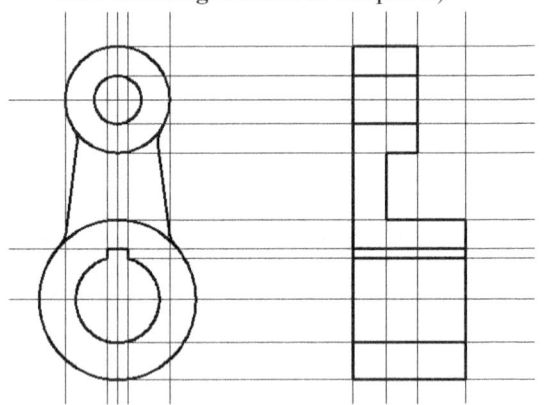

- Turn OFF the **Construction** layer.
- Activate the **Centerlines** layer and create center marks and centrelines.

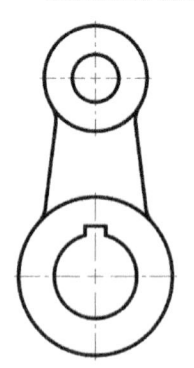

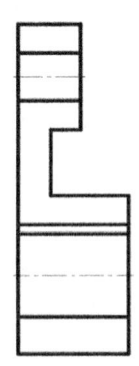

- Activate the **Cutting Plane** layer.
- Activate the **Ortho Mode** icon on the Status bar, if not already active.
- Click the **Polyline** button on the **Draw** panel and pick a point below the front view, as shown.

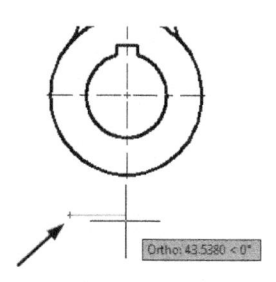

- Right-click and select the **Width** option from the shortcut menu.
- Type 0 as the starting width and press RETURN.
- Type 10 as the ending width and press RETURN.
- Move the pointer horizontally toward the right and enter 20.
- Right-click and select the **Width** option.
- Set the starting and ending width to 0.
- Move the pointer horizontally and click when trace lines are displayed, as shown below.

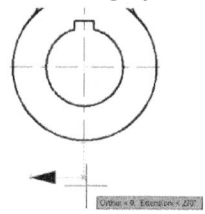

- Move the pointer vertically up and click.
- Move the pointer to the endpoint of the lower horizontal line.

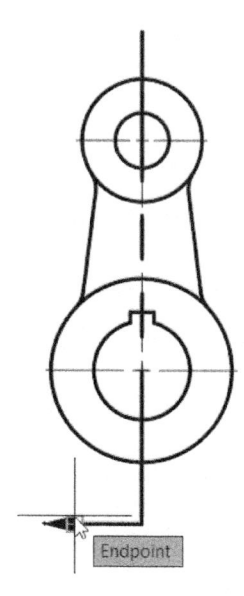

- Move the pointer upward.
- Move the pointer toward the left and click when trace lines are displayed from the endpoint of the lower horizontal line.

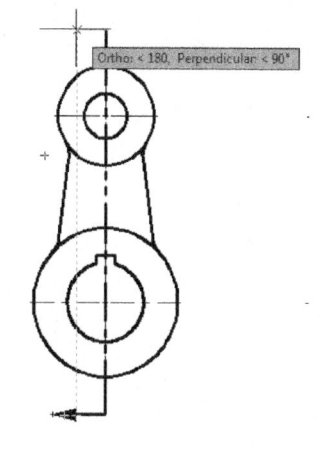

- Right-click and select the **Width** option.
- Type 10 and press RETURN.
- Type 0 and press RETURN.
- Move the pointer toward the left, type 20, and then press RETURN.

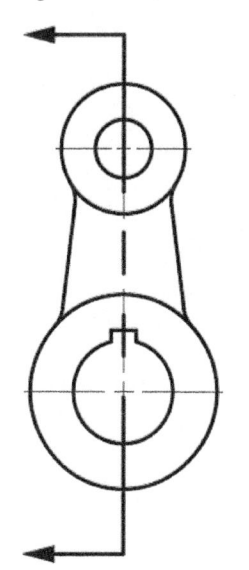

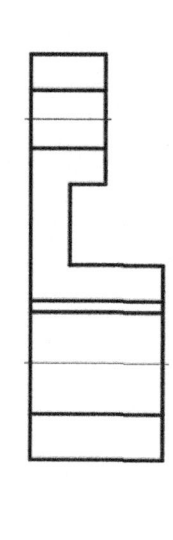

- Press Esc to deactivate the **Polyline** tool.
- Activate the **Hatch lines** layer.
- Type **H** in the command line and press RETURN.
- Right-click and select the **seTtings** option; the **Hatch and Gradient** dialog appears.
- Click in the **Swatch** box under the **Type and pattern** group; the **Hatch Pattern Palette** dialog appears.

189 | Section Views

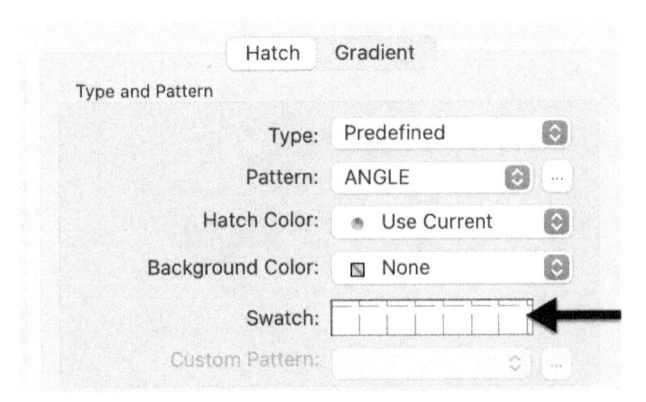

- Doouble-click on the **ANSI31** hatch on the Hatch Library.
- Set the **Scale** value to **2**.
- Click the **Add Pick Points** button from the **Boundaries** group and click in Region 1, Region 2, and Region 3. 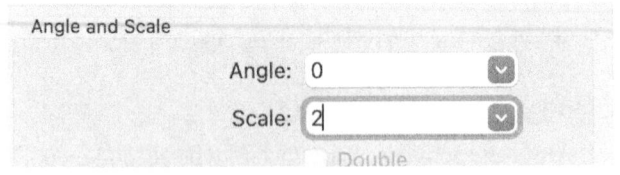
- Press RETURN to create hatch lines. 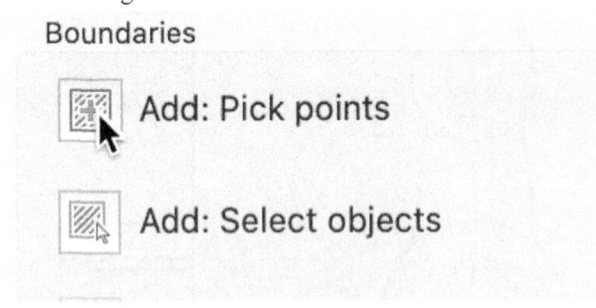 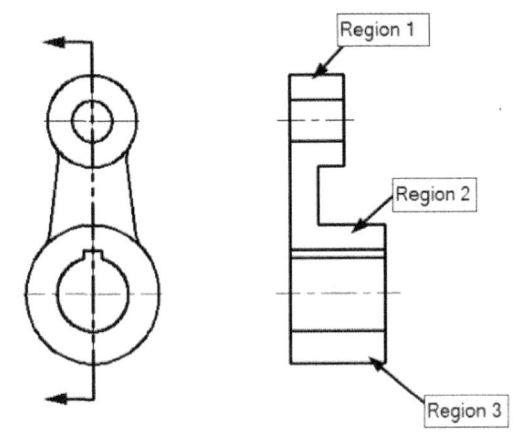
- Save the drawing as **Crank.dwg** and close. 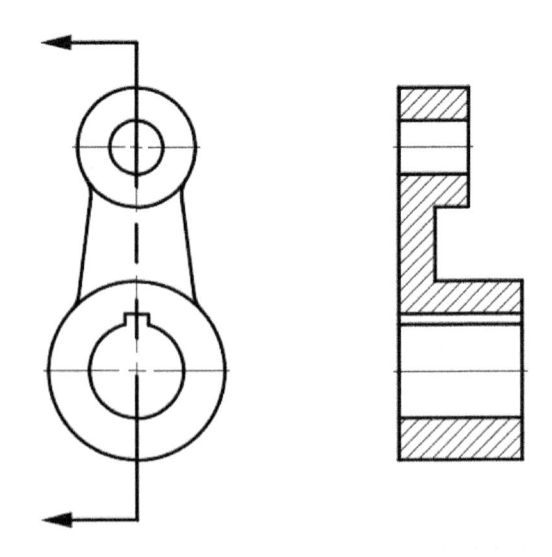

Setting the Properties of Hatch lines

You can set the properties of the hatch lines such as angle, scale, and transparency on the **Hatch Pattern Palette** dialog.

Example:
- Create four layers with the following settings.

Layer	Lineweight	Linetype
Construction	0.00 mm	Continuous
Object	0.30 mm	Continuous
Centerline	0.00 mm	CENTER2
Hatch lines	0.00 mm	Continuous

- Create the following drawing in different layers. Do not apply dimensions. 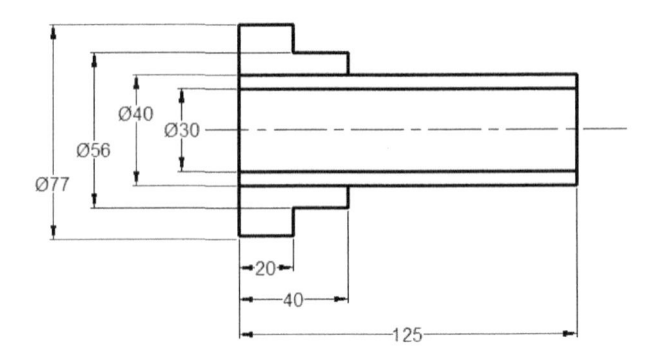
- Type **H** and press RETURN; the **Hatch Creation** tab appears in the tool set.
- Select the **Hatches** option from the **Hatch Type** drop-down in the **Hatch Editor** visor.

AutoCAD 2023 For Beginners (For Mac Users)

You can also select a different hatch type, such as Solid, Gradient, and User-defined.

- Select **ANSI31** from the **Hatch library**.
- Select **Blue** from the **Hatch Color** drop-down.

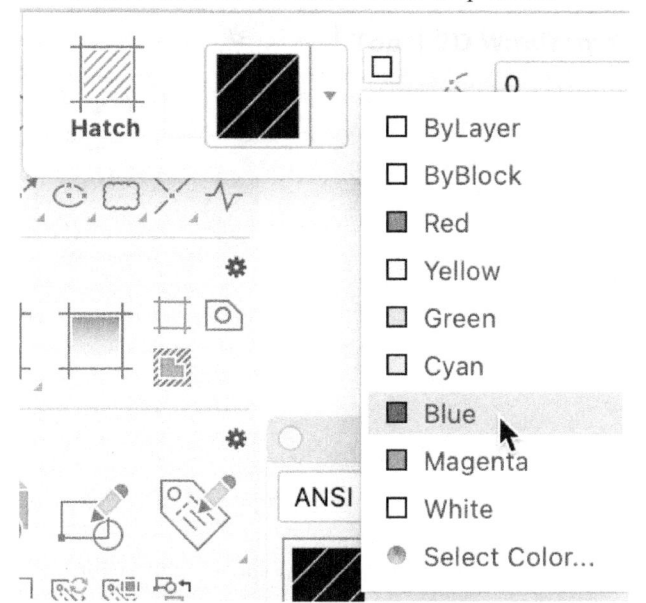

- Right-click and select **seTtings**.
- Select the **Hatch lines** from the **Layers** drop-down in the **Options** section.

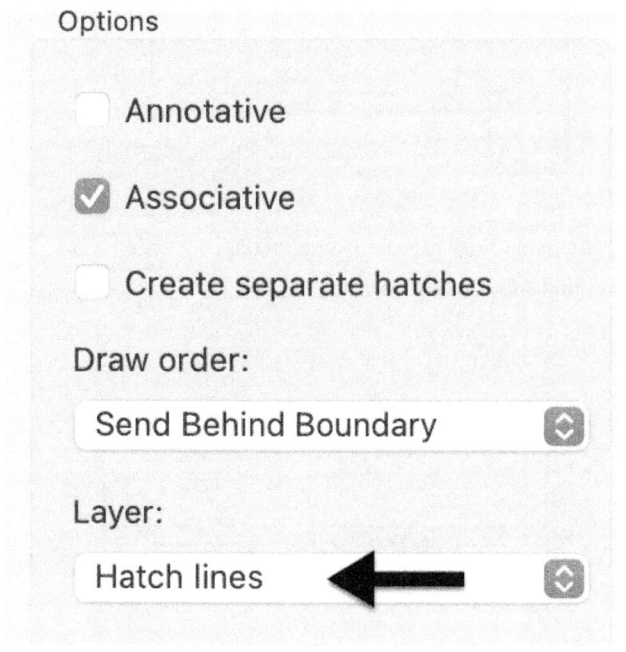

- Click **OK** on the dialog.

- Click the **Pick Points** button from the **Hatch Editor** visor.

- Pick points in the outer areas of the drawing, as shown below.

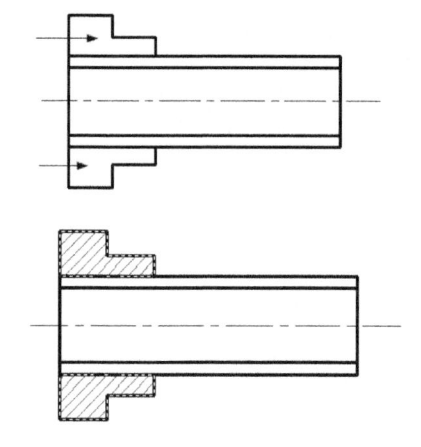

- Adjust the **Hatch Pattern Scale** to **1.5**; you will notice that the distance between the hatch lines changes.

- Press RETURN.
- Press the SPACEBAR to activate the **HATCH** command again.
- Change the **Hatch Angle** value to **90** in the **Hatch Editor** visor.

- Click the **Pick Points** button from the **Hatch Editor** visor.
- Pick points in the area, as shown below.

191 | Section Views

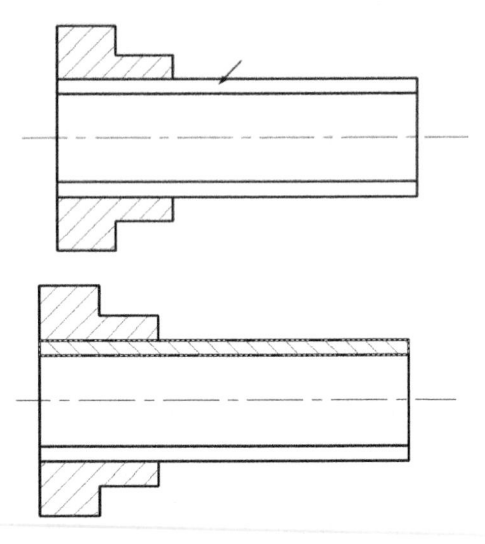

On zooming into the hatch lines, you may notice that they are not aligned properly. It is because the **Use Current Origin** button activated in the **Hatch Origin** section on the **Hatch and Gradient** dialog. As a result, the origin of the drawing will act as the origin of the hatch pattern. However, you can change the origin of the hatch pattern.

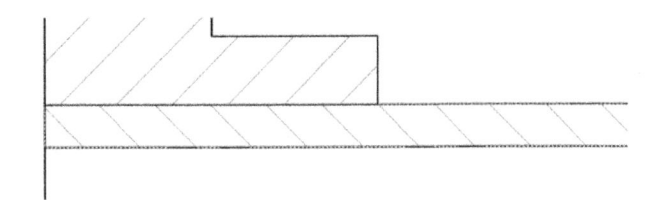

- Right-click and select **seTtings** option.
- Select the **Specified Origin** option from the **Hatch Origin** section.
- Click the **Click to set new origin** icon.

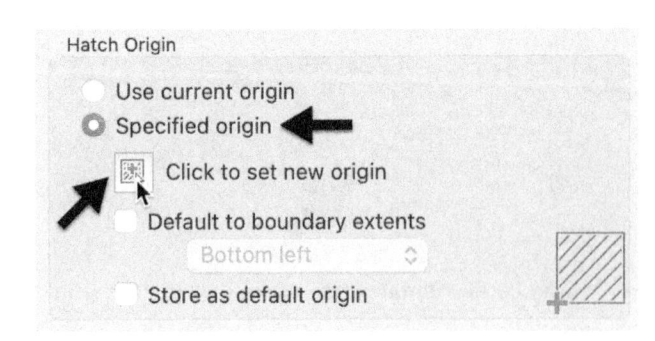

- Set the origin point, as shown below.

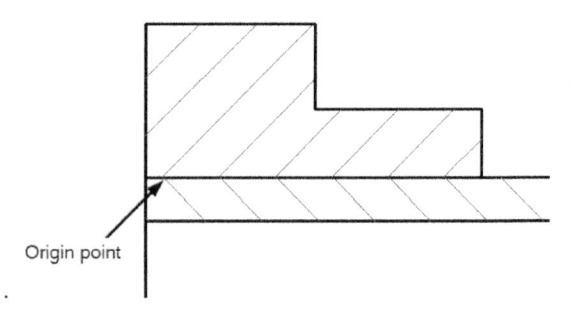

- Click **OK** on the dialog.
- Click **Exit the Hatch editor and close the visor**.
- Activate the **Hatch** tool and click **Match Hatch Properties** on the **Hatch Editor** visor.

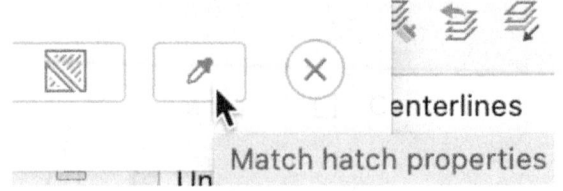

The **Match hatch Properties** tools are used to create new hatch lines by using the properties of an existing one.

- Select the source hatching, as shown in the figure.
- Pick a point in the empty area, as shown below.

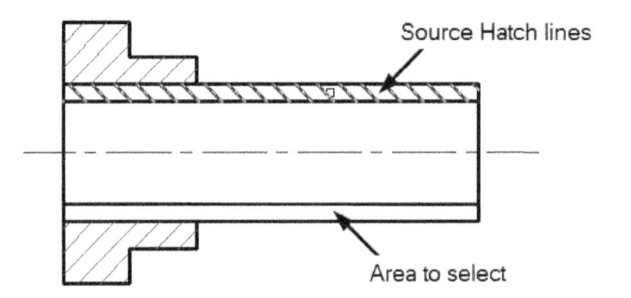

New hatch lines are created using the properties and origin of the source hatching.

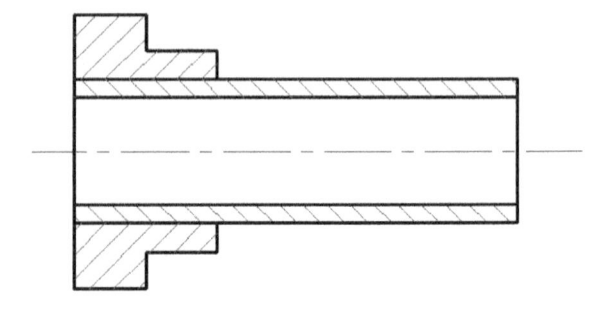

- Save and close the file.

192 | Section Views

Island Detection tools

While creating hatch lines, the island detection tools help you to detect the internal areas of a drawing.

Example:

- Create the drawing, as shown below. Do not apply dimensions.

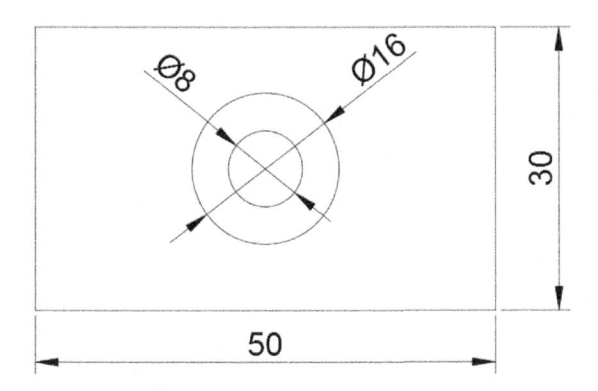

- Click **Drafting > Hatch > Hatch** on the tool set.
- Right-click and select **seTtings**.
- Select **ANSI31** using the **Swatch** box.
- Click the **More Options** icon on the bottom-right corner of the **Hatch and Gradient** dialog.

- Select the **Normal** option from the **Islands** section.

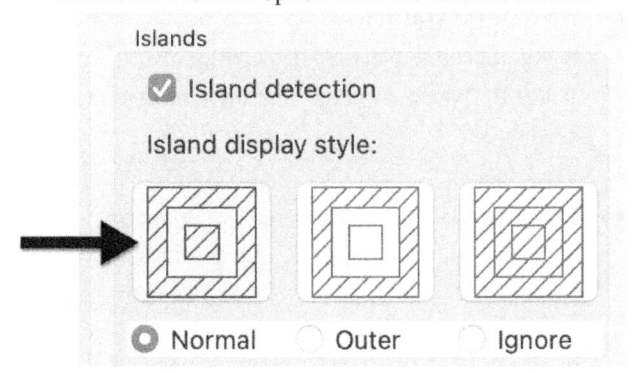

- Click **OK** on the **Hatch and Gradient** dialog.
- Pick a point in the area outside the large circle; you will notice that the area inside the small circle is detected automatically. Also, hatch lines are created inside the small circle.

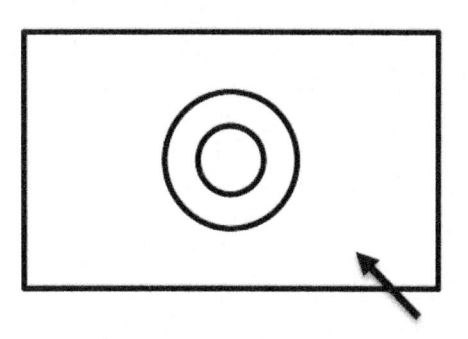

- Press RETURN.

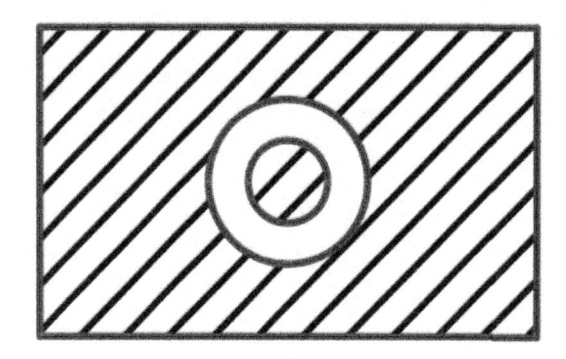

- Click **Undo** on the **Toolbar**.

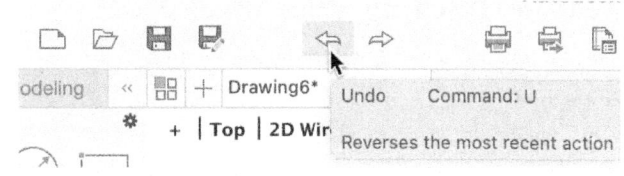

- Activate the **Hatch** tool.
- Right-click and select **seTtings**.
- Select **ANSI31** using the **Swatch** box.
- Click the **More Options** icon on the bottom-right corner of the **Hatch and Gradient** dialog.
- Select the **Outer** option from the **Islands** section.

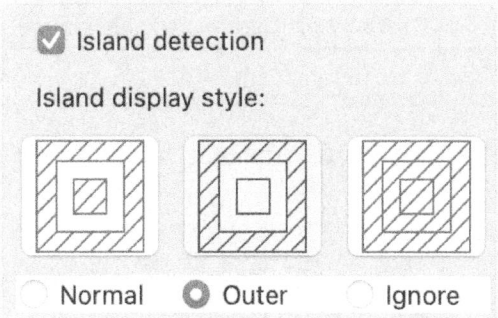

- Pick a point in the area outside the large circle and press RETURN; you will notice that hatch lines are created only outside the large circle. The **Outer Island Detection** tool will enable you to create hatch lines only in the outermost level of the drawing.

- Repeat the process using the **Ignore** option. You will notice that the internal loops are ignored while creating the hatch lines.

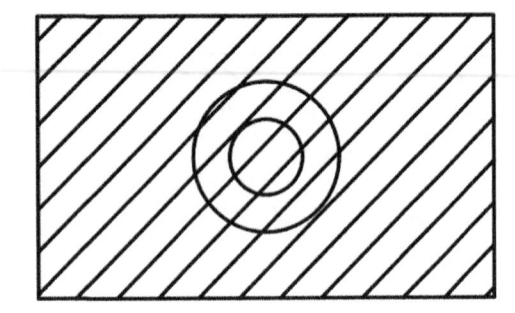

Text in Hatching

You can create hatching without passing through the text and dimensions.

- Create a drawing, as shown in the figure.

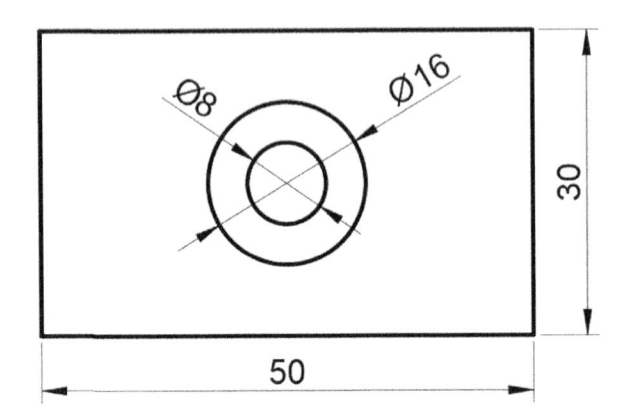

- Click **Drafting > Text > Multiline Text** on the tool set.

- Specify the first and second corners of the text editor, as shown below.

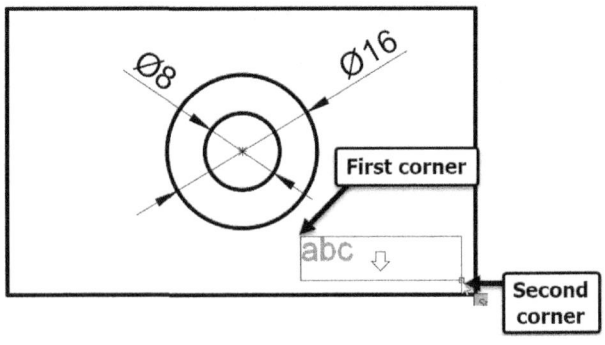

- Select **Arial** from the **Font** drop-down of the **Text Editor** visor.
- Ensure that **Text Height** is set to **2.5**.

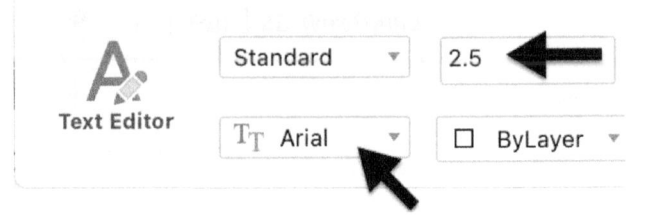

- Type **AutoCAD** in the text editor. Left-click in the space of the graphics window.

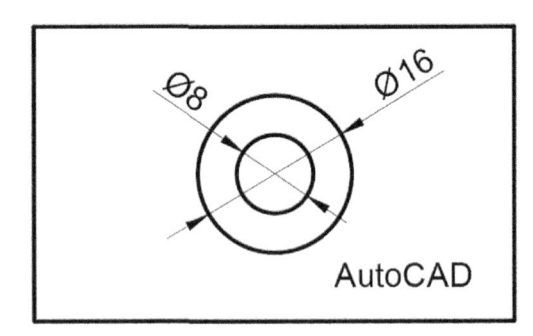

- Activate the **Hatch** tool.
- Right-click and select seTtings option.
- Select the **Normal** option from the **Island detection** section.
- Click **OK**.
- Pick a point in the area covered by the outside boundary and press RETURN; hatch lines are created.
  You will notice that hatch lines do not pass through the text and dimension.

194 | Section Views

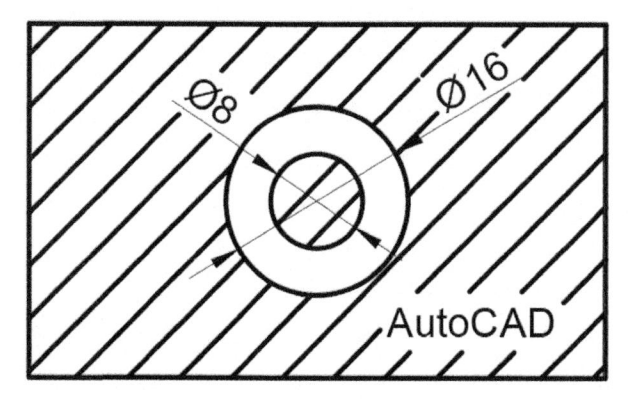

Exercises

Exercise 1

Create the half-section view of the object shown below.

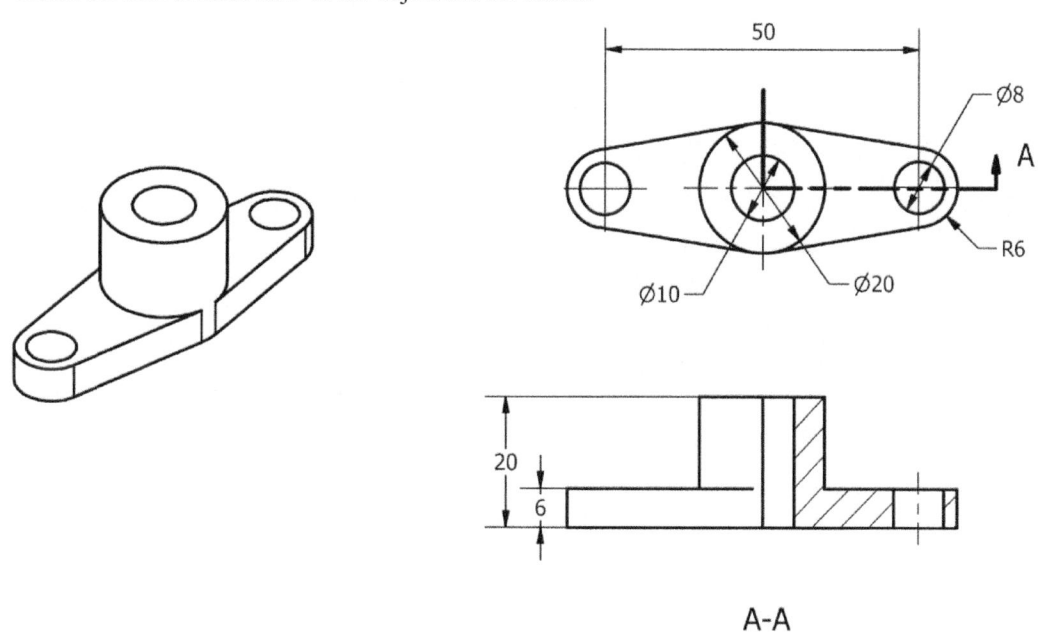

Exercise 2

In this exercise, the top, front, and right-side views of an object are given. Replace the front view with a section view. The section plane is given in the top view.

AutoCAD 2023 For Beginners (For Mac Users)

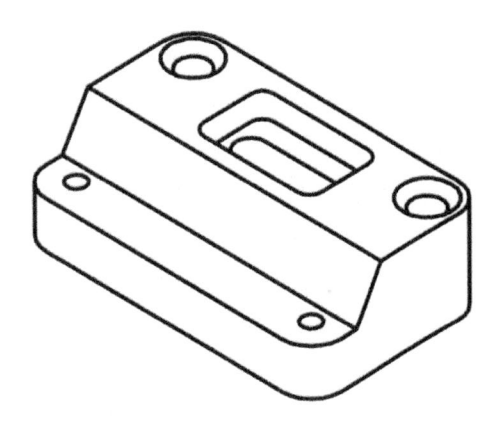

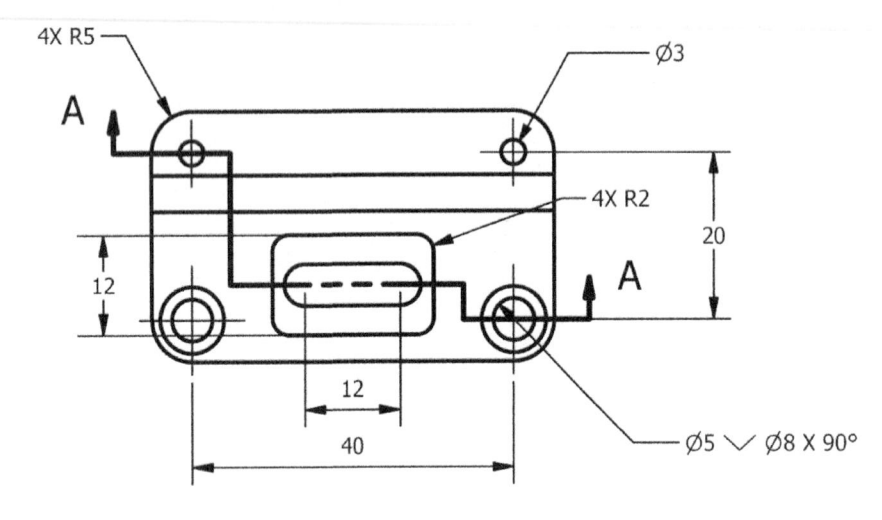

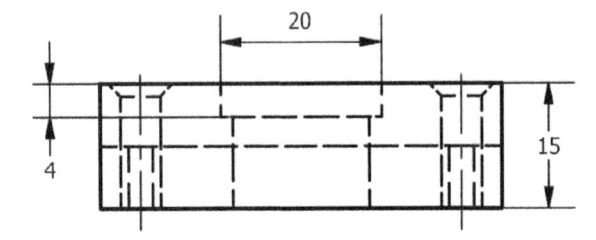

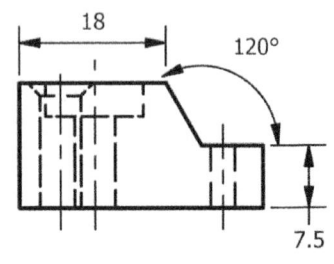

196 Section Views

Chapter 9: Blocks, Attributes, and Xrefs

In this chapter, you will learn to do the following:
- **Create and insert Blocks**
- **Create Annotative Blocks**
- **Explode and purge Blocks**
- **Use the Divide tool**
- **Insert Multiple Blocks**
- **Edit Blocks**
- **Create Blocks using the Write Block tool**
- **Define and insert Attributes**
- **Work with Xrefs**

Introduction

In this chapter, you will learn to create and insert Blocks and Attributes in a drawing. You will also learn to attach external references to a drawing. The first part of this chapter deals with Blocks. A Block is a group of objects combined and saved together. You can later insert it in drawings. The second part of this chapter deals with Attributes. An Attribute is an intelligent text attached to a block. It can be any information related to the block such as description, part name, and value, and so on. The third part of the chapter deals with the Xrefs (external references). External references are drawing files, images, PDF files attached to a drawing.

Creating Blocks

To create a block, first, you need to create shapes using the drawing tools and use the BLOCK command to convert all the objects into a single object. The following example shows the procedure to create a block.

Example 1
- Create the drawing, as shown below. Do not apply dimensions. Assume the missing dimensions.

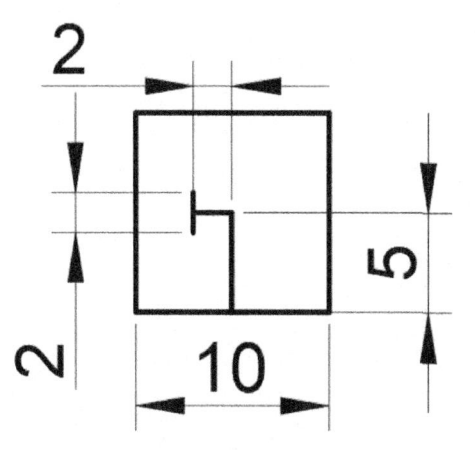

- Click **Drafting > Block > Block, Make** on the tool set; the **Define Block** dialog appears.

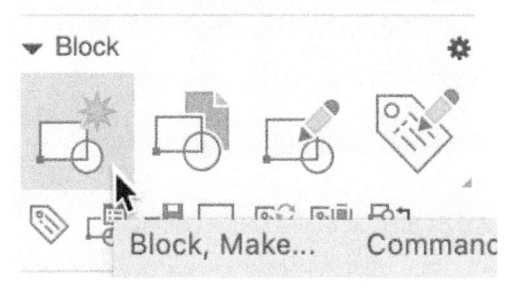

- Enter **Target** in the **Name** field.

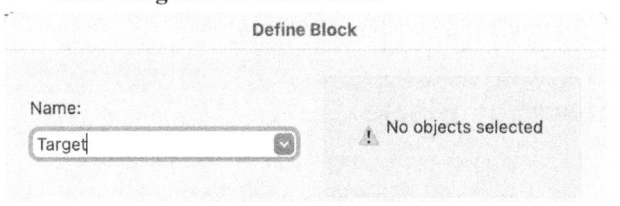

- Click the **Select Objects** button on the dialog. Drag a window and select all the objects of the drawing.
- Right-click to accept; the dialog appears again. You can choose to retain or delete the objects after defining the block. The **Retain objects** option under the **Source objects** section retains the objects in the graphics window after defining the block. The **Convert to block** option deletes the objects and displays the block in place of them. The **Delete objects** option completely deletes the objects from the graphics window.
- Select the **Delete objects** option under the **Source objects** section.
- Click the **Pick point** button on the dialog.

- Select the midpoint of the left vertical line. The selected point will be the insertion point when you insert this block into a drawing.

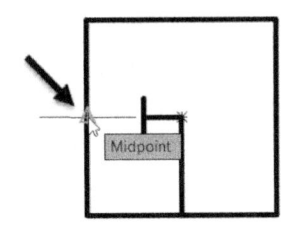

You can also add a description to the block in the **Description** box. In addition to that, you can set the behavior of the block such as scalability, annotative, and explode ability using the options in the **Block Behavior** section. The options in the **Units** area can be used to set the units of the block.

- Uncheck the **Scale uniformly** option (for this example).
- Uncheck the **Open in block editor** option, if selected.
- Click **Create Block** on the dialog; the block will be created and saved in the database.

Inserting Blocks

After creating a block, you can insert it at the desired location inside the drawing using the INSERT command. The procedures to insert blocks are explained in the following examples.

Example 1
- Click the **Blocks** tab on the palettes area.
- Right-click on the **Target** block and select **Insert in Drawing**.

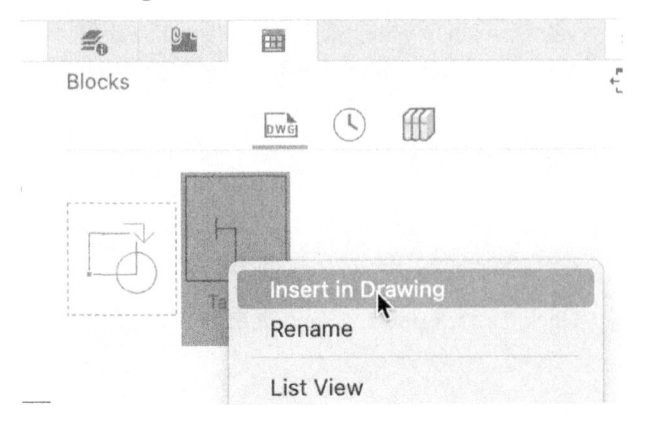

- Pick a point in the graphics window to place the block.

Example 2 (Scaling the block)

The **Blocks** palette can be used to access a large number of blocks. There are three tabs on this palette: **Blocks in current Drawing**, **Recent blocks**, and **Block Libraries**. The **Blocks in current Drawing** tab displays the blocks available in the current drawing. The **Recent blocks** tab displays the recently used blocks. The **Block libraries** tab displays the blocks available in the selected drawing files. To do this, click the **Block libraries** tab, and then click the **Browse block libraries** button. Next, browse to the required location and select the drawing file; the blocks in the drawing file are displayed on the palette. Note that you can also insert an entire drawing file as a block.

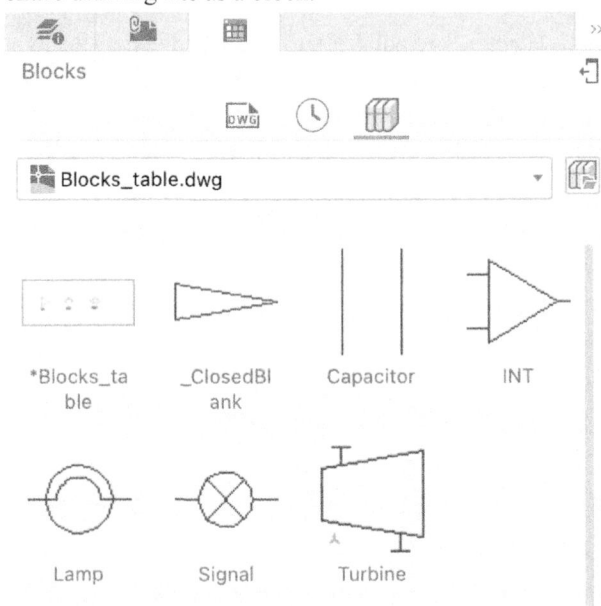

If you want to select another drawing file, then click the **Browse block libraries** icon next to the **File** drop-down. Next, select the required drawing file.

You can use the options in the **Scale** drop-down available in the **Insertion Options** section to scale the block. The **Uniform Scale** option can be used to scale the block uniformly. You can select the **Scale** option to specify the scale factor separately in the X, Y, and Z boxes. If you select the checkbox next to the **Scale** drop-down, the block can be scaled dynamically in the graphics window.

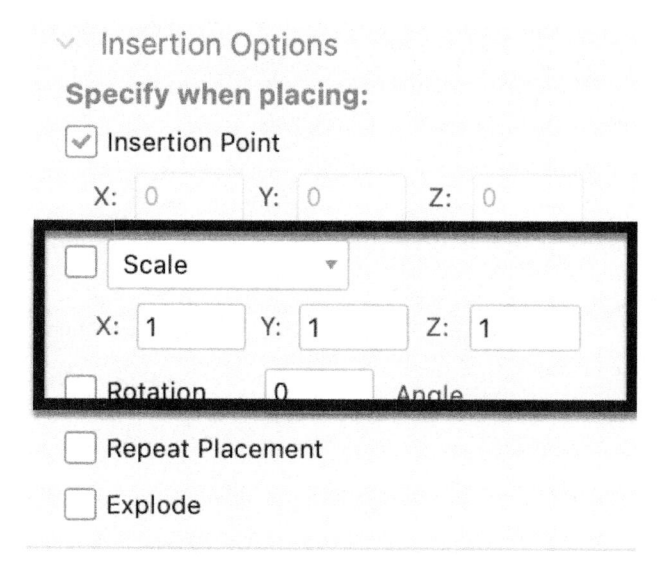

AutoCAD 2023 For Beginners (For Mac Users)

Insertion Options

Specify when placing:
- ☑ Insertion Point
  - X: 0   Y: 0   Z: 0
- ☐ Scale
  - X: 1   Y: 1   Z: 1
- ☐ Rotation   0   Angle
- ☐ Repeat Placement
- ☐ Explode

- Make sure that the **Insertion Point** option is checked.
- Select the checkbox next to the **Scale** drop-down.
- Select the **Scale** option from the **Scale** drop-down.
- Double-click on the **Target** block in the **Recent blocks** tab; the block is attached to the pointer.
- Pick a point in the graphics window; the message, "Enter X scale factor, specify opposite corner, or [Corner/XYZ]:" appears in the command line. Also, as you move the pointer, the block automatically scales.
- Type 3 and press RETURN; the message, "Enter Y scale factor <use X scale factor>:" appears.
- Type 2 as the Y scale factor and press RETURN; the block will be scaled, as shown below.

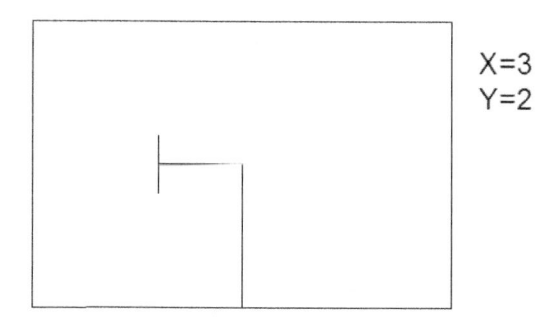

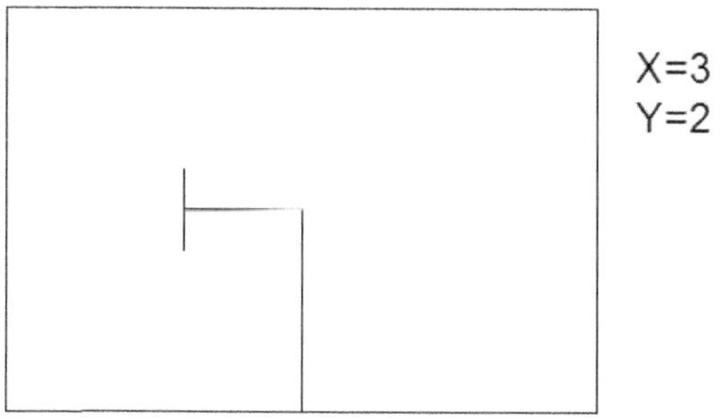

X=3
Y=2

Example 3 (Rotating the block)
- Click **Block** on the palette; the **Blocks** palette appears.
- Clear the checkbox next to the **Scale** drop-down.
- Select the **Uniform scale** option from the **Scale** drop-down.

The **Rotation** option can be used to rotate the block. You can enter the rotation angle in the **Angle** box. You can dynamically rotate the block by selecting the checkbox next to the **Rotation** option.

- Select the checkbox next to the **Rotation** option.
- Double-click on the **Target** block in the **Recent Blocks** tab; the block is attached to the pointer.
- Pick a point in the graphics window; the message, "Specify rotation angle <0>:" appears in the command line. As you rotate the pointer, the block also rotates. You can dynamically rotate the block and pick a point to orient the block at an angle or type a value and press RETURN to specify the angle.
- Type **45** and press RETURN; the block will be rotated by **45** degrees.

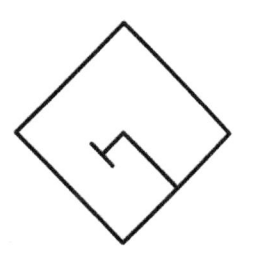

- Save and close the drawing file.

Redefining Blocks

AutoCAD allows you to redefine an already-created block.

- Download the Redefining Blocks.dwg file from the companion website.
- Open the downloaded drawing file.

- On the tool set, click **Drafting > Block > Block, Make**.
- Click the **Select Objects** button on the **Define Block** dialog.
- Create a selection window across the objects located on the left side, as shown.

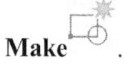

199 | Blocks, Attributes, and Xrefs

AutoCAD 2023 For Beginners (For Mac Users)

- Press RETURN to accept the selection.
- On the **Define Block** dialog, click the **Pick Point** button in the **Base point** section.
- Select the center point of the circle to define the base point of the block.

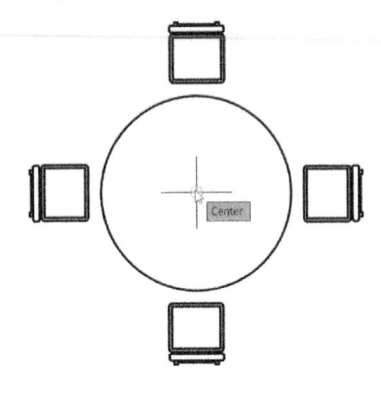

- Type **Dining Table** in the **Name** box.
- Select the **Retain objects** option in the **Source Objects** section.
- Click **Create Block** on the **Define Block** dialog; the block is created.
- Click the **Block** tab on the palettes.
- Double-click on the **Dining Table** block on the Blocks palette.
- Uncheck the **Rotation** option in the **Insertion Options** section of the **Blocks** palette.
- Click in the graphics window to insert the block.

Now, you need to redefine the Dining Table block with the objects located on the right side.

- On the **Drafting** tool set, click **Block > Block, Make**.
- Click on the down-arrow located next to the **Name** box.
- Select **Dining Table** from the list.

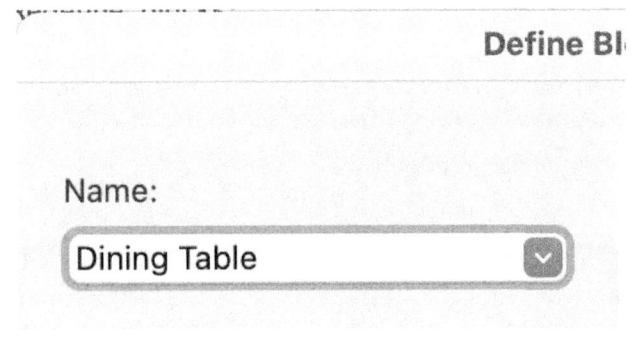

- Click the **Select Objects** button on the **Define Block** dialog.
- Create a selection across the objects located on the right side.

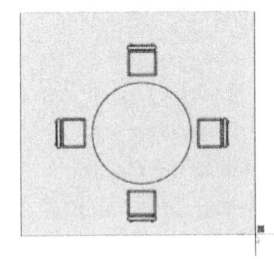

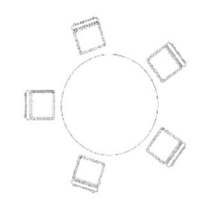

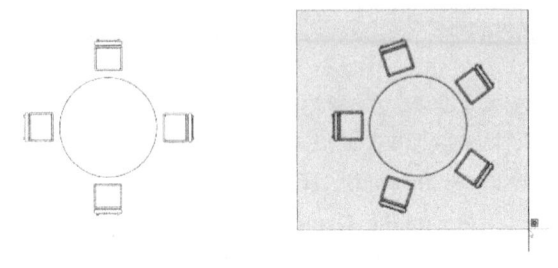

- Press RETURN to accept the selection.
- On the **Define Block** dialog, click the **Pick Point** button in the **Base point** section.
- Select the center point of the circle to define the base point of the block.

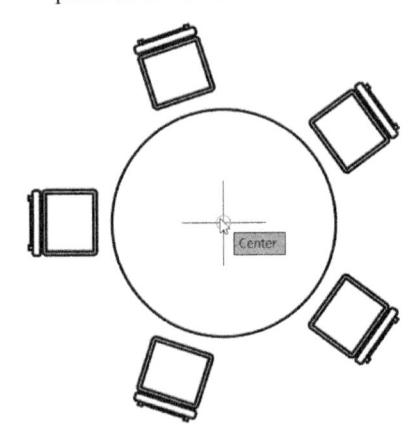

- Click **Create Block** on the **Define Block** dialog; the **Block – Redefine Block** message box appears.
- Click the **Redefine Block** option; the block is redefined and updated in the graphics window.

200 | Blocks, Attributes, and Xrefs

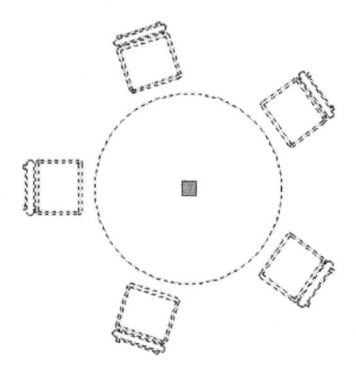

- Close the Drawing file without saving.

Creating Annotative Blocks

Annotative blocks possess annotative properties. They will be scaled automatically depending upon the scale of the drawing sheet. The procedure to create and insert annotative blocks is explained in the following example.

Example:
- Create the drawing shown in the figure. Assume the missing dimensions.

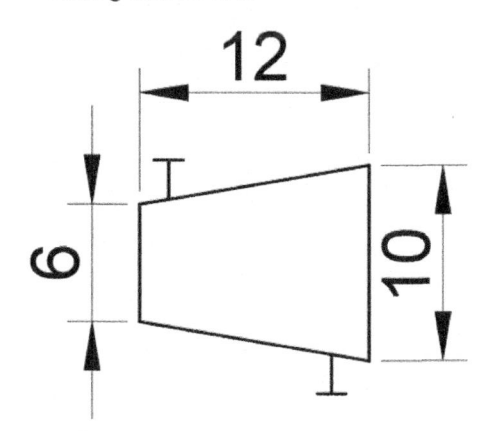

- On the **Drafting** tool set, click **Block > Block, Make**; the **Define Block** dialog appears.
- Enter **Turbine Driver** in the **Name** field.
- Click the **Select Objects** button on the dialog. Create a window and select all the objects of the drawing. Right-click to accept the selection.
- Select the **Delete objects** option under the **Source Objects** section.
- Click the **Pick Point** button and select the midpoint of the left vertical line.

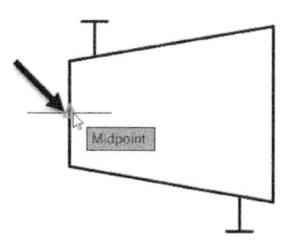

- Check the **Annotative** option under the **Block Behavior** section. Click the **Create Block** button on the dialog.
- Activate the **Automatically add scales to automated objects** button located on the right side of the Status Bar.

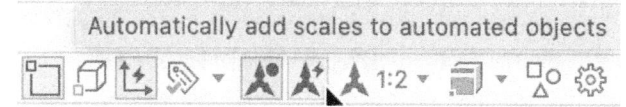

- Set the **Annotation Scale** to **1:10**.

- Double-click on the **Turbine Driver** block in the **Blocks** palette.
- Pick a point in the graphics window; the block will be inserted with the scale factor 1:10.
- Click **View > Zoom > All** on the **Menu Bar** to view the block.
- Change the **Annotation Scale** to **1:2**; you will notice that the block is automatically scaled to **1:2**.

Exploding Blocks

When you insert a block into a drawing, it will be considered as a single object, even though it consists of numerous individual objects. At many times, you may require to break a block into its parts. Use the **Explode** tool to break a block into its individual objects.

- To explode a block, click **Drafting > Modify > Explode** on the tool set (or) type EXPLODE in the command line and press RETURN.
- Select the block and press RETURN; the block will be broken into individual objects. You can select the individual objects by clicking on them. (Refer to the Explode Tool section of Chapter 4).

Using the Purge tool

You can remove the unused blocks and other unwanted drawing items from the database using the **Purge** tool. This tool also allows you to find non-purgeable items from the current drawing.

- To activate the **Purge** tool, click **Purge** on the toolbar; the **Purge** dialog appears.

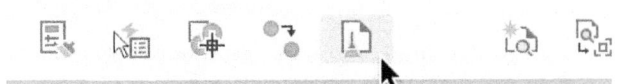

- Click the **Find Non-Purgeable Items** button on the dialog to view the items that cannot be purged. The items that are currently displayed in the drawing cannot be purged. Also, the items such as styles, layers, and linetypes that are currently used in the drawing cannot be purged. You can expand the node under the All items tree to view the individual items that cannot be purged. Next, select the item to view the possible reasons not to purge in the **Reasons** tab.

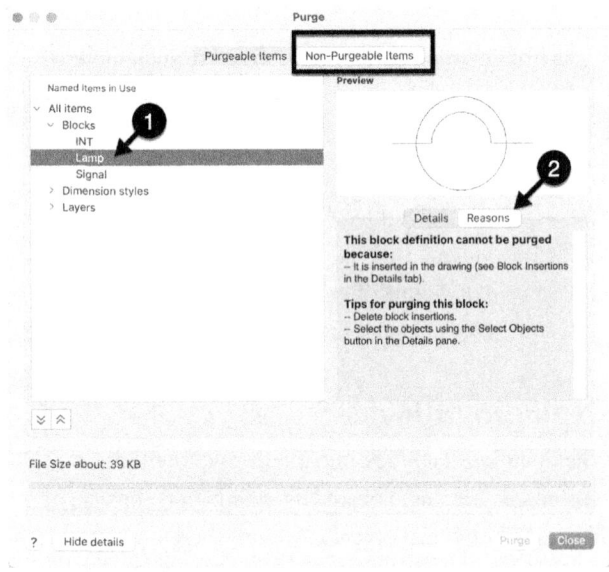

- Click the **Purgeable Items** button to view the items in the drawing that can be purged.
- To remove unwanted blocks from the database, expand the **Blocks** tree, and select the blocks.

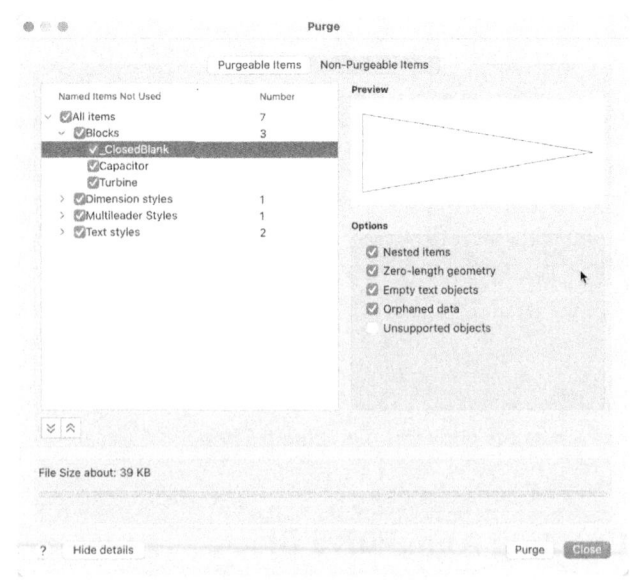

- Click the **Purge** button on the dialog
- Click **Close** on the **Purge** dialog.

Using the Divide tool

The **Divide** tool is used to place many instances of an object equally spaced on a line segment. You can also place blocks on a line segment. The following example shows you to divide a line using the **Divide** tool.

Example:
- Create the object, as shown in the figure.

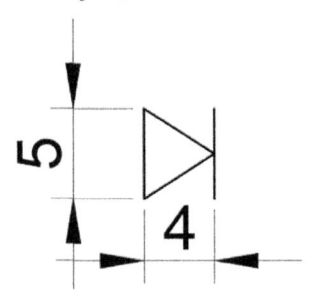

- Create a block with the name **Diode**. Specify the midpoint of the left vertical line as the base point.

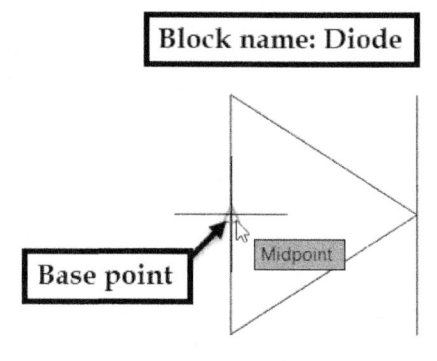

- Create a line of 50 mm length and 45 degrees inclination.

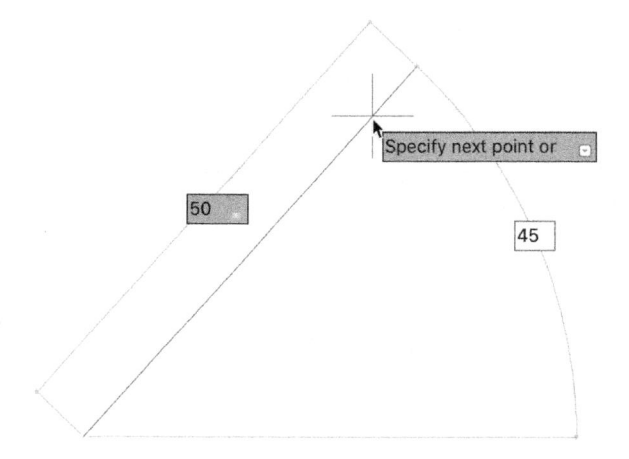

- On the **Drafting** tool set, click **Draw** panel > **Point** drop-down > **Divide**.

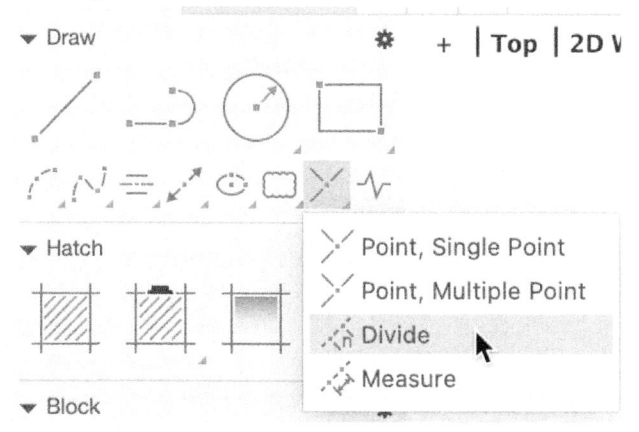

- Select the line segment; the message, "Enter the number of segments or [Block]:" appears.
- Right-click and select the **Block** option from the shortcut menu; the message, "Enter name of block to insert," appears.
- Type **Diode** and press RETURN; the message, "Align block with object? [Yes/No] <Y>:" appears.
- Type Y and press RETURN; the message, "Enter the number of segments:" appears.
- Type **5** and press RETURN; the line segment will be divided into five segments, and four instances of blocks will be placed.

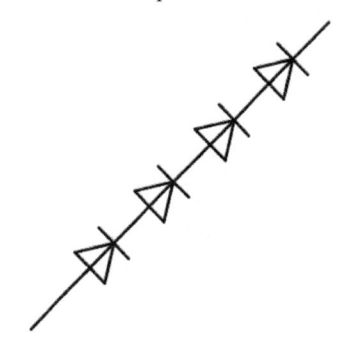

- Trim the unwanted portions, as shown below.

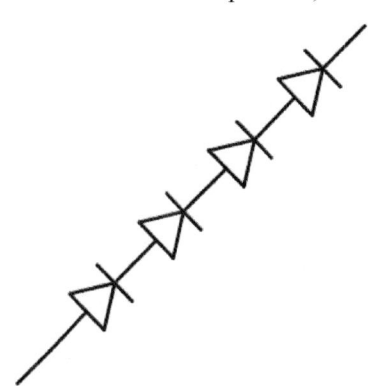

Renaming Blocks

You can rename blocks at any time. The procedure to rename blocks is discussed next.

- On the Menu bar, click **Format** > **Rename** or type **RENAME** in the command line and press RETURN; the **Rename** dialog appears.
- In the **Rename** dialog, select **Blocks** from the **Named Objects** list.
- Select the block to be named from the **Items** list.

203 | Blocks, Attributes, and Xrefs

AutoCAD 2023 For Beginners (For Mac Users)

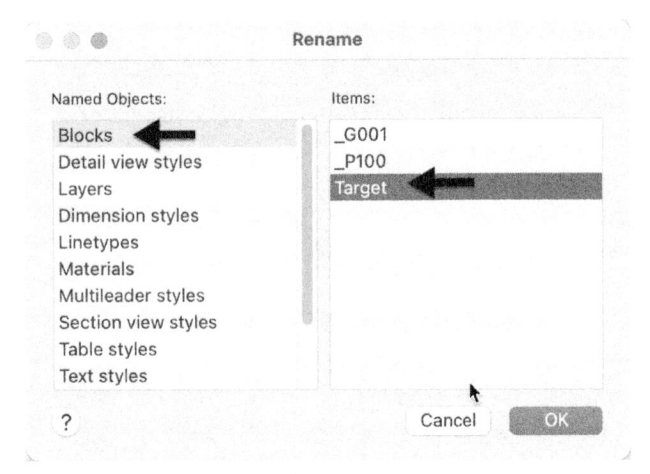

- Enter a new name.

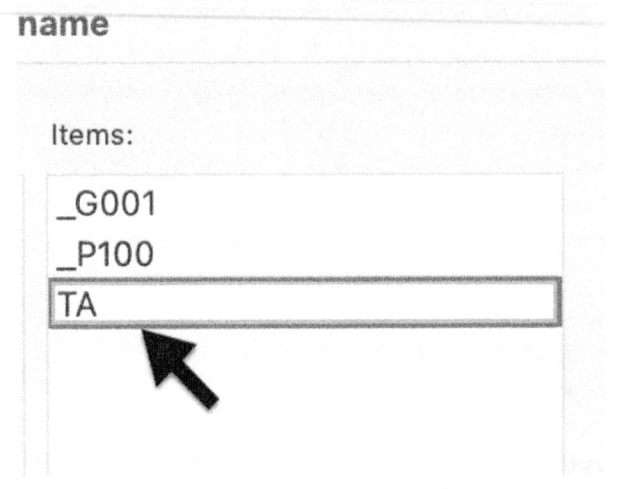

- Click **OK**; the block will be renamed.

Inserting Blocks in a Table

You can insert blocks in a table and fit inside the table cells. Note that you cannot insert Annotative blocks in a table. The following example shows you to insert a block in a table.

Example:
- Create three blocks, as shown below. You can also download them from the companion website.

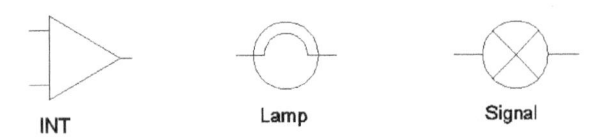

  INT   Lamp   Signal

- On the **Drafting** tool set, click **Table > Table**.

- Click in the drawing area to specify the first corner of the table.
- Move the pointer toward right such that two columns are displayed.
- Move the pointer downward such that four rows and a header row is displayed.
- Click to create the table.

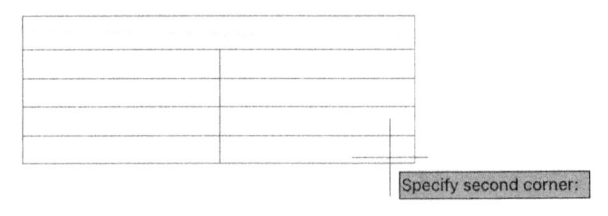

- Type-in text in the table cells (double-click in the cells and type), as shown below.

Electronic/Electrical Symbols	
Symbol	Name
	INT
	Lamp
	Signal

- Select the first cell in the **Symbol** row.
- Click the **Insert Block** icon on the **Table Cell** visor.

- In the **Insert Block in Table Cell** dialog, select **INT** from the **Name** drop-down.
- Set **Overall cell alignment** to **Middle Center**.

204 Blocks, Attributes, and Xrefs

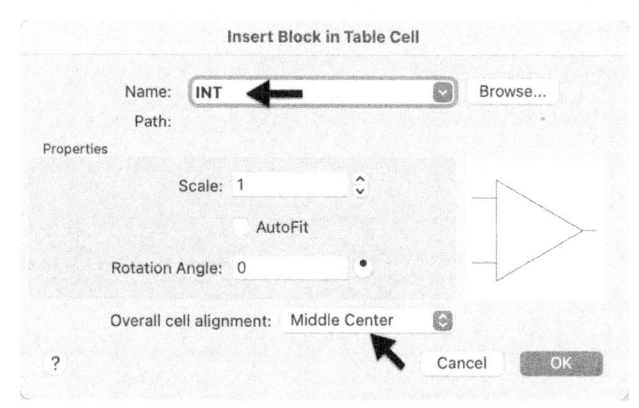

- Click **OK**; the **INT** symbol will be placed in the selected cell.

Electronic/Electrical Symbols	
Symbol	Name
	INT
	Lamp
	Signal

- Likewise, insert the other symbols in the corresponding cells.

Electronic/Electrical Symbols	
Symbol	Name
	INT
	Lamp
	Signal

Inserting Multiple Blocks

You can insert multiple instances of a block at a time by using the **MINSERT** command. This command is similar to the **ARRAY** command. The following example explains the procedure to insert multiple blocks at a time.

Example:

- Create two blocks, as shown below.

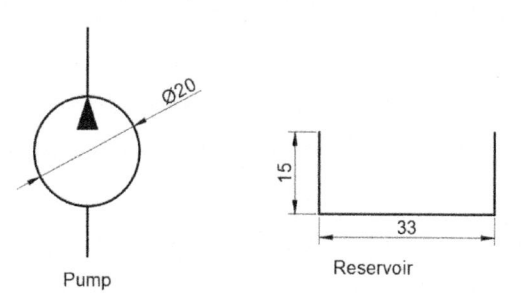

- Type **MINSERT** in the command line and press RETURN; the message, "Enter block name or [?]:" appears.
- Type **Pump** and press RETURN; the Pump is attached to the pointer.
- Pick a point in the graphics window.
- Enter 1 as the scale factor.
- Enter 0 as the rotation angle; the message, "Enter number of rows (---) <1>:" appears.
- Enter 1 as the row value; the message, "Enter number of columns (|||) <1>:" appears.
- Enter 4 as the column value; the message, "Specify distance between columns (|||):" appears.
- Type 60 and press RETURN; the pumps will be inserted as shown below.

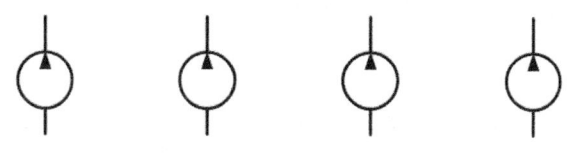

- Likewise, insert the reservoirs and create lines, as shown below.

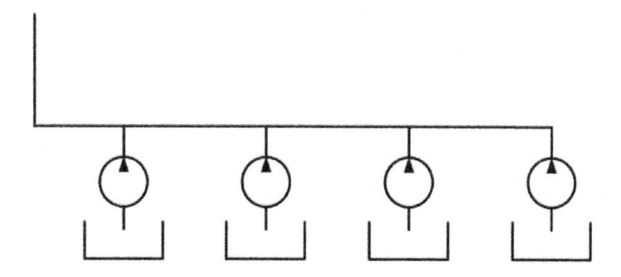

Editing Blocks

During the design process, you may need to edit blocks. You can easily edit a block using the **Block Editor** window. As you edit a block, all the instances of it will be automatically updated. The procedure to edit a block is discussed next.

- Click **Block > Block Editor** on the **Drafting** tool set; the **Edit Block Definition** dialog appears.

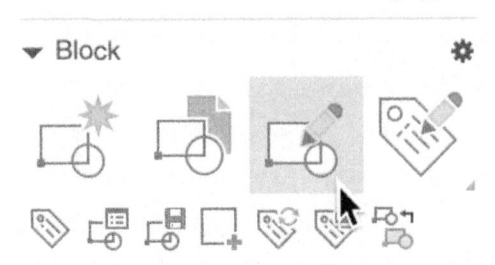

- In the **Edit Block Definition** dialog, select **Pump** from the list and click **Edit Block**; the **Block Editor** visor appears.

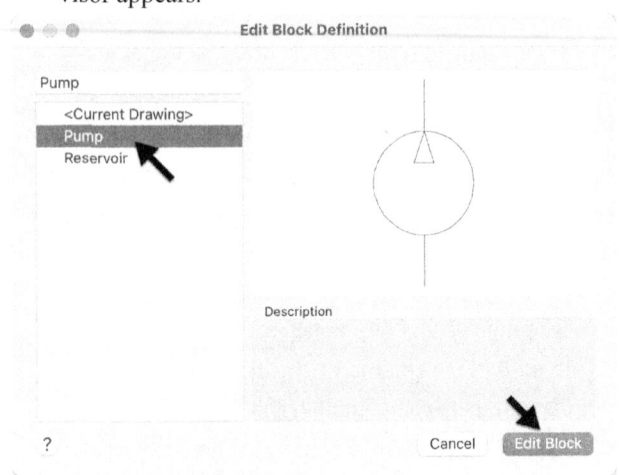

- Click **Drafting > Draw > Polyline** on the tool set and draw a polyline, as shown below.

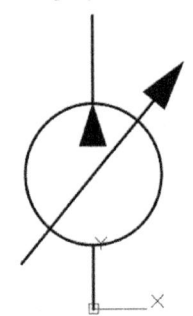

- Click **Save** on the **Block Editor** visor.

- Click **Exit Block Editor and close visor**.

All the instances of the block will be updated automatically.

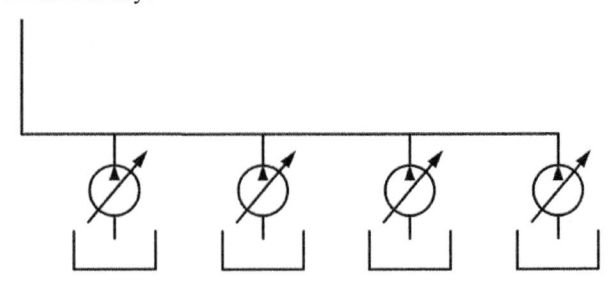

Using the Write Block tool

Using the **Write Block** tool, you can create a drawing file from a block or objects. You can later insert this drawing file as a block into another drawing. The procedure to create a drawing file using blocks is discussed in the following example.

Example:

- Start a new drawing file and create two blocks, as shown below. You can also download them from the companion website.

- Insert the blocks and create the drawing, as shown below.

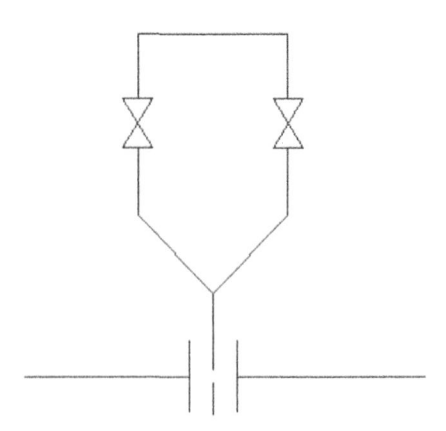

- Click the **Base** icon on the **Block** panel on the **Drafting** tool set.

206 | Blocks, Attributes, and Xrefs

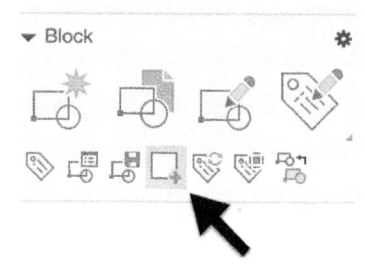

- Select the endpoint of the lower horizontal line, as shown.

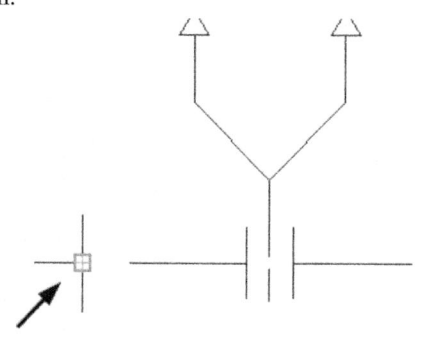

- Click **Write Block** on the **Block** panel of the **Drafting** tool set; the **Write Block** dialog appears.

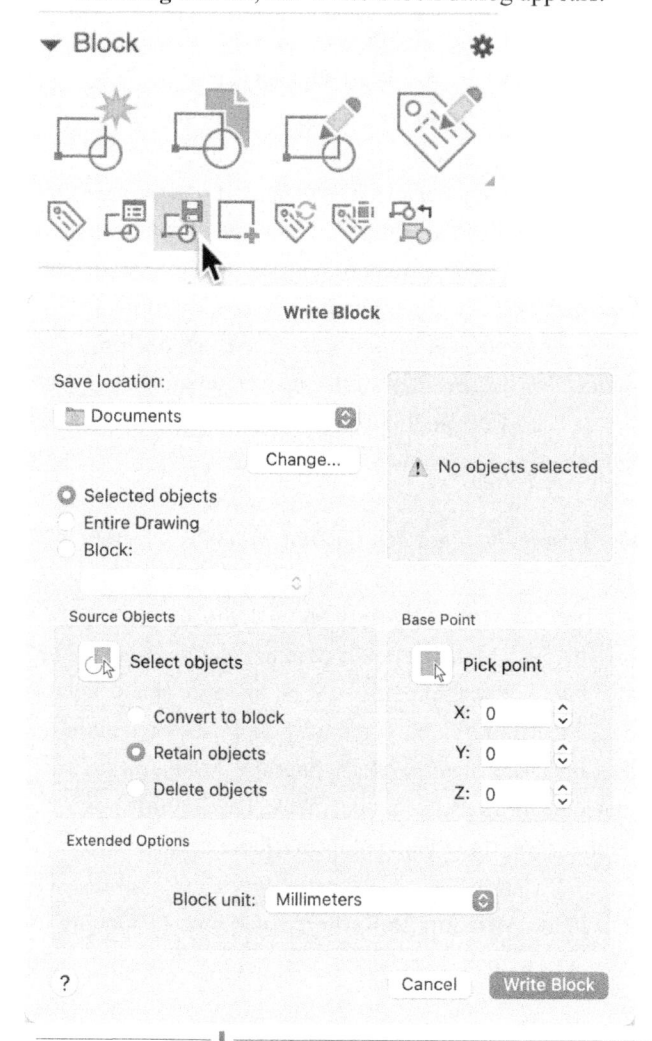

In the **Write Block** dialog, you can select three different types of sources (Block, Entire drawing, or Selected objects) to create a block. If you select the **Block** option, you can select blocks present in the drawing from the drop-down.

- Select the **Entire drawing** option.
- Specify the location of the file.
- Click the **Write Block** button.
- Type **Tap-in line** in the **Save As** box.
- Click **Save**.
- Close the drawing file.
- Open a new drawing file, and then type **I** in the command line and press RETURN; the **BLOCKS** palette appears.
- Click the **Recent Blocks** tab and double-click on the **Tap-in Line** file.

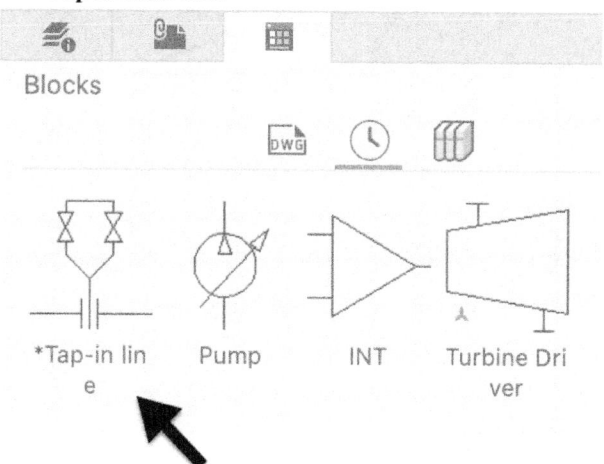

- Pick a point in the graphics window to insert the block.

Defining Attributes

An attribute is a line of text attached to a block. It may contain any type of information related to a block. For example, the following image shows a Compressor symbol with an equipment tag. The procedure to create an attribute is discussed in the following example.

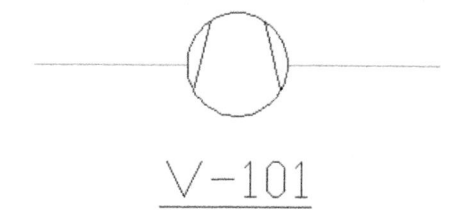

Blocks, Attributes, and Xrefs

AutoCAD 2023 For Beginners (For Mac Users)

Example 1:
- Open a new drawing file.
- Create the symbols, as shown below.

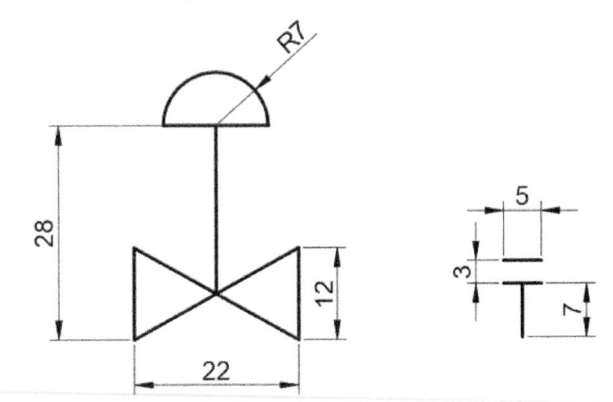

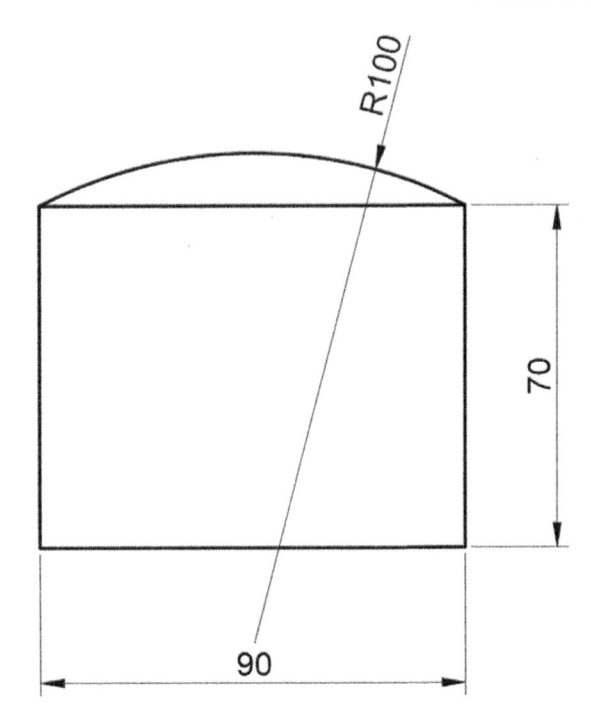

- Click **Define Attribute** on **Block** panel of the **Drafting** tool set; the **Attribute Definition** dialog appears.

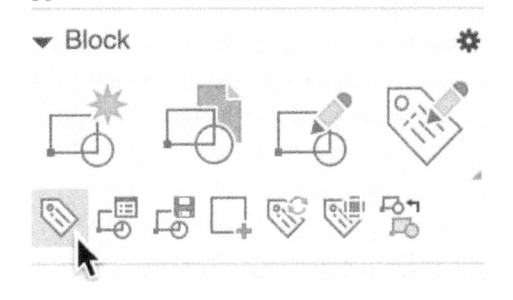

- Click the **Show Advanced Options** arrow.

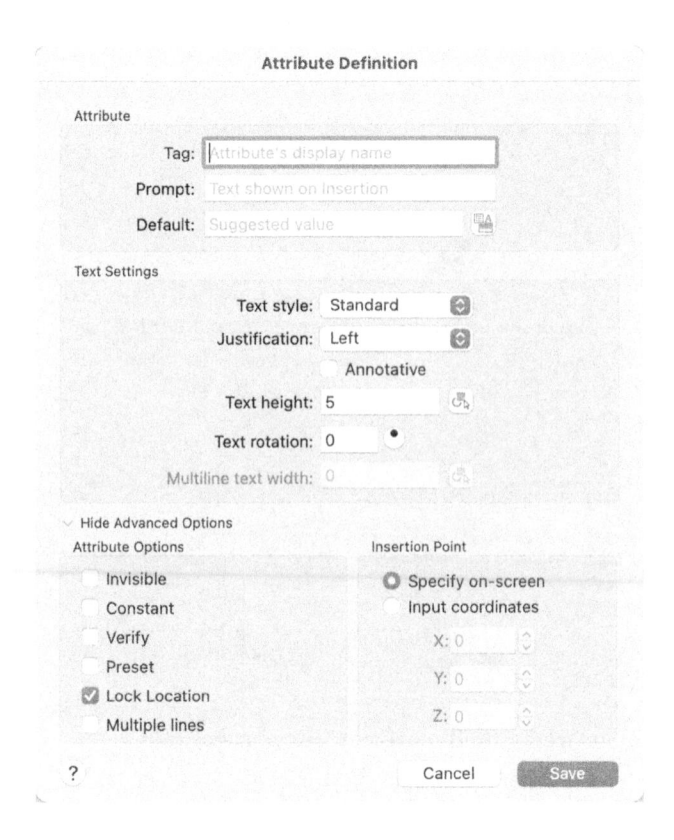

The options in the **Attribute Options** group of the **Attribute Definition** dialog define the display mode of the attribute. If you check the **Invisible** option, the attribute will be invisible. The **Constant** option makes the value of the attribute constant. You cannot change the value. The **Verify** option prompts you to verify after you enter a value. The **Preset** option can be used to set a predefined value for the attribute. The **Lock position** option fixes the position of the attribute to a selected point. The **Multiple lines** option allows typing the attribute value in single or multiple lines.

- Ensure that the **Lock position** option is selected.

The options in the **Attribute** group define the values of the attribute. The **Tag** box is used to enter the label of the attribute. For example, if you want to create an attribute called RESISTANCE, you must type **Resistance** in the **Tag** box. The **Prompt** box defines the prompt message that appears after placing the block. The **Default** box defines the default value of the attribute.

- In the **Attribute Definition** dialog, enter **Valvetag** in the **Tag** box.

208 | Blocks, Attributes, and Xrefs

AutoCAD 2023 For Beginners (For Mac Users)

The **Text Settings** options define the display properties of the text, such as style, and height. Observe the other options in this dialog. Most of them are self-explanatory.

- Enter **5** in the **Text height** box.
- Set the **Justification** to **Middle** and click **Save**.
- Specify the location of the attribute, as shown below.

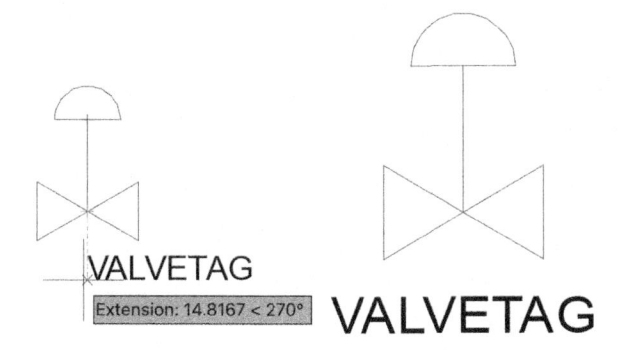

- Click the **Block, Make** button on the **Block** panel; the **Define Block** dialog appears.
- On the dialog, click the **Select objects** button.
- Drag a window and select the control valve symbol and attribute — next, press RETURN.
- Select the **Delete objects** option from the **Source Objects** group.
- Click the **Pick Point** button under the **Base point** group and select the point, as shown below.

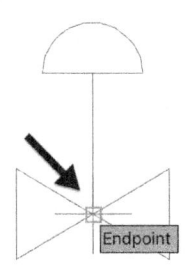

- Enter **Control Valve** in the **Name** box and click **Create Block**.
- Likewise, create the **Equipmenttag** attribute and place it inside the tank symbol.
- Create a block and name it as **Tank**.

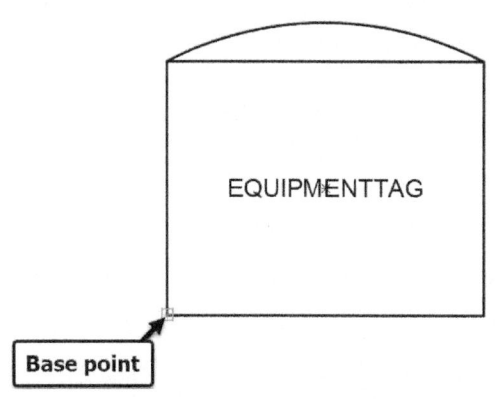

- Also, create a block of the nozzle symbol and name it **Nozzle**.

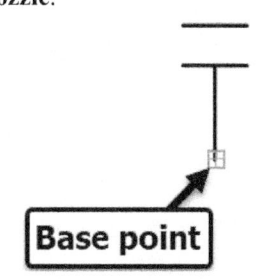

Inserting Attributed Blocks

You can use the INSERT command to insert the attributed blocks into a drawing. The procedure to insert attributed blocks is discussed next.

- On the **Drafting** tool set, click **Block > Blocks Palette**.
- Double-click on the **Tank** block.
- Click in the graphics window to define the insertion point. The **Edit Attributes** dialog appears.
- Enter **TK-001** in the **EQUIPMENTTAG** field and click **Confirm**; the block will be placed along with the attribute.

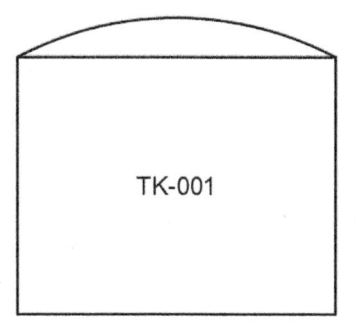

- Likewise, place the control valves, as shown below.

Blocks, Attributes, and Xrefs

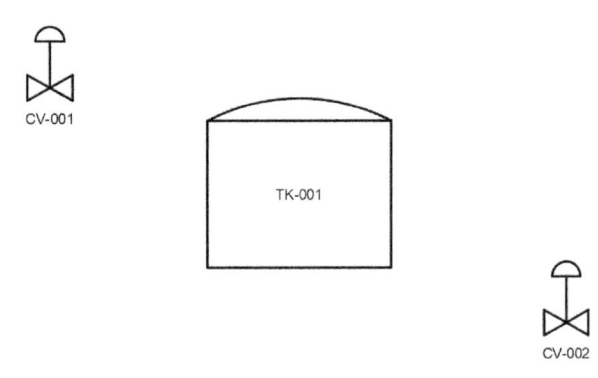

- Place and rotate the nozzles on the tank, as shown below.

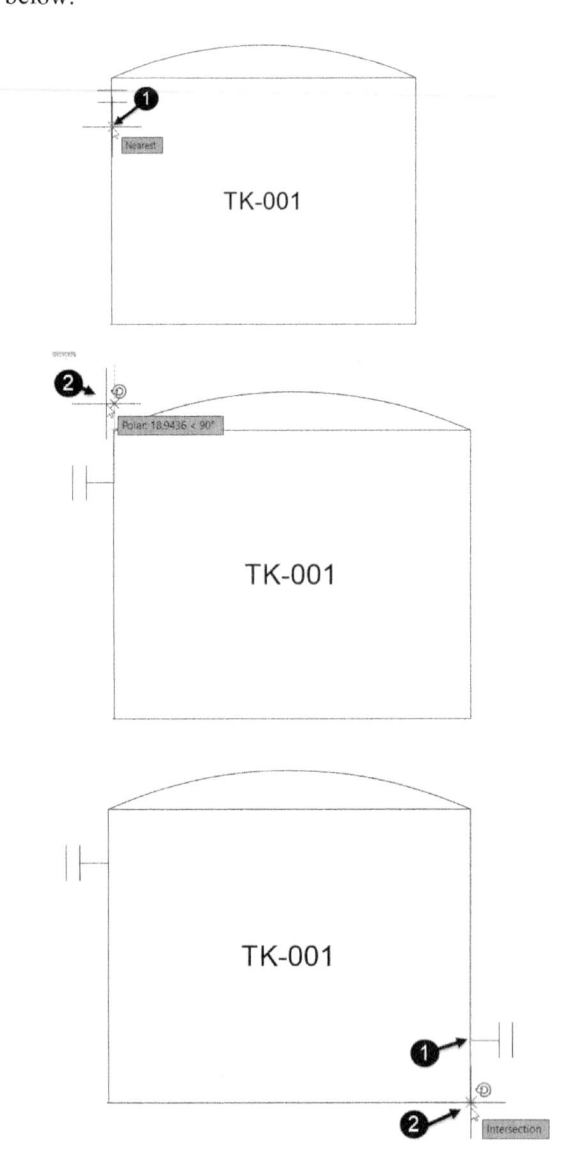

- Use the **Polyline** tool and connect the control valves and tank.

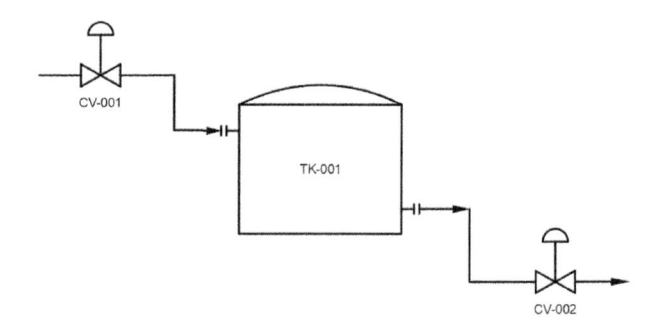

Working with External references

In AutoCAD, you can attach a drawing file, image, or pdf file to another drawing. These attachments are called External References (Xrefs). They are dynamic in nature and update when changes are made to them. In the following example, you will learn to attach drawing files to a drawing.

Example 1:
- Create the drawing shown below.

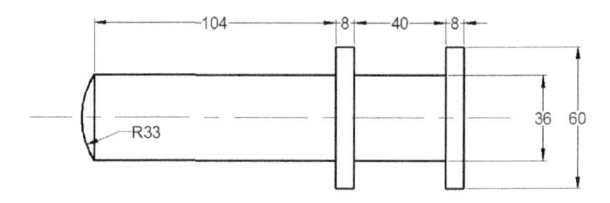

- Type **BASE** in the command line and press RETURN.
- Select the midpoint of the vertical line as the base point, as shown.

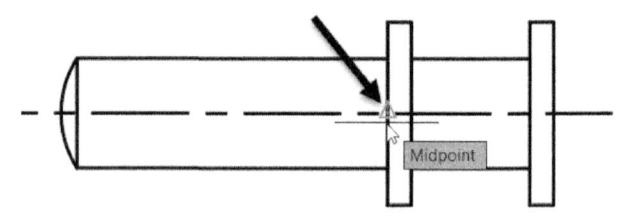

- Save the drawing as **Crank pin.dwg**
- Create another drawing as shown below (For help, refer to the **Multi View Drawings** section in Chapter 5).

210 | Blocks, Attributes, and Xrefs

AutoCAD 2023 For Beginners (For Mac Users)

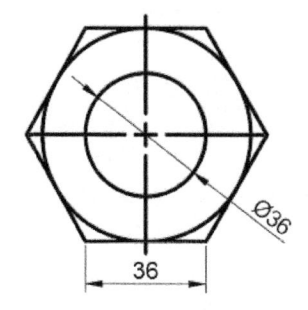

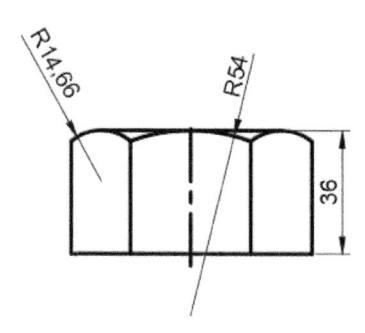

- Use the **Base** tool and specify the base point, as shown below.

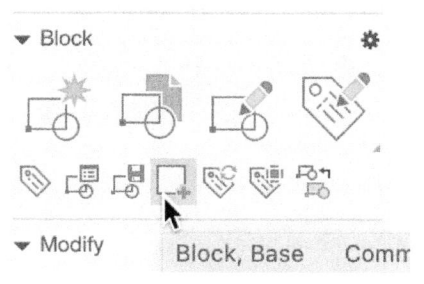

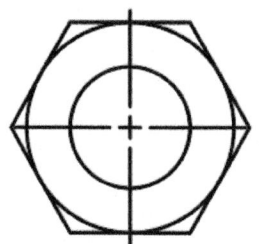

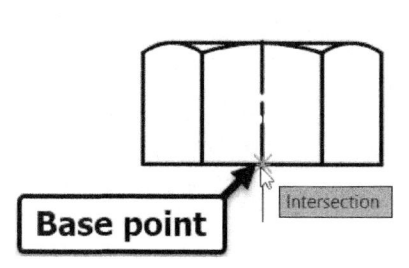

- Save the drawing as **Nut.dwg** and close it.

- Open the **Crank.dwg** file created in Chapter 8.
- Click the **Reference Manager** tab on the palettes.

- Click **Attach Reference** on the **Reference Manager** palette.

- Browse to the location of the **Crankpin.dwg** and double-click on it; the **Attach External Reference** dialog appears.

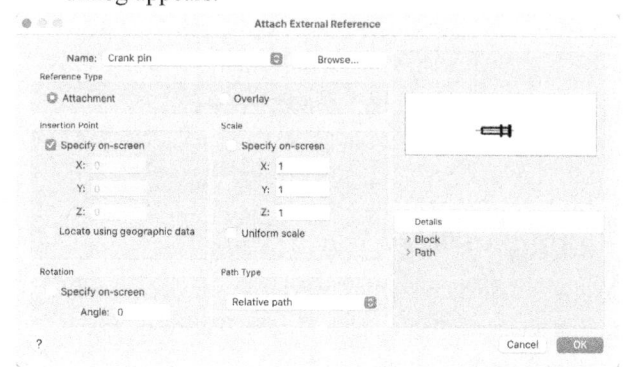

The options on this dialog include the insertion point, scale, and rotation angle of the external reference.

- Accept the default settings in this dialog and click **OK**; the crankpin will be attached to the pointer.
- Select the point on the hatched view, as shown below.

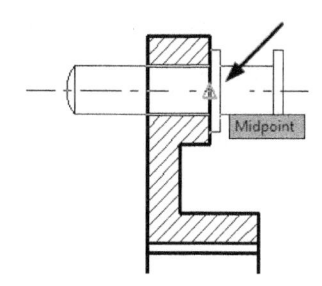

211 | Blocks, Attributes, and Xrefs

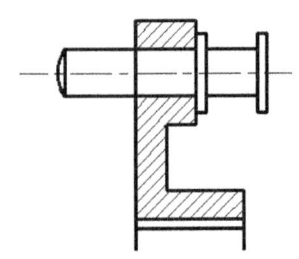

- In the **Reference Manager** palette, click the **Attach Reference**  icon.
- Browse to the location of the **Nut.dwg** and double-click on it; the **Attach External Reference** dialog appears.
- In the **Attach External Reference** dialog, enter **90** in the **Angle** box under the **Rotation** group and click **OK**.
- Select the insertion point on the section view, as shown below.

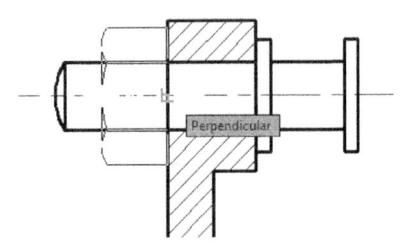

Fading an Xref

You can change the fading of Xref by using the Xref fading slider available in the **Look & Feel** page of the **Application Preferences** dialog.

- Right-click in the drawing area and select Preferences.
- Click the Look & Feel tab on the left-side of the dialog.
- Drag the XRefs slider in the Fading Control section.

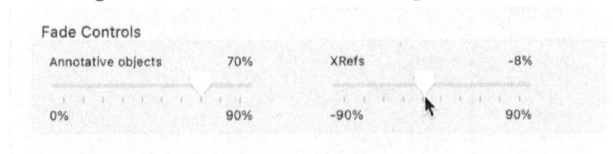

Clipping External References

You can hide the unwanted portion of an external reference by using the **Clip** tool.

- Select the **Nut.dwg** from the graphics window. 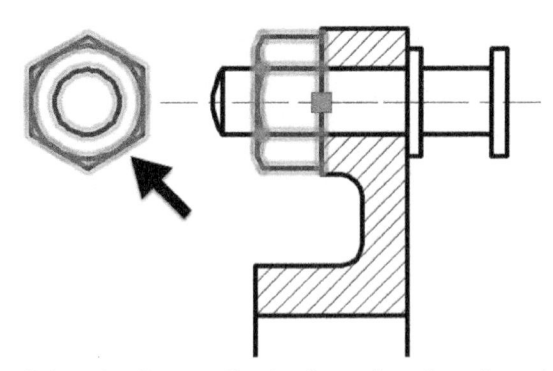
- Select the **Create clipping boundary** icon from the **External Reference** visor. 
- Right-click and select the **Rectangular** option from the shortcut menu.
- Draw a rectangle as shown below; only the front view of the nut is visible, and the top view is hidden. Also, the clipping frame is visible. 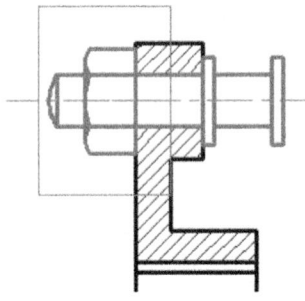
- To hide the clipping frame, type XCLIPFRAME in the command line
- Type 0 and press RETURN.
- You can also hide the frame by clicking **Modify > Object > External reference > Frame** on the Menu Bar. 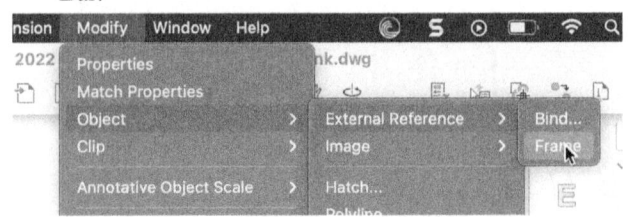
- Attach another instance of the **Nut.dwg** file.

212 | Blocks, Attributes, and Xrefs

- Use the **Rotate** and **Move** tools to position the top view, as shown below.

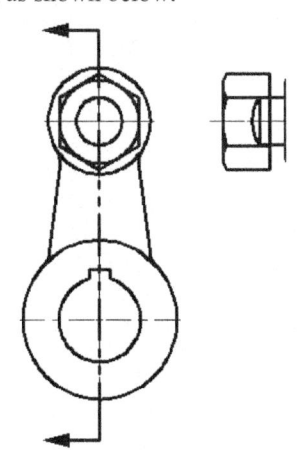

- Use the **Create clipping boundary** tool and clip the Xref.

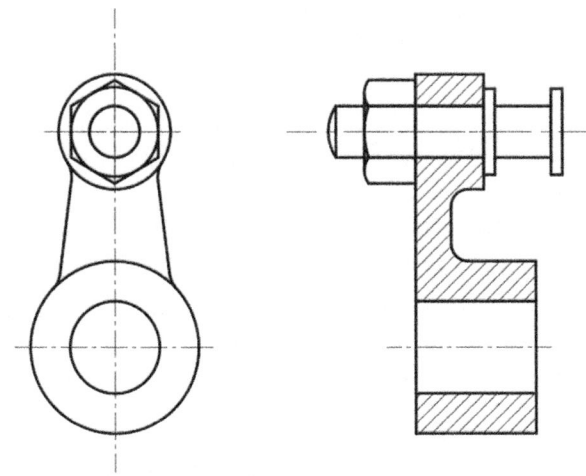

Editing the External References

AutoCAD allows you to edit the external references in the file to which they are attached. You can also edit them by opening their drawing file. The procedure to edit an external reference is discussed next.

- Select **Nut** from the drawing; the **External Reference** visor appears
- Click the **Edit Reference in Place** button on the **External Reference** visor.
- Select the **Automatically select all nested objects** option.
- Click **Edit** to get into the reference editing mode.

- In the drawing, the centerlines of the nut are overlapping on the centerlines of the crank. Delete the centerlines and center marks of the nut.
- Click **Save** on the **External Reference** visor; the **Alert** message box appears.

- Click **OK**.

Binding the External References

If you want to share a drawing file consisting external references, you need to package the drawing along with the reference files or bind the external references into the drawing. The Package Drawing tool is explained in Chapter 11. The procedure the bind the drawing is explained next.

- On the **Reference Manager** palette, click the right mouse button on the **Nut** attachment.
- Select the **Bind** option; the **Nut** attachment is binded to the drawing.

Notice that the layers of the Nut file are listed in the Layers list. However, the name of the Xref file is added at the beginning the layer name.

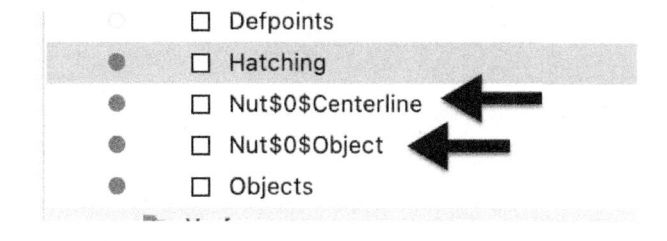

Also, notice that the **Nut** file is removed from the Reference Manager palette. It becomes the part of the drawing.

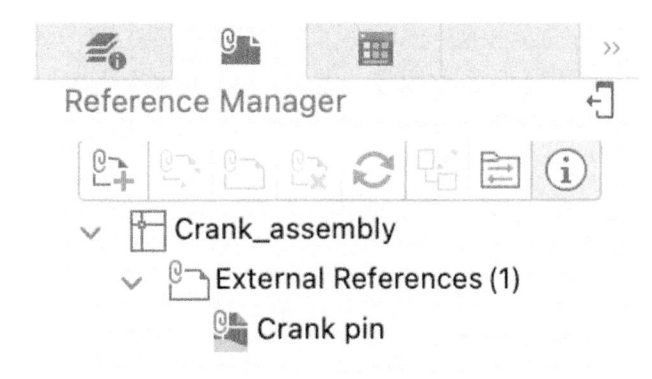

- On the **Reference Manager** palette, click the right mouse button on the **Crank pin** attachment.
- Select the **Bind-Insert** option.

Notice that the layers of the **Crank pin** file are added to the Layers list without any prefix.

Adding Balloons

- Click **Drafting > Leader > Multileader Style Manager** button on the tool set; the **Multileader Style Manager** dialog appears.
- Click the **Plus** button on the dialog.
- In the **Create New Multileader Style** dialog, enter **Balloon Callout** in the **New Style name** box and click **Continue**. 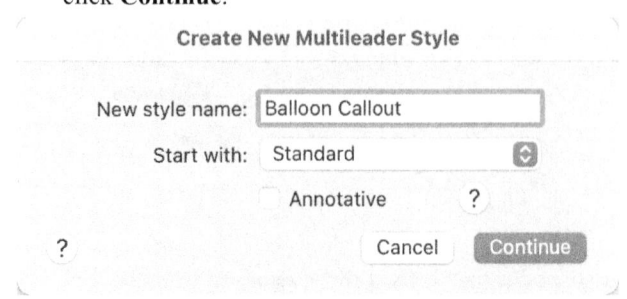
- In the **Modify Multileader Style** dialog, click the **Content** tab, and set the **Type** to **Block**.
- Under **Block options**, set the **Source block** to **Circle**.
- Set the **Scale** to **3**. 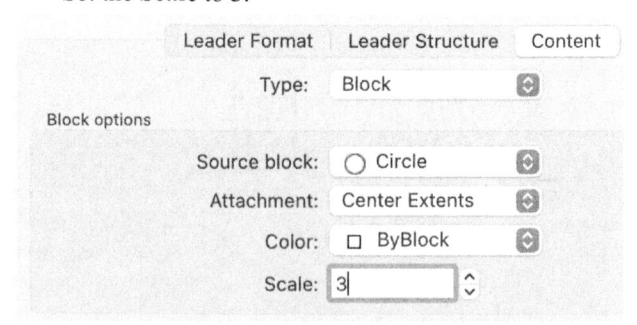
- Click the **Leader Format** tab and set the Arrowhead **Size** to 8. 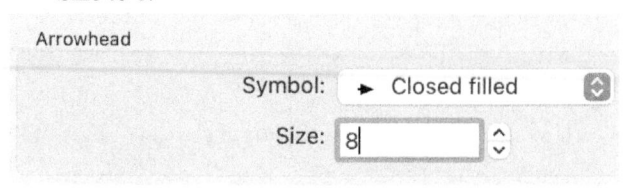
- Click **OK** and set the **Balloon Callout** style as current.
- Click **Close**.
- Click **Drafting > Leader > Multileader** on the tool set.
- Click the down arrow next to the **Polar Tracking** icon on the status bar and select **45** from the menu. Activate the **Polar Tracking**.
- Select a point on the section view of the crank.
- Move the pointer along the polar trace lines and click; the _TagCircle dialog appears. 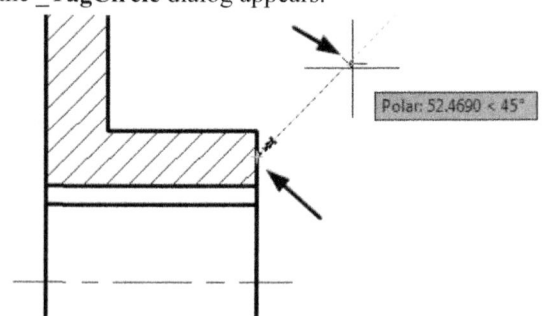
- In the _TagCircle dialog, enter 1 in the **Enter tag number** field. 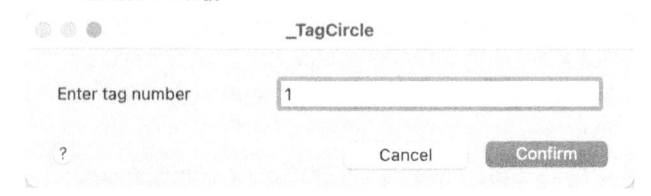
- Click **Confirm**; the balloon will be created.

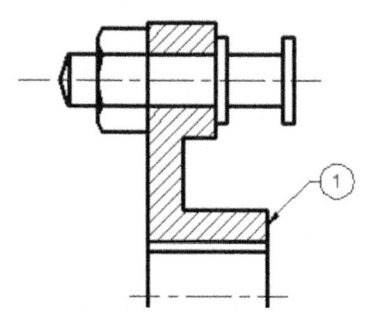

- Likewise, create other balloons.

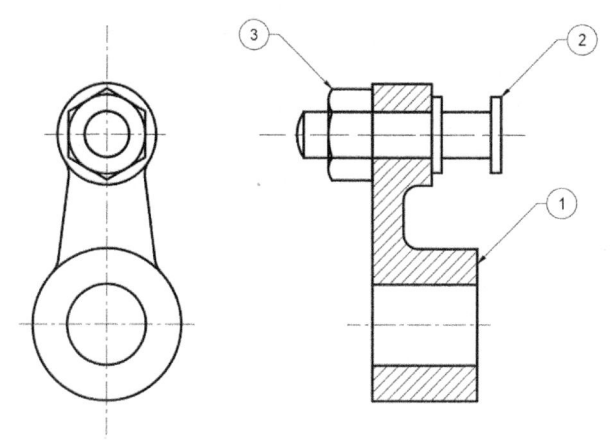

Creating the Part List

- Click **Drafting > Table > Table** on the tool set.
- On the **Insert Table** dialog, type **4** and **3** in the **Columns** and **Data rows** boxes, respectively.
- Select **First row cell style > Title**.
- Select **Second row cell style > Header**.
- Select **All other row cell style > Data**.
- Select **Insertion behavior > Specify Insertion point**.

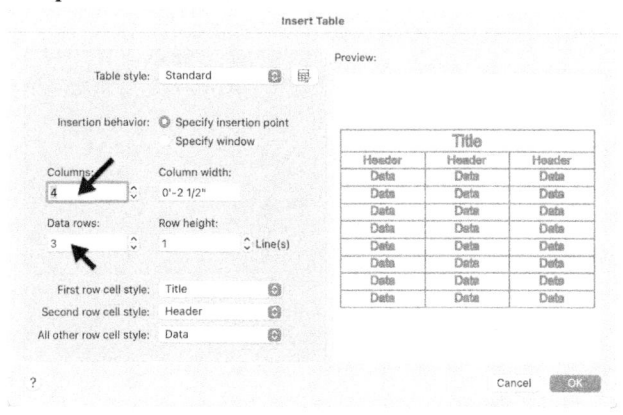

- Click **OK**.
- Click in the drawing area to create the table.

- Type **Parts List** in the title row.
- Press the TAB key and type **Part No.** in the first column of the Header row.
- Likewise, type-in text in the table cells (double-click in the cells and type), as shown below.

Parts List			
Part No.	Name	Material	Quantity
1	Crank	Forged Steel	1
2	Crank pin	45C	1
3	Nut	MS	1

- Click on any one of the edges of the table; you will notice that grips are displayed on it. You can edit the table using these grips.

- Click and drag the square grip above the MATERIAL cell; the width of the cell will be changed.

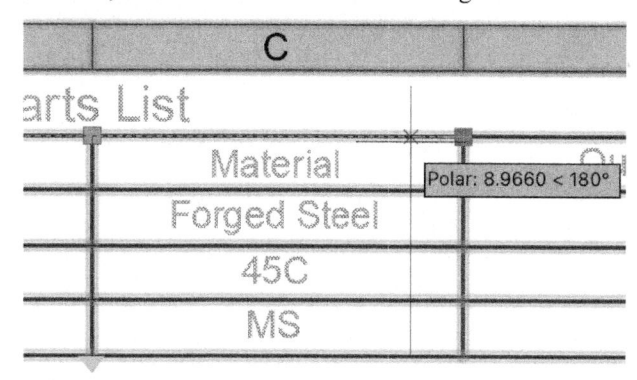

- Likewise, change the width of the other columns, as shown.

Parts List			
Part No.	Name	Material	Quantity
1	Crank	Forged Steel	1
2	Crank pin	45C	1
3	Nut	MS	1

- Click on the anyone of the edges of the table.
- Click and drag the triangular grip located at the bottom left corner of the table; the height of the rows will be increased uniformly.

Blocks, Attributes, and Xrefs

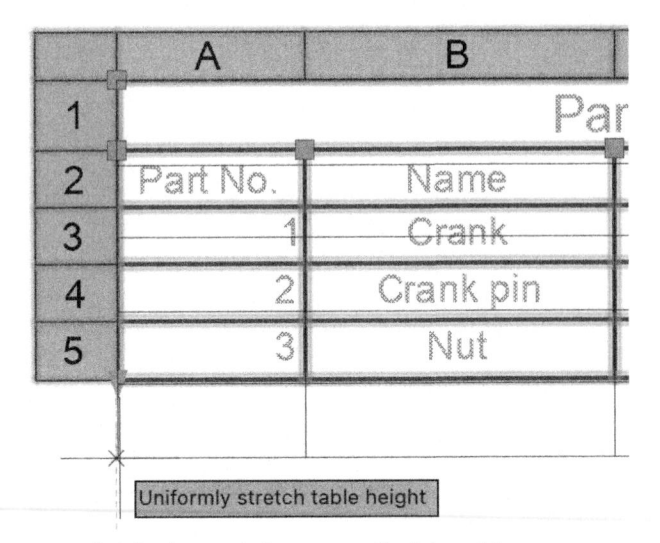

- Click in the top left corner cell of the table.
- Press and hold the SHIFT key and click in the lower right corner of the table; all the cells in the table will be selected.

- Click the **Layers and Properties** tab on the palettes.

- In the **Properties** palette, click **Alignment > Middle Center**; the data in all the cells will appear in the middle center of the cells.

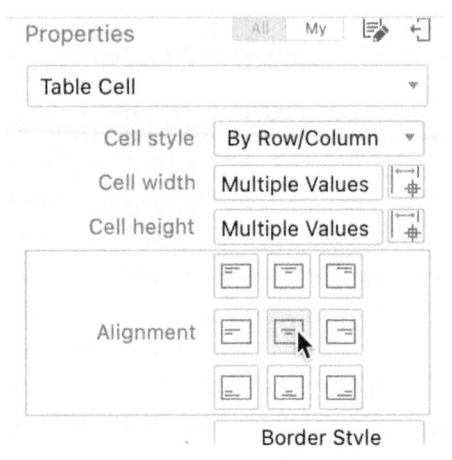

Exercise

216 | Blocks, Attributes, and Xrefs

Blocks, Attributes, and Xrefs

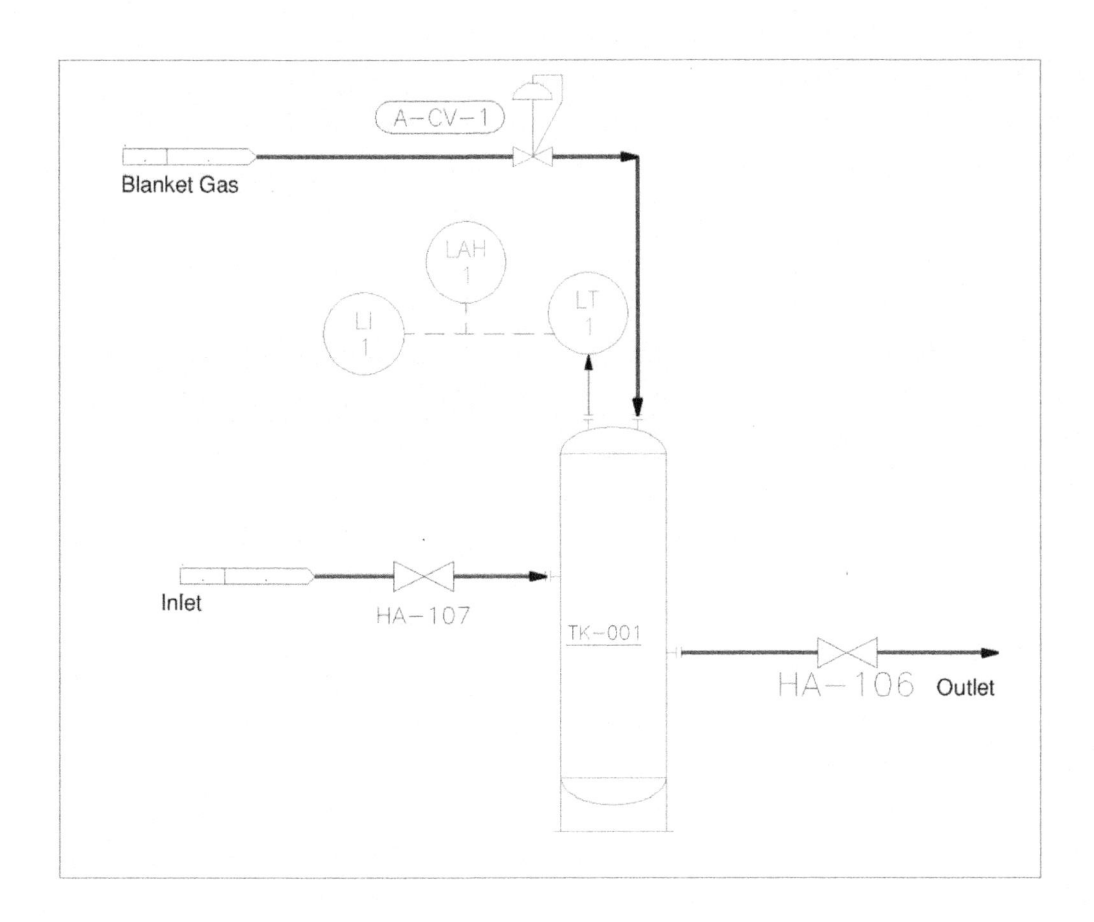

AutoCAD 2023 For Beginners (For Mac Users)

Chapter 10: Layouts & Annotative Objects

In this chapter, you will learn to do the following:

- **Create Layouts**
- **Specify the Paper space settings**
- **Create Viewports in Paper space**
- **Change Layer properties in Viewports**
- **Create a Title Block on the layout**
- **Use Annotative objects in Viewports**

Drawing Layouts

There are two workspaces in AutoCAD: The Model space and the Paper space. In the Model space, you create 2D drawings and 3D models. You can even plot drawings from the model space. However, it is difficult to plot drawings at a scale or if a drawing consists of multiple views arranged at different scales. For this purpose, we use Layouts or paper space. In Layouts or paper space, you can work on notes and annotations and perform the plotting or publishing operations. In Layouts, you can arrange a single view or multiple views of a drawing or multiple drawings by using Viewports. These viewports display drawings at specific scales on layouts. They are mainly rectangular in shape, but you can also create circular and polygonal viewports. In this chapter, you will learn about viewports and various annotative objects.

Working with Layouts

Layouts represent the conventional drawing sheet. They are created to plot a drawing on a paper or in electronic form. A drawing can have multiple layouts to print in different sheet formats. By default, there are two layouts available: Layout 1 and Layout 2. You can also create new layouts by clicking the plus (+) symbol next to the layout. Next, select **New layout** from the shortcut menu. In the following example, you will create two layouts, one representing the ISO A1 (841 X 594) sheet and another representing the ISO A4 (210 X 297) sheet.

Example:
- Open a new drawing file.
- Create layers with the following settings:

Layer	Linetype	Lineweight
Construction	Continuous	Default
Object Lines	Continuous	0.6mm
Hidden Lines	Hidden	0.3 mm
Center Lines	CENTER	Default
Dimensions	Continuous	Default
Title Block	Continuous	1.2mm
Viewport	Continuous	Default

- Create the drawing, as shown next. Do not add dimensions.

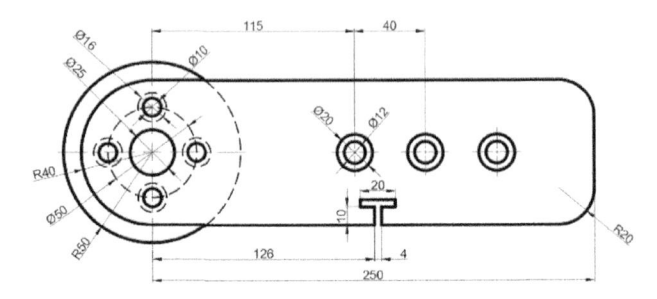

- Click the **Layout 1** tab at the bottom of the graphics window.

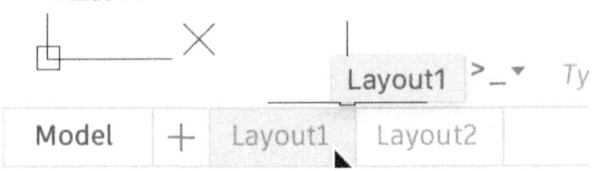

You will notice that a white paper is displayed with the viewport created automatically. The components of a layout are shown in the figure below.

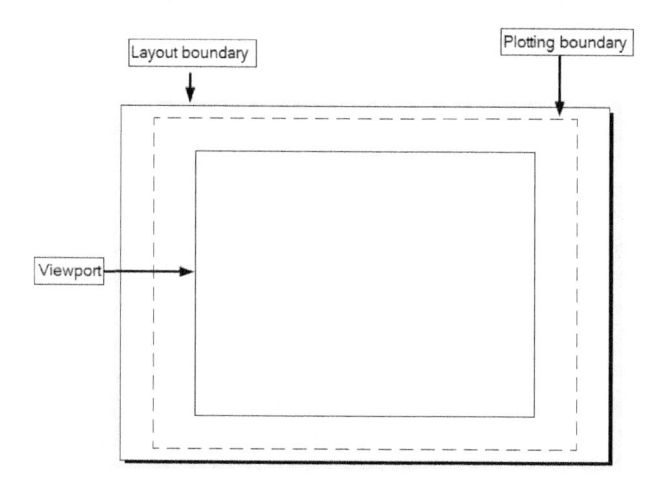

AutoCAD 2023 For Beginners (For Mac Users)

- Click **Page Setup Manager** on the toolbar; the **Page Setup Manager** dialog appears.

- In the **Page Setup Manager** dialog, select the **Edit** option from the drop-down, as shown.

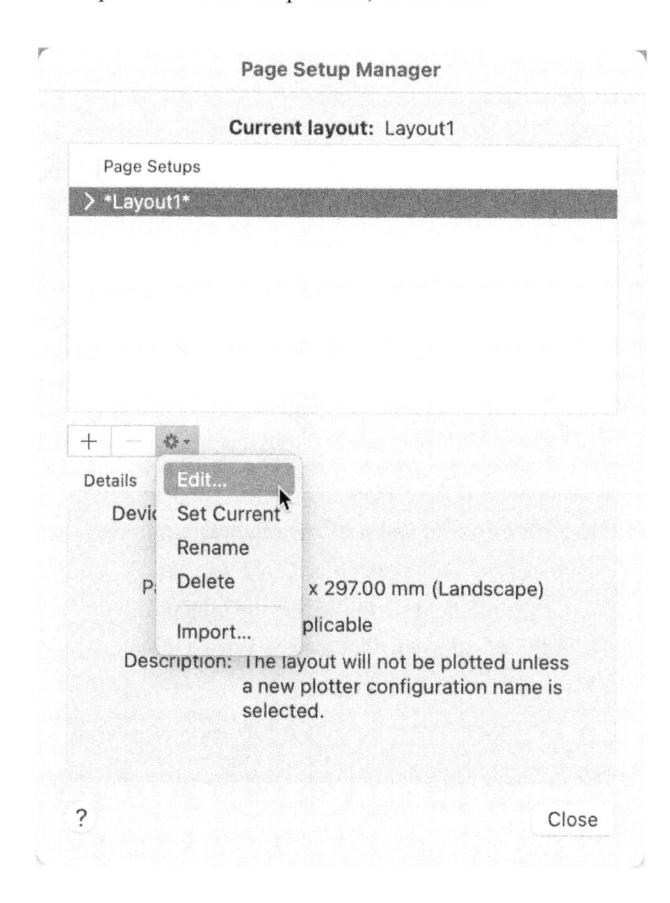

- In the **Page Setup** dialog, select **DWG to PDF.pc3** from the **Printer** drop-down.

- Set the **Plot Style** to **acad.stb**.
- Set the **Paper size** to ISO A1 (841.00 x 594.00 MM).
- Set the **Scale** to **1:1**.

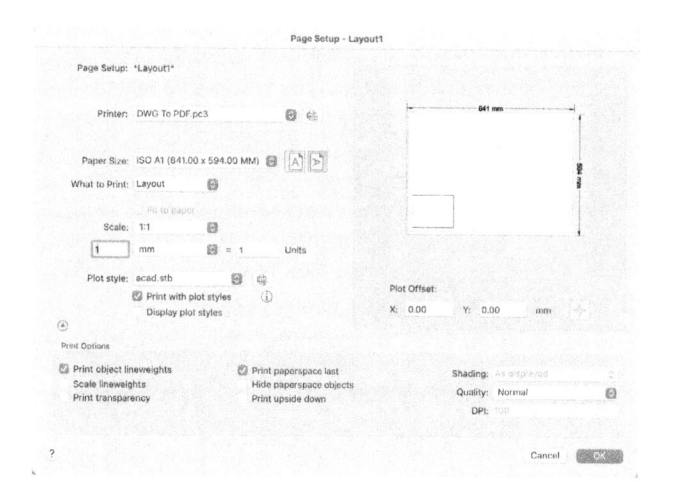

- Click **OK**, and then click **Close** on the **Page Setup Manager** dialog.
- Click the **Layout2** tab below the graphics window.
- Double-click on the **Layout1** tab and enter **ISO A1**; the **Layout1** is renamed. 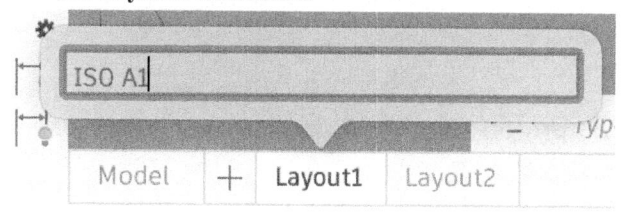
- Similarly, rename the **Layout2** to **ISO A4**.
- Click **Page Setup Manager** on the toolbar; the **Page Setup Manager** dialog appears.
- Select **ISO A4** from the list.
- Select **Edit** from the drop-down on the dialog, as shown.

219 | Layouts & Annotative Objects

AutoCAD 2023 For Beginners (For Mac Users)

- In the **Page Setup** dialog, select **Printer > DWG to PDF.pc3**
- Select **acad.stb** from the **Plot style** drop-down.
- Set the **Paper Size** to **ISO A4 (210 x 297 MM)** and **Scale** to **1:1**.
- Click the **Portrait** button next to the **Paper size** drop-down and click **OK**; you will notice that the size of the Layout is changed to A4 size.

- Close the **Page Setup Manager** dialog.

Creating Viewports in the Paper space

The viewports that exist in the paper space are called floating viewports. It is because you can position them anywhere in the layout and modify their shape and size with respect to the layout.

Creating a Viewport in the ISO A4 layout

- Open the **ISO A4** layout, if not already open.
- Select the default viewport that exists in the **ISO A4** layout.
- Press the DELETE key; the viewport will be deleted.
- Right-click on the toolbar, and select Customize toolbar.
- Drag the **Viewports** sub-toolbar and release it on the toolbar.

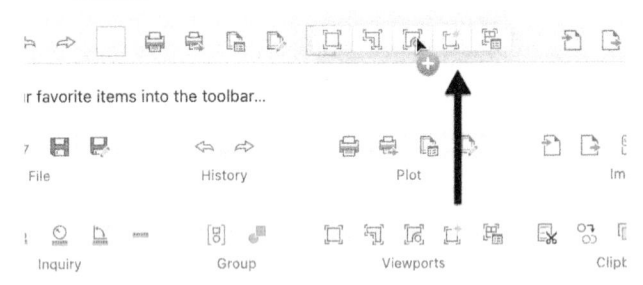

- Click **Done**.
- Click the **Single Viewport** icon on the toolbar.

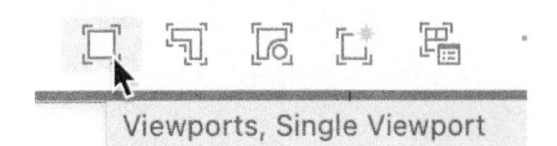

- Create the rectangular viewport by picking the first and second corner points, as shown in the figure.

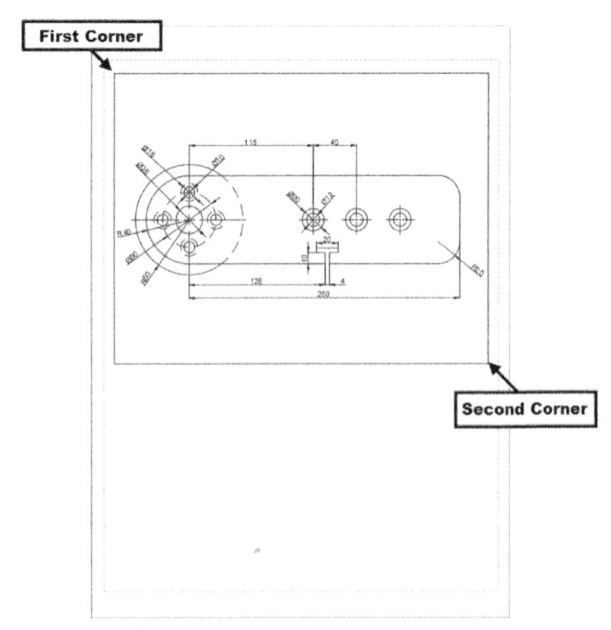

- Click the **Toggle viewport between Model space and Paper space** button on the status bar; the model space inside the viewport will be activated. Also, the viewport frame will become thicker when you are in model space.

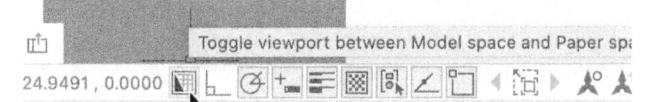

- Click the **Viewport Scale** button and select **1:2** from the menu; the drawing will be zoomed out.

- Use the **Pan** tool and position the drawing in the center of the viewport.
- After fitting the drawing inside the viewport, you can lock the position by clicking the **Lock/Unlock Viewport** button on the status bar.

After locking the viewport, you cannot change the scale or position of the drawing.

AutoCAD 2023 For Beginners (For Mac Users)

- Click the **Toggle viewport between Model space and Paper space** button on the status bar to switch back to paper space.

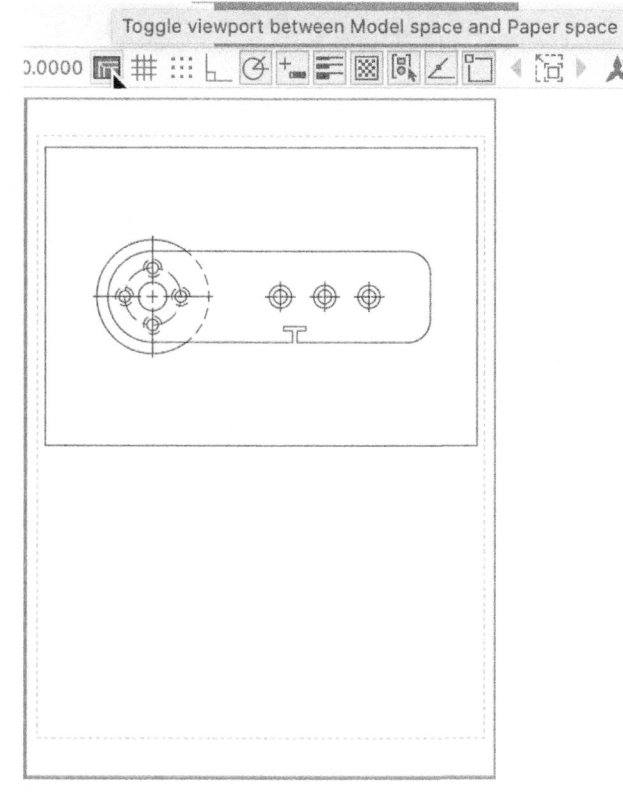

Creating Viewports in the ISO A1 layout

- Click the **ISO A1** tab below the graphics window.
- Select the viewport frame and modify the viewport using the grips, as shown below.

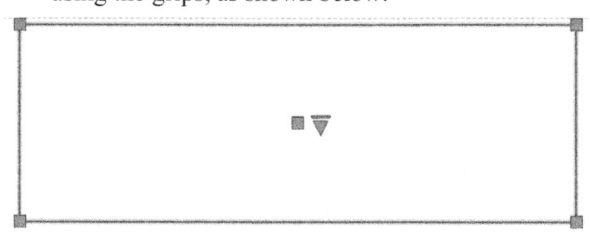

- Double-click inside the viewport to switch to the model space.
- Use the **Zoom** and **Pan** tools and drag the drawing to the center of the viewport.
- Click the **Viewport Scale** button and select **2:1** from the menu.
- Use the **Pan** tool and position the drawing, as shown in the figure.
- Click the **Lock/Unlock Viewport** button on the status bar.
- Double-click outside the viewport to switch to the paper space.
- Use the **Circle** tool and create a 180 mm diameter circle on the layout, as shown below.

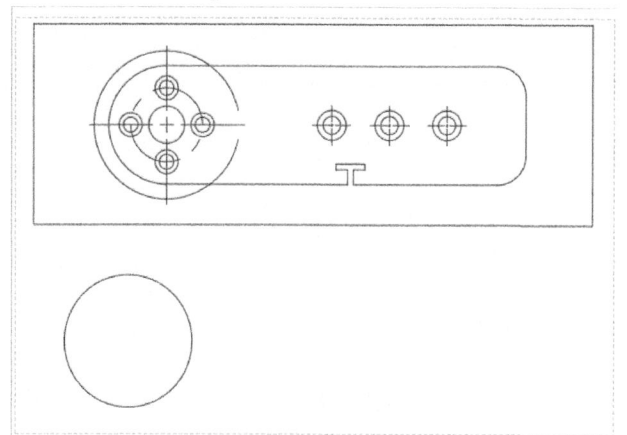

- Click **Viewports, Object** on the toolbar.

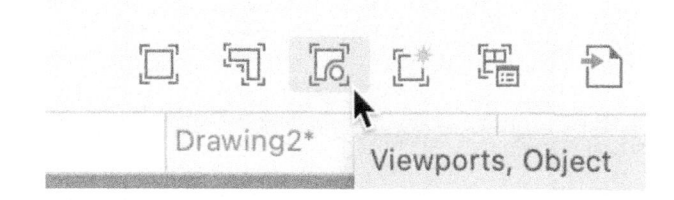

- Select the circle from the layout; it will be converted into a viewport.

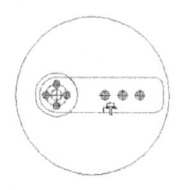

- Double-click in the circular viewport to switch to the model space.
- Click the **Viewport Scale** button on the status bar and select **4:1** from the menu; the drawing will be zoomed in to its center.
- Use the **Pan** tool and adjust the drawing, as shown below.

221 | **Layouts & Annotative Objects**

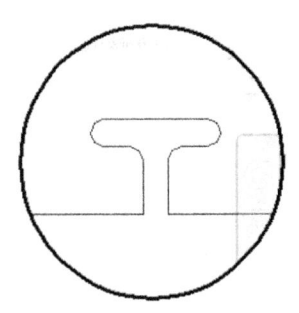

- Click the **Lock/Unlock Viewport** button on the status bar.
- Click **Plot** on the toolbar. 
- Click the **Preview** button located at the lower left corner of the **Plot** dialog; the plot preview will be displayed. You will notice that the viewport frames are also displayed in the preview.
- Close the preview window, and then click **Cancel** on the **Plot** dialog. 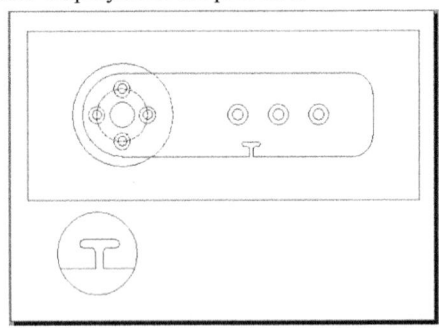

To hide viewport frames while plotting a drawing, follow the steps given below.

- In the **Layers** palette, create a new layer called **Hide Viewports** and activate it. 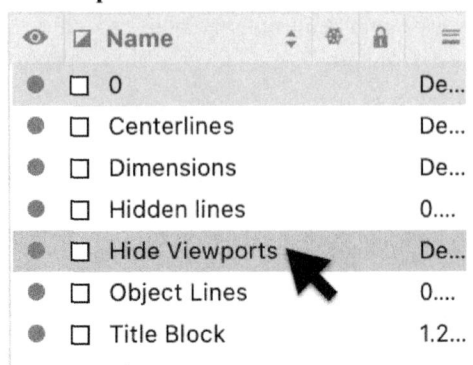
- Right-click on the **Hide Viewports** layer and select **Layer Status > Print**. 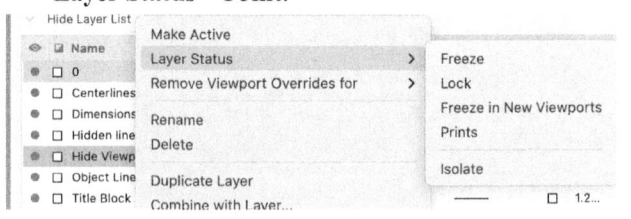
- Select the two viewports from the layout. 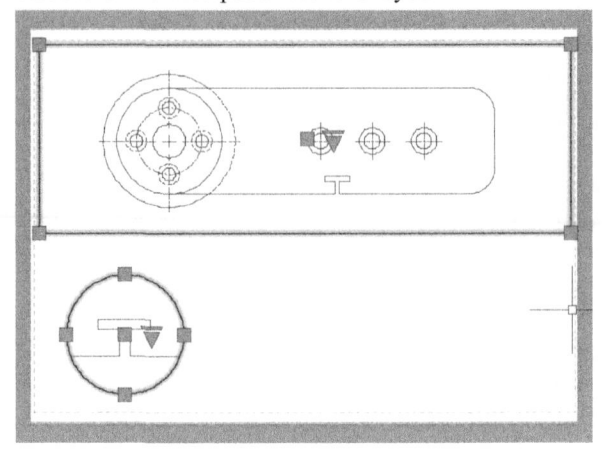
- On the **Layers** palette, select the **Hide Viewports** from the **Layers** drop-down.

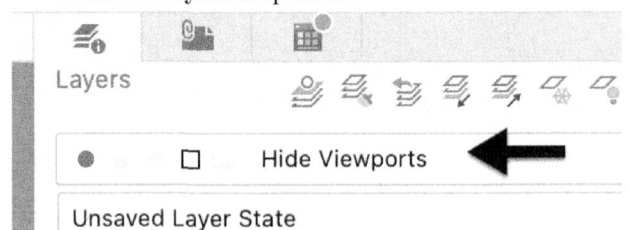

The viewport frames will become unplottable. To check this, click the **Preview** button on the **Plot** dialog; the plot preview will be displayed as shown below.

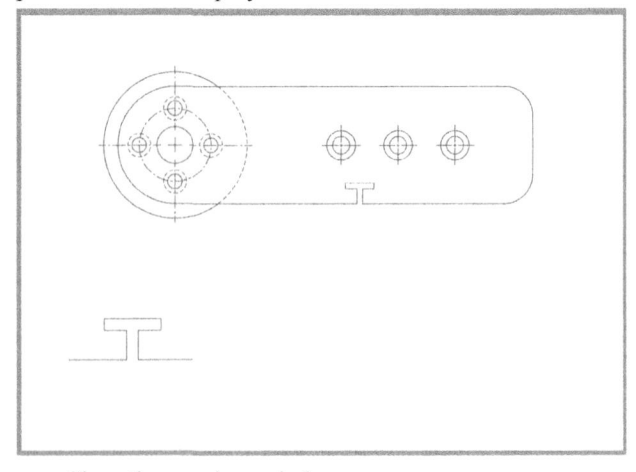

- Close the preview window.

222 | Layouts & Annotative Objects

Changing the Layer Properties in Viewports

The layer properties in viewports are not related to the layer properties in model space. You can change the layer properties in viewports without any effect in the model space.

- Double-click inside the larger viewport to activate the model space.
- In the **Layers** palette, click the icon in the **VP Freeze** column of the **Hidden lines** layer; the hidden lines will disappear in the viewport, as shown below.

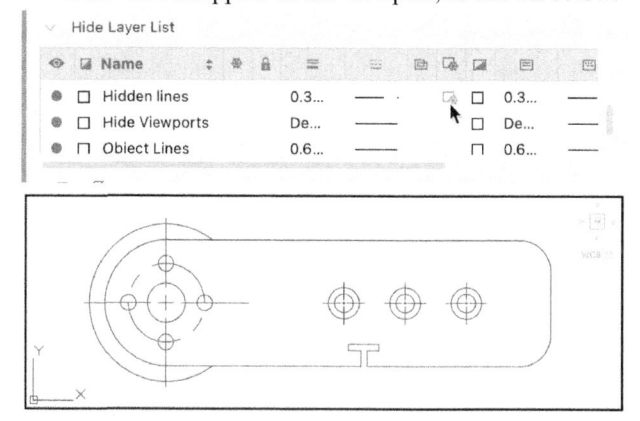

- Double-click outside the viewport to switch to paper space.
- Click the **Model** tab below the graphics window; you will notice that the hidden lines are retained in the model space.

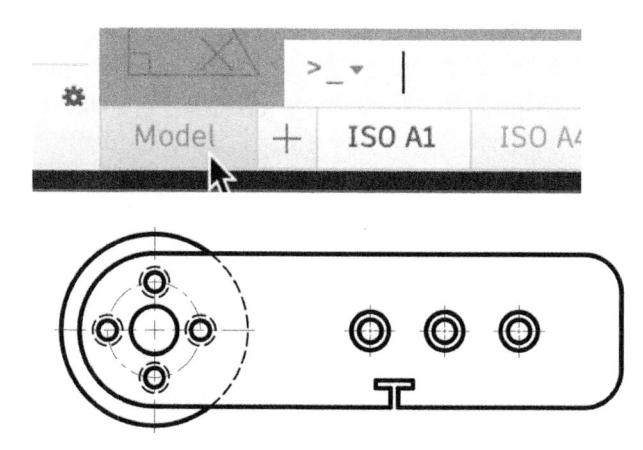

Creating the Title Block on the Layout

You can draw objects on layouts to create a title block, borders, and viewports. However, it is not recommended to draw the actual drawing on layouts. You can also create dimensions on layouts.

Example1:
- Click the **ISO A1** layout tab.
- Activate the **Title Block** layer.
- Click the **Rectangle** button on the **Draw** panel.
- Pick a point at the lower right corner of the layout.
- Right-click and select the **Dimensions** option shortcut menu.
- Specify the length of the rectangle as **820** and width as **550**.
- Click in the upper area of the layout; a rectangular border will be created.
- Create a title block at the lower right corner, as shown below (Use the **Line** and **Multiline Text** tools).

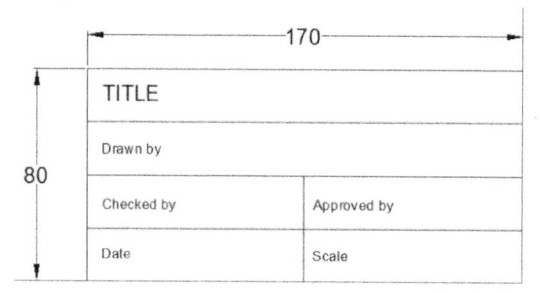

- Create attributes and place them inside the title, as shown below (refer to *Chapter 9: Blocks, Attributes, and Xrefs* to learn how to create attributes).

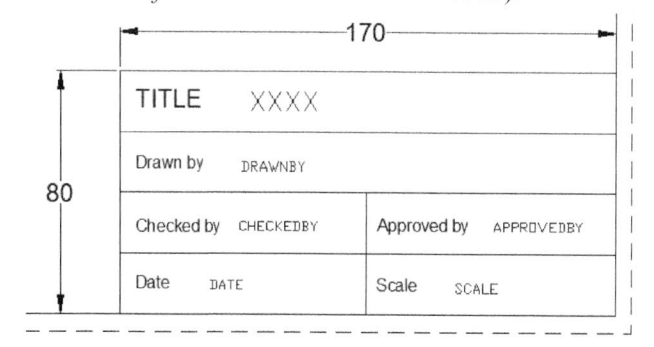

- Use the **Block, Make** tool and convert it into a block.
- Use the **Block** palette and insert it at the lower right corner of the layout.
- Save the drawing file as **Viewports-Example.dwg**.

Working with Annotative Dimensions

In AutoCAD, you create drawings at their actual size. However, when you scale a drawing to fit inside a viewport, the size of the dimensions will not be appropriately scaled. For example, in the following figure, the first viewport is scaled to 1:2, and the second viewport is scaled to 1:1. The dimensions in the first viewport appear much smaller.

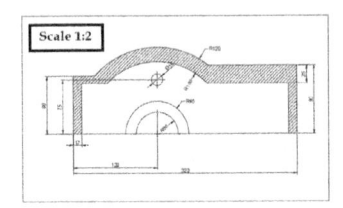

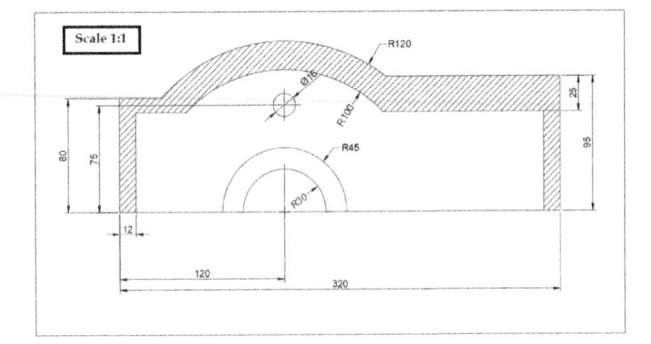

You can fix this problem by applying the Annotative property to dimensions.

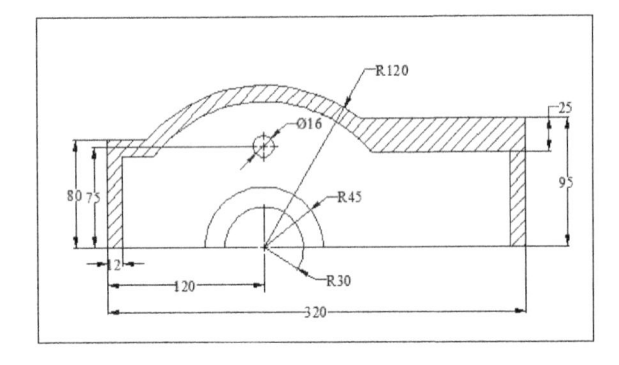

- Open the **Viewports-Example.dwg**, if not already opened.
- Activate the **Dimensions** layer.
- Type **D** in the command line and press RETURN.
- In the **Dimension Style Manager**, click the **Plus** button.
- In the **Create New Dimension Style** dialog, enter **New style name** as **Dim_Anno** and select the **Annotative** checkbox. Click **Continue**.

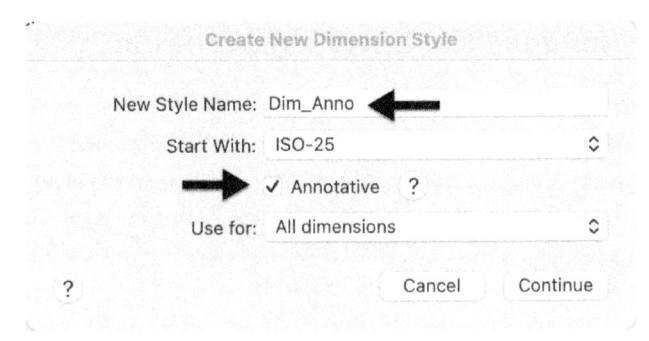

- Set the following settings in the **New Dimension Style** dialog.

  Lines tab: Offset from origin 1.25
  Symbols and Arrows tab: Arrow size 2.5, Center Marks-Line.
  Text tab: Text height – 2.5, Placement - Vertical-Centered, Alignment - Horizontal
  Primary Units tab: Units Format – Decimal, Precision – 0, Decimal separator – '.' period

- In the **Fit** tab, ensure that the **Annotative** checkbox is selected.

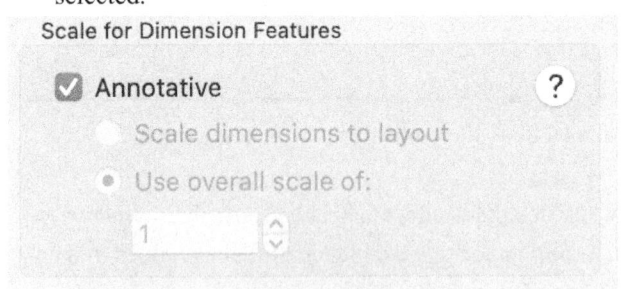

- Click **OK** on the **New Dimension Style** dialog; you will notice that the **Dim_Anno** style is listed in the **Dimension Style Manager**. Also, the annotation symbol is displayed next to it. It indicates that all dimensions created using this style will have annotative property.
- Right-click on the **Dim_Anno** style and select **Set current**.
- Click on the **Close** button.

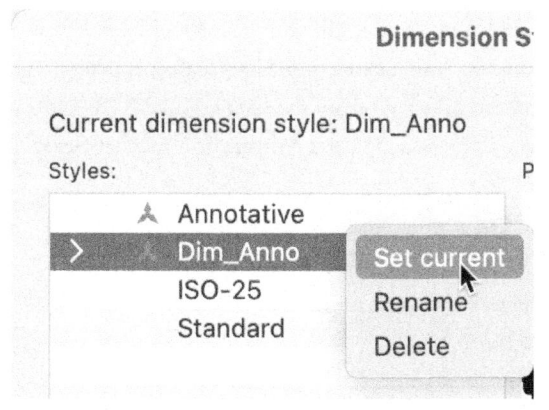

- Activate the **Dimension** tool and set the Annotation Scale to **1:1**. Click **OK**.

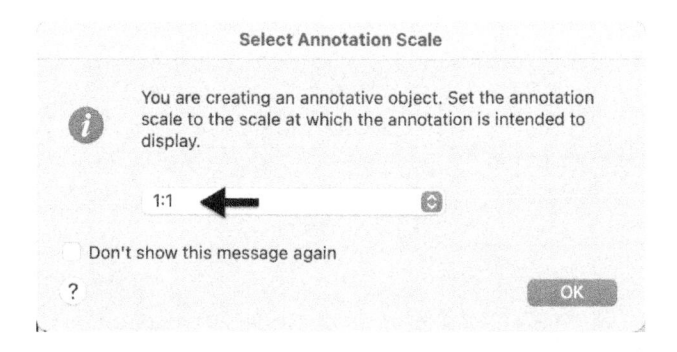

- Create a linear dimension, as shown below.

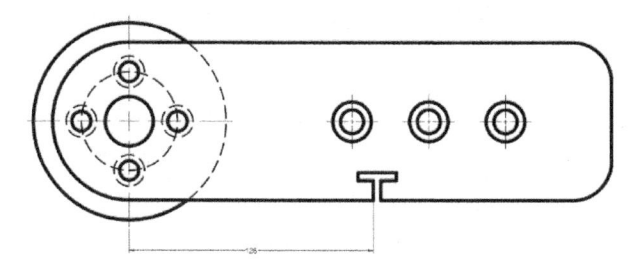

- Activate **Automatically add scales to annotative objects when the annotation scale changes** on the status bar.

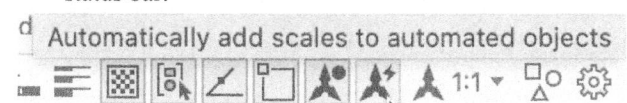

- Set the **Annotation Scale** to **1:2**; the size of the dimension will automatically increase by two times.

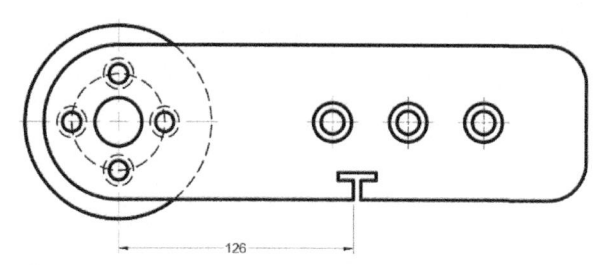

Example 2:

- Ensure that the **Annotation Scale** is set to **1:2** and create another linear dimension, as shown in the figure.

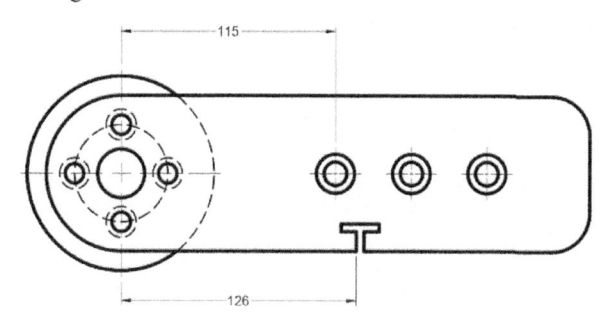

- Click the **ISO A4** layout in which the viewport scale is set to 1:2; you will notice that the dimensions are scaled with respect to the viewport.

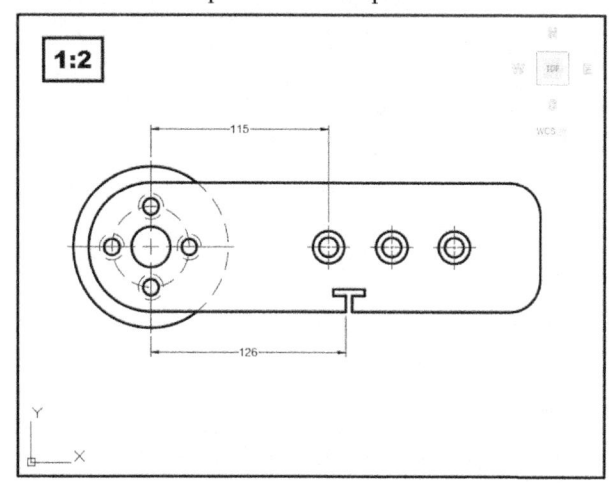

- Click the **ISO A1** layout; you will notice that the dimensions are not displayed in the 2:1 viewport. To display dimensions in the 2:1 viewport, you need to add 2:1 scale to dimensions.

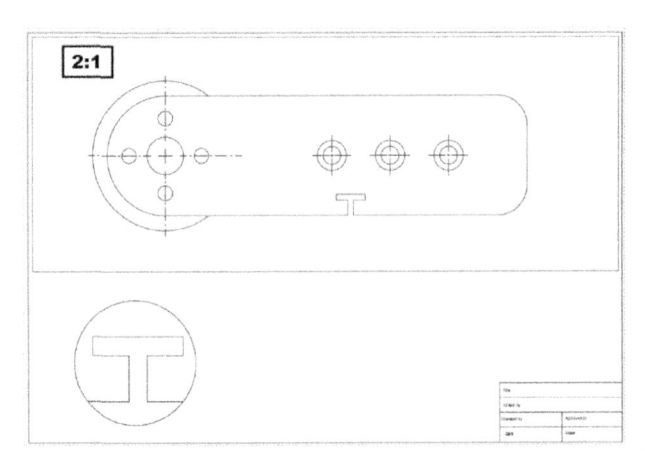

- Click the **Model** tab below the graphics window to switch to the model space.
- Click **Modify > Annotative Object Scale > Add/Delete Scales** on the menu bar. 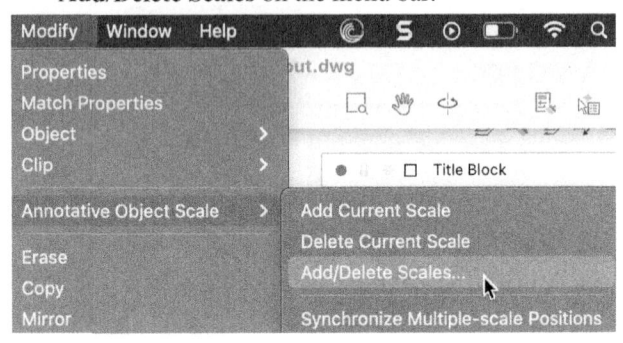
- Select the dimensions from the graphics window and right-click; the **Annotation Object Scale List** dialog appears. The scales applied to the selected dimensions are displayed on this dialog. You need to add a 2:1 scale to the dimensions so that they will be visible in the 2:1 viewport. 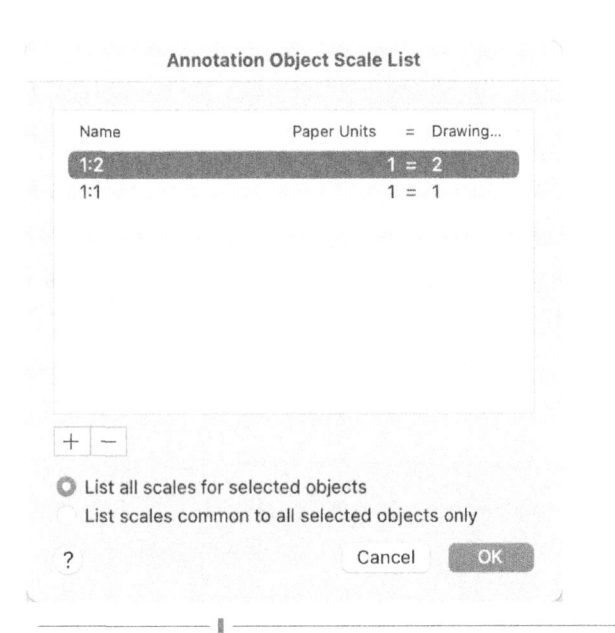
- To add a new scale to the dimensions, click the **Plus** button; the **Add Scales to Object** dialog appears.
- Select the **2:1** scale from the list and click **OK**; the scale will be added to the **Annotation Object Scale list** dialog.
- Click **OK** on the **Annotation Object Scale** dialog.
- Click the **ISO A1** layout; the dimensions are displayed in both 2:1 and 1:2 viewports. 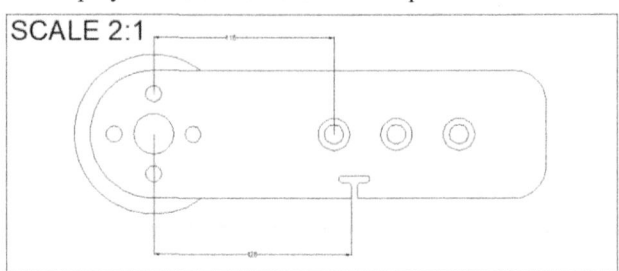 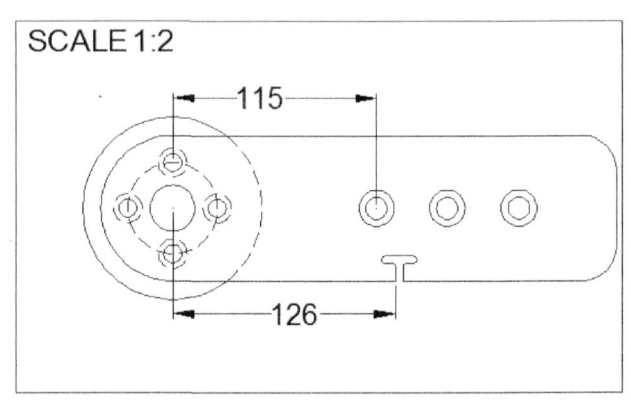
- Similarly, create other dimensions, as shown below. Add 2:1 and 1:2 scales to dimensions and check the drawing in two different layouts.

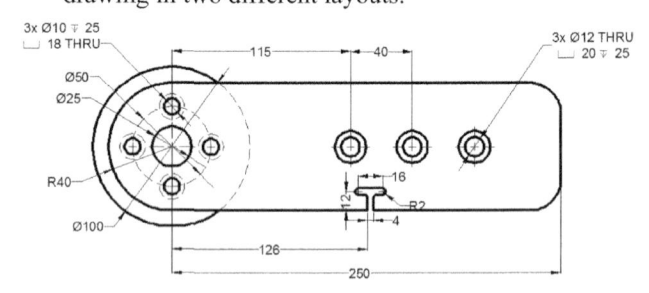

Scaling Hatches relative to Viewports

While working in layouts, you may also need to scale the hatch with respect to the viewport scale. The following figure shows a drawing in two different viewports 1:2 and 1:1. The hatch in the left viewport is smaller than that in the right side viewport. You can correct this problem by using the **Relative to Paper Space** option.

226 | Layouts & Annotative Objects

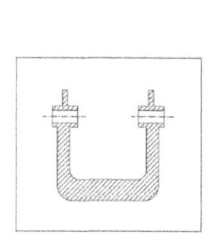

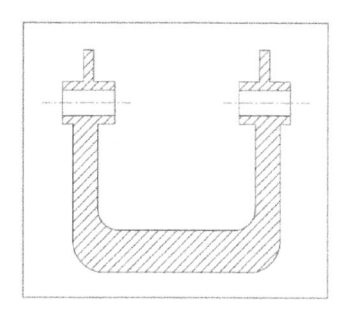

- Double-click inside a viewport; the model space will be activated.
- Double-click on the hatch patterns from the drawing; the **Hatch Edit** dialog appears.
- In the **Hatch Edit** dialog, select the **Relative to Paper Space** option from the **Angle and Scale** section.

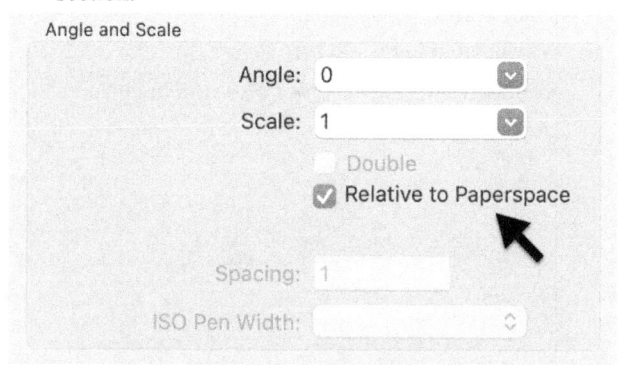

- Click the **OK** button; you will notice that the hatch will be scaled with respect to the viewport scale. Double-click outside the viewport to switch to the paper space.

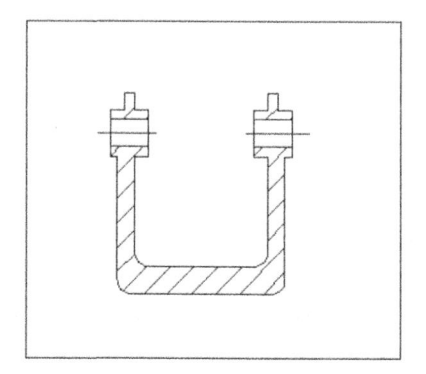

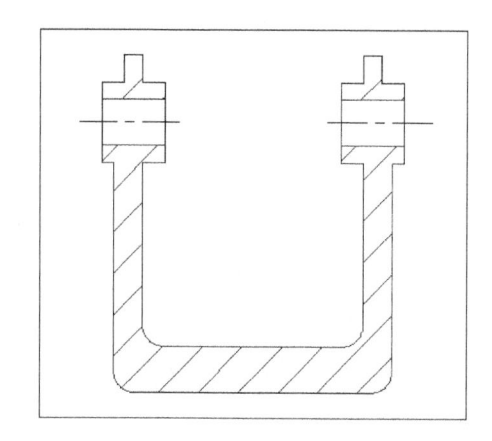

Working with Annotative Text

Annotative property can also be assigned to text. The annotative text will be scaled with respect to the viewport scale.

- Open the **Viewports-Example.dwg**, if not already opened.
- Click **Text > Text Style** on the **Drafting** tool set; the **Text Style** dialog appears.
- Click the **Add or remove text styles** button on the **Text Style** dialog. 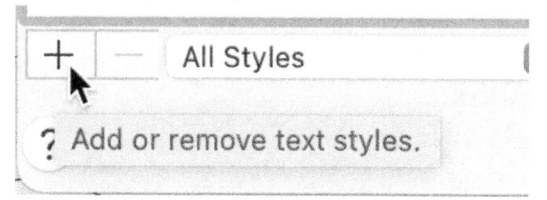
- Enter **Text_Anno** as the **Style name**. 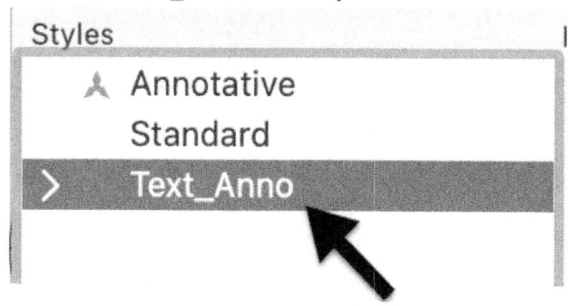
- Select the **Text_Anno** style from the **Styles** list.
- Set **Family** to **Arial**.
- Click the **Annotative** button.
- Set **Paper Text Height** to **2.5** and **Width Factor** to **1**.
- Click **Apply** and **Close**.
- Select **1:1** from the **Viewport Scale** menu at the status bar.

- Click **Text > Multiline Text** on the **Drafting** tool set.
- Specify the first corner of the text editor by picking an arbitrary point.
- Right-click and select the **Justify** option from the shortcut menu.
- Right-click and select the **MC** option.
- Move the pointer toward the right and specify the second corner of the text editor.
- Type **All dimensions are in mm** and click the **Save** button on the **Text Editor** visor.
- Move the text and place it at the bottom left corner of the drawing, as shown below. You can also add a frame to the text. To do this, first select the text. On the **Properties** palette, under the **Text** section, check the **Text Frame** option.

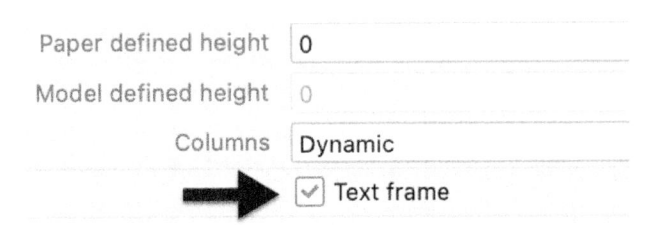

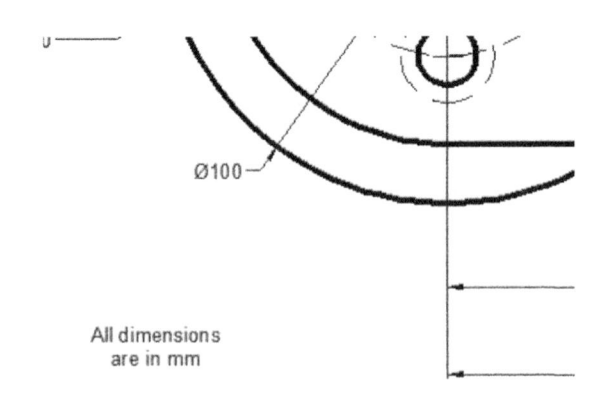

- View the drawing in the **ISO A4** layout; you will notice that the text is not displayed. It is because the text is set to a 1:2 scale.
- On the status bar, click the **Show annotation objects for all scales** button.

The text is visible in the ISO A4 layout.

- Save the drawing as **Layout Example.dwg** and close.

Exercises

Exercise 1

Create the drawing, as shown below. After creating the drawing, perform the following tasks:
- Create a layout of the A3 size and then create a viewport.
- Set the viewport scale to 1:2.
- Set the scale of the dimensions and hatch lines with respect to the viewport.

AutoCAD 2023 For Beginners (For Mac Users)

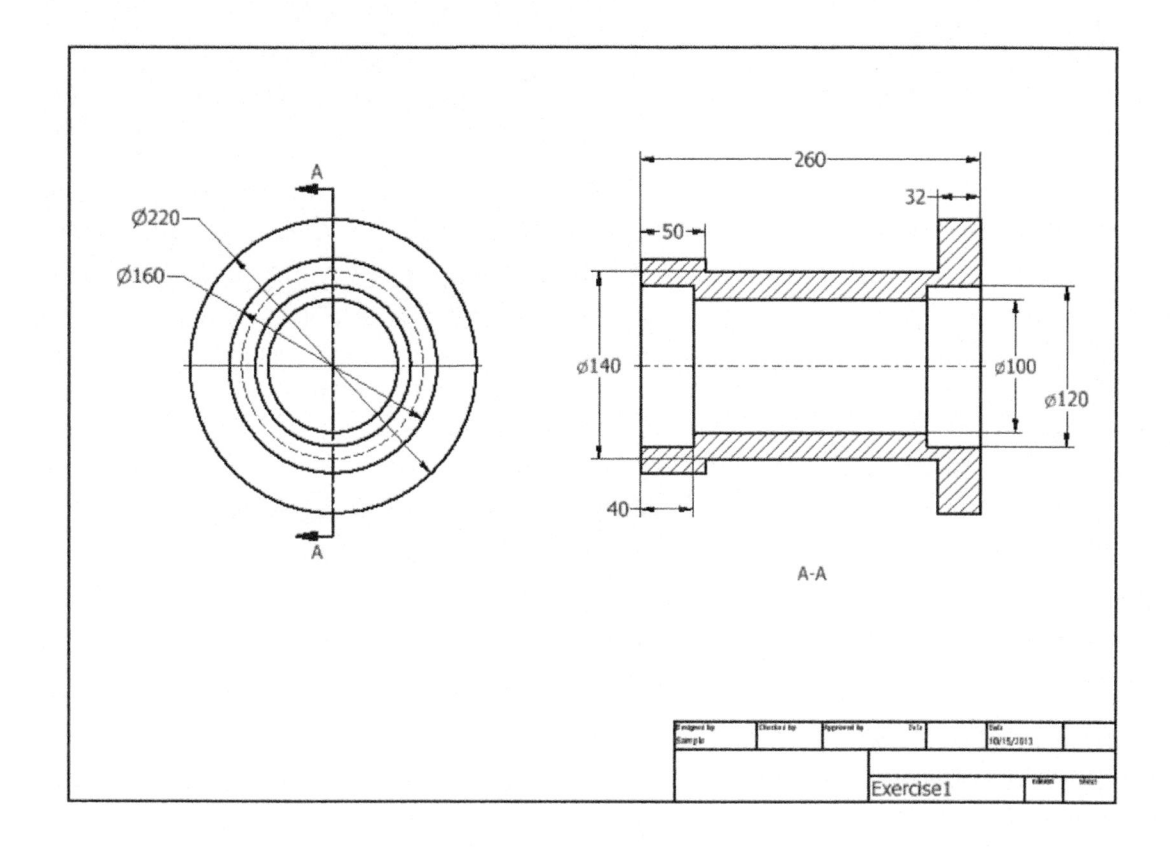

AutoCAD 2023 For Beginners (For Mac Users)

Chapter 11: Templates and Plotting

In this chapter, you will learn to do the following:

- **Create Plot Style Tables**
- **Create Templates**
- **Plot/Print the drawing**
- **Compare Drawings**
- **Batch Publish**
- **Package Drawing**

Plotting Drawings

Plotting is the process of producing a physical copy of the drawing using a printer or plotter. The printer may be directly connected to an AutoCAD workstation or on the network of workstations. Although the process of plotting is straightforward, it is essential to know how to establish communication between AutoCAD and the plotter. In this chapter, you will learn to connect a plotter with AutoCAD, define plotting style, and produce professional prints of drawings. You will also learn to print and publish drawings in digital format.

Creating Plot Style Tables

Plot styles determine the final look of the plotted drawing. They are used to override the layer properties such as color, linetype, and lineweight when the drawing is printed. There are two types of plot styles: **Color-dependent** and **Named** plot style. **Color-dependent** plot styles are assigned based on the object color, whereas the **Named** plot styles are assigned based on layer or by an object.

- On the Menu bar, click **File > Plot styles** or type STYLESMANAGER in the command line; the **Plot Styles** folder appears.

- Double-click on the acad.stb plot style; the **Plot Style Table Editor** dialog appears.
- Right-click on the **Style 1** plot style and select **Rename style**.

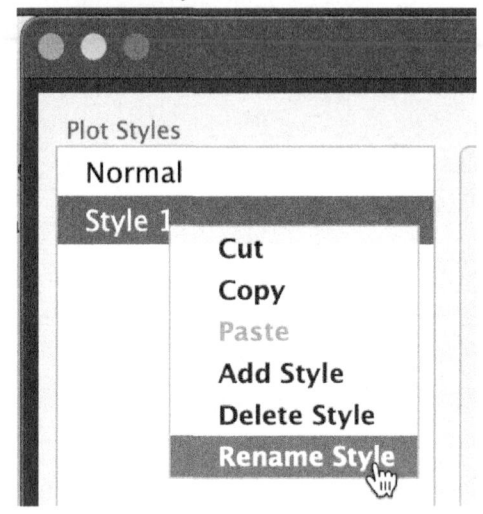

- Enter **PS1** in the **Name** box.
- Select **Black** from the **Color** drop-down.
- Set the **Screening** value to 70. The screening factor will fade objects in the printed output. A 20% screening factor will result in more fading of objects than a 50% screening factor.

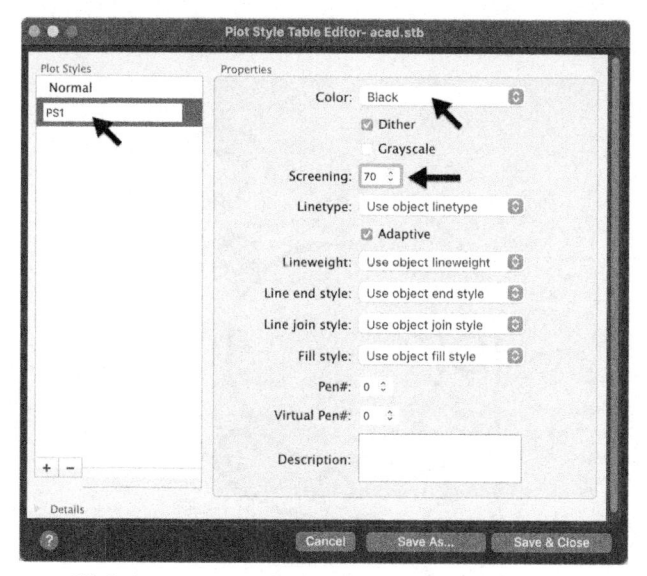

AutoCAD 2023 For Beginners (For Mac Users)

Layer	Linetype	Lineweight	Plot Style
Construction	Continuous	Default	PS1
Object	Continuous	0.7 mm	PS1
Hidden Lines	Hidden	0.3 mm	PS1
Center Lines	CENTER	0.25 mm	PS1
Dimensions	Continuous	0.25 mm	PS1
Section Lines	Continuous	0.5 mm	PS1
Cutting Plane	Phantom	0.6mm	PS1
Title Block	Continuous	1mm	PS1
Viewport	Continuous	0.25 mm	PS1
Text	Continuous	Default	PS1
Title block text	Continuous	Default	PS1

- Click **Save As** on the **Plot Style Table Editor** dialog.
- Type **Sample** in the **Save As** box and click the **Save** button.
- Click **Save & Close** to close the **Add Plot Style Table** dialog; the **Sample** plot style will be added to the **Plot Styles** folder.

- Dock the **Layers** palette.
- Click the **Layout 1** tab to activate the paper space.
- Click **Page setup Manager** on the toolbar; the **Page Setup Manager** dialog appears.
- Click the **Gear** drop-down > **Edit**; the **Page Setup** dialog appears.
- Select the plotter from the **Printer** drop-down.
- Set the **Paper Size** to **A3** and **Drawing orientation** to **Landscape**.
- Click **OK** and **Close** to exit both the dialogs.
- Draw a title block in the paper space, as shown below.

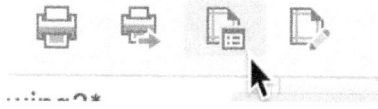

Creating Templates

After specifying the required settings in a drawing file, you can save those settings for future use. You can do so by creating a template. Template files have settings such as units, limits, and layers already created, which will increase your productivity.

- Click the **New** button on the **Toolbar**; the **Select Template** dialog appears.
- Double-click on the **acadiso.dwt** file; a drawing file will be opened.
- Undock the **Layers** palette and create the layers shown in the table below:

231 | Templates and Plotting

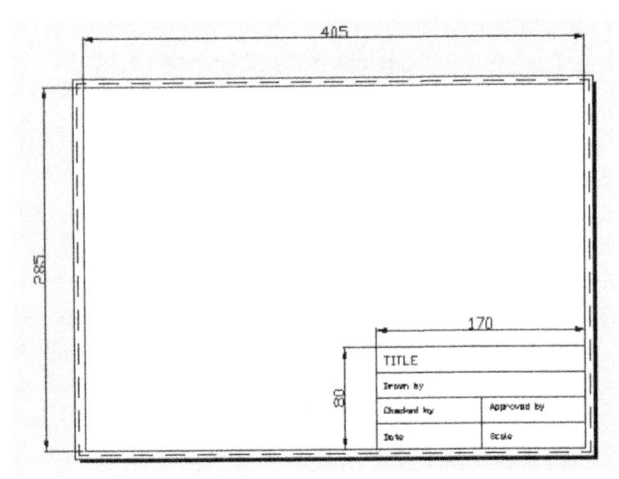

- Create a viewport inside the title block (refer to the **Creating Viewports in the Paper space** section discussed earlier in this chapter).

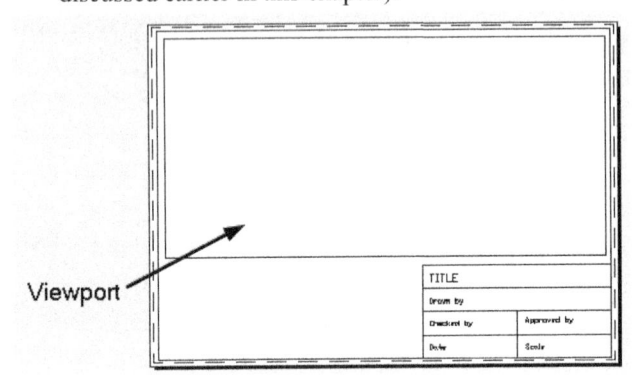

- On the Toolbar, click the **Save** button; the **Save Drawing As** dialog appears.
- In the **Save Drawing As** dialog, set **Files of type** to **AutoCAD Drawing Template (*.dwt).**
- Type **ISOA3** in the **File name** box and click **Save**.
- Right-click and select Metric.
- Type **ISO-A3 Horizontal layout with title block** as the description and press RETURN.
- Close the **ISOA3** file.

Plotting/Printing the drawing

- Click the **New** button.
- Double-click on **ISOA3**. A new drawing will be started with the selected template.
- Undock the **Layers** palette; you will notice that the layers saved in the template file are loaded automatically.
- Dock the **Layers** palette.
- Create a drawing, as shown below. You can also download the drawing from the companion website.

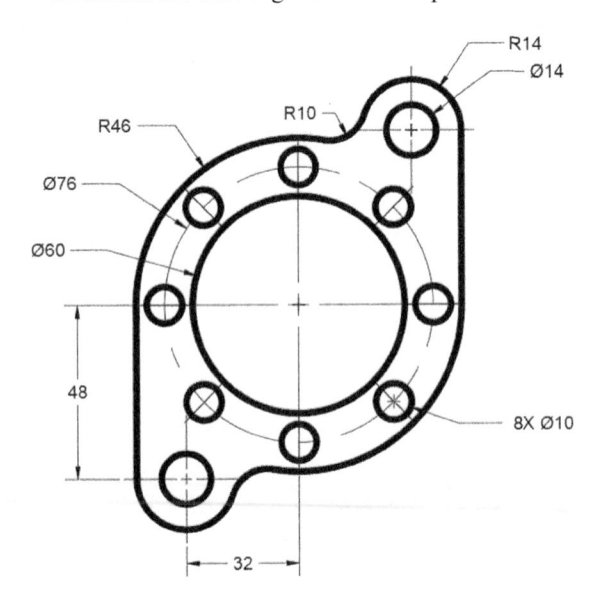

- Click the **Layout 1** tab to activate the paper space.
- Double-click inside the viewport to activate the model space.
- Set the **Viewport Scale** to 1:1 on the status bar.
- Use the **Pan** tool and position the drawing at the center of the viewport.
- Double-click outside the viewport to activate the paper space.
- Hide the viewport frame by freezing the **Viewport** layer.

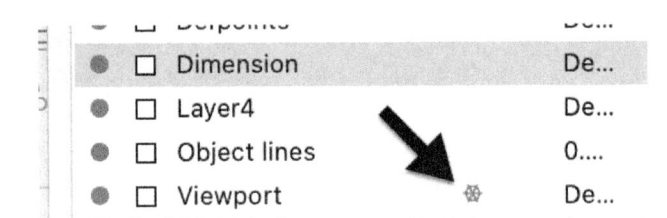

- Click the **Plot** button on the **Toolbar**; the **Plot** dialog appears.

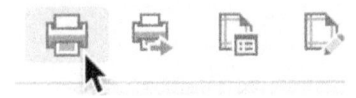

- Make sure that the options in this dialog are the same as that you specified while creating the template.
- Select the printer from the **Printer** drop-down.
- Click the **Preview** button located at the bottom left corner; the preview window appears.
- Examine the print preview for the desired output and close it.

232 | Templates and Plotting

- Click the **Plot** button on the **Plot** dialog; the drawing will be plotted.

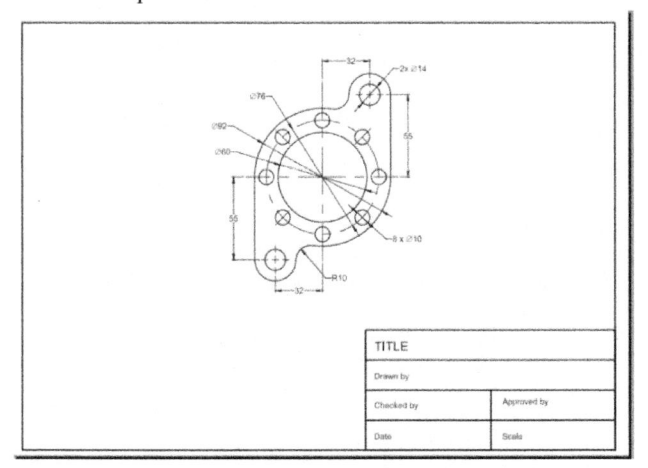

- Save and close the drawing file.

Exporting to PDF

The PDF and DWF files are one of the commonly used file formats to exchange drawings between designers and clients. AutoCAD makes it easy to export the drawing to the PDF or DWF formats.

- On the menu bar, click **File > Export to PDF**.
- On the Plot dialog, select **AutoCAD PDF (High Quality Print).pc3** option from the **Printer** drop-down.
- Click the **Printer Options** icon next to the **Printer** drop-down. 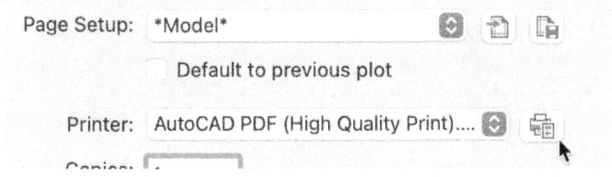
- On the **PDF Options** dialog, set the Vector quality, Raster image quality, line merge control, and Data options.

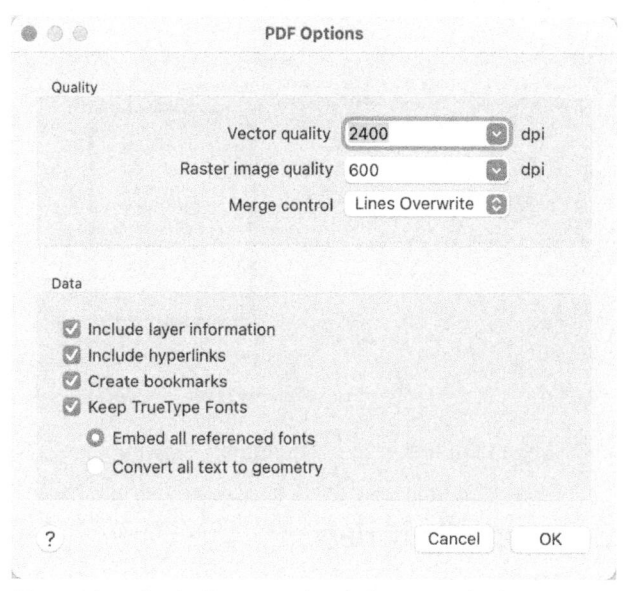

The options in the **Data** section help you to include layer information, hyperlinks, and create bookmarks. Also, you can capture fonts used in the drawing.

- Click **OK**.
- Click the **Plot** button.
- Specify the location of the PDF file and click **Save**. **Plot and Publish Job complete** dialog appears after exporting the PDF file.
- Click **Open the PDF file** to view the PDF viewer and notice the layers, bookmarks, hyperlinks in the drawing. Also, you can find any text in the drawing using the text search option in the PDF viewer.

Importing a PDF

AutoCAD allows you to import a PDF into a drawing file.

- Click the **Import** icon on the toolbar.

- Browse to the location of the PDF file.
- Select the PDF file, and a preview appears in the **Preview** area of the **Import PDF** dialog.
- On the **Import PDF** dialog, specify the **Scale** factor.
- Under the **PDF data to import** section, check the **TrueType text** option.
- Under the **Layers** section, check the **Use PDF Layers** option.

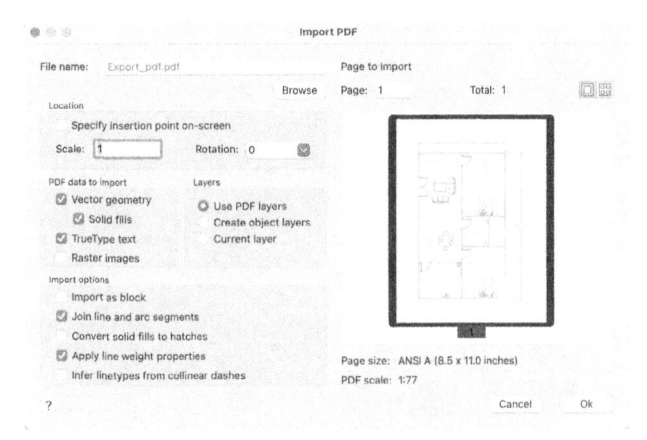

- Click **OK** to insert the PDF into the drawing.

Compare Drawings

The **DWG Compare** command compares two revisions of a drawing or two different drawings.

- Download the DWG_compare1 and DWG_compare2 drawing files from the companion website.
- Open the DWG_compare1 drawing.

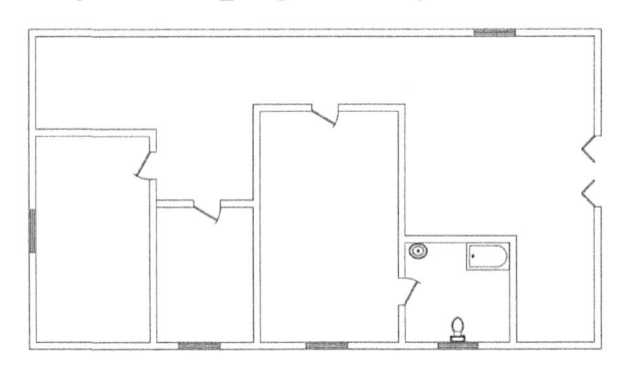

- Click the **DWG Compare** on the toolbar.

- Browse to the location of the DWG_compare2 file and double click on it; The differences between the two drawings are highlighted by a revision cloud. Also, the DWG Compare toolbar is displayed below the tool set.

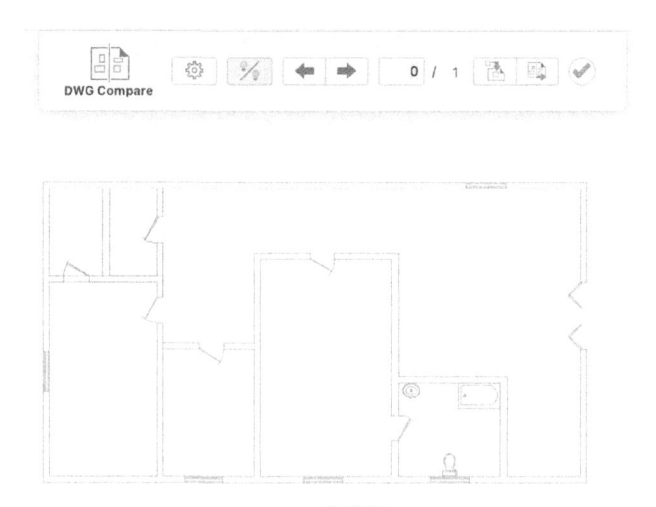

You can click the **On or off** icon to turn ON or OFF the comparisons.

Use the **Next Diff** and **Previous Diff** icons to zoom to different results.

On the **DWG Compare** toolbar, click the **Settings** drop-down to specify the color settings, revision cloud settings, and objects to be filtered.

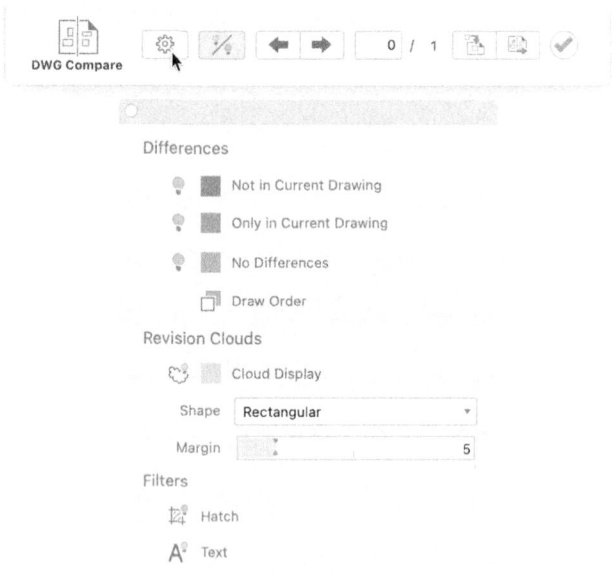

- Select the **Polygonal** option from the **Shape** drop-down in the **Revision Clouds** section.
- Click and drag the **Margin** dragger to change the margin between the revision cloud and highlighted objects.

234 | **Templates and Plotting**

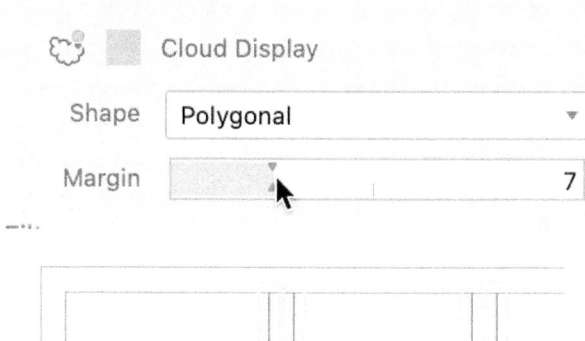

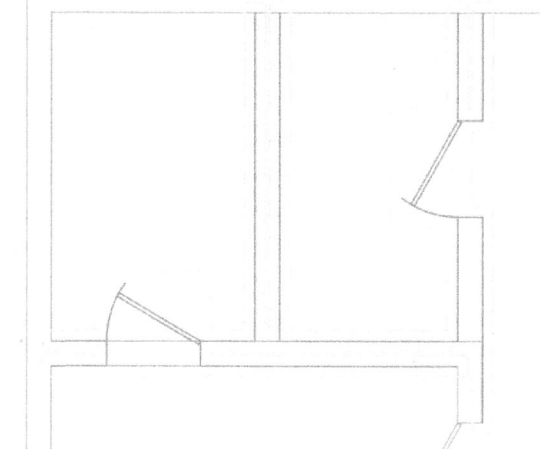

- Close the dialog.

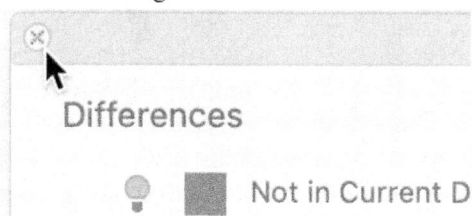

- Click the **Import Objects** icon on the **DWG Compare** toolbar.

- Select the objects highlighted in red color.

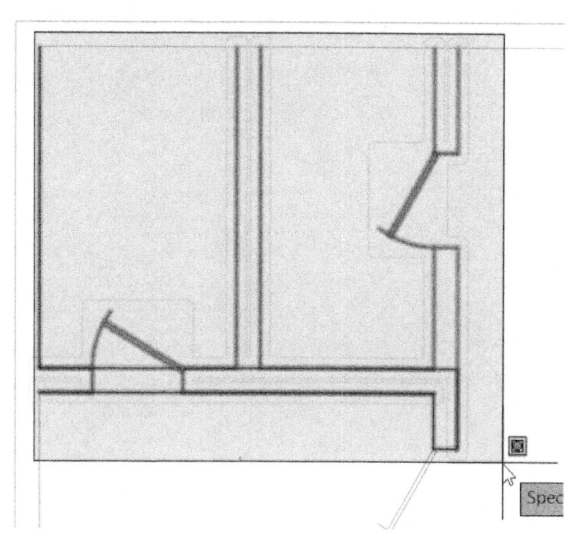

- Press RETURN; the selected objects are imported into the current drawing.

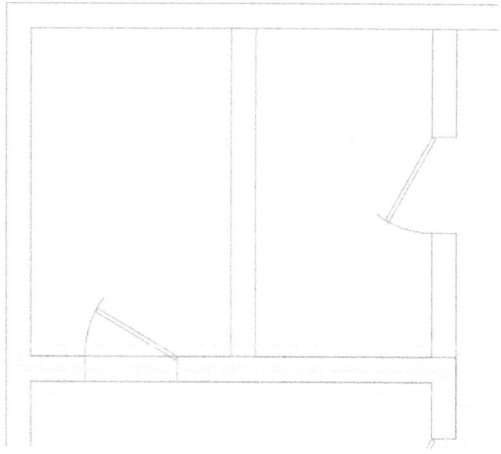

Notice that there is a revision cloud still displayed around the objects highlighted in green. These objects exist only in the current drawing.

- Select the objects highlighted in green color and press Delete on your keyboard; the revision clouds disappear.

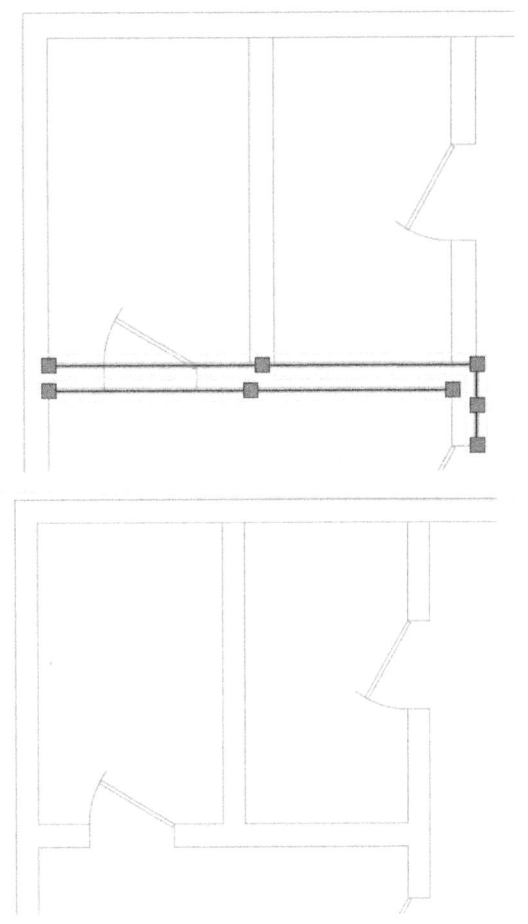

- Click the **Exit DWG Compare Mode** icon on the **DWG Compare** toolbar.

- Close the DWG_compare1 file without saving.

Exporting the Compared results to a new drawing

- Open the DWG_compare1 drawing.

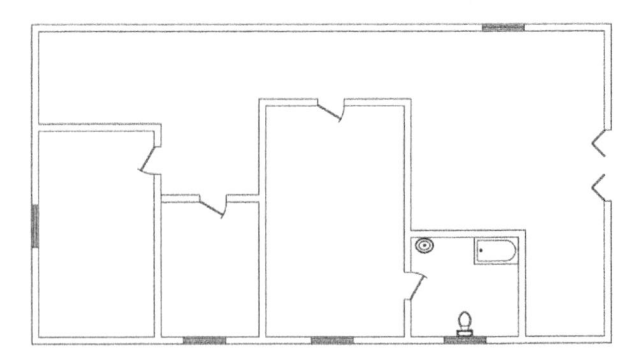

- Click the **DWG Compare** on the toolbar.
- Browse to the location of the DWG_compare2 file and double click on it; The differences between the two drawings are highlighted by a revision cloud. Also, the DWG Compare toolbar is displayed below the tool set.
- Click the **Export Snapshot** icon on the **DWG Compare** toolbar.

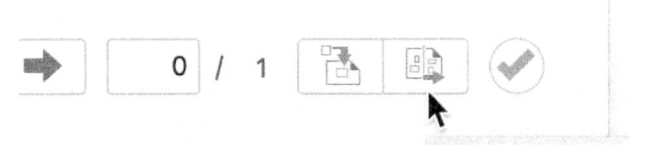

- Click **Continue** on the **Compare – Export a Comparison Snapshot** message box.

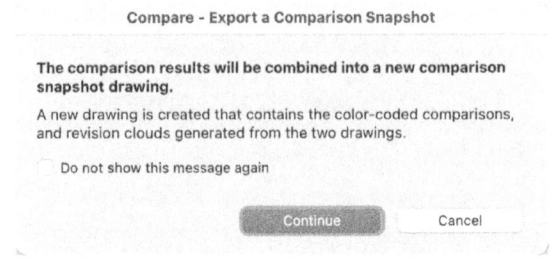

- Specify the location of the export file and click **Save**; the exported file is opened in another tab.

You can examine the DWG compare results using the **DWG Compare Snapshot** toolbar.

AutoCAD 2023 For Beginners (For Mac Users)

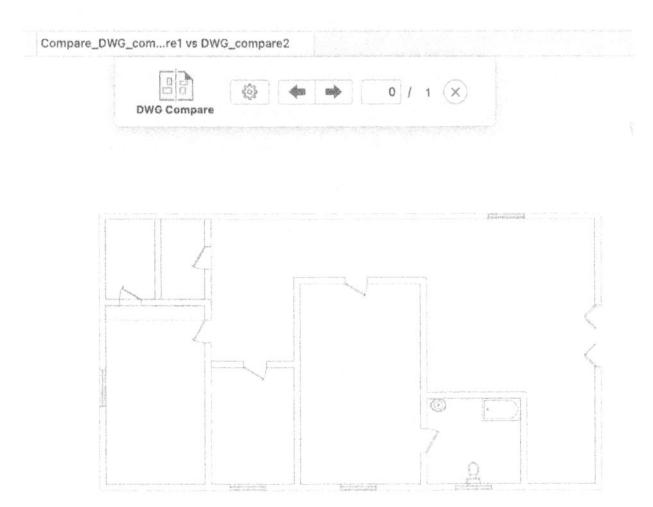

- Close all the files.

Batch Publish

The **Batch Publish** tool is used to publish multiple drawings or entire project quickly and accurately.

- Open the DWG_compare1 drawing.
- Click the **PUBLISH** icon on the toolbar (or) click **File > Batch Publish** on the menu bar.

- Click the **Add current drawing** button on the **Batch Publish** dialog. You can also click the **Add open drawings** button to add all the opened drawings.
- Select the Model space sheet and click the Minus button; the model space sheet is removed from the list. You can also click the **Remove model space sheet from the sheet list** icon to remove all the model space sheets.

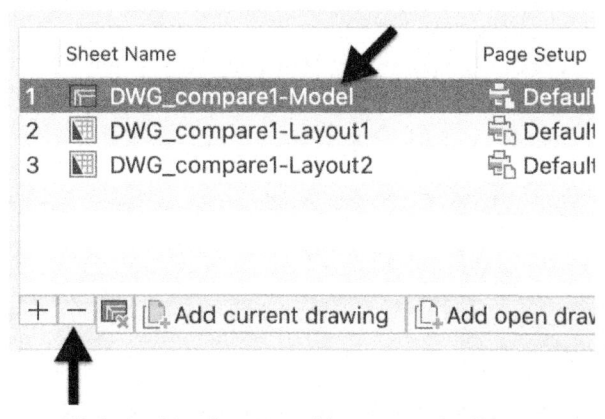

- Click the **Plus** button and browse to the location of the DWG_compare2 file and double click on it.
- Press and hold the COMMAND key on your keyboard and select the DWG_compare1_Layout2 and DWG_compare1_Layout2.
- Click the **Minus** button.

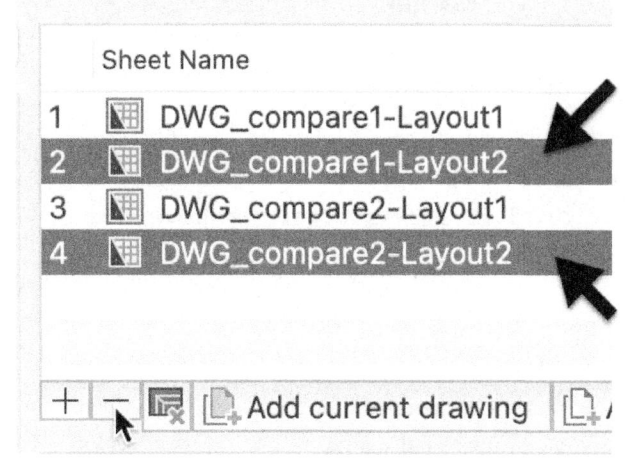

- Select **Publish to > PDF** from the top-left corner of the dialog.

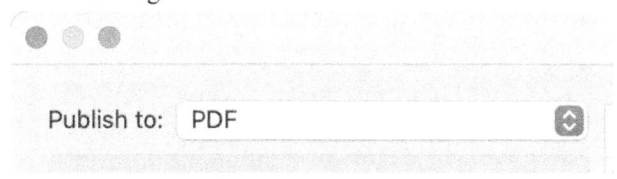

- Under the **Publish Output** section, select **Preset > AutoCAD PDF (High Quality Print)**.
- Specify the location of the output file using the **Location** drop-down.
- Make sure that the **Single PDF with multiple sheets** option is checked.
- Check the **Open when complete** option and click the **Publish** button.
- Specify the location of the output file and type the its name in the **Save As** box.

237 | Templates and Plotting

- Click the **Save** button; the PDF is opened in the **Previewer** application. Notice the layouts of two different drawings in a single PDF.

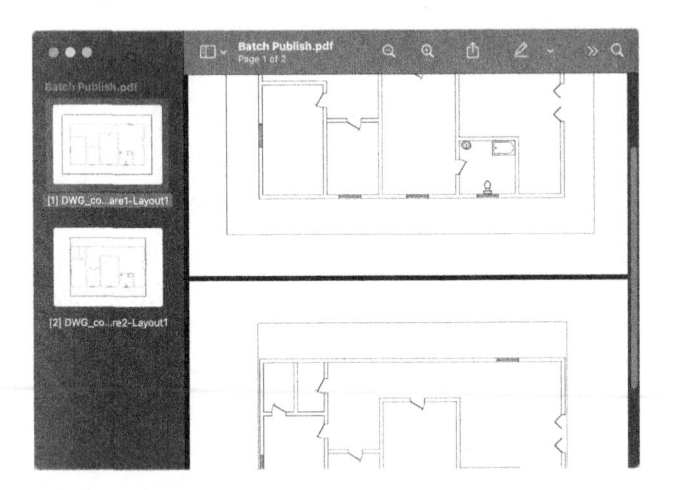

Package Drawing

The Package Drawing tool is used to package a drawing including all its external references, fonts, and shapes.

- Download and open the Crank _assembly file.
- Click the **Package Drawing** icon on the toolbar (or) click **File** > **Package Drawing** on the menu bar.

The **Package Drawing** dialog displays all the external references, fonts, and shapes.

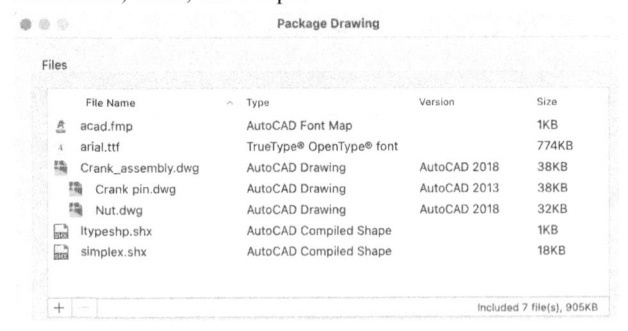

- Click the **Package Settings** button.
- Specify the **Package Type** and **File Compatability**.
- Select the required options from the **Advanced Options** section.

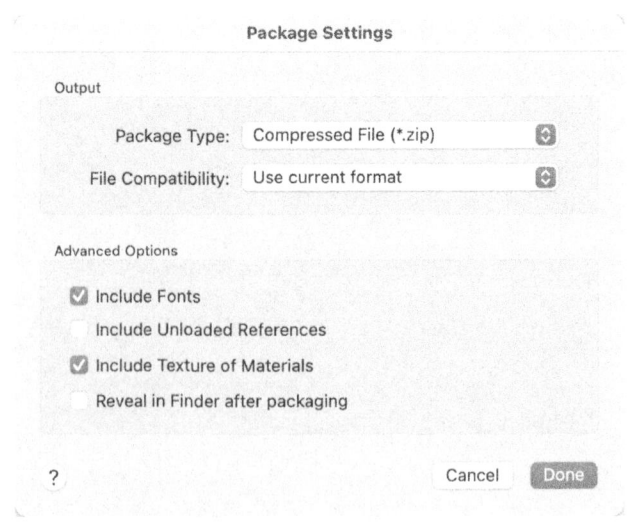

- Click the **Done** button.

Next, you can use the **Plus** button to add additional files that are not associated with drawing such as image files, spreadsheets, Bill of materials, or any relevant data. You can also add some notes in the **Package Notes** box.

- Click the Package files button.
- Specify the location of the package file and click **Save**. Next, you can send the Zip file to your colleague or other CAD users.

Exercise

Create and plot the drawing, as shown in the figure.

AutoCAD 2023 For Beginners (For Mac Users)

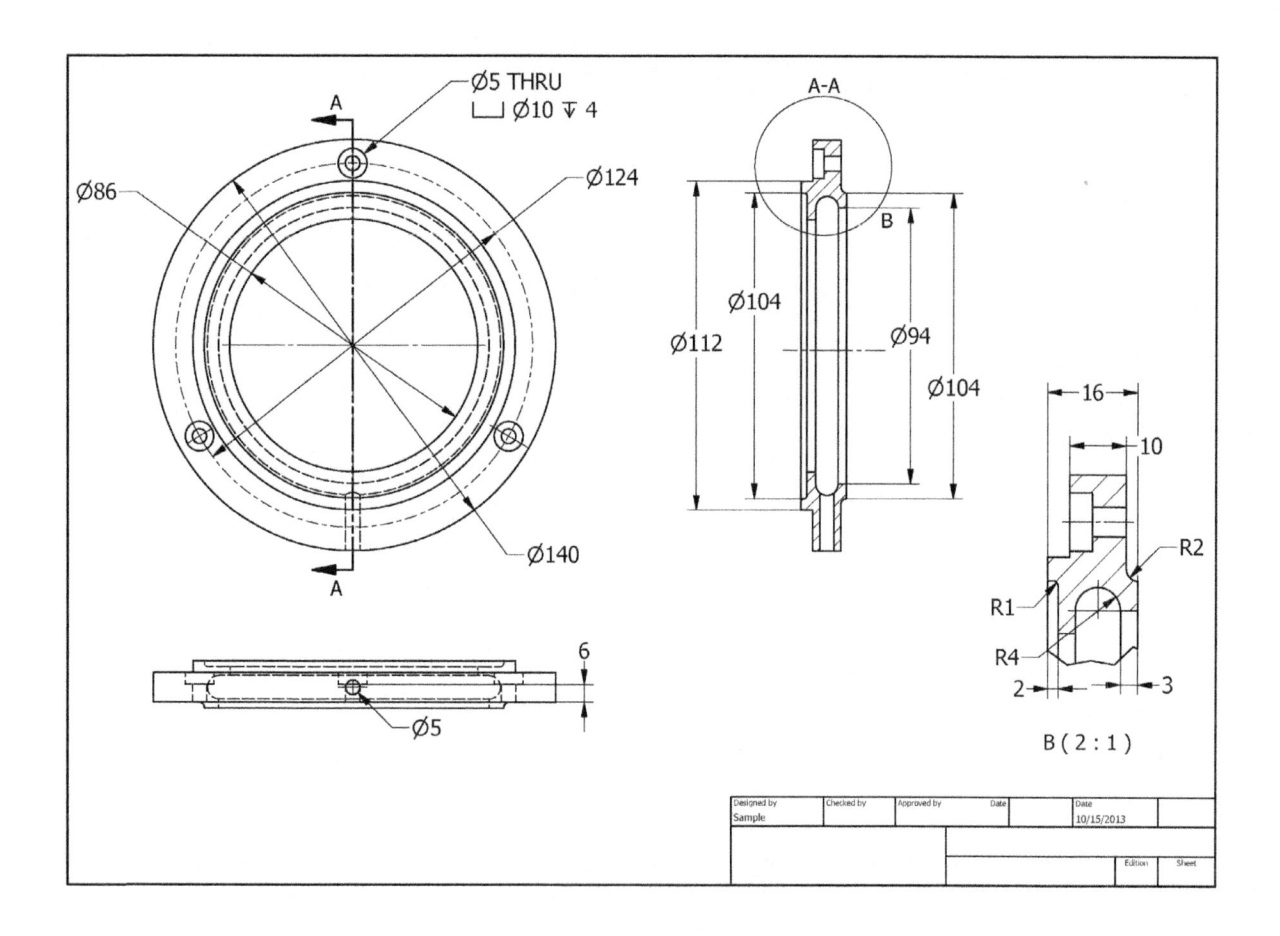

239 | **Templates and Plotting**

Chapter 12: 3D Modeling Basics

In this chapter, you will learn to do the following:

- **Create boxes, cylinders, wedges, cones, pyramids, spheres, and torus**
- **Create User Coordinate Systems**
- **Work with Dynamic UCS**
- **Change the View Style of objects**
- **Create Viewports in model space**
- **Create walls using the Polysolid tool**
- **Change the current UCS**
- **Create extruded, revolved, swept, lofted, and press-pulled objects**
- **Perform Boolean operations**
- **Align objects**
- **Create spiral and helical curves**

Introduction

In AutoCAD, you can create three types of 3D models: surfaces, solids, and meshes. Solids are used to create 3D models of engineering components and assemblies, and surfaces are used to create complex shapes such as plastic parts and meshes that are used for games and movies. Solids are three-dimensional models of actual objects that possess physical properties such as mass properties, the center of gravity, surface area, and moments of inertia. Surfaces are construction features without any thickness. They do not possess any physical properties. Meshes are similar to solids without mass and volume properties. In this chapter, you will learn the basics of 3D modeling, such as creating, navigating, and visualizing solid models.

The Modeling tool set

It contains the tools related to 3D modeling. You can access the tools for creating and editing solids and meshes, modifying the model display, working with coordinate systems, and sectioning 3D models.

AutoCAD 2023 For Beginners (For Mac Users)

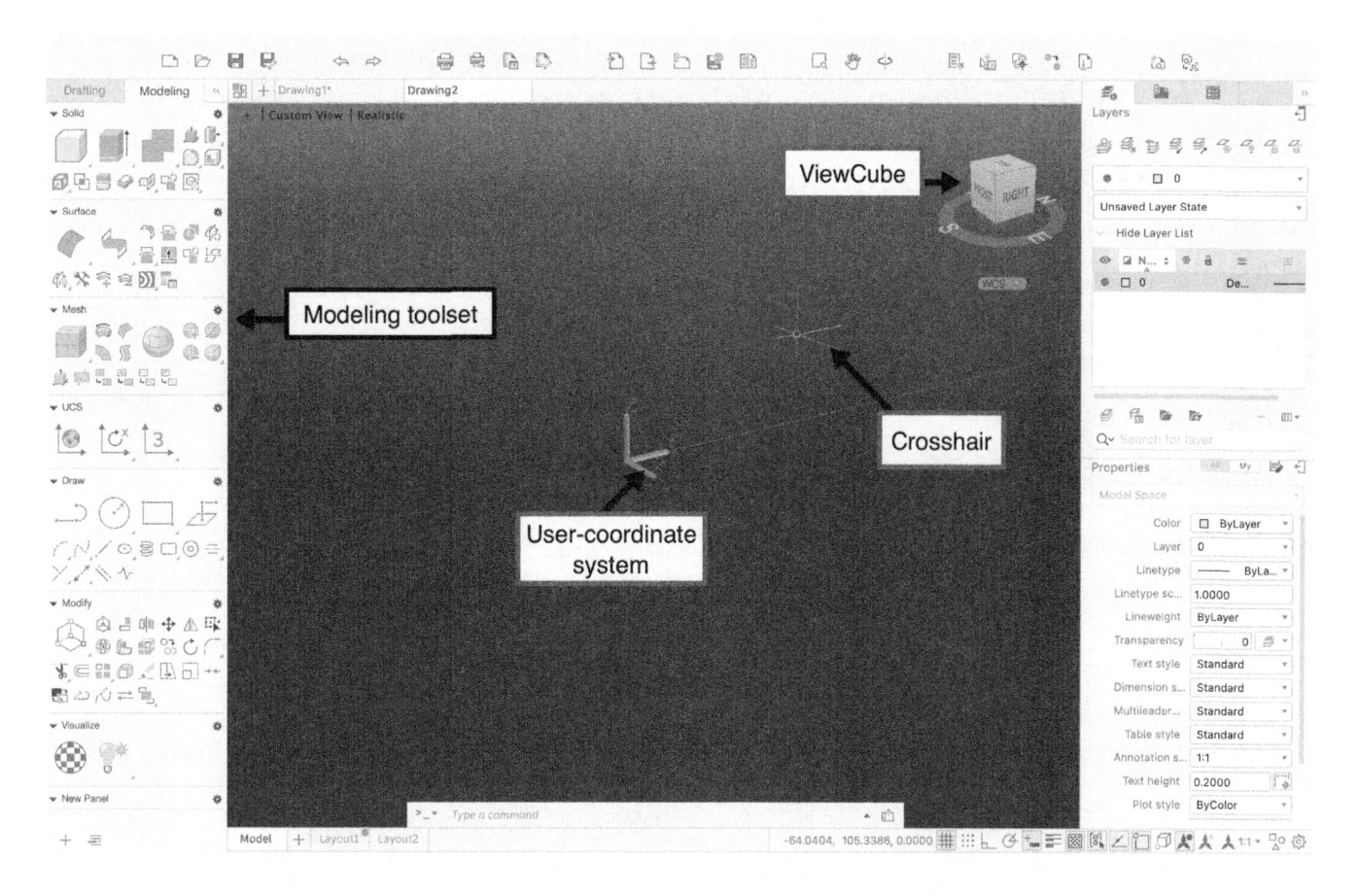

The **ViewCube** can be used to modify the view of the model quickly and easily. It is located at the top right corner of the graphics window. Using the **ViewCube**, you can switch between the standard and isometric views, rotate the model, switch to the **Home** view of the model, and create a new user coordinate system. You can also change the way the ViewCube functions by using the **ViewCube Settings** dialog. Right-click on the ViewCube, and then select the **ViewCube Settings** option; the **ViewCube Settings** dialog will be opened.

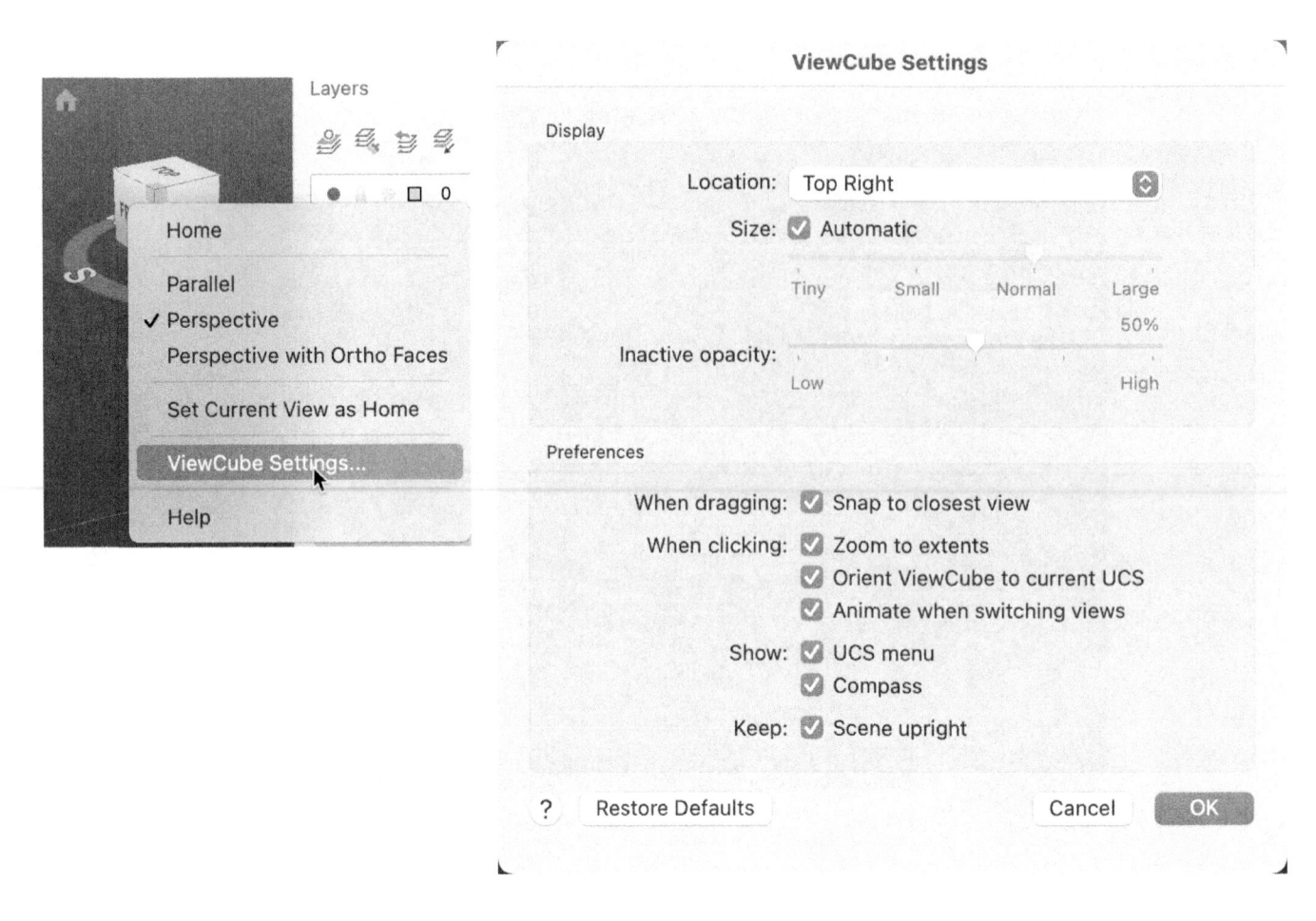

You can also modify the model view by using the Viewport Label menus. In addition to that, you can also change the view style of the model and control the display of other tools in the graphics window using the Viewport Label menus.

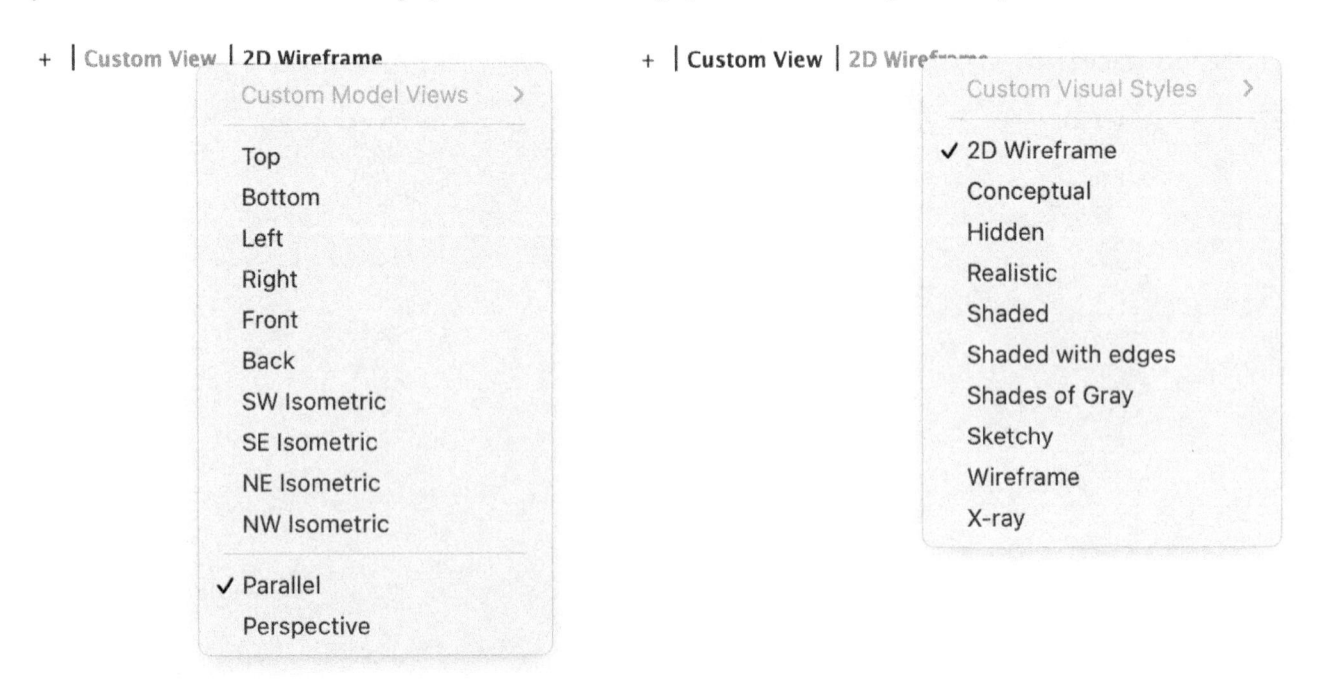

Now, you will create 3D models using the tools available in AutoCAD.

242 | 3D Modeling Basics

AutoCAD 2023 For Beginners (For Mac Users)

The Box tool

The **Box** tool is used to create boxes having six rectangular or square faces. It is the most commonly used tool, as many 3D objects are made of boxes.

- Click the **AutoCAD 2023** icon on your desktop.
- On the Welcome window, click **Create** > **New** > **acadiso3D**. Next, click **Open**. A new file will be started.
- Click **Modeling** > **Solid** > **Box** on the tool set or type **BOX** in the command line; the message, "Specify the first corner," appears in the command line.

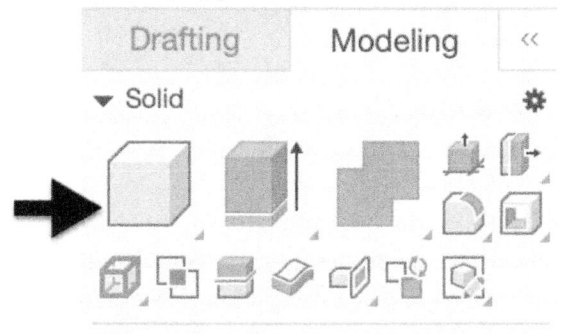

- Pick an arbitrary point in the graphics window; the message, "Specify the other corner," appears in the command line.
- Ensure that the **Dynamic Input** icon is active on the status bar. You will notice the two value boxes to specify the length and width of the box.
- Type 100 in the length box and press the TAB key.
- Type 70 in the width box and press RETURN.
- Move the pointer upward, type 60 as height, and press RETURN; the box will be created as shown.
- Click **View** > **Zoom** > **All** on the Menu Bar.
- On the **Viewport Label Menus**, click **Visual Style Controls** > **Shades of Grey**.
- Right click on the **Home** icon above the ViewCube and select **Parallel**.

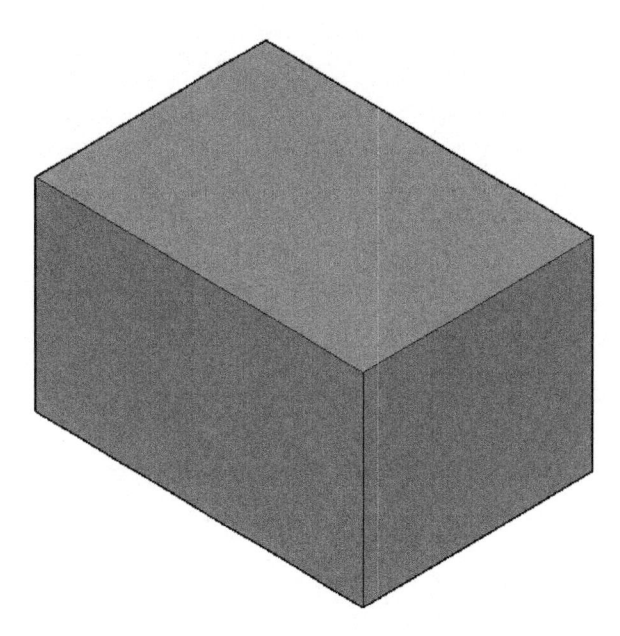

Creating the User Coordinate System

User Coordinate Systems assist you while creating 3D models. They are used to create construction planes on which you can add additional features to the model. Various methods to create User coordinate systems are discussed next.

Example1:

- On the status bar, click the **Customization** button and select **Dynamic UCS** from the menu. Also, select **3D Object Snap** from the menu.
- Deactivate the **Dynamic UCS** icon on the status bar. You will learn about this option later in this chapter.

- Select the UCS displayed at the bottom left corner of the modelspace.
- Place the pointer on the origin of the UCS.

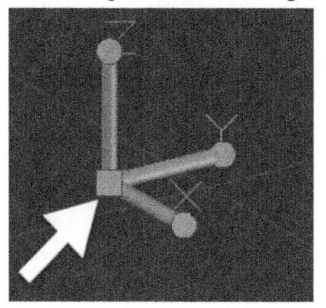

3D Modeling Basics

- Select the **Move and Align** option from the menu.

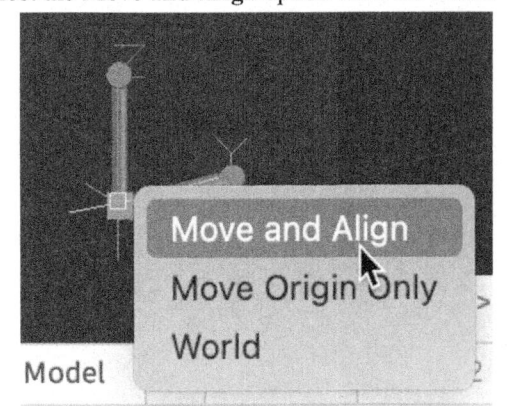

- Activate the **3D Object Snap** icon on the status bar.

- Select the vertex point on the top left corner of the box as shown below; the message, "Specify point on X-axis or <accept>:" appears in the command line.

- Select the endpoint of the top face of the box, as shown in the figure; the message, "Specify other corner or [Cube Length]:" appears in the command line.

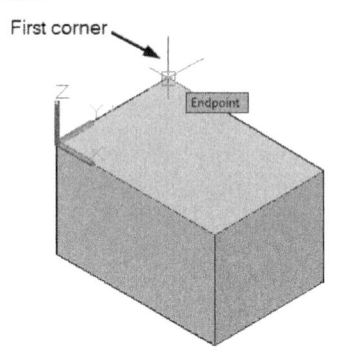

- On the Status bar, click the right-mouse button on the **3D Object Snap** icon, and select **Midpoint on edge**.

- Select the midpoint of the front edge of the box, as shown below.

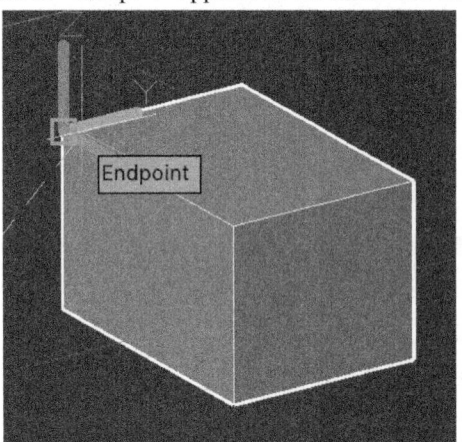

Creating a Wedge

When you slice a box diagonally, it results in a wedge. A wedge has five faces, three rectangular and two triangular.

- Click **Modeling > Solid > Primitives drop-down > Wedge**  on the tool set or type **WE** in the command line and press RETURN; the message, "Specify first corner or [Center]" appears in the command line.

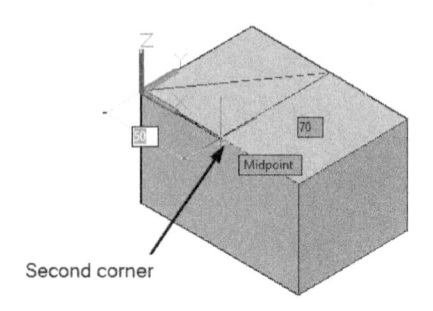

- Move the pointer upward and enter 40 as the height; the wedge will be created, as shown below.

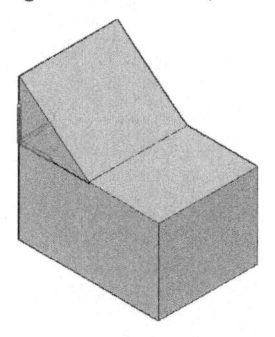

Example2: (Creating UCS by selecting 3-points)

You can create a UCS by selecting three points. The first point will be the origin of the UCS, the second point will define the X-axis, and the third point defines the Y-axis.

- Click **Modeling > UCS > 3 Point** on the tool set; the UCS is attached to the pointer and the message, "Specify new origin point <0,0,0>:" appears.

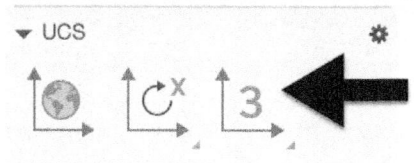

- Select the lower endpoint of the wedge, as shown in the figure.

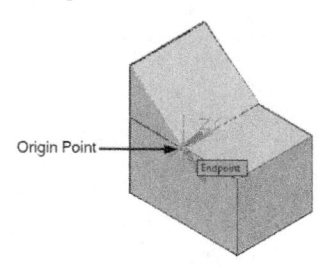

- Move the pointer toward the right.
- Select the other endpoint of the bottom edge of the wedge, as shown in the figure.

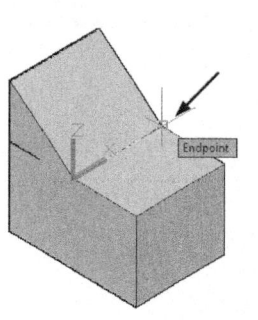

- Move the pointer along the diagonal edge of the wedge
- Select the endpoint on the top edge, as shown. The UCS will be created and aligned to the inclined face of the wedge.

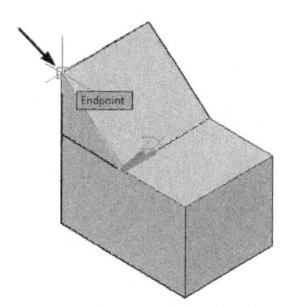

Creating a Cylinder

Cylinders are commonly used features after boxes. In AutoCAD, you can create cylinders easily by using the **Cylinder** tool. You can create a circular or elliptical cylinder by using this tool.

- Click **View > Visual Styles** drop-down > **Wireframe** on the menu bar; the view style of the model will be changed to the wireframe style.

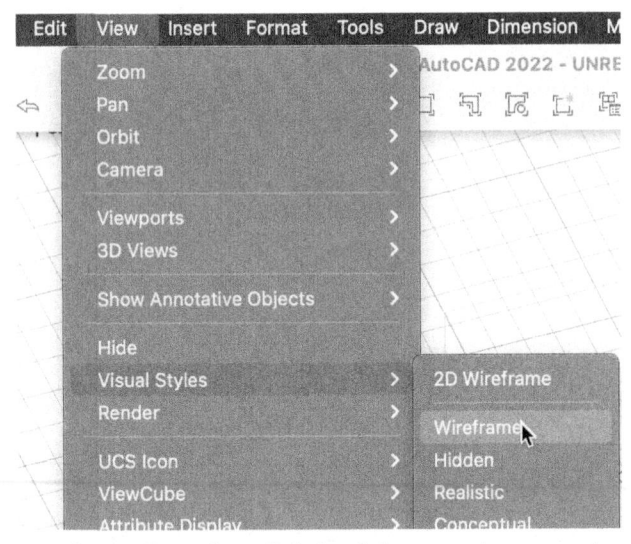

- On the Status bar, click the right mouse button on the **3D Object Snap** icon and select the **Center of face** option, if not already selected.
- Click **Modeling > Solid > Primitives** drop-down > **Cylinder** on the tool set or type **CYL** in the command line. 
- Snap to the center point of the inclined face, and then click to select it; the center point of the cylinder is specified on the inclined face of the wedge. 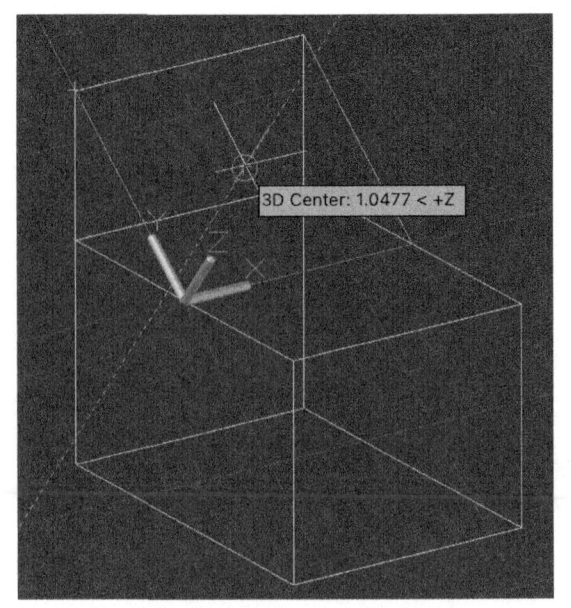
- Type 20 as the base radius and press RETURN.
- Move the pointer upward; you will notice that the pointer moves along the Z-axis of the UCS.
- Type 25 as height and press RETURN; the cylinder will be created as shown below.

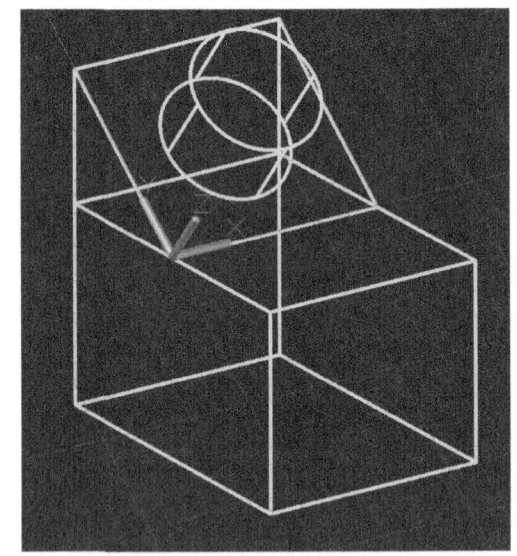

Example 3: (Returning to the previous position of the UCS)

- Click **Modeling > UCS > UCS, Previous** on the tool set; the UCS will return to its previous position.

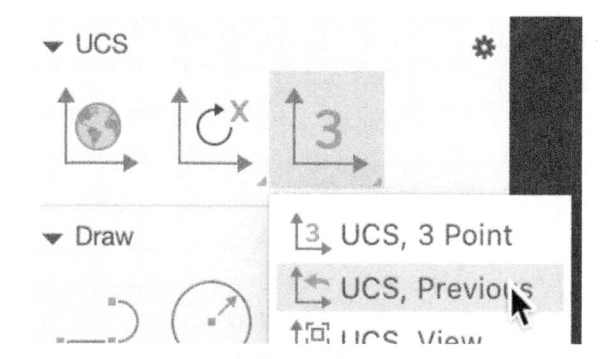

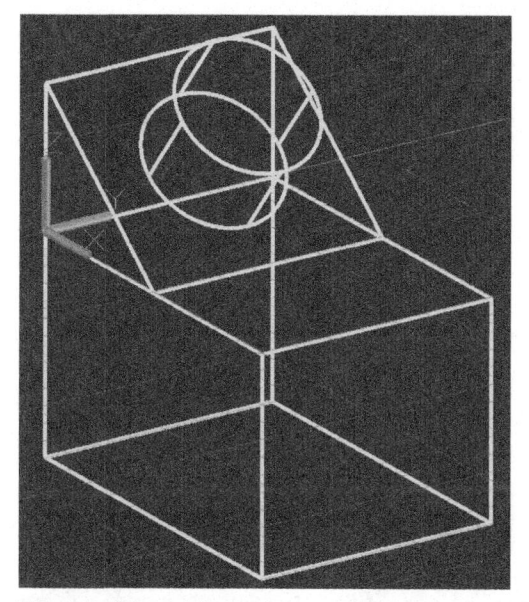

Example 4: (Creating a UCS by specifying its origin)

- Select the UCS and place the pointer on its origin.
- Select the **Move Origin Only** option; the UCS will be attached to the pointer.

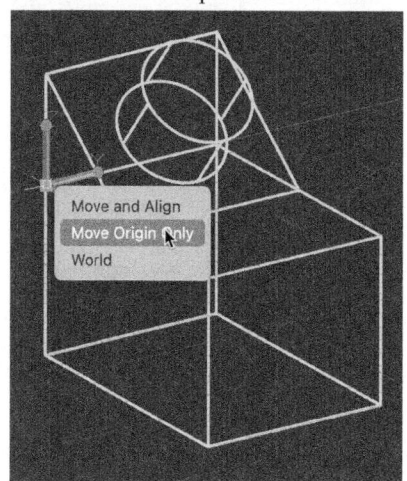

- Select the lower-left corner point of the box; the UCS will be placed at that point. Note that the orientation will not change.

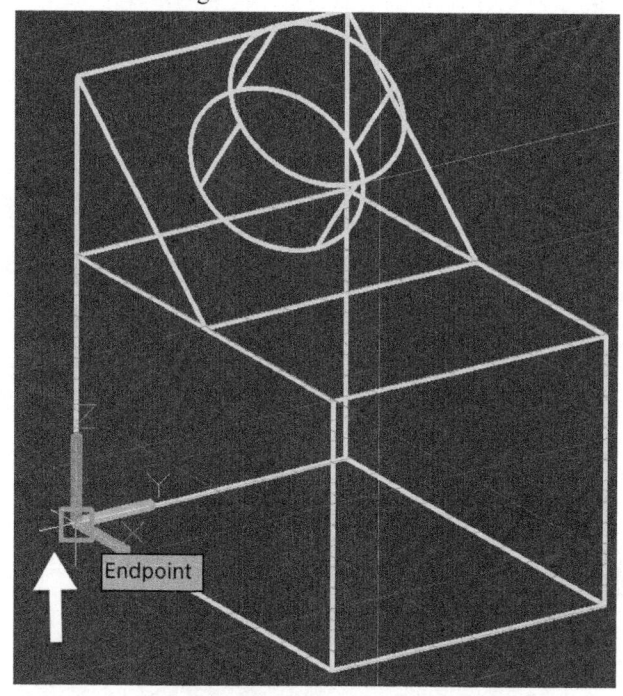

Example 5: (Rotating the UCS about X, Y, and Z axes)

You can rotate a UCS about X, Y, or Z axes by using the drop-down available in the **UCS** panel, as shown below.

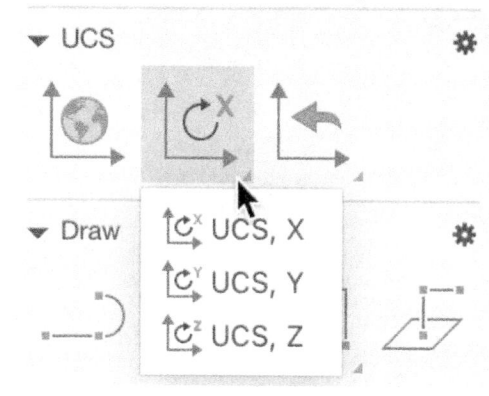

- Click the **X** option from the drop-down shown in the above figure; the message, "Specify rotation angle about X axis <90>:" appears in the command line.
- Type in the rotation angle in the command line.
- Similarly, you can rotate the UCS about the Y and Z axes using the respective options from the drop-down.

247 | **3D Modeling Basics**

Example 6: (Creating the UCS by specifying the Z-axis)

Using the **ZAxis** option, you can create a UCS by specifying its Z-axis.

- Type **UCS** in the command line and press RETURN.
- Type **ZA** or **ZAaxis** in the command line and press RETURN.
- Select the bottom right endpoint as the origin; the message, "Specify point on positive portion of Z-axis:" appears in the command line. Also, a rubber band line originating from the Z-axis is attached to the pointer. Now, as you move the pointer, you will notice that the Z-axis also moves.

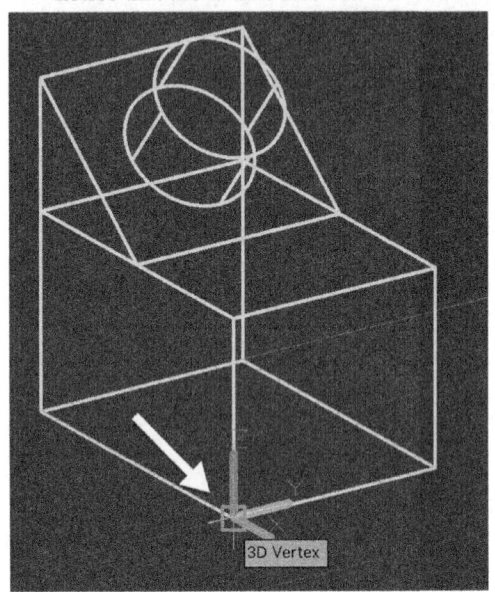

- Move the pointer and select the left endpoint of the bottom edge, as shown below; the Z-axis will be aligned to the bottom edge.

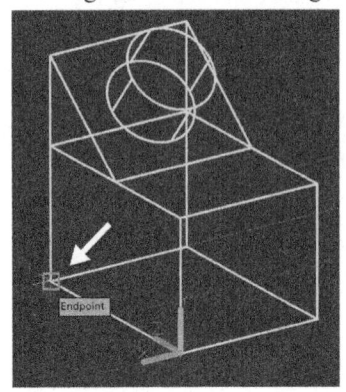

Example 7: (Creating UCS parallel to the screen)

Using the **View** tool in the **UCS** panel, you can create a UCS which is parallel to the screen.

- Click **Modeling > UCS > UCS, View** on the tool set; the XY plane of the UCS will become parallel to the screen. The UCS origin will not change. This option is useful if you want to use the current view and add a title block or any other annotation.

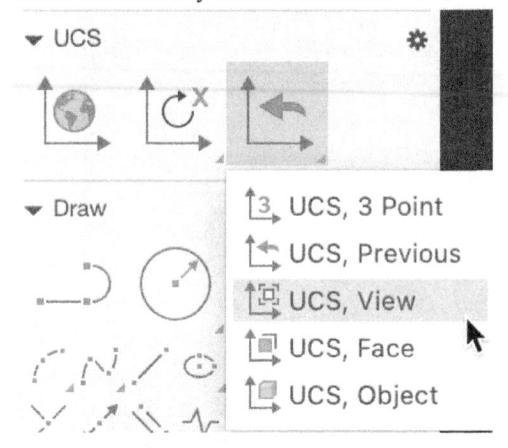

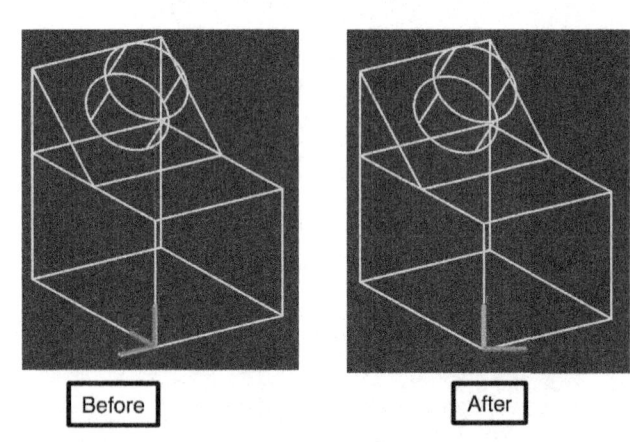

Before / After

Example 8: (Creating UCS aligned to an object)

You can create a UCS aligned to an object. The origin of the UCS will be aligned to the nearest endpoint of the object.

- Click **Modeling > UCS > UCS, Object** on the tool set; the message, "Select object to align UCS:" appears in the command line.
- Select the cylindrical object from the model; the UCS will be aligned to it.

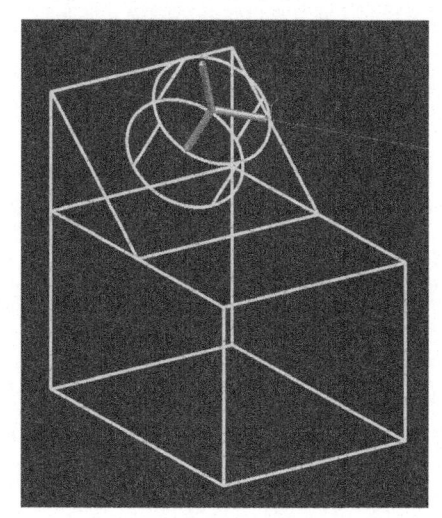

Example 9: (Creating UCS aligned to a face)

You can align a UCS to a planar or curved face of a model using the **Face** tool.

- Click **Modeling > UCS > UCS, Face** on the tool set; the message, "Select face of solid, surface, or mesh:" appears in the command line.
- Move the pointer over the faces of the model; you will notice that the UCS is displayed on the faces.

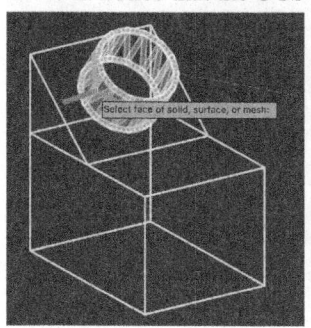

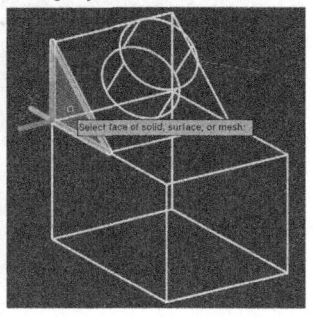

- Select the top face of the box; the message, "Enter an option [Next/Xflip/Yflip] <accept>:" appears in the command line.
  If you select the **Next** option, the adjacent face will be highlighted. The **Xflip** option is used to rotate the UCS 180 degrees about the X axis. The **Yflip** option is used to rotate the UCS 180 degrees about the Y axis.
- Press RETURN to accept; the UCS will be aligned to the selected face.

Using Dynamic User Coordinate System

In the previous section, you have learned to create various types of static user coordinate systems. They are active until you define another user coordinate system. You can also create dynamic user coordinate systems. A Dynamic User Coordinate System is a temporary UCS that appears automatically when you place your pointer over the face of a 3D solid object. Note that the Dynamic User Coordinate system appears only when you use tools that create objects directly (For example, drawing tools and primitive tools). To create a Dynamic UCS, you need to activate the **Dynamic UCS** option on the status bar.

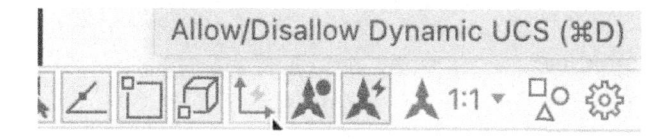

- Click the **Cylinder** button on the **Modeling** panel.
- Ensure that the **Dynamic UCS** button is active on the status bar.
- Move the pointer over the faces of the model; they will be highlighted.
- Click on the front face of the box and create the cylinder, as shown below.

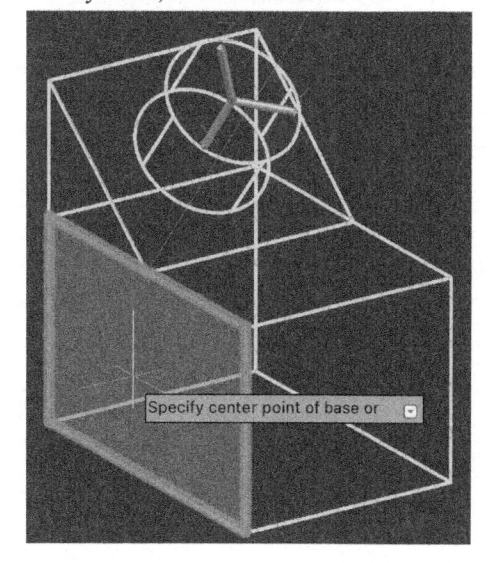

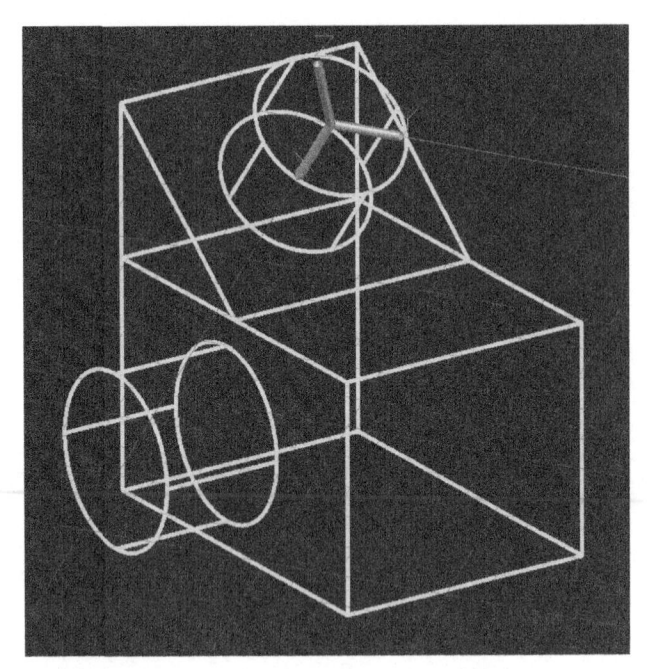

Model Space Viewports for 3D Modeling

While creating 3D models, it is useful to have a look at your model from several different orientations at the same time. For this purpose, you need to create different viewports in model space. You can create multiple viewports in model space using the **Viewport** drop-down available in the **View** tab of the menu bar. It can also be done by using the **Viewports** dialog. To load this dialog, click the Named Viewports icon on the toolbar (or) click **View > Viewports > New Viewports**; the **Viewports** dialog appears. In the dialog, select the **New Viewports** tab and then select **Four: Equal** from the **Standard viewports** list. Next, select **3D** from the **Setup** drop-down. Click the **OK** button; four tiled viewports are displayed on the screen. You can notice that each viewport has a different view and a different UCS. Click inside any viewport to activate it and perform any operation.

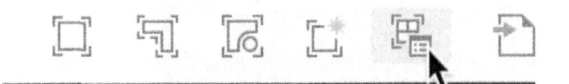

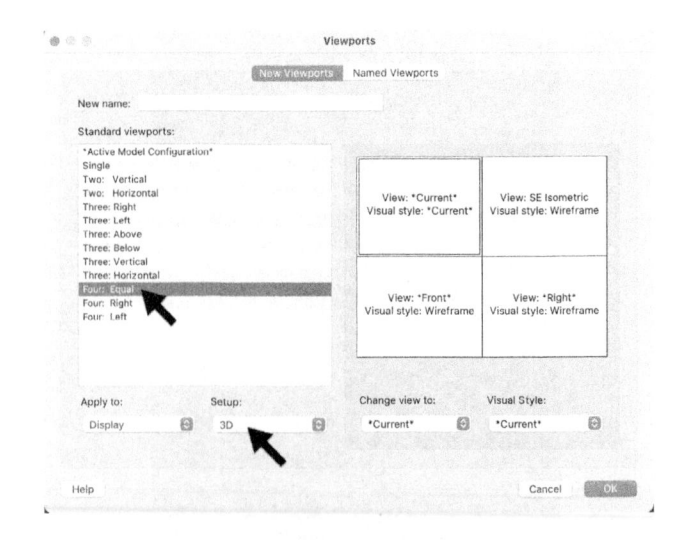

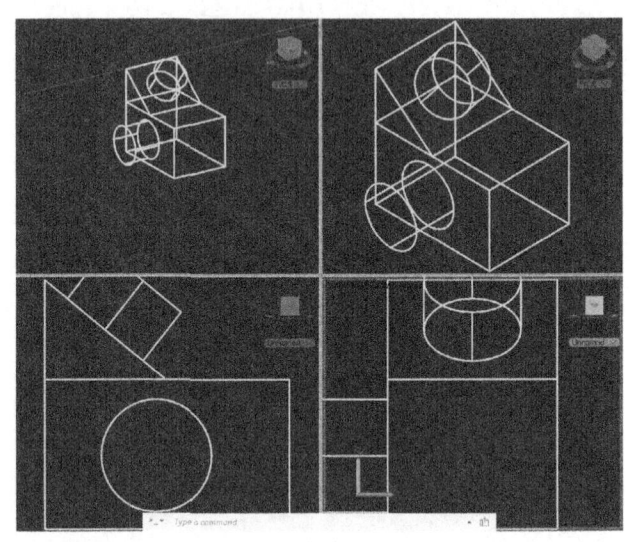

To return to the single viewport, click **View > Viewports > 1 Viewport**; the currently active viewport will fill the screen area.

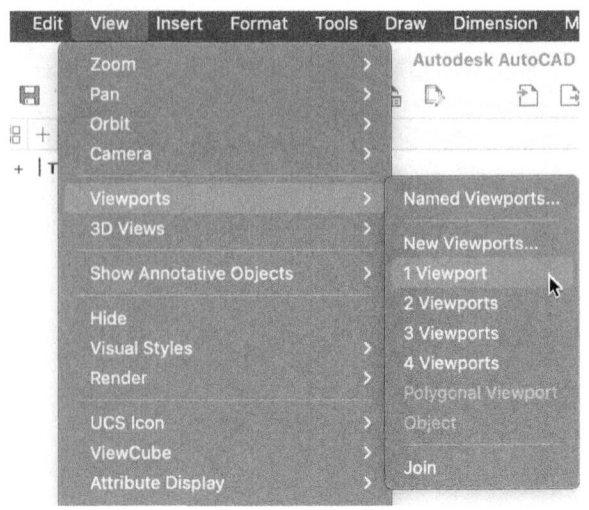

3D Modeling Basics

Creating Other Primitive Shapes

In AutoCAD, there is a set of tools to create basic geometric shapes. In earlier sections, you have learned to create boxes, wedges, and cylinders. Now, you will learn to create other primitive shapes.

Creating Cones

Creating a cone is similar to creating a cylinder. It has a similar shape compared to a cylinder, but it is tapered on one side.

Example 1:

- To create a cone, click **Modeling** > **Solid** > **Primitives** drop-down > **Cone** on the tool set; the message, "Specify center point of base or [3P/2P/Ttr/Elliptical]:" appears in the command line.
- Pick an arbitrary point from the graphics window; the message, "Specify base radius or [Diameter]:" appears.
- Type a radius value in the command line and press RETURN. You can also right-click and select the **Diameter** option to specify the diameter of the base.
- Move the pointer in the vertical direction and pick a point to specify the height of the cone. You can also type in the height value in the command line and press RETURN; the cone will be created.

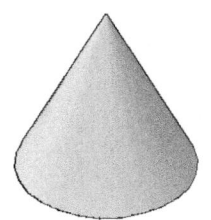

Example 2:

- Type **CONE** in the command line and press RETURN.
- Right-click and select the **Elliptical** option; the message, "Specify endpoint of first axis or [Center]:" appears in the command line.
- Pick a point to specify the endpoint of the first axis.
- Move the pointer and click to specify the other endpoint of the first axis. You can also type in the length of the first axis and press RETURN; the message, "Specify endpoint of second axis:" appears.
- Pick a point or type-in the radius value to specify the second axis.
- Move the pointer upward and pick a point to specify the height. You can also enter the value of height in the command line or the **Dynamic Input** box.

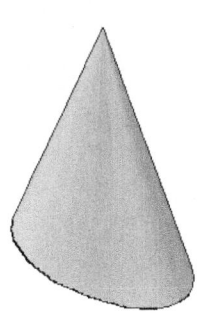

Example 3:

- Click **Modeling** > **Solid** > **Primitives** drop-down > **Cone** on the tool set.
- Select the center point and specify the base radius as 20; the message, "Specify height or [2Point/Axis endpoint/Top radius]," appears in the command line.
- Right-click and select the **Top radius** option; the message, "Specify top radius:" appears.
- Type 10 as the top radius value and press RETURN.
- Move the pointer upward and enter 40 as the height.

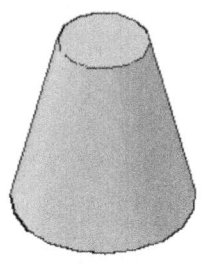

Creating a Sphere

- Click **Modeling** > **Solid** > **Primitives** drop-down > **Sphere** on the tool set.
- Specify the center point of the sphere.
- Move the pointer outward and enter the radius value. You can also right-click and select the **Diameter** option to specify the diameter of the sphere.

251 | 3D Modeling Basics

Creating a Torus

Torus is a donut-shaped solid primitive. To create a torus, you need to specify the center of the torus, radius or diameter of the torus, and radius or diameter of the tube.

- Click **Modeling** > **Solid** > **Primitives** drop-down > **Torus** on the tool set or type **TOR** in the command line and press RETURN.
- Specify the center point of the torus.
- Move the pointer outward and enter the radius of the torus. You can also right-click select the **Diameter** option to specify the diameter of the torus.
- Type the tube radius and press RETURN; the torus will be created.

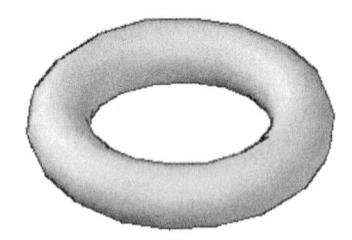

Creating a Pyramid

Pyramids are similar to cones except that the base of the pyramid is not circular in shape.

- To create a pyramid, click **Modeling** > **Solid** > **Primitives** drop-down > **Pyramid** on the tool set or type **PYR** in the command line and press RETURN.
- Type S and press RETURN.
- Type 4 and press RETURN to specify the number of sides of the pyramid.
- Specify the center point of the base.
- Specify the base radius of the circumscribed circle. You can also right-click and select **Inscribed** to specify the base radius of the inscribed circle.
- After creating the base, move the pointer in a vertical direction and pick a point to specify the height of the pyramid. You can also type the value of the height and press RETURN; the pyramid will be created.

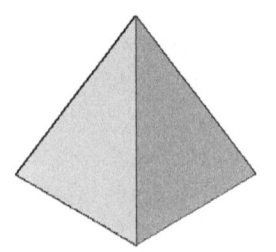

The other options displayed in the command line while creating the pyramid are the same as in the **Cone** tool.

Using the Polysolid tool

The **Polysolid** tool is used to create a 3D wall. It can also be used to convert a line, polyline, arc, or a circle to a wall. The **Polysolid** tool is similar to the **Polyline** tool except that you create a rectangular-shaped wall that has a pre-defined height and width.

- Click **Modeling** > **Solid** > **Primitives** drop-down > **Polysolid** on the tool set; the message, "Specify start point or [Object/Height/Width/Justify] <Object>:" appears in the command line.
- Activate the **Ortho Mode** on the status bar.
- Pick an arbitrary point in the graphics window and move the pointer in the X-direction.
- Type 200 in the command line and press RETURN; a 3D wall of 200 length is created.
- Right-click and select the **Arc** option.
- Move the pointer in the Y-direction.
- Type 100 as the arc diameter and press RETURN.
- Type L in the command line and press RETURN.
- Move the pointer in the –X-direction.
- Type 100, and press RETURN.
- Move the pointer in the Y-direction and enter 150 as the wall length.
- Move the pointer in –X-direction and enter 100 as the wall length.
- Right-click and select the **Close** option; the wall will be closed.

252 | 3D Modeling Basics

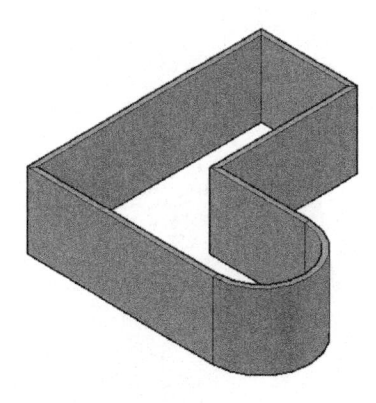

Using the Extrude tool

The **Extrude** tool is used to add a third dimension (height) to an existing 2D shape. If you extrude a closed shape such as circle and closed polylines, a solid is created. If you extrude an open sketch such as lines and arcs, a surface is created.

Example 1:
- Start a new AutoCAD file using the **acadiso3D** template.
- Click **View > 3D Views > Front** on the menu bar; the front view will become parallel to the screen.

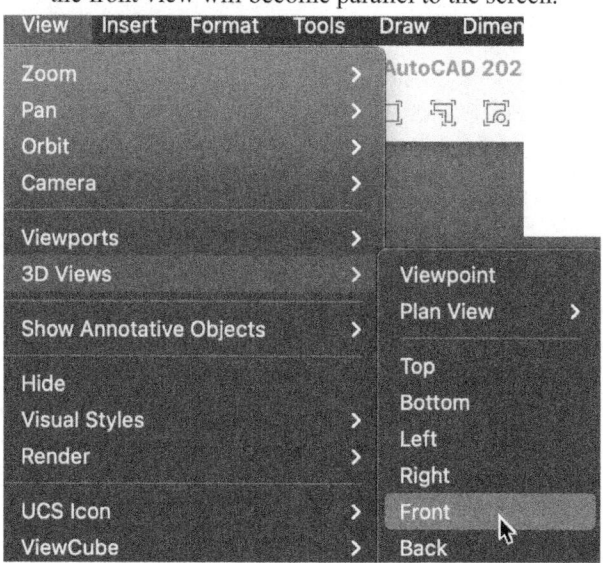

- Click **Modeling > Draw > Polyline** on the tool set and create the sketch, as shown below.

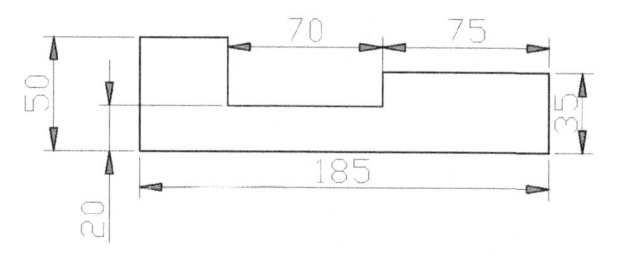

- Select **SE Isometric** from the **Viewport Label Menus**; the view orientation will be changed to Southeast Isometric.

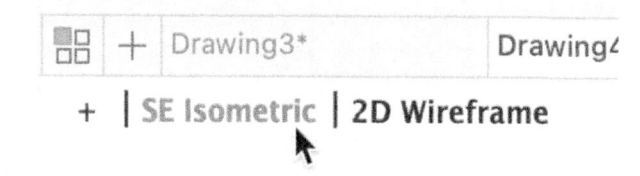

- Click **Modeling > Solid > Extrude.**
- Select the polyline sketch and press RETURN.
- Move the pointer toward the right.
- Type **100** in the command line or **Dynamic Input** box and press RETURN; the polyline sketch will be extruded.

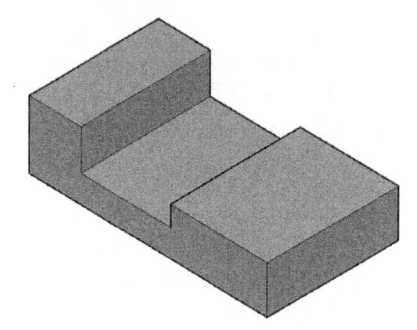

Example 2:
- Start a new AutoCAD file using the **acadiso3D** template.
- Click **View > 3D Views > Top** on the menu bar; the view will become parallel to the screen.
- Click **Modeling > Draw > Line** on the tool set and create the sketch, as shown below.

253 | 3D Modeling Basics

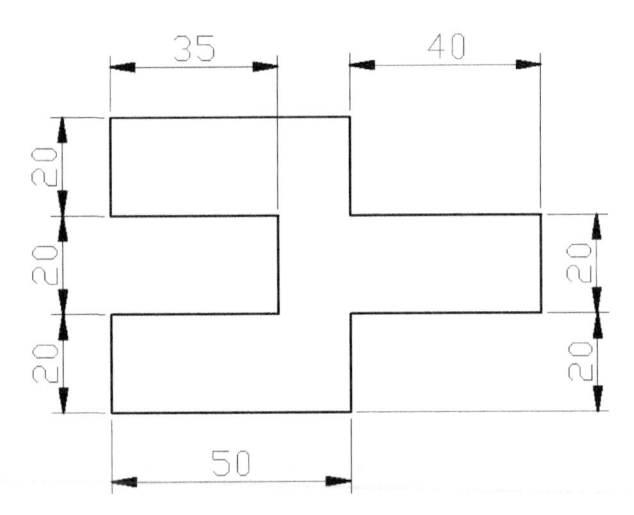

- Click **View > 3D Views > SE Isometric** on the menu bar; the view orientation will be changed to southeast Isometric.
- Click **Drafting > Hatch > Region** on the tool set. 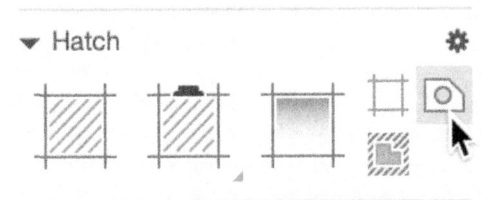
- Press and hold the left mouse button. Next, drag a window across all the objects of the sketch.
- Press RETURN; the sketch will be converted into a region. Now, you can extrude the region to create a solid. If you try to extrude the lines without creating a region, it will result in a surface. 
- Click **Modeling > Solid > Extrude**  on the tool set.
- Select the region created from the sketch, and then press RETURN; the message, "Specify height of extrusion or [Direction/Path/Taper angle/Expression]:" appears in the command line.
- Right-click and select the **Taper angle** option.
- Type 5 as the taper angle and press RETURN.
- Move the pointer upward, type 40 in the command line and press RETURN; the extruded solid will be created with a taper.

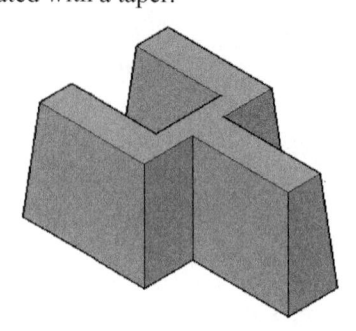

Example 3:
- Type **EXT** in the command line and press RETURN.
- Press and hold the CONTROL key and select the top face of the model.
- Press RETURN and move the pointer upward.
- Type 25 as the extrusion height and press RETURN; the extruded solid will be created.

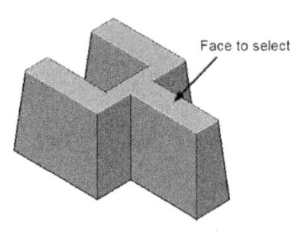

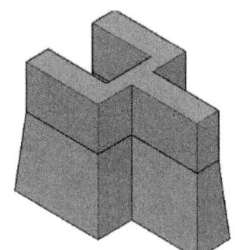

Using the Revolve tool

The **Revolve** tool is used to revolve an open or closed 2D sketch about a selected axis. If you revolve a closed profile such as a polyline sketch, polygon, circle, or a sketch region, a solid object is created. An open profile results in a surface. The sketch is deleted after revolving it. If you want to retain the sketch, you need to set the **DELOBJ** system variable to 0.

- Start a new AutoCAD file using the **acadiso3D** template.
- Set the current UCS to front and create the sketch using the **Line** tool. Do not add dimensions.

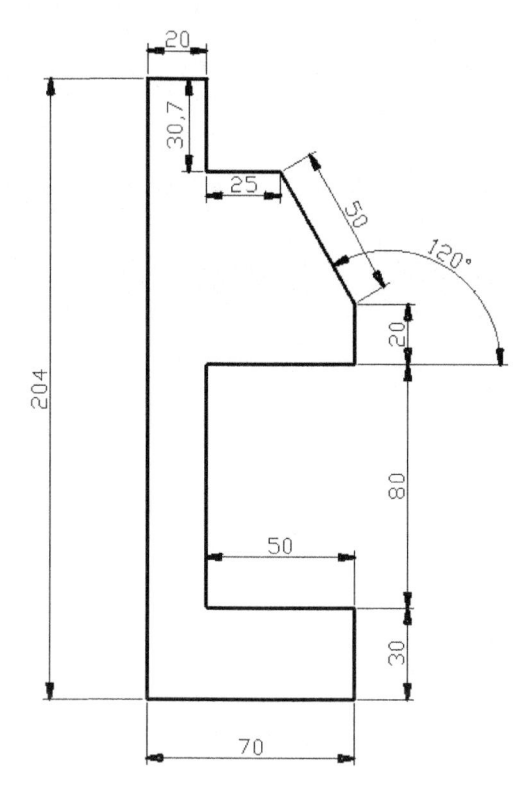

- Convert the sketch into the region using the **Region** tool.

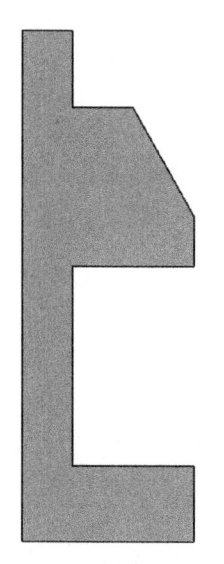

- Create a vertical line at a distance of 10 mm from the left vertical edge of the region.

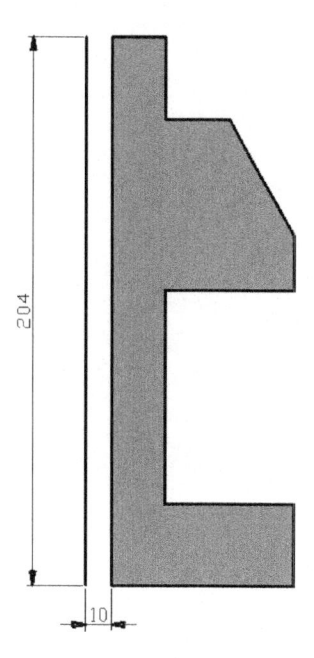

- Click **Modeling > Solid > Solid** drop-down > **Revolve** on the tool set or type REV in the command line.

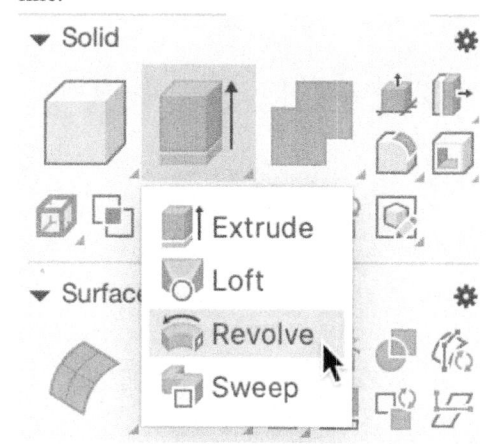

- Select the sketch region and press RETURN; the message, "Specify axis start point or define axis by [Object/X/Y/Z] <Object>:" appears in the command line.
- Right-click and select the **Object** option
- Select the vertical line created at an offset; the message, "Specify angle of revolution or [STart angle/Reverse/EXpression] <360>:" appears.

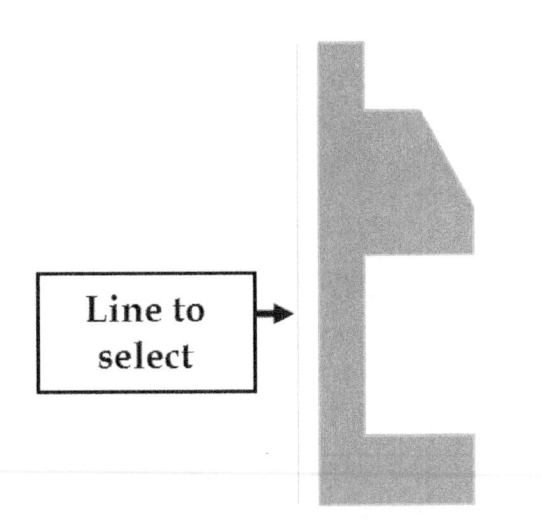

- Press RETURN to specify 360 as the revolution angle.

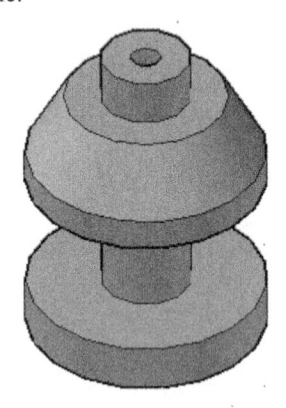

Using the Sweep tool

The **Sweep** tool is used to create a new solid or surface by sweeping a closed or open planar profile along an open or closed 2D or 3D path. The procedure to create a solid by using the **Sweep** tool is discussed next.

Example:
- Start a new AutoCAD file using the **acadiso3D** template.
- Set the current UCS to **Front**.

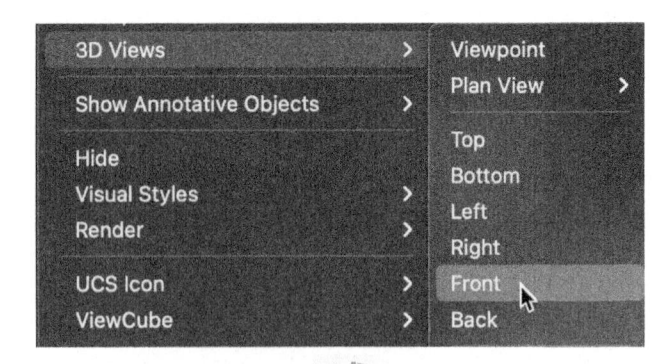

- Activate the **Polyline** tool.
- Deactivate the **Ortho Mode** icon on the Status bar, if already active.
- Specify the start point of the polyline.
- Move the pointer vertically downward.
- Type 38 and press the TAB key.
- Type 270, and press RETURN.

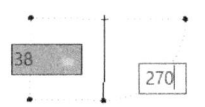

- Move the pointer toward the bottom-left corner.
- Type 83 and press the TAB.
- Type 229, and press RETURN.

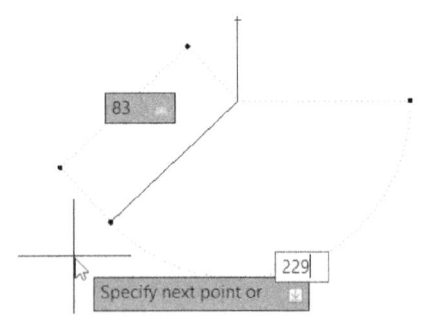

- Move the pointer downward.
- Type 66 and press the TAB key.
- Type 270, and press RETURN.

AutoCAD 2023 For Beginners (For Mac Users)

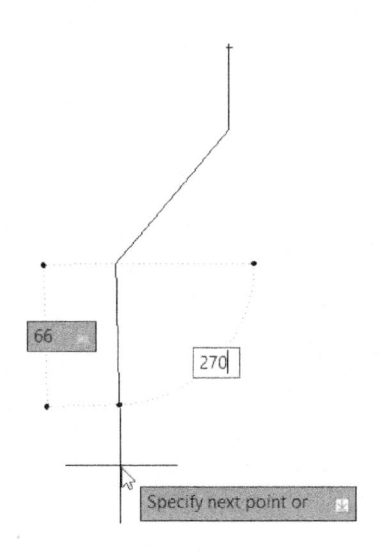

- Right-click and select the **Arc** option.
- Move the pointer toward right.
- Type 108 and press TAB.
- Type 0 and press RETURN.

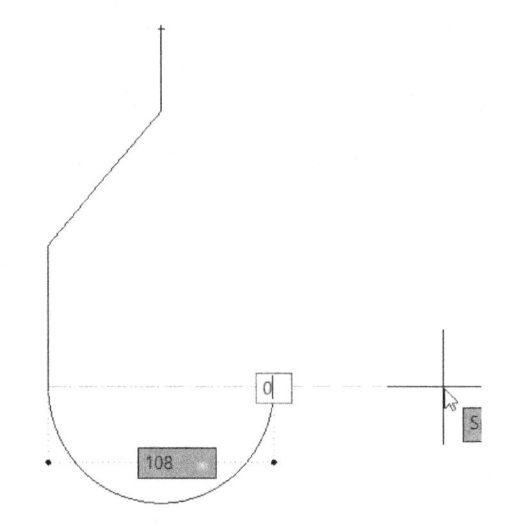

- Press Esc to deactivate the **Polyline** tool.
- Use the **Fillet** tool and apply fillets of 25 mm radius.

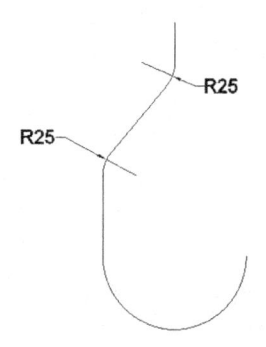

- Change the view orientation to SE Isometric.
- Type UCS and press RETURN.
- Type ZA and press RETURN.
- Select the endpoint of the top vertical line as the UCS origin.
- Move the pointer downward and select the endpoint of the vertical line; the Z-axis is aligned to the vertical line.

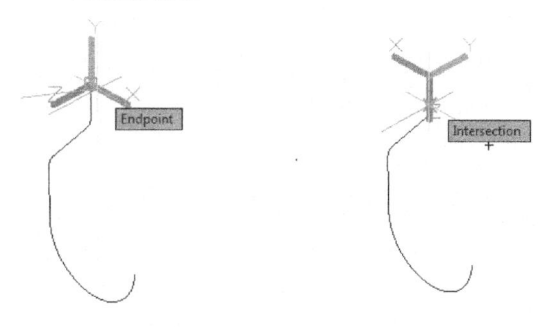

- Click the **Circle > Center, Radius** button on the **Draw** panel.
- Select the endpoint of the vertical line to specify the center point of the circle. Specify 5 mm as the radius of the circle.
- Click the **UCS, World** button on the **UCS** panel; the User Coordinate System will be set to World Coordinate System (0,0,0).

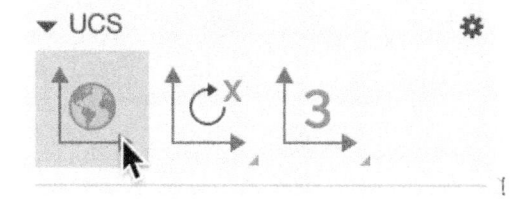

257 | 3D Modeling Basics

- Click **Modeling > Solid > Solids** drop-down > **Sweep** on the tool set.

- Select the circle as the profile and press RETURN; the message, "Select sweep path or [Alignment/Base point/Scale/Twist]:" appears in the command line.

The **Alignment** option aligns the profile perpendicular to the direction of the sweep path. By default, the profile is aligned to the path.

The **Base point** specifies the base point of the profile. By default, the center of the profile is used as the base point. You can select any other point on the profile to define the base point.

The **Scale** option scales the profile along the path.

The **Twist** option twists the profile as it is swept along the length of the path.

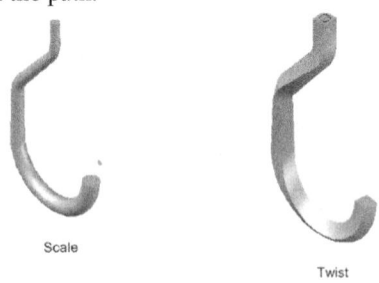

- Select the path to create the swept solid object.

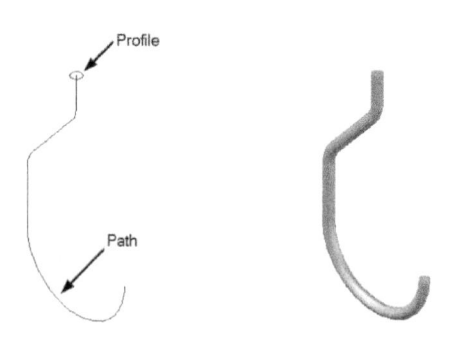

Using the Loft tool

Using the **Loft** tool, you can create a solid or surface by selecting a series of cross-sections. The selected cross-sections will define the shape of the lofted solid.

Example 1:
- Deactivate the **Dynamic Input** icon on the status bar.
- Type CIRCLE in the command line and press RETURN.
- Type 0,0,0 in the command line and press RETURN.
- Type 25 as the radius value and press RETURN.
- Type CIRCLE in the command line.
- Type 0,0,70 in the command line and press RETURN.
- Type 50 as the radius value and press RETURN.
- Type CIRCLE in the command line.
- Type 0,0,140 in the command line and press RETURN.
- Type 25 as the radius value and press RETURN.

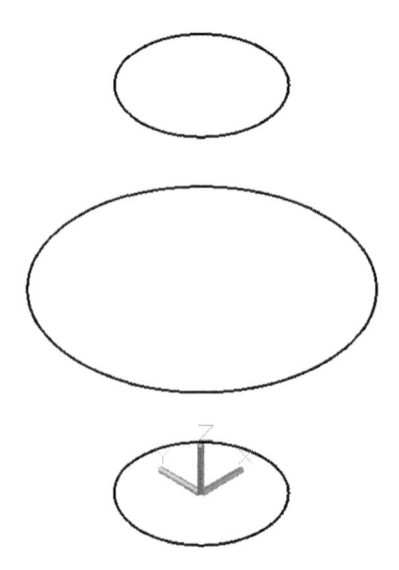

- Click **Modeling > Solid > Solids** drop-down > **Loft**

258 | 3D Modeling Basics

on the tool set (or) type **LOFT** in the command line and press RETURN.

- Select the first, second, and third cross-sections one by one; the preview of the lofted solid appears.
- Press RETURN to accept the selection; the message, "Enter an option [Guides/Path/Cross sections only/Settings] <Cross sections only>:" appears in the command line.
- Right-click and select the **Settings** option; the **Loft Settings** dialog appears. In this dialog, the **Smooth Fit** option creates a smooth connection between the cross-sections. If you select the **Ruled** option, the lofted solid or surface has sharp edges.

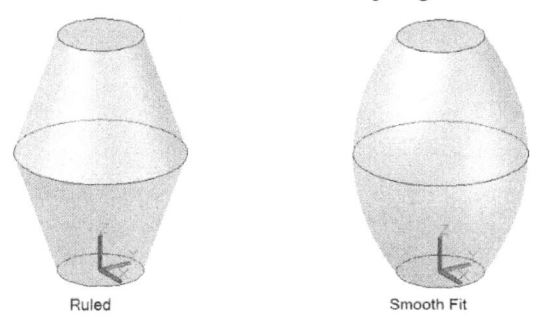

The **Normal to** option creates a solid or surface normal to the cross-section. You can select the loft solid or surface to be normal to **All cross sections**, or **Start Cross Section** or **End Cross Section** or **Start and End Cross Sections**.

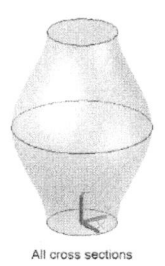

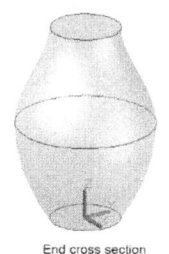

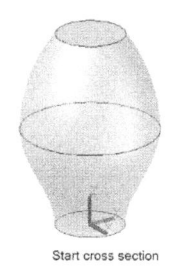

The **Draft angles** option defines the draft angle and magnitude at start and end cross-sections. The draft angle is the beginning direction of the loft surface. If you set the draft angle to 90 degrees, the loft surface starts vertically from the cross-section, and the 0-draft angle starts loft surface horizontally. The Magnitude is the relative distance up to which the loft surface will follow the draft angle before it bends.

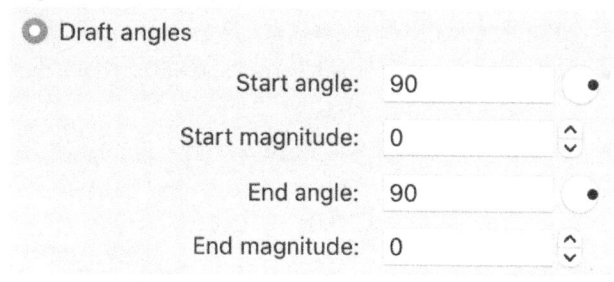

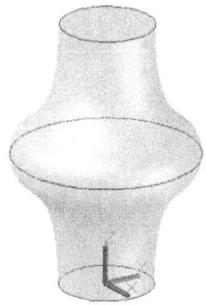

The **Close surface or solid** option connects the start and end section of the lofted object.

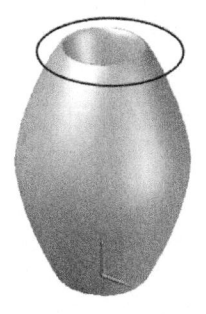

- Select the **Normal to** option and select **All cross sections**. Click **OK**; the loft solid will be created, as shown below.

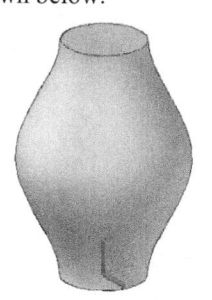

259 | 3D Modeling Basics

Using the Presspull tool

The **Presspull** tool is used to create and modify solid models with greater ease and speed. It can be used to accomplish two types of operations: extruding closed 2D shapes and add or remove material from a solid object based on whether you "pull" or "push" the extrusion.

- Start a new file.
- Create two layers called **Sketch** and **Solid**. Make the **Sketch** layer as current.
- Set the Current UCS to **Right** and draw the sketch, as shown below.

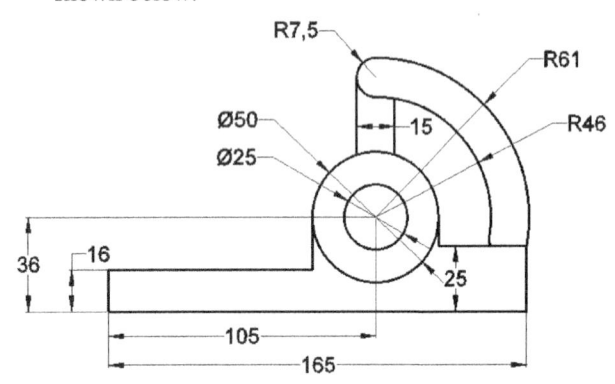

- Change the view orientation to SE Isometric.
- Ensure that the **Dynamic Input** icon is activated on the status bar.
- Activate the **Solid** layer.
- Click **Modeling > Solid > Presspull** on the tool set.
- Click inside the bottom region of the sketch and move the pointer backward. Type 60 in the Dynamic input box and press RETURN; the extruded feature will be created.

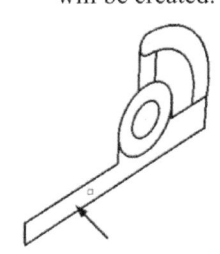

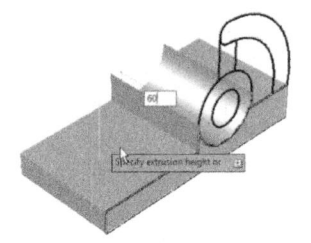

- Click on the region enclosed by the larger circle and extrude it up to 64 mm distance.

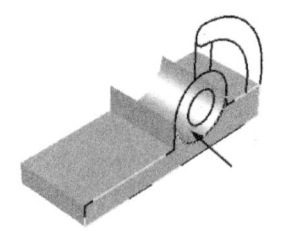

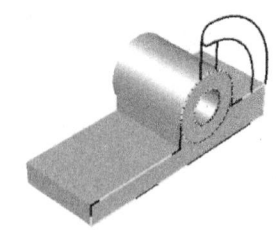

- Press and hold the CONTROL key and select the front face of the cylindrical object. Move the pointer forward. Type 4 in the dynamic input box and press RETURN.

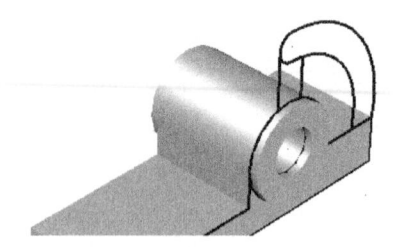

- Click in the curved slot region and move the pointer backward; the message, "Specify extrusion height or [Multiple]:" appears in the command line.
- Right-click and select the **Multiple** option.
- Click in the region enclosed by the two vertical lines.

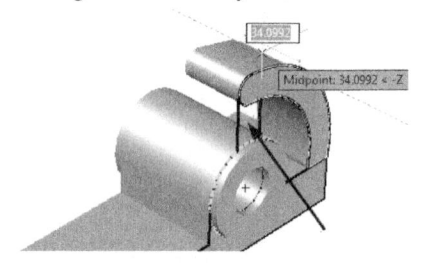

- Right-click and move the pointer backward. Type **12** in the dynamic input box and press RETURN.

- Activate the **Presspull** tool.
- Press and hold the COMMAND key and select the front face of the slot and move the pointer forward — type 4 in the dynamic input box and press RETURN.

260 | 3D Modeling Basics

- Activate the **Sketch** layer.
- Activate the **Dynamic UCS** icon on the status bar.
- Click the **Circle > Center, Radius** on the **Draw** panel of the **Modeling** tool set.
- Press and hold the SHIFT key. Right-click and select the **Center** option from the shortcut menu.
- Select the center point of the slot end cap and create a circle of 4 mm radius.

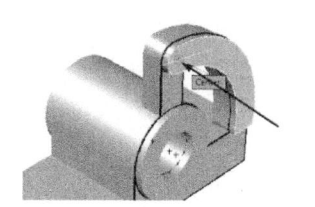

- Click **Modeling > Modify > Array** drop-down > **Path Array** on the tool set.
- Select the circle created in the previous step and press RETURN.
- Select the arc as the path curve; the preview of the path array is displayed.

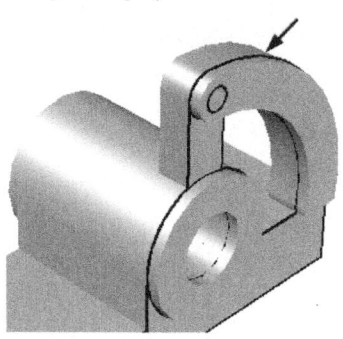

- In the **Path Array** visor, set the **Spacing between items** value to 25; the item count is automatically adjusted.
- Click the **Create array and close visor** button; the polar array is created.

- Activate the **Solid** layer.

- Activate the **Presspull** command.
- Click in any one of the circles.
- Right-click and select the **Multiple** option.
- Click inside the rest of the circles of the polar array. Right-click to accept.
- Move the pointer backward and click; the holes will be created, as shown in the figure.
- Turn Off the **Sketch** layer; the sketches will be hidden.

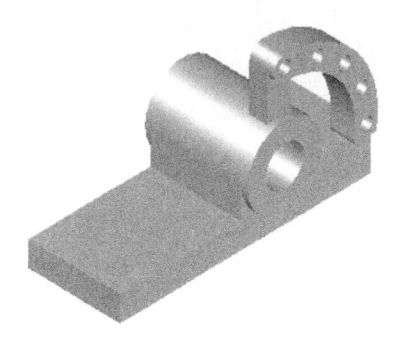

- Click the **Orbit** button on the toolbar.
- Press and drag the left mouse button to rotate the model.

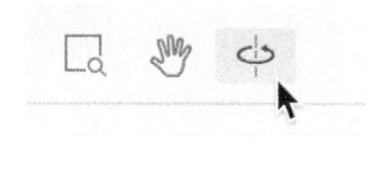

Performing the Boolean Operations

Boolean operations are performed to add two or more solids together, subtract a single solid or group of solids from another, or form a common portion when two solids are combined. You must have at least two solids to perform a Boolean operation. There are three tools available to perform Boolean Operations- **Union Subtract** and **Intersect**. These tools are discussed next.

The Union tool

The **Union** tool joins two or more solids together into a single solid. For example, when you try to select the complete model, its individual objects are selected. But, after performing the Union operation, all the solid objects are combined and act as one object.

- To perform the Union operation, click **Solid > Boolean > Union** on the **Modeling** tool set.

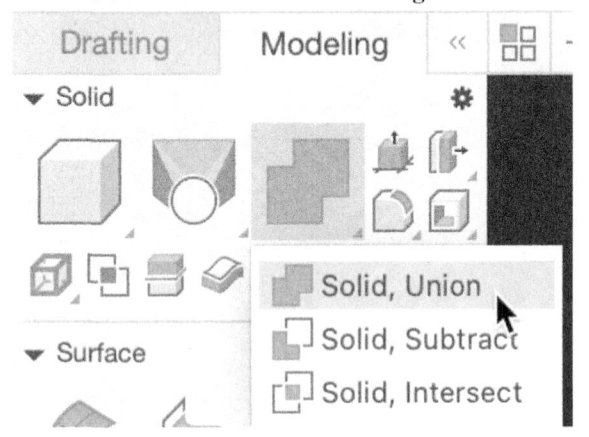

- Click the left mouse button and create a selection window across the model; all the objects of the model will be selected.
- Press RETURN; all the solid objects of the model will be combined.
  Now, when you select an individual object, the complete model will be selected.

The Subtract tool

The **Subtract** tool is used to subtract one or more solid objects from another object.

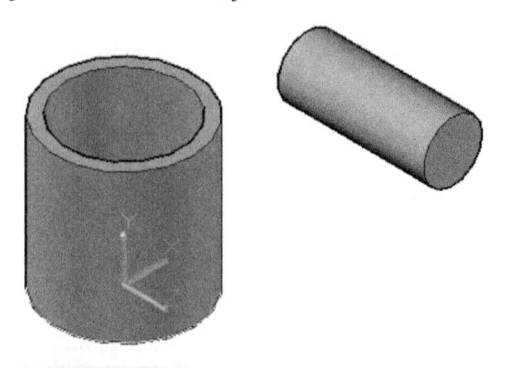

- Open a new drawing file.
- Select **View > 3D Views > Top** on the menu bar.
- Create two concentric circles of 240 and 200 mm in diameter.

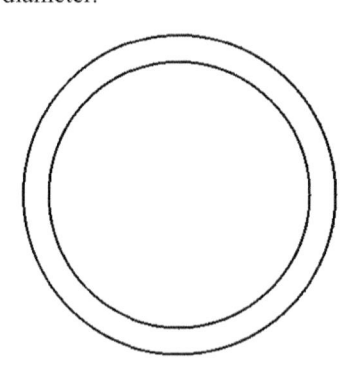

- Change the view orientation to SE Isometric.
- Activate the **Presspull** tool.
- Click inside the region between the large and small circles.

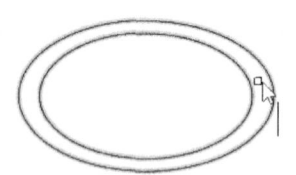

- Move the pointer upward, type 250, and then press RETURN.

262 | 3D Modeling Basics

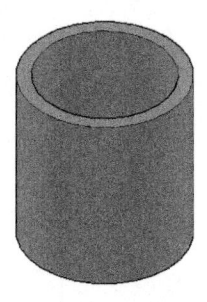

- Press Esc to deactivate the **Presspull** tool.
- Select **View > 3D Views > Right** on the menu bar.
- Click **Modeling > Solid > Primitive** drop-down > **Cylinder** on the tool set.
- Select an arbitrary point in the graphics window.
- Move the pointer outward, type 50, and then press RETURN.
- Type 240 and press RETURN.
- Change the view orientation to **SE Isometric**.
- Click the **Align** button on the **Modify** panel.

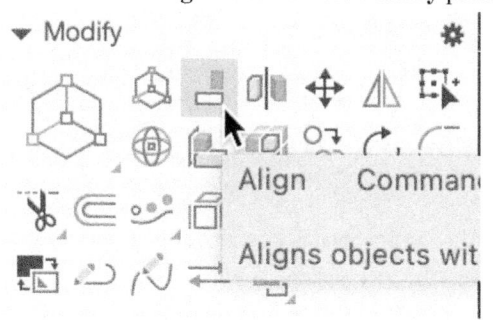

- Select the horizontal cylinder and press RETURN; the message, "Specify first source point:" appears in the command line.
- Press and hold the SHIFT key. Right-click and select the **Center** option.
- Select the center point of the front face of the horizontal cylinder; the message, "Specify first destination point:" appears in the command line.

- Press and hold the SHIFT key. Right-click and select the **Quadrant** option.

- Select the quadrant point of the outer circle on the top face of the hollow cylinder.

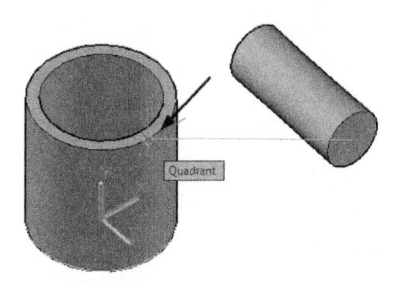

- Press RETURN; the horizontal cylinder will be aligned with the hollow cylinder.

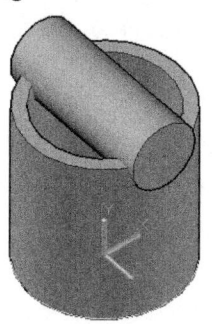

- Click **Solid > Boolean > Subtract** on the **Modeling** tool set; the message, "Select objects," appears in the command line.

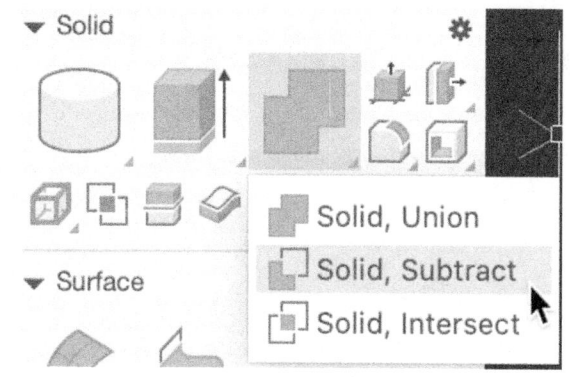

- Select the hollow cylinder and press RETURN; the message, "Select objects," appears in the command line.
- Select the horizontal cylinder and press RETURN; it will be subtracted from the hollow cylinder, as shown next.

3D Modeling Basics

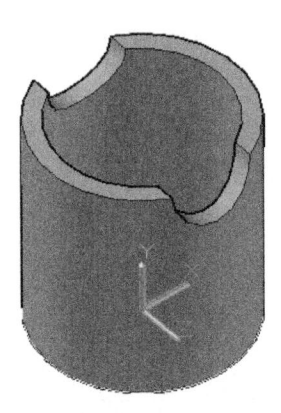

The Intersect tool

The **Intersect** tool is used to create a composite solid by finding common volume shared by the selected objects.

- Start a new file.
- Select **View > 3D Views > Front** on the menu bar.
- Create the sketch, as shown below. 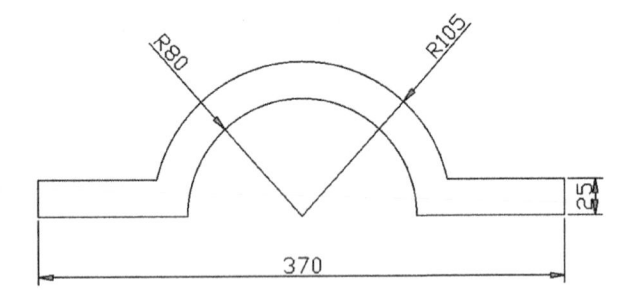
- Change the view orientation to **SE Isometric**.
- Use the **Presspull** tool and extrude the sketch up to 150 mm distance. 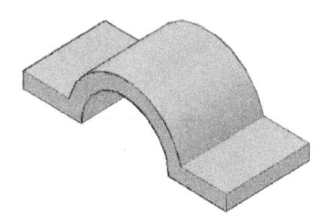
- Select **View > 3D Views > Top** on the menu bar.
- Activate the **Circle** tool and create three circles, as shown. 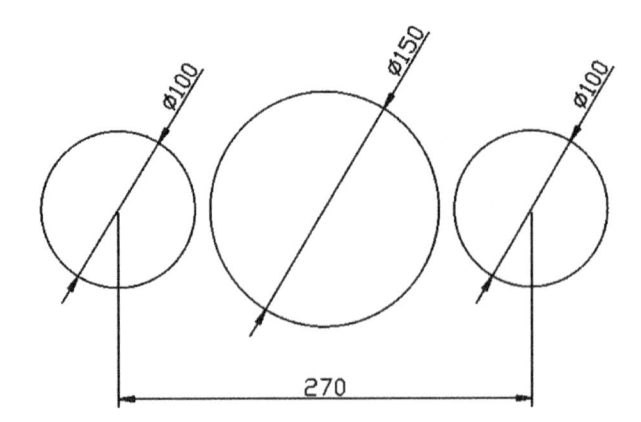
- Click **Modeling > Draw > Line** on the tool set.
- Press and hold the SHIFT key, and then right-click.
- Select the **Tangent** option.
- Select the small circle by clicking at the location, as shown. 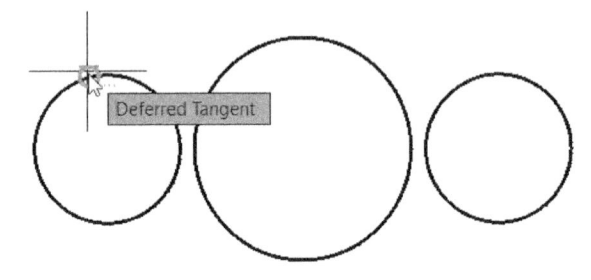
- Press and hold the SHIFT key, and then right-click.
- Select the **Tangent** option.
- Select the large circle by clicking at the location, as shown. 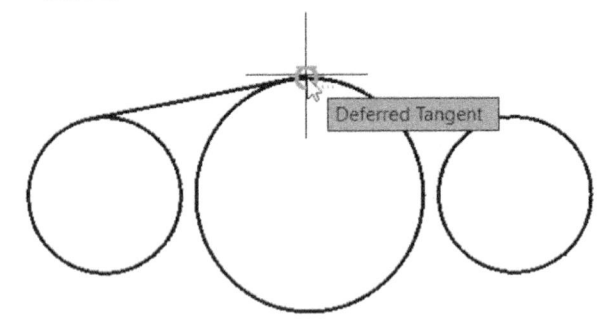
- Right-click and select Enter.
- Likewise, create three more lines tangent to the circles, as shown.

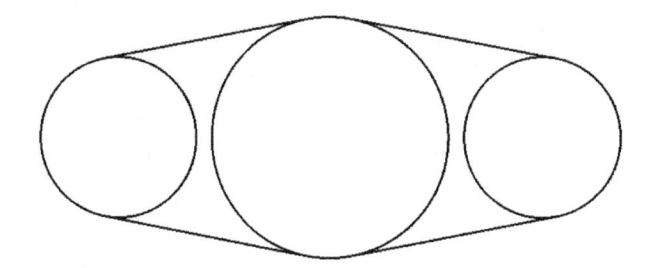

- Click **Modeling > Modify > Trim** on the tool set.
- Select the entities to trim, as shown.
- Press Esc. 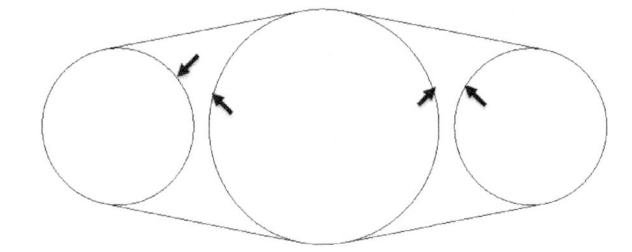
- Change the view orientation to SE Isometric. 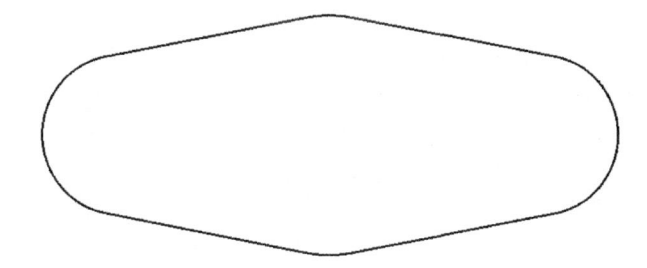
- Use the **Presspull** tool and extrude the sketch up to 200 mm height, as shown below.
- Click **View > Visual styles > Wireframe** on the menu bar. 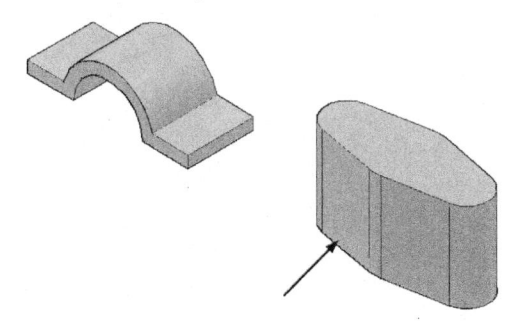
- Deactivate the **3D Object Snap** option on the status bar.
- Type **DS** in the command line and press RETURN; the **Drafting Settings** dialog appears.

- Click the **Object Snap** tab and **Clear All** the **Object Snap** modes.
- Now, select the **Quadrant** and **Midpoint** options and click **OK**.

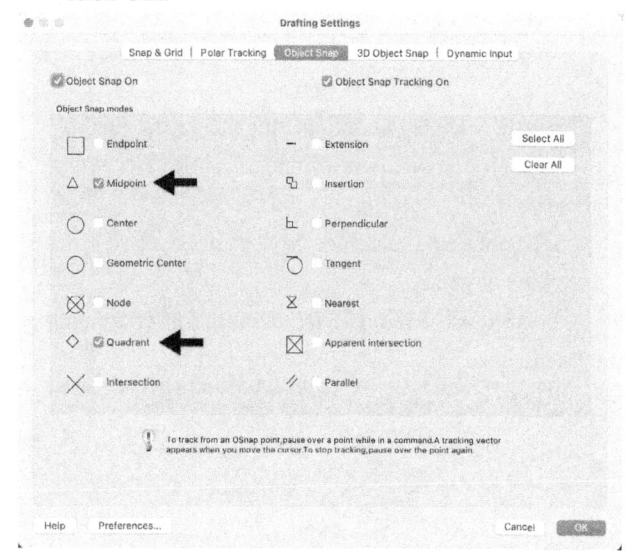

- Type **AL** in the command line and press RETURN.
- Select the second extrusion and press RETURN; the message, "Specify first source point:" appears.
- Select the point on the source object as shown below; the message, "Specify first destination point:" appears.
- Select the point on the destination object as shown below; the message, "Specify second source point:" appears.

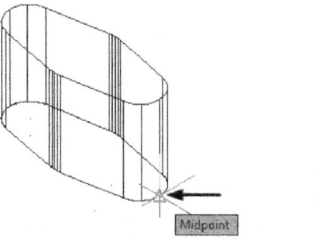

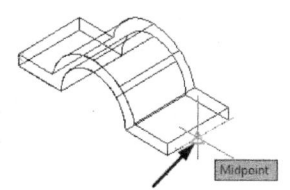

- Select another point on the source object, as shown below; the message, "Specify second destination point:" appears.
- Select another point on the destination object, as shown below; the message, "Specify third source point or <continue>:" appears.

265 | 3D Modeling Basics

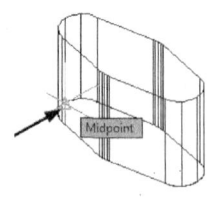

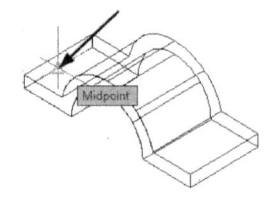

- Press RETURN to continue; the message, "Scale objects based on alignment points? [Yes/No] <N>:" appears.
- Right-click and select the **NO** option; the two objects will be aligned.
- Click **View** > **Visual styles** > **Shades of Gray** on the menu bar.

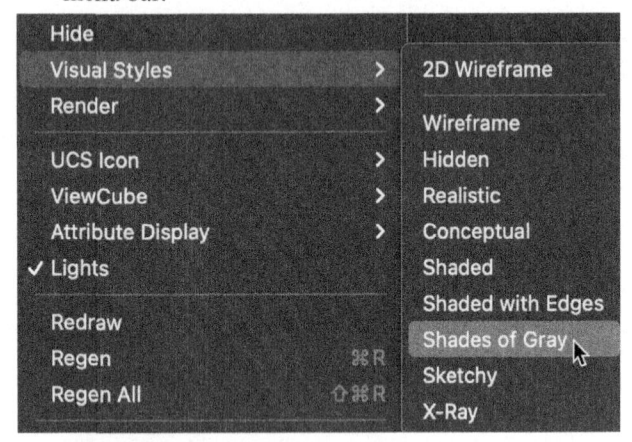

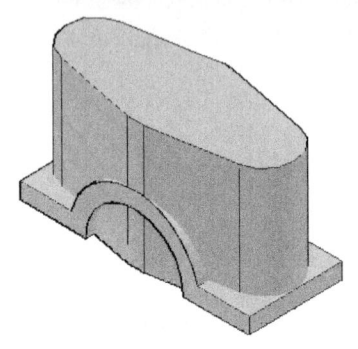

- Click **Solid** > **Boolean** > **Intersect** on the **Modeling** tool set.

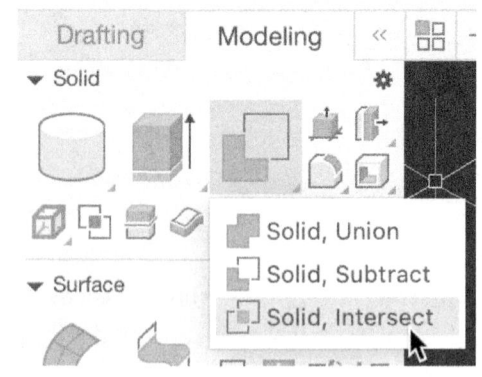

- Select the two objects and press RETURN; the intersection object will be created as shown below.

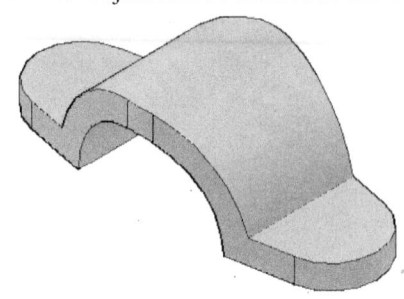

Using the Helix tool

The **Helix** tool is used to create a spiral or helix object. You can use this helix object as a path for a swept solid object.

Example 1:
- Start a new file.
- Click **Modeling** > **Draw** > **Helix** on the tool set.

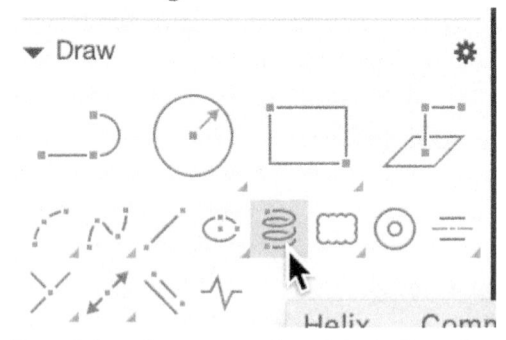

- Type 0,0 as the center point of the helix and press RETURN; the message, "Specify base radius or [Diameter]:" appears in the command line.
- Type 50 and press RETURN; the message, "Specify top radius or [Diameter] <50.0000>:" appears.
- Type 0 and press RETURN; the message, "Specify helix height or [Axis endpoint/Turns/turn

266 | 3D Modeling Basics

Height/tWist] <1.0000>:" appears.
- Right-click and select the **Turns** option.
- Type 8 as the number of turns and press RETURN; the message, "Specify helix height or [Axis endpoint/Turns/turn Height/tWist] <1.0000>:" appears.
- Type 0 as the height and press RETURN; the spiral curve will be created as shown in the figure.

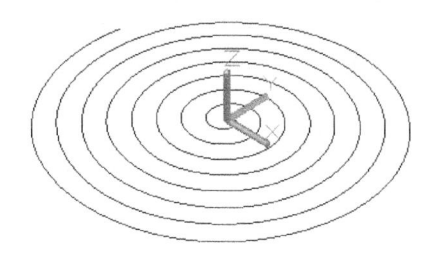

Example 2:
- Start a new file.

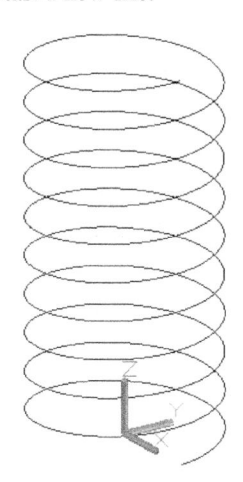

- Type HELIX in the command line and press RETURN.
- Type 0, 0 as the center point of the helix.
- Type 50 as the base radius and press RETURN.
- Press RETURN to accept 50 as the top radius.
- Right-click and select the **turn Height** option.
- Type 20 as the turn height (pitch) and press RETURN.
- Type 200 as the total height of the helix and press RETURN; the helix will be created as shown in the figure.

Exercises
Create 3D models using the drawing views and dimensions.

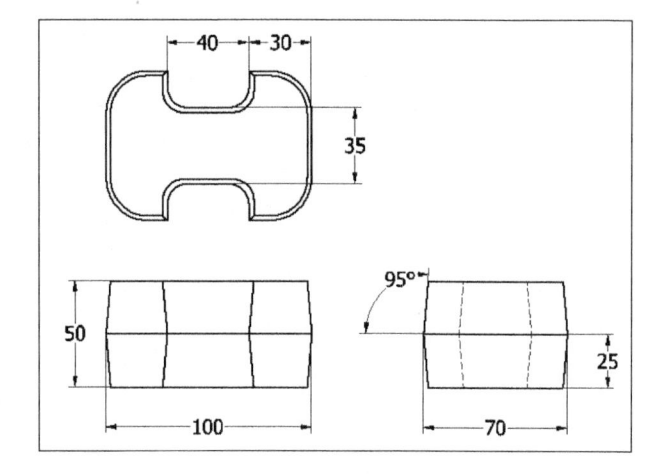

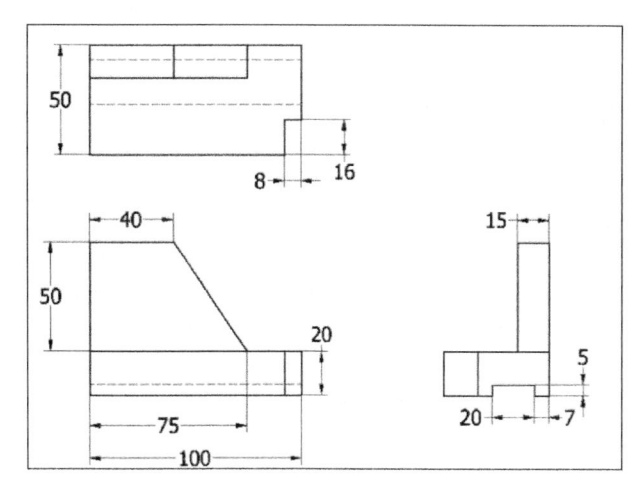

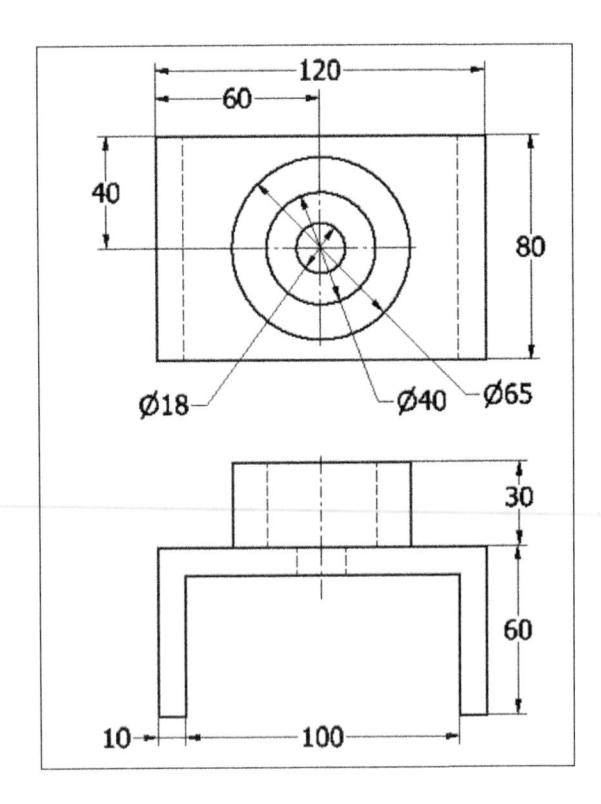

Chapter 13: Solid Editing & generating 2D views

In this chapter, you will learn to do the following:

- Move objects in 3D space
- Create 3D Arrays
- Mirror objects in 3D space
- Fillet edges
- Taper faces of a solid object
- Offset faces
- Rotate objects
- Create 3D Polylines
- Shell objects
- Chamfer edges
- Create Live sections
- Generate 2D views of a 3D model
- Create section and detailed views

Introduction

In the previous chapter, you have learned to create simple solid objects. Now, you will learn to use the solid editing tools to create complex models. You will also learn to generate orthographic views of 3D models.

Using the Move tool

The **Move** tool that you used in 2D drawings can also be used in 3D modeling. You can change the position of an object using the **Move** tool. The application of this tool in 3D modeling is discussed next.

Example:

- Start a new AutoCAD file using the **acadiso3D** template.
- Click **View > 3D Views > Front** from the menu bar.
- Create the sketch on the front view and presspull it up to 100 mm distance.

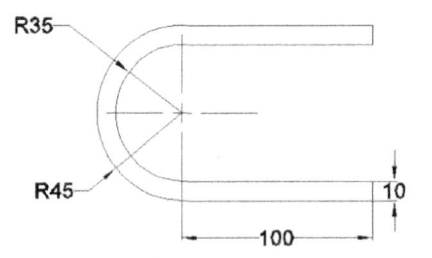

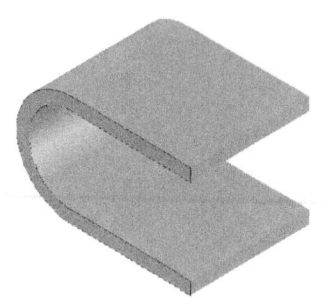

- Click **View > 3D Views > Top** from the menu bar.
- Create a cylinder of 20 mm diameter and 20 mm in height.
- Change the view orientation to SE Isometric.

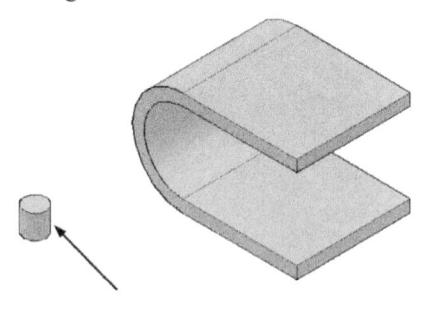

- Type **M** in the command line and press RETURN; the **Move** tool is activated.
- Select the cylinder and press RETURN.
- Select the center point of the cylinder to define the base point.

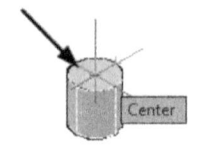

- Select the endpoint of the base object, as shown; the cylinder will be aligned to it.

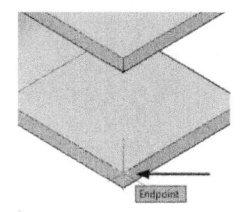

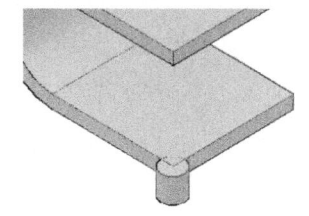

Using the 3D Move tool

The **3D Move** tool is similar to the **Move** tool. You can use this tool to move objects in 3D space. By default, the **3D Move** tool is activated, and the **Move gizmo** is displayed when you select an object. You can use the **Move gizmo** to move the object along a particular axis.

- Select the cylinder to display the **Move gizmo** tool.
- Select the X-axis (Red arrow) of the gizmo and move the pointer reverse direction.

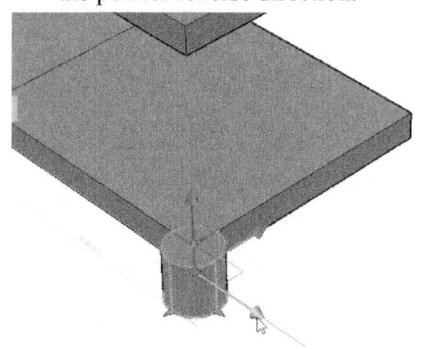

- Type 20 and press RETURN; the cylinder will be moved through a 20 mm distance along the X-axis.

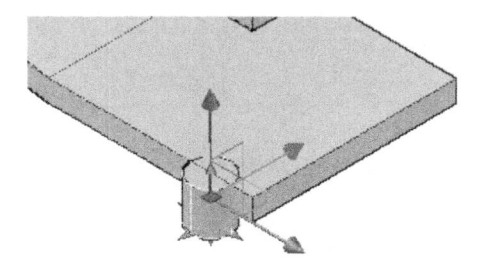

- Select the Y-axis (Green arrow) of the gizmo and move the pointer toward the right.
- Type 20 and press RETURN; the cylinder will be moved, as shown below.

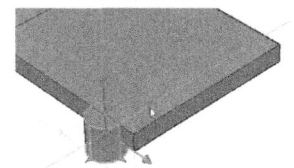

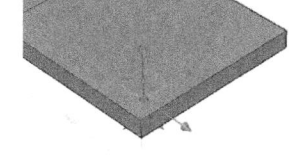

Using the Array tool

The **Array** tool is used to create Rectangular, path, and polar arrays. You can create a rectangular array by specifying the item count and distance along the X, Y, and Z directions.

Example 1 (Rectangular Array)

- Type **ARRAY** in the command line and press RETURN.
- Select the cylinder from the model and press RETURN; the message, "Enter array type [Rectangular/PAth/POlar] <Path>:" appears in the command line.
- Right-click and select the **Rectangular** option.
- Type **COL** in the command line and press RETURN.
- Type 2 in the command line and press RETURN.
- Type -40 in the command line and press RETURN.
- Type **R** in the command line and press RETURN.
- Type 2 in the command line and press RETURN.
- Type 60 in the command line and press RETURN.
- Press RETURN to accept 0 as the incrementing elevation between rows.
- Type **L** in the command line and press RETURN.
- Type 2 in the command line and press RETURN.
- Type 80 in the command line and press RETURN.
- Type **AS** in the command line and press RETURN.
- Type **NO** in the command line and press RETURN.
- Deactivate the **Associative** icon on the **Array Creation** tab.
- Press RETURN to create the rectangular array.

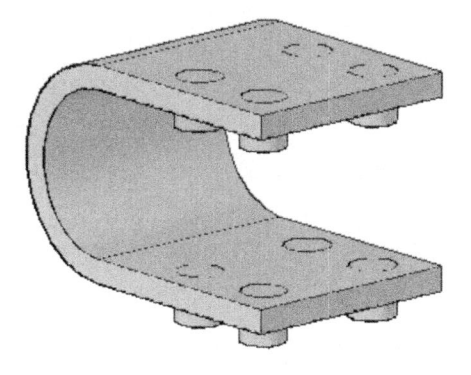

- Type **SU** in the command line and press RETURN; the **Subtract** tool will be activated.
- Select the base object and press RETURN; the

271 | Solid Editing & generating 2D views

message, "Select solids, surfaces, and regions to subtract" appears.
- Select all the cylinders and press RETURN; holes will be created on the model.

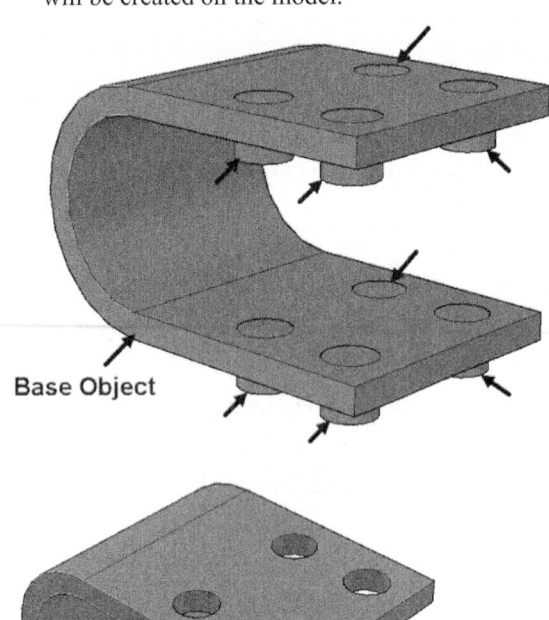

- Click **View > 3D Views > Front** from the menu bar.
- Draw the sketch as shown below and extrude it up to 12 mm using the **Presspull** tool.
- Change the view orientation to SE Isometric.

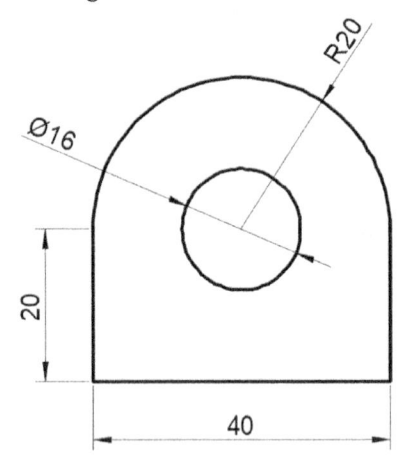

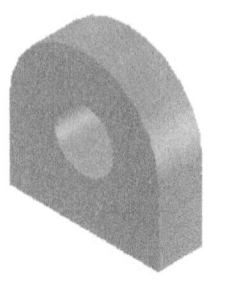

Using the 3D Align tool

The **3D Align** tool aligns one solid with another. It translates and rotates the object to align with the destination object. You need to select three points on the source object and destination object to align them together. An example of the **3D Align** tool is given next.

Example 2:
- Start a new AutoCAD file using the **acadiso3D** template.
- Click **View > 3D Views > Front** on the menu bar.
- Create a solid object, as shown below. The extrusion distance is 40 mm.

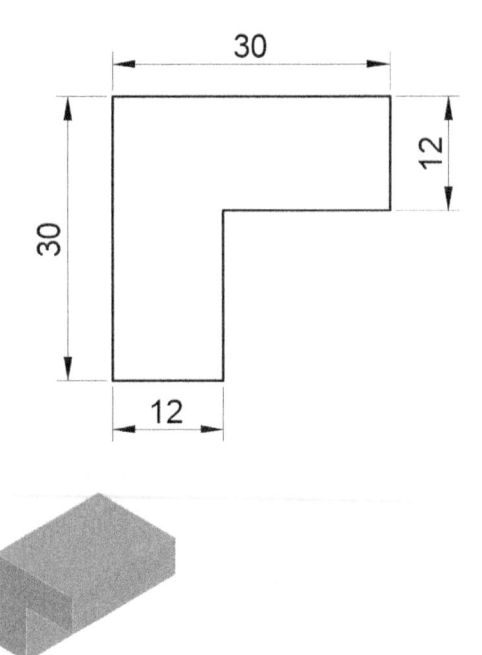

- Deactivate the **3D Object Snap** button on the status bar.

- Type **DS** in the command line and press RETURN; the **Drafting Settings** dialog appears.
- Click the **Object Snap** tab and **Clear All** the **Object Snap** modes.
- Now, select the **Endpoint** option and click **OK**.

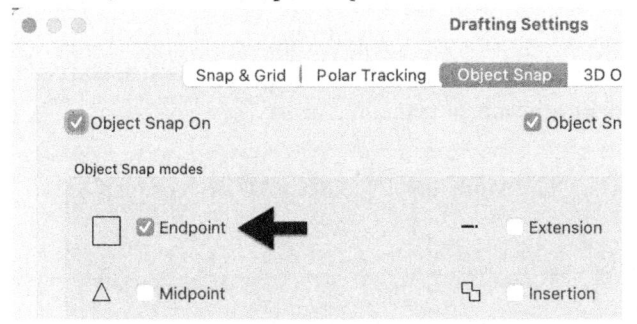

- Click **Modeling > Modify > 3D Align** on the tool set.

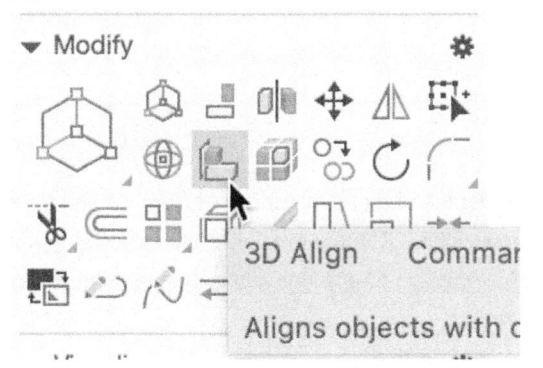

- Select the second solid object from the graphics window and press RETURN; the message, "Specify base point or [Copy]:" appears in the command line.

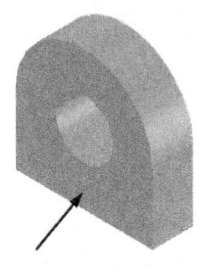

- Right-click and select the **Copy** option.
- Select three endpoints on the source object, as shown below.

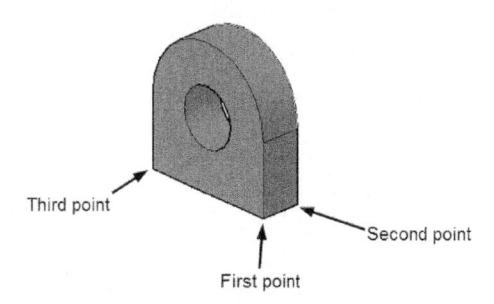

- Select three endpoints on the destination object as shown below; a copy of the source object will be aligned to the destination object.

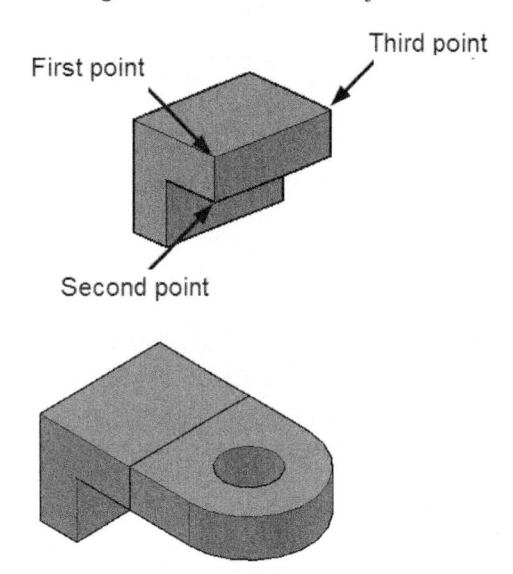

- Activate the **Ortho Mode** button on the status bar.
- Type **3DALIGN** in the command line and press RETURN.
- Select the second solid object. Press RETURN to accept the selection.

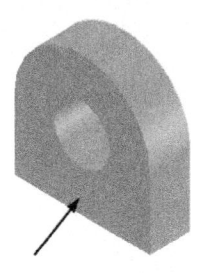

- Select the base point on the object as shown in the figure; the message, "Specify second point or [Continue] <C>:" appears in the command line.

273 | Solid Editing & generating 2D views

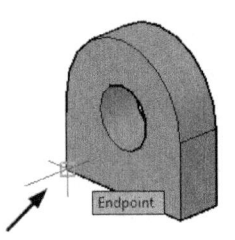

- Right-click and select the **Continue** option; the message, "Specify first destination point:" appears in the command line.
- Select the endpoint on the destination object, as shown below.

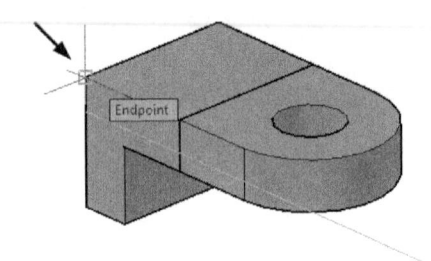

- Move the pointer along the X-direction and select the endpoint as shown in the figure; the message, "Specify third destination point or [eXit] <X>:" appears in the command line.

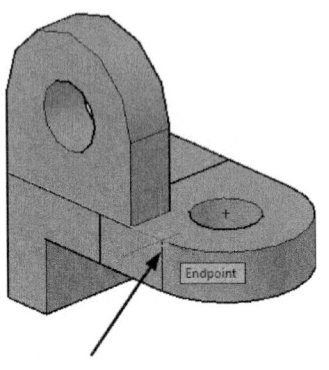

- Right-click and select the **eXit** option; the source object will be aligned, as shown below.

Using the 3D Mirror tool

The **3D Mirror** tool is similar to the **Mirror** tool. Using the **Mirror** tool, you can create a mirrored replica of an object in a 2D drawing. The objects are mirrored about an axis lying on a plane. But, with the **3D Mirror** tool, you need to define a plane about which the object will be mirrored. The **3D Mirror** tool provides many options to define the mirror plane.

- Click **Modeling > Modify > 3D Mirror** on the tool set.

- Select the object to be mirrored from the model and press RETURN; the message, "Specify first point of mirror plane (3 points)," appears above the command line.

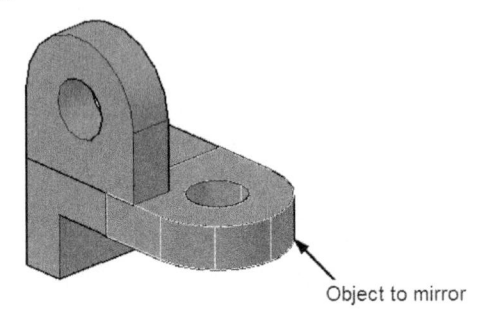

The **3points** option is selected by default to create the mirror plane. You need to specify three points to create a mirror plane. The mirror plane will pass through the selected points.

- Select the first and second points of the mirror plane, as shown below.

274 | Solid Editing & generating 2D views

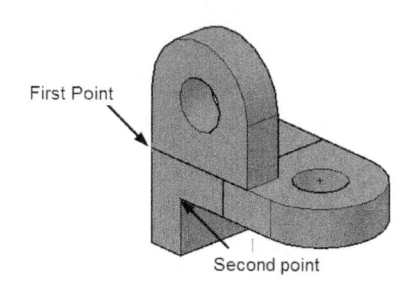

- Click the **Orbit** button on the toolbar and rotate the model, as shown below.

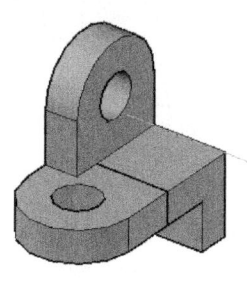

- Right-click and select **Exit** from the shortcut menu.
- Select the third point to define the mirror plane; the message, "Delete source objects? [Yes/No] <N>:" appears in the command line.

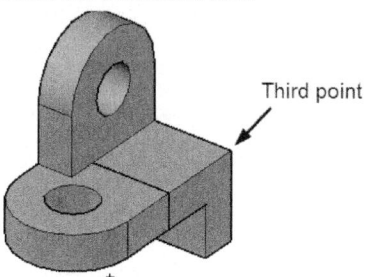

- Right-click and select the **No** option; the object will be mirrored.

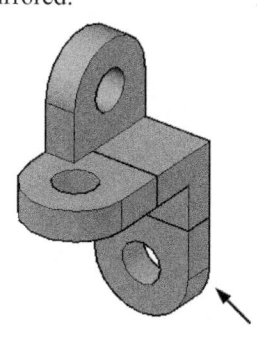

- Click the right-mouse button on the **Object Snap** icon on the status bar and select **Center**.
- Type **3DMIRROR** in the command line and press RETURN.
- Select the object to be the mirror from the model and press RETURN.

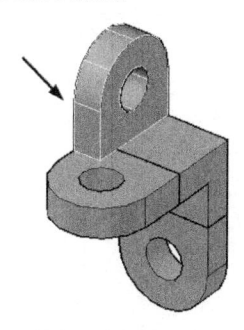

- Right-click and select the **XY** option; the message, "Specify point on XY plane <0,0,0>:" appears in the command line.

    The **XY** option creates a plane parallel to the XY plane. You need to specify a point at which the plane parallel to the XY plane will be created.

- Select the center point of the horizontal hole to define the mirror plane; the message, "Delete source objects? [Yes/No] <N>:" appears in the command line.

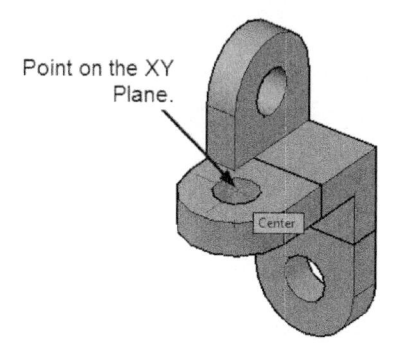

- Right-click and select the **No** option; the object will be mirrored, as shown below.

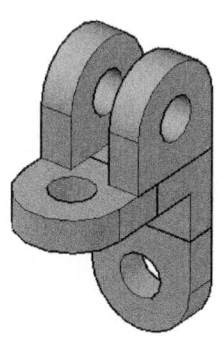

- Click **Boolean** drop-down > **Union** on the **Solid** panel and select all the objects of the model.
- Press RETURN; the objects will be combined into a single object.
- Change the view to SE Isometric.

275 | Solid Editing & generating 2D views

Using the Fillet Edge tool

The **Fillet Edge** tool is used to create rounds (convex corners) or fillets (concave corners) on solid objects, just as in 2D drawings.

- Click **Solid > Fillet Edge** on the **Modeling** tool set (or) type **FILLETEDGE** in the command line and press RETURN; the message, "Select an edge or [Chain/Loop/Radius]:"

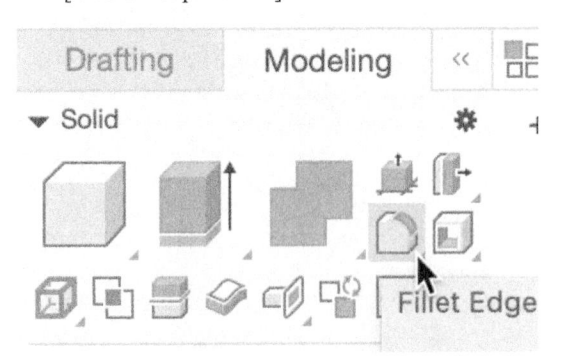

- Right-click and select the **Chain** option; the message, "Select an edge chain or [Edge/Radius]:" appears.
- Select the edges from the model, as shown below; you will notice that a chain of edges is selected.

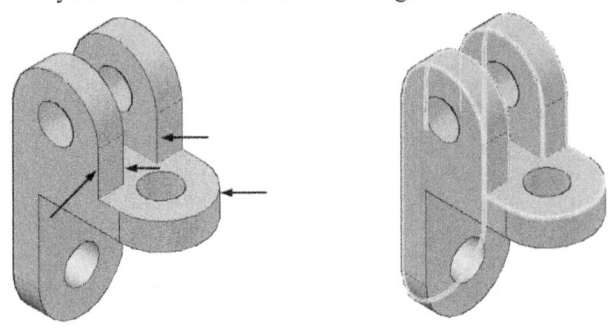

- Right-click and select the **Radius** option; the message, "Enter fillet radius or [Expression] <1.0000>:" appears.
- Type 2 in the command line and press RETURN.

- Press RETURN; the message, "Press Enter to accept the fillet or [Radius]:" appears. Also, a grip displayed on the fillets. You can use this grip to change the fillet radius dynamically.

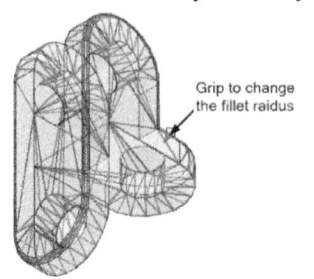

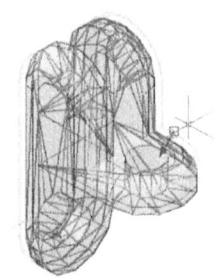

- Press RETURN to create rounds, as shown in the figure.

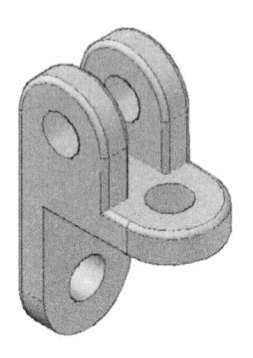

- Click the **Fillet Edge** button on the **Solid** panel.
- Right-click and select the **Loop** option.
- Select the edge from the model, as shown in the figure; the edges on the front face of the model are highlighted. Also, the message, "Enter an option [Accept/Next] <Accept>:" appears in the command line.

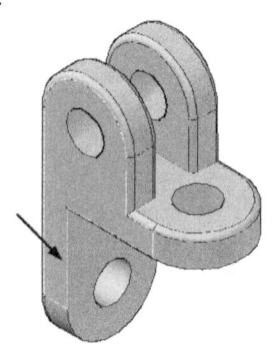

- Right-click and select the **Next** option; the edges on the side face will be highlighted.
- Select the **Accept** button; rounds and fillets are displayed on the side face.

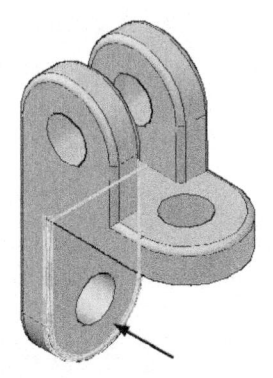

- Likewise, select the round edge, as shown in the figure,
- Right-click and select the **Next** option; the edges on the bottom face of the model will be highlighted.
- Click the **Orbit** button on the toolbar and rotate the model.
- Right-click and select **Exit**.
- Right-click and select the **Accept** option to view rounds and fillets on the bottom face.
- Right-click and select the **Radius** option and type 2. Press RETURN to accept.
- Press RETURN twice to create rounds, as shown in the figure.

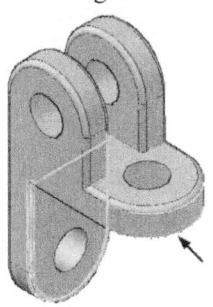

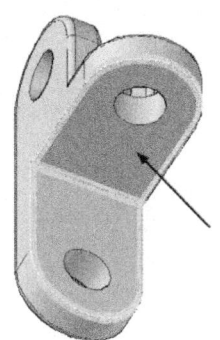

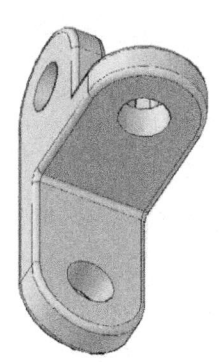

- Similarly, create fillets on the remaining edges by using the **Chain** option.

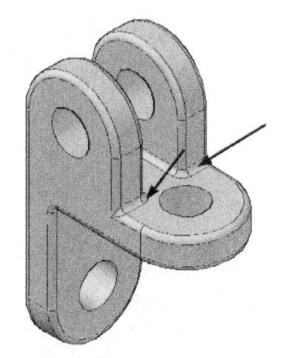

- Save and close the file.

Using the Taper Faces tool

The **Taper Faces** tool is used to taper faces. You can use this tool to change the angle of planar or curved faces.

Example 3:

In this example, you will create a cylinder and taper the outer face.

- Start a new AutoCAD file.
- Click **View > 3D Views > Front** on the menu bar.
- Create a hollow cylinder with an inner and outer diameter as 140 and 150, respectively. The cylinder height is 50.

- Click **Solid > Solid** drop-down > **Taper Faces** on the **Modeling** tool set.

277 Solid Editing & generating 2D views

- Select the outer cylindrical face and press RETURN to accept; the message, "Specify the base point:" appears in the command line.
- Press and hold the SHIFT key and right-click to display the shortcut menu. Select the **Center** option from the shortcut menu.
- Move the pointer over the circular edge on the front face; the center point of the circular edge will be highlighted.
- Select the center point of the circular edge.
- Move the pointer along the Z-direction in the direction, as shown in the figure.
- Click to specify the axis of the taper; the message, "Specify the taper angle:" appears in the command line.

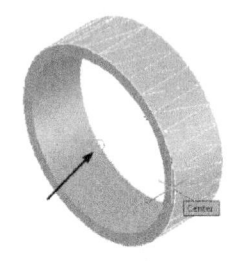

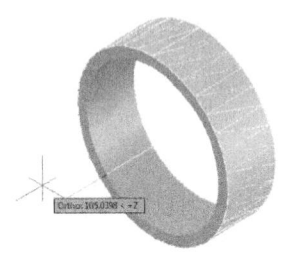

- Type 10 as the taper angle and press RETURN; the outer cylindrical face will be tapered as shown in the figure.

- Right-click and select eXit.
- Right-click and select eXit.

Using the Offset Faces tool

The **Offset Faces** tool is used to move the faces of a 3D object in the perpendicular direction.

- Right-click and select **Subobject Selection Filter > Face**.

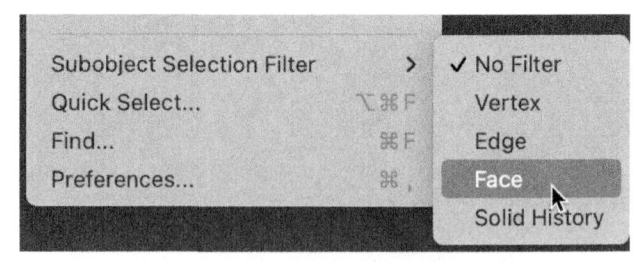

- Click **Solid > Solid drop-down > Offset Faces** on the **Modeling** tool set.

- Select the front face of the model and press RETURN; the message, "Specify the offset distance:" appears in the command line.

Note: By mistake, if you have selected the side faces, then click the Remove option in the command line. Next, click on the side faces, and then press RETURN to remove them from the selection.

- Type -20 in the command line and press RETURN; the face will be offset.

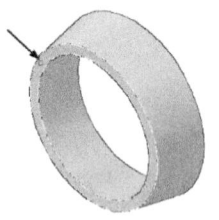

- Right-click and select eXit.
- Right-click and select eXit.
- Right-click and select **Subobject Selection Filter > No Filter**.
- Create a cylinder of 40 mm diameter and 30 mm length at the center of the hollow cylinder.

AutoCAD 2023 For Beginners (For Mac Users)

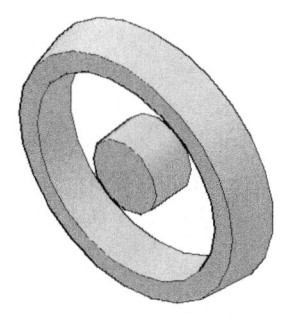

- Create a truncated cone with the following dimensions.
    - Base radius: 8 mm
    - Top radius: 5 mm
    - Height: 65mm

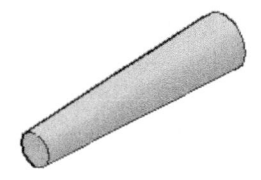

Using the 3D Rotate tool

The **3D Rotate** tool is used to rotate objects about an axis. You can define the axis of rotation by using the **Rotate Gizmo** tool. The **Rotate Gizmo** tool will be displayed when you activate the **3D Rotate** tool and select an object.

- Click **Modify > 3D Rotate** on the **Modeling** tool set.

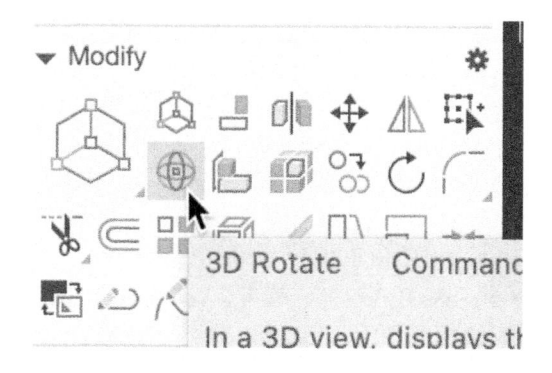

- Select the truncated cone and press RETURN; the **Rotate Gizmo** tool will be displayed.
- Select the center point of the front face as the base point; the **Rotate Gizmo** tool will be moved to the selected point.

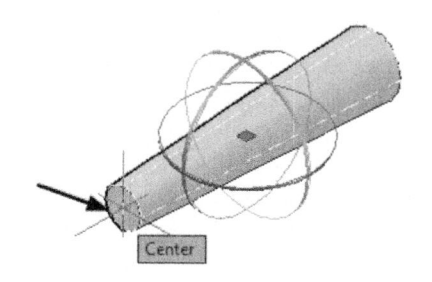

- Select the Z axis (Blue ring) of the **Rotate Gizmo**; an axis line is displayed along the Z-axis.
- Type **270** as the rotation angle and press RETURN; the cone will be rotated by 270 degrees.

- On the status bar, click the right-mouse button on the **Object Snap** icon, and then select the **Quadrant** option, if not already selected.
- Click the **Move** button on the **Modify** panel and select the cone. Press RETURN to accept.
- Select the base point and the destination point, as shown below; the cone will be placed at the destination point.

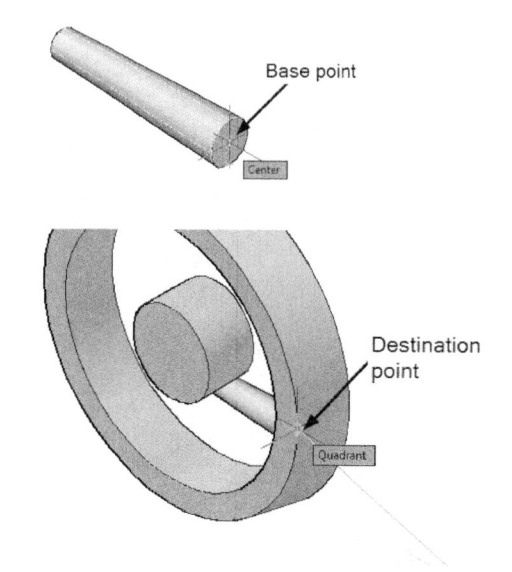

- Select the cone; the **Move Gizmo** tool will be displayed on it.

279 | Solid Editing & generating 2D views

- Select the Y-axis (Green arrow) of the **Move Gizmo** tool and move the pointer toward the right.
- Type 22 in the command line and press RETURN; the cone will be moved through 22 mm.

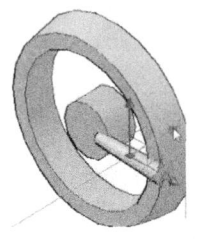

Using the 3D Polyline tool

The **3D Polyline** tool is similar to the **Polyline** tool, except that you can create a polyline by specifying coordinate points in three dimensions. Also, you can only create straight lines using this tool.

- Change the **Visual Style** of the model to **Wireframe**.
- Click **Draw > 3D Polyline** on the **Modeling** tool set.

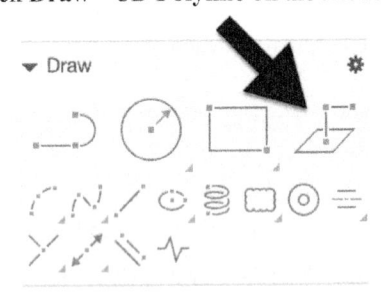

- Select the center point on the front face of the cylindrical object.
- Move the pointer toward the right and select the center point on the back face of the cylindrical object.

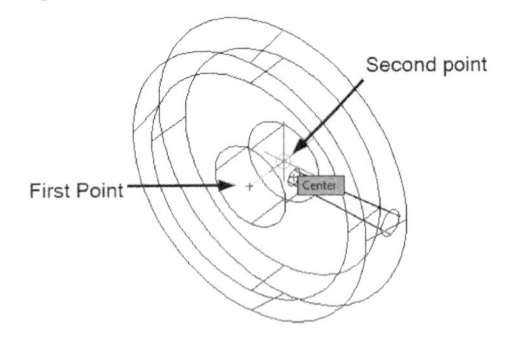

- Press RETURN; the 3D polyline will be created.

Creating a 3D Polar Array

You can create a 3D polar array by using the **Polar** option of the **3DARRAY** command. This option is similar to the 2D Polar Array tool. The only difference between these two tools is that you need to specify an axis of rotation in 3D polar array, whereas in 2D Polar array, you need to specify an axis point. The axis of rotation in a 3D polar array can be specified by selecting two points. It allows you to create a 3D polar array about an axis in the 3D workspace.

- Type **3A** in the command line and press RETURN.
- Select the truncated cone from the model and press RETURN.
- Right-click and select the **Polar** option; the message, "Enter the number of items in the array:" appears.
- Type 6 in the command line and press RETURN; the message, "Specify the angle to fill (+=ccw, -=cw) <360>:" appears in the command line.
    Type + and press RETURN to create the polar array in counter-clockwise direction and type – to create it in the clockwise direction.
- Press RETURN to accept 360 as the fill angle; the message, "Rotate arrayed objects? [Yes/No] <Y>:" appears in the command line.
- Right-click and select the **Yes** option; the message, "Specify center point of array:" appears.
- Select the first and second points of the axis, as shown in the figure; the polar array will be created.

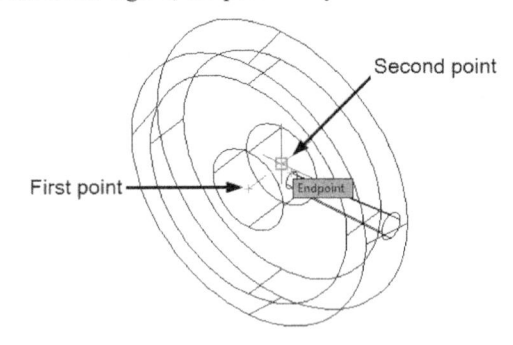

- Change the **Visual Style** to **Shades of Grey**.
- Perform the **Union** operation to combine all the objects.

280 | Solid Editing & generating 2D views

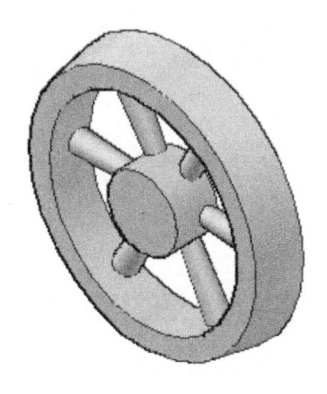

Using the Shell tool

The **Shell** tool converts a solid object into a thin-walled hollow object. You need to first select the object to be shelled, and then select the faces to be removed and enter the thickness of the walls.

- Click **Solid** > **Solid** drop-down > **Shell** on the **Modeling** tool set.

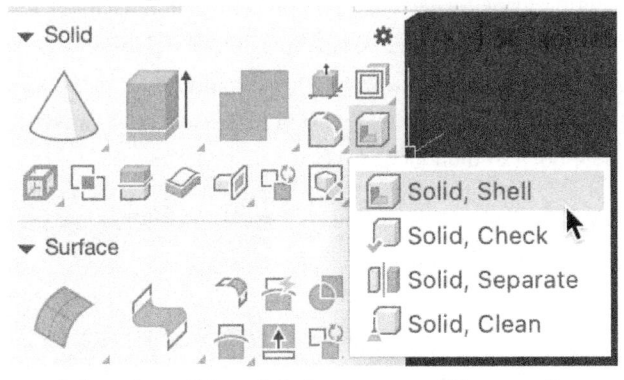

- Select the solid model; the message, "Remove faces or [Undo/Add/ALL]:" appears.
- Select the front face of the cylindrical object.
- Click the **Orbit** icon on the toolbar.
- Press and hold the left mouse button and drag; the model will be rotated.
- Right-click and select **Exit**.
- Select the back face of the cylindrical object.

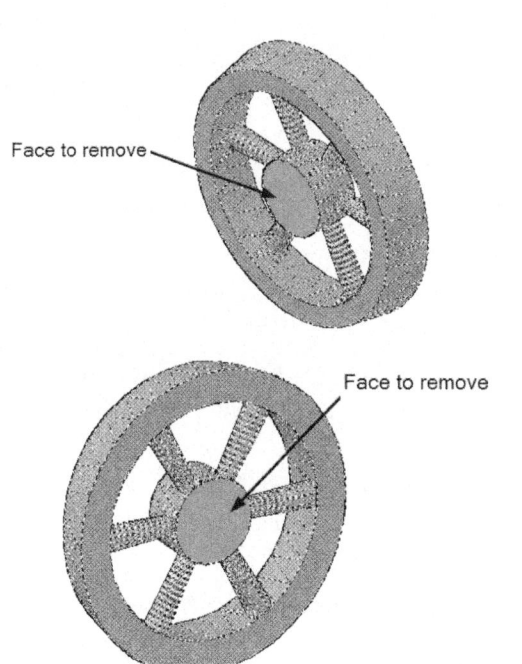

- Press RETURN; the message, "Enter the shell offset distance:" appears.
- Type 10 in the command line and press RETURN; the cylindrical object will be shelled.
- Right-click and select the **eXit** option.

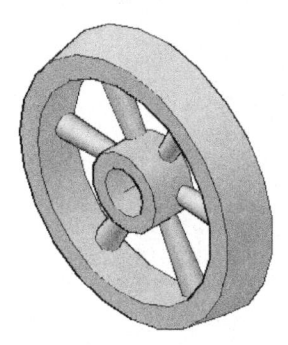

Using the Chamfer Edge tool

The **Chamfer Edge** tool is used to bevel sharp edges of a solid object. When you chamfer an edge, a wedge is created automatically, and the Boolean operation is performed to subtract it from the solid object.

- Click **Solid** > **Fillet Edge** drop-down > **Chamfer Edge** on the **Modeling** tool set.

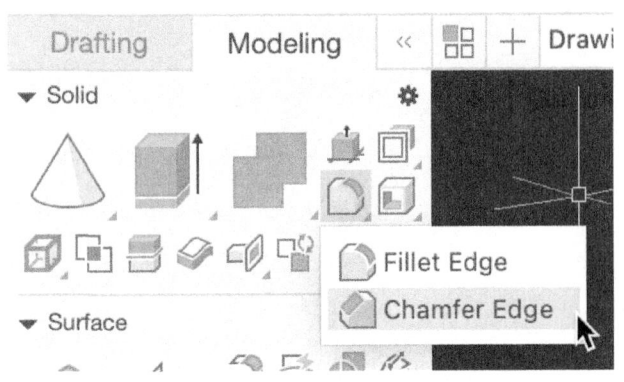

- Select the outer circular edge of the cylindrical object.
- Right-click and select the **Distance** option; the message, "Specify Distance1 or [Expression] <1.0000>:" appears.
- Type 4 in the command line and press RETURN; you will notice that the preview of the chamfer changes. Also, the message, "Specify Distance2 or [Expression] <1.0000>:" appears in the command line.
- Type 2 in the command line and press RETURN.
- Press RETURN twice to create the chamfer, as shown in the figure.

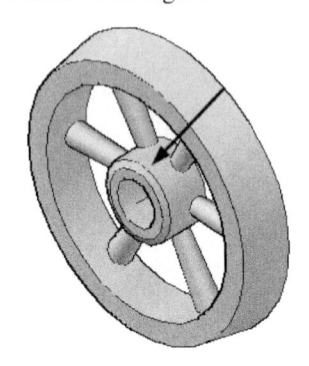

Using the Section Plane tool

The **Section Plane** tool creates a translucent cutting plane passing through a solid object to show the inside portion of it. This tool is handy when the inside portion of the solid is not visible. You can move this cutting plane dynamically to view the inside portion at different locations of the solid.

- To create a section plane, click **Solid > Modeling > Section Plane** on the **Modeling** tool set; the message, "Select face or any point to locate section line or [Draw section/Orthographic]:" appears.

- Right-click and select the **Orthographic** option.
- Right-click and select **Right**.

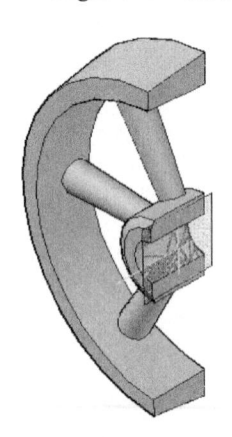

Using the Live Section tool

The **Livesection** tool is used to make a side of the section plane invisible or visible. When you create a section plane by selecting a plane, one side of the section plane will be invisible automatically. However, when you create a section plane by selecting points, you need to use the **Live Section** tool to make one side invisible. Click **Solid > Modeling > Livesection** on the **Modeling** tool set. Next, select the section plane; one side of the section plane will be hidden or unhidden, as shown in the figure.

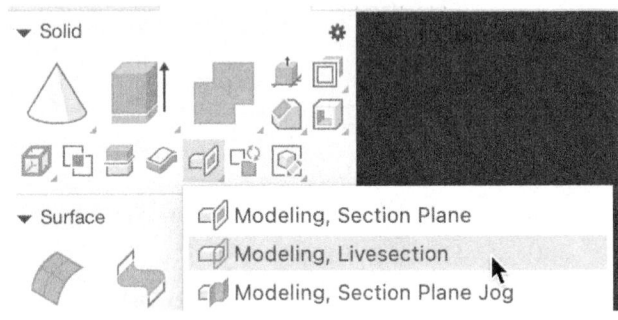

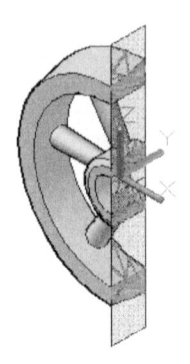

- Save the file as **Example 3**.

Exercises

Create 3D models using the drawing views and dimensions.

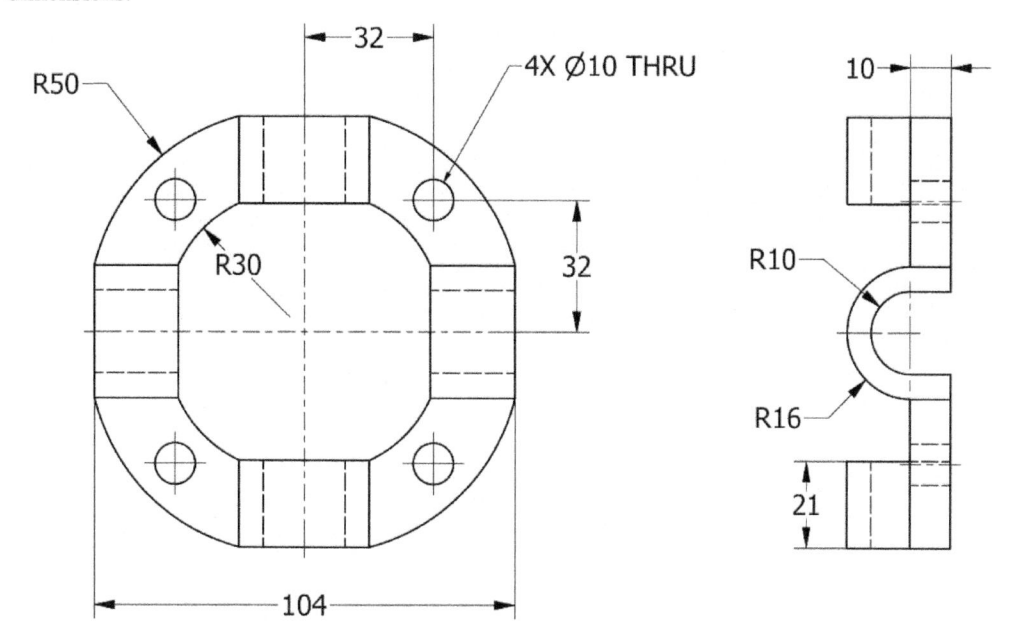

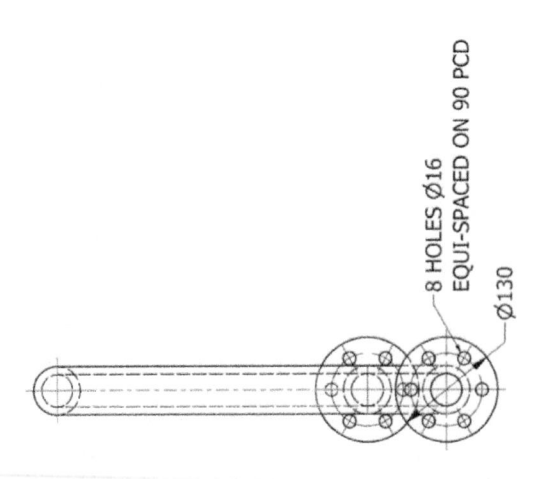

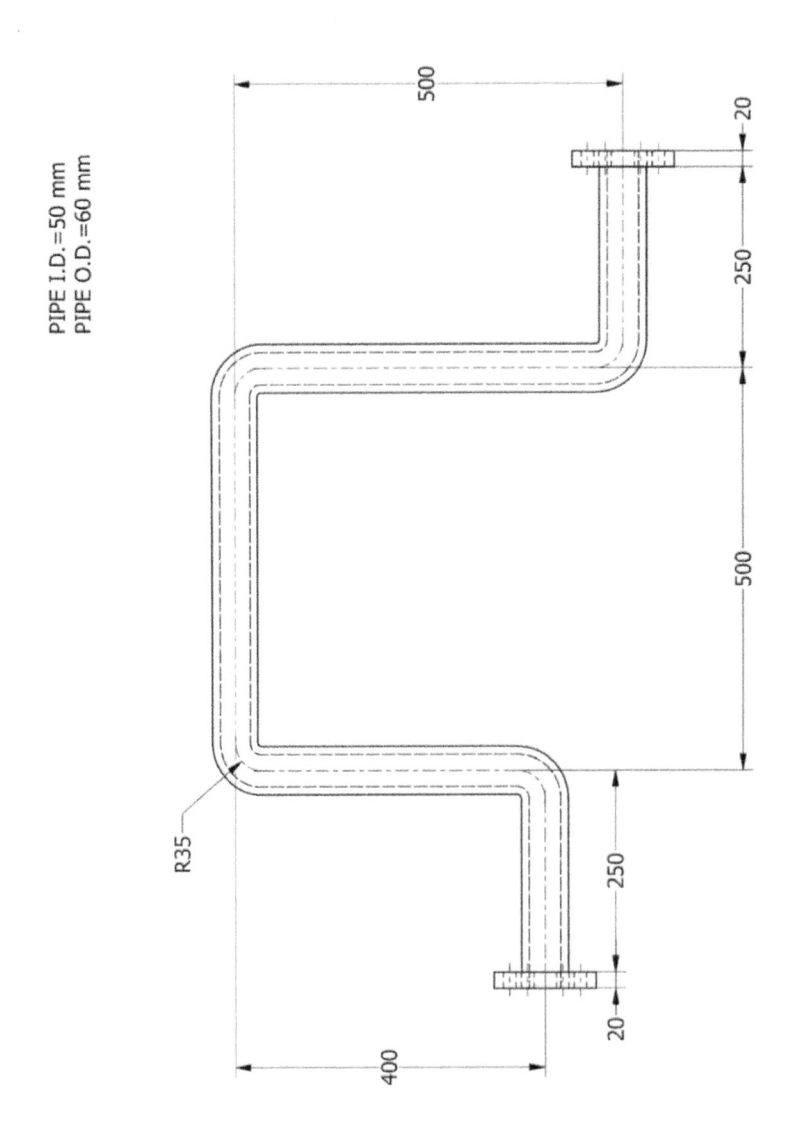

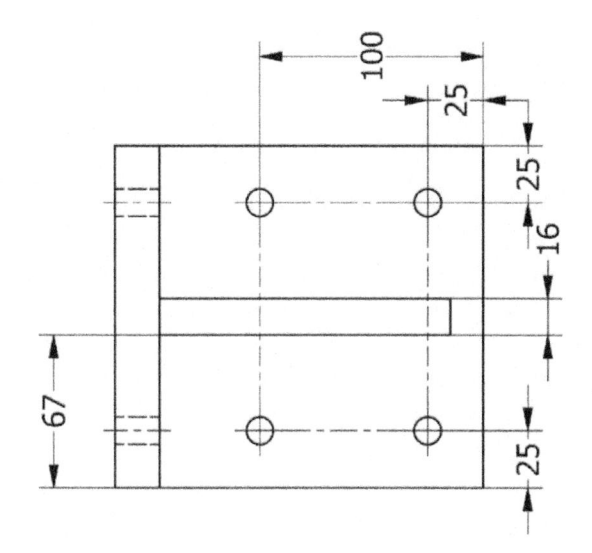

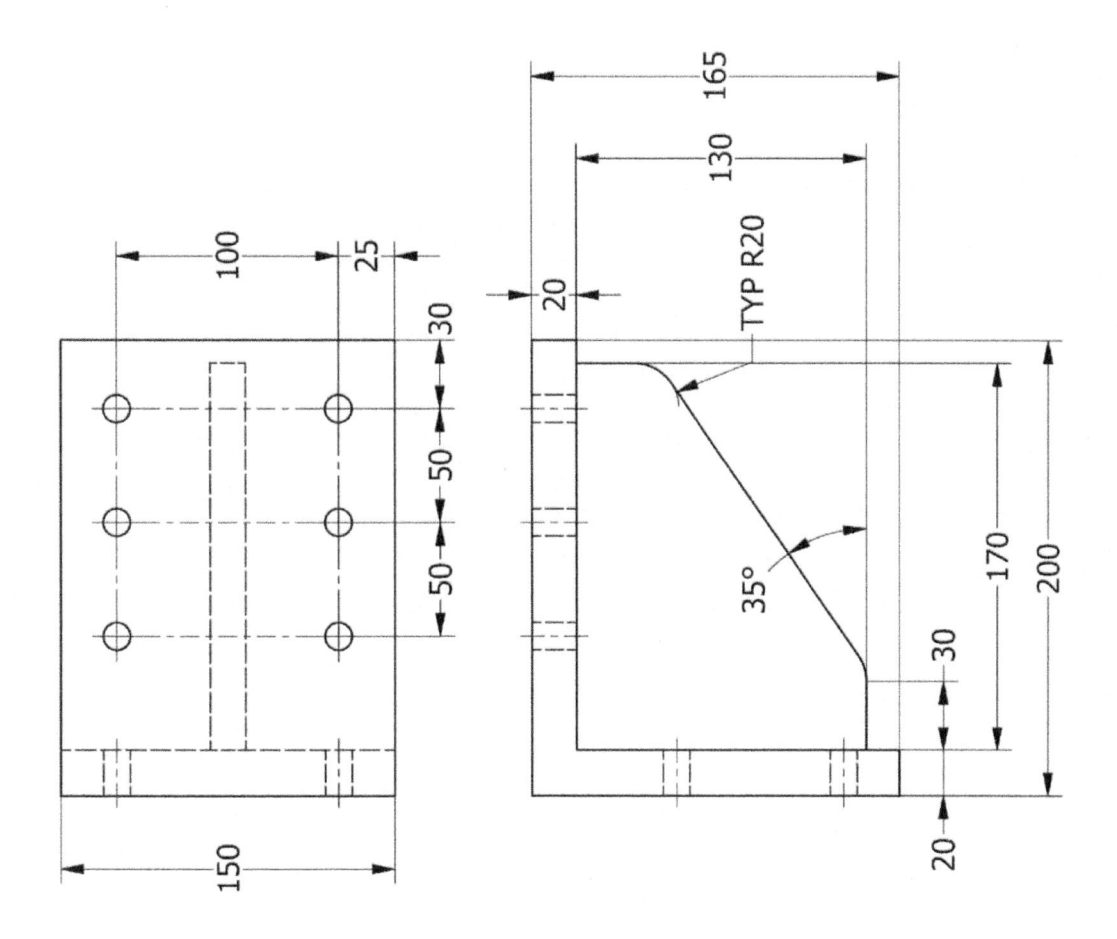

SHELL THICKNESS = 2 mm

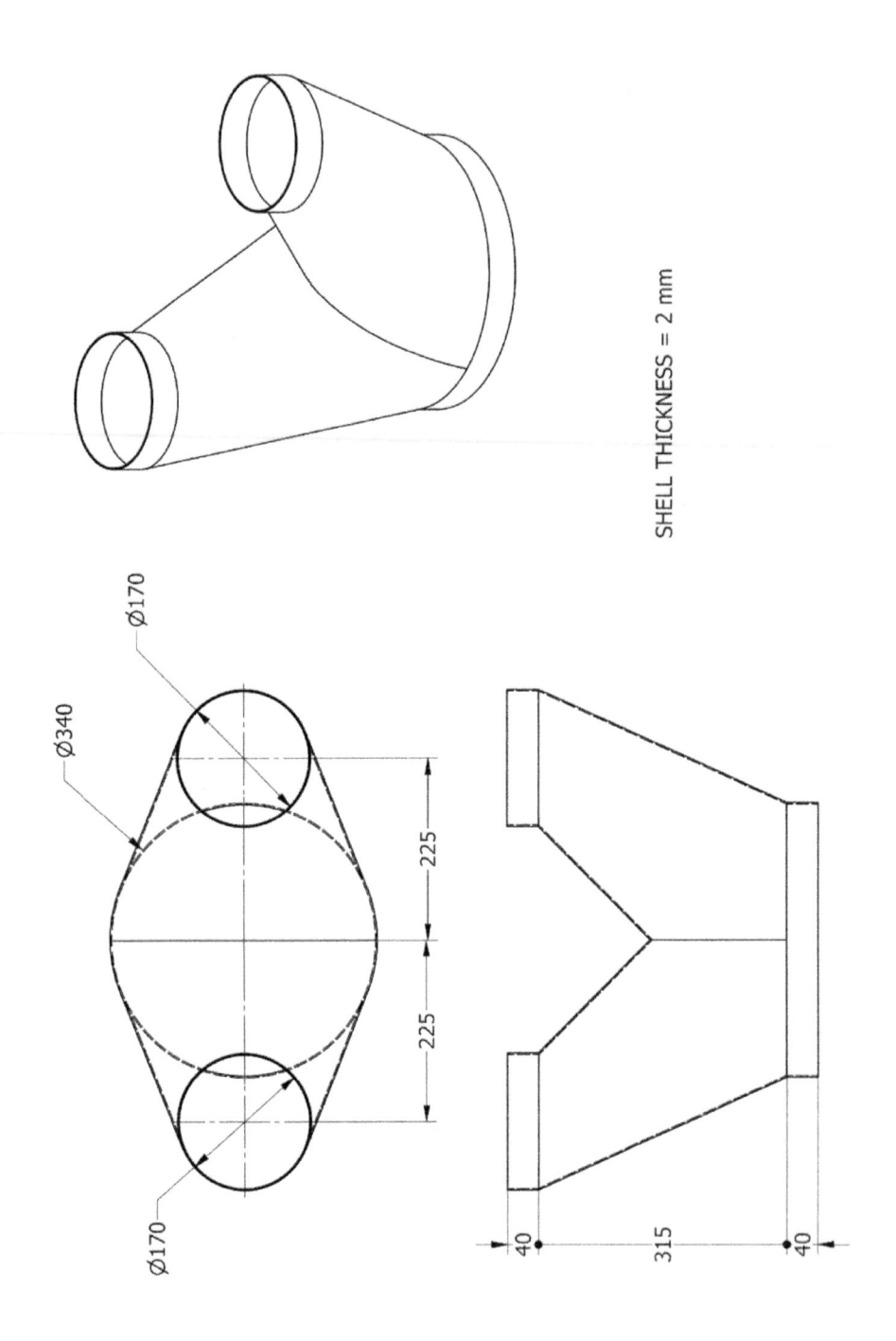

Ø170
Ø340
Ø170

225
225

40
315
40

Chapter 14: Creating Architectural Drawings

In this chapter, you will learn to do the following:

- **Defining Settings for Architectural Drawings**
- **Creating Inner Walls**
- **Creating Openings and Doors**
- **Creating Kitchen Fixtures**
- **Creating Bathroom Fixtures**
- **Adding Furniture using Blocks**
- **Adding Windows**
- **Arranging Objects of the drawing in Layers**
- **Creating Grid Lines**
- **Adding Dimensions**
- **Create Stair Details**
- **Elevation View**
- **Roof Plan**
- **Wall and Roof details**

Example 1

In this example, you will learn to create an architectural drawing.

Creating Outer Walls

- Start **AutoCAD 2023** and click **Create > New > acad.dwt**.
- Type **UNITS** in the command line and press RETURN.
- On the **Drawing Units** dialog, select **Type > Architectural**.
- Select **Precision > 0-01/16**.
- Set the **Insertion Scale** to **Inches** and click **OK**.
- Type **LIMITS** in the command line and press RETURN.
- Press RETURN to accept 0, 0 as the lower limit.
- Type 100', 80' in the command line, and press RETURN. The program sets the upper limit of the drawing.
- Turn OFF the Grid Display icon on the status bar.
- Select **View > Zoom > All** on the Menu Bar.
- On the Status bar, turn ON the **Ortho Mode** icon.
- On the **Drafting** tool set, click **Draw > Line**, and then select an arbitrary point. It defines the start point of the line.
- Move the pointer toward right horizontally and type-in 412 — press RETURN.
- Move the pointer vertically and type-in 338 — press RETURN.
- Move the pointer onto the starting point of the drawing, and then move it upwards. You will notice that a dotted line appears.

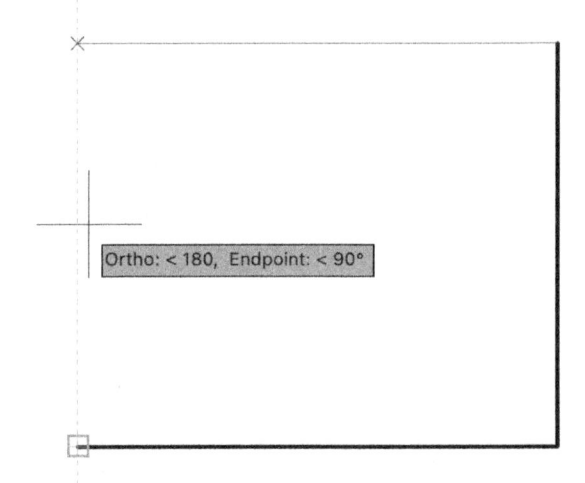

- Click to create a horizontal line. You will notice that the two horizontal lines are of the same length.
- Click the right mouse button and select **Close**.

- On the **Drafting** tool set, click **Modify > Offset**.
- Type-in 6 as offset distance and press RETURN.
- Select the left vertical line of the drawing.
- Move the pointer inside the drawing and click to create an offset line.
- Likewise, offset the other lines, as shown below.

- On the menu bar, click **View > Zoom > Window**.

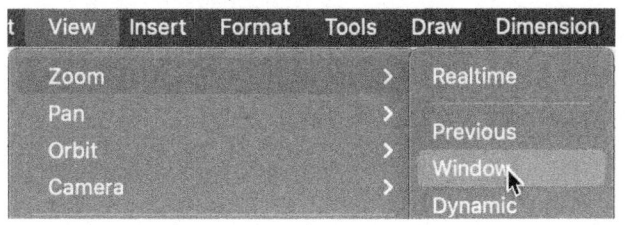

- Create a window on the top left corner of the drawing. The corner portion will be zoomed in.

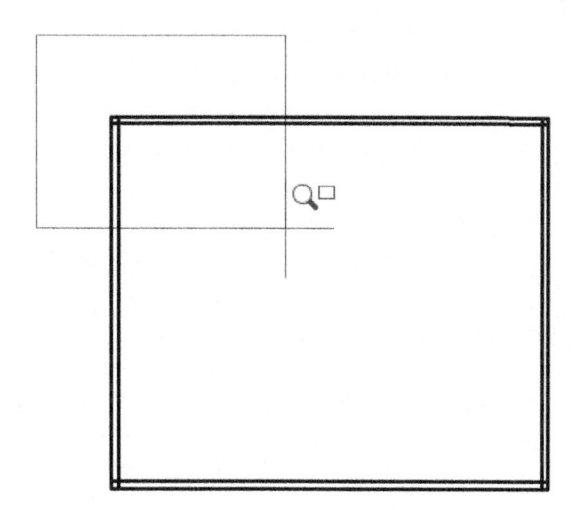

- On the **Drafting** tool set, click **Modify > Fillet**.
- Right-click and select the **Radius** option.
- Type in 0 — press RETURN.
- Select the inner offset lines, as shown below.

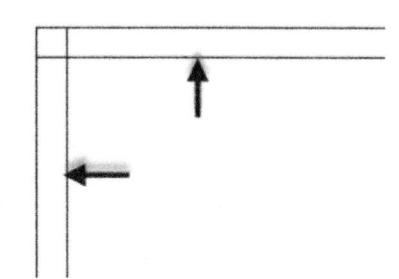

- Likewise, fillet the other corners.

- Save the drawing. Make sure that you save the drawing after each section.

Creating Inner Walls

- Activate the **Offset** command and type in **130** in the command line, and then press RETURN.
- Select the inner line of the right side wall and click inside the drawing.
- Press Esc.

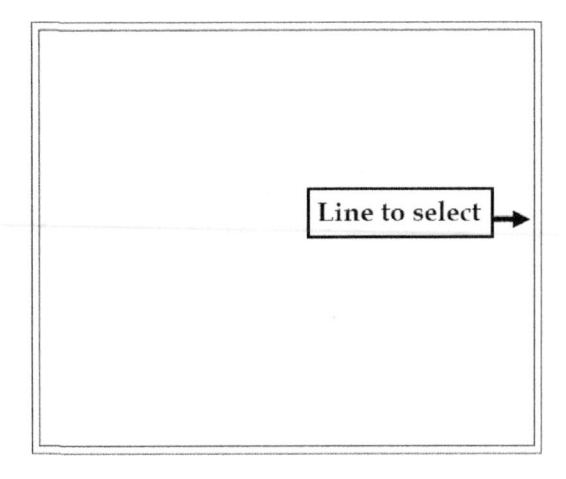

- Select the new offset line. You will notice that three grips are displayed on the line.
- Click the right mouse button and select **Copy Selection**.

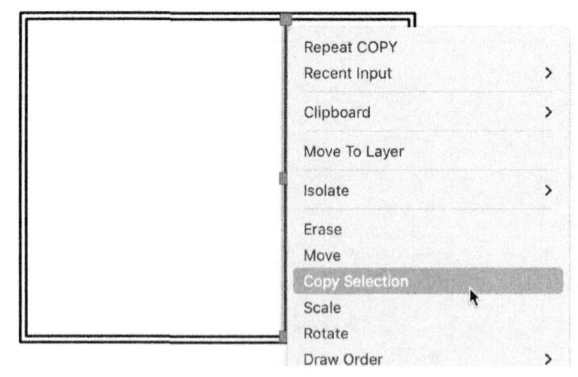

- Select the endpoint of the selected line as a base point.
- Move the pointer toward the left and type in 4, and then press RETURN. A new line is created, and another line is attached to the pointer.
- Move the pointer toward the left and type in 118, and then press RETURN.

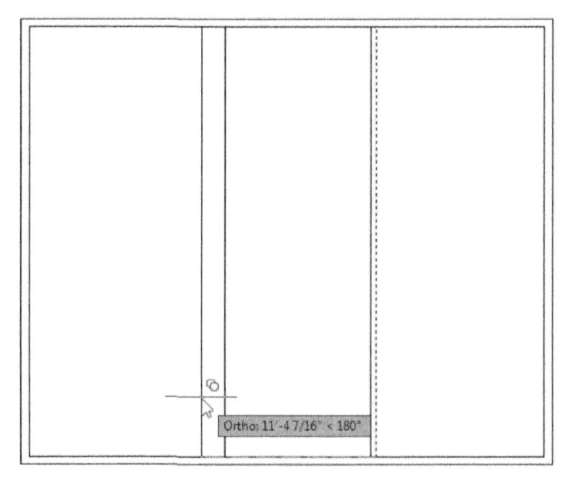

- Move the pointer toward the left and type in 122, and then press RETURN.
- Press Esc to come out of the **Copy** command.

- Likewise, create horizontal offset lines, as shown below.

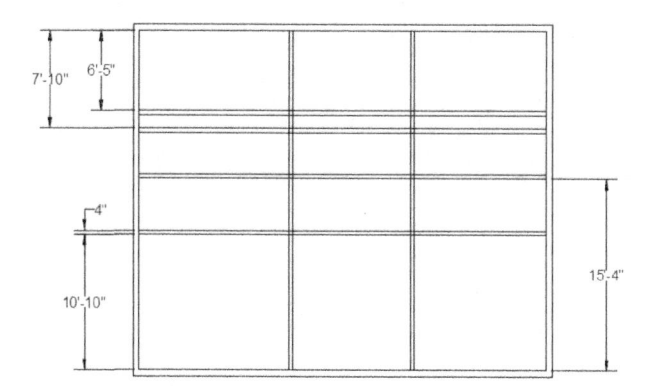

- On the **Drafting** tool set, click **Modify > Trim**.
- Click on the lines at the locations shown below.

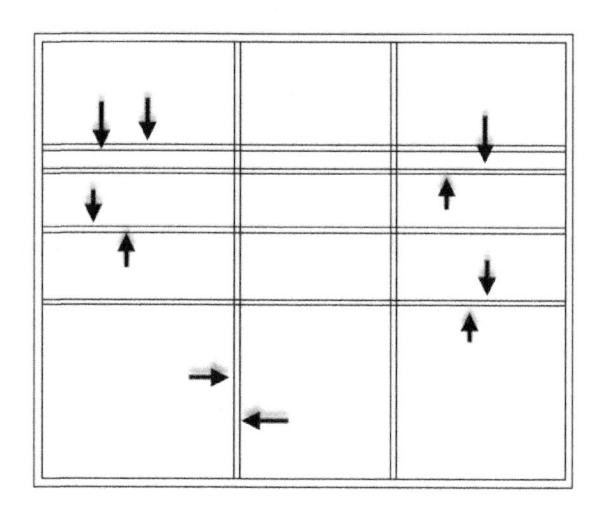

- Specify the fence points across the horizontal lines, as shown below.

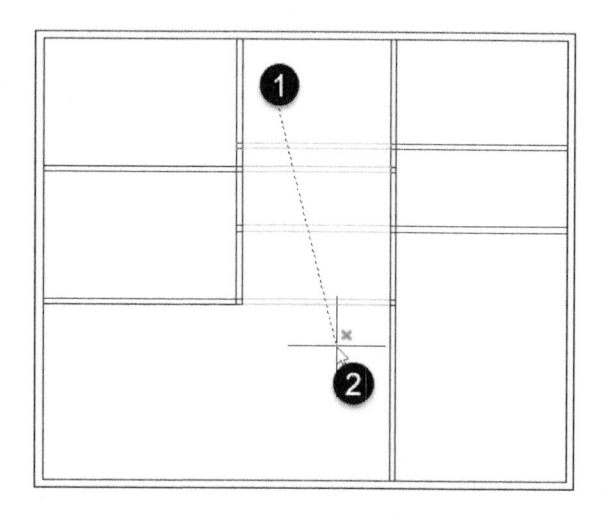

- Right-click and select the **Crossing** option.
- Create the selection window, as shown.

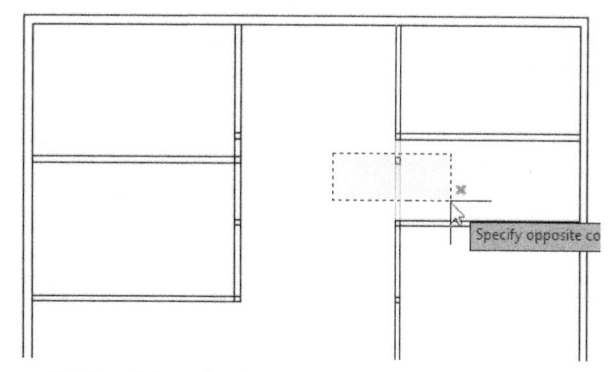

- Right-click and select the **Crossing** option.
- Create the selection window, as shown.

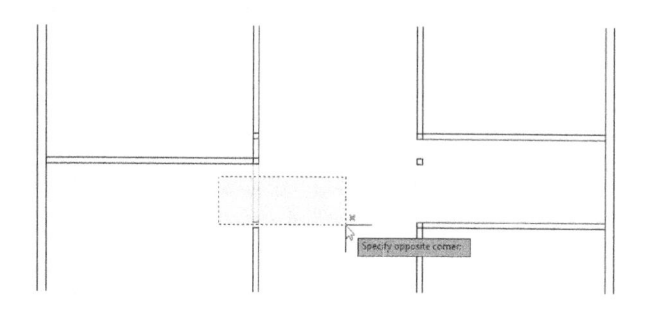

- Zoom to the top portion of the drawing by placing the pointer in the top portion and rotating the mouse scroll in the forward direction.
- Select the portion of the horizontal line that lies between the lines of the inner wall. The selected portions will be trimmed.

291 | Creating Architectural Drawings

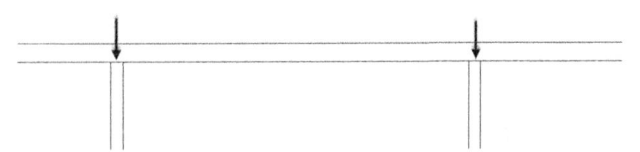

- Press and hold the mouse scroll wheel and drag downwards until the lower portion of the drawing is visible.
- Trim the unwanted portion, as shown below.

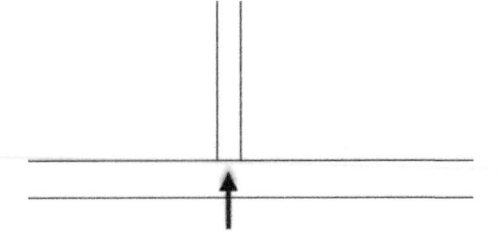

- Trim the unwanted portions, as shown below.

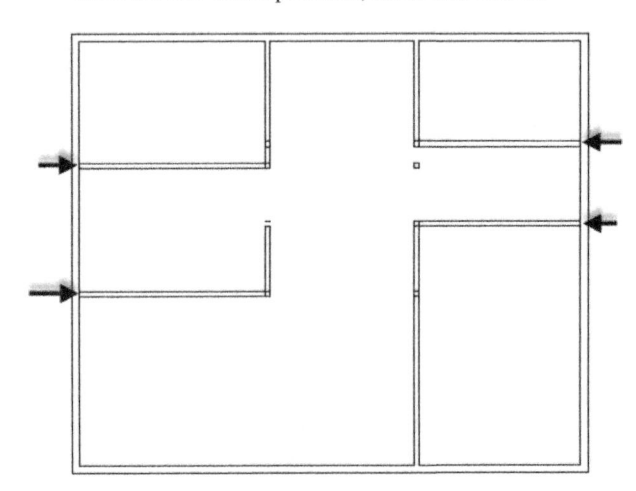

- Trim the unwanted portions at the corners.

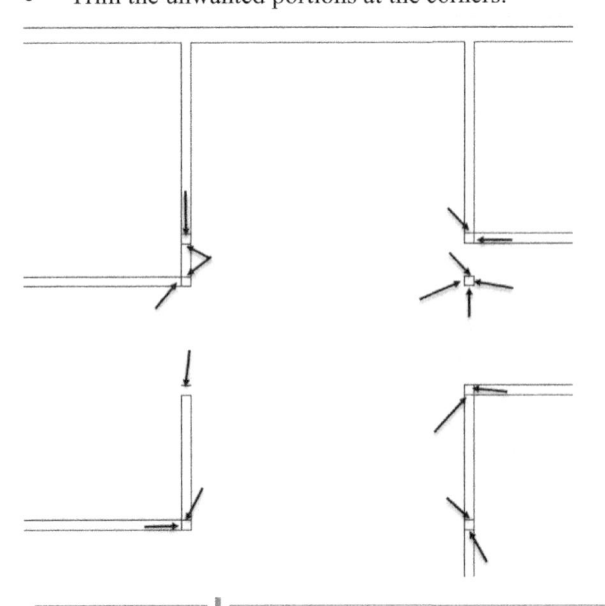

- Press Esc to deactivate the **Trim** command.

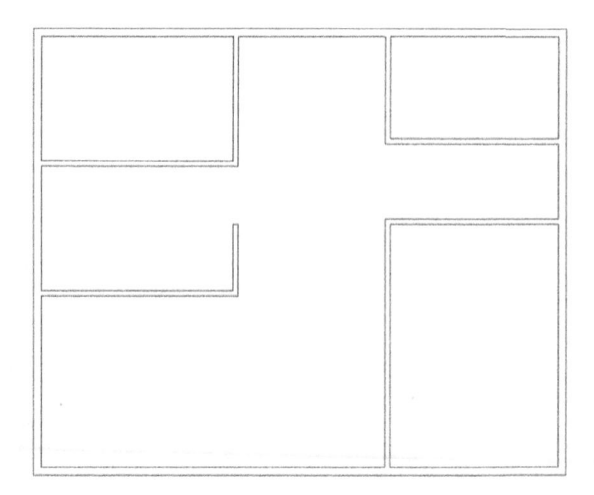

Creating Openings and Doors

- Activate the **Line** command and select the corner of the inner wall, as shown below.
- Move the pointer downward and select the other corner point.

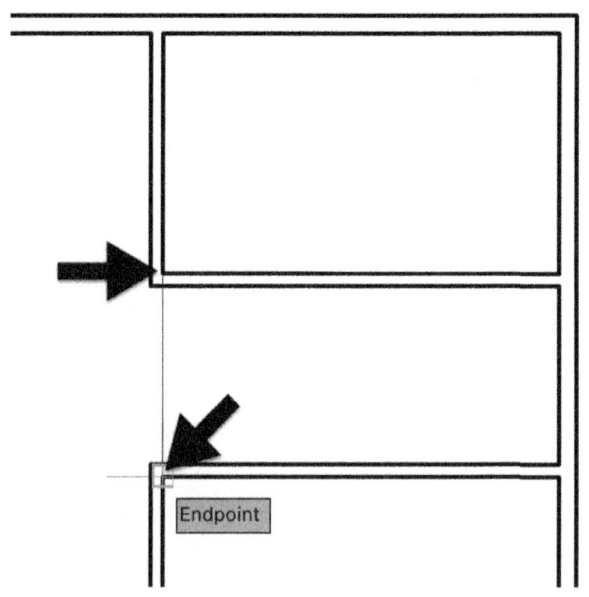

- Deactivate the **Line** command and select the new line.
- Select the middle point of the new line and move the pointer toward the right.
- Type-in 6 and press RETURN.

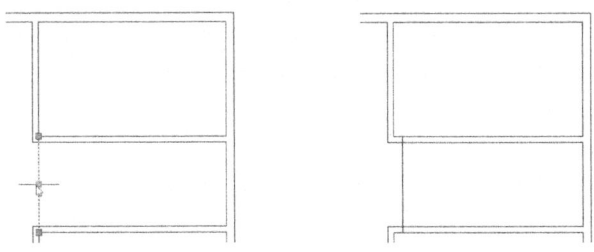

- Activate the **Offset** command and specify 32 as the offset distance.
- Select the new line and move rightwards, and then click. 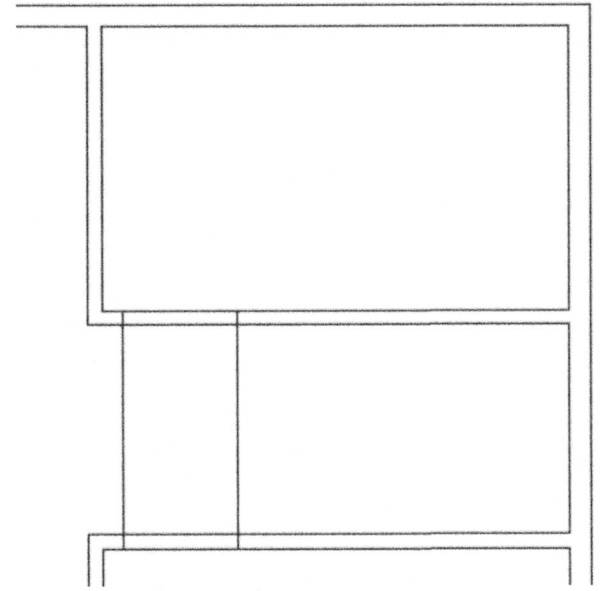
- Activate the **Trim** command and trim the unwanted portions. 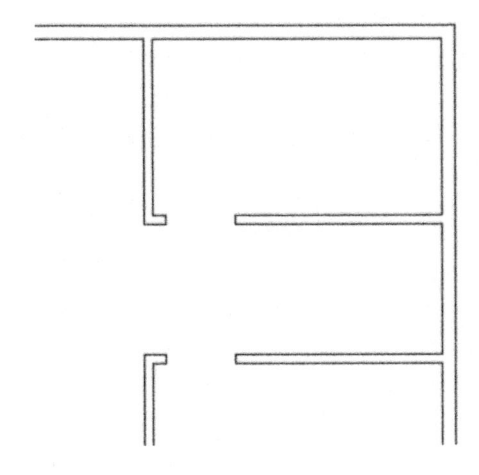
- Likewise, create other openings, as shown below (use the method described in the earlier step).

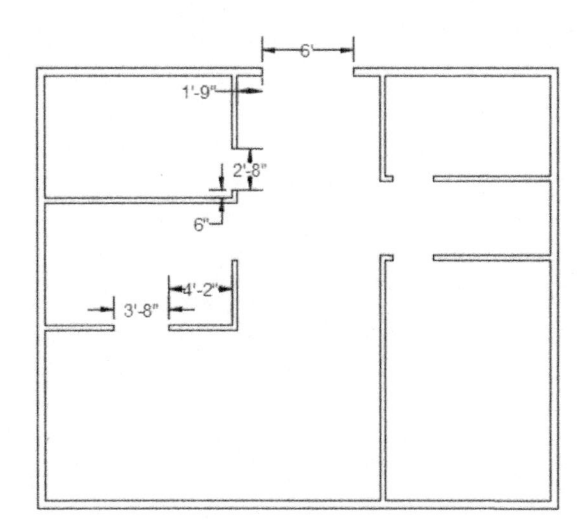

- On the tool set, click **Drafting > Draw > Rectangle**.
- Select the endpoint of the opening, as shown below.
- Right-click and select **Dimensions**. 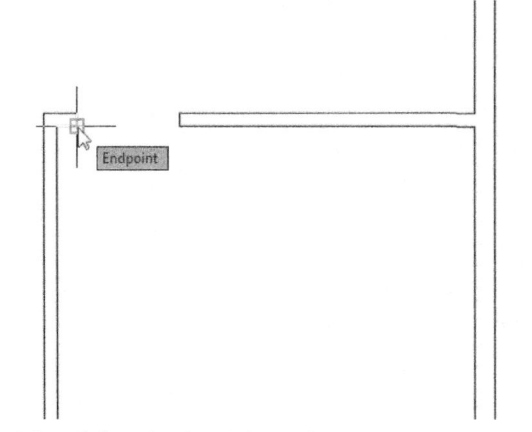
- Type-in 1 and press RETURN. It defines the length of the rectangle.
- Type-in 32 and press RETURN. It defines the width of the rectangle.
- Move the pointer down and click to create the door. Now, you need to create the door swing.
- On the tool set, click **Drafting > Draw > Arc** drop-down > **Start, Center, End**. 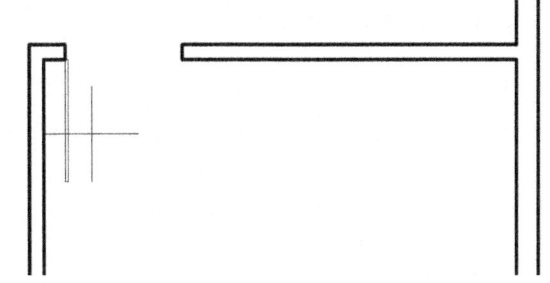

293 | Creating Architectural Drawings

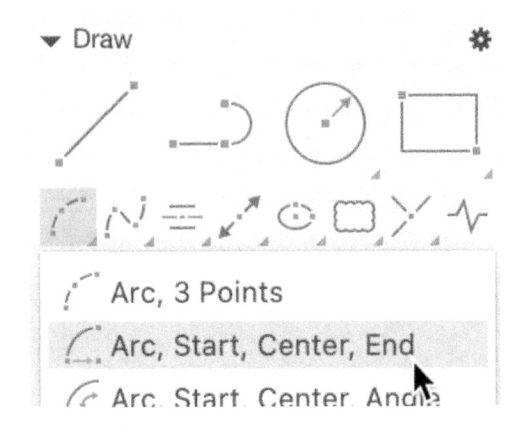

- Select the start, center, and end of the arc in the sequence shown below.

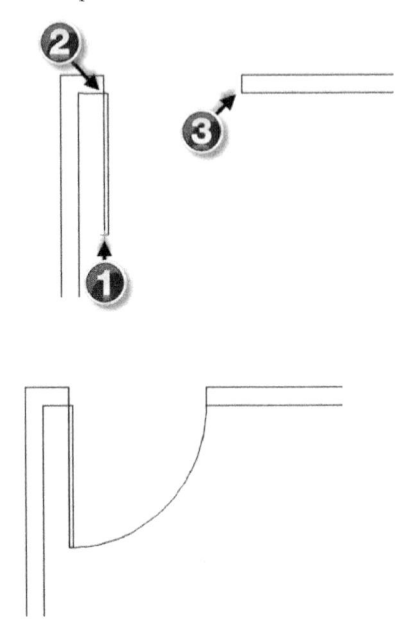

- Select the door and door swing.
- Click the right mouse button and select **Copy Selection**.
- Select the corner point of the rectangle as the base point.

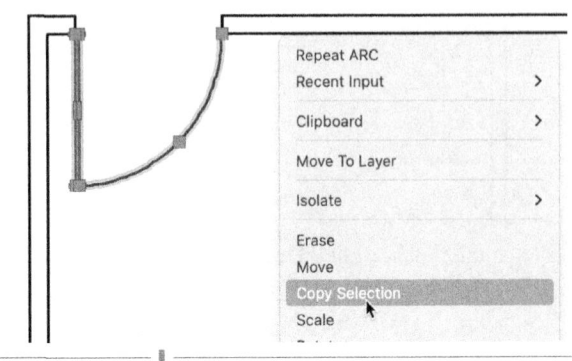

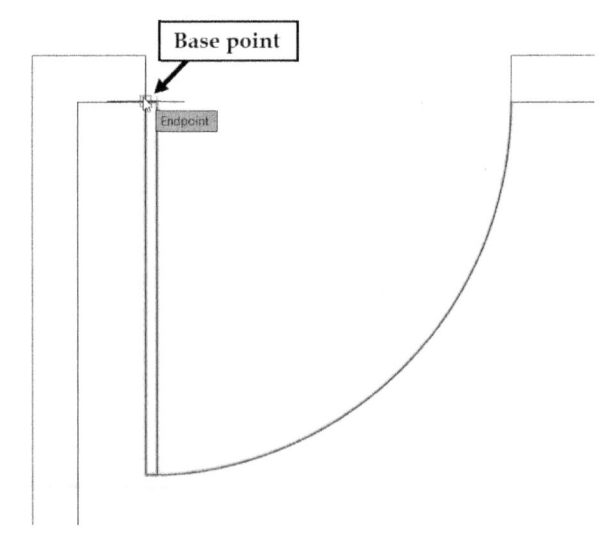

- Select the corner points of openings, as shown below.

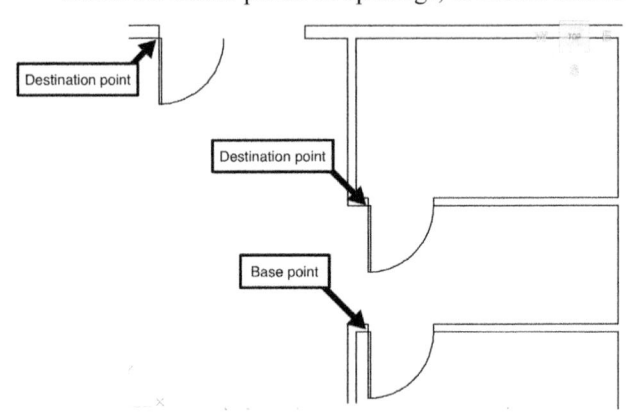

- Press Esc to deactivate the **Copy** command.
- Click the right-mouse button to the **Object Snap** icon on the status bar.
- Make sure that the **Midpoint** option is selected.
- On the **Drafting** tool set, click **Modify > Mirror**, and then select the door and swing of the bathroom, as shown. Press RETURN to accept the selection.

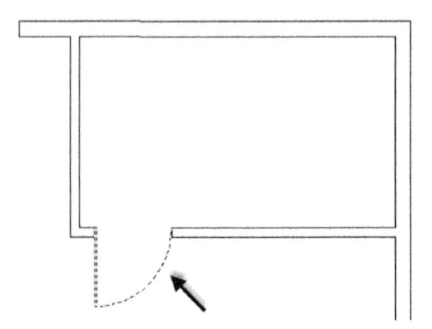

- Define the mirror line by selecting the points, as shown below.

294 | Creating Architectural Drawings

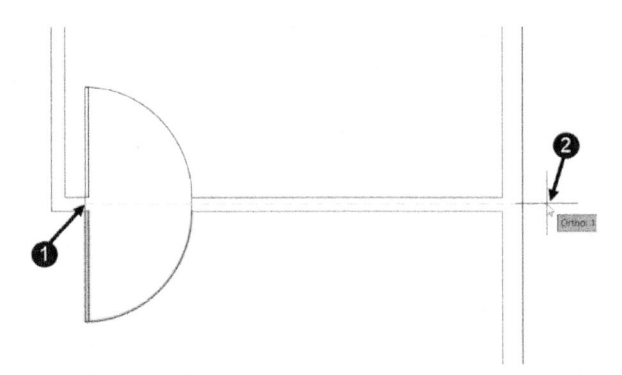

- Right-click and select **Yes**. It deletes the original object.
- On the **Drafting** tool set, click **Modify > Scale**, and then select the door & swing at the main entrance — press RETURN.
- Select the base point, as shown below.

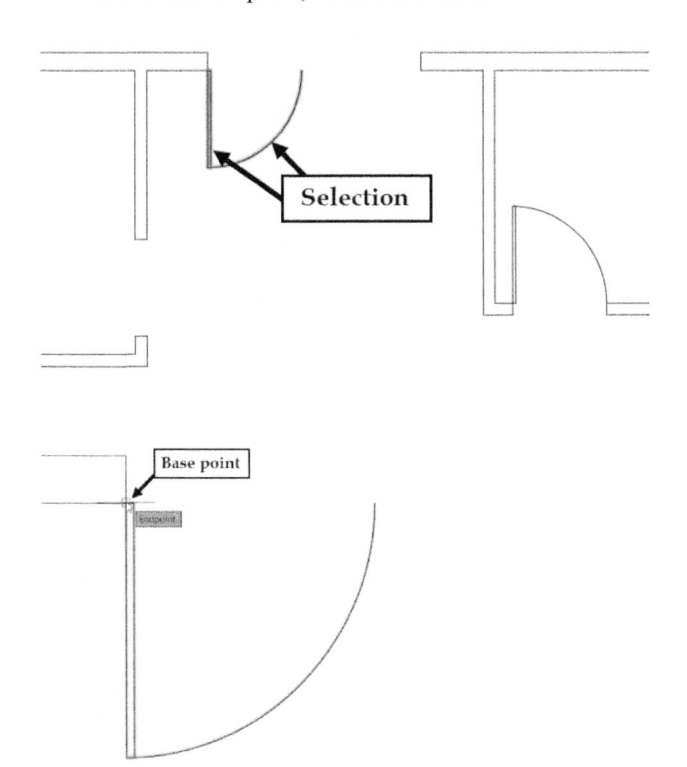

- Right-click and select the **Reference** option.
- Select the two endpoints, as shown below. It defines the reference length of the objects. Now, you need to define the length up to which you want to scale the objects.
- Type-in 36 and press RETURN. The objects will be scaled.

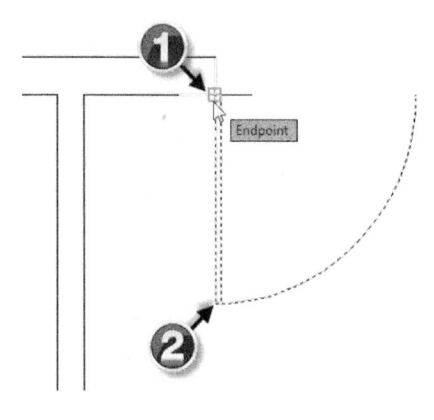

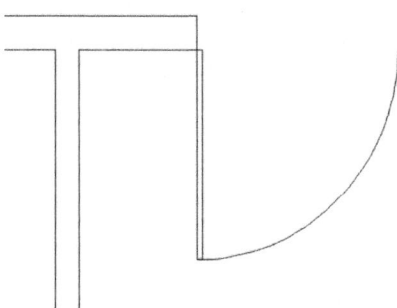

- Activate the **Mirror** command and select the door & swing at the entrance. Press RETURN to accept the selection.
- Define the mirror line by selecting the points, as shown below.

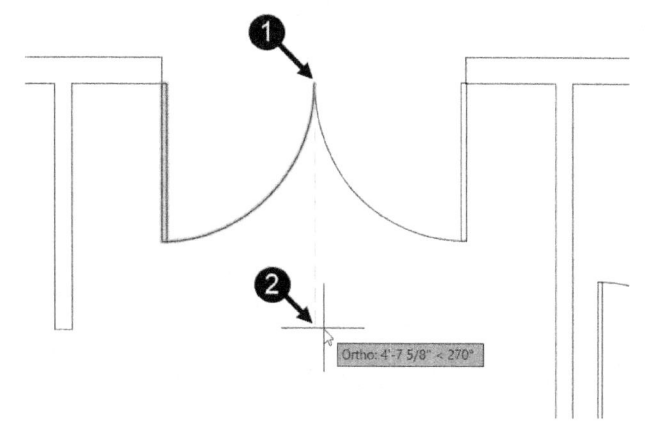

- Right-click and select **No**. It keeps the original object.
- Copy the door & swing of the bathroom and place it at the opening, as shown below.
- Press Esc.

295 | Creating Architectural Drawings

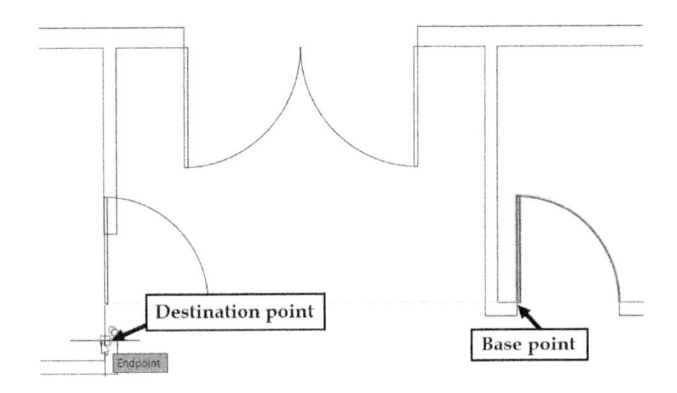

- On the **Drafting** tool set, click **Modify > Rotate**, and then select the copied object. Next, press RETURN.
- Select the base point, as shown.

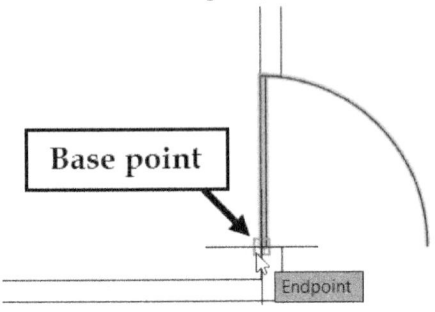

- Move the pointer vertically upward, and then click.

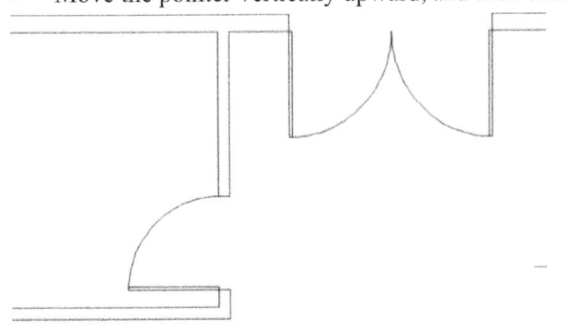

- Create an opening on the rear side of the plan, as shown below.

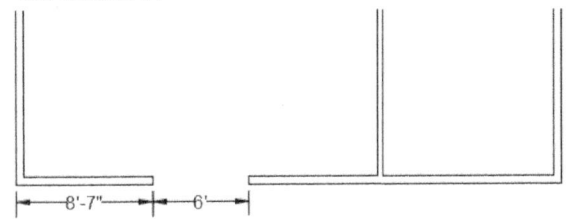

Now, you will create a sliding door in the opening.
- Activate the **Rectangle** command and select the corner point of the opening, as shown below.

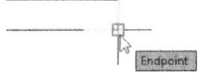

- Right-click and select the **Dimensions** option.
- Specify 37 and 2 as the length and width of the rectangle, respectively.
- Move the pointer upward and click to create the rectangle.

- Type **M** in the command line and press RETURN. Select the rectangle, and then press RETURN.
- Select its lower-left corner point to define the base point. Move the pointer upward and type-in 1 in the command line, and then press RETURN.

- On the **Drafting** tool set, click **Modify > Explode**, and select the rectangle. Press RETURN to explode the rectangle.
- Activate the **Offset** command and specify 2 as the offset distance.
- Offset the left and right vertical lines of the rectangle.

- Press **Esc** to deactivate the **Offset** command.
- Activate the **Line** command and select the midpoints of the offset lines. It creates a line connecting the offset lines. It creates one part of the sliding door.

- Press **Esc** to deactivate the **Line** command.
- Type-in **CO** in the command line and press RETURN.
- Drag a selection window covering all the elements of the sliding door. Press RETURN.

296 | Creating Architectural Drawings

AutoCAD 2023 For Beginners (For Mac Users)

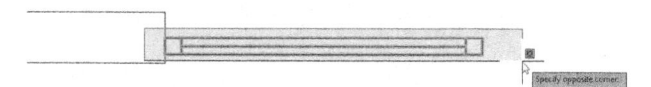

- Select the lower-left corner of the sliding door as the base point.
- Move the pointer and select the endpoint of the offset line, as shown.

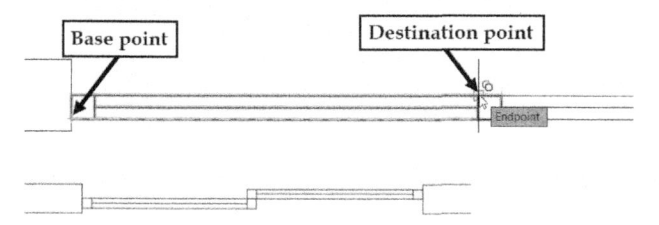

- Press **Esc** to deactivate the **Copy** command.

Now, you need to draw thresholds on the door openings.

- Zoom to the front door area using the **Zoom Window** tool.

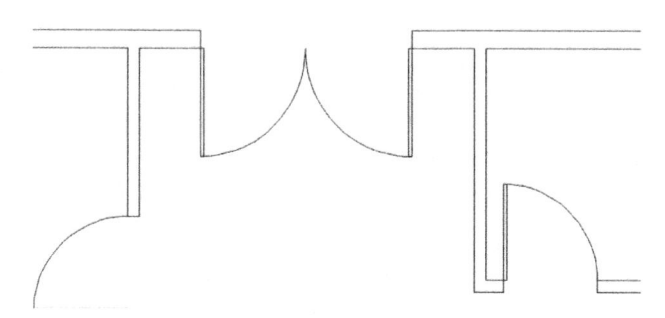

- On the status bar, click the right mouse button on the **Object Snap** button and make sure that **Endpoint**, **Nearest,** and **Perpendicular** options are selected.

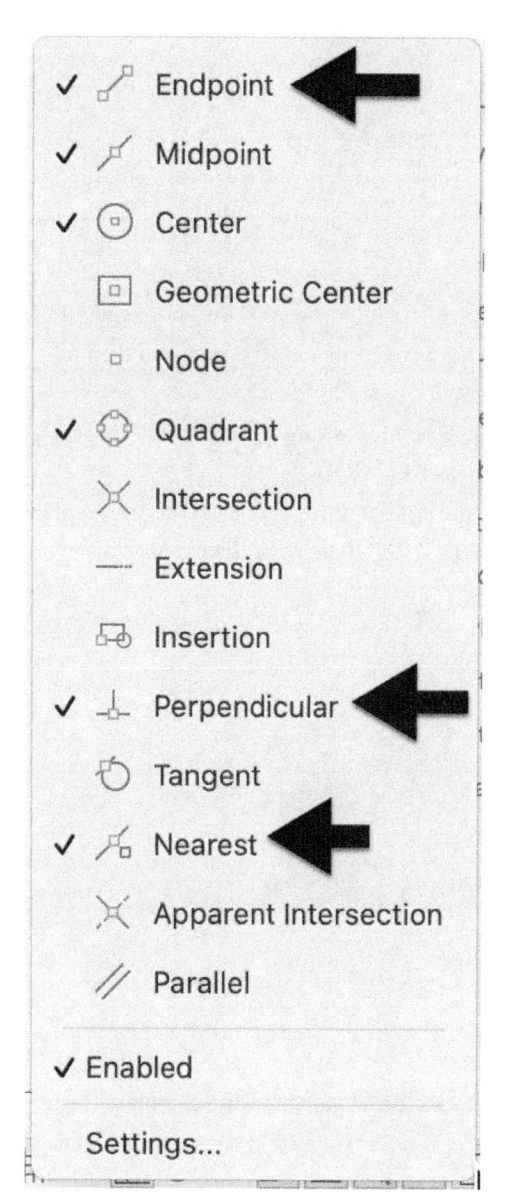

- Type-in **L** in the command line and press RETURN.
- Press and hold the **Shift** key and click the right mouse button.
- Select **From** from the shortcut menu and click the endpoint of the door opening, as shown below.
- Move the pointer on the horizontal line and type in 3, and then press RETURN. It defines the start point of the line at 3 distance from the endpoint.

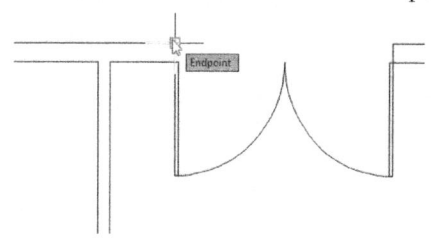

297 Creating Architectural Drawings

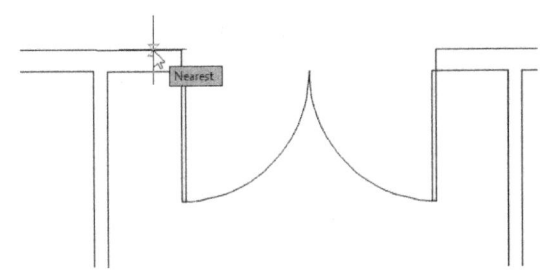

- Move the pointer up and type-in 2, and then press RETURN.
- Move the pointer toward the right and type in 78, and then press RETURN.
- Move the pointer downward and type in 2, and then press RETURN. It creates a threshold. 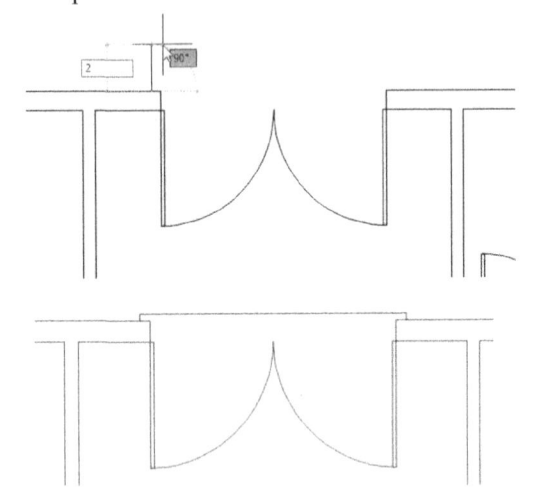
- Press Esc to deactivate the **Line** command.
- Likewise, create a threshold on the sliding glass door.

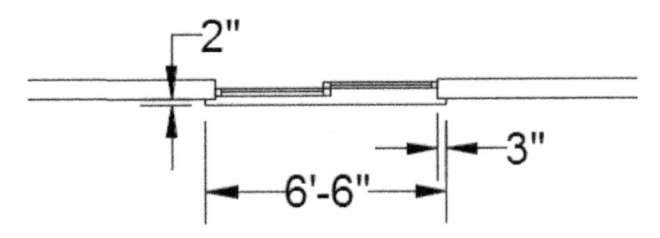

Creating Kitchen Fixtures

- Zoom to the kitchen area by using the **Zoom Window** tool. 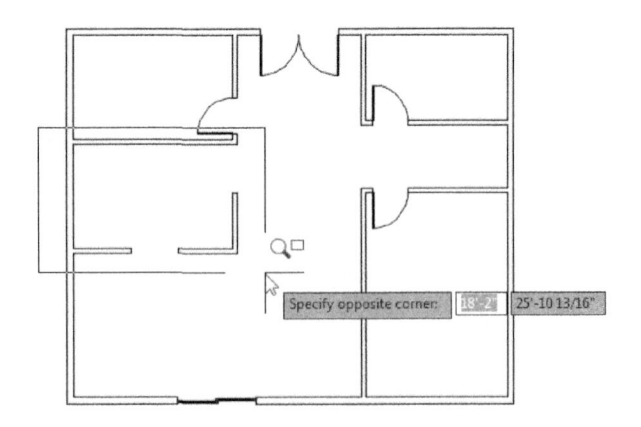
- Activate the **Offset** command and specify 26 as the offset distance.
- Offset the lines shown below. 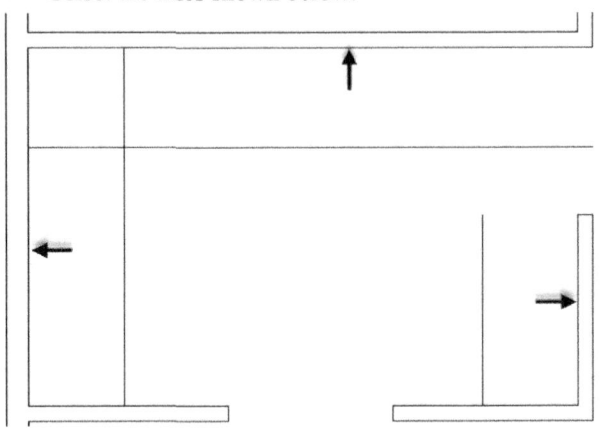
- Trim the unwanted portions. 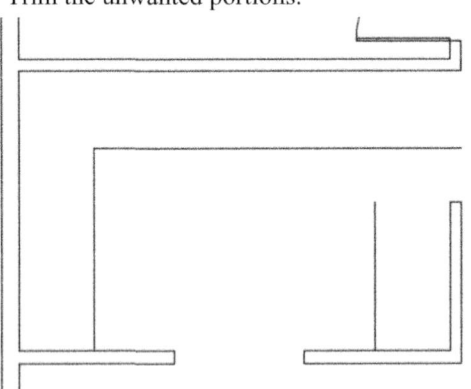
- Create another offset line at 54 distance, and then trim the unwanted elements.

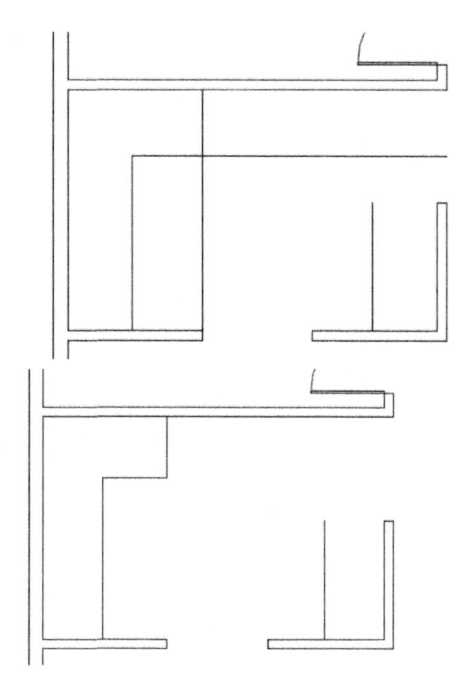

- Create another line, as shown below.

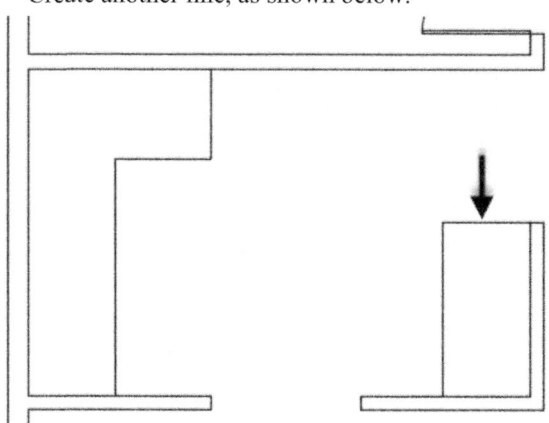

Now, you have finished drawing the counters. You need to draw a refrigerator, stove and sink.

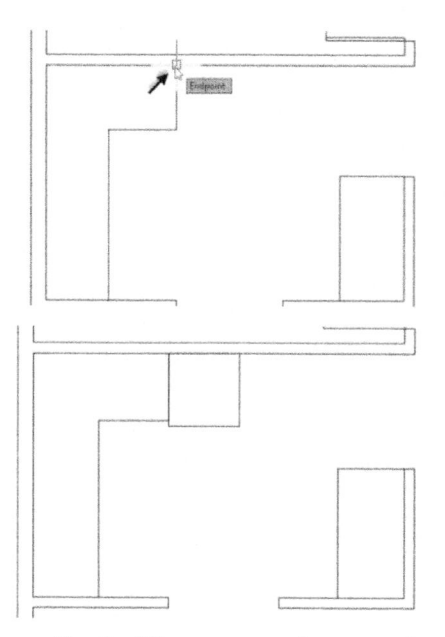

- Type-in **REC** in the command line and press RETURN. It activates the **Rectangle** command.
- Select the corner point of the counter.
- Right-click and select the **Dimensions** option.
- Specify 28 as length and width of the rectangle. Move the pointer toward the right and click to create the rectangle.
- Use the **Move** command to move the rectangle 2 inches rightwards and downwards. 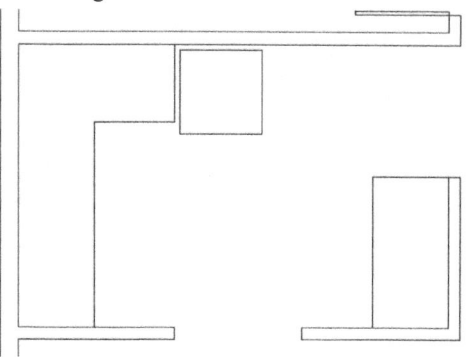
- Create the outline of the stove using the **Offset** and **Trim** commands.

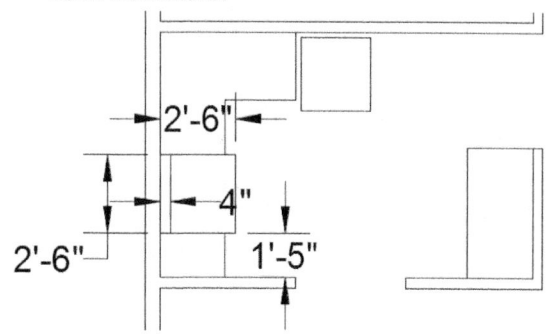

Now, you need to create the sink.

- Use the **Offset** command and create offset lines, as shown below.

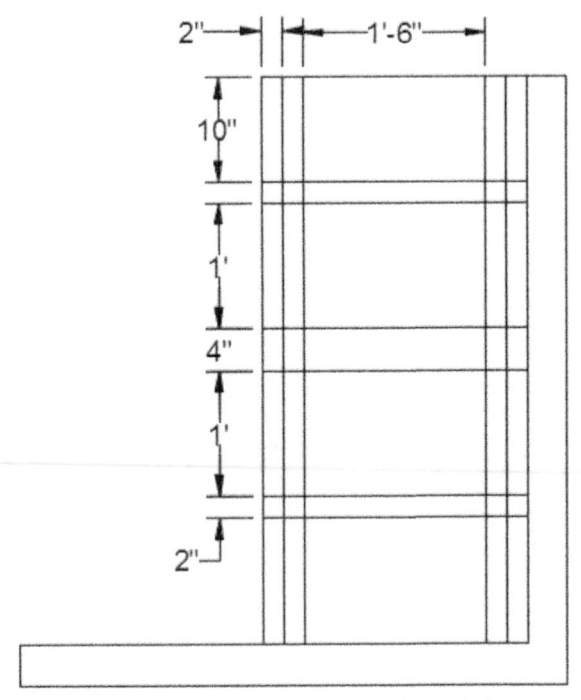

- Trim the unwanted elements, as shown below.

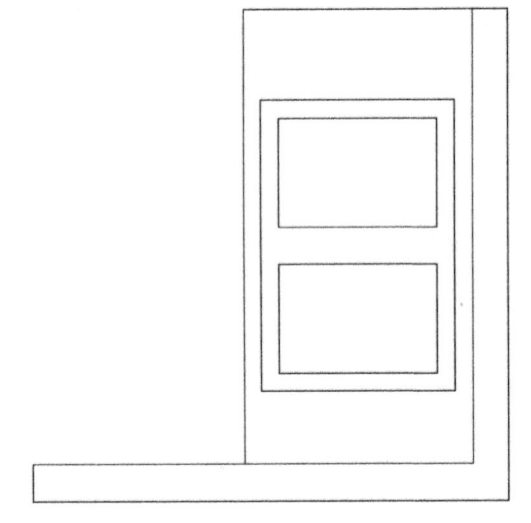

- Fillet the corners, as shown below.

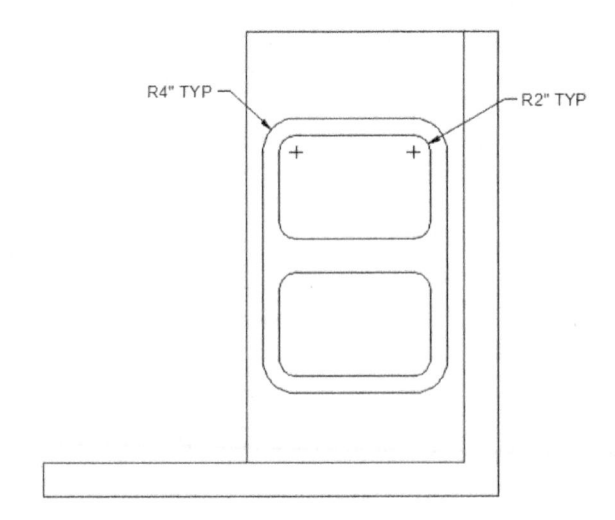

- Activate the **Circle** command and hover the pointer on the midpoints of the sink edges and move, as shown below.

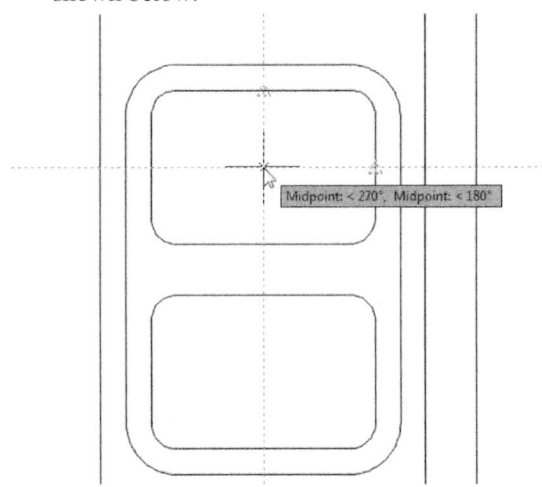

- Create the circles at the intersection points of the trace lines.

300 | Creating Architectural Drawings

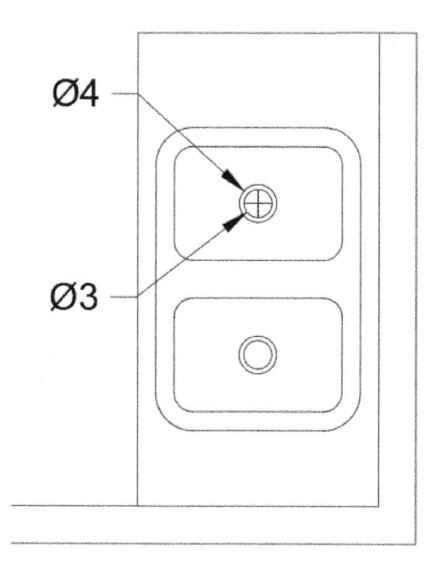

Creating Bathroom Fixtures

- Zoom into the bathroom area and create offset lines, as shown below.

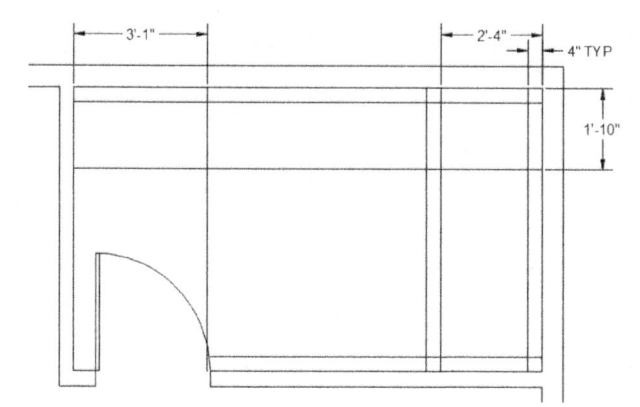

- Trim the unwanted elements, as shown below.

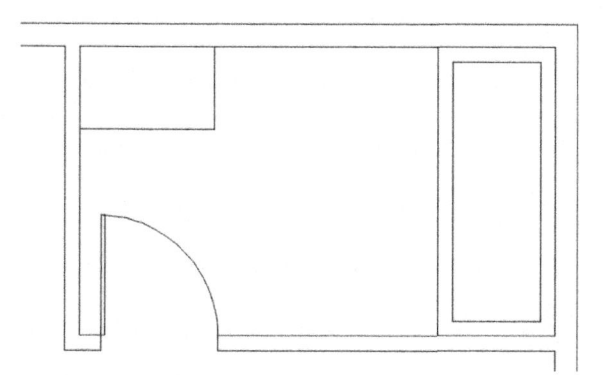

- Fillet the corners, as shown below. The fillet radius is 4.

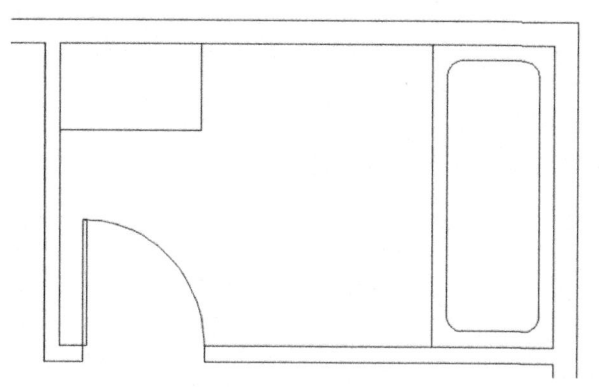

- On the tool set, click **Drafting** > **Draw** > **Ellipse** drop-down > **Center**.

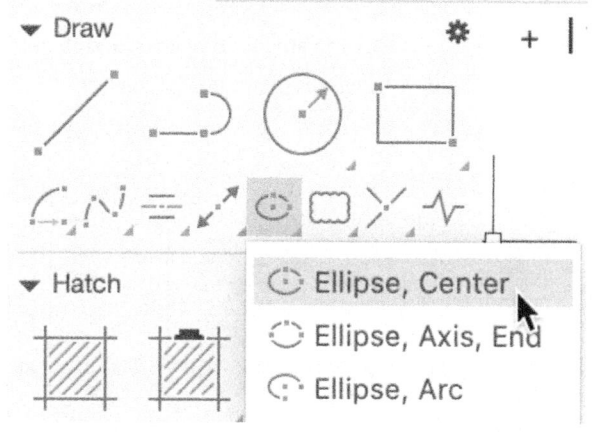

- Hover the pointer on the midpoints of the vertical and horizontal lines, as shown below.

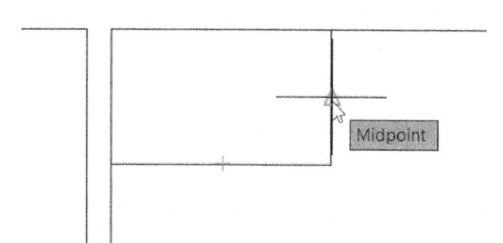

- Move the pointer and click at the intersection point of the trace lines.

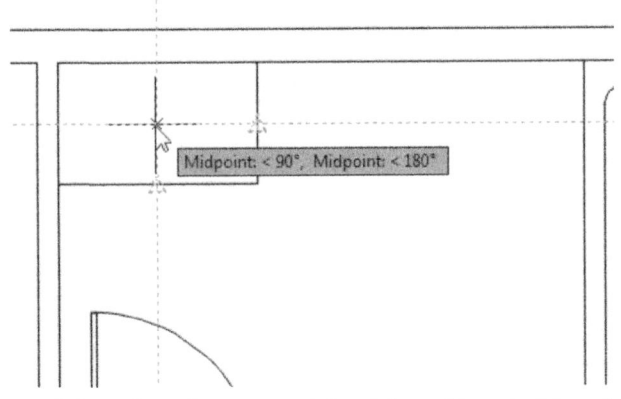

- Move the pointer toward the right and type in 10, and then press RETURN. It defines the major radius of the ellipse.
- Move the pointer downward and type in 5, and then press RETURN. It defines the minor radius of the ellipse.

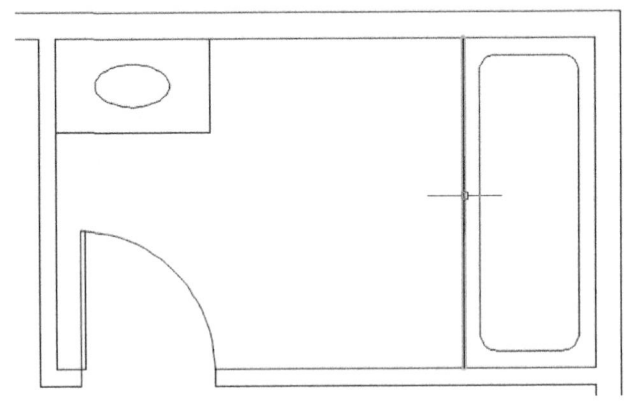

- Likewise, create another ellipse of 11 major radius and 7 minor radius.

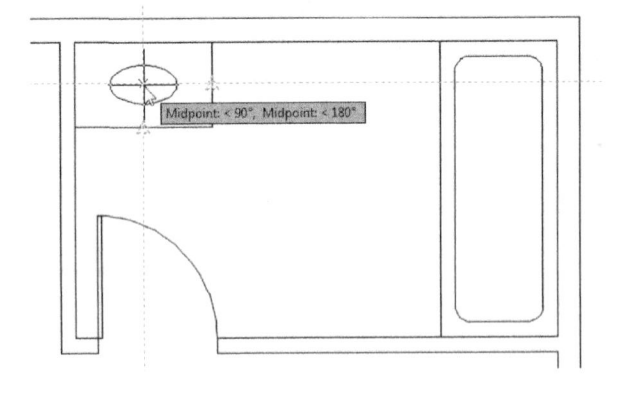

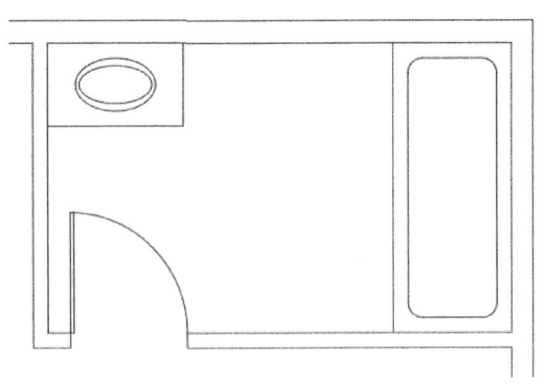

- Select the outer ellipse, and then click on the center point of the ellipse.
- Move the pointer up and type-in 1, and then press RETURN. The outer ellipse moves up.

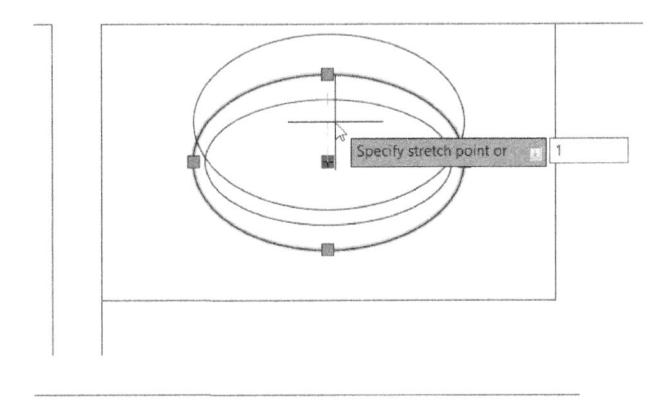

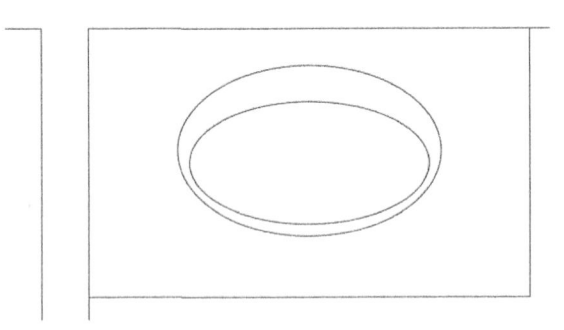

- Activate the **Rectangle** command and create a 22 x 9 rectangle, as shown below.

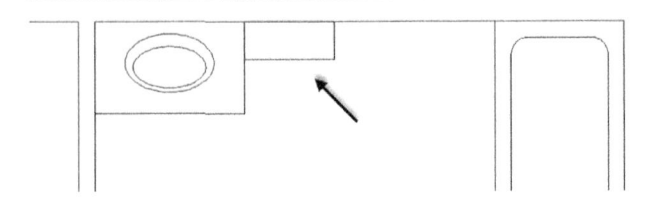

- Move the rectangle up to 19.5 rightwards and 1 downwards.

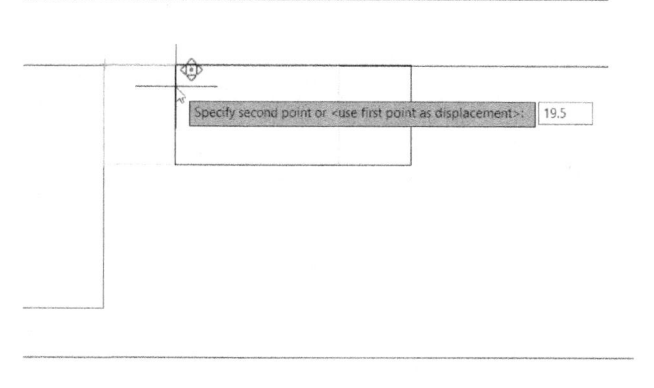

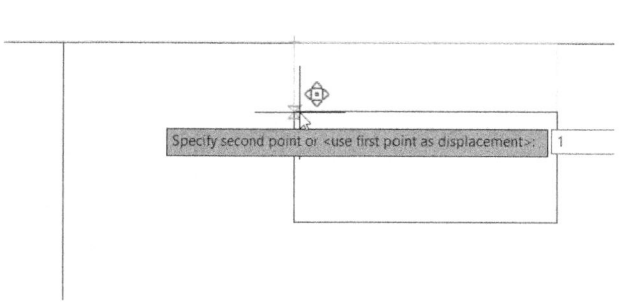

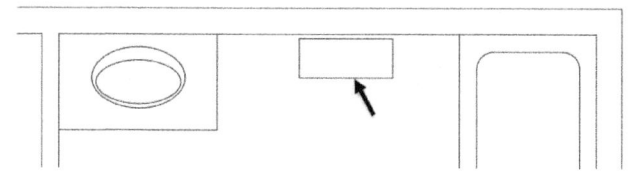

- Type-in 6 as the minor radius and press RETURN.

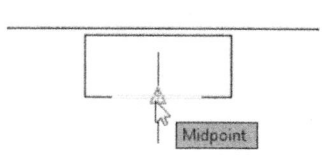

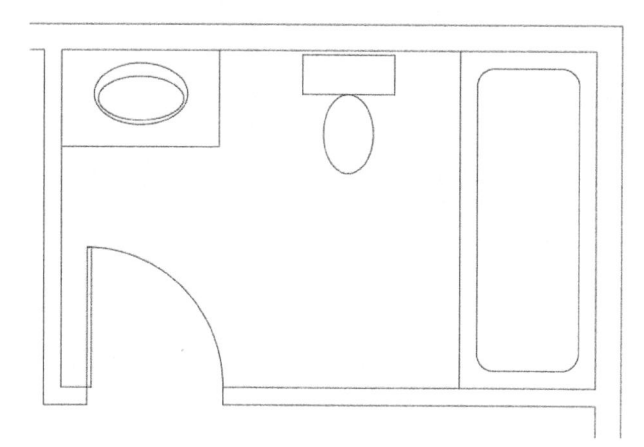

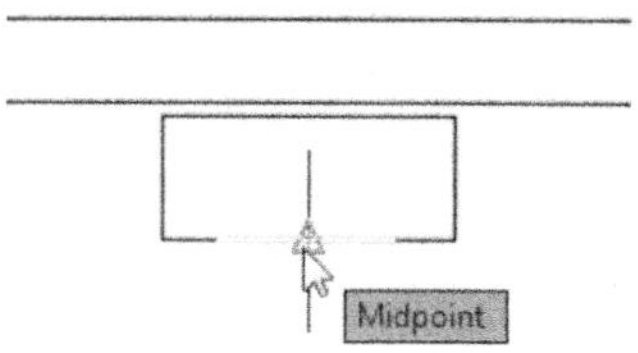

- On the tool set, click **Drafting > Draw > Ellipse** drop-down > **Axis, End**.

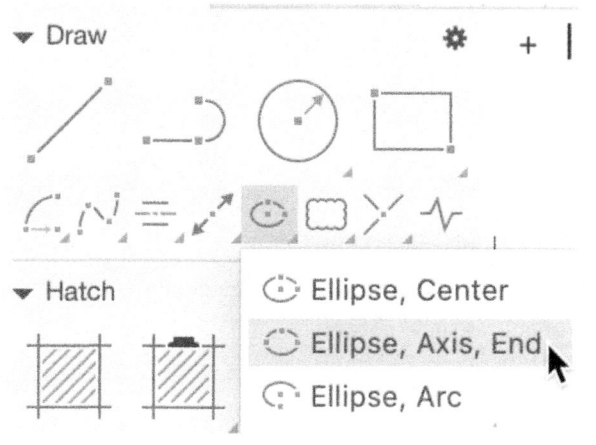

- Select the midpoint of the lower horizontal line of the rectangle.
- Move the pointer downward and type in 18, and then press RETURN.

Adding Furniture using Blocks

- Download the *Home_Space_Planner_Symbols.dwg* file from the companion website.
- Click the **Blocks** tab on the palettes.
- On the **Blocks** palette, click the Library tab.
- Click the **Open Block Libraries** button.
- Browse to the location of the downloaded file and double-click on it. It displays all the blocks available in the selected drawing file.
- Click and drag the highlighted blocks into the graphics window.

- Select the Dining set block, and then click on the point located at its center.
- Move the block and place it at the location shown below.

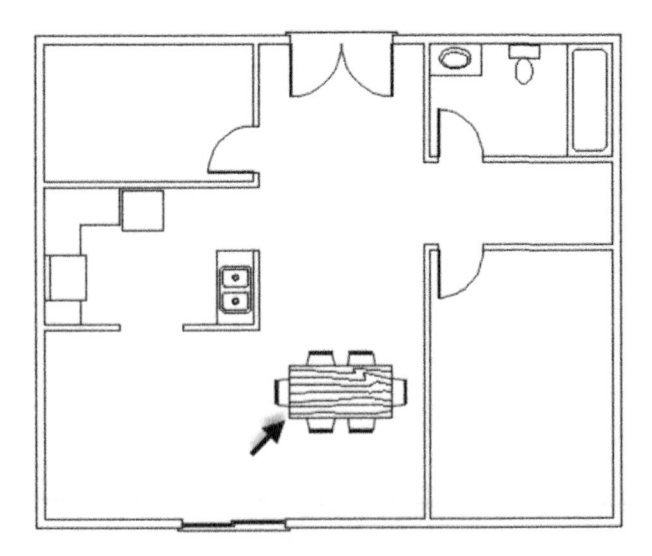

- Activate the **Rectangle** command and select the corner point of the bedroom, as shown.
- Right-click and select the **Dimensions** option. 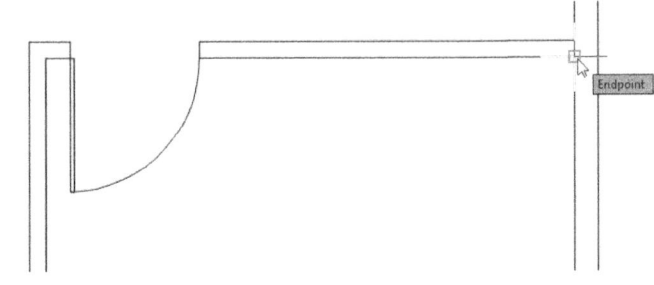
- Specify 86 and 27.5 as the length and width of the rectangle, respectively.
- Move the pointer downward and click to create the rectangle.
- Create another rectangle by selecting the corner points, as shown below. 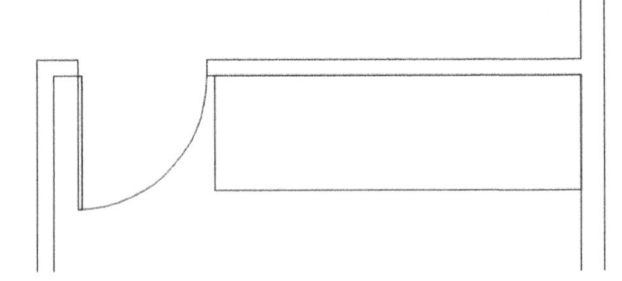

304 | Creating Architectural Drawings

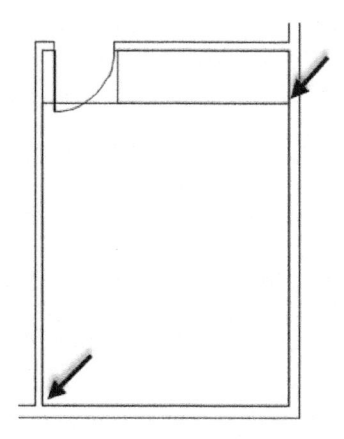

- Offset the rectangle by a distance of 47.5 inwards.
- Delete the original rectangle.

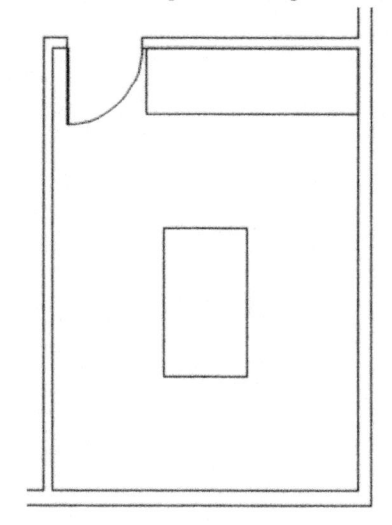

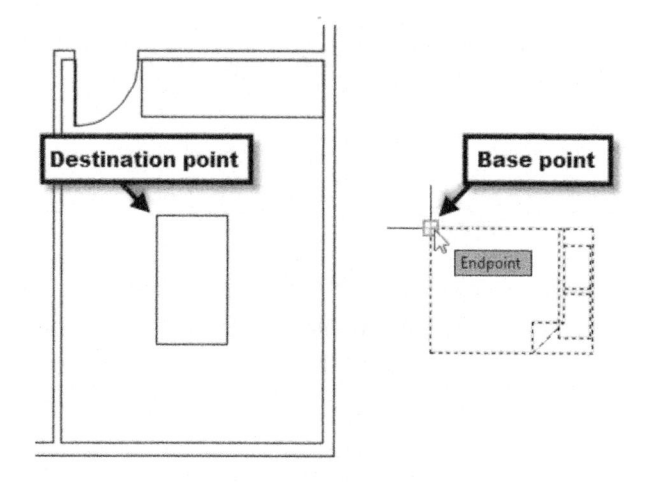

- Delete the offset rectangle.

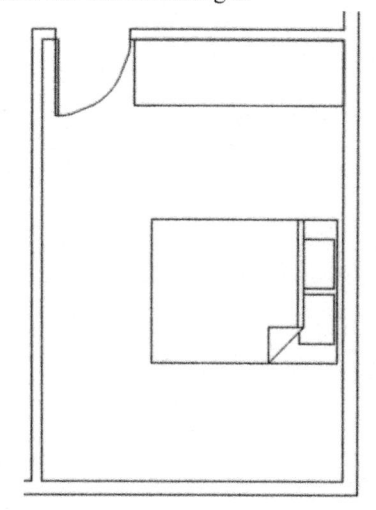

- Rotate the bed by **90** degrees.
- Activate the **Move** command and select the bed. Press RETURN to accept the selection.
- Select the top left corner of the bed to define the base point.
- Select the top left corner of the offset rectangle to define the destination point.

Adding Windows

- In the empty space, create the window using the **Line** command, as shown below.

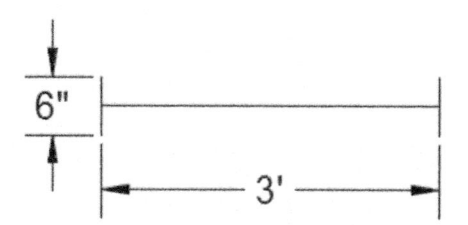

- On the **Drafting** tool set, click **Block > Make**.
- On the **Define Block** dialog, type-in **Window** in the **Name** box.
- Click the **Select Objects** button and select all the elements of the window by dragging a selection window.
- Press RETURN.

- Click the **Pick point** button and select the lower-left corner of the window.

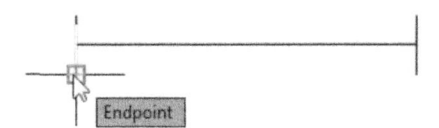

- On the dialog, check the **Open in block editor** option and click **Create Block**. It creates the block and opens it in the **Block Editor**.
- On the **Block Editor** visor, click **Parameters** drop-down > **Linear**.

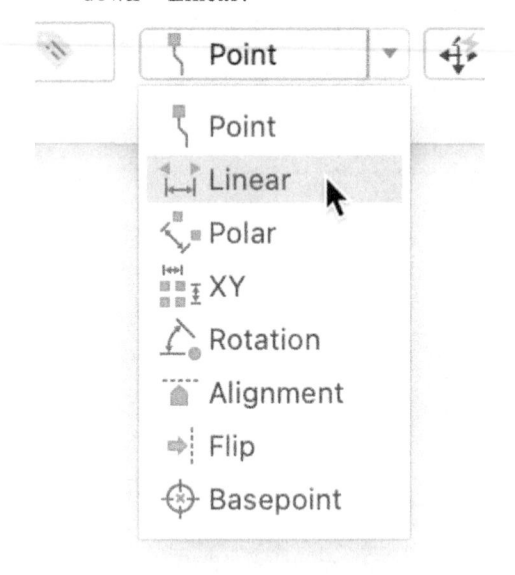

- Click the endpoints of the horizontal line.
- Move the pointer downward and click to define the parameter location.

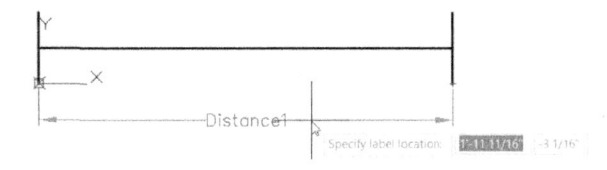

- Press RETURN to specify 2 as the number of the grips to be displayed when you select the parameter.
- On the **Block Editor** visor, click **Actions** drop-down > **Stretch**.

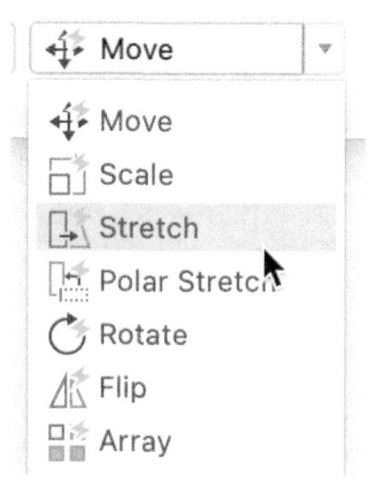

- Select the **Distance1** parameter.
- Select the right endpoint of the horizontal line. It defines the point that can be used to stretch the block.

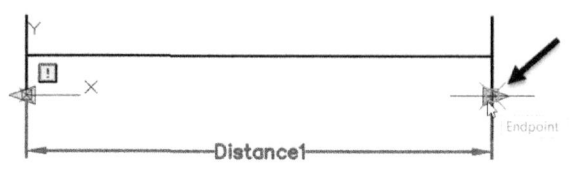

- Create a window around the selected endpoint.

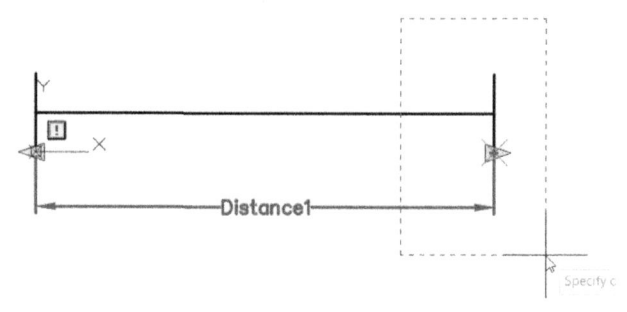

- Select the horizontal and right vertical lines, and then press RETURN. It defines the elements that can be stretched.

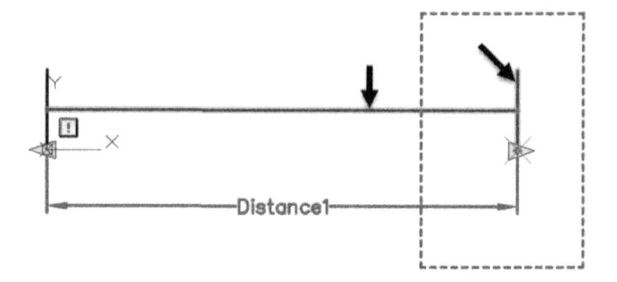

- On the **Block Editor** visor, click the **Save** button.
- Click the **Exit Block Editor and close the visor** button.

306 | Creating Architectural Drawings

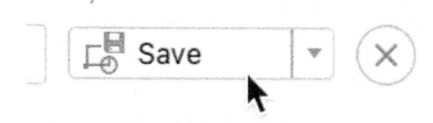

- Select the block and click the arrow grip. Drag the pointer to stretch the block.

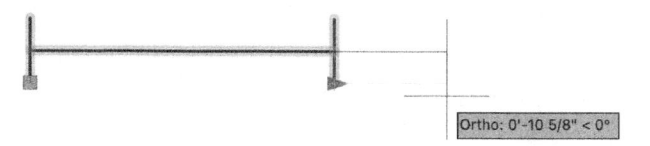

- Click the **Blocks** tab on the palette.
- Click the **Blocks in current drawing** tab on the **Blocks** palette.
- Double-click on the **Window** block.

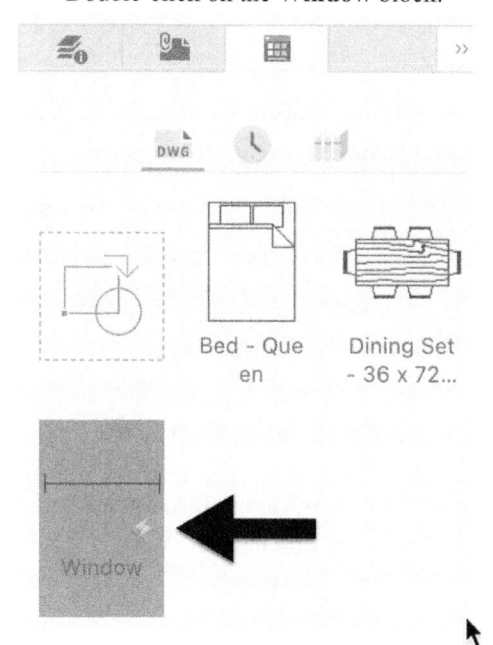

- Select the lower right corner of the bedroom.

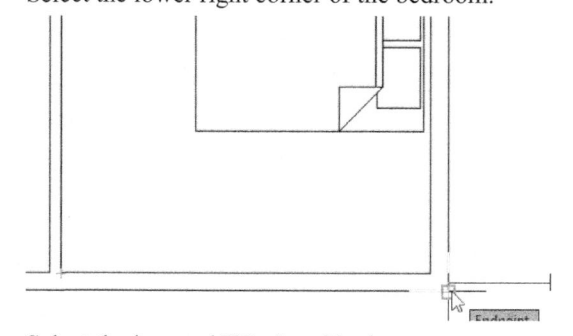

- Select the inserted **Window** block.
- Select the base point of the **Window** block.
- Move the pointer on the horizontal wall and type in 95, and then press RETURN. The **Window** block will be moved to the specified location.

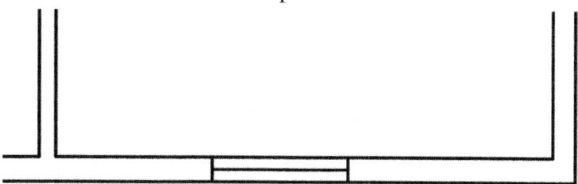

- Activate the **Dynamic Input** icon on the Status bar.
- Select the **Window** block and drag the arrow grip.
- Type-in **54** and press RETURN. It changes the window size to 54.

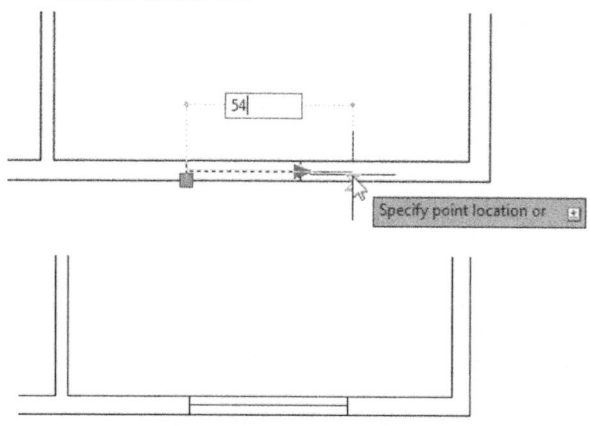

- Double-click on the **Window** block in the **Blocks** palette.
- Right-click and select the **Rotate** option.
- Type-in **90** and press RETURN.
- Place the **Window** block on the kitchen wall, as shown below.

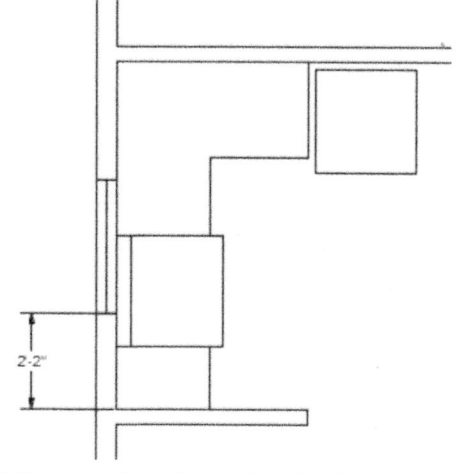

- Likewise, place the window blocks, as shown below.

307 | Creating Architectural Drawings

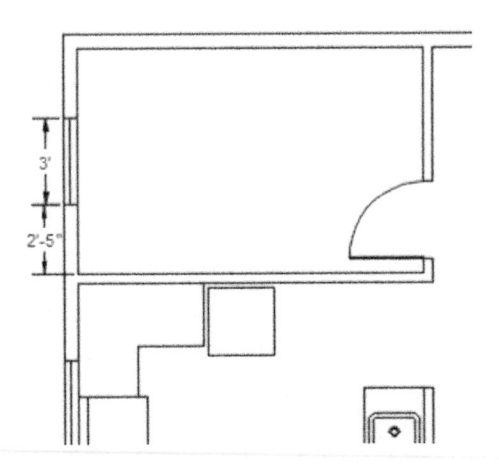

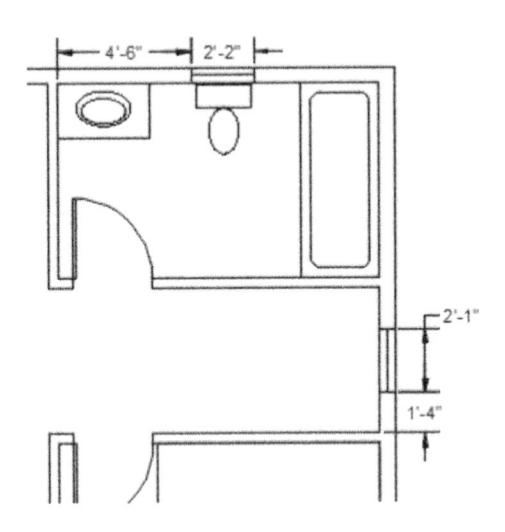

AutoCAD 2023 For Beginners (For Mac Users)

- Create another layer, and then type-in **Door** — press RETURN.
- Likewise, create other layers and define the layer properties, as shown below. Refer to Chapter 3 to learn more about layers.

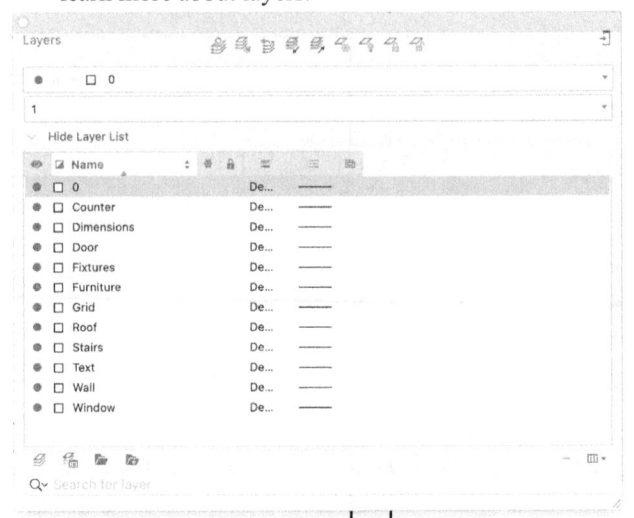

- Click the **Layer States Manager** button on the **Layers** palette.

Arranging Objects of the drawing in Layers

- Click the **Layers and Properties** tab on the palette.
- Click the **Undock** icon located at the top-right corner of the palette.

- On the **Layers** palette, click the **New Layer** button.

- Type **Wall** in the layer **Name** box and press RETURN.

- Click the **Plus** + button on the **Layer States Manager** dialog.
- Type **Architectural Floor Plan** in **Layer State Name** box and click the **Add** button.

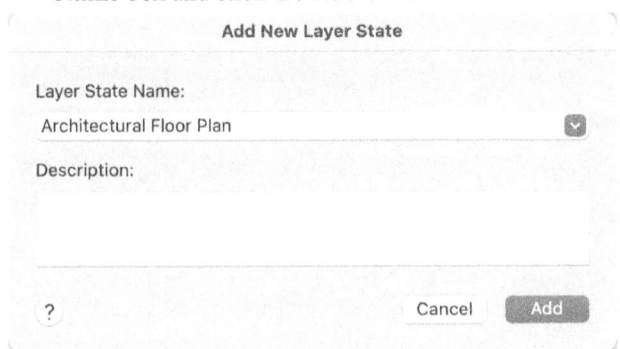

- Click the gear drop-down and select the **Edit** option.

308 Creating Architectural Drawings

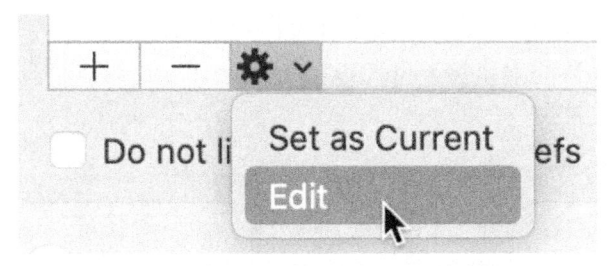

- Change the Linetypes and colors of the layers, as shown.

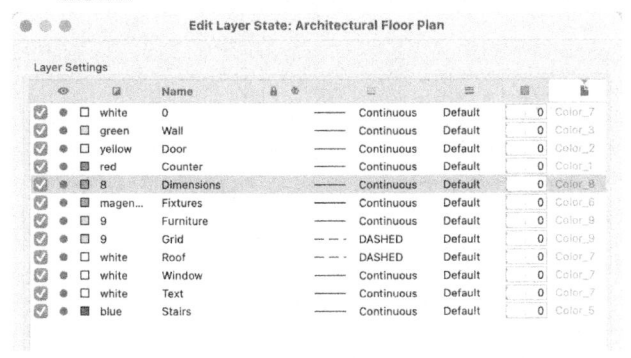

- Click **OK** and **Save & Close**.
- Select the **Architectural Floor Plan** from the **Layer State** drop-down. 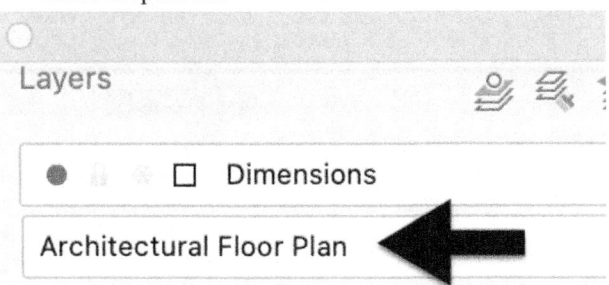
- Click the **Dock** icon on the top-right corner of the **Layers** palette.

- Select the Dining set, cupboard, and bed.
- On the Layers palette, click **Layer** drop-down > **Furniture**. The selected objects will be transferred to the Furniture layer.

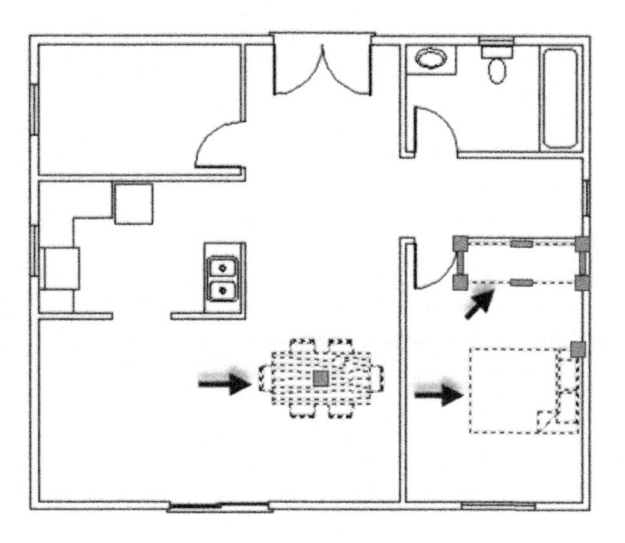

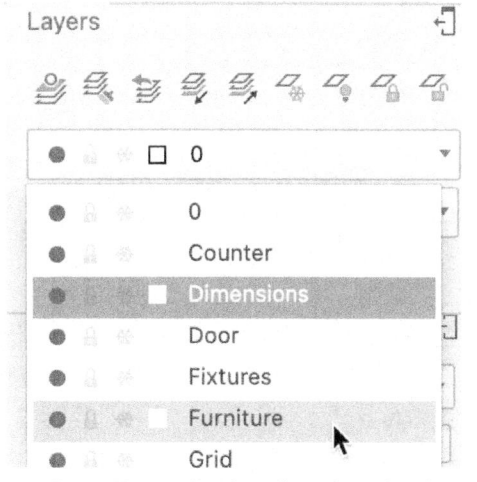

- Press Esc to deselect the selected objects.
- Likewise, transfer the other objects to their respective layers.

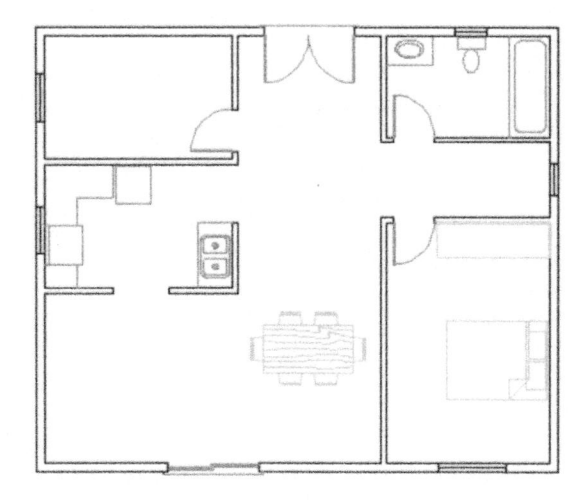

- Undock the **Layers** palette.

309 | **Creating Architectural Drawings**

- Click the **Layer States Manager** button on the **Layers** palette.
- Click the **Plus** + button on the **Layer States Manager** dialog.
- Type **Walls** in **Layer State Name** box and click the **Add** button.
- Click the gear drop-down and select the **Edit** option.
- Click the round dots associated with all the layers except the **0** and **Wall** layers. It will hide the corresponding layers.

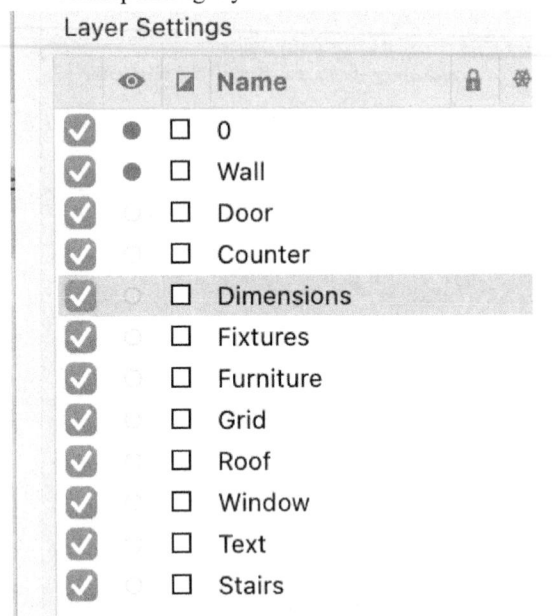

- Click **OK** and **Save & Close**.
- Select the **Walls** from the **Layer State** drop-down.
- Click the **Dock** icon on the top-right corner of the **Layers** palette.

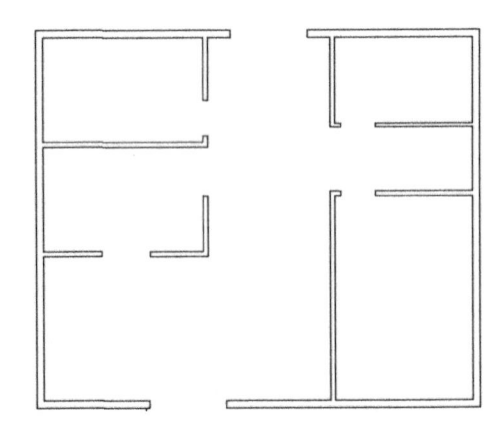

- Create a selection window and select all the walls.

- On the **Layers** palette, click **Layer** drop-down > **Wall**. All the walls will be transferred to the **Wall** layer.

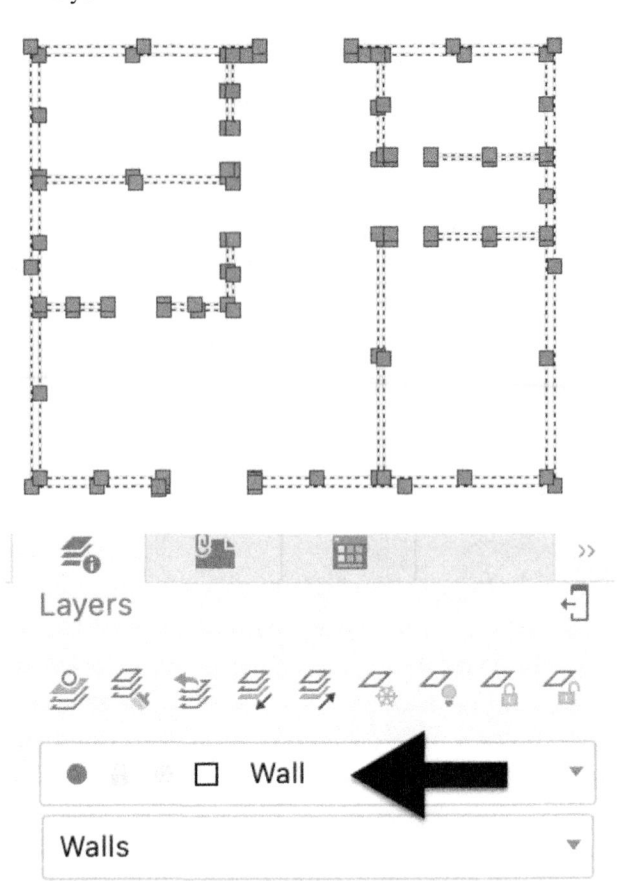

- Select the **Architectural Floor Plan** option from the **Layer state** drop-down; all the layers are the displayed.

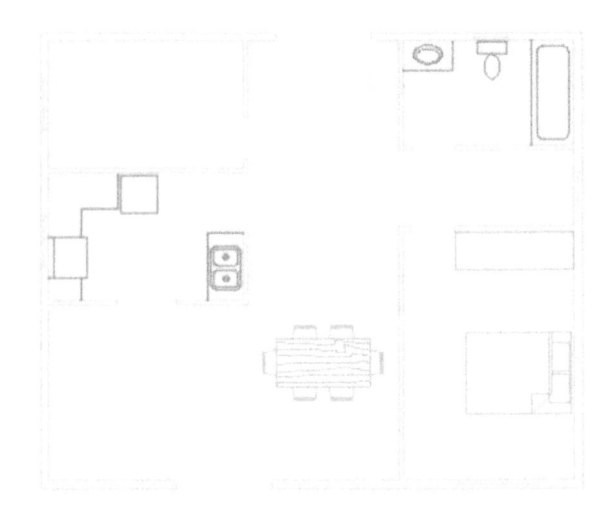

310 | Creating Architectural Drawings

Creating Grid Lines

- On the Layers palette, click **Layer** drop-down > **Grid**. The Grid layer becomes active.

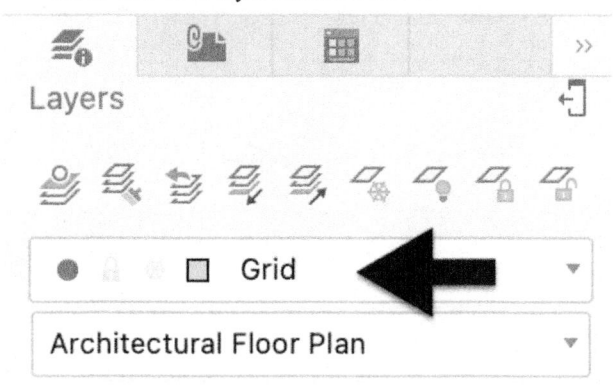

- Activate the **Line** command.
- Press and hold the Shift key and right-click, and then select the **Mid Between 2 Points** option.
- Select the endpoints of the wall, as shown below.

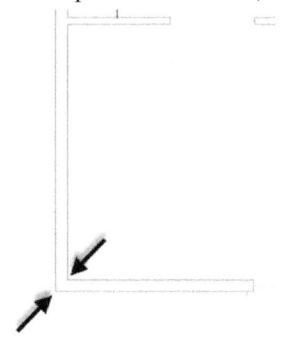

- Move the point upward and click to draw a vertical line of arbitrary length.

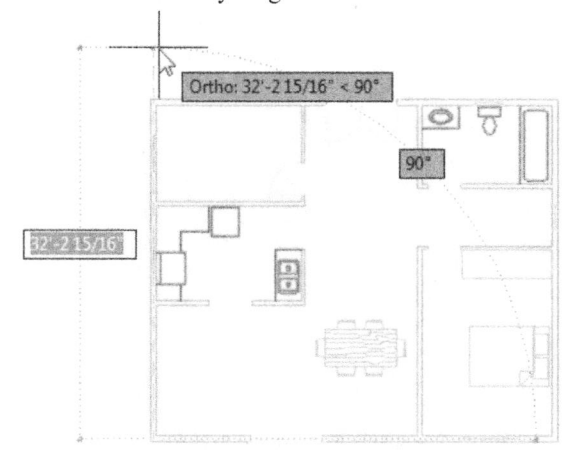

- Press Esc to deactivate the **Line** command.
- Select the line to display grips on it.
- Click the lower end grip and drag the pointer to increase the length of the line.

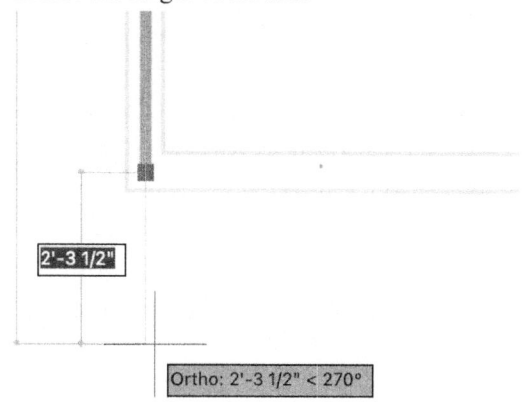

- Activate the **Offset** command and offset the grid line up to 406.
- Create other grid lines, as shown below.

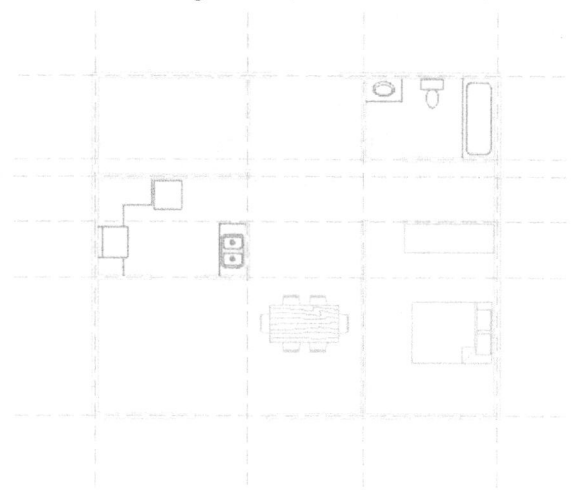

- Create a new layer called **Grid Bubbles** and make it active.

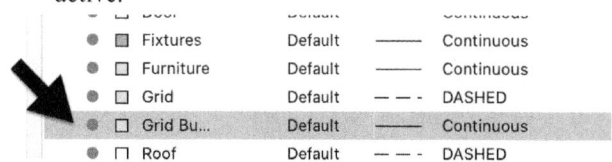

- Create a circle of 12 diameter.
- On the **Drafting** tool set, click **Block** > **Define Attribute**.

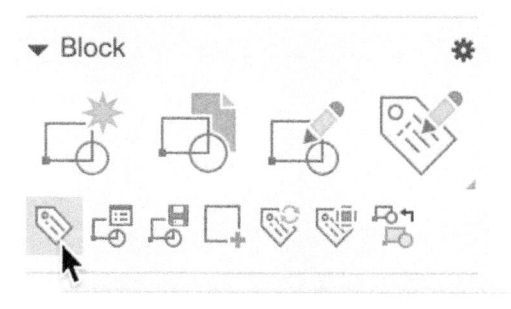

311 | Creating Architectural Drawings

- On the **Attribute Definition** dialog, type-in GRIDBUBBLE in the **Tag** box and select **Justification > Middle center**.
- Type-in 6" in the **Text height** box and click **Save**.
- Select the center point of the circle. The attribute text will be placed at its center.

- On the **Drafting** tool set, click **Block > Make**.
- Type-in Grid bubble in the **Name** box and click the **Select objects** button.
- Draw a crossing window to select the circle and attribute. Press RETURN to accept the selection.
- Click the **Pick point** icon under the **Base point** section.
- Select the lower quadrant point of the circle to define the base point of the block.

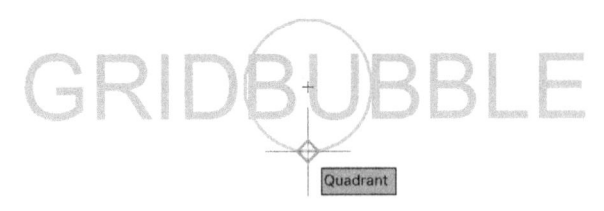

- Uncheck the **Open in block editor** option and click **Create Block**.
- Click the **Blocks** tab on the palettes
- Double-click on the **Grid Bubble** block on the **Blocks** palette.

- Select the top endpoint of the first vertical grid line. The **Grid Bubble** dialog pops up.
- Type-in **A** in the GRIDBUBBLE box and click **Confirm**.

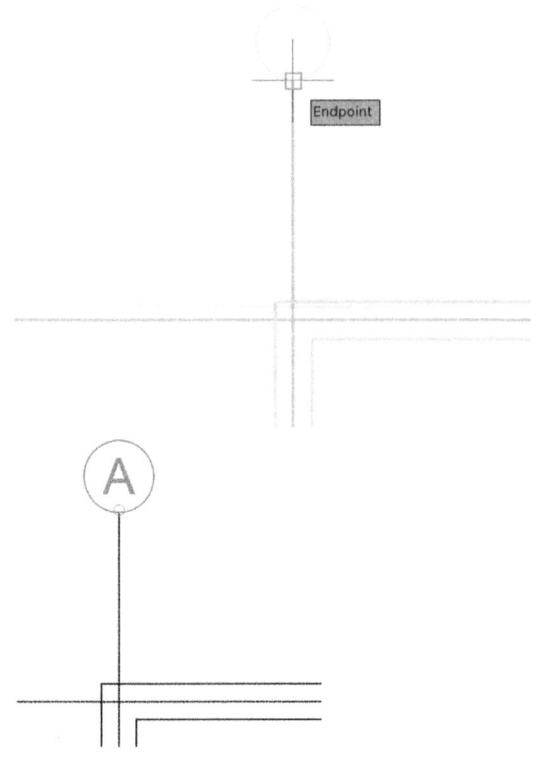

- Likewise, add other grid bubbles to the vertical grid lines.

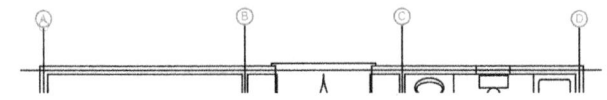

- Create another block with the name Vertical Grid bubble. Make sure that you select the right quadrant point of the circle as the base point.

- Insert the vertical grid bubbles, as shown below.

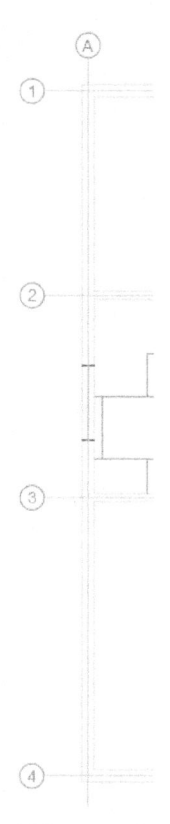

Adding Dimensions

- On the **Layers** palette, click **Layer** drop-down > **Dimensions** to make it active.
- Type **D** in the command line and press RETURN.
- On the **Dimension Style Manager** dialog, select the **Standard** dimension style and click the **Plus** 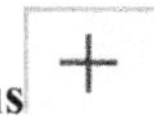 button.
- Type-in Floor Plan in the **New Style Name** box and click **Continue**.
- Click the **Primary Units** tab and select **Unit format** > **Architectural**.
- Set **Precision** to **0'-01/16"**.
- Set **Fraction format** to **Horizontal**.
- Under the **Zero Suppression** section, uncheck the **0 inches** option.
- Click the **Symbols and Arrows** tab.
- Under the **Arrowheads** section, select **First** > **Architectural tick**. The second arrowhead is automatically changed to **Architectural tick**.
- Select **Leader** > **Closed Filled** and enter 1/4' in the **Arrow Size** box.
- Click the **Lines** tab and set **Extend beyond dim lines** and **Offset from origin** to 3".
- Click the **Text** tab and **Text height** to 6".
- In the **Placement** section, set the following settings.
  Vertical-Centered
  Horizontal-Centered
  View Direction-Left-to-Right
- In the **Alignment** section, select the **Aligned with dimension line** option.
- Click the **Fit** tab and select **Either text or arrows (best fit)** option from the **Fit Options** section.
- In the **Text placement** section, select the **Over dimension line, without Leader** option.
- Click **OK**.
- Right-click on the **Floor Plan** dimension style and select **Set Current** on the **Dimension Style Manager**.
- Click **Close**.
- On the **Drafting** tool set, click **Dimension** > **Dimension**.
- Select the points on the vertical grid lines, as shown below.
- Move the pointer and click to locate the dimension. 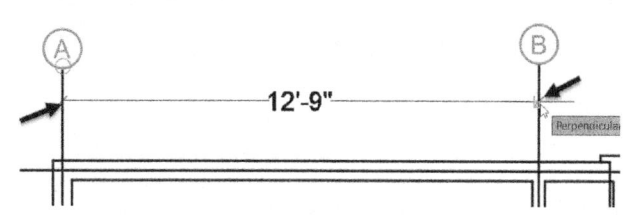
- On the **Drafting** tool set, click **Dimension** > **Dimension** drop-down > **Continue**. You will notice that a dimension is attached to the pointer
- Move the pointer and click on the next grid line.
- Likewise, move the pointer and click on the next grid line. 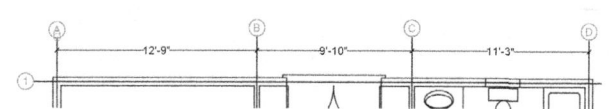
- Activate the **Dimension** command and create the overall horizontal dimension. 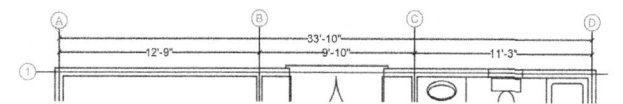
- Likewise, add vertical dimensions to the grid lines.

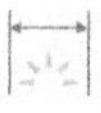

313 | Creating Architectural Drawings

AutoCAD 2023 For Beginners (For Mac Users)

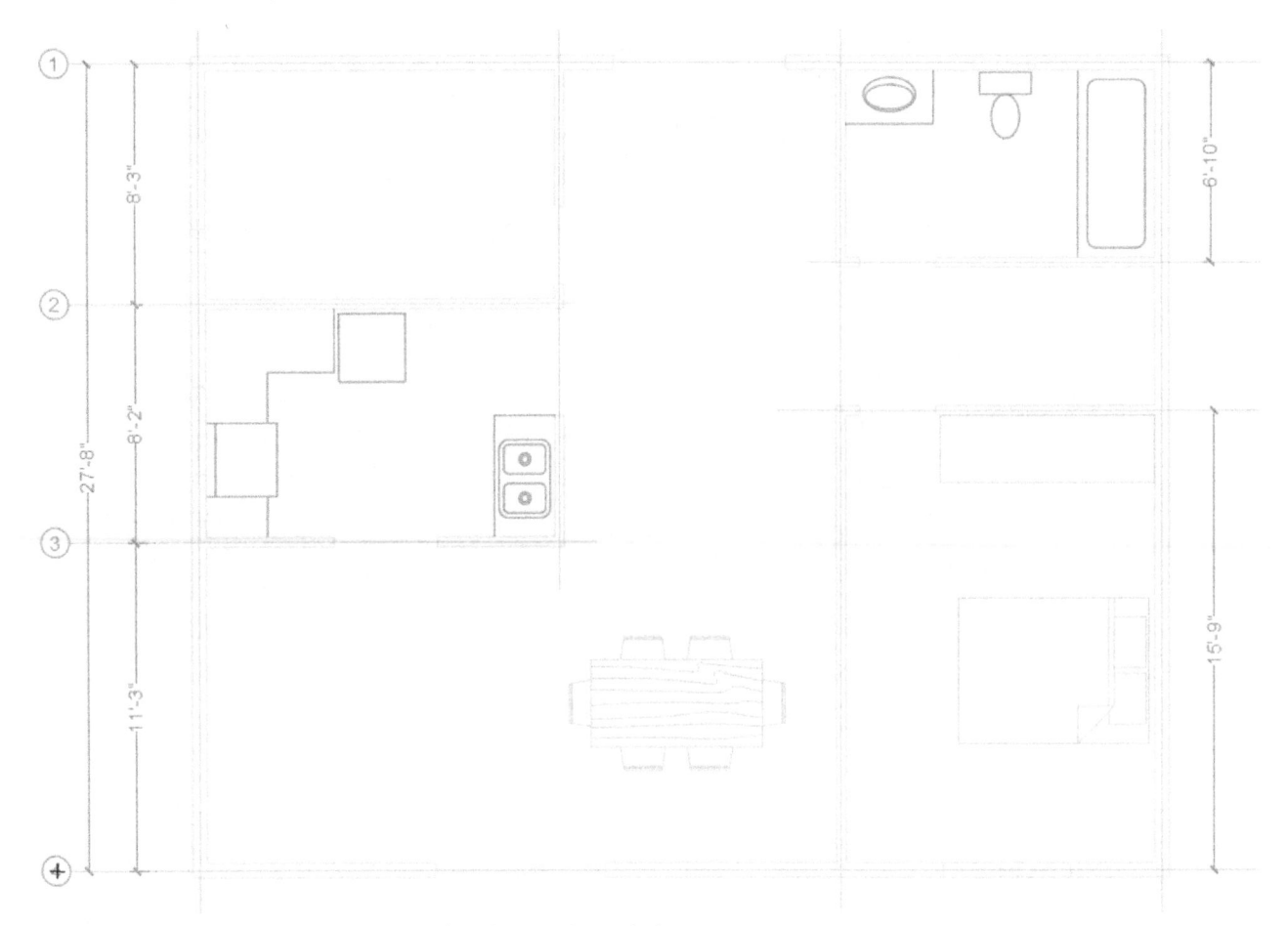

- Complete adding dimensions to the drawing, as shown below.

AutoCAD 2023 For Beginners (For Mac Users)

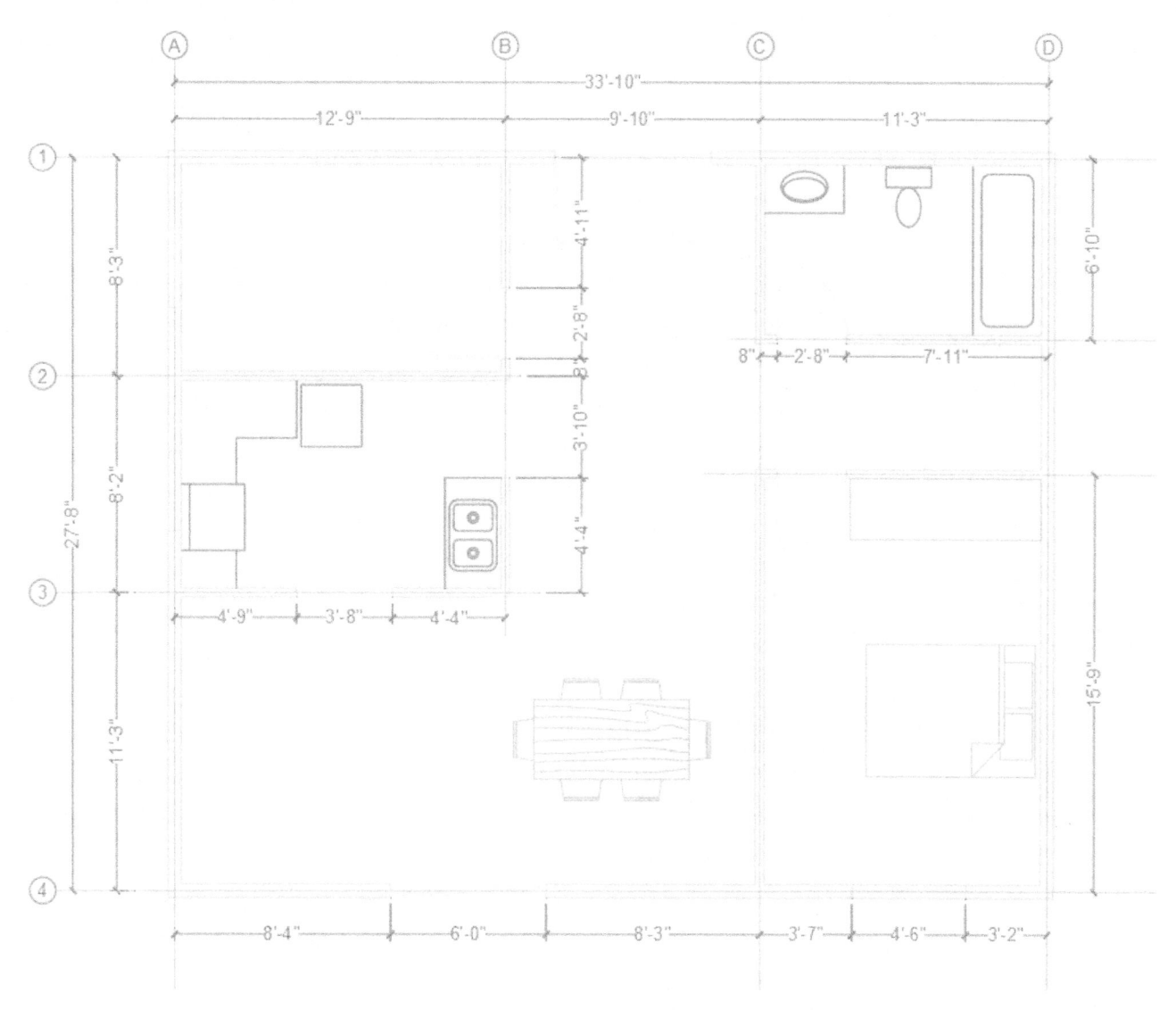

- On the toolbar, click the **Count** icon.

- Create a window by specifying the two corner points, as shown.
- Press ENTER.

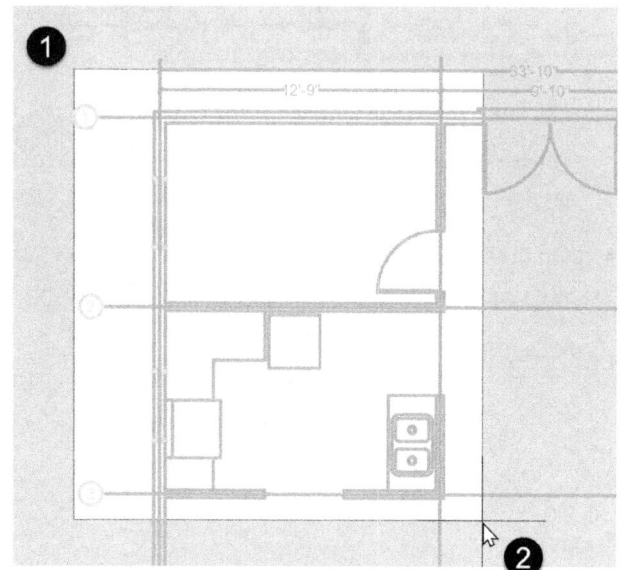

The blocks available in the specified region are displayed

315 | **Creating Architectural Drawings**

on the **Count** palette.

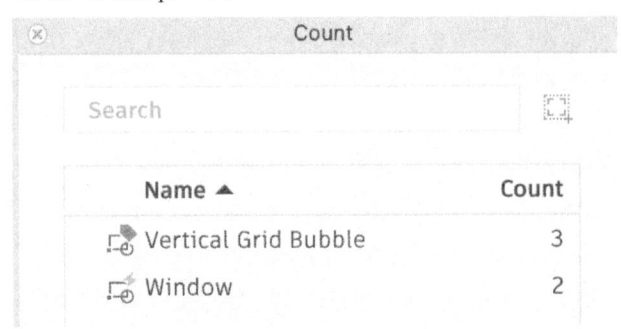

You can click the **Specify Area** icon on the Count toolbar and specify another area in the drawing.

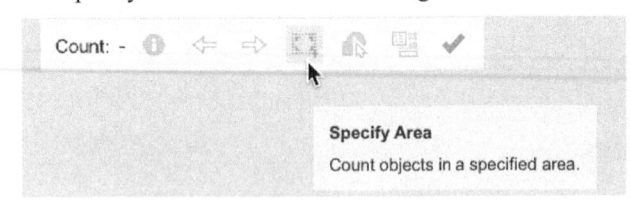

- Select the rectangular selection box and press DELETE.

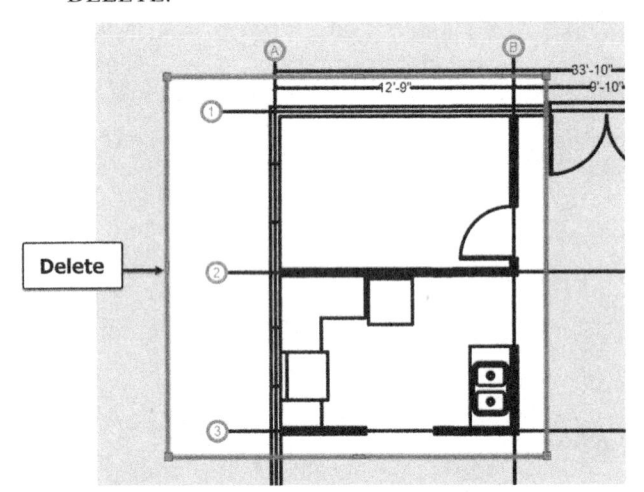

- Click the **Continue and count the entire model space** option on the **Count – Invalid Area** message box.
- On the **Count** palette, click the right mouse button on the **Window** block and select **Review Count Details**.

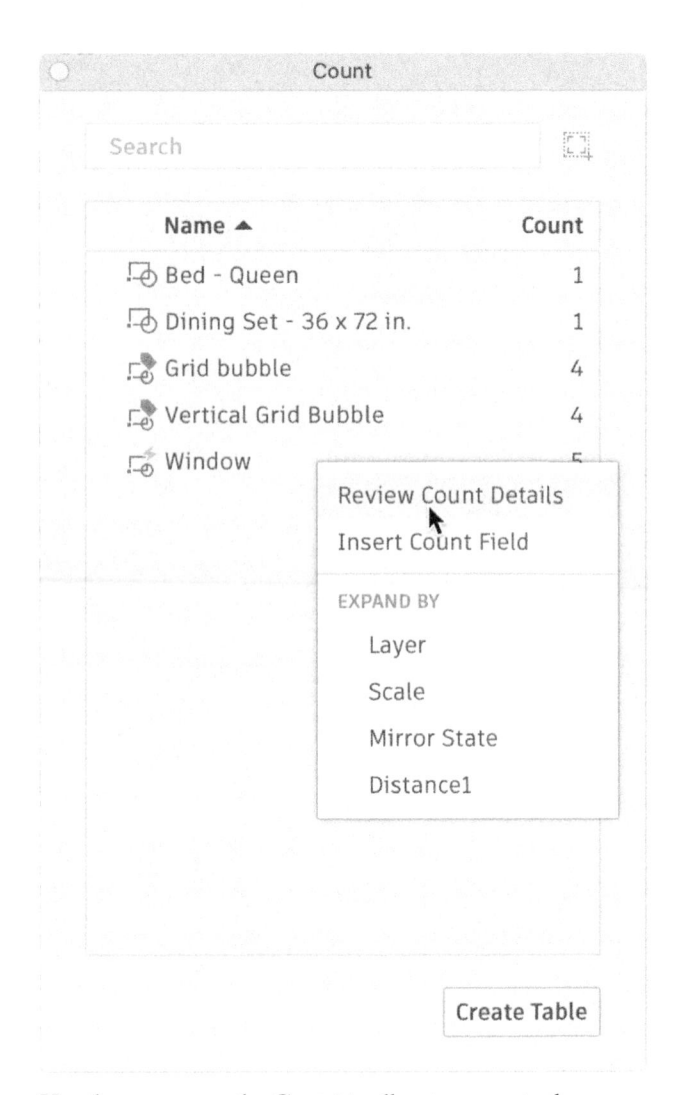

Use the arrows on the **Count** toolbar to zoom to the instances of the Window blocks.

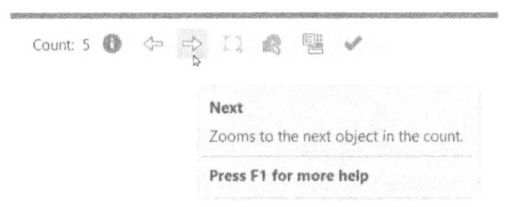

316 | **Creating Architectural Drawings**

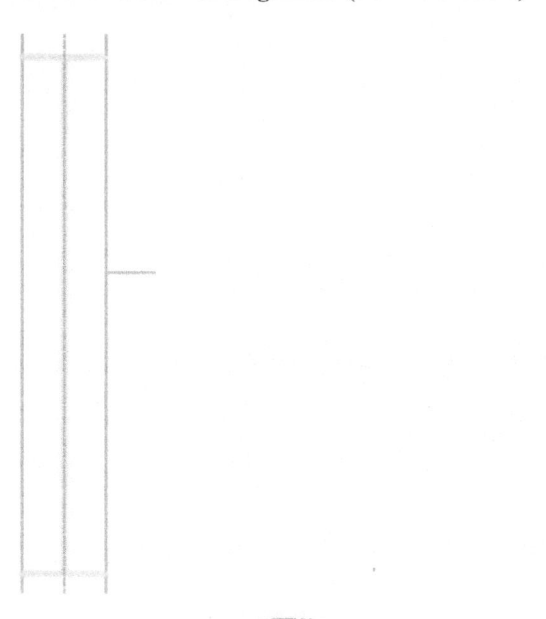

Item	Count
Window	5
Vertical Grid Bubble	4
Grid bubble	4
Dining Set - 36 x 72 in.	1
Bed - Queen	1

- Save and close the drawing.

Use the **Insert Count Field** icon on the **Count** toolbar, if you want to insert the count into the drawing.

- Click the **End Count** icon on the **Count** toolbar to close it.
- Click the **Create table** button on the **Count** palette.

- Check the **Select all** box to select all the blocks.

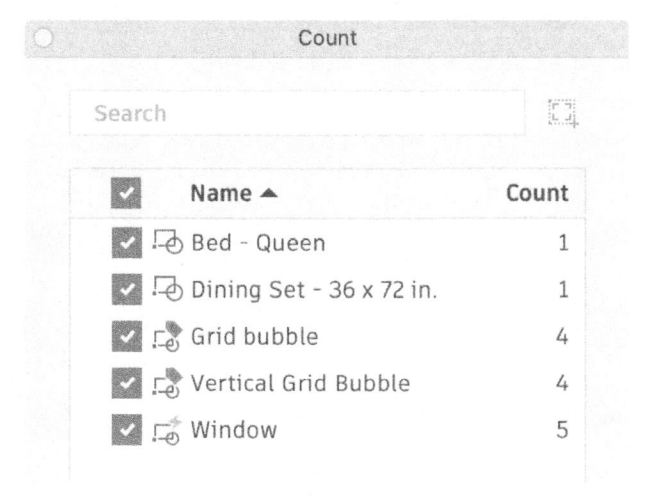

Name	Count
Bed - Queen	1
Dining Set - 36 x 72 in.	1
Grid bubble	4
Vertical Grid Bubble	4
Window	5

- Click the **Insert** button.
- Click in the graphics window to place the count table.

Example 2

In this tutorial, you will draw stairs.

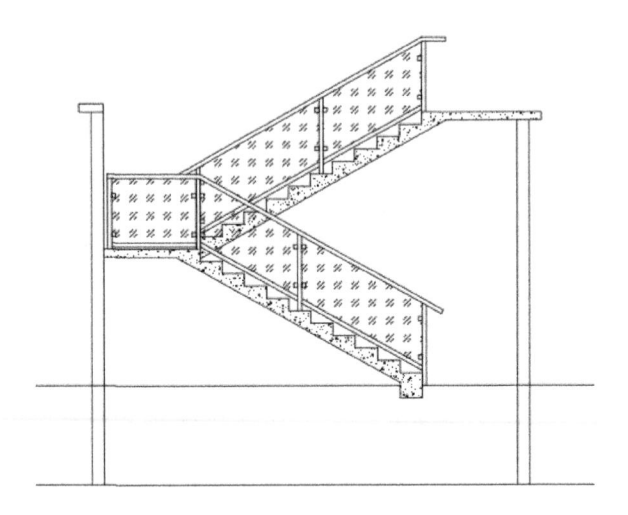

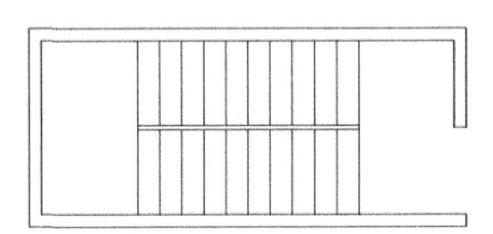

Staircase Nomenclature

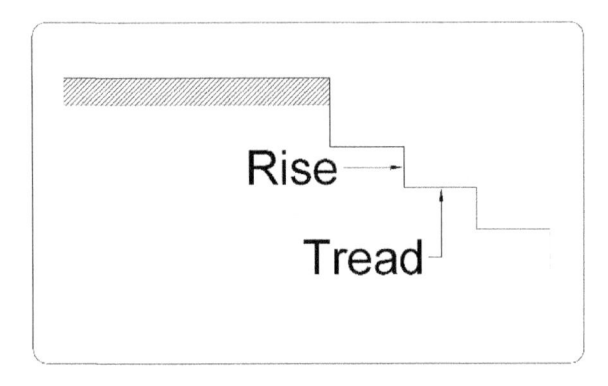

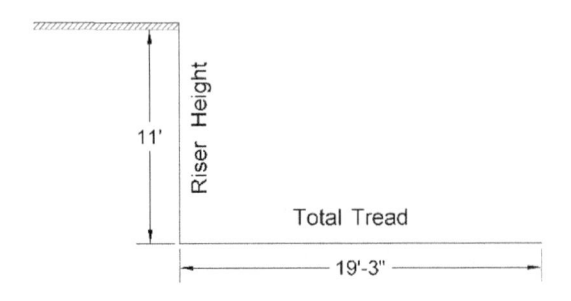

Creating the Stairs

- Start a new AutoCAD file using the **acad.dwt** template.
- Type **UNITS** in the command line and press RETURN.
- On the **Drawing Units** dialog, select **Type > Architectural**.
- Select **Precision > 0-01/16**.
- Set the **Insertion scale units** to **Inches**, and click **OK**.
- Type LIMITS in the command line and press RETURN.
- Press RETURN to accept 0, 0 as the lower limit.
- Type 50', 40' in the command line, and press RETURN. The program sets the upper limit of the drawing.
- Click the **View > Zoom > All** on the Menu Bar.
- Turn OFF the grid.
- Click the **Ortho Mode** icon on the Status bar.
- Click the **Polyline** tool on the **Draw** panel of the **Drawing** tool set.
- Click to define the start point of the line.
- Move the pointer toward left.
- Type 17'8" and press RETURN.
- Move the pointer upward.
- Type 7' and press RETURN.
- Move the pointer toward the right.
- Type 17'2" and press RETURN.
- Move the pointer downward.
- Type 3'6" and press RETURN.
- Press Esc.

- Click the **Offset** icon on the **Modify** panel of the **Drafting** tool set.
- Type 6" and press RETURN.
- Select the polyline.

318 Creating Architectural Drawings

- Move the pointer outward and click.

- Click the **Line** tool and close the open ends of the drawing, as shown.

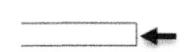

- Create a selection window across all the elements of the drawing.

- Click the **Explode** icon on the **Modify** panel of the **Drafting** tool set. The polylines are exploded into lines.
- Click the **Offset** icon on the **Modify** panel of the **Drafting** tool set.
- Type 4' and press RETURN.
- Select the left vertical inner edge.
- Move the pointer toward right and click.

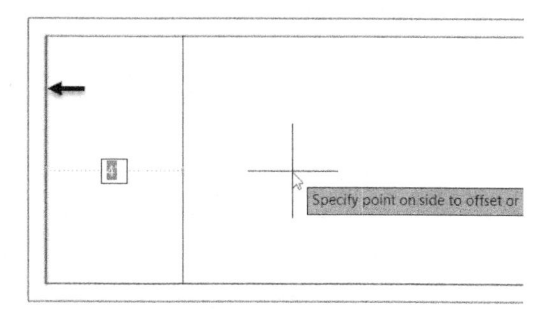

- Press RETURN.
- On the **Drafting** tool set, click **Modify** panel > **Array** drop-down > **Path Array**.
- Select the offset line and press RETURN.
- Click on the inner horizontal line at the location, as shown.

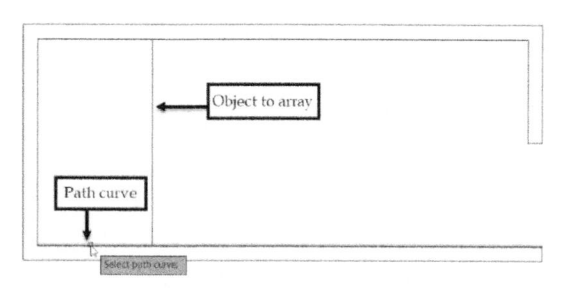

- On the **Path Array** visor, select **Measure** from the **Method** drop-down.

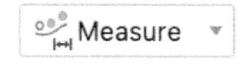

- Uncheck the **Fill entire path** option.
- Type 11 in the **Number of Items** and **Spacing between items** boxes, respectively.

- Type AS in the command line and press RETURN.
- Type N in the command line and press RETURN.
- Click the **Close Array and close visor** icon.

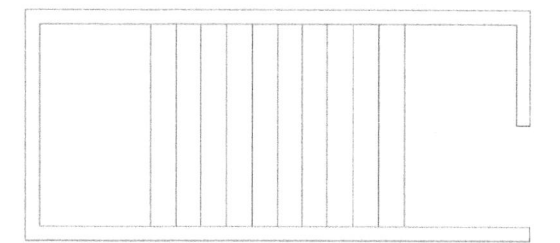

AutoCAD 2023 For Beginners (For Mac Users)

- Offset the inner horizontal lines by 3'5" distance in the inward direction.

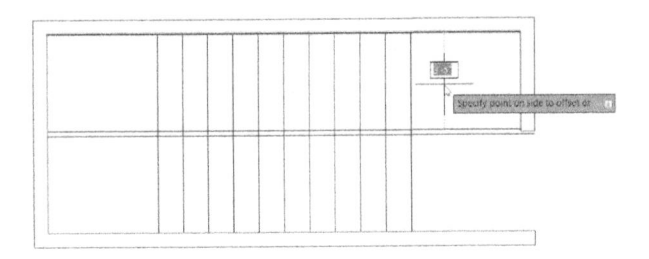

- On the **Drafting** tool set, click **Modify** panel > **Trim/Extend** drop-down > **Trim**.
- Select the portions of the horizontal lines, as shown.

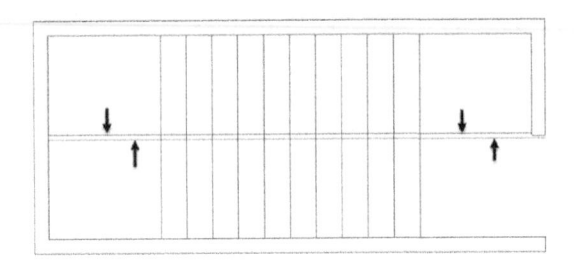

- Zoom-in to the center portion of the stairs.
- Click on the portions of the vertical lines, as shown.

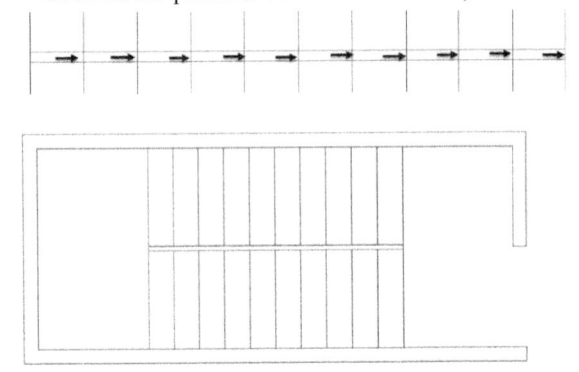

Creating the Section elevation of the Staircase

- Create a horizontal line above the staircase, as shown.

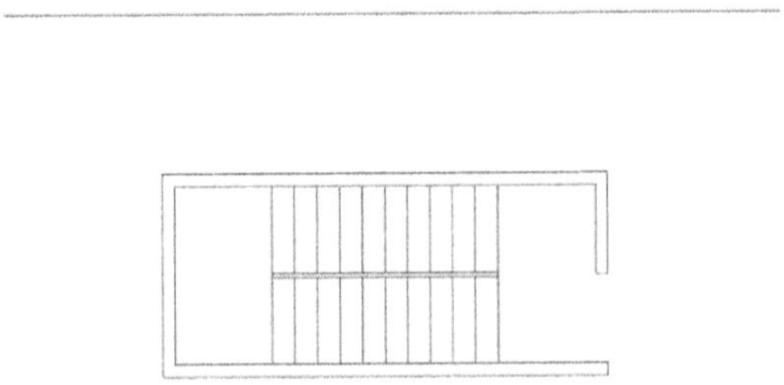

- Click the **Offset** icon on the **Modify** panel of the **Drafting** tool set.

- Type 4' and press RETURN.
- Select the newly created horizontal line.
- Move the pointer upward and click.

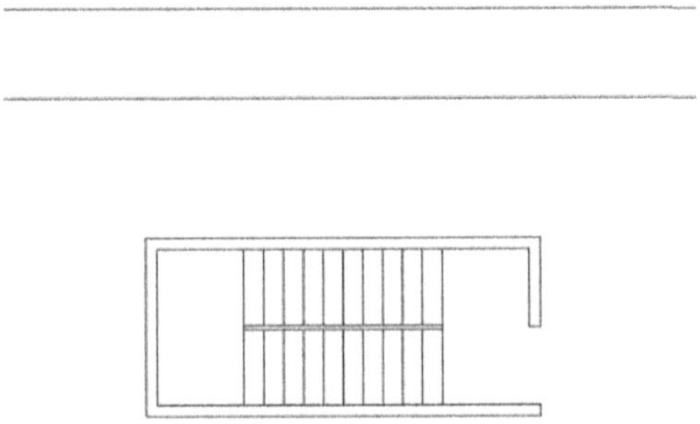

- On the **Drafting** tool set, click the **Draw** panel > **Construction line** icon.
- Right-click and select the **Ver** option.
- Select the corners of the drawing, as shown.

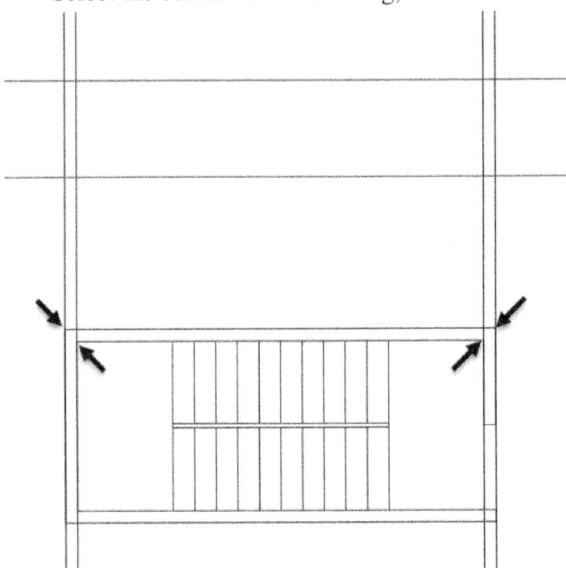

- Click the **Offset** icon on the **Modify** panel of the **Drafting** tool set.
- Type 11' and press RETURN.
- Select the offset horizontal line.
- Move the pointer upward and click.

320 | Creating Architectural Drawings

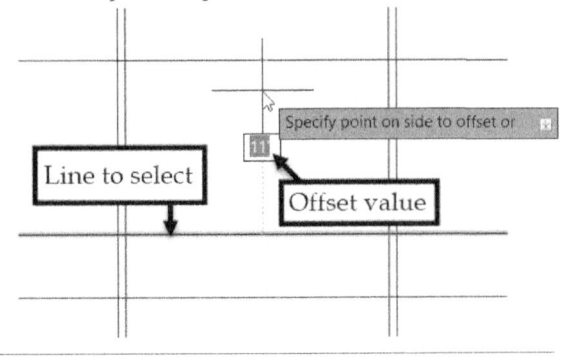

AutoCAD 2023 For Beginners (For Mac Users)

- Press RETURN twice to deactivate the **Offset** tool and then activate it again.
- Type 4" and press RETURN.
- Select the newly created offset line.
- Move the pointer upward and click.

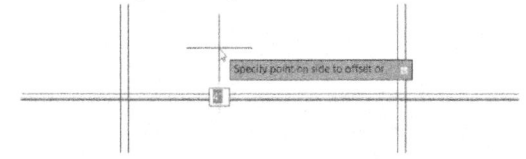

- On the **Drafting** tool set, click **Modify** panel > **Trim/Extend** drop-down > **Trim**.
- Press and hold the left mouse button and drag the pointer across the portions of the construction lines, as shown.

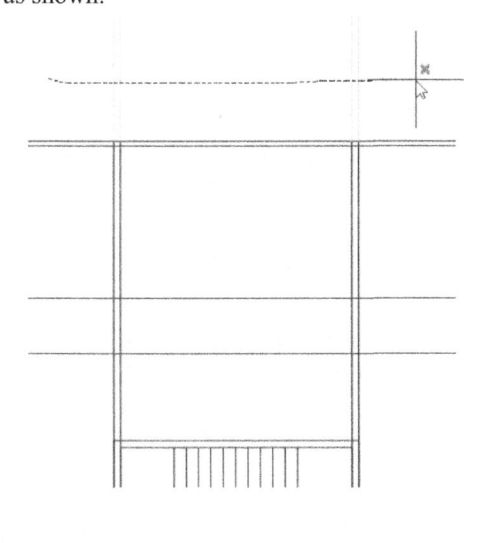

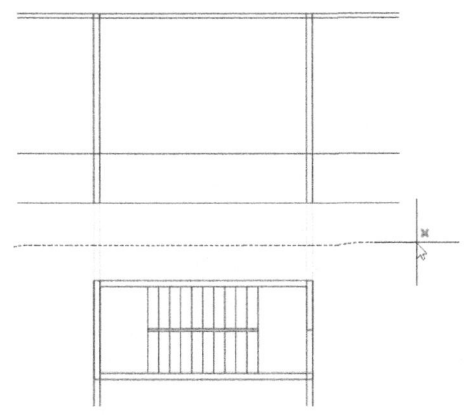

- On the **Drafting** tool set, click **Modify** panel > **Trim/Extend** drop-down > **Trim**.
- Trim the portions of the vertical and horizontal lines, as shown.

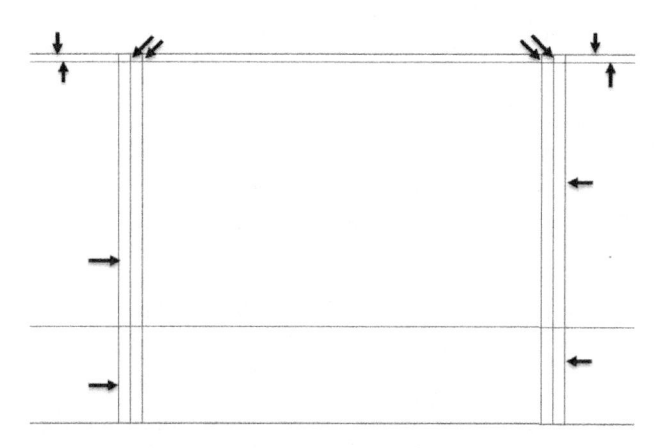

- On the **Drafting** tool set, click **Modify** panel > **Trim/Extend** drop-down > **Extend**.
- Right-click and select the **Boundary edges** option.
- Select the lower horizontal edge of the roof, as shown.

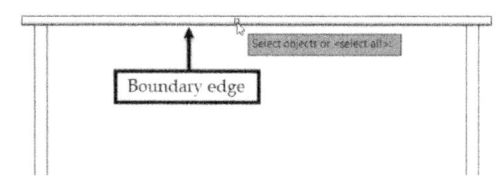

- Press RETURN.
- Press and hold the left mouse button.
- Drag the pointer across the staircase lines; the lines are extended up to the boundary edge.

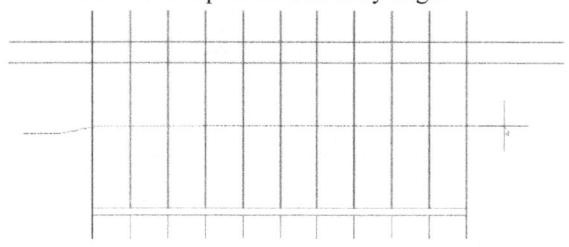

- Click the **Offset** icon on the **Modify** panel of the **Drafting** tool set.
- Type 6" and press RETURN.
- Offset the outer vertical lines on both sides.

321 | Creating Architectural Drawings

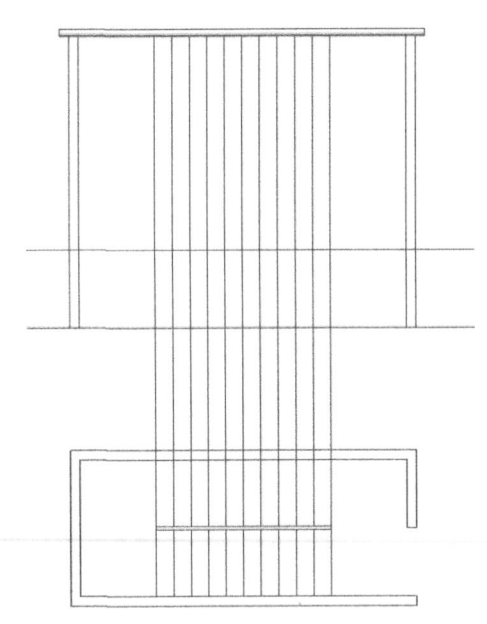

- On the **Drafting** tool set, click **Modify** panel > **Trim/Extend** drop-down > **Trim**.
- Right-click and select the **cuTting edges** option.
- Select the horizontal lines, as shown.
- Press RETURN.

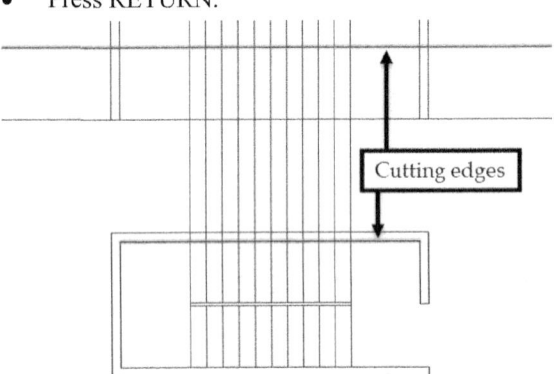

- Click and drag the pointer across the vertical lines, as shown.

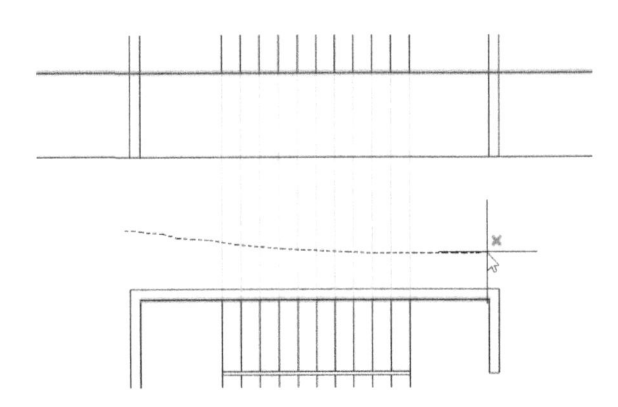

- On the **Drafting** tool set, click **Draw** panel > **Polyline**.

- Select the first point of the polyline.
- Move the pointer upward.
- Type 6" and press RETURN.

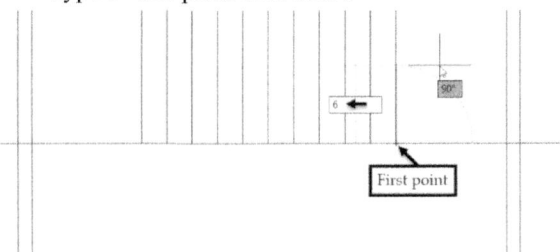

- Move the pointer toward left.
- Type 11" and press RETURN.
- Press Esc.

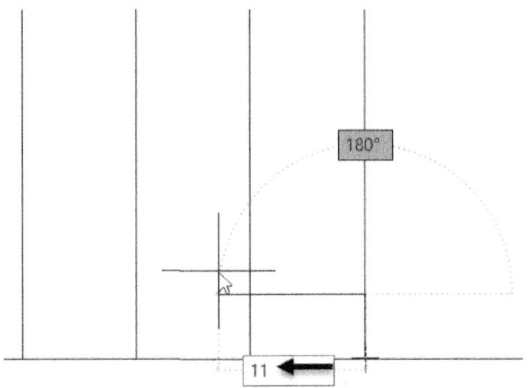

- Select the polyline and click the **Copy** icon on the **Modify** panel of the **Drafting** tool set.
- Select the first point of the polyline as the base point.

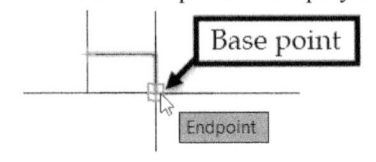

- Move the pointer upward and select the endpoint of the polyline. The polyline is copied.

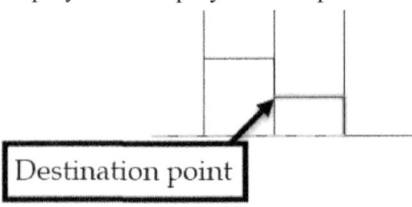

- Likewise, create copies of the polylines, as shown.

322 | Creating Architectural Drawings

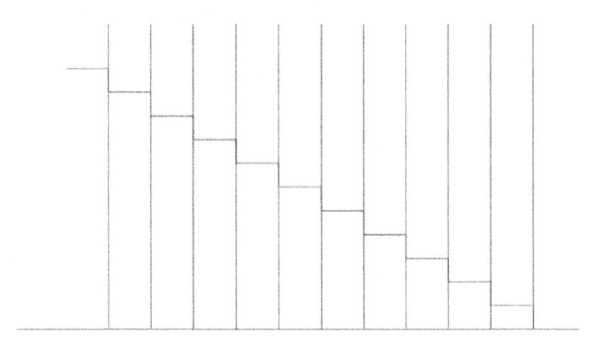

- On the **Drafting** tool set, click **Modify** panel > **Join** icon.

- Select all the polylines and press RETURN. All the polylines are joined.

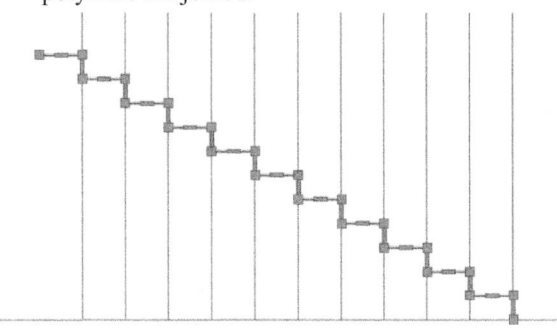

- On the **Drafting** tool set, click **Modify** panel > **Trim/Extend** drop-down > **Extend**.
- Click on the end portion of the polyline to extend it up to the left vertical line.

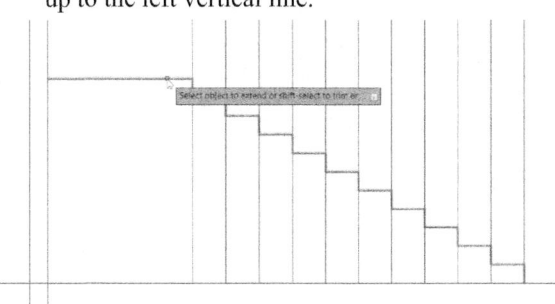

- Press Esc.
- Select the stairs and click the **Mirror** icon on the **Modify** panel of the **Drafting** tool set.
- Specify the start point of the mirror line, as shown.

- Move the pointer toward the left and specify the endpoint of the mirror line, as shown.

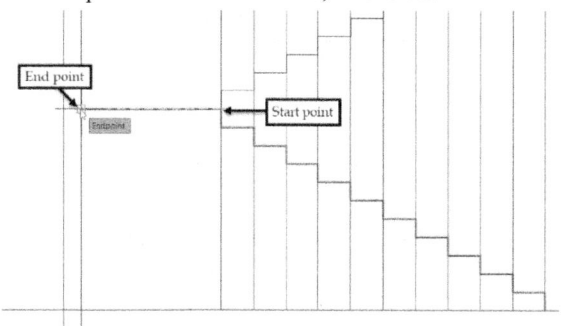

- Right-click and select **No**.
- Select the mirrored polyline.
- Click on the endpoint of the polyline.

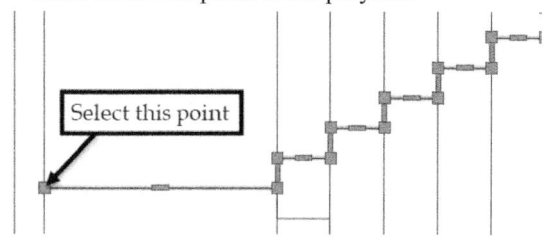

- Move the pointer toward the right and select the vertex point, as shown. The polyline is shortened.

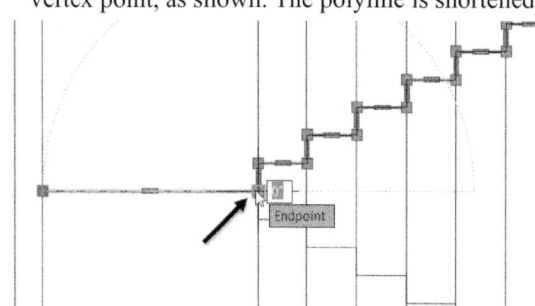

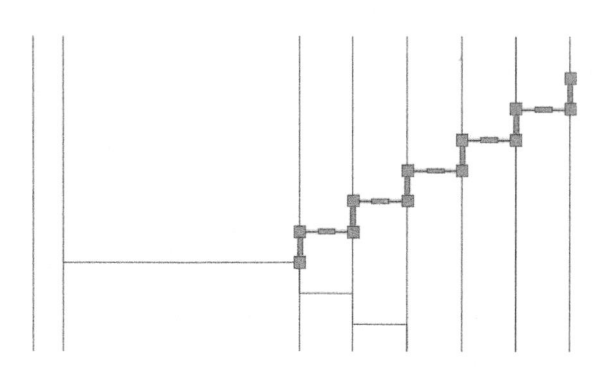

- Press Esc to deselect the mirrored polyline.
- Drag a selection window across the vertical lines from right to left, as shown.

323 | **Creating Architectural Drawings**

AutoCAD 2023 For Beginners (For Mac Users)

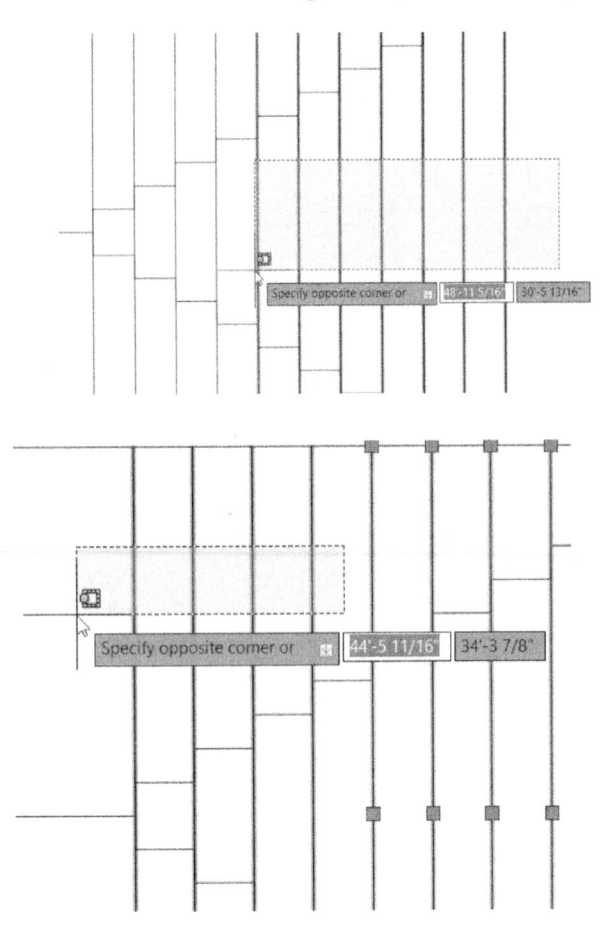

- Press Delete on your keyboard.
- On the **Drafting** tool set, click **Draw** panel >**Line**.
- Select the corner points, as shown.

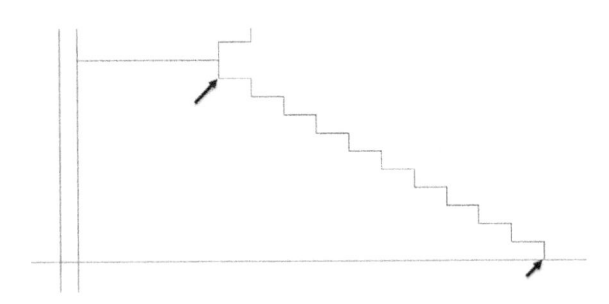

- Offset the newly created line by 4".

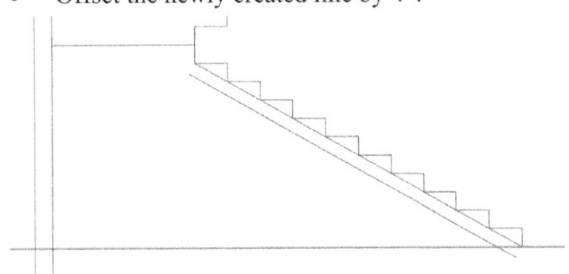

- On the **Drafting** tool set, click **Draw** panel > **Line**.

- Press and hold the Shift key and right click.
- Select the **From** option from the **Object Snap** menu.
- Select the point, as shown.

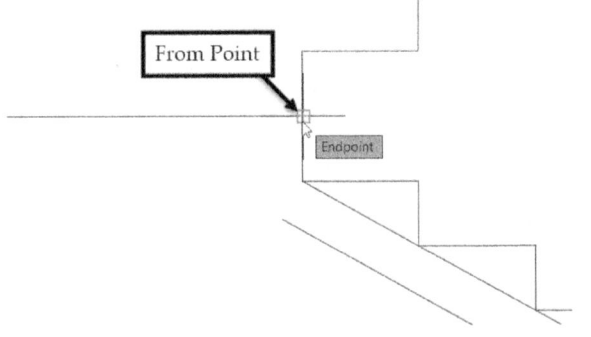

- Move the pointer downward and type 4".
- Press RETURN to specify the start point of the line.
- Move the pointer toward the left and click to create a horizontal line.

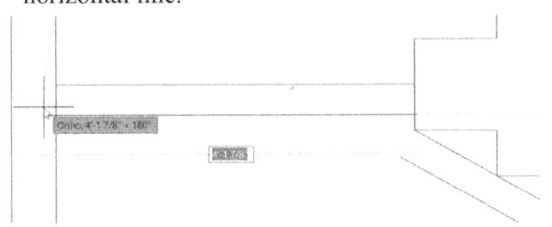

- Click the **Fillet** icon on the **Modify** panel.
- Select the horizontal and inclined lines, as shown.

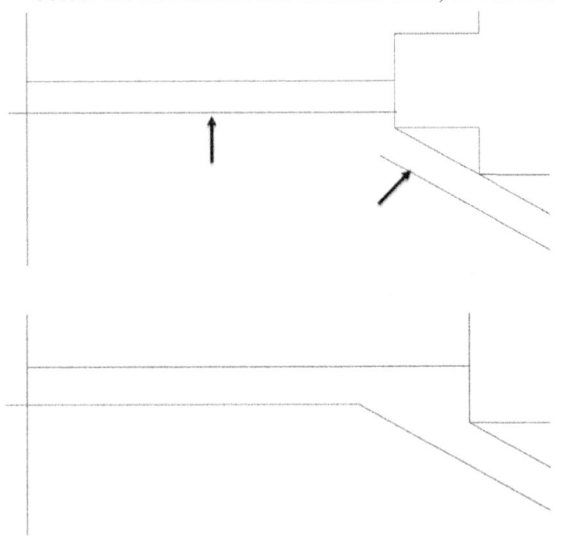

- Delete the inclined line, as shown.

324 | Creating Architectural Drawings

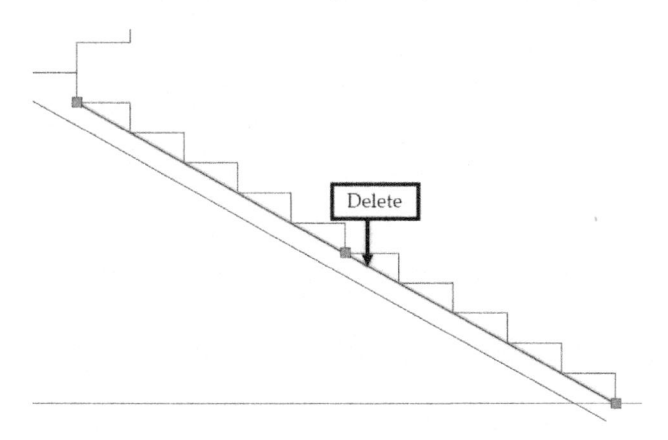

- On the **Drafting** tool set, click **Draw** panel > **Line**.
- Select the corner point of the stair, as shown.

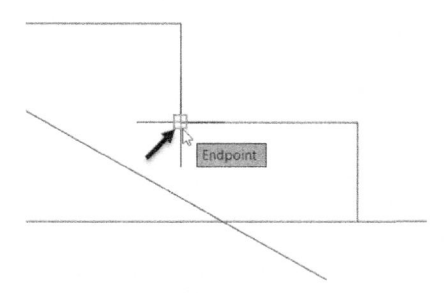

- Move the pointer downward.
- Type 1' and press RETURN.
- Move the pointer toward the right.
- Type 11" and press RETURN.
- Move the pointer upward.
- Type 6" and press RETURN.

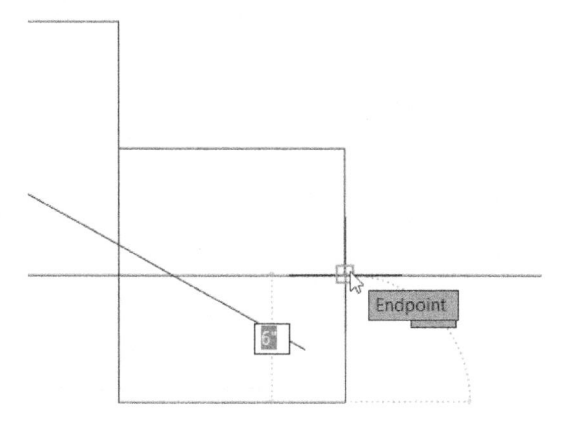

- On the **Drafting** tool set, click **Modify** panel > **Trim/Extend** drop-down > **Trim**.
- Select the portions of the lines, as shown.

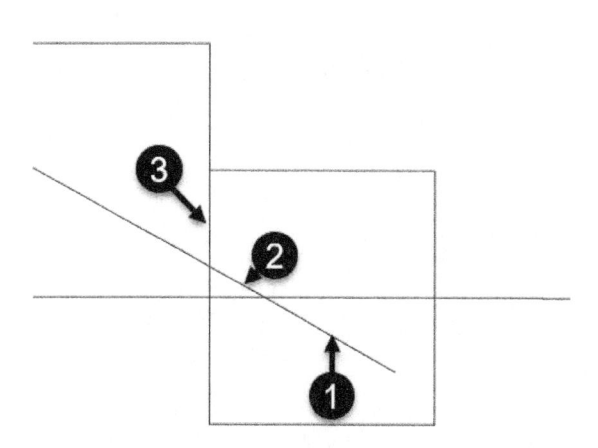

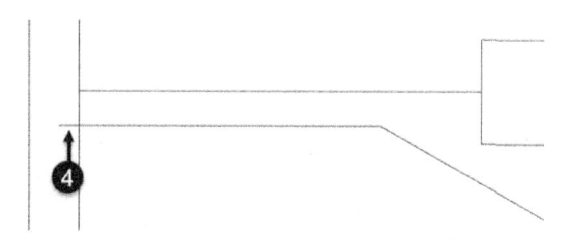

- On the **Drafting** tool set, click **Draw** panel >**Line**.
- Select the corner points, as shown.

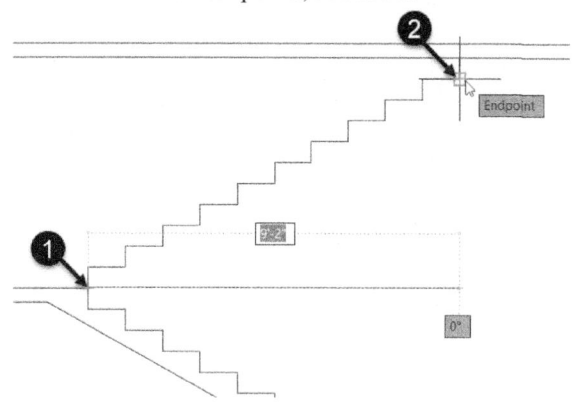

- Offset the newly created line by 4".

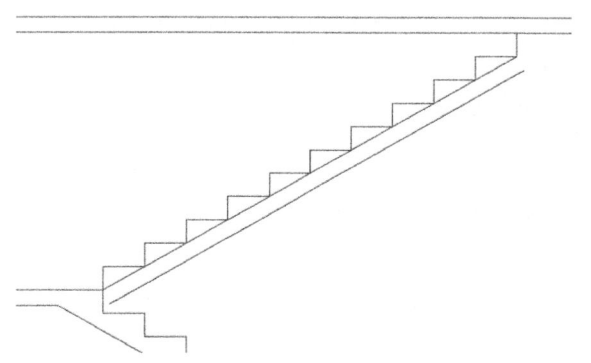

- On the **Drafting** tool set, click **Modify** panel > **Trim/Extend** drop-down > **Extend**.

Creating Architectural Drawings

- Select the inclined line, as shown.

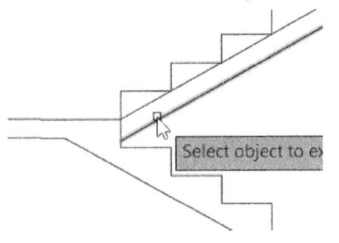

- Extend the inclined line up to the horizontal line, as shown.

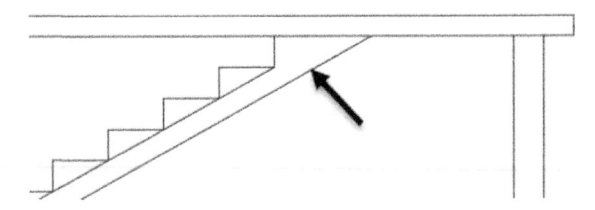

- Extend the vertical lines, as shown. Next, press Esc.

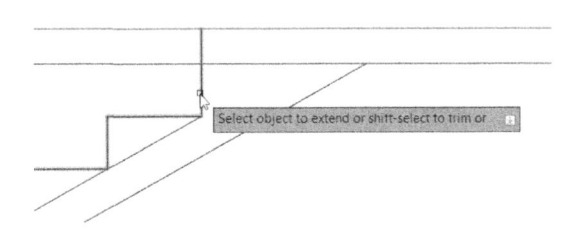

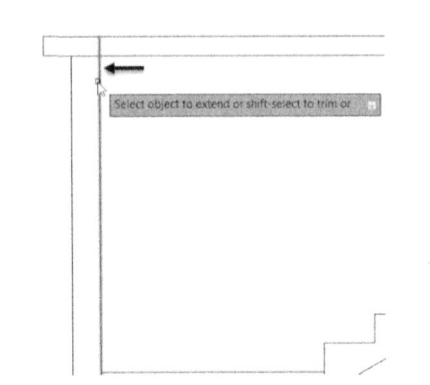

- Select the inclined line, as shown.

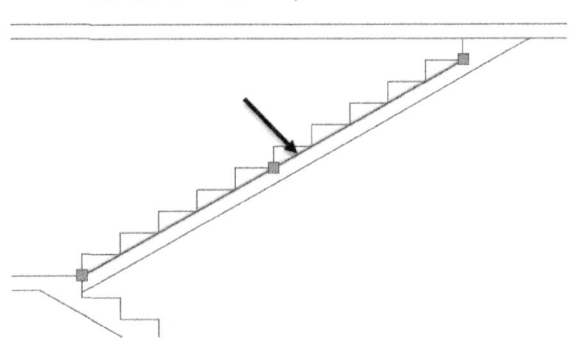

- Press Delete.
- On the **Drafting** tool set, click **Modify** panel > **Trim/Extend** drop-down > **Trim**.
- Select the horizontal lines, as shown.

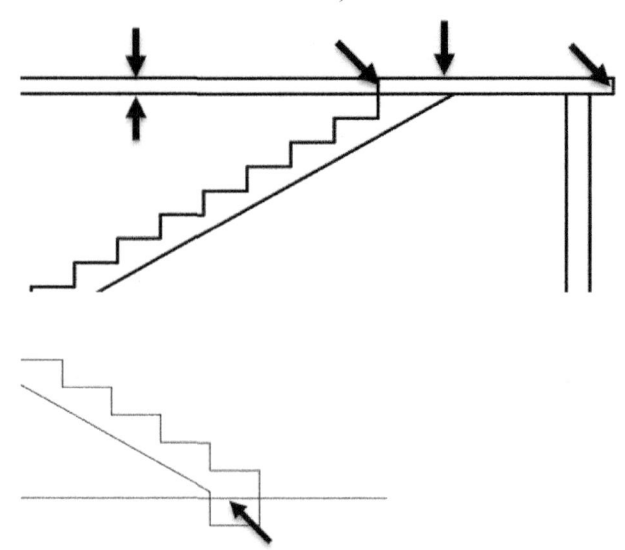

- Offset the horizontal line by 4" in the downward direction.

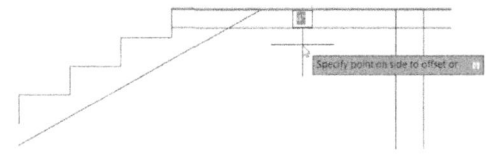

- Trim the elements, as shown.

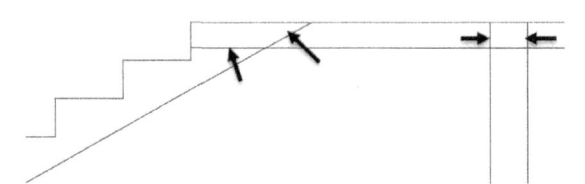

- Close the end of the offset line.

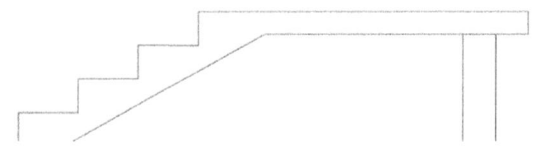

- On the **Drafting** tool set, click **Hatch** panel > **Hatch**.
- On the **Hatch** visor, click the **Pattern** drop-down > **Open Library**.

AutoCAD 2023 For Beginners (For Mac Users)

- Type AR in the search bar and double-click on the **AR-CONC** pattern.

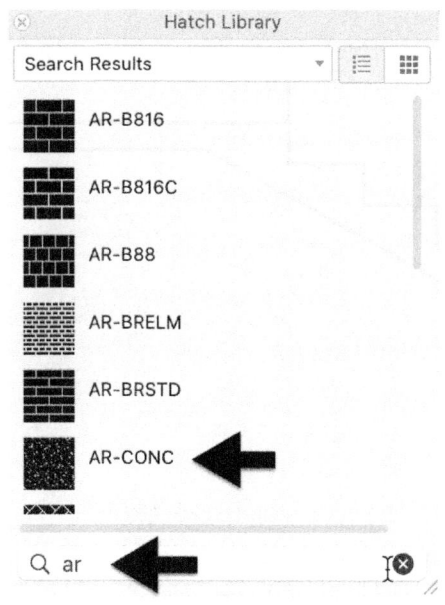

- Pick points in the areas, as shown.

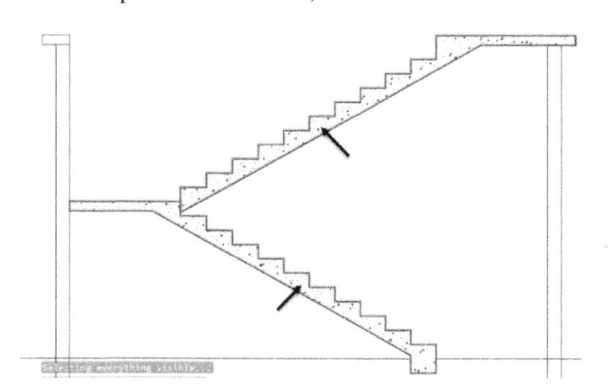

- Click the **Exit the Hatch Editor and close the visor** icon on the visor.

Creating the Handrail

- On the **Drafting** tool set, click **Draw** panel > **Line**.
- Create two vertical lines of 3' length each at the locations, as shown.

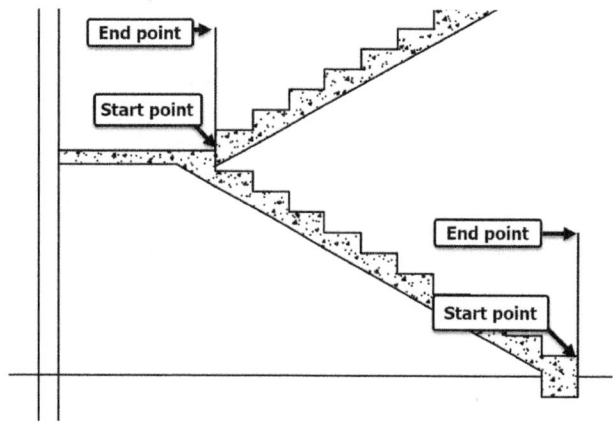

- Activate the **Line** tool and connect the endpoints of the two vertical lines, as shown.

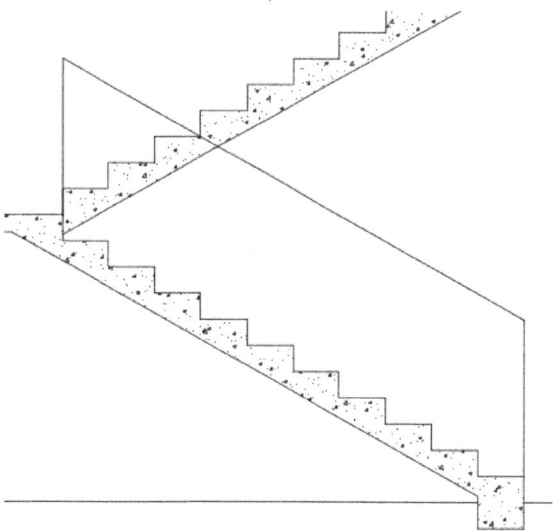

- Click the **Customize** panel icon on the **Modify** panel and check the Lengthen option.
- Click the **Lengthen** icon on the **Modify** panel.

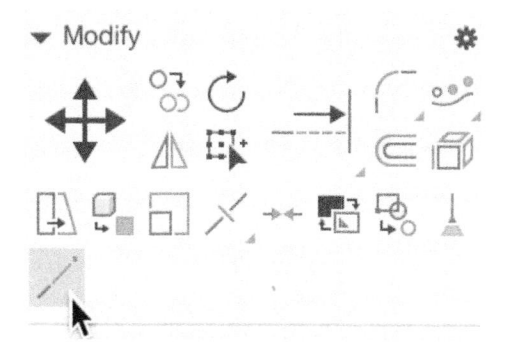

327 | Creating Architectural Drawings

- Right-click and select **DElta**.
- Type 12" and press RETURN.
- Click near the endpoint of the inclined line.

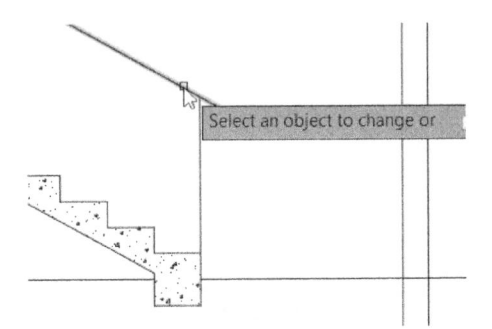

The inclined line is lengthened.

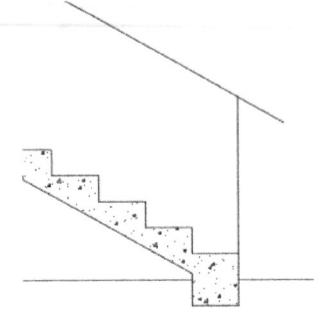

- Create a horizontal line, as shown.

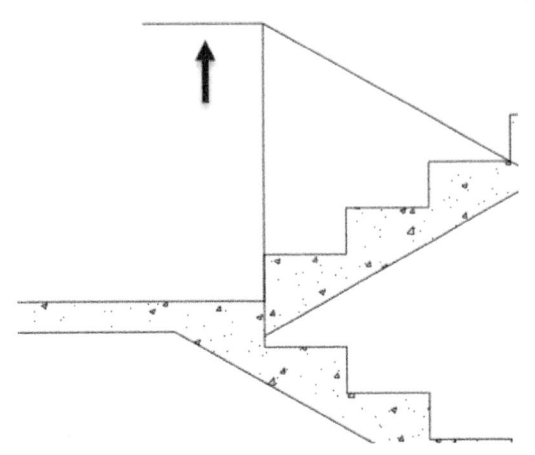

- Click the **Offset** icon on the **Modify** panel.
- Offset the newly created lines by 2" distance, as shown.

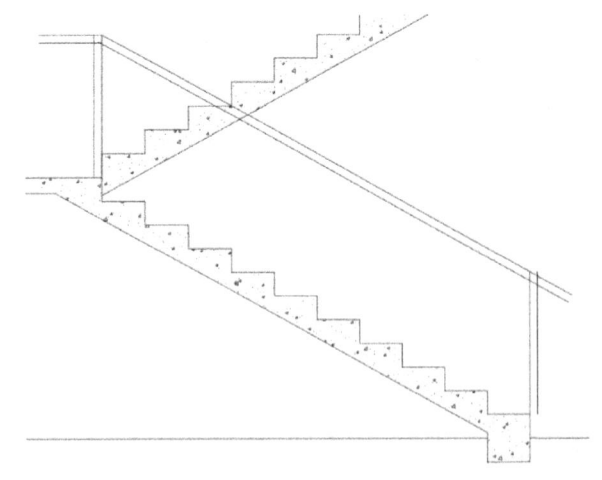

- On the **Drafting** tool set, click **Modify** panel > **Trim/Extend** drop-down > **Extend**.
- Extend the two vertical lines up to the bottom horizontal edge, as shown.

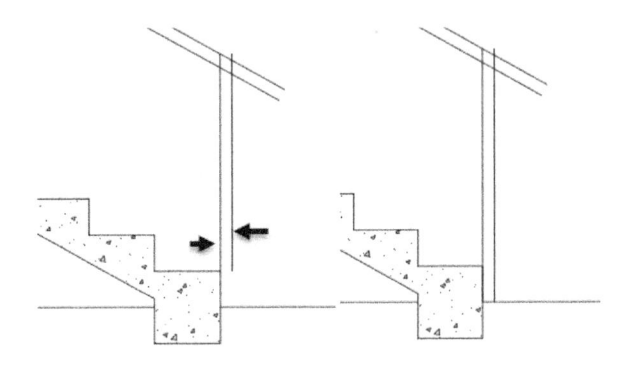

- Activate the **Line** tool.
- Zoom to the fifth step from the top.
- Press and hold the Shift key and right click.
- Select the **Mid between 2 Points** option.
- Select the two endpoints of the step; the start point of the line is specified at the midpoint.

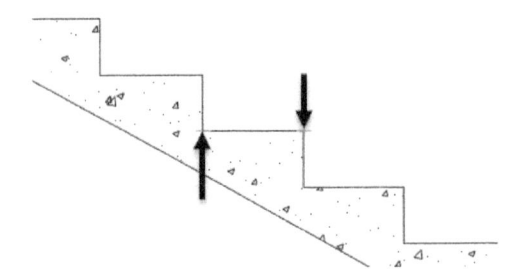

- Move the pointer upward and click.

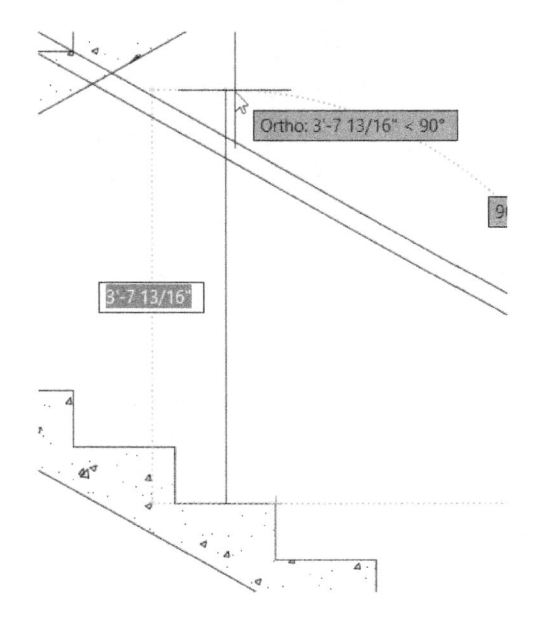

- Click the **Offset** icon on the **Modify** panel.
- Offset the newly created line by 1" on both sides, as shown.
- Delete the middle line.

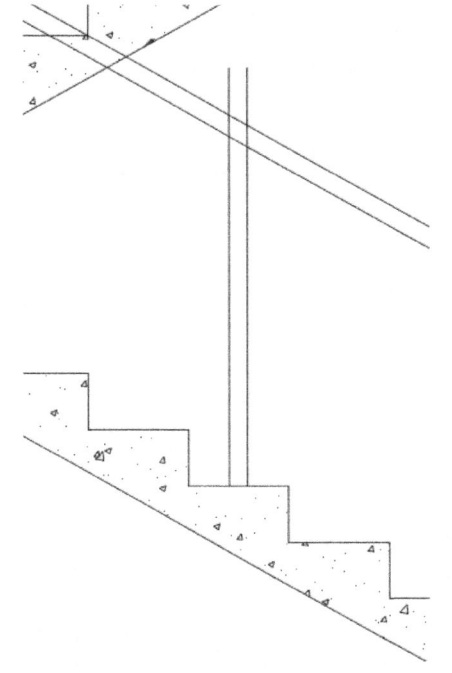

- On the **Drafting** tool set, click **Modify** panel > **Trim/Extend** drop-down > **Trim**.
- Right-click and select the **cuTting edges** option.
- Select the lower inclined and horizontal lines of the handrail.
- Press RETURN.

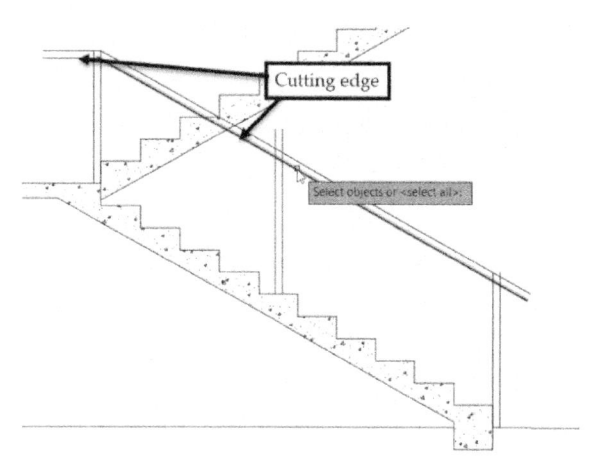

- Trim the portions of the vertical lines, as shown.

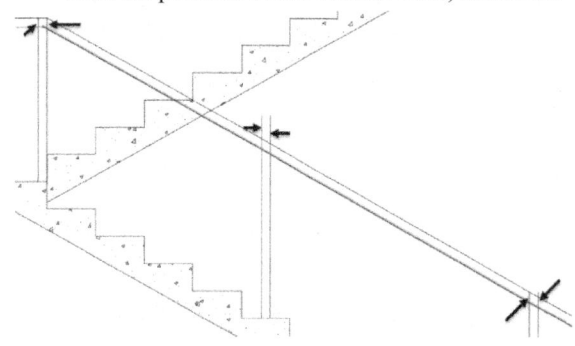

- On the **Drafting** tool set, click **Modify** panel > **Trim/Extend** drop-down > **Trim**.
- Select the unwanted portions of the lines, as shown.

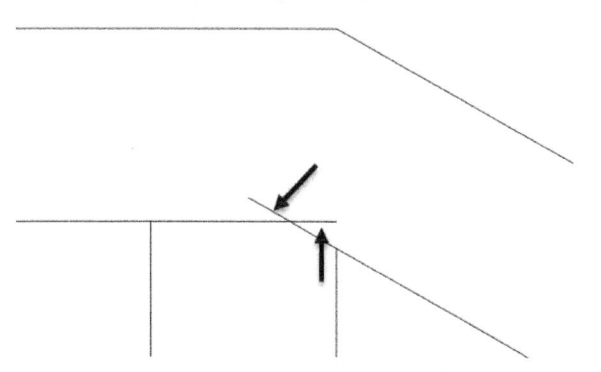

- On the **Drafting** tool set, click **Modify** > **Break at Point**.

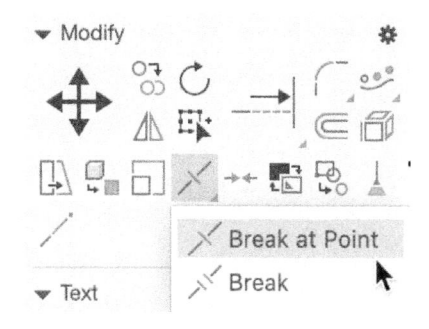

329 | **Creating Architectural Drawings**

AutoCAD 2023 For Beginners (For Mac Users)

- Select the vertical line, as shown.
- Press and hold the Shift key and right click.
- Select the **Midpoint** option.
- Select the midpoint of the vertical line, as shown. The vertical line is broken at the midpoint.

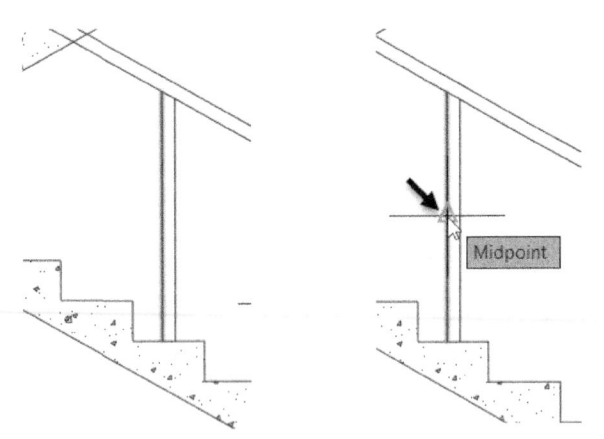

- Click the **Object Snap** drop-down on the status bar and select the **Midpoint** option.
- On the **Drafting** tool set, click **Draw** panel > **Rectangle/Polygon** drop-down > **Rectangle**.
- Select the midpoint of the lower portion of the broken line, as shown.

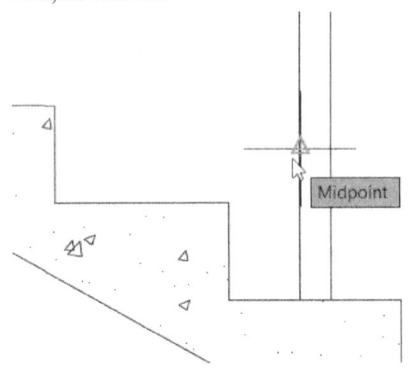

- Right-click and select the **Dimensions** option.
- Type 2 and press RETURN.
- Type 2 and press RETURN.
- Move the pointer upward and click.

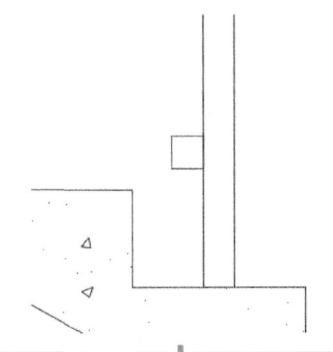

- Select the rectangle and click the **Copy** icon on the **Modify** panel.
- Select the top right corner point of the rectangle.
- Move the pointer upward.
- Select the midpoint of the upper portion of the broken line, as shown.

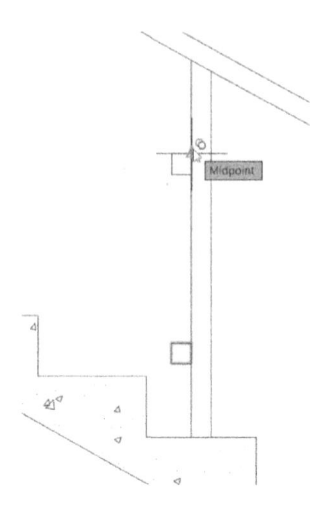

- Select the two rectangles and click the **Copy** icon on the **Modify** panel.
- Select the top right corner point of anyone of the rectangles.

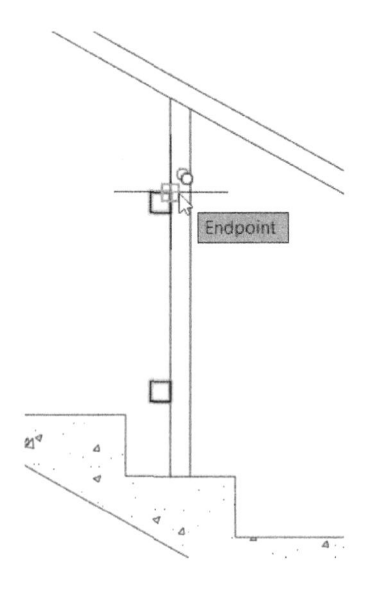

- Move the pointer toward the right.
- Type 4" and press RETURN.

330 | Creating Architectural Drawings

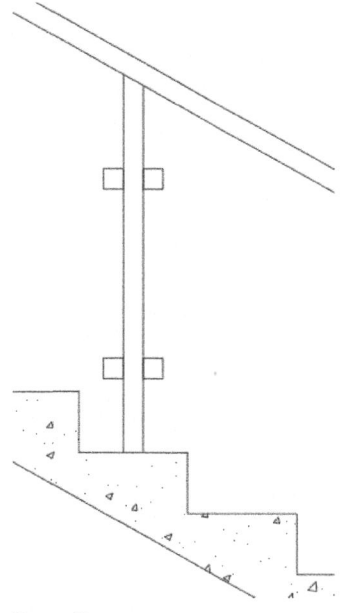

- Press Esc.
- Select the four rectangles and click the **Copy** icon on the **Modify** panel.
- Select the midpoint of the right vertical line.

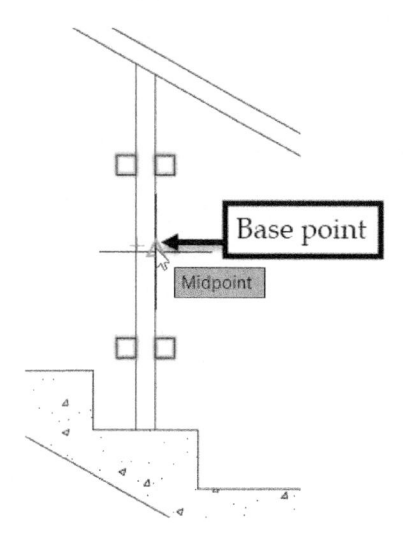

- Move the pointer toward right and select the midpoint of the vertical line, as shown.

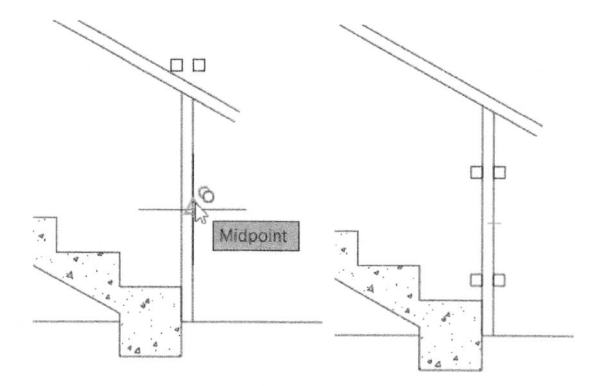

- Move the pointer toward the left and select the midpoint of the vertical line, as shown.

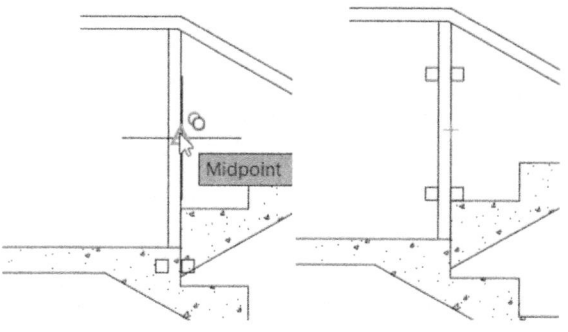

- Press ESC.
- Delete the two rectangles, as shown.

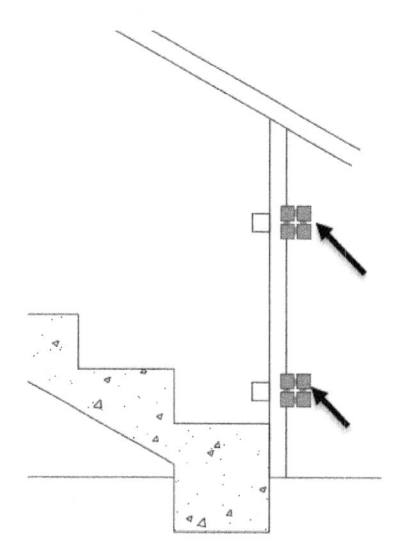

- Select the vertical line and click the **Offset** icon on the **Modify** panel.
- Type 3'8" and press RETURN.
- Move the pointer toward the left and click.

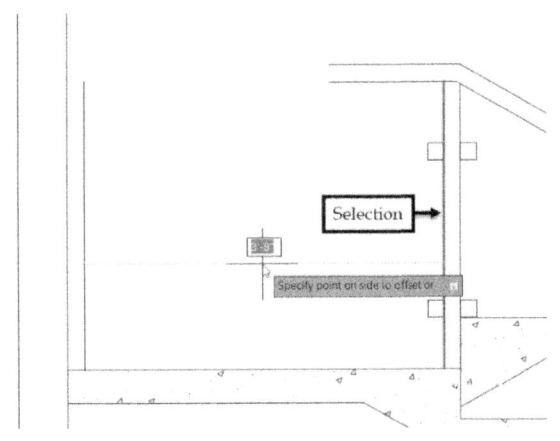

- Press RETURN twice.
- Type 2" and press RETURN.
- Select the newly offset line.
- Move the pointer toward right and click.

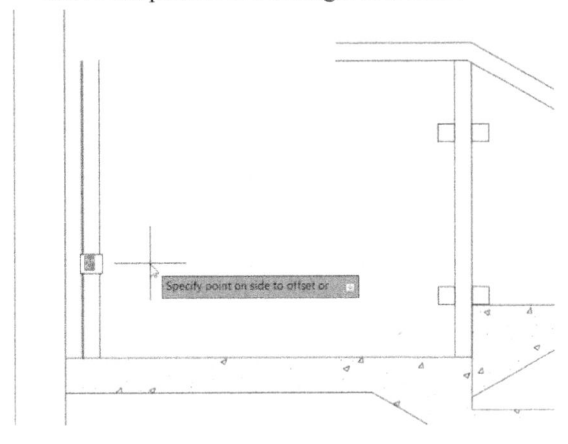

- Click the **Fillet** icon on the **Modify** panel.
- Select the left vertical and top horizontal line, as shown.

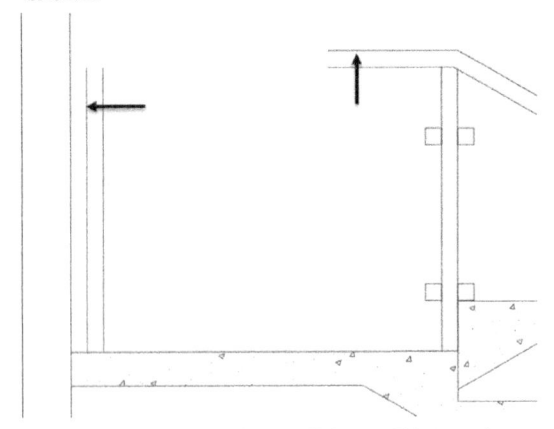

- On the **Drafting** tool set, click **Modify** panel > **Trim/Extend** drop-down > **Extend**.
- Extend the horizontal line up to the vertical line.

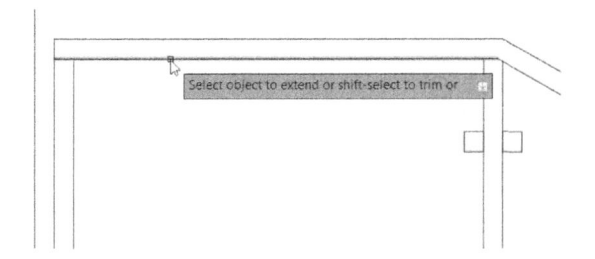

- Press Esc.
- Select the two rectangles and click the **Copy** icon on the **Modify** panel.
- Specify the base and destination points, as shown.

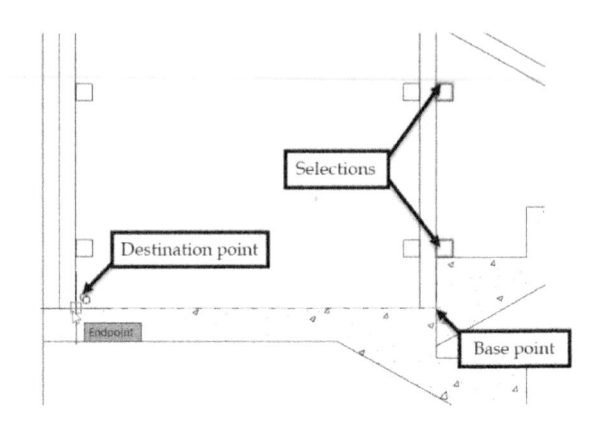

- Click the **Line** icon on the **Draw** panel.
- Select the corner points of the top and bottom steps, as shown.
- Press Esc.

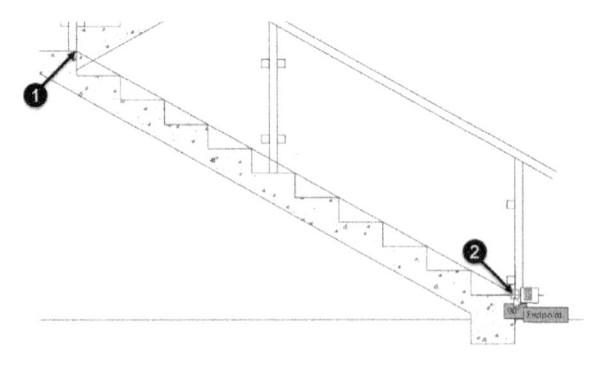

- Select the newly created line and click the **Offset** icon on the **Modify** panel.
- Type 1" and press RETURN.
- Move the pointer upward and click.

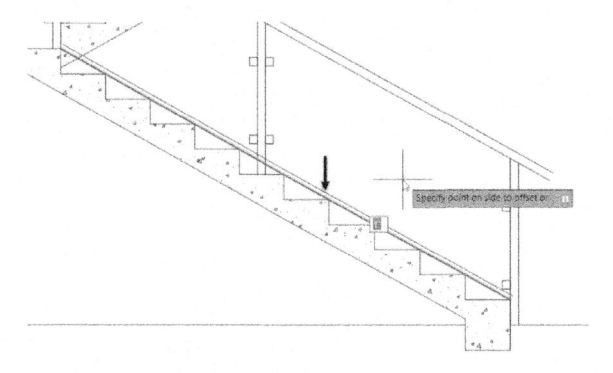

- Press RETURN twice.
- Type 2" and press RETURN.
- Select the newly offset line.
- Move the pointer upward and click.

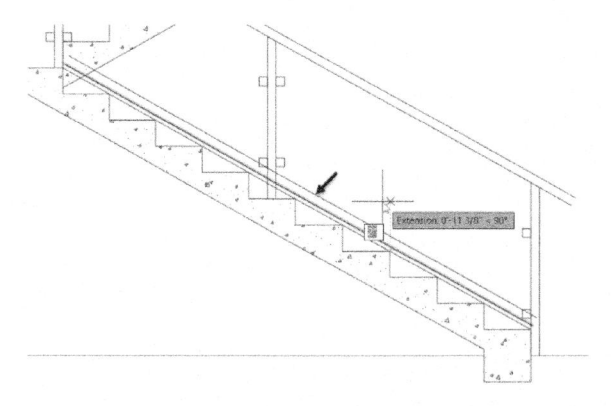

- On the **Drafting** tool set, click **Modify** panel > **Trim/Extend** drop-down > **Trim**.
- Trim the intersecting portions of the lines, as shown.

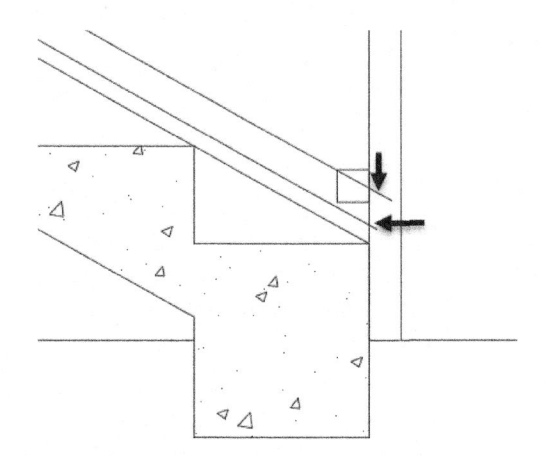

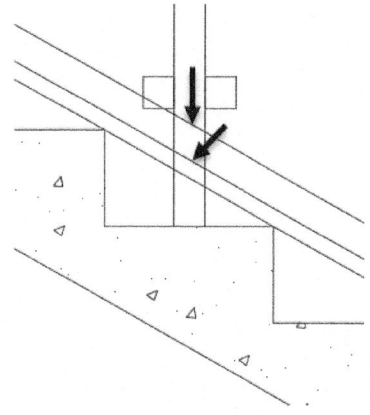

- Press Esc.
- Select the rectangles and click the **Move** icon on the **Modify** panel.
- Specify the base point, as shown.

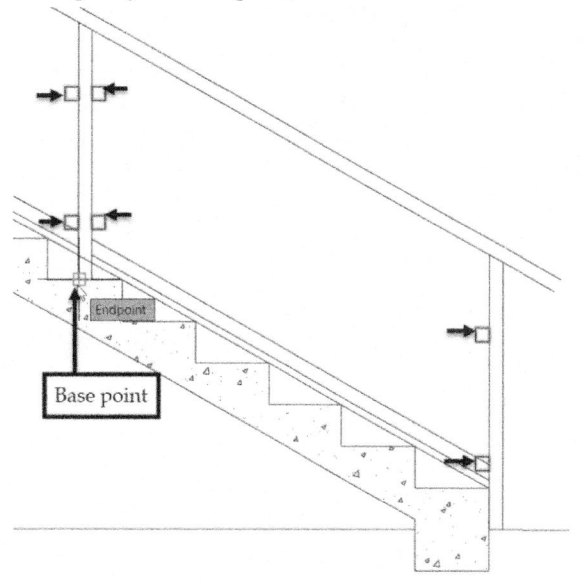

- Move the pointer upward.
- Type 4" and press RETURN.

333 | Creating Architectural Drawings

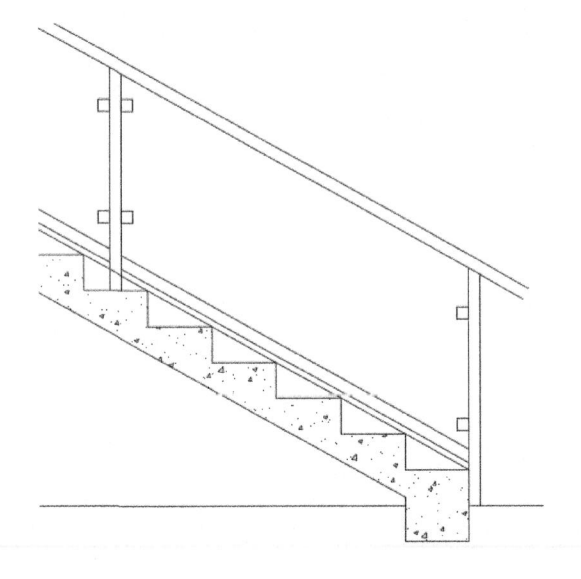

- Select the horizontal line, as shown.
- Click the **Offset** icon on the **Modify** panel.
- Type 33" and press RETURN.
- Move the pointer downward and click.

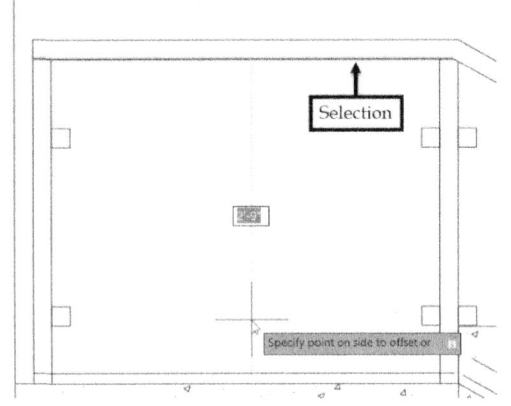

- Press RETURN twice.
- Type 2" and press RETURN.
- Select the newly offset line.
- Move the pointer upward and click.

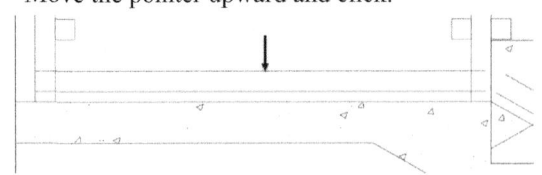

- Click the **Fillet** icon on the **Modify** panel.
- Select the horizontal and inclined lines, as shown.
- Press RETURN and select the horizontal and inclined lines, as shown.

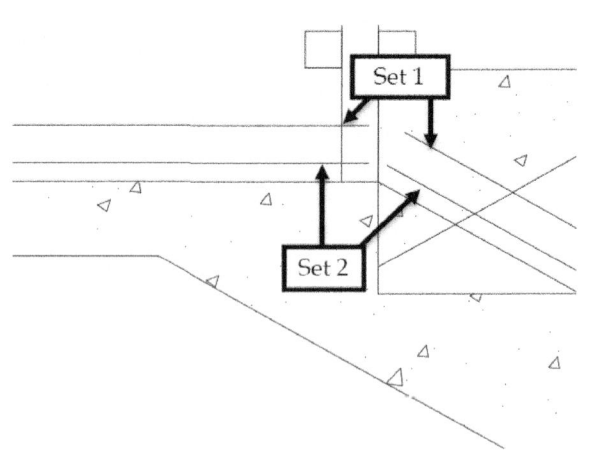

- Click the **Trim** icon on the **Modify** panel.
- Select the portions of the horizontal and inclined line, as shown.

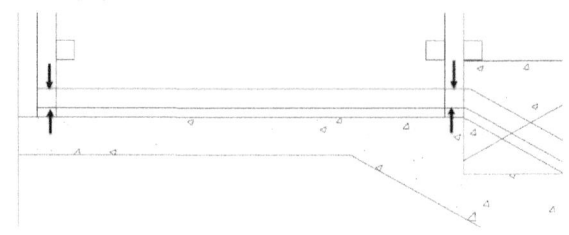

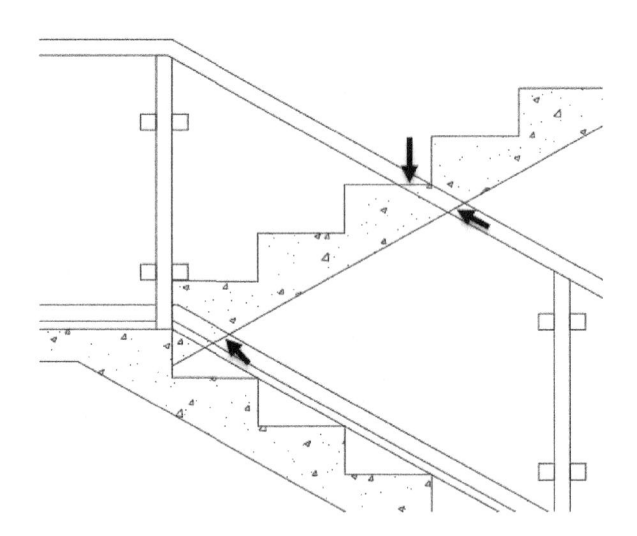

- Right-click and select the **eRase** option.
- Select the inclined line, as shown.
- Press RETURN.

334 | Creating Architectural Drawings

AutoCAD 2023 For Beginners (For Mac Users)

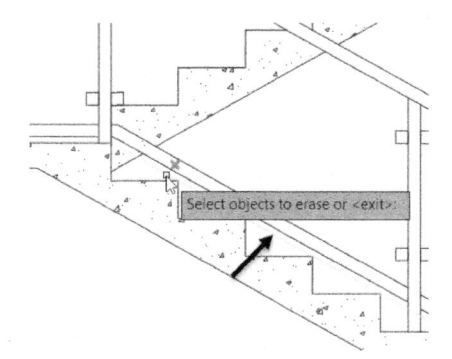

- Close the end of the offset lines using the **Line** tool.

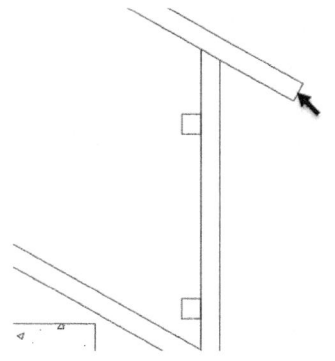

- Select the elements of the handrail.

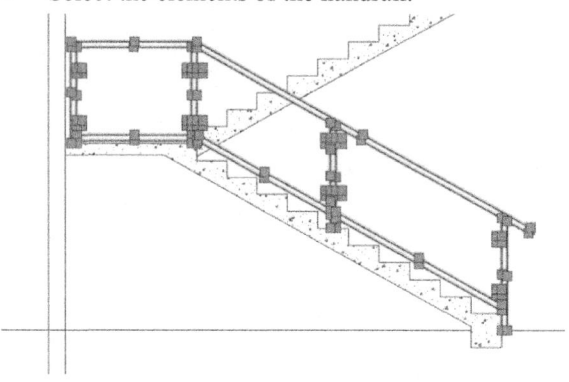

- Click the **Copy** icon on the **Modify** panel.
- Specify the base point, as shown.
- Move the pointer toward the right and click to create the copy.

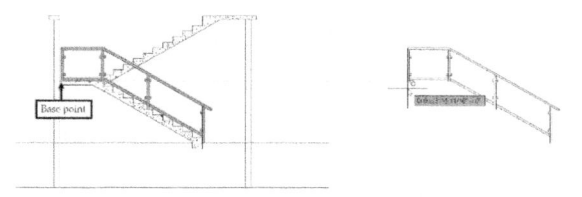

- Click the **Mirror** icon on the **Modify** panel.
- Create a selection window covering all the copied entities of the handrail.

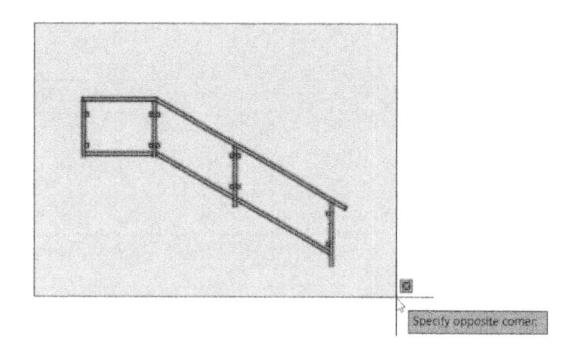

- Press RETURN.
- Select the base point, as shown.
- Move the pointer vertically upward and click.

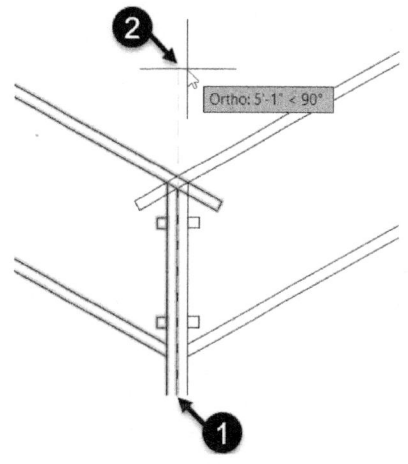

- Right-click and select **Yes**.
- Create a selection window across all the mirrored entities.
- Click the **Move** icon on the **Modify** panel.
- Specify the base point, as shown.

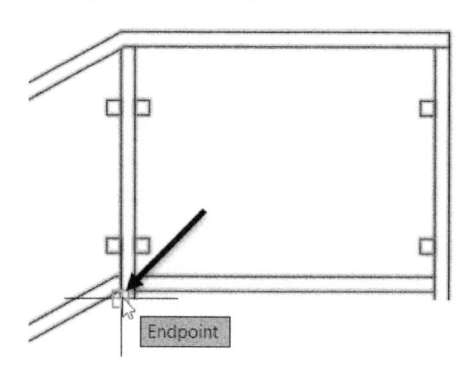

- Move the pointer toward the right and select the destination point.

335 | Creating Architectural Drawings

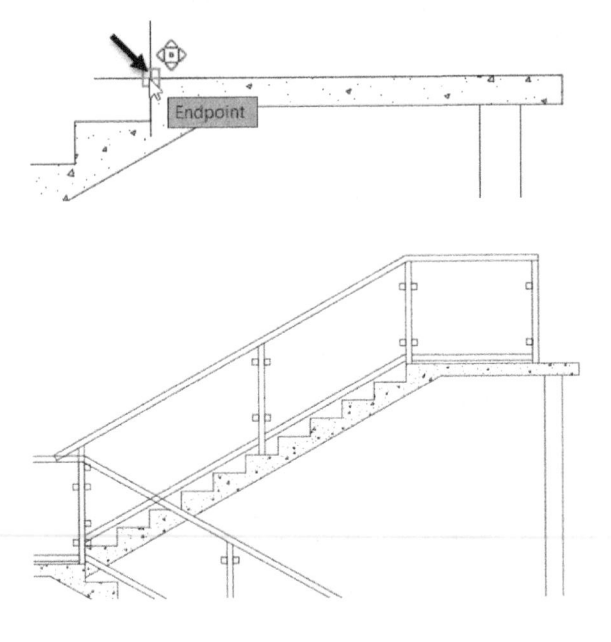

- Select the elements of the handrail, as shown.

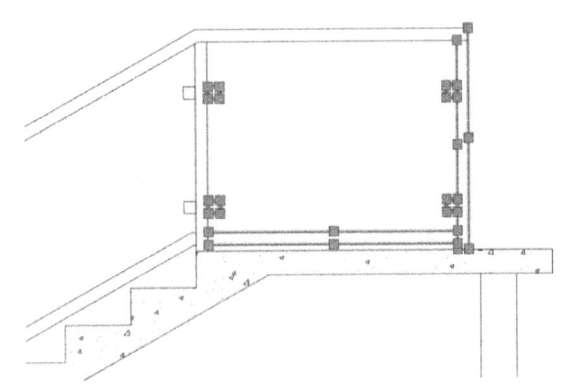

- Press Delete.
- Click the **Line** icon on the **Draw** panel.
- Press and hold the Shift key.
- Right click and select **From** from the **Object Snap** menu.
- Select the corner point of the handrail, as shown.

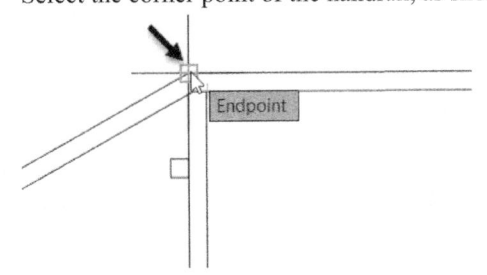

- Move the pointer along the horizontal line, as shown.

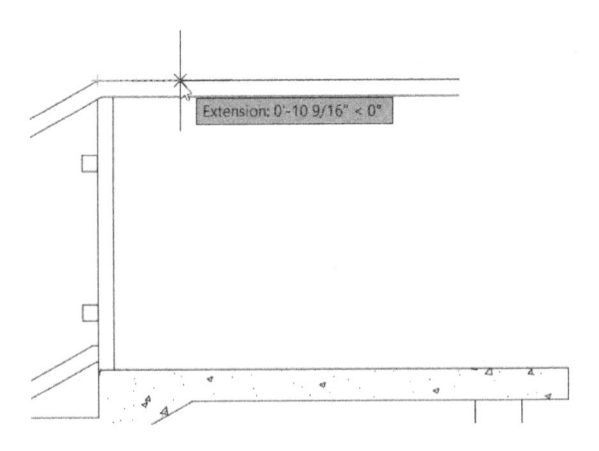

- Type 12 and press RETURN.
- Move the pointer downward and click.
- Click the **Trim** icon on the **Modify** panel.
- Trim the unwanted elements.

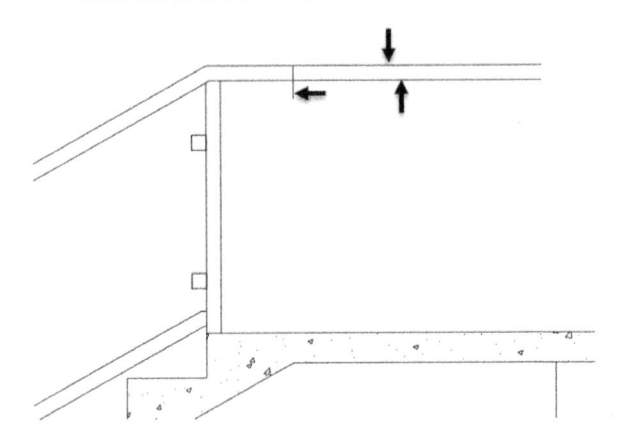

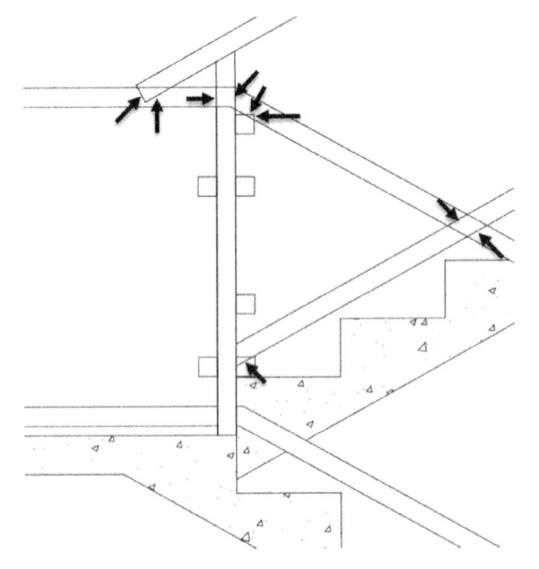

- On the **Drafting** tool set, click **Hatch** panel > **Hatch**.
- On the **Hatch** visor, click the **Pattern** drop-down > **Open Library**.

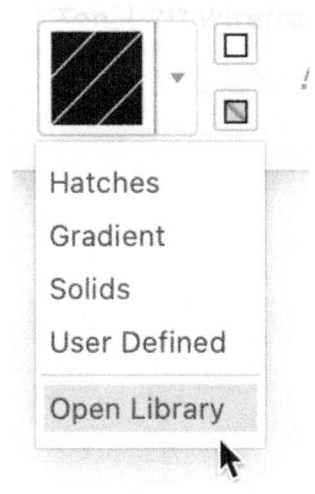

- Type GOS in the search bar and double-click on the **GOST-GLASS** pattern.

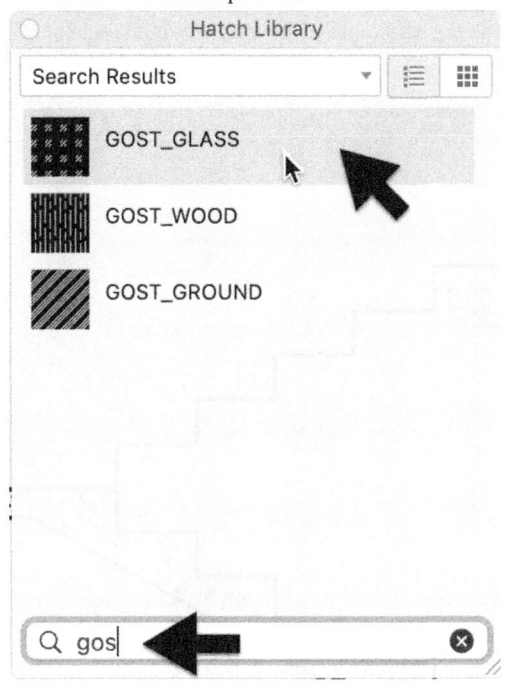

- Pick points in the areas, as shown.

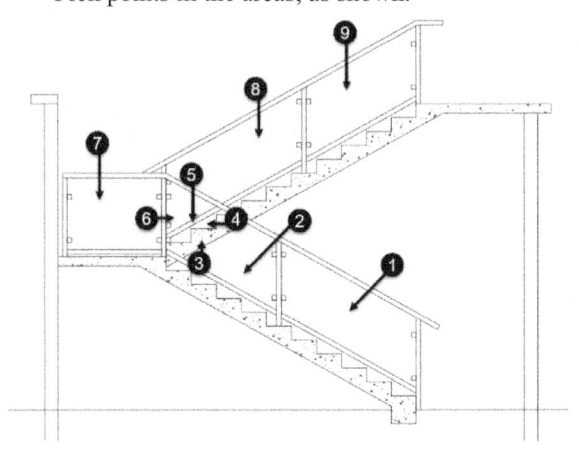

- Right click and select RETURN.

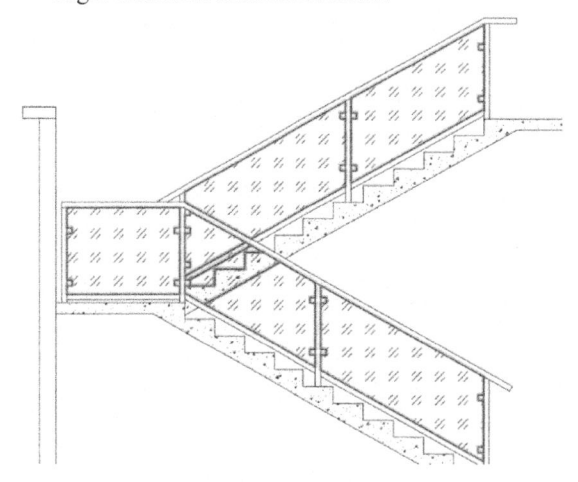

- Delete the construction lines, as shown.

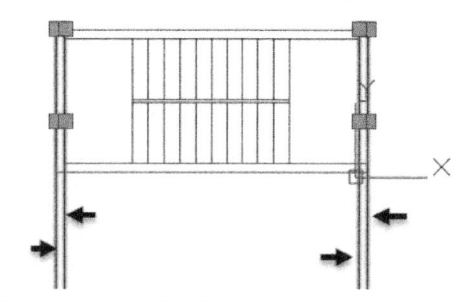

- Save and close the file.

Example 3

In this tutorial, you will create the elevation view using the floor plan.

- Download the Elevation_plan from the companion website and open it.
- Click the **Undock** icon on the **Layers** palette.
- Click the **New Layer** icon on the Layers palette.
- Type Elevation as the layer name.
- Double-click on the Elevation layer.

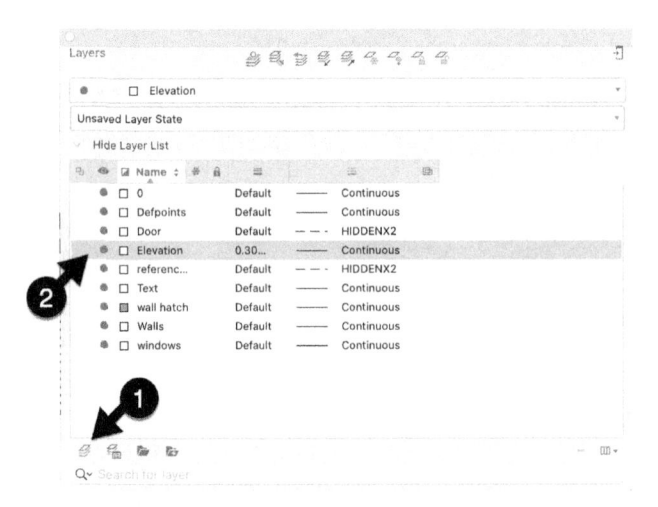

- Dock the **Layers** palette.
- Draw a horizontal line above the floor plan, as shown.

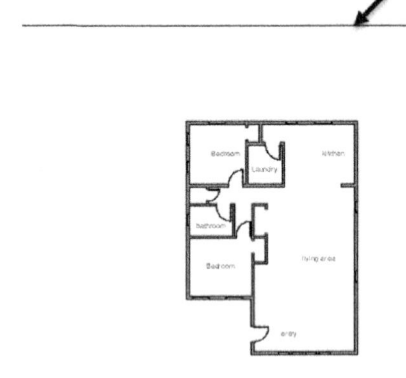

- On the **Drafting** tool set, click **Draw** panel > **Construction Line** > **Ray** tool.

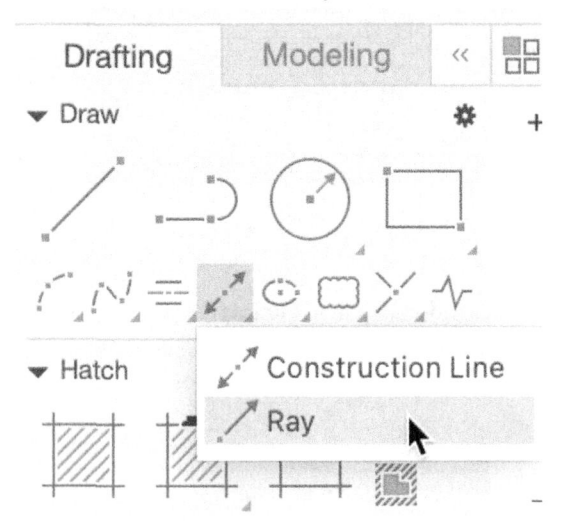

- Select the top-left corner of the floor plan.
- Move the pointer upward and click.

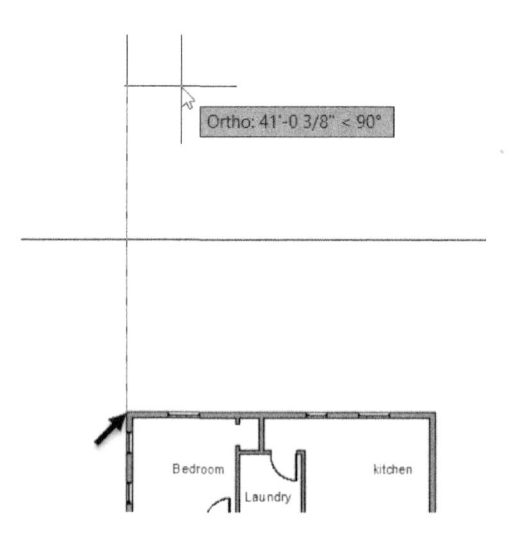

- Press RETURN twice.
- Select the top-right corner of the floor plan.
- Move the pointer upward and click.

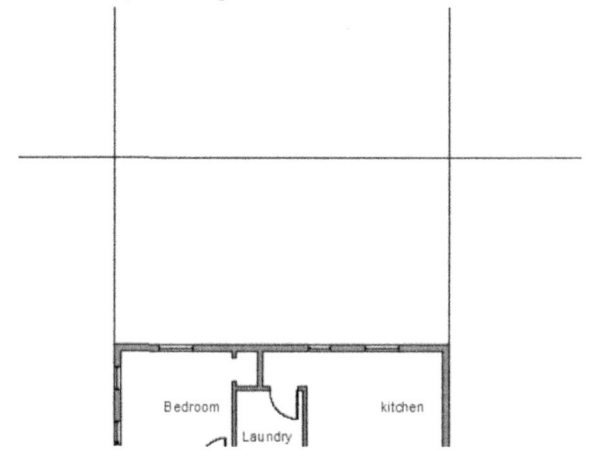

- Click the **Offset** tool on the **Modify** panel of the **Drafting** tool set.
- Type 6" and press RETURN.
- Select the horizontal line.
- Move the pointer upward and click to create an offset line.

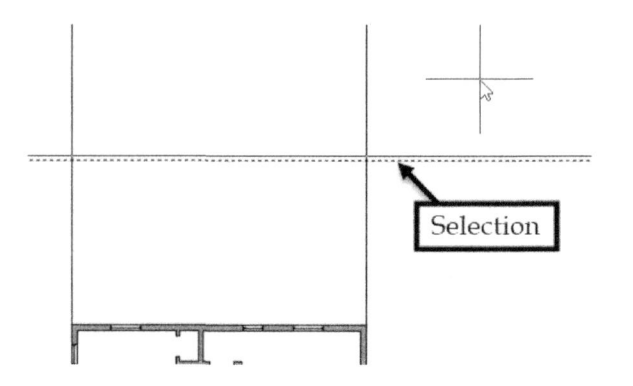

338 | Creating Architectural Drawings

- Press RETURN twice.
- Type 9' as the offset distance. Next, press RETURN.
- Select the offset line created previously.
- Move the pointer upward and click.

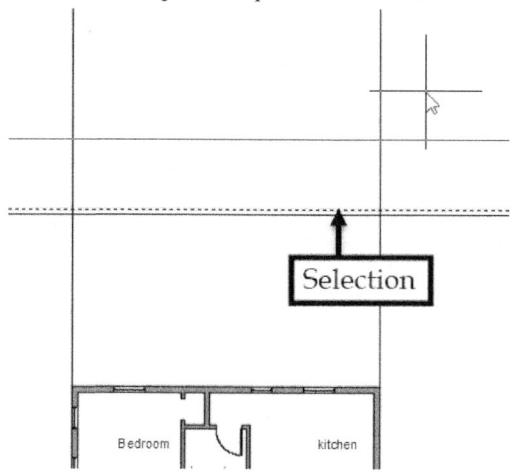

- Press RETURN twice.
- Type 10" as the offset distance. Next, press RETURN.
- Select the offset line created previously.
- Move the pointer upward and click.

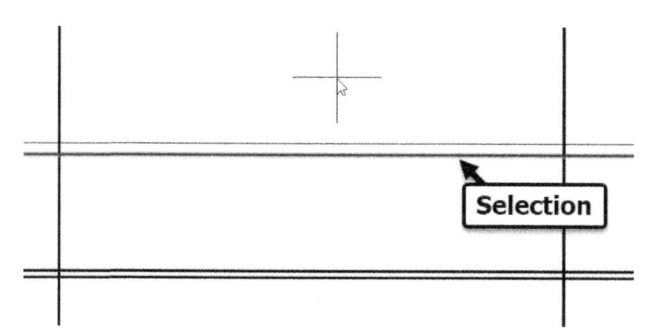

- Press RETURN twice.
- Type 6' as the offset distance. Next, press RETURN.
- Select the offset line created previously.
- Move the pointer upward and click.

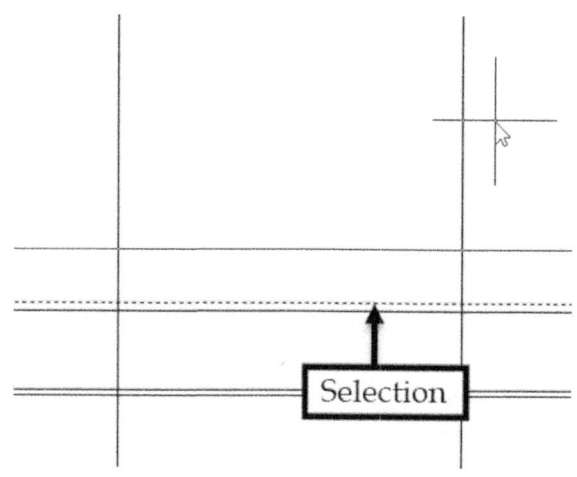

- On the **Drafting** tool set, click **Draw** panel > **Construction Line** tool.
- Right-click and select the **Offset** option.
- Type 16" as the offset distance. Next, press RETURN.
- Select the right exterior wall.
- Move the pointer toward right and click.
- Select the left exterior wall.
- Move the pointer toward the left and click.

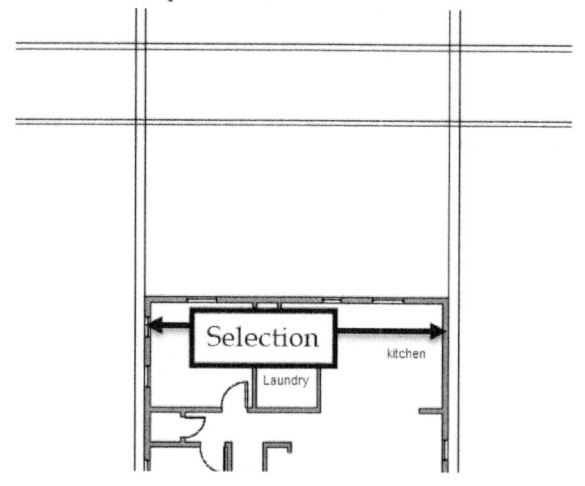

- Press RETURN twice.
- Right-click and select the **Ver** option.
- Select the corner point of the exterior wall, as shown.

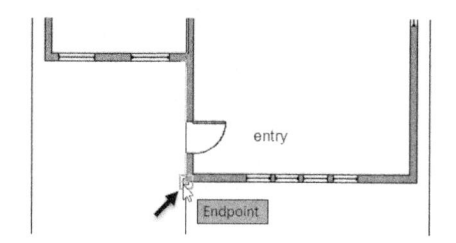

- Press RETURN twice.
- Right-click and select the **Offset** option.
- Type 16" as the offset distance. Next, press RETURN.
- Select the construction line created in the last step.
- Move the pointer toward the left and click.

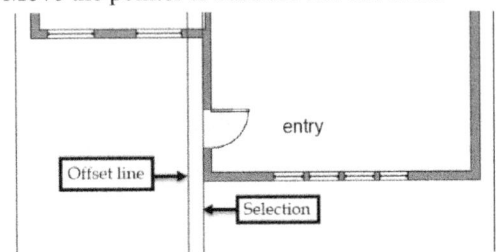

- On the **Drafting** tool set, click **Modify** panel > **Break at Point** tool.

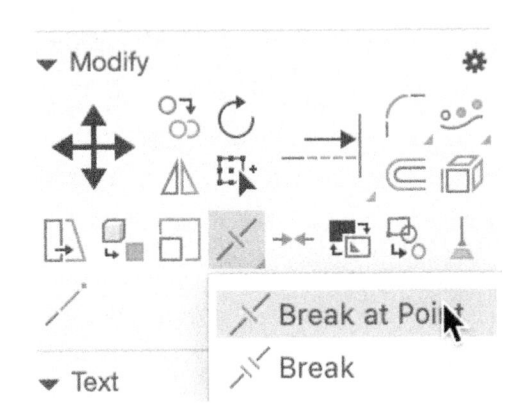

- Select the horizontal line, as shown.

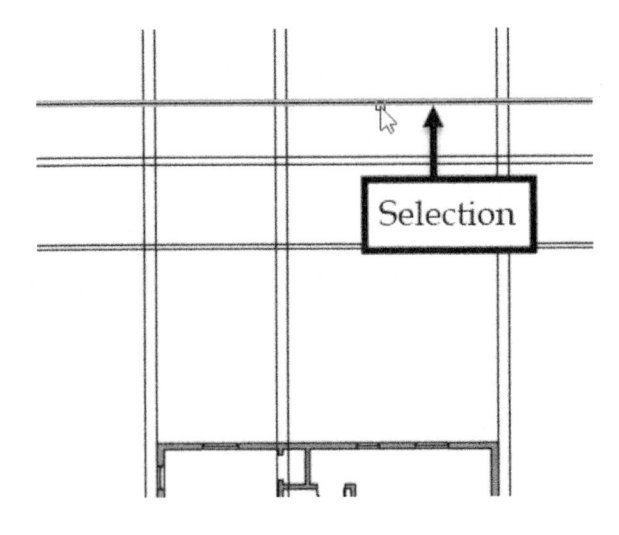

- Select the intersection point between the horizontal and vertical lines, as shown.

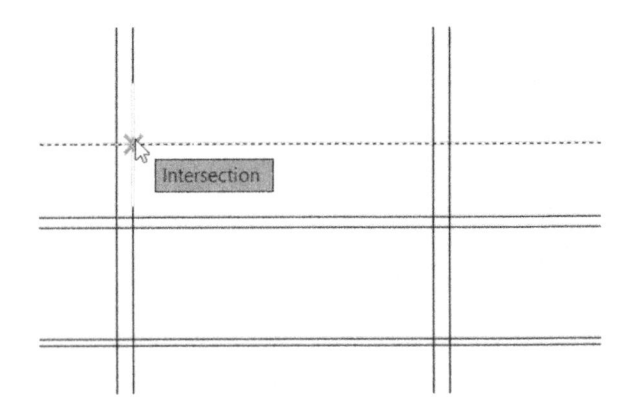

- Press RETURN to activate the **Break at Point** tool.
- Select the right portion of the broken line.
- Select the intersection point between the horizontal and vertical lines, as shown.

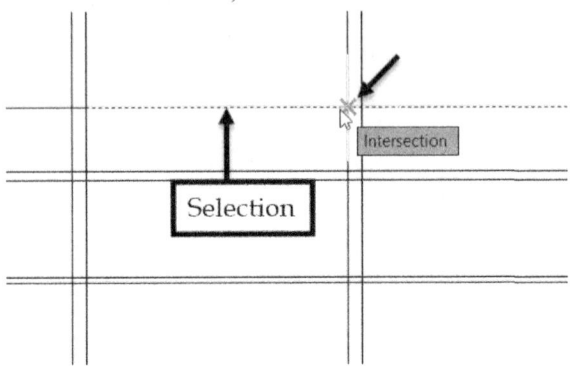

- Click the **Line** tool on the **Draw** panel of the **Drafting** tool set.
- Select the midpoint of the broken line, as shown.

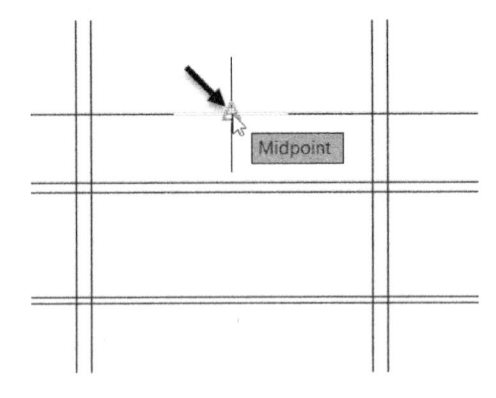

- Select the intersection point between the horizontal and vertical lines, as shown.

340 | Creating Architectural Drawings

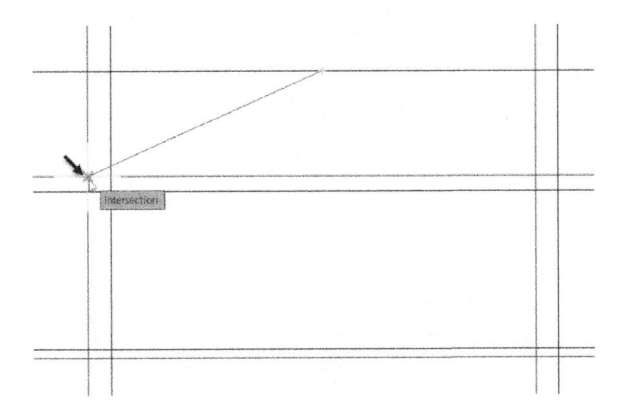

- Press RETURN twice.
- Select the start point of the line created in the last step.
- Select the intersection point between the horizontal and vertical lines, as shown.

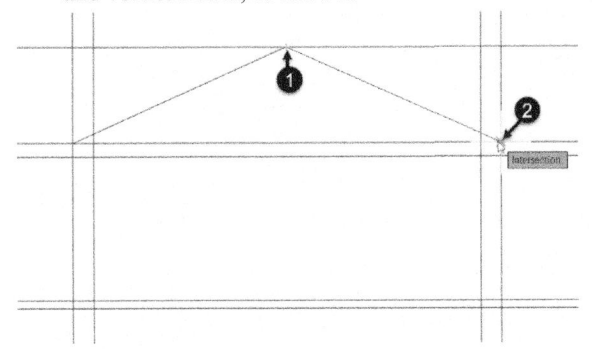

- Click the **Trim** tool on the **Modify** panel of the **Drafting** tool set.
- Select the portions of the vertical lines, as shown.

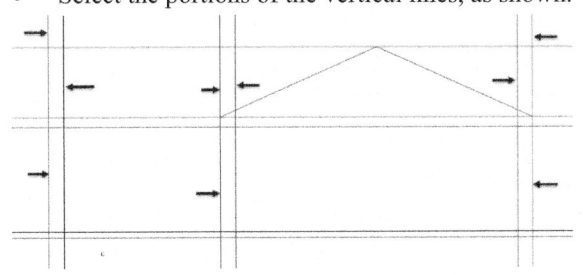

- Click and drag the mouse pointer across the vertical lines, as shown.

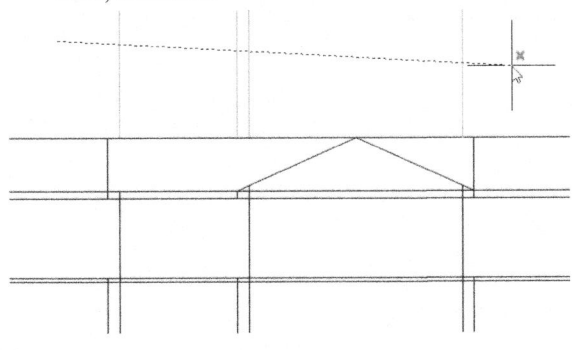

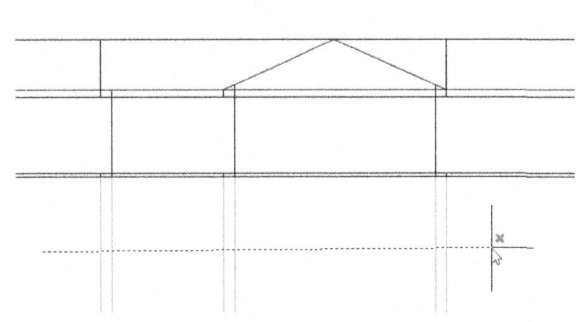

- Trim the horizontal and vertical lines, as shown.

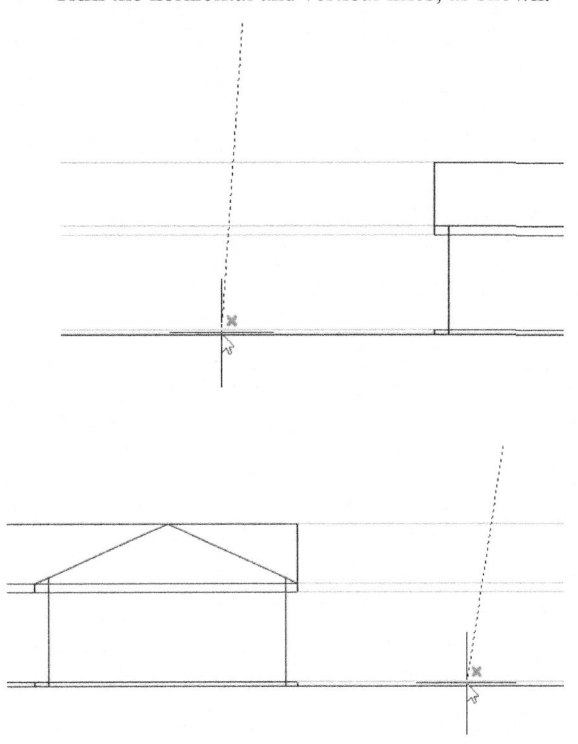

- Trim the small portions, as shown.

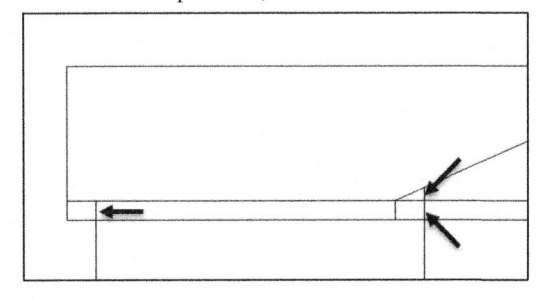

341 | **Creating Architectural Drawings**

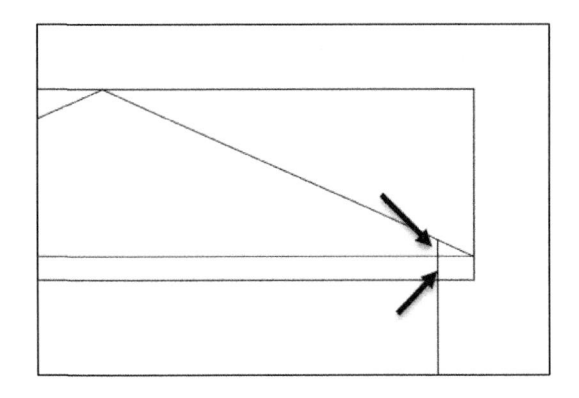

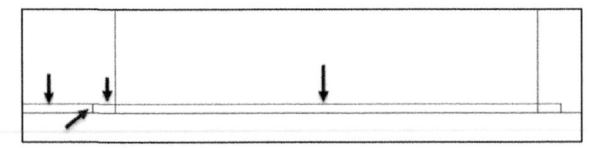

- Press Esc.
- Select the inclined line, as shown. 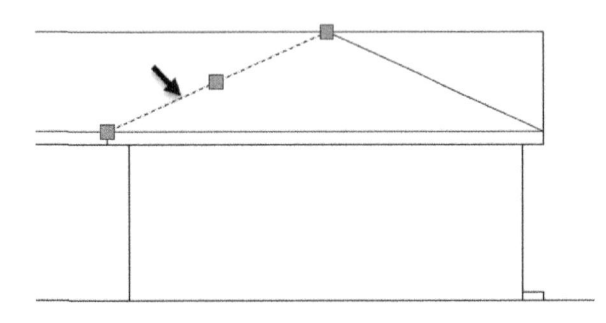
- Click the **Copy** tool on the **Modify** panel of the **Drafting** tool set.
- Specify the base point, as shown.
- Move the pointer downward and select the intersection point, as shown. 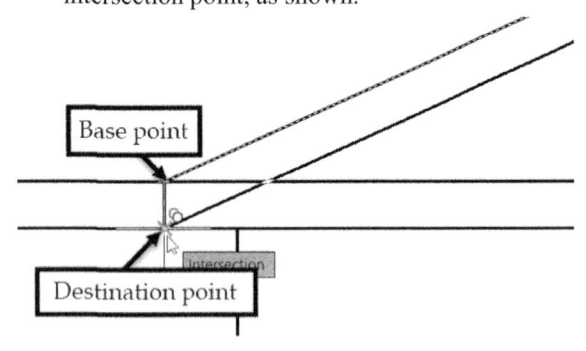
- Press Esc.
- Likewise, copy the other inclined line, as shown.

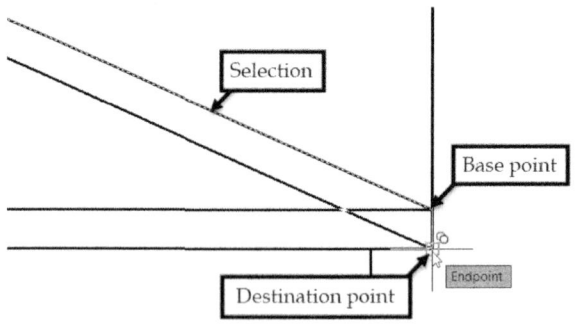

- Click the **Trim** tool on the **Modify** panel of the **Drafting** tool set.
- Select the portions of the horizontal line, as shown.

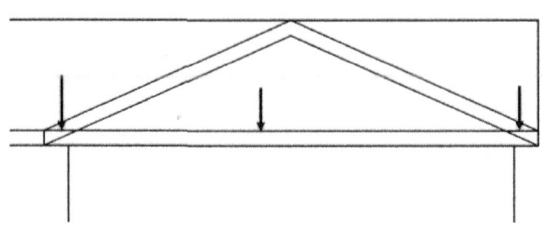

- On the **Drafting** tool set, click **Modify** panel > **Break at Point** tool.
- Select the horizontal line, as shown.
- Select the intersection point, as shown.

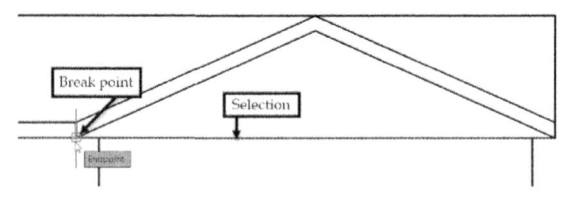

- On the **Drafting** tool set, click **Modify** panel > **Break at Point** tool.
- Select the vertical line, as shown.
- Select the intersection point, as shown.

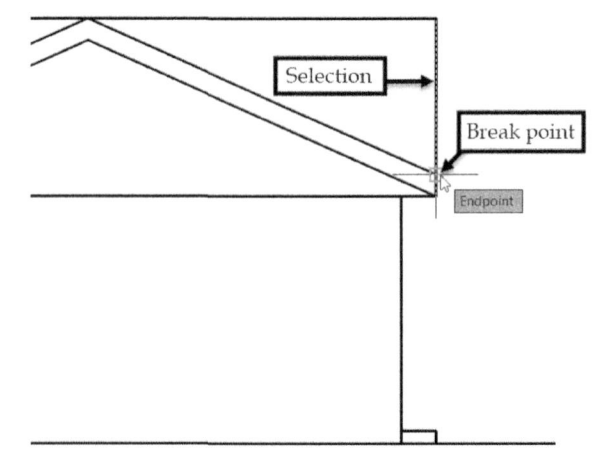

- On the **Drafting** tool set, click **Modify** panel > **Break at Point** tool.
- Select the vertical line, as shown.
- Select the intersection point, as shown.

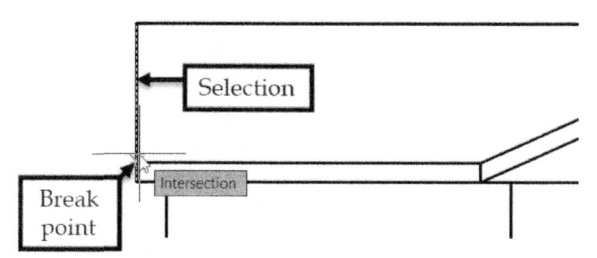

- Select the horizontal line, as shown.
- Press Delete.

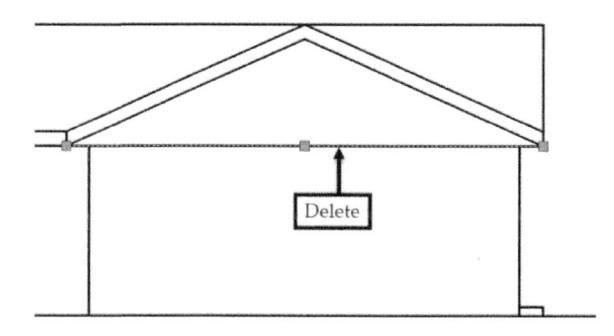

- Click the **Trim** drop-down > **Extend** on the **Modify** panel of the **Drafting** tool set.
- Select the two vertical lines, as shown.

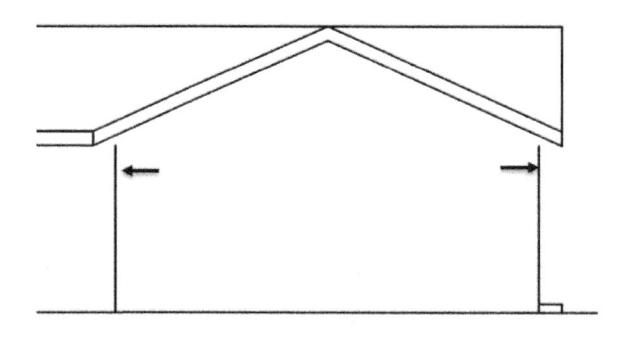

- Create a horizontal line connecting the endpoints of the two vertical lines.

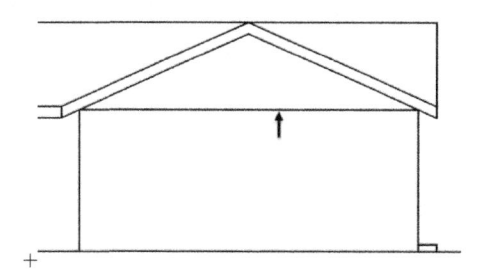

- Select the two construction lines, as shown.

- Press Delete.

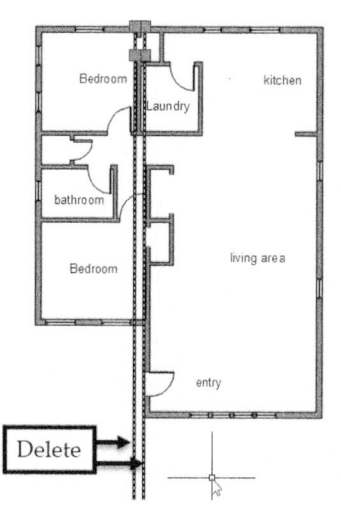

- On the **Drafting** tool set, click **Draw** panel > **Construction Line** tool.
- Right-click and select the **Ver** option.
- Zoom to the lower portion of the floor plan and select the vertex points on the window, as shown.

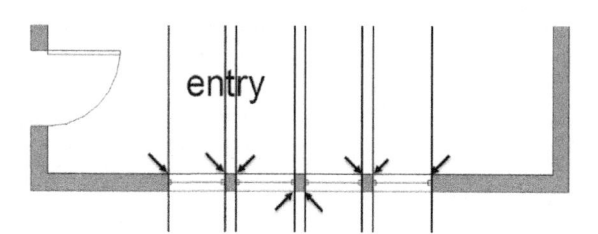

- Click the **Offset** tool on the **Modify** panel of the **Drafting** tool set.
- Type 3' as the offset distance. Next, press RETURN.
- Select the horizontal line, as shown.
- Move the pointer upward and click.

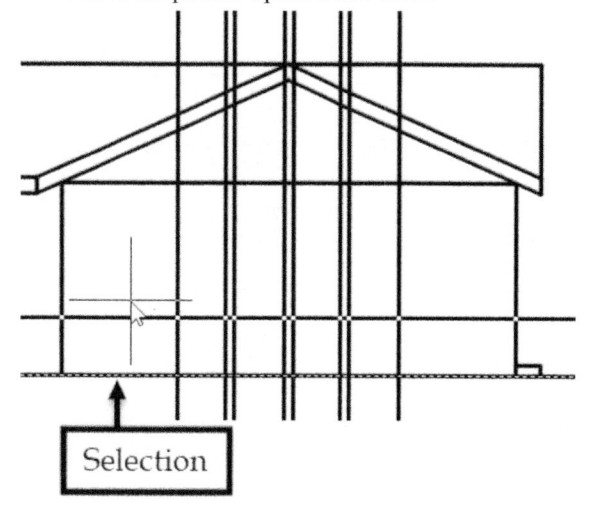

- Click the **Rectangle** tool on the **Draw** panel of the **Drafting** tool set.

- Select the intersection point, as shown.

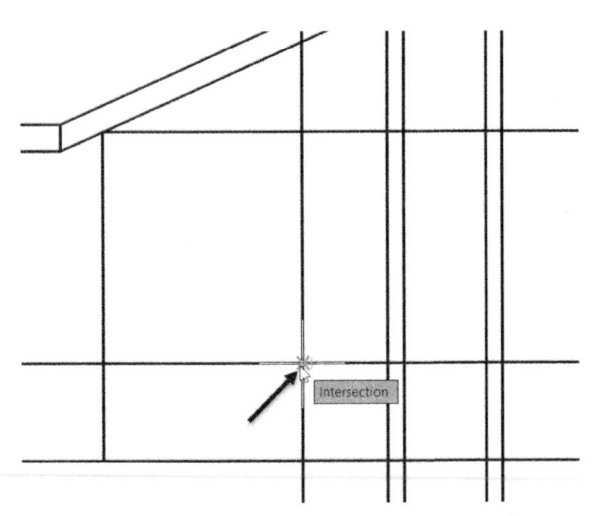

- Right-click and select the **Dimensions** option.
- Select the two intersection points, as shown.

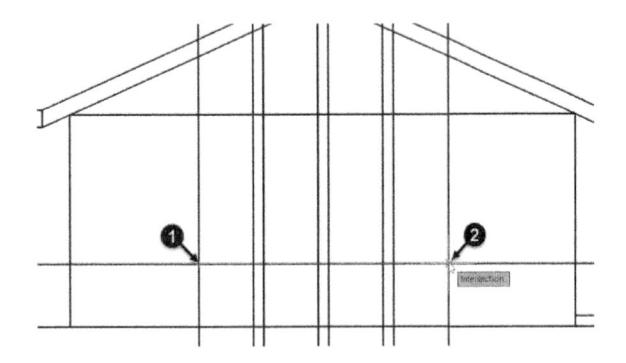

- Type 54 as the rectangle width and press RETURN.
- Move the pointer upward and click.

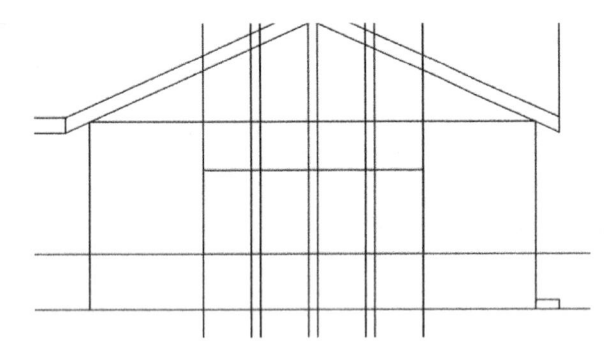

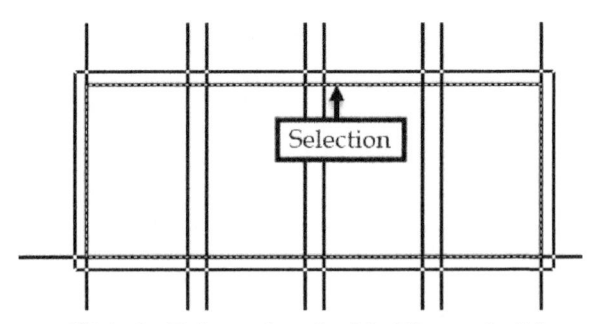

- Click the **Trim** tool on the **Modify** panel of the **Drafting** tool set.
- Click and drag the pointer across the vertical lines, as shown.

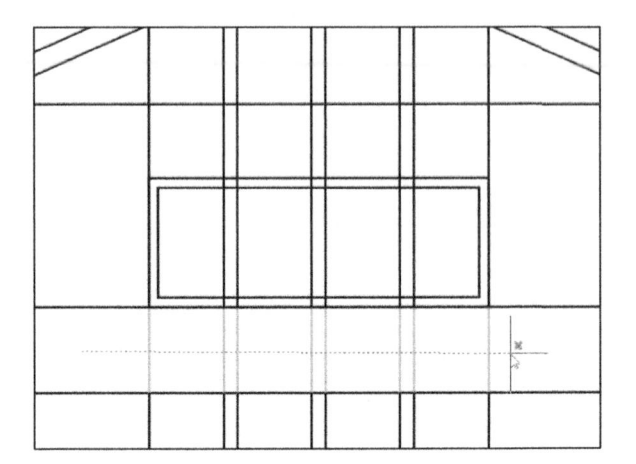

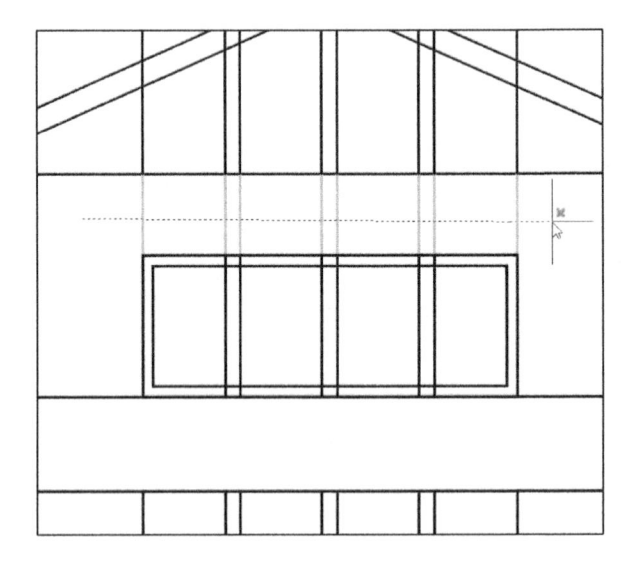

- Click the **Offset** tool on the **Modify** panel of the **Drafting** tool set.
- Type 4" as the offset distance. Next, press RETURN.
- Select the rectangle.
- Move the pointer outward and click.

344 | Creating Architectural Drawings

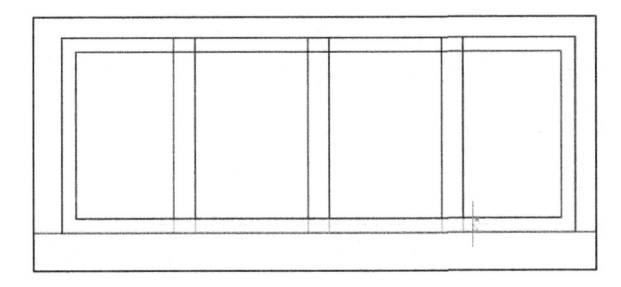

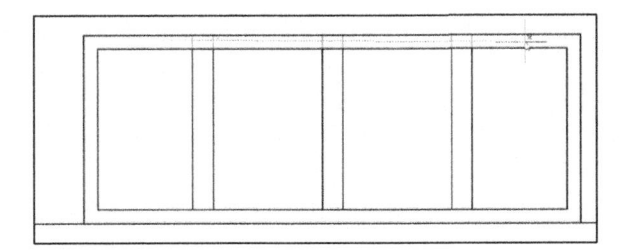

- Select the **Mid between 2 Points** option.
- Select the two points, as shown.
- Move the pointer downward and click.

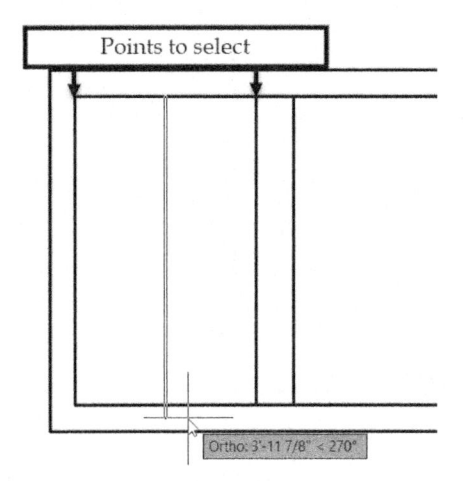

- Press RETURN.
- Select the vertical and horizontal construction lines, and then press Delete.

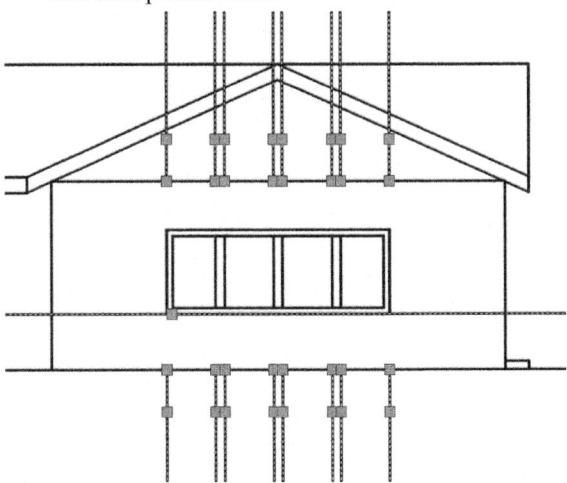

- Press RETURN twice.
- Select the midpoint of the vertical line, as shown.

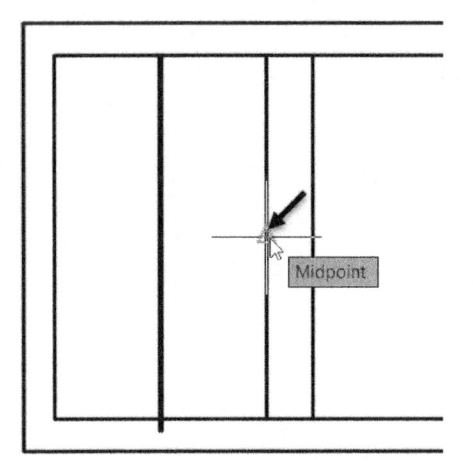

- Select the two rectangles and click the **Explode** tool on the **Modify** panel of the **Drafting** tool set.

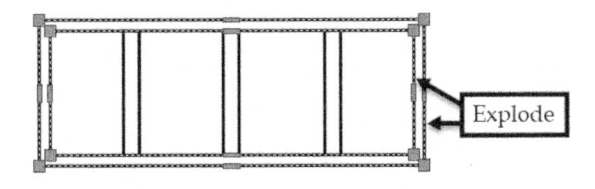

- Move the pointer toward the left and select the midpoint of the vertical line.

- Type **MLINE** in the command line and press RETURN.
- Right-click and select the **Justification** option.
- Right-click and select the **Zero** option.
- Right-click and select the **Scale** option.
- Type 0.25 and press RETURN.
- Press and hold the Shift key, and then right click.

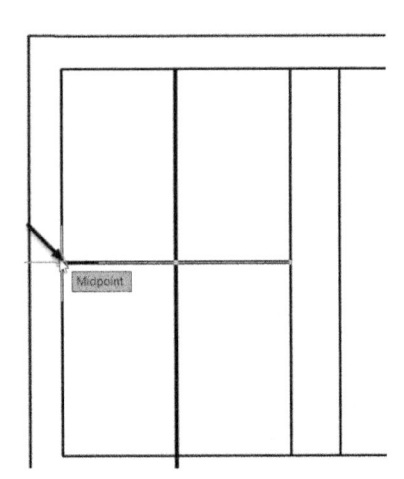

- Press Esc.
- Type **MLEDIT** in the command line and press RETURN.
- Right-click and select **OC**.
- Select the two multilines; the open cross is created at the intersection of the two multilines.

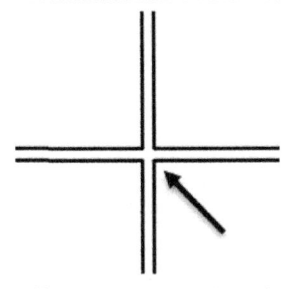

- Click the **Trim** tool on the **Modify** panel of the **Drafting** tool set.
- Click and drag the pointer across the unwanted portions of the multilines, as shown.

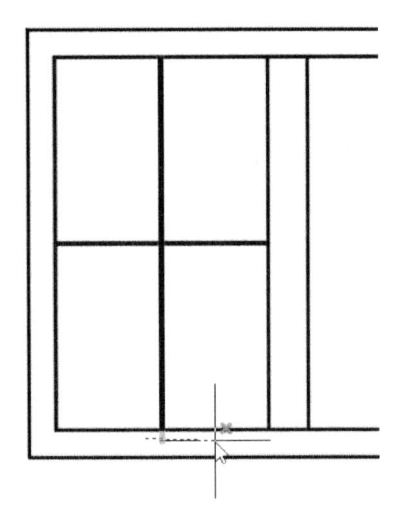

- Click the **Copy** tool on the **Modify** panel of the **Drafting** tool set.

- Select the two multilines and press RETURN.
- Select the lower-left corner point.
- Move the pointer toward right and select the corner point, as shown.

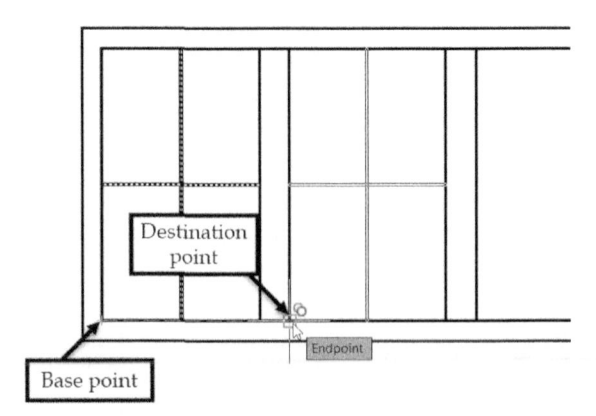

- Likewise, create two more copies of the multi-lines, as shown.

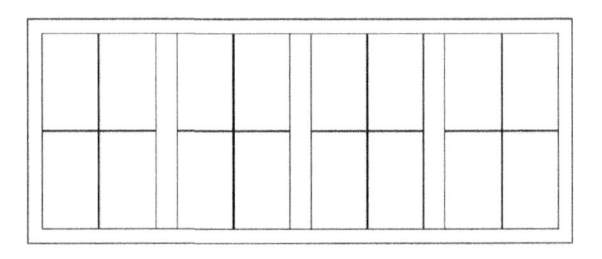

- Likewise, create two windows on the left side.

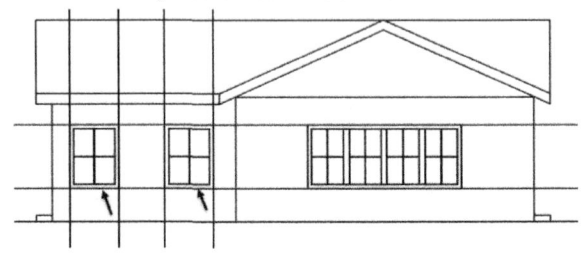

- Delete the construction lines.

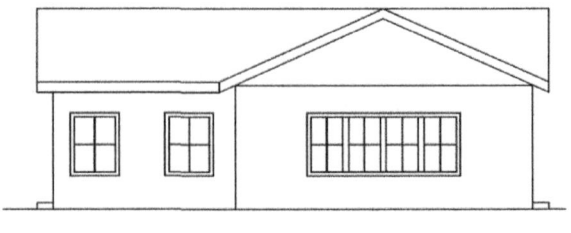

- Click the **Hatch** tool on the **Hatch** panel of the **Drafting** tool set.
- On the **Hatch** visor, click **Pattern** drop-down > **Open Library**.
- Type **AR** in the search bar, and then double-click on the **AR-RSHKE** pattern.

346 | Creating Architectural Drawings

AutoCAD 2023 For Beginners (For Mac Users)

- Click in the regions, as shown.

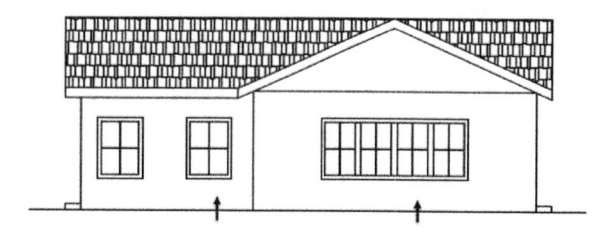

- Press RETURN twice.
- On the **Hatch** visor, click **Pattern** drop-down > **Open Library**.
- Type **ANSI** in the search bar, and then double-click on the **ANSI31** pattern.
- On the **Hatch** visor, enter **135** and **50** in the **Hatch angle** and **Hatch pattern scale** boxes, respectively.

- Click in the region, as shown.

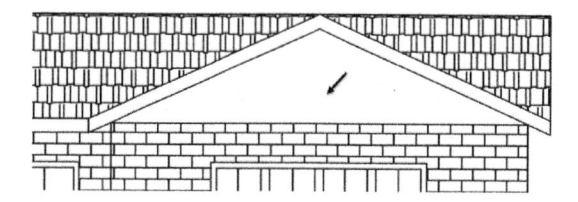

- Press RETURN.
- Save and close the file.

- Click in the regions, as shown.

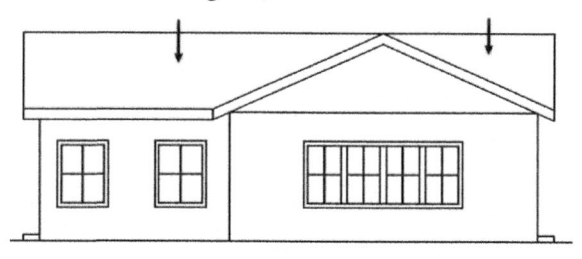

- Press RETURN twice.
- On the **Hatch** visor, click **Pattern** drop-down > **Open Library**.
- Type **AR** in the search bar, and then double-click on the **AR-B816** pattern.

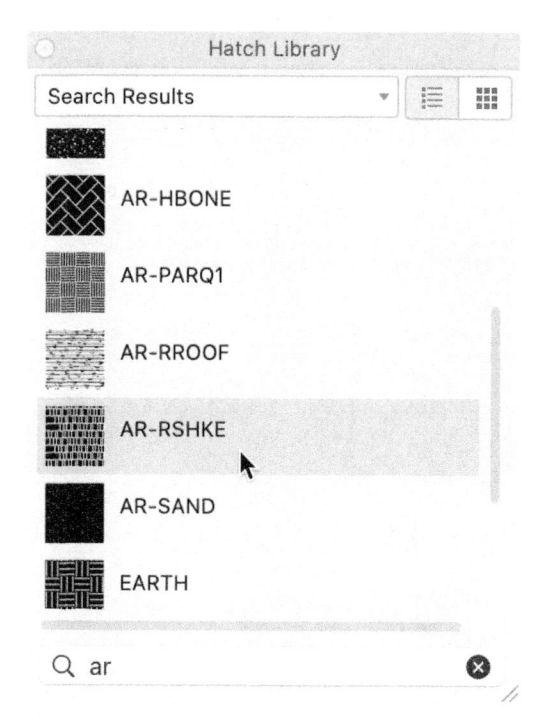

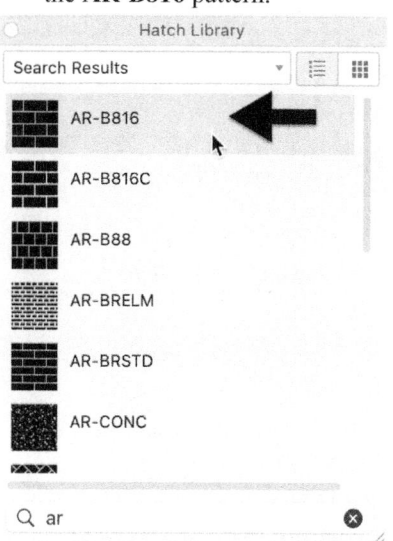

Example 4

In this tutorial, you will create the Roof plan using the floor plan.

347 Creating Architectural Drawings

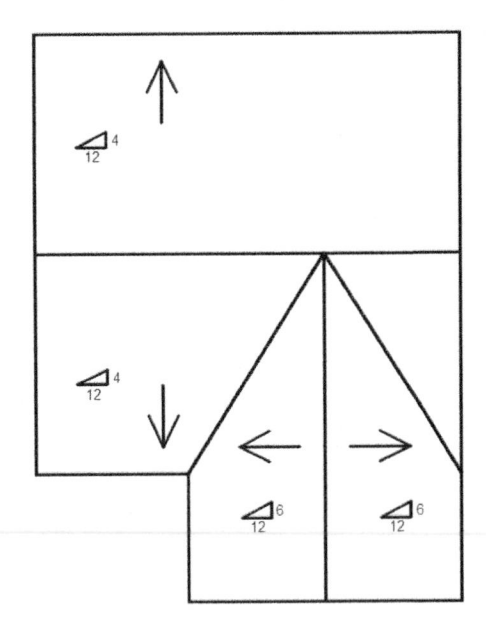

- Download the Floor_plan.dwg from the companion website.
- Start a new drawing using the acad.dwt template.
- Click the **Reference Manager** tab on the palettes.
- Click the **Attach References** tool on the **Reference Manager** palette.
- Go to the location of the Floor_plan.dwg file and double-click on it.
- Click **OK** on the **Attach External Reference** dialog.
- Click in the graphics window.
- Click **View > Zoom > All** on the menu bar.
- Click the **Polyline** tool on the **Draw** panel of the **Drafting** tool set.
- Select the corner points of the floor plan.

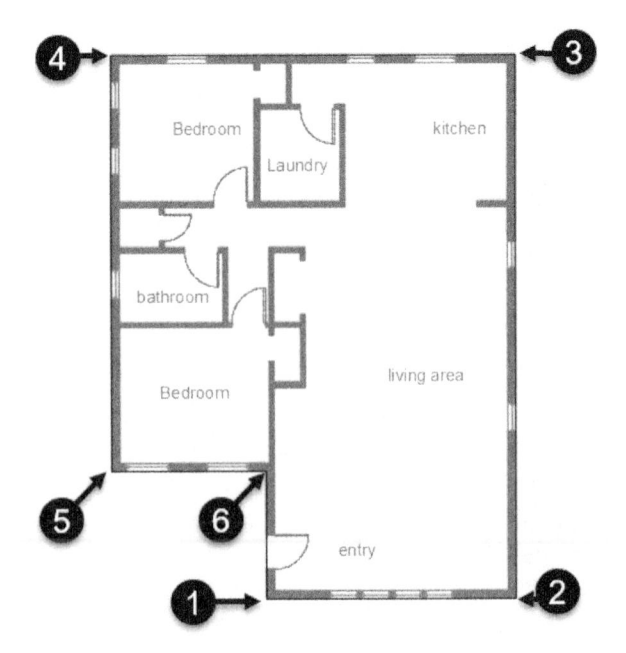

- Right-click and select the **Close** option.
- Click the **Offset** tool on the **Modify** panel of the **Drafting** tool set.
- Type 16 and press RETURN.
- Select the newly created polyline.
- Move the pointer outward and click.

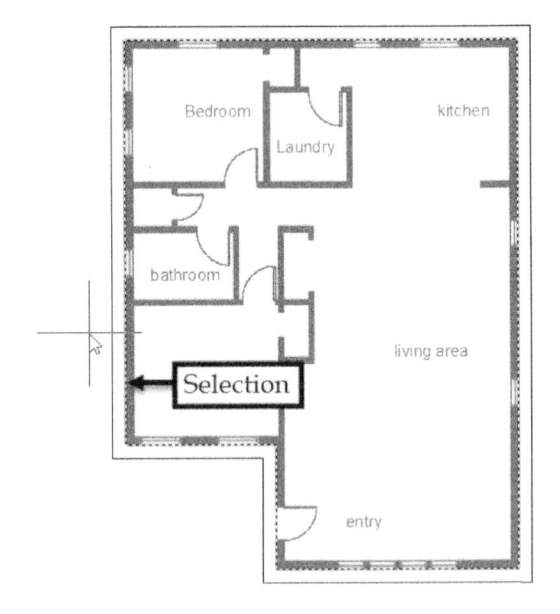

- Click the **Erase** tool on the **Modify** panel of the **Drafting** tool set.
- Select the polyline used to create the offset.

Creating Architectural Drawings

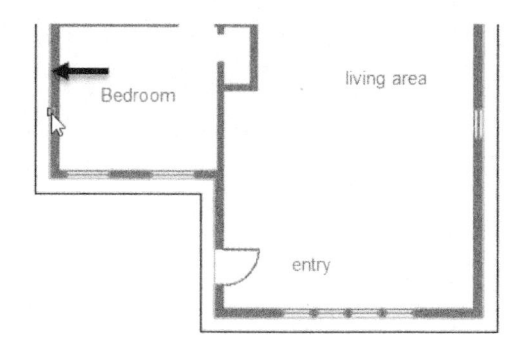

- Press RETURN.
- Click the **Line** tool on the **Draw** panel of the **Drafting** tool set.
- Select the midpoint of the left vertical line.

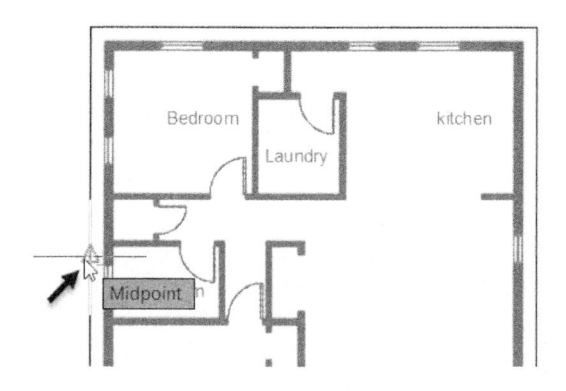

- Make sure the **Ortho Mode** icon is active on the status bar.
- Move the pointer toward right and click.

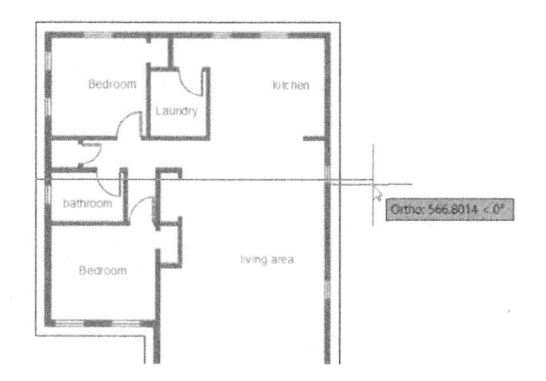

- Press RETURN twice.
- Select the midpoint of the lower horizontal line, as shown.

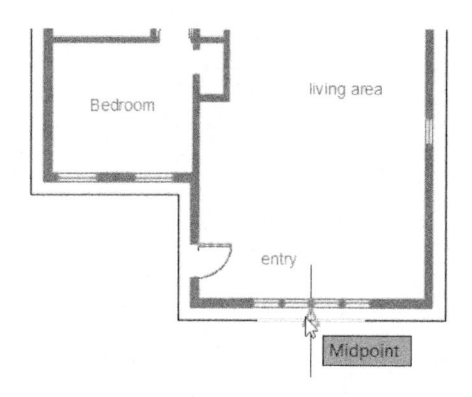

- Move the pointer upward and click.

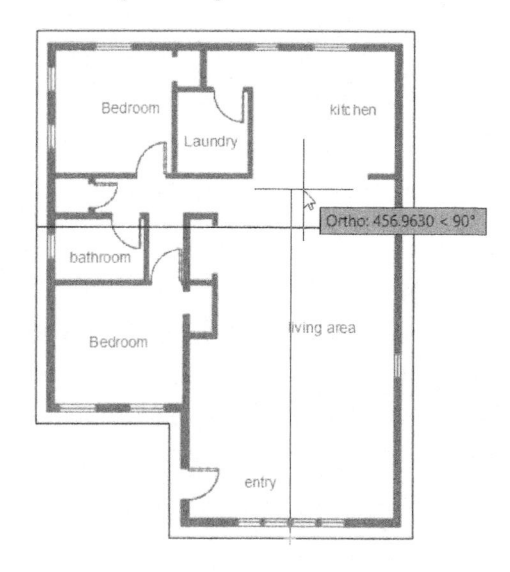

- Click the **Trim** tool on the **Modify** panel of the **Drafting** tool set.
- Select the unwanted portions of the lines, as shown.

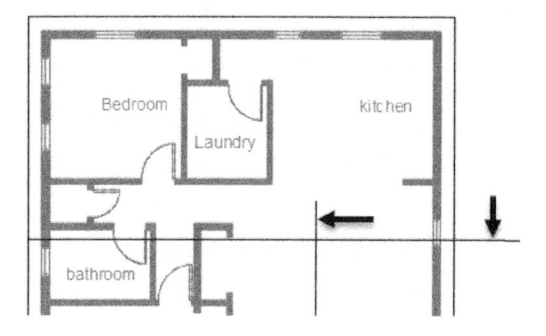

- Click the **Line** tool on the **Draw** panel of the **Drafting** tool set.
- Select the corner point of the polyline.
- Select the intersection point of the vertical and horizontal lines.

349 | Creating Architectural Drawings

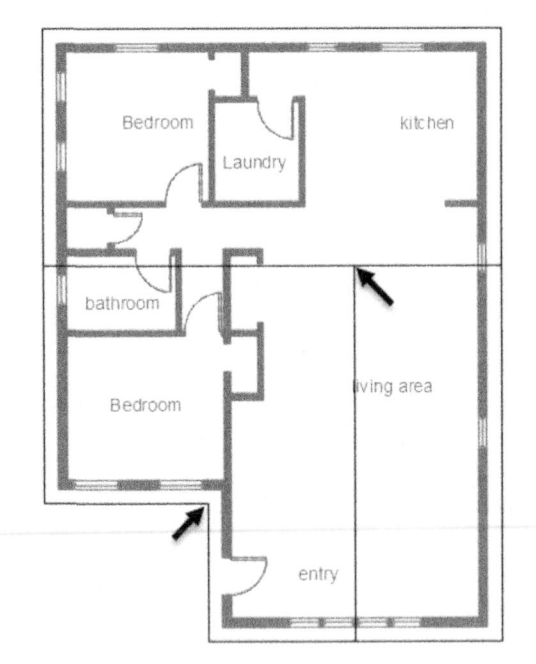

- Press Esc.
- Select the inclined line.
- Click the **Mirror** tool on the **Modify** panel of the **Drafting** tool set.
- Select the endpoints of the vertical line.
- Right-click and select the **No** option.

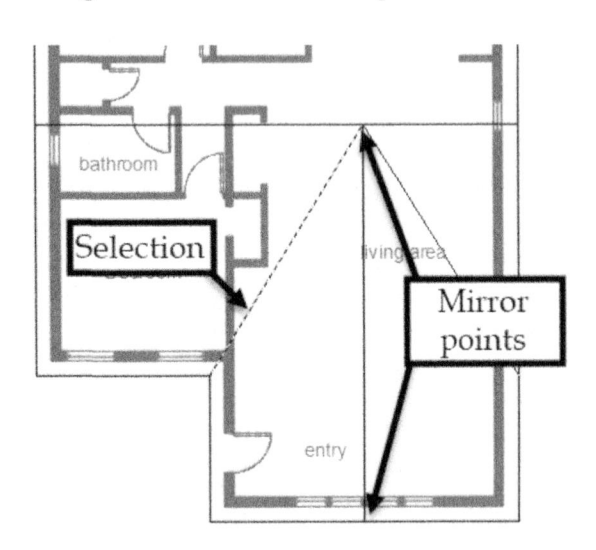

- Select the attachment.
- Click on the origin point of the attachment, and then move the pointer upward.

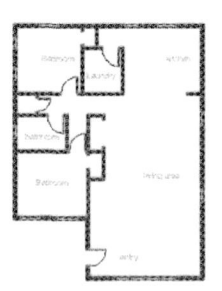

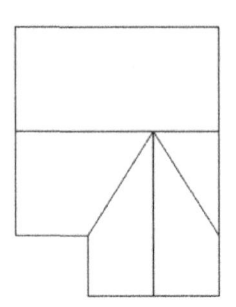

- Click the **Line** tool on the **Draw** panel of the **Drafting** tool set.
- Click in the graphics window.
- Move the pointer toward the right.
- Type 36 and press RETURN.
- Move the pointer upward.
- Type 18 and press RETURN.

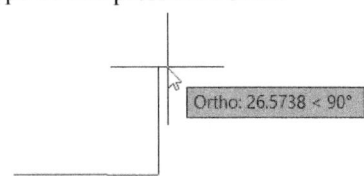

- Select the start point of the horizontal line.

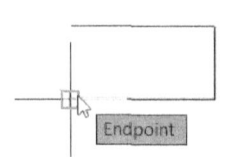

- Press ESC.

350 | Creating Architectural Drawings

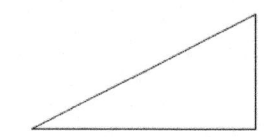

- Click the **Single Line Text** on the **Text** panel of the **Drafting** tool set.

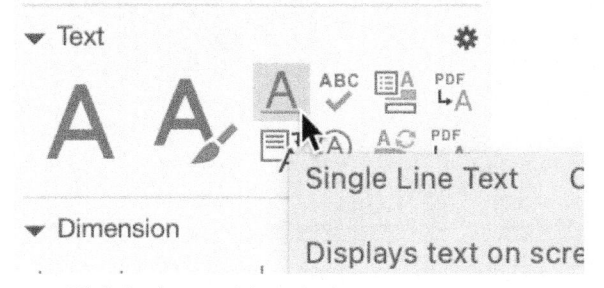

- Click in the graphics window.
- Type **12** as the text height. Next, press RETURN.
- Type 0 as the rotation angle, and then press RETURN.
- Type 4 and click in the graphics window.
- Type 12 and click in the graphics window.
- Press ESC.
- Position the texts at the locations, as shown.

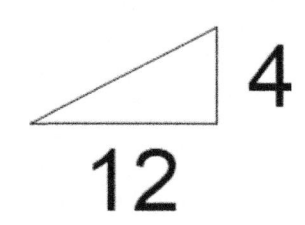

- Create a selection window across the triangle and the texts.
- Click the **Copy** tool on the **Modify** panel of the **Drafting** tool set.
- Select the base point, as shown.

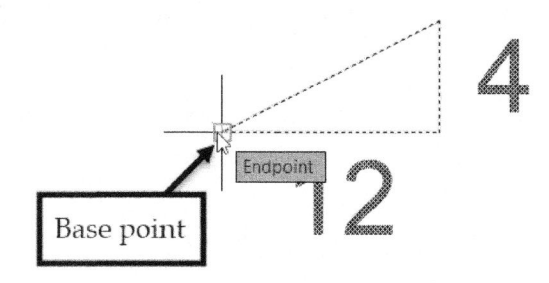

- Place the copies at the locations, as shown.

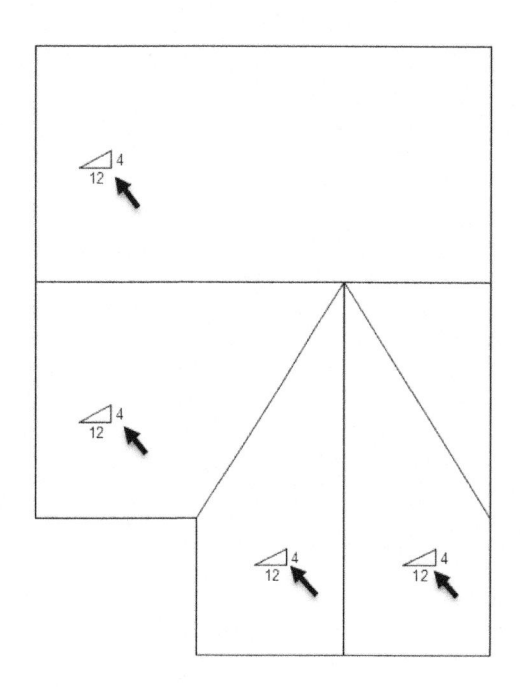

- Zoom the lower portion of the drawing.
- Double-click on 4.
- Type 6 and click in the graphics window.
- Likewise, change the text on the right side to 6.

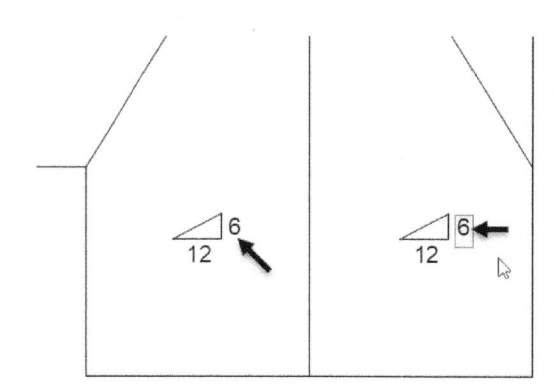

- Press ESC.
- Click the **Rectangle** tool on the **Draw** panel of the **Drafting** tool set.
- Click at the location, as shown.
- Right-click and select the **Dimensions** option.
- Type 36 and press RETURN.
- Type 72 and press RETURN.
- Move the pointer downward and click.

351 | Creating Architectural Drawings

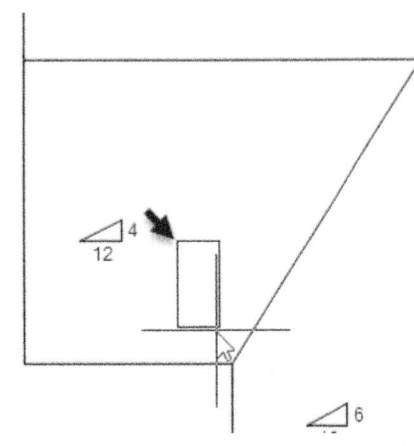

- Click the **Line** tool on the **Draw** panel of the **Drafting** tool set.
- Select the midpoints of the horizontal edges of the rectangle. 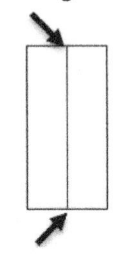
- Press RETURN twice.
- Select the midpoint of the left vertical edge of the rectangle.
- Select the lower endpoint of the vertical line.
- Select the midpoint of the right vertical edge of the rectangle. 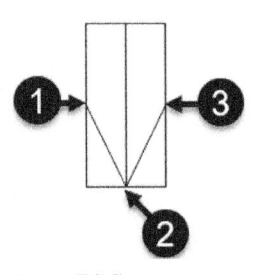
- Press ESC.
- Select the rectangle and press Delete.

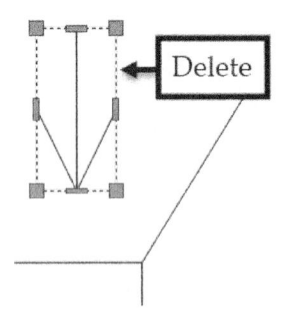

- Create a selection window across all the elements of the arrow.
- Click the **Mirror** tool on the **Modify** panel of the **Drafting** tool set.
- Select the endpoints of the horizontal line to define the mirror line.
- Right-click and select **NO**. 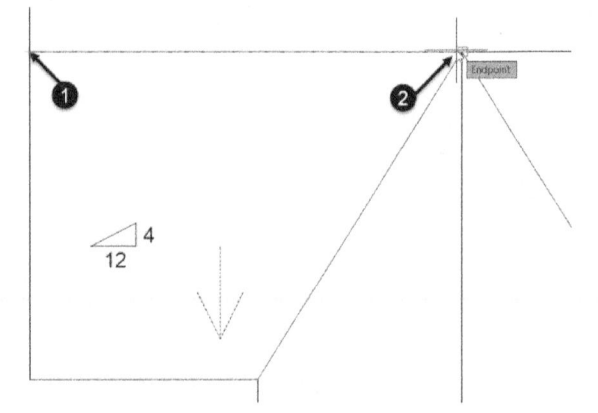
- Create a selection window across all the elements of the arrow.
- Click the **Rotate** tool on the **Modify** panel of the **Drafting** tool set.
- Select the base point, as shown.
- Right-click and select the **Copy** option. 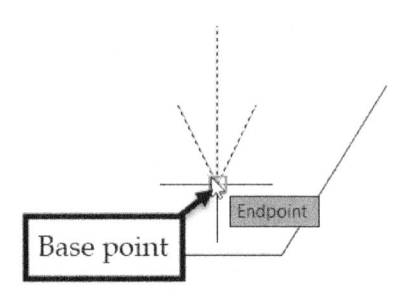
- Move the pointer vertically downward and click.
- Select the elements of the rotated arrow.

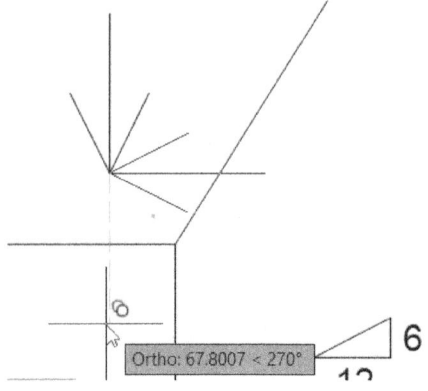

- Click the **Move** tool on the **Modify** panel of the **Drafting** tool set.
- Select the base point, as shown. 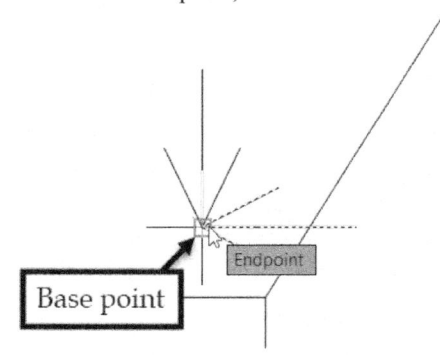
- Move the pointer toward right and click. 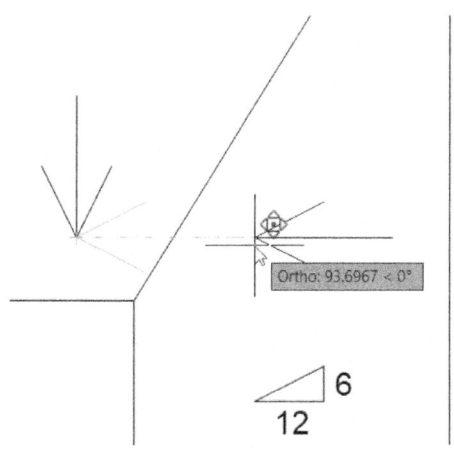
- Select the elements of the arrow moved in the previous step.
- Click the **Mirror** tool on the **Modify** panel of the **Drafting** tool set.
- Select the endpoints of the vertical line, as shown. 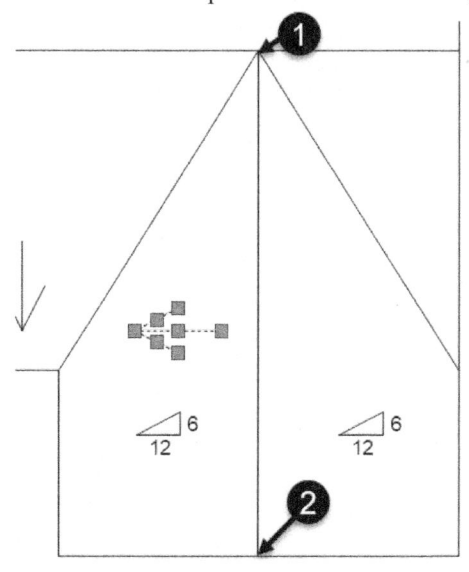
- Right-click and select **No**.
- Save and close the drawing file.

Example 5

In this tutorial, you will create the Roof and wall detail.

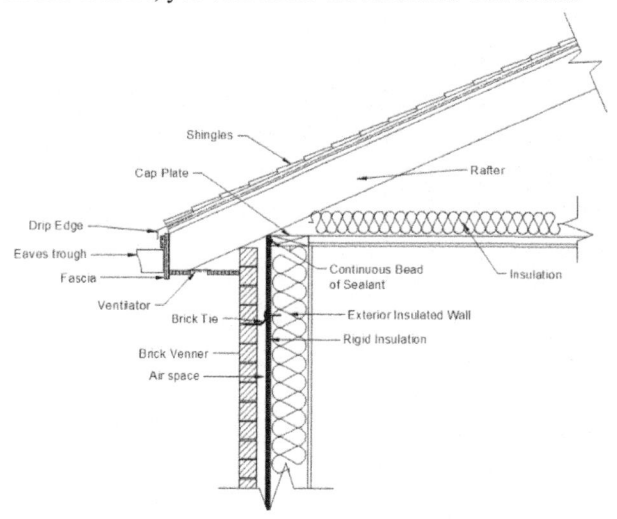

- Download the Roof_&_wall_detail.dwg file and open it.
- Click the **Undock** button on the **Layers** palette.
- Create a new layer and name it as Roof_wall_detail.
- Make the new layer are current.
- Click the Dock button on the **Layers** palette. 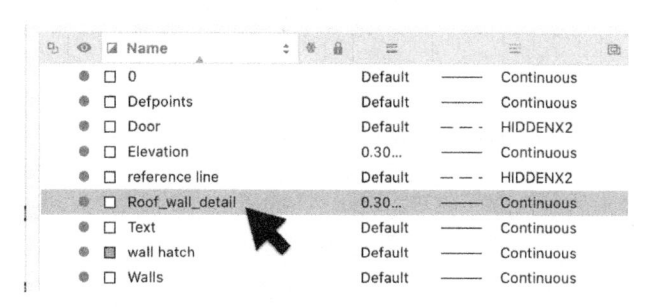
- On the **Drafting** tool set, click **Draw** panel > **Construction Line** drop-down > **Ray** tool.
- Create the projection lines from the elevation view, as shown.

353 | Creating Architectural Drawings

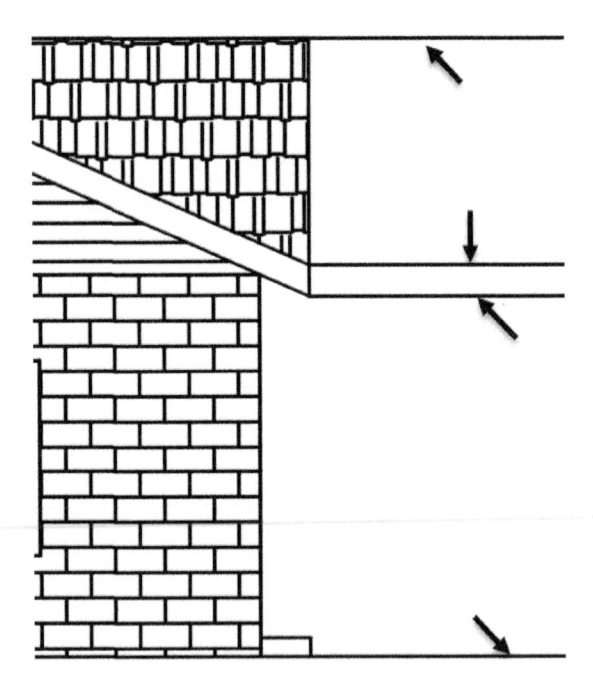

- Create a vertical line, as shown.

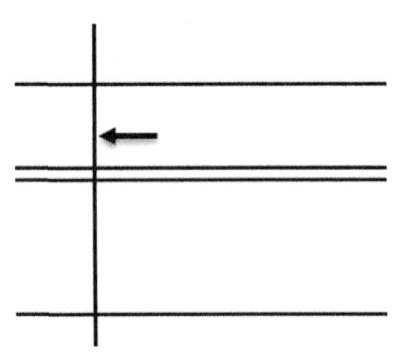

- Select the two inclined lines of the roof, as shown.
- Select the two vertical lines, as shown.

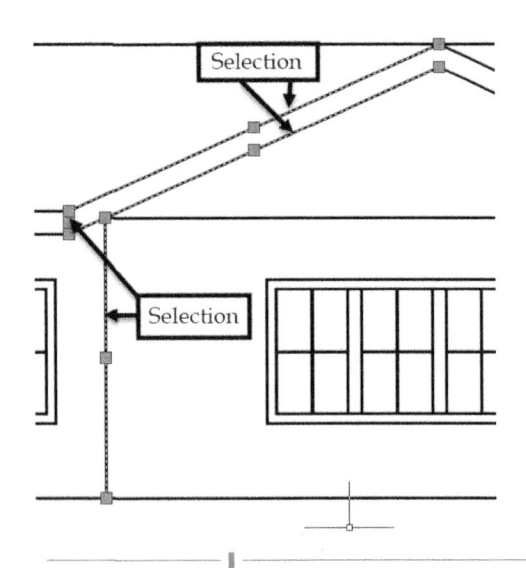

- Click the **Copy** tool on the **Modify** panel of the **Drafting** tool set.
- Select the base point, as shown.

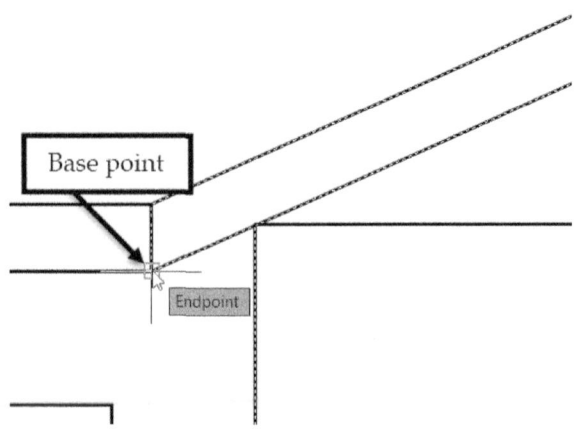

- Move the pointer toward right and select the intersection point, as shown.

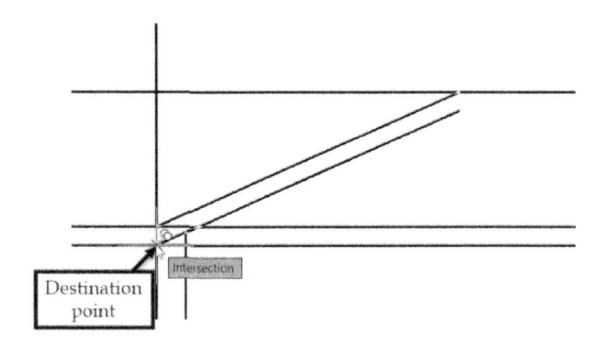

- Delete the reference lines, as shown.

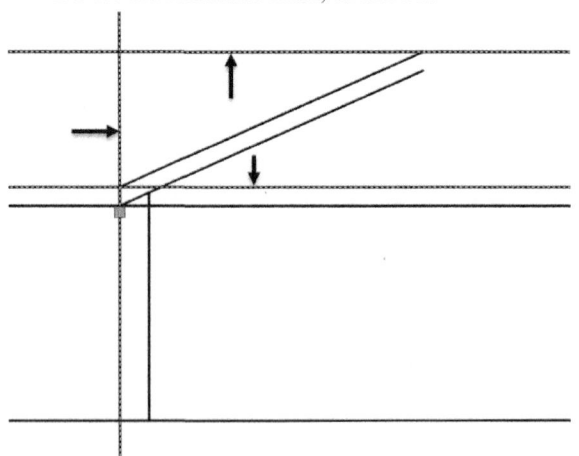

- Click the **Trim** tool on the **Modify** panel of the **Drafting** tool set.
- Select the portion of the horizontal line, as shown.

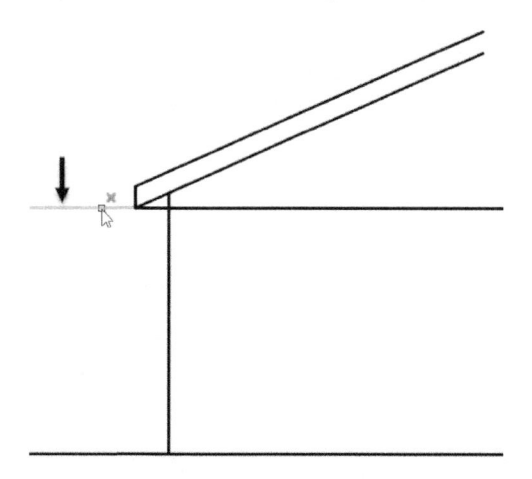

- Click the **Offset** tool on the **Modify** panel of the **Drafting** tool set.
- Type 4 and press RETURN.
- Select the vertical line.
- Move the pointer toward right and click.

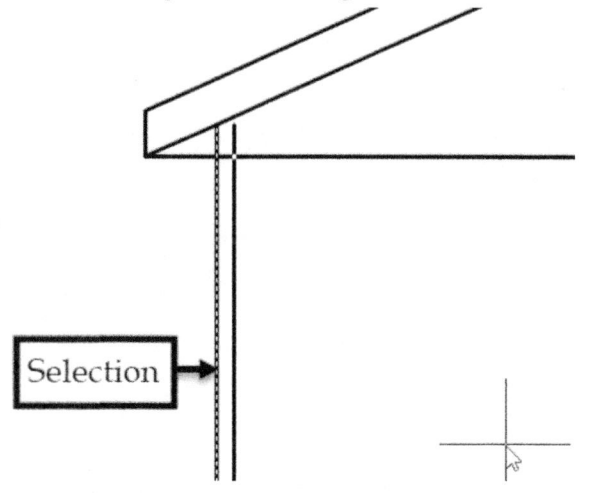

- Press RETURN twice.
- Type 2 and press RETURN.
- Select the offset line.
- Move the pointer toward the right and click.

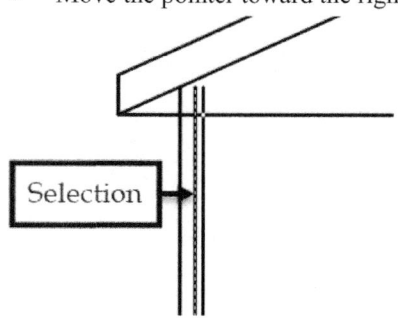

Creating the Brick Venner

- Click the **Rectangle** tool on the **Draw** panel of the **Drafting** tool set.

- Specify the corner point, as shown.

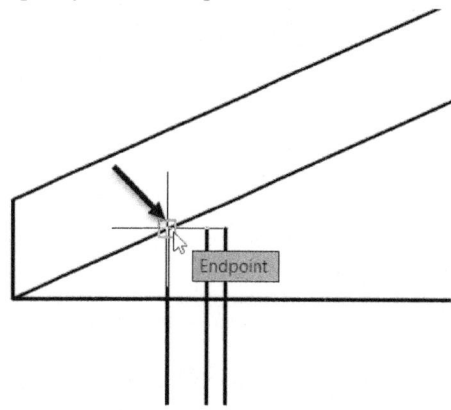

- Right-click and select the **Dimensions** option.
- Type 4 and press RETURN.
- Type 4 and press RETURN.
- Move the pointer downward and click.

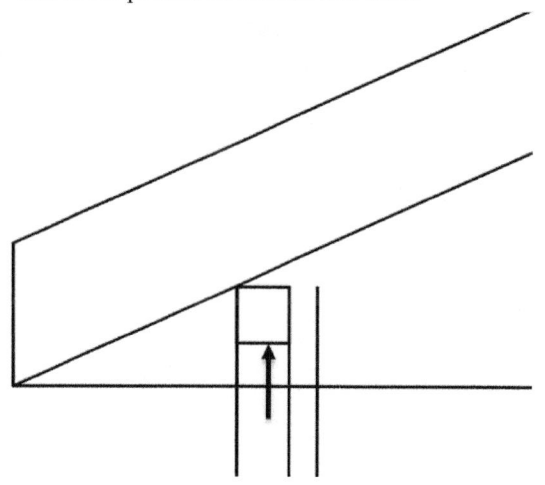

- Select the rectangle and click **Array** drop-down > **Path Array** on the **Modify** panel of the **Drafting** tool set.

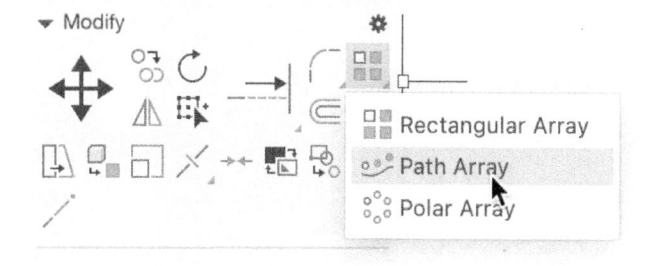

- Select the left vertical line to define the path.

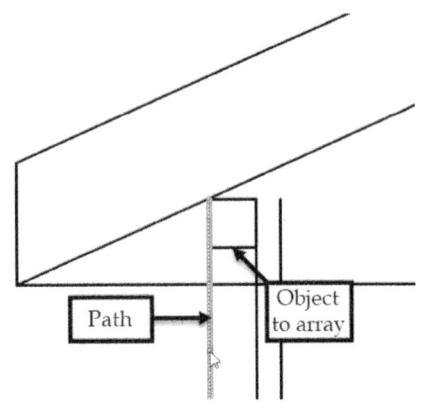

- On the **Path Array** visor, uncheck the **Fill entire path** option.
- Type **14** in the **Number of Items** box.
- Type **4.25** in the **Spacing between items** box.

- Type AS and press RETURN.
- Type No and press RETURN.
- Press RETURN.

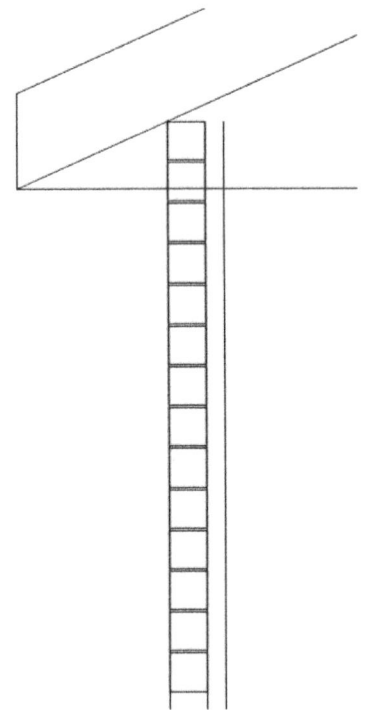

- Select anyone of the rectangles.

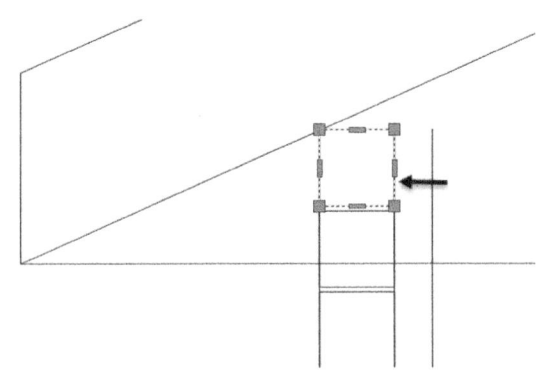

- Click the **Select Similar** icon on the toolbar.

- Click the **Explode** tool on the **Modify** panel of the **Drafting** tool set. All the rectangles are exploded into individual objects.
- Click the **Line** tool on the **Draw** panel of the **Drafting** tool set.
- Zoom to the top portion of the drawing.
- Create a line by selecting the two points, as shown.

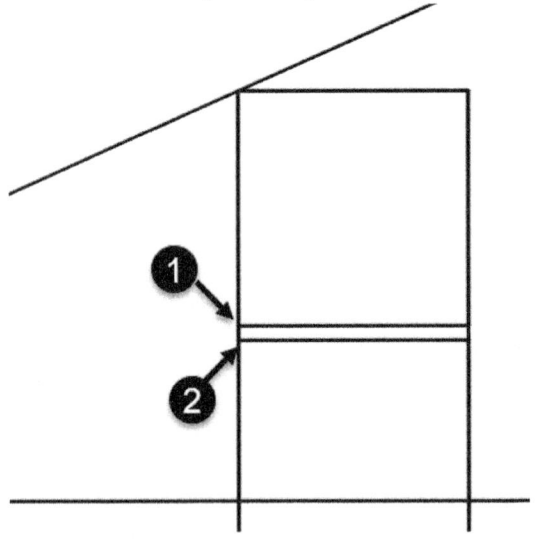

- Press ESC.
- Select the newly created line.
- Click the **Move** tool on the **Modify** panel of the **Drafting** tool set.
- Select the top endpoint of the selected line.
- Move the pointer toward the right.

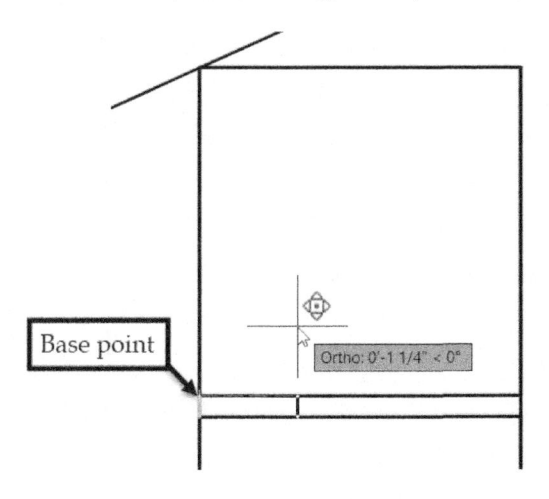

- Type 0.125, and press RETURN.
- Select the line moved in the last step.
- Click **Array** drop-down > **Rectangular Array** on the **Modify** panel of the **Drafting** tool set.
- Type **2** in the **Number of columns** box.
- Type **13** in the **Number of rows** box.

- Right-click and select **Spacing**.
- Type **3.75** and press RETURN.
- Type **-4.25** and press RETURN.
- Type **AS** and press RETURN.
- Type **NO** and press RETURN.
- Press RETURN.
- Select the two vertical lines, as shown.

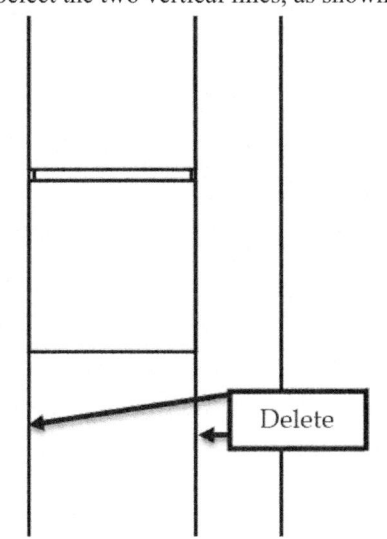

- Press Delete.

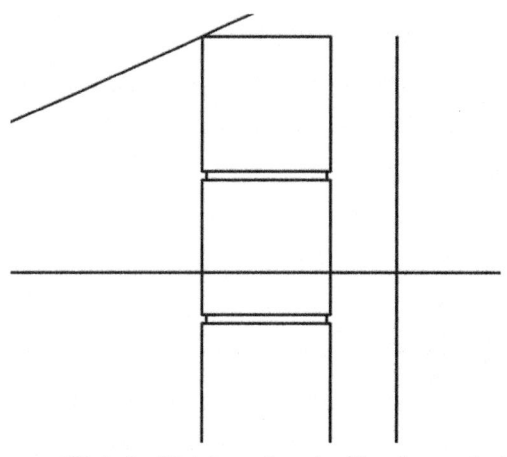

- Click the **Hatch** tool on the **Hatch** panel of the **Drafting** tool set.
- On the **Hatch** visor, click **Pattern** drop-down > **Open Library**.
- Type **ANSI** in the search bar, and then double-click on the **ANSI31** pattern.
- On the **Hatch** visor, enter **8** in the **Hatch pattern scale** box.

- Click in the region, as shown.

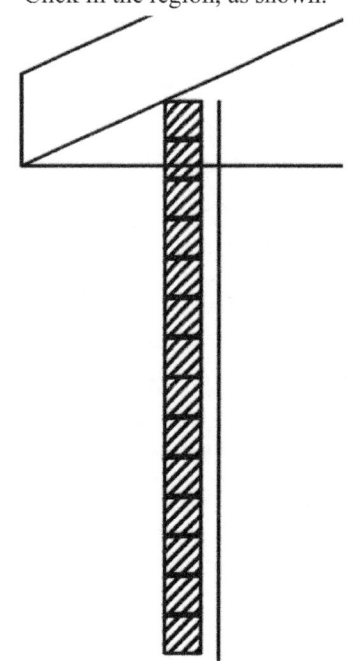

- Press RETURN.

Creating the Brick Tie

- On the Menu bar, click **View** > **Zoom** > **Window**.
- Create a zoom window at the location, as shown.

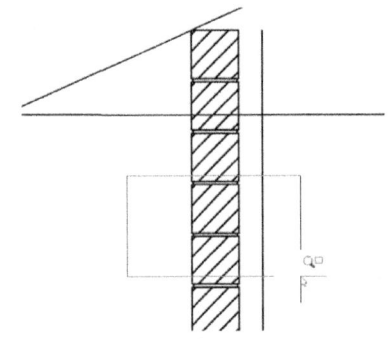

- Click the **Offset** tool on the **Modify** panel of the **Drafting** tool set.
- Type 0.025, and press RETURN.
- Offset the two horizontal lines in the inward direction.

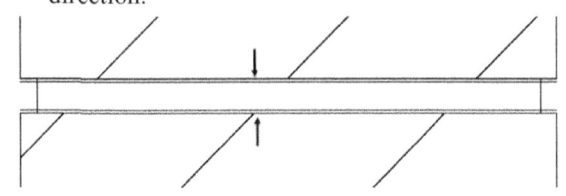

- Press RETURN twice.
- Type 1 and press RETURN.
- Offset the left vertical line towards the right.

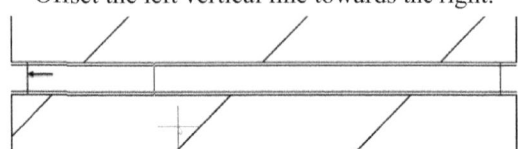

- Click the **Trim** tool on the **Modify** panel of the **Drafting** tool set.
- Trim the portions of the lines, as shown.

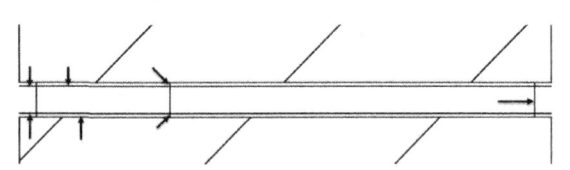

- Click the **Trim** drop-down > **Extend** on the **Modify** panel of the **Drafting** tool set.
- Select the ends of the horizontal lines, as shown.

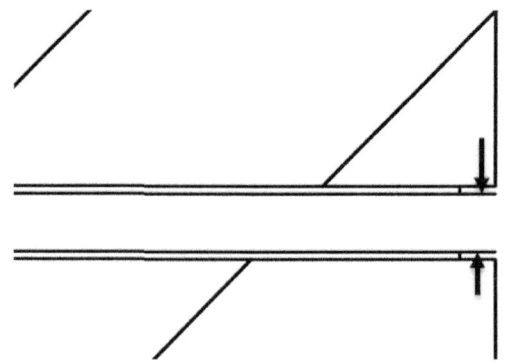

The horizontal lines are extended up to the right vertical line.

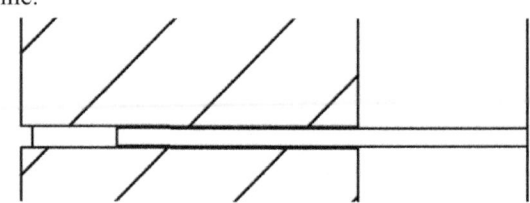

- Click the **Line** tool on the **Draw** panel of the **Drafting** tool set.
- Select the endpoint of the lower horizontal line.
- Move the pointer vertically upward.
- Type 3 and press RETURN.
- Click the **Offset** tool on the **Modify** panel of the **Drafting** tool set.
- Type 0.2 and press RETURN.
- Select the vertical line created in the last step.
- Move the pointer toward the left and click.

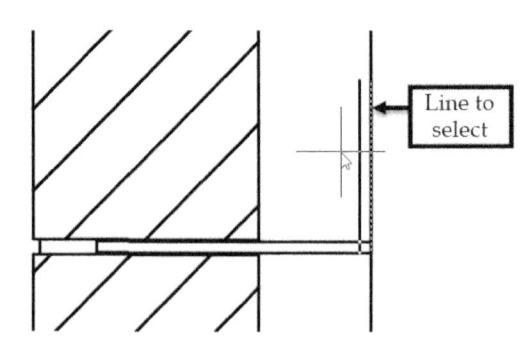

- Click the **Fillet** drop-down > **Chamfer** on the **Modify** panel of the **Drafting** tool set.
- Right-click and select the **Angle** option.
- Type 1 as the chamfer length and press RETURN.
- Type 45 as the chamfer angle and press RETURN.
- Select horizontal and vertical lines, as shown.

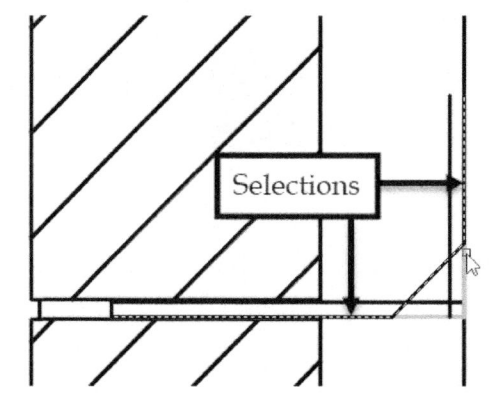

- Likewise, create another chamfer, as shown.

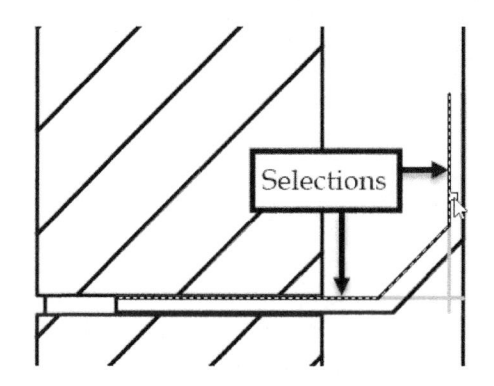

- Click the **Line** tool on the **Draw** panel of the **Drafting** tool set.
- Cap the ends of the offset lines, as shown.

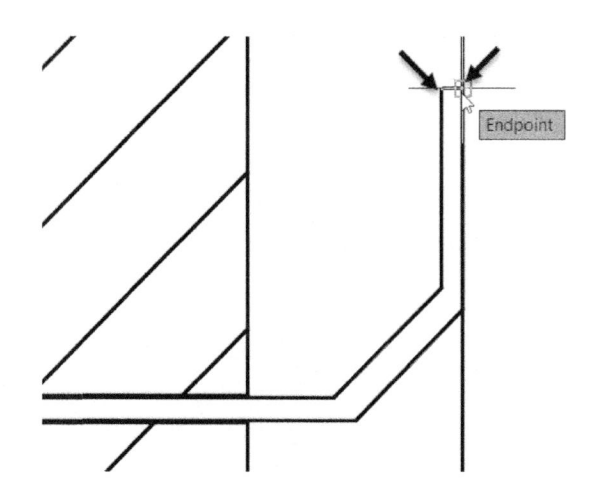

- Click the **Rectangle** tool on the **Draw** panel of the **Drafting** tool set.
- Click in the graphic window.
- Right-click and select the **Dimensions** option.
- Type 0.2 and press RETURN.
- Type 0.5 and press RETURN.
- Click to create a rectangle.

- Select the rectangle and click the **Move** tool on the **Modify** panel of the **Drafting** tool set.
- Select the midpoint of the right vertical edge of the rectangle.

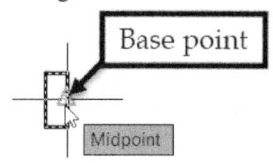

- Move the pointer and select the midpoint of the vertical line, as shown.

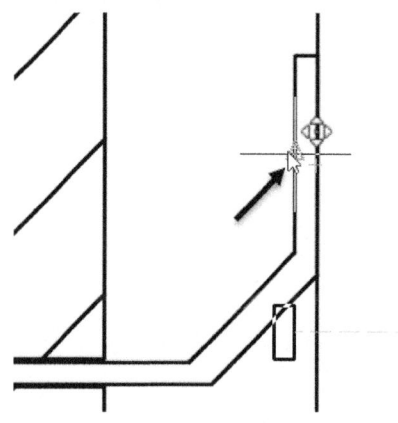

- Click the **Line** tool on the **Draw** panel of the **Drafting** tool set.
- Select the midpoint of the right vertical edge of the rectangle.
- Move the pointer toward the right.

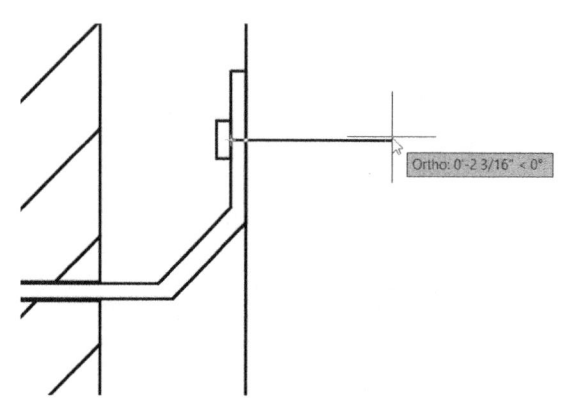

- Type 3.5 and press RETURN.
- Click the **Offset** tool on the **Modify** panel of the **Drafting** tool set.
- Type 0.1 and press RETURN.
- Offset the newly created horizontal line on both sides.

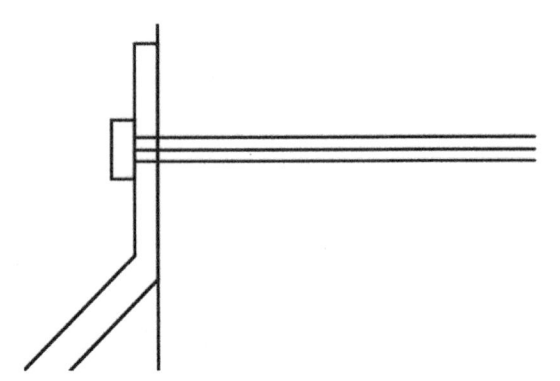

- Press ESC.
- Select the center line and press Delete.
- Click the **Arc** drop-down > **Start, End, Direction** on the **Draw** panel of the **Drafting** tool set.
- Select the endpoints of the offset lines.
- Move the pointer toward right and click.

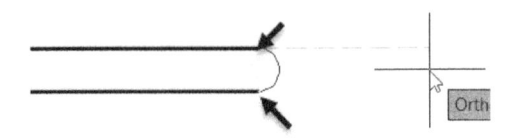

- Click the **Trim** tool on the **Modify** panel of the **Drafting** tool set.
- Trim the portion of the vertical line, as shown.

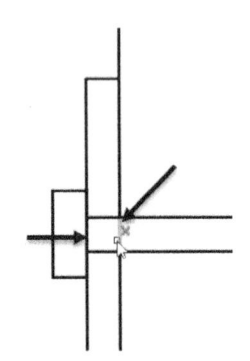

- Click the **Hatch** tool on the **Hatch** panel of the **Drafting** tool set.
- Select the **Solids** option from the **Pattern** drop-down.

- Click in the regions, as shown.

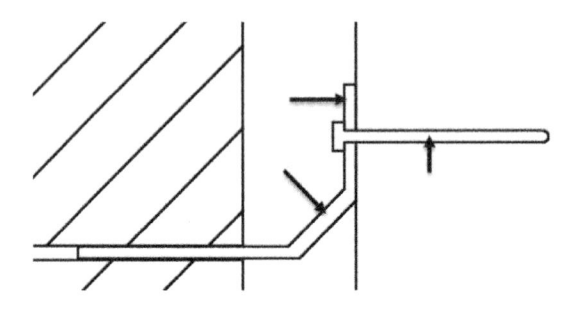

- Click **Close Hatch Creation** on the tool set.

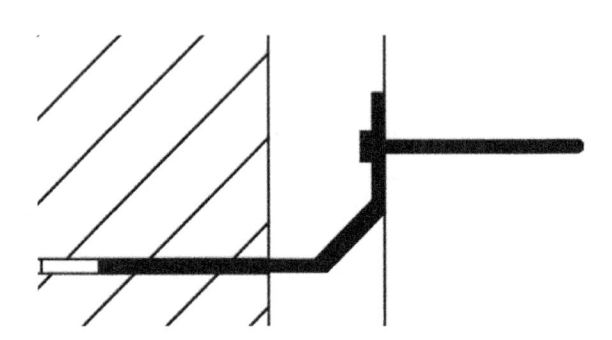

Creating the Insulation

- Click the **Offset** tool on the **Modify** panel of the **Drafting** tool set.
- Type 1 and press RETURN.
- Select the vertical line, as shown.
- Move the pointer toward right and click.
- Likewise, offset the bottom vertical line.

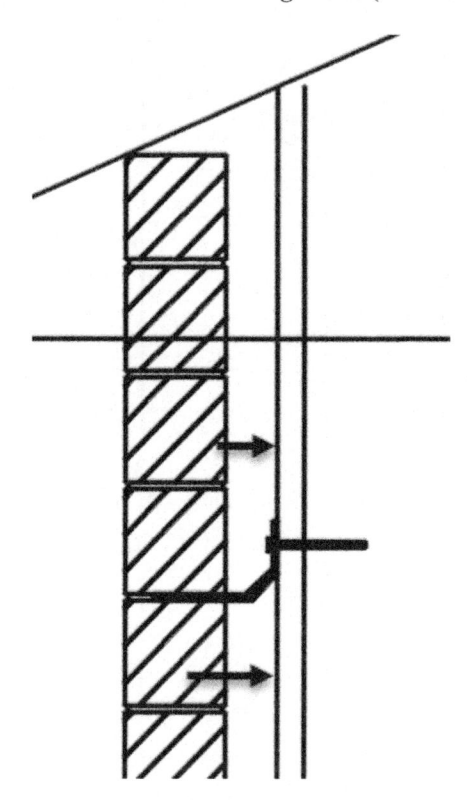

- Press RETURN twice.
- Type 9 and press RETURN.
- Select the offset line.
- Move the pointer toward right and click.

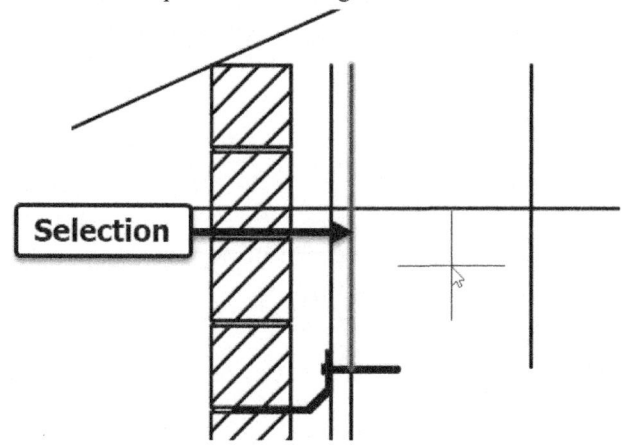

- Click the **Trim** drop-down > **Extend** on the **Modify** panel of the **Drafting** tool set.
- Click on the lower portion of the newly offset line.

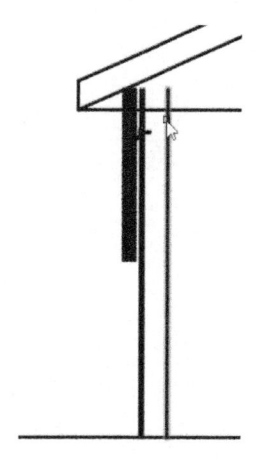

- Click the **Offset** tool on the **Modify** panel of the **Drafting** tool set.
- Type 0.75 and press RETURN.
- Select the offset line.
- Move the pointer toward right and click.

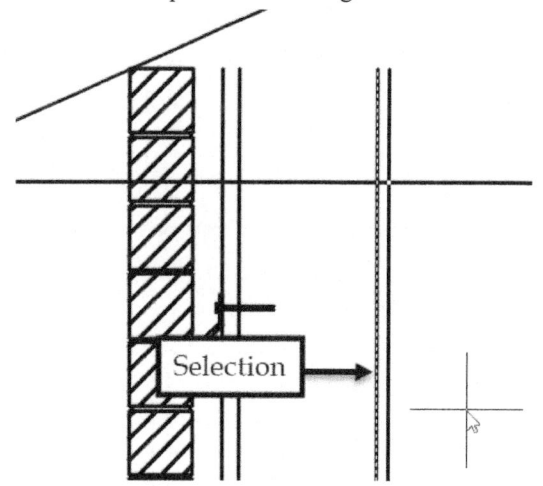

- Click the **Trim** drop-down > **Extend** on the **Modify** panel of the **Drafting** tool set.
- Click and drag the pointer across the ends of the vertical lines, as shown.

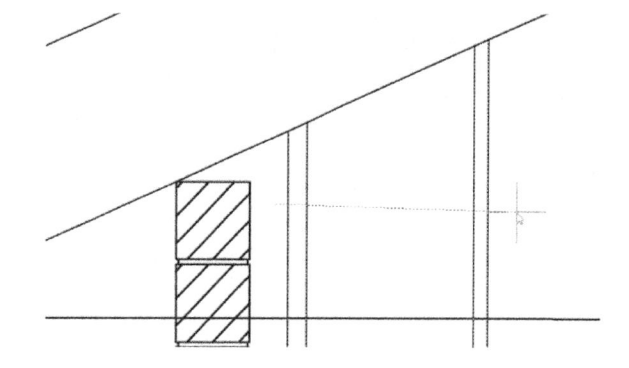

361 Creating Architectural Drawings

AutoCAD 2023 For Beginners (For Mac Users)

- Create the two horizontal lines, as shown.

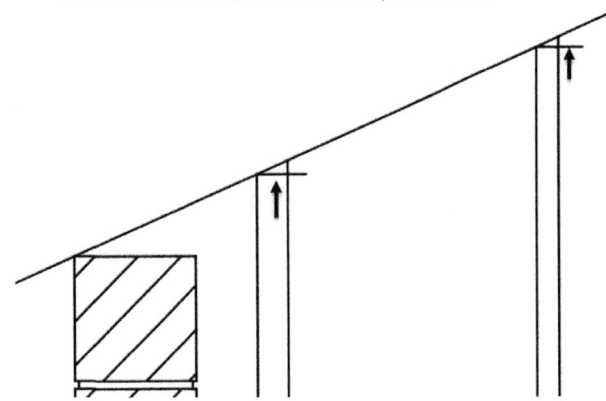

- Trim the extending portions.

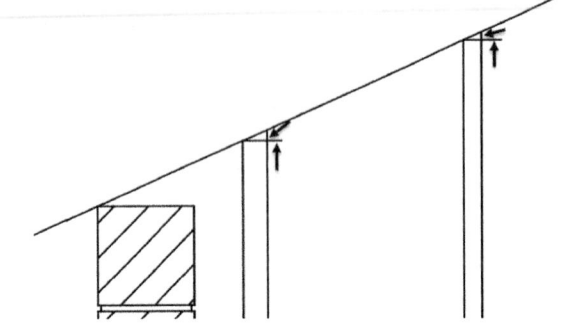

- Click the **Rectangle** tool on the **Draw** panel of the **Drafting** tool set.
- Select the corner point, as shown.

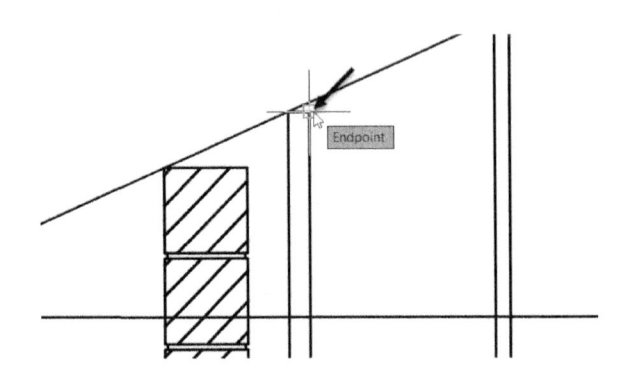

- Right-click and select the **Dimensions** option.
- Type 9 and press RETURN.
- Type 2.25 and press RETURN.
- Move the pointer downward and click.
- Click the **Line** tool on the **Draw** panel of the **Drafting** tool set.
- Create the diagonal lines by selecting the corner points of the rectangle.

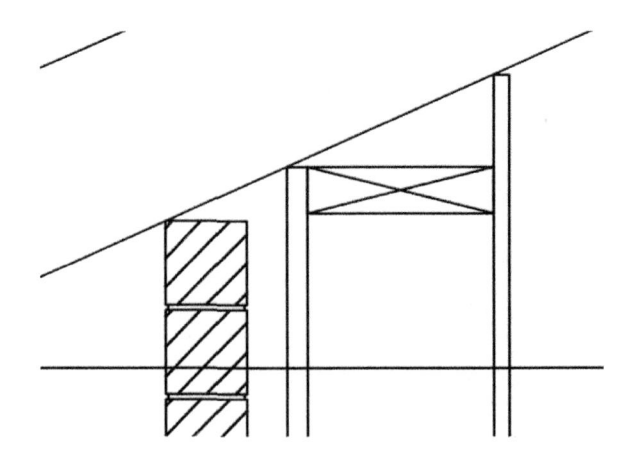

- Click the **Custom panel** icon on the **Draw** panel on the **Drafting** tool set, and then check the **Donut** tool.

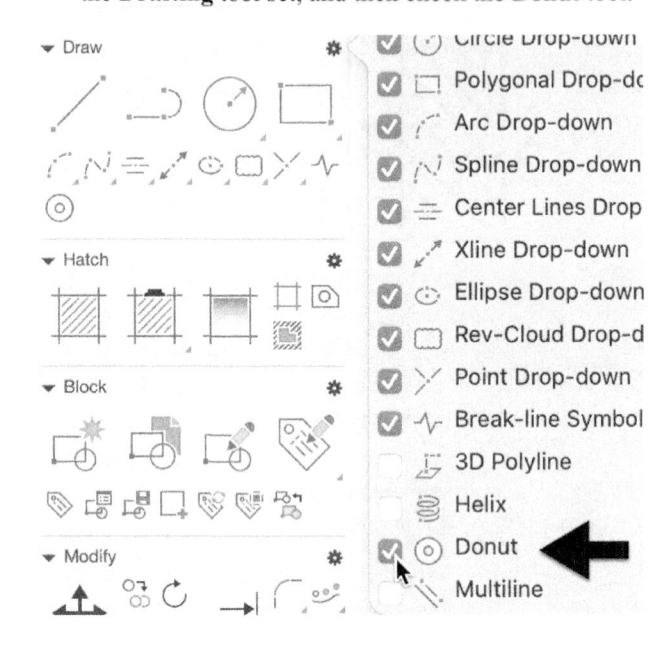

- Click the **Donut** icon on the **Draw** panel.
- Type 0 as the internal diameter, and then press RETURN.
- Type 1 as the external diameter, and then press RETURN.
- Select the midpoint of the left vertical edge of the rectangle.

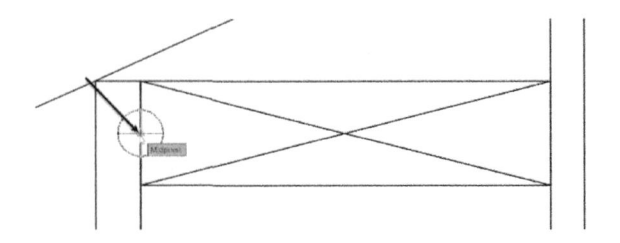

362 | Creating Architectural Drawings

- Press Esc.
- Click the **Line** tool on the **Draw** panel of the **Drafting** tool set.
- Create a horizontal line, as shown.

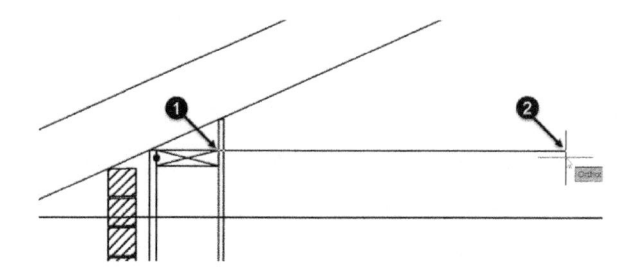

- Click the **Offset** tool on the **Modify** panel of the **Drafting** tool set.
- Type 1.5 and press RETURN.
- Select the newly created line.
- Move the pointer downward and click.

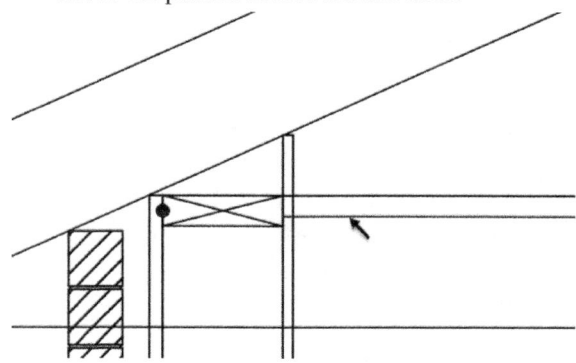

- Press RETURN twice.
- Type 0.75 and press RETURN.
- Select the offset line.
- Move the pointer downward and click.

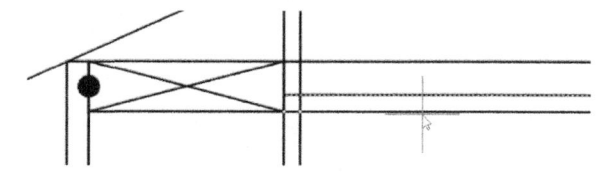

- Press RETURN.
- Click the **Trim** tool on the **Modify** panel of the **Drafting** tool set.
- Trim the elements, as shown.

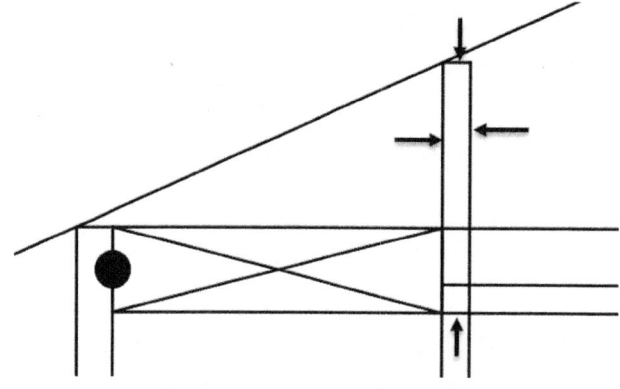

- Click the **Hatch** tool on the **Hatch** panel of the **Drafting** tool set.
- On the **Hatch** visor, click **Pattern** drop-down > **Open Library**.
- Type **ANSI** in the search bar, and then double-click on the **ANSI37** pattern.
- On the **Hatch** visor, enter **2** in the **Hatch pattern scale** box.
- Type 45 in the **Hatch angle** box.

- Click in the regions, as shown.

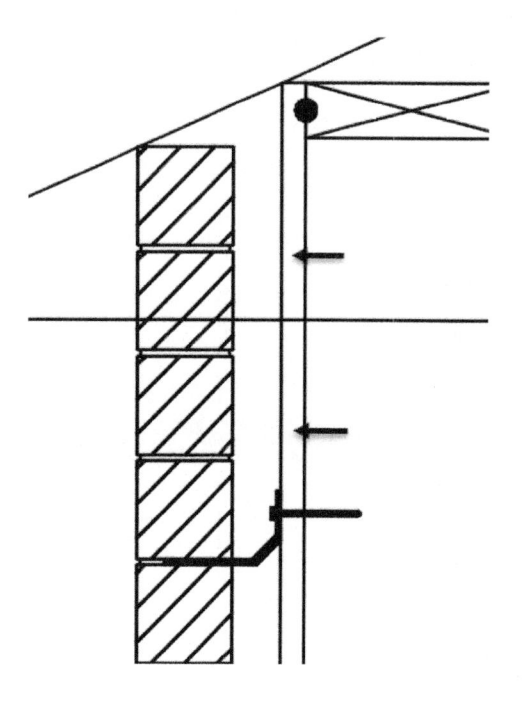

- Click in the area below the brick tie; the **Hatch – Boundary Definition Error** message box appears.

- Click **Close** on the message box.
- Press **ESC**.
- Click the **Line** tool on the **Draw** panel of the **Drafting** tool set.
- Select the end points of the line, as shown.

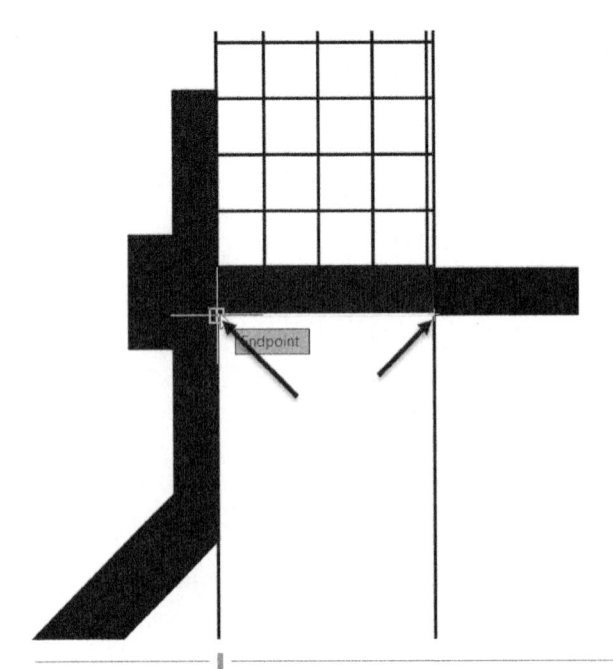

- Press RETURN twice.
- Zoom to the lower portion of the and select the lower endpoints of the vertical lines, as shown.

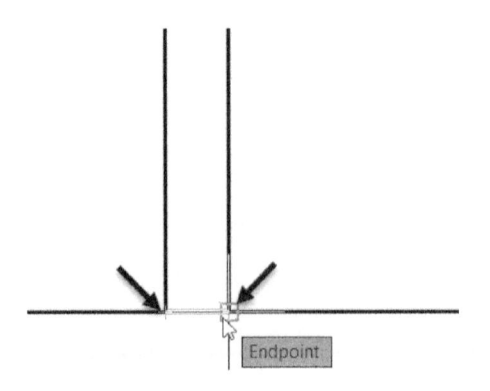

- On the **Drafting** tool set, click the **Region** tool on the **Hatch** panel.
- Select the vertical and horizontal lines, as shown.

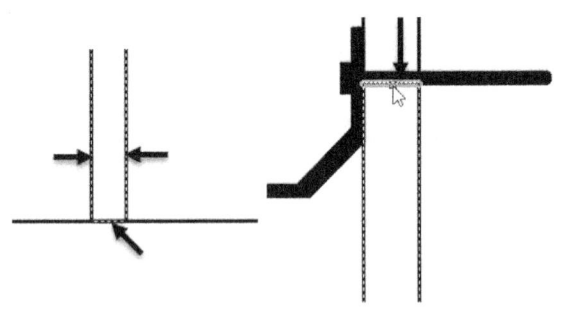

- Press RETURN.
- Click the **Hatch** tool on the **Hatch** panel of the **Drafting** tool set.
- Click in the area below the brick tie.
- Press RETURN.

364 | Creating Architectural Drawings

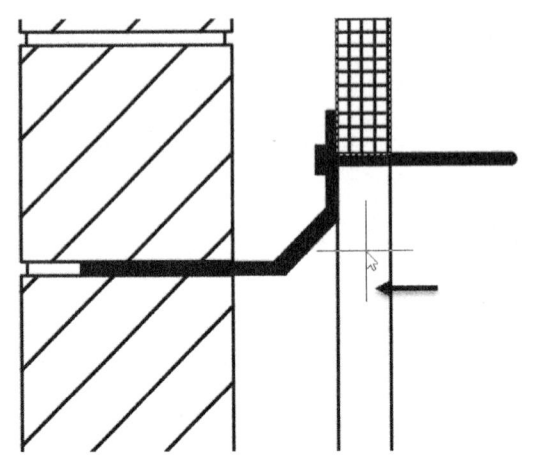

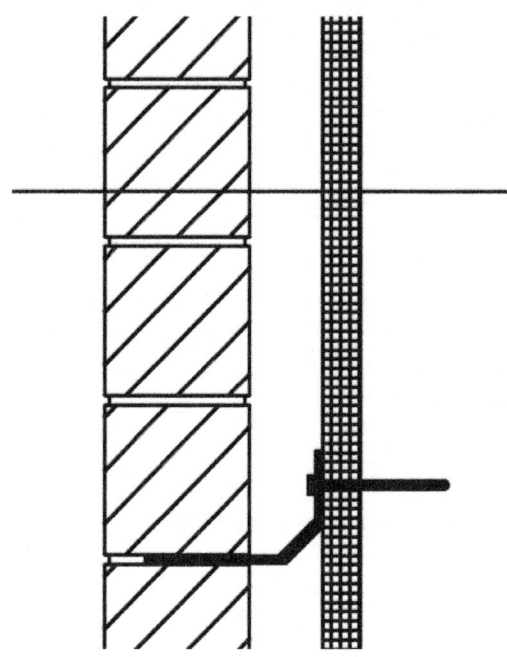

- Click the **Line** tool on the **Draw** panel of the **Drafting** tool set.
- Select the midpoint of the horizontal line, as shown.
- Move the pointer downward and click.

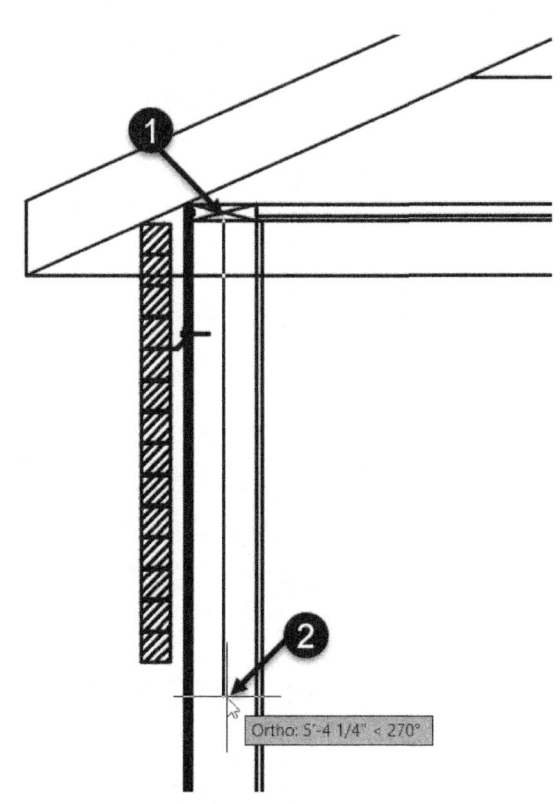

- Click the **Undock** icon on the **Layers** palette.
- Click the **New Layer** icon on the **Layers** palette.
- Type **Insulation** as the layer name.

- Click in the **Linetype** drop-down > **Manage** on the **Layers** palette.

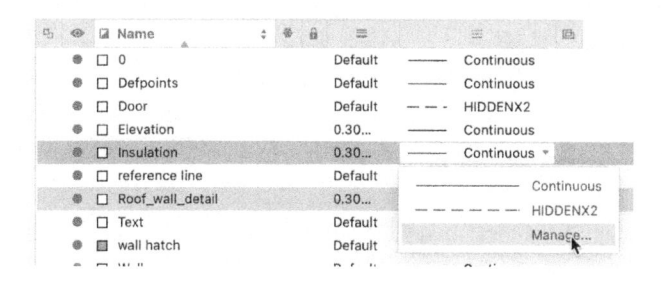

- Click the **Load** button on the **Select Linetype** dialog.
- Select the **BATTING** linetype from the linetype list.
- Click **Add**.

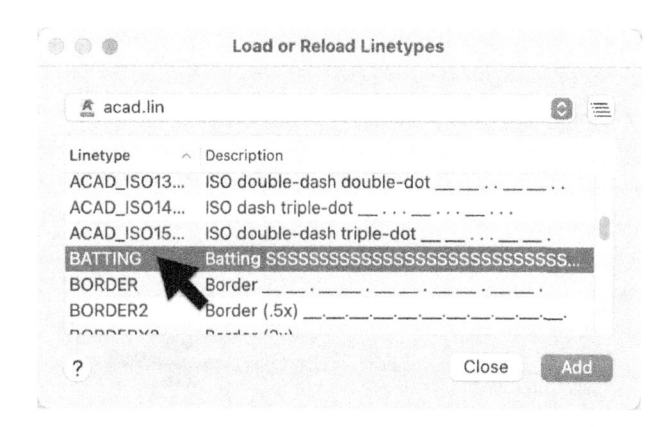

- Select the **BATTING** linetype from the **Select Linetype** dialog.

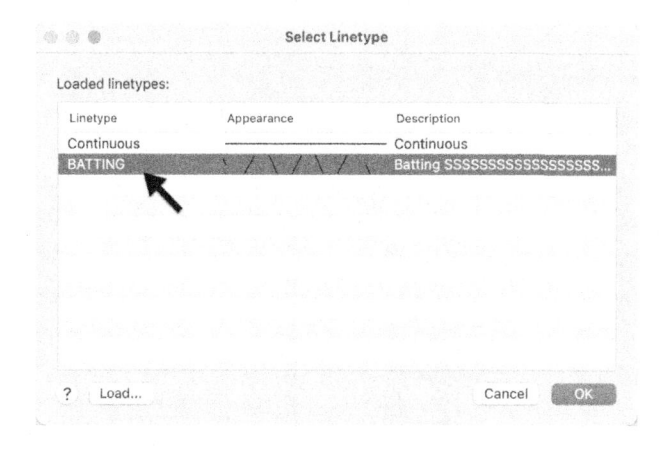

- Click **OK**.
- Click the **Dock** icon on the **Layers** palette.
- Select the newly created line.
- Select **Insulation** from the **Layer** drop-down on the **Layers** palette.

365 | Creating Architectural Drawings

AutoCAD 2023 For Beginners (For Mac Users)

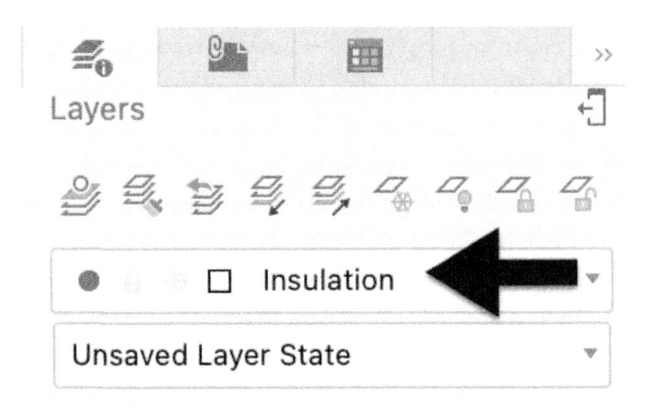

- Select the newly created line.
- Type 10 in the **Linetype Scale** box and press RETURN.

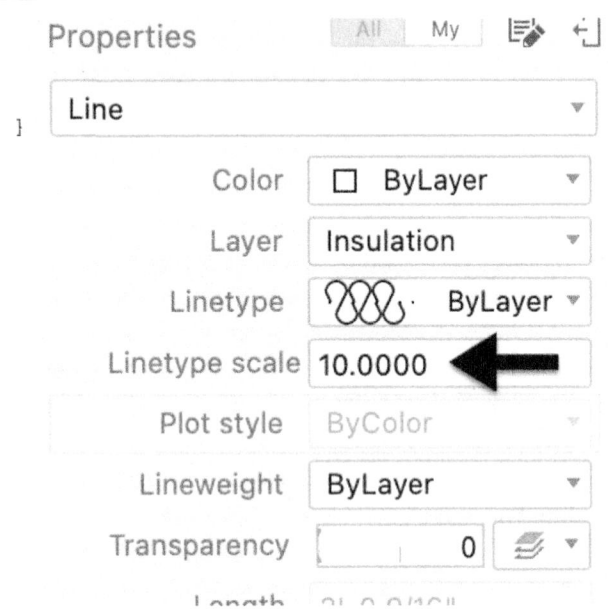

- Press ESC.

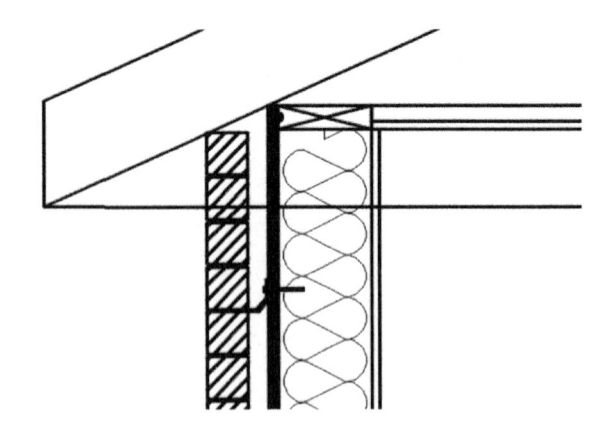

- Click the **Offset** tool on the **Modify** panel of the **Drafting** tool set.
- Type 3 and press RETURN.

- Select the horizontal line, as shown.
- Move the pointer upward and click.

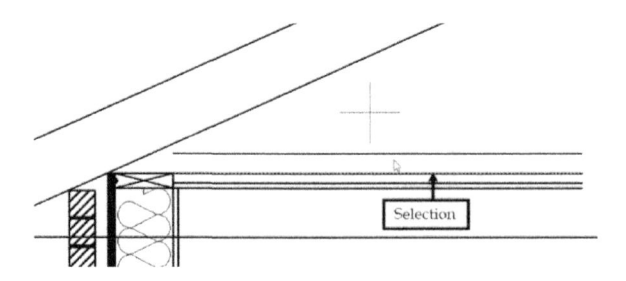

- Press ESC.
- Select the newly created line.
- Select **Insulation** from the **Layer** drop-down on the **Layers** palette.
- Type 6 in the **Linetype Scale** box and press RETURN.
- Press ESC.

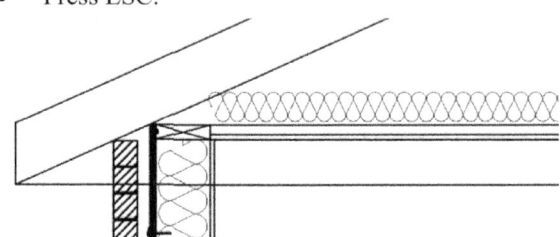

Creating the Roof Detail

- Offset the inclined line by 1".

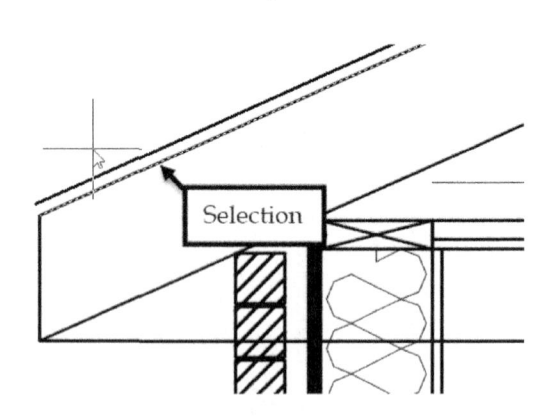

- Close the end of the offset lines.

366 | Creating Architectural Drawings

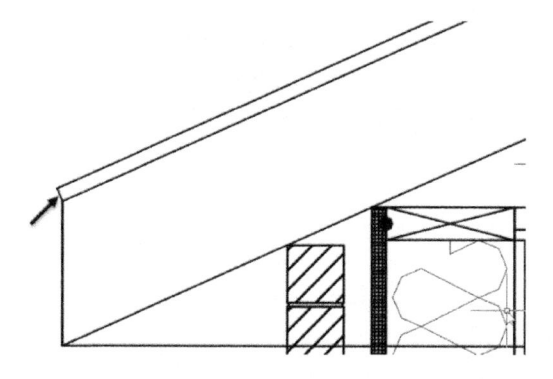

- Offset the new line by 0.5".

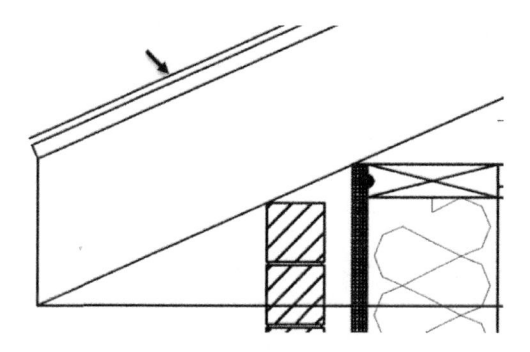

- Select the newly created offset line.
- Select HIDDENX2 from the **Linetype** drop-down on the **Properties** palette.

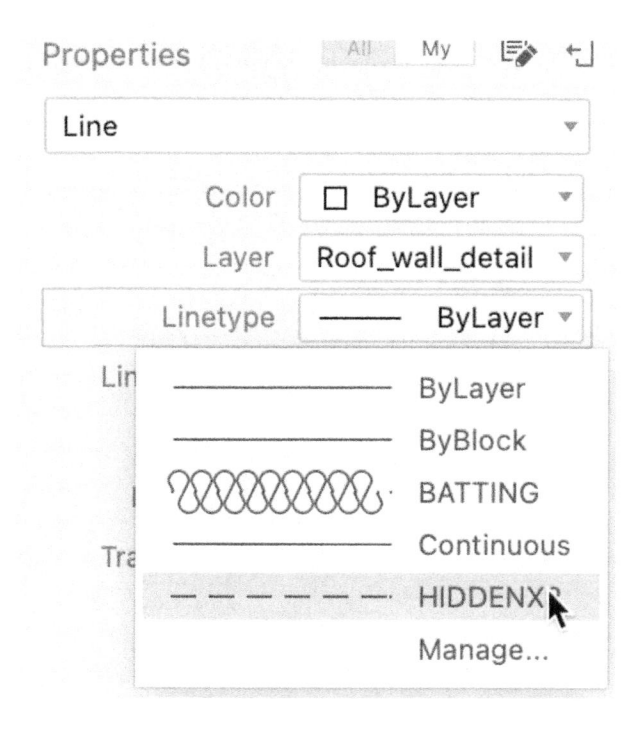

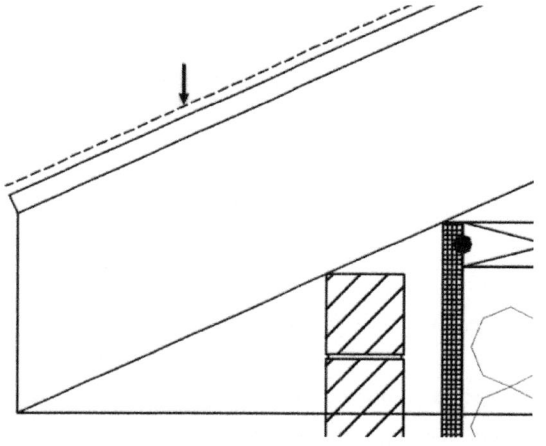

- Create another line with the offset distance of 0.75".

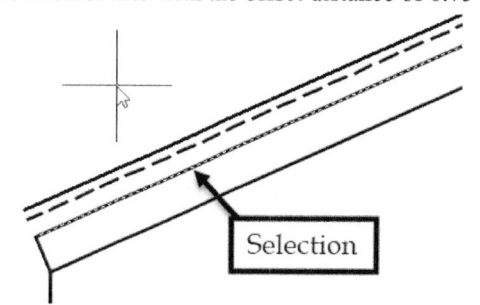

- Click the **Lengthen** tool on the **Modify** panel.
- Right-click and select the **DElta** option.
- Type 2.5 and press RETURN.
- Select the newly offset line.

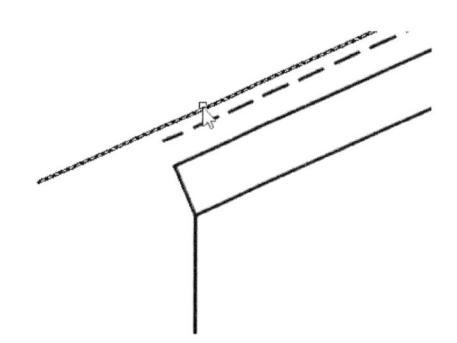

- Deactivate the **Ortho Mode** icon on the status bar.
- Click the **Line** tool on the **Draw** panel of the **Drafting** tool set.
- Select the endpoint of the inclined line, as shown.

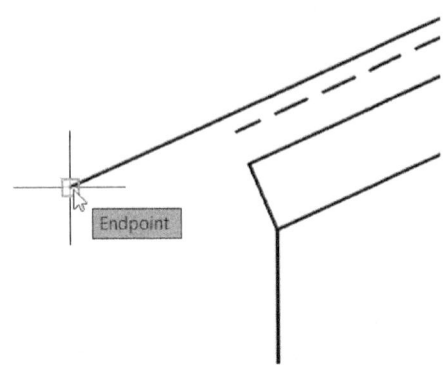

- Press and hold the SHIFT key, and then right click.
- Select the **Parallel** option from the shortcut menu.

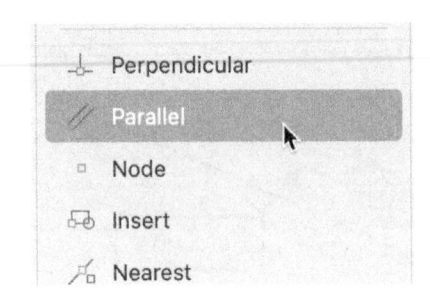

- Move the pointer and hover it on the inclined line, as shown.

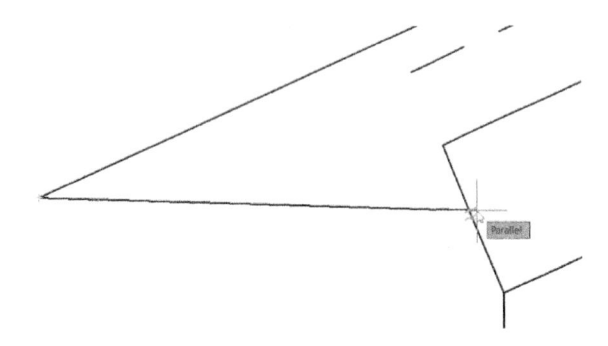

- Move the pointer inline to the start point of the line; a tracking line appears with a parallel symbol, as shown.

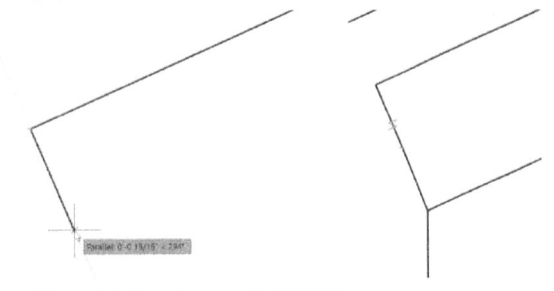

- Type 0.25 and press RETURN.
- Press and hold the SHIFT key, and then right click.

- Select the **Parallel** option from the shortcut menu.
- Move the pointer toward the right and hover the pointer on the endpoint of the hidden line; the tracking line appears from the endpoint.

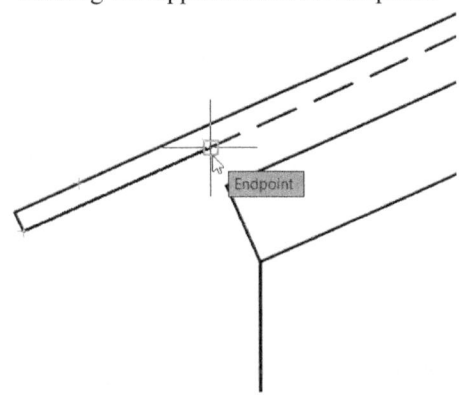

- Type 0.375, and press RETURN.

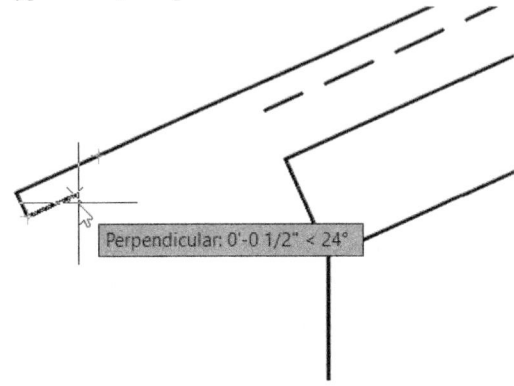

- Hover the pointer on the endpoint of the previous line and move the pointer downward; a tracking line appears from the endpoint.

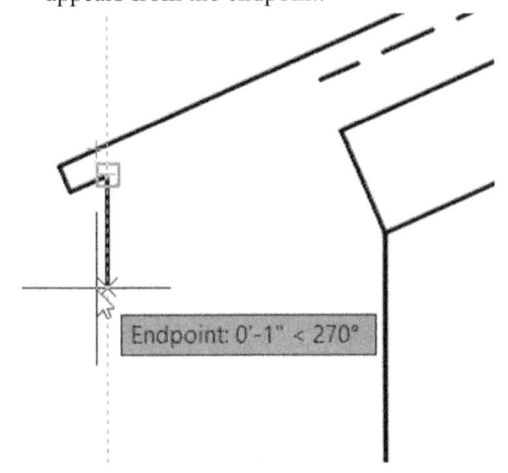

- Type 1.5 and press RETURN.
- Type @.375<225 in the command line and press RETURN.
- Press Esc.

368 | Creating Architectural Drawings

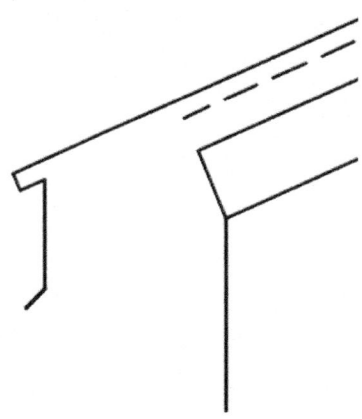

- On the **Draw** panel, click **Arc** drop-down > **Start, End, Direction**.
- Select the end points of the line, as shown.
- Press and hold the Ctrl key and select the endpoint, as shown.

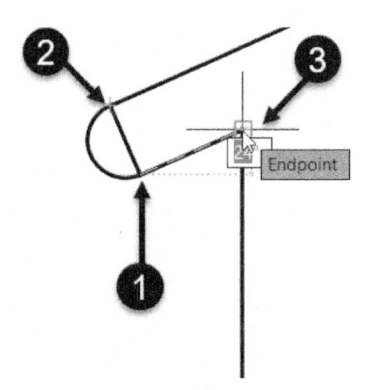

- Delete the line between the endpoints of the arc.

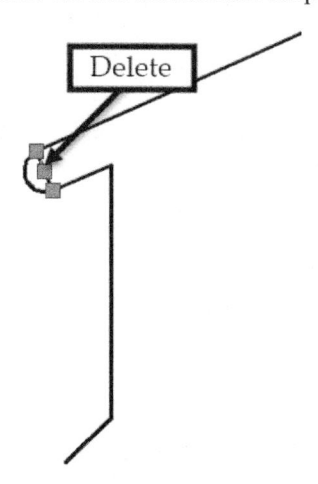

- On the **Modify** panel, click the **Break at point** tool.

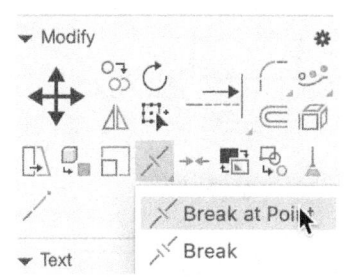

- Select the inclined line.

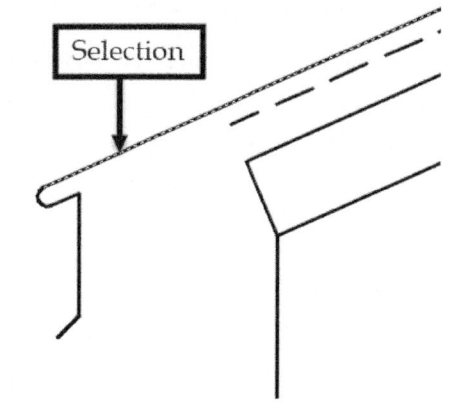

- Press and hold the SHIFT key, and then right click.
- Select the **From** option from the shortcut menu.
- Select the endpoint of the selected line.

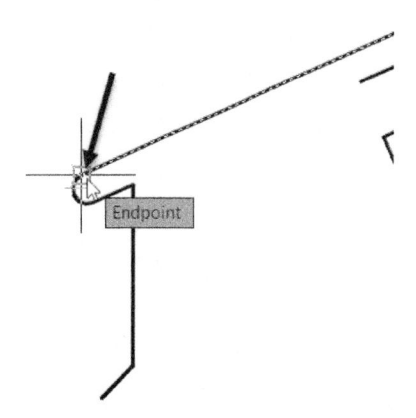

- Move the pointer on the selected line.
- Type 9 and press RETURN; the line is broken at the specified distance.
- Delete the right-side portion of the line.

369 | **Creating Architectural Drawings**

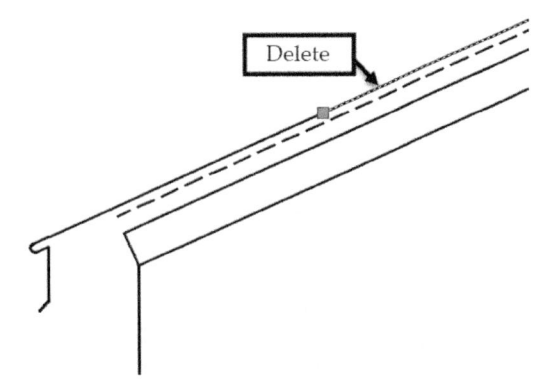

- Click the **Rectangle** tool on the **Draw** panel of the **Drafting** tool set.
- Select the corner point, as shown.
- Right-click and select the **Dimensions** option.
- Type 1 and press RETURN.
- Type 10 and press RETURN.
- Move the pointer toward the left and click.

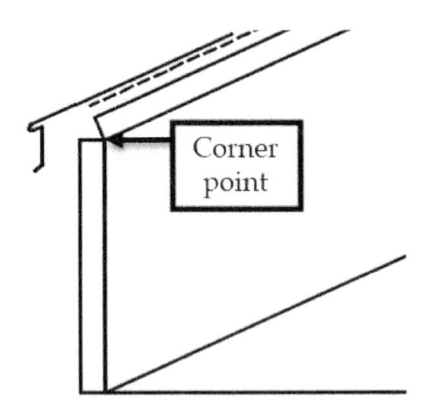

- Click the **Rectangle** tool on the **Draw** panel of the **Drafting** tool set.
- Select the top-left corner of the rectangle, as shown.
- Right-click and select the **Dimensions** option.
- Type 1 and press RETURN.
- Type 2.5 and press RETURN.
- Move the pointer toward the left and click.

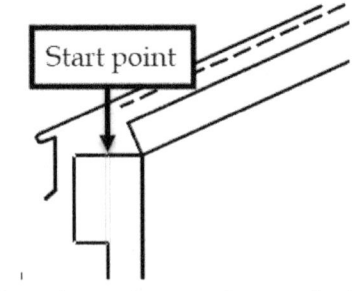

- Move the newly created rectangle downward by 0.5".

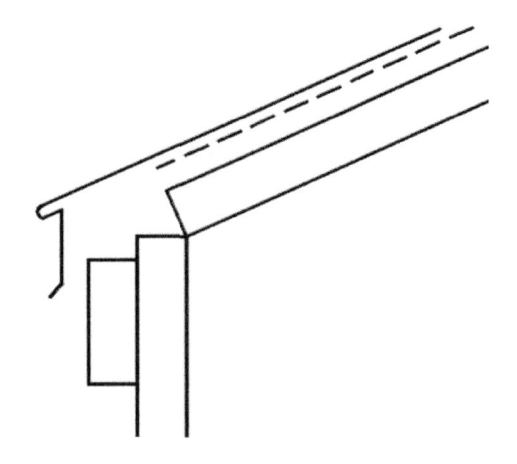

- Click the **Trim** tool on the **Modify** panel of the **Drafting** tool set.
- Right-click and select the **cuTting edges** option.
- Select the vertical edge of the brick, as shown.
- Press RETURN.
- Click on the horizontal line on the right side.

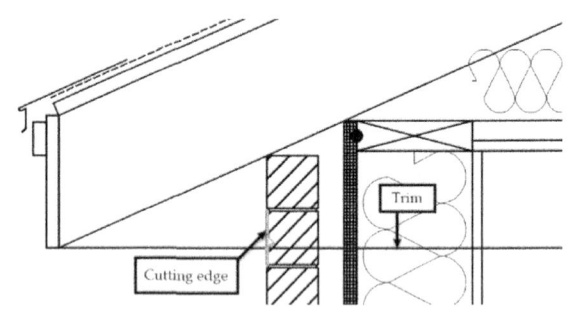

- Click the **Offset** tool on the **Modify** panel of the **Drafting** tool set.
- Type 1 and press RETURN.
- Select the horizontal line trimmed in the last step.
- Move the pointer upward and click.

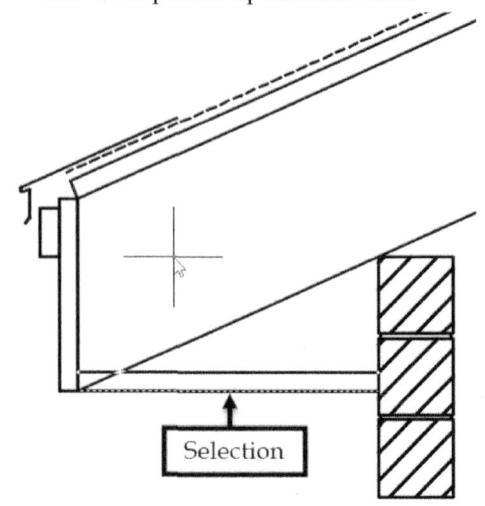

370 | Creating Architectural Drawings

- Select the offset line.
- Move the pointer upward and click.

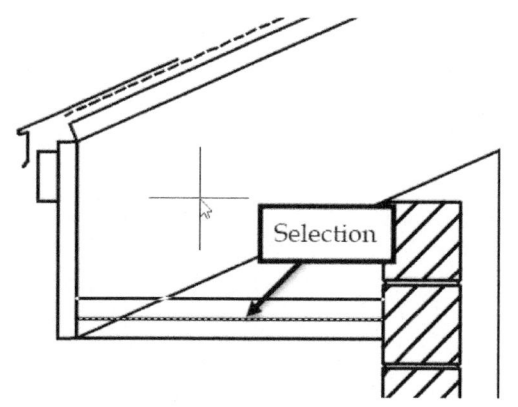

- Click the **Trim** tool on the **Modify** panel of the **Drafting** tool set.
- Select the portions of the lines, as shown.

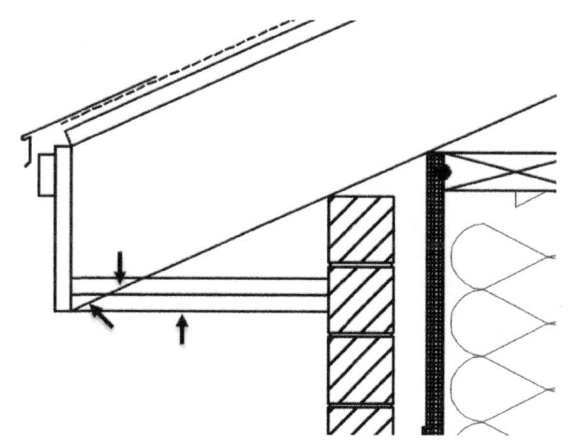

- Click the **Offset** tool on the **Modify** panel of the **Drafting** tool set.
- Type 7 and press RETURN.
- Select the left vertical line of the veneer brick.
- Move the pointer toward the left and click.

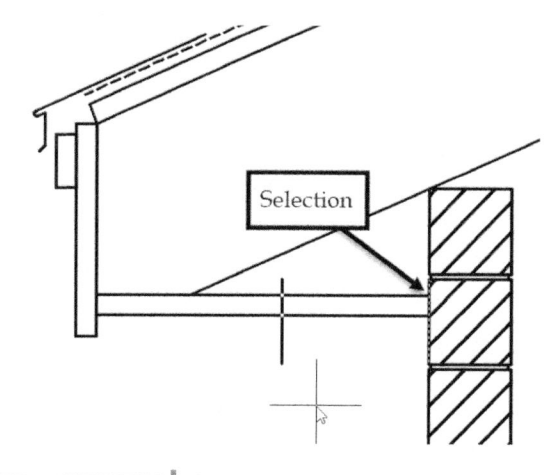

- Press RETURN twice.
- Type 4 and press RETURN.
- Select the offset line.
- Move the pointer toward the left and click.

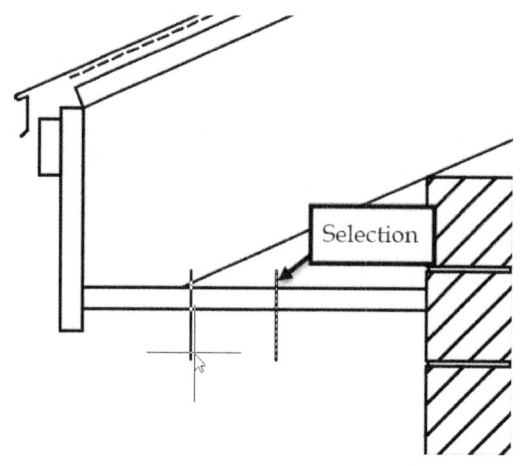

- Click the **Trim** tool on the **Modify** panel of the **Drafting** tool set.
- Select the portions of the lines, as shown.

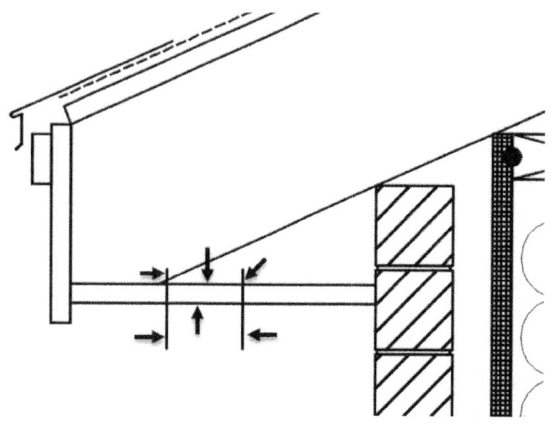

- Create a line by selecting the corner points of the opening, as shown.

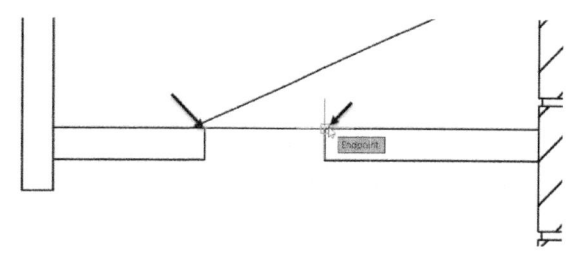

- Press ESC.
- Activate the **Ortho Mode** icon on the status bar.
- Select the newly created line and click the **Scale** tool on the **Modify** panel of the **Drafting** tool set.
- Select the midpoint.

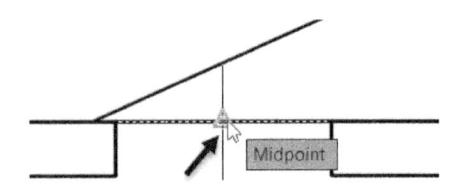

- Move the pointer vertically downward.
- Type 1.25 as the scale factor, and then press RETURN.
- Select the horizontal line and click on its midpoint grip.
- Move the pointer upward.

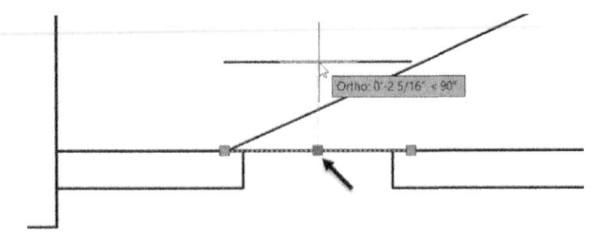

- Type 0.2 and press RETURN.
- Create an inclined line and pattern it, as shown.

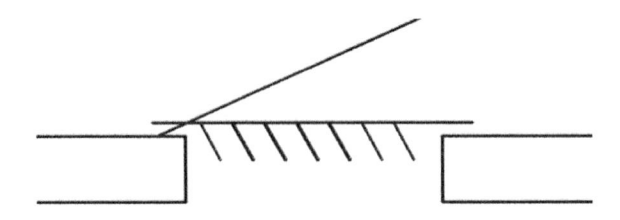

- On the **Drafting** tool set, click **Hatch** panel > **Hatch**.
- On the **Hatch** visor, click the **Pattern** drop-down > **Open Library.**
- Type **GOST** in the search bar and double-click on the **GOST_WOOD** pattern.

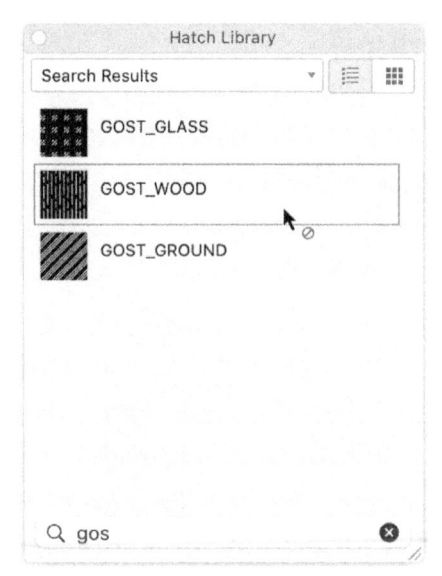

- Pick points in the areas, as shown.

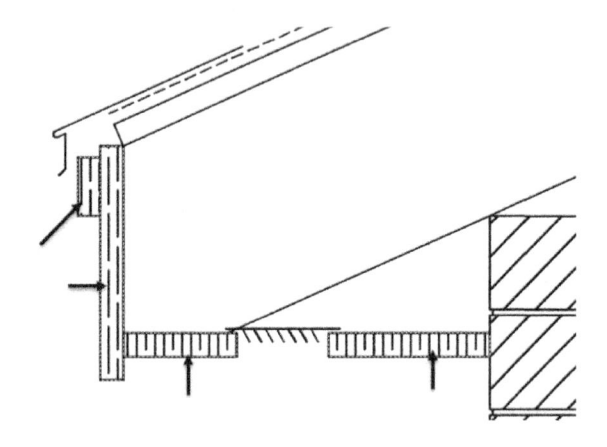

- Type 0.2 in the **Pattern Hatch Scale** box and press RETURN.
- Press RETURN.
- On the **Drafting** tool set, click **Draw** panel > **Rectangle/Polygon** drop-down > **Rectangle**.
- Select the lower right corner of the rectangle, as shown.
- Right-click and select the **Dimensions** option.
- Type 6 and press RETURN.
- Type 5 and press RETURN.
- Move the pointer downward and click.

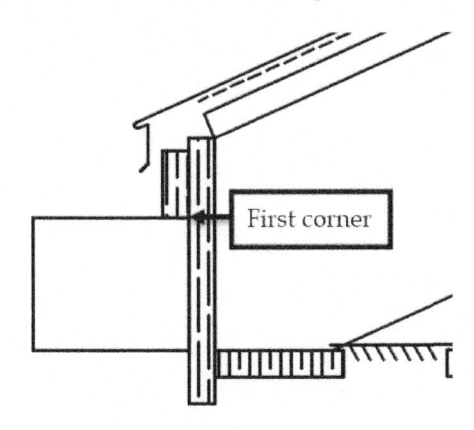

- Select the rectangle and click the **Move** tool on the **Modify** panel.
- Select the top right corner point of the rectangle.
- Move the pointer downward.
- Type 0.5 and press RETURN.
- Select the rectangle and click the **Move** tool on the **Modify** panel.
- Select the top right corner point of the rectangle.
- Move the pointer toward left.
- Type 0.25 and press RETURN.

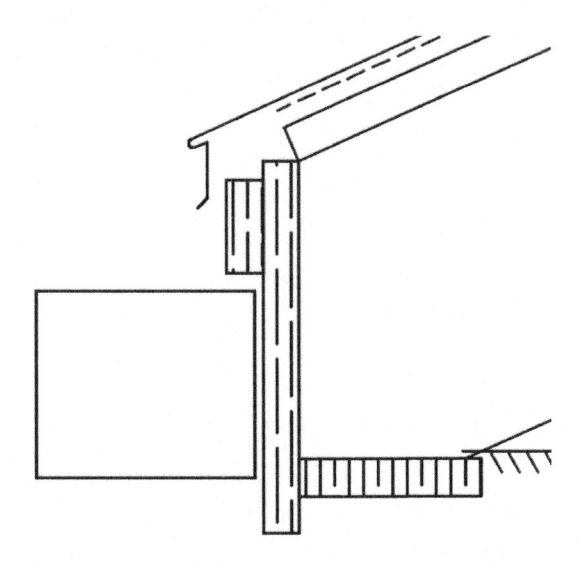

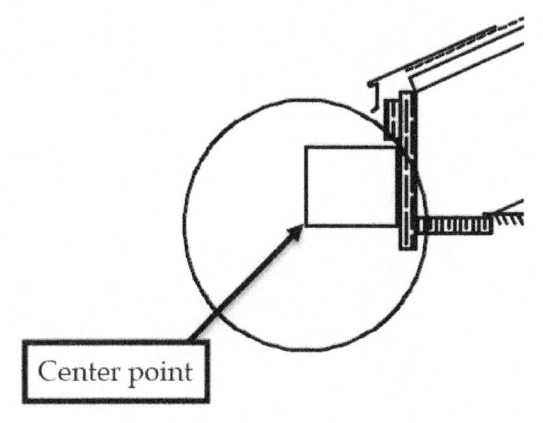

- Select the circle.
- Click on the centerpoint of the circle.
- Move the pointer toward left.
- Type 7 and press RETURN.

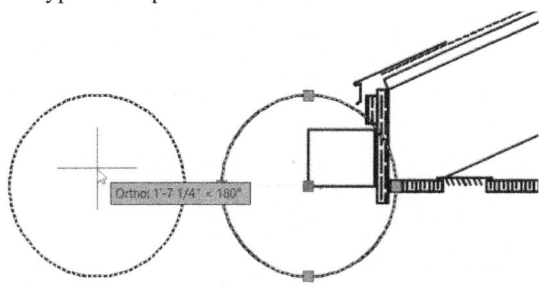

- Click the **Trim** tool on the **Modify** panel.
- Trim the edges of the circle and rectangle, as shown.

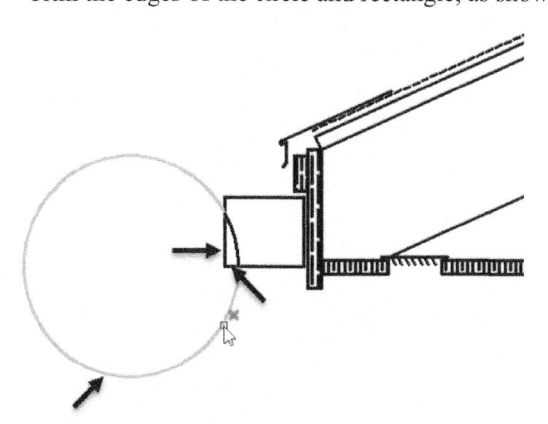

- Click **Circle** drop-down > **Center, Radius** on the **Draw** panel of the **Drafting** tool set.
- Select the lower-left corner of the rectangle.
- Type 8 and press RETURN.

- Press ESC.
- Select the rectangle and click the **Explode** tool on the **Modify** panel.

373 | Creating Architectural Drawings

AutoCAD 2023 For Beginners (For Mac Users)

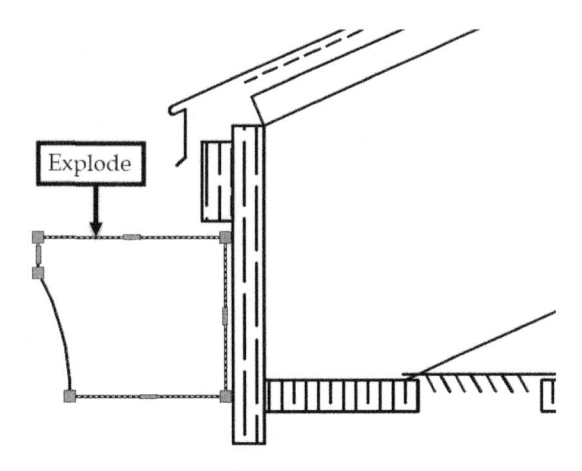

- Select the lines and arcs, as shown in the figure.

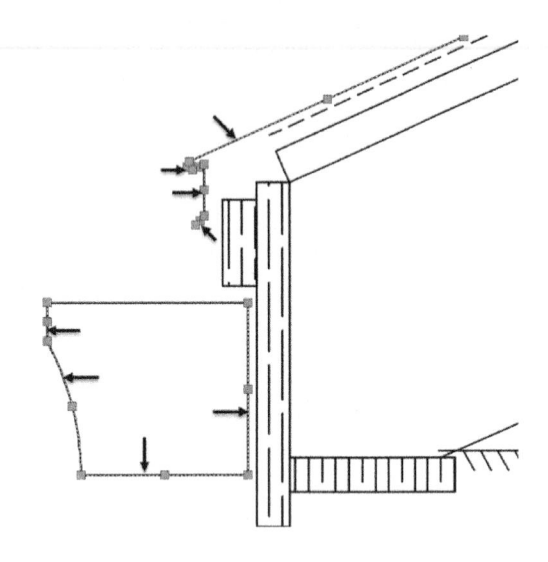

- On the **Drafting** tool set, click the **Lineweight** drop-down on the **Properties** palette, and then select 0.70.

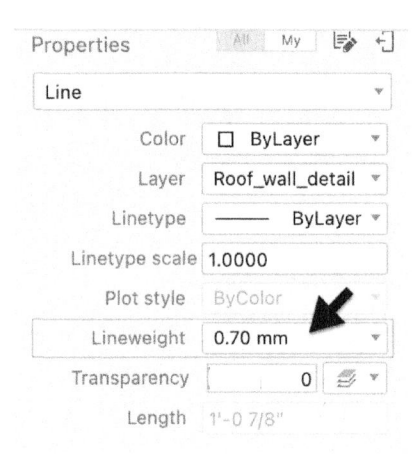

- Press Esc.
- Click the **Offset** tool on the **Modify** panel.
- Type 1.25 and press RETURN.

- Select the offset line, as shown in the figure.
- Move the pointer upward and click.

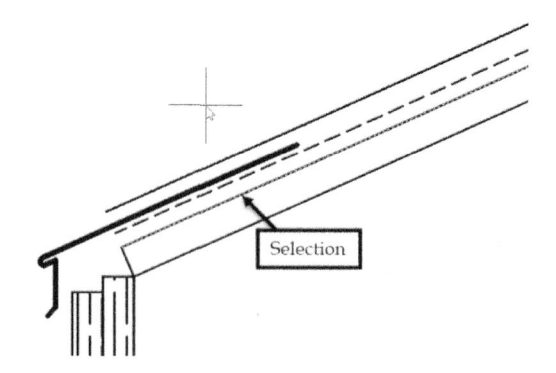

- Deactivate the **Ortho Mode** icon on the Status bar.
- Click the **Line** tool on the **Draw** panel.
- Select the endpoint of the offset line.
- Press and hold the SHIFT key and right click.
- Select the **Parallel** option from the shortcut menu.
- Hover the pointer on the line, as shown.

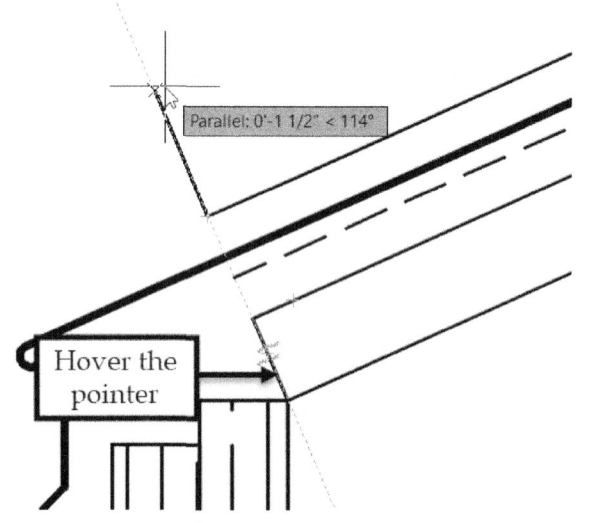

- Move the pointer along the tracking line.
- Type 2 and press RETURN.
- Type @7<20 and press RETURN.
- Press Esc.

374 | Creating Architectural Drawings

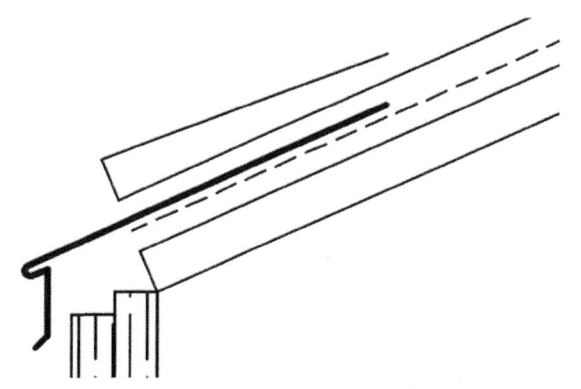

- Select the two newly created lines.
- Click the **Array** drop-down > **Path Array** tool on the **Modify** panel.
- Select the inclined line, as shown.

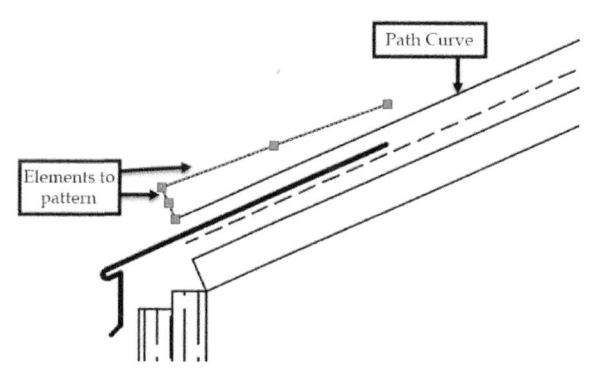

- Type 7 in the **Spacing between items** box on the **Path array** visor.

- Click **Close array and close visor**.

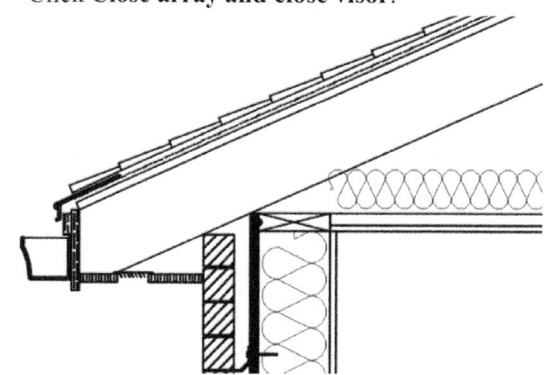

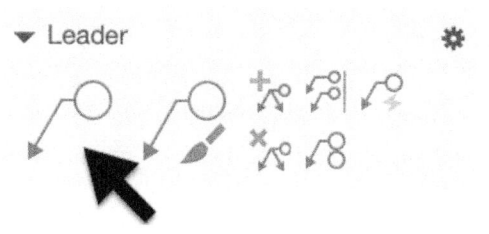

- Deactivate the **Ortho Mode** icon on the status bar.
- Specify the start point of the leader on the insulation, as shown.
- Move the pointer diagonally toward the bottom right corner, and then click.
- Type **Insulation** and click in the graphics area.

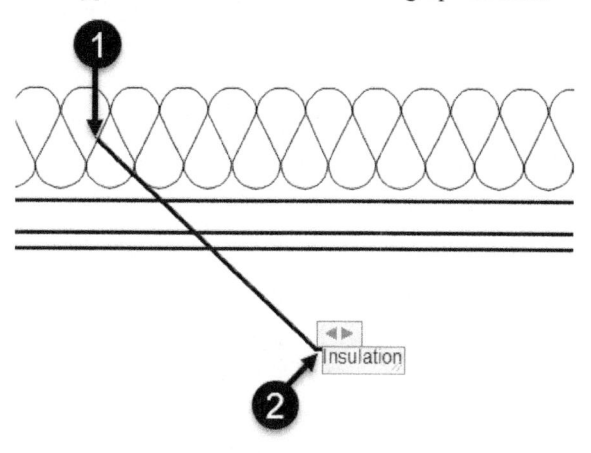

- Select the leader.
- On the **Properties** palette, click the **All** tab.
- Scroll to the **Leaders** section and enter 2 in the **Arrowhead size** and **Landing distance** boxes, respectively.

Adding Annotations

- On the **Drafting** tool set, click **Leader** > **Leader**.

Creating Architectural Drawings

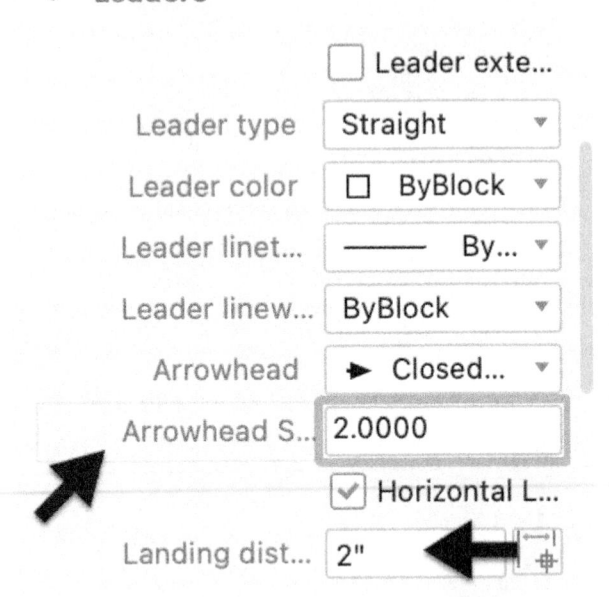

- Type **Continuous Bead of Sealant** and click in the graphics area.

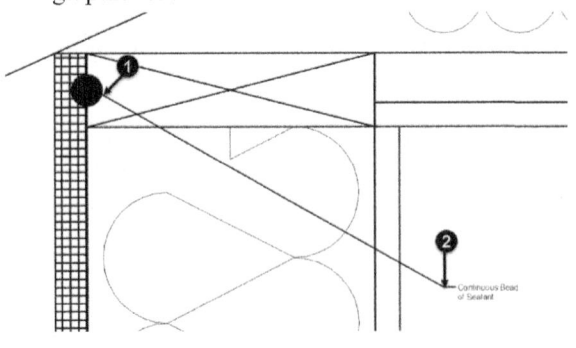

- Click the **Match Properties** tool on the toolbar.
- Select the **Insulation** leader to specify the source object.

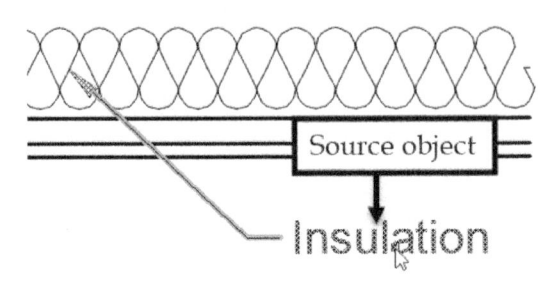

- Scroll to the **Text** section, and then enter **2** and **1** in the **Height** and **Landing gap** boxes, respectively.

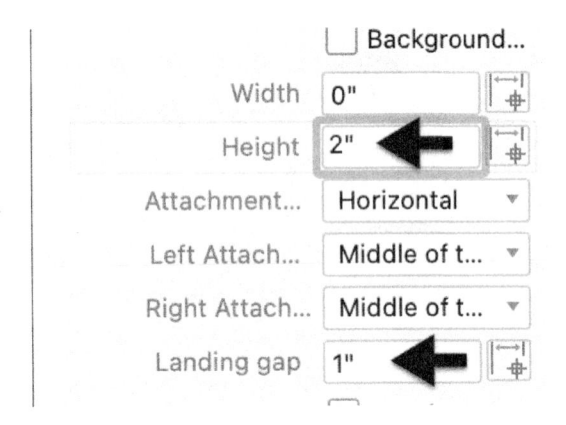

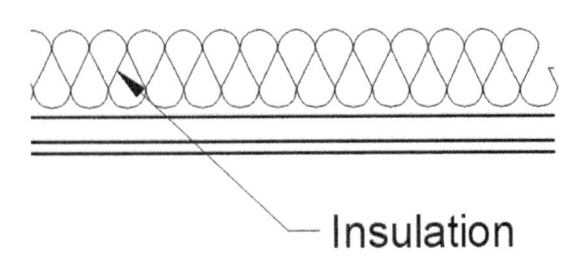

- Select the newly created leader; the properties of the source object are matched with the destination object.

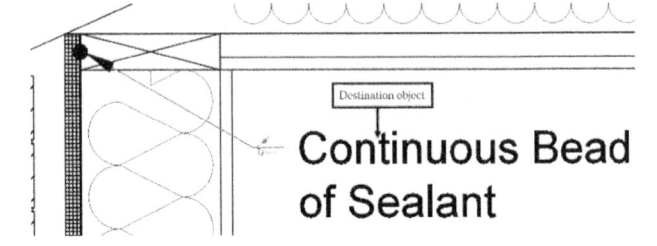

- On the **Drafting** tool set, click **Text** > **Multiline Text**.
- Click at the location, as shown.

- On the **Drafting** tool set, click **Leader** drop-down > **Leader** on the **Annotation** panel.
- Specify the start point of the leader on the donut, as shown.
- Move the pointer diagonally toward the bottom right corner, and then click.

376 | Creating Architectural Drawings

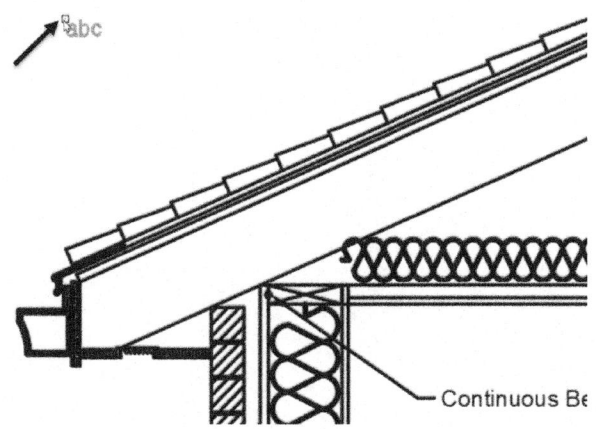

- Right-click and select the **Height** option from the shortcut menu.
- Type 2" and press ENTER.
- Specify the second corner of the text box, as shown.

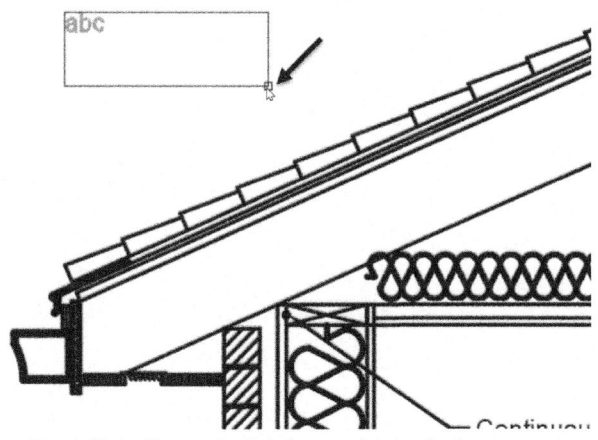

- Type **Shingles** and click in graphics window.
- On the **Drafting** tool set, click **Leader** drop-down > **Leader** on the **Annotation** panel.
- Right-click and select the **select Mtext** option from the shortcut menu.
- Select the multiline text from the graphics window.

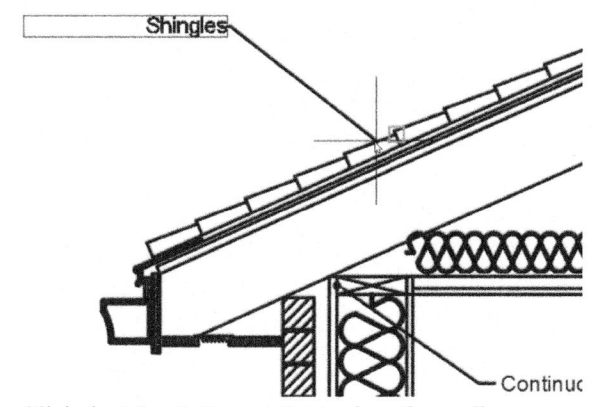

- Click the **Match Properties** tool on the toolbar.

- Select the **Insulation** leader to specify the source object.
- Select the newly created leader.
- Likewise, create the remaining leaders, as shown.

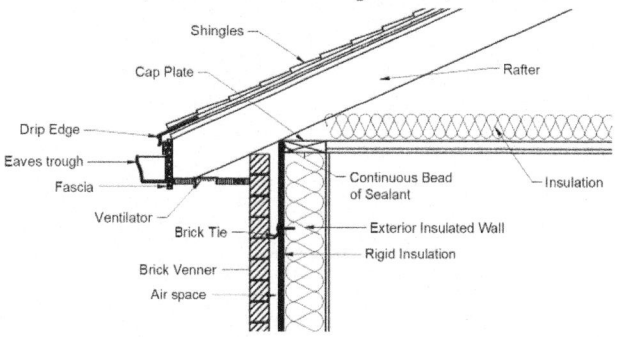

- Activate the **Ortho Mode** icon on the status bar.
- On the **Drafting** tool set, click **Draw > Break-line Symbol**.

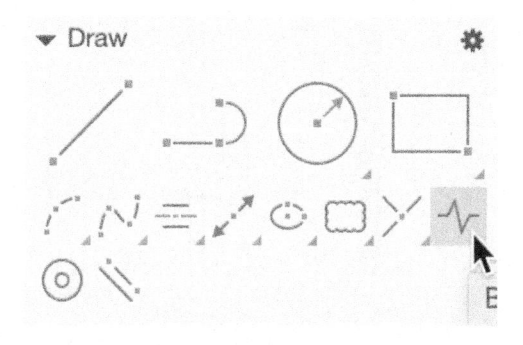

- Right-click and select the **Size** option.
- Type **8** and press RETURN.
- Zoom to the bottom portion and specify the start and endpoints of the break line.

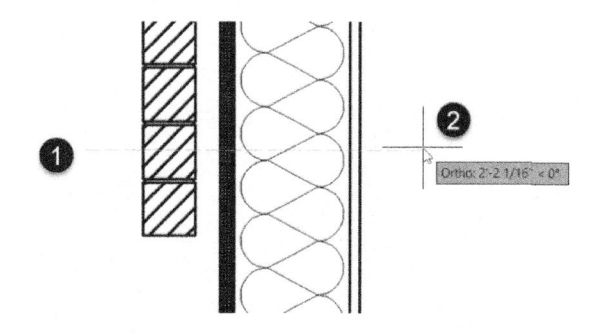

- Select the midpoint of the break line; the break line symbol is placed.

377 | Creating Architectural Drawings

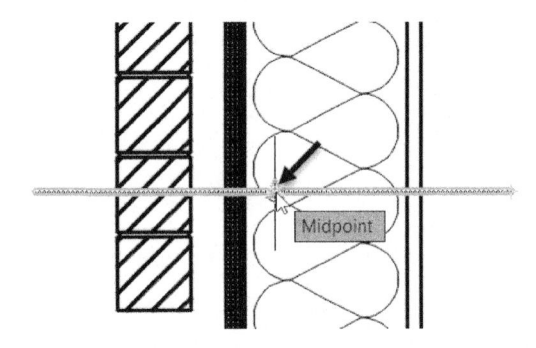

- On the **Drafting** tool set, click **Trim** drop-down > **Trim** on the **Modify** panel.
- Right-click and select the **cuTting edges** option.
- Select the break line and press RETURN.

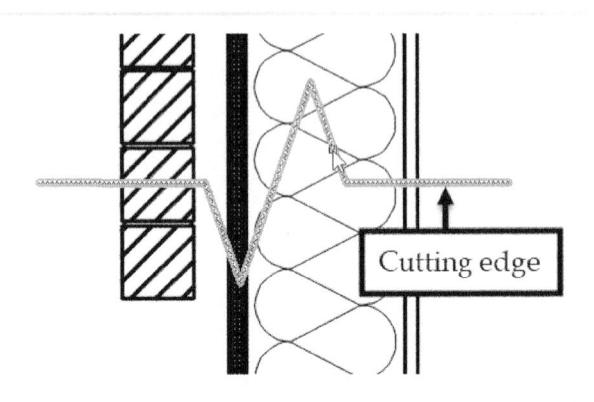

- Trim the elements on the bottom side of the drawing.
- Select the region below the break line and click the **Explode** tool on the **Modify** panel of the **Drafting** tool set.

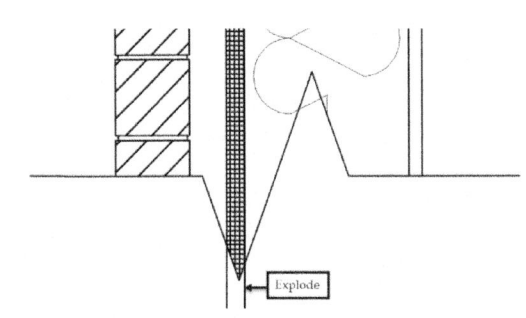

- Save and close the drawing file.

- Trim the vertical lines.

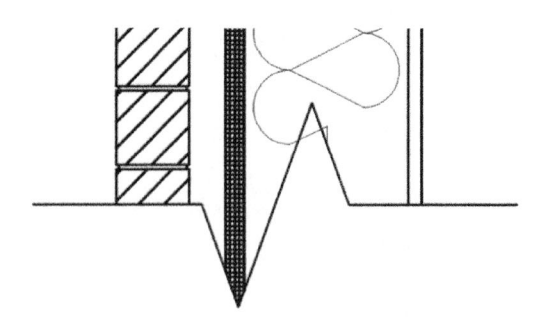

- Likewise, create the break lines and trim the elements, as shown.

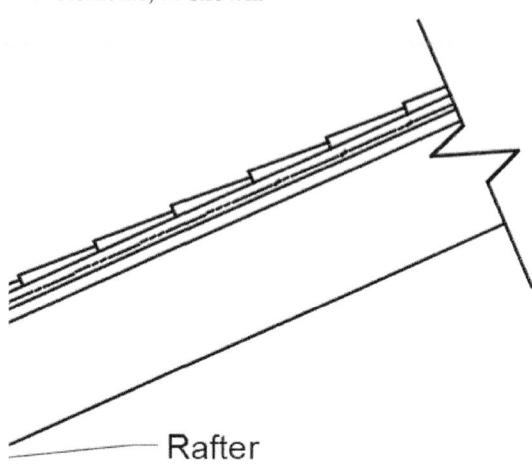

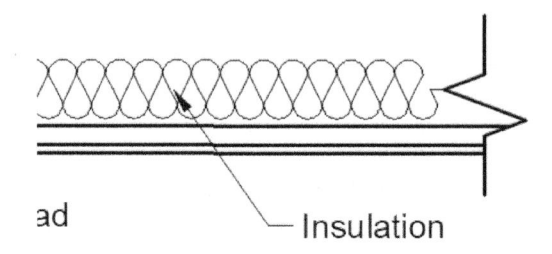

378 | Creating Architectural Drawings

Exercise

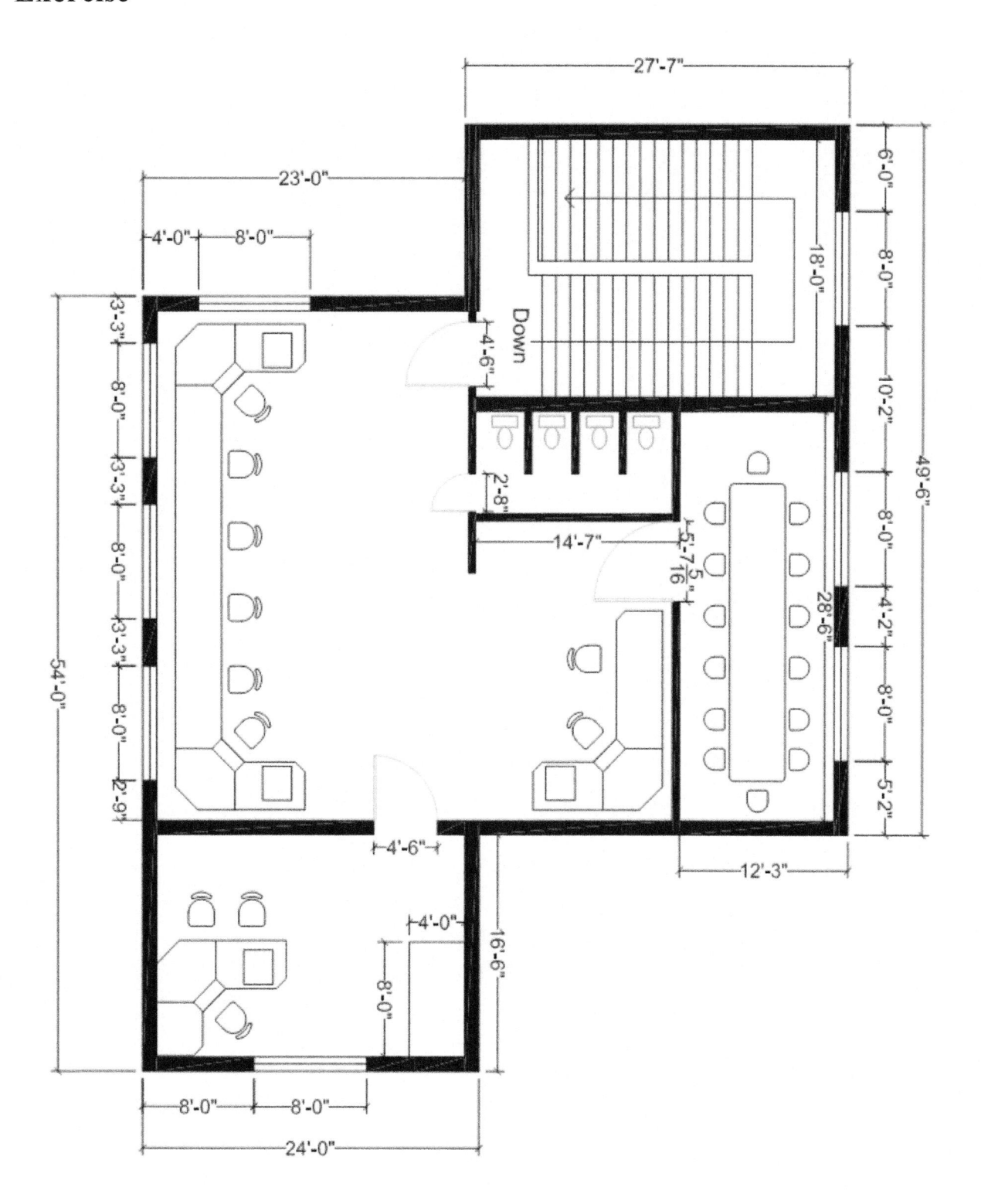

Index

2-Point, 43
3 Point, 245
3D Commands, 31
3D Mirror, 274
3D Object Snap, 244
3D polar array, 280
3D Rotate, 279
3-Point, 44, 46
Add/Delete Scales, 226
Adjust Space, 145
Aligned, 136
Angular, 140
Annotation Scale, 201
Annotative Dimensions, 223
Annotative Text, 227
Arc, 46
Arc Length, 137
Array, 271
Attach, 211
Auto Constrain, 174
Automatically add scale to automated Objects, 201
Auxiliary Views, 122
Axis, End, 53
Baseline, 139
Block Editor, 205, 306
Box, 243
Break, 145
Center, 301
Center Mark, 143, 149
Center, Diameter, 43
Center, Radius, 43
Center, Start, Angle, 150
Centerline, 143
Chamfer, 80
Chamfer Edge, 281
Circle, 42
Coincident, 170
Collinear, 170

Color Theme, 3
Command line, 8
Command List, 20
Cone, 251
Constraint Settings, 179
Construction, 116
Continue, 138
Copy, 75
Copy Selection, 290
Customization, 38
Cylinder, 246
Define Attributes, 208, 311
Dialogs and Palettes, 14
Diameter, 141
DIMEDIT, 158
Dimension, 133
Dimension Style, 147
Dimension, Dimjogline, 142, 144
Dimensional Constraints, 179
Dimensions, 313
Divide, 202
Drafting Settings, 66
Drawing area, 7
DWG Compare, 234
Dynamic Input, 39
Dynamic UCS, 243
Ellipse, 53
Elliptical Arc, 54
Erase, 42
Explode, 83
Export Snapshot, 236
Extend, 79, 157
Extrude, 253
File tabs, 7
Fillet, 79
Fillet Edge, 276
From, 119
Grid, 58

Hatch, 185
Hatch Pattern Scale, 191
Help, 20
Ignore Island Detection, 194
Infer Constraints, 181
insert blocks in a table, 204
Inspect, 146
Intersect, 264
Isometric snap, 160, 161
Jogged, 141
Limits, 59
Limmax, 80
Line, 38
Linear, 135, 179
Linetype gap selection, 69
LineWeight, 59
Live Section, 282
Loft, 258
Match Properties, 164
Menu Bar, 13
Mirror, 81, 294
Move, 74, 270
Move gizmo, 271
Multileader Style, 151
Multiline Text, 194
Multiple Points, 45
Named views, 128
New Layer, 62
Object snap, 63
Object Snap Tracking, 68
Oblique, 159
Offset, 86
Offset Faces, 278
Ordinate, 144
Ortho Mode, 60
Page Setup Manager, 219
Pan, 72
Parameter Manager, 180
Path Array, 87, 261
Plot, 222, 232

Plot styles, 230
Polar Array, 84
Polar Tracking, 60
Polygon, 50
Polyline, 47
Polysolid, 252
Presspull, 260
Properties palette, 163
Purge, 202
Pyramid, 252
Radius, 141
Rectangle, 48
Rectangular Array, 88
Redo, 42
Relative to Paper Space, 226
rename blocks, 203
Revolve, 254, 255
Rotate, 75
Rotate Gizmo, 279
Running Object Snaps, 66
Scale, 76
SE Isometric, 253
Section Plane, 282
Selection Window, 16
Shell, 281
Shortcut Menus, 14
Show annotation objects, 228
Snap Mode, 58
Sphere, 251
Spline CV, 52
Spline Fit, 51
Start Center End, 293
Start, Center, End, 46
Start, End, Direction, 47
Status Bar, 9
Stretch, 83, 156
Subtract, 262
Sweep, 256, 258
System requirements, 1
Table, 215

Tan, Tan, Tan, 45
Taper Faces, 277
Templates, 231
Tolerances, 152
Tool sets, 4
Toolbar, 7
Torus, 252
Trim, 77
UCS, Previous, 246
UCS, View, 248
Undo, 42
Union, 261
Update, 158
user interface, 2
ViewCube, 8
ViewCube Settings, 241

VP Freeze, 223
Wedge, 244
Wireframe, 245
Write Block, 206
Zoom Dynamic, 70
Zoom Extents, 69
Zoom Window, 289
Zoom-All, 70
Zoom-Center, 71
Zoom-In, 72
Zoom-Object, 71
Zoom-Out, 72
Zoom-Previous, 70
Zoom-Realtime, 70
Zoom-Scale, 71
Zoom-Window, 70

Printed in Great Britain
by Amazon